Shelby County, Tennessee Newspaper Abstracts through 1859

Helen Rowland

Heritage Books
2024

HERITAGE BOOKS
AN IMPRINT OF HERITAGE BOOKS, INC.

Books, CDs, and more—Worldwide

For our listing of thousands of titles see our website
at
www.HeritageBooks.com

A Facsimile Reprint
Published 2024 by
HERITAGE BOOKS, INC.
Publishing Division
5810 Ruatan Street
Berwyn Heights, MD 20740

Originally published 2002

International Standard Book Number
Paperbound: 978-0-7884-8751-4

FOREWORD

This book contains a collection of abstracts from Memphis and Shelby County, Tennessee newspapers. I have included many clippings about events in other counties in Tennessee as well as Mississippi and Arkansas. In some cases these articles were in the newspaper due to their close proximity to Memphis; in other cases there may have been family or friends in Memphis who would be interested in the news. That is why I have included these clippings in this book.

American Eagle is a Ft. Pickering newspaper. Somerville Reporter is a Somerville paper. The Pioneer, Jackson Gazette and Southern Statesman are Jackson, Madison County, newspapers. All others are Memphis newspapers.

Instant (inst.) means within the current month. Ultimo (ult.) means in the previous month; however, this may not hold true in the editions of the Weekly Appeal. There were many issues missing from the first half of 1854. 1855 was extremely hard to read. Several editions were missing from 1856. You will notice many question marks, which I used whenever I was not sure of the content or spelling. Also, there are obvious errors in some articles. These were copied as written in the newspapers. There were many spelling errors in the newspapers, so check the index for various spellings of the surnames you are researching.

Remember that the list of interments at the end is only persons who were *buried* in the city of Memphis. As you will see, the percentage of obituaries for the deceased is very low.

Somewhere in time...........

Wm. **ABBEY**, son of Col. Richard **ABBEY**, of Tunica county, Miss., died on Saturday night last, after a short illness of fever, aged 24 years. His remains were brought up on the *Laughlin,* to be transferred to the *City of Huntsville,* for Nashville, where he will be interred in the family burying ground. Memphis Daily Appeal, Thurs., 4/17/1856.

Died, At Grenada, Miss., on the 18th instant, of typhoid fever, Miss Sarah, eldest daughter of John C. and Elizabeth **ABBOTT**. She was for several years an exemplary member of the Presbyterian Church. She was a dutiful and affectionate daughter, a kind sister and devoted friend—beloved by all who knew her. Memphis Daily Appeal, 1/26/1856.

All my interest being in Memphis, I respectfully offer my services to my friends and the public, as a Commission Merchant, in the coming season. I was engaged all last season in the cotton trade...My office will be on Front Row, near the corner of Union Street...Jas. **ABERNATHY**. Daily Enquirer, 1/8/1847.

Married, On the 4th(?) of November, at the residence of the bride's father, (Col. W. __. **DICKENS**) in Panola county, Miss., by Rev. James ___, Mr. Robert S. **ABERNATHY**, of Coahoma County, and Miss A. Fisher **DICKENS**. Memphis Daily Appeal, 11/10/1857.

Married, On the 27th, at the residence of the bride's father, by Rev. W. F. **TALLEY**, Mr. Joseph H. **ABINGTON** to Miss F. D. **TALLEY**, all of Collierville, Tenn. Memphis Daily Appeal, 7/31/1857.

Married, On the 30th ult. by Rev. J. H. **GRAY**, D.D., Mr. John **ABLE** to Miss Caroline **DOEBLER**, all of this city. Memphis Daily Appeal, 11/1/1855.

Died – In the 19th year of her age, of chronic affection of the stomach, in Fort Pickering, May the 21st (?), 1842, Mrs. Sarah Ann, consort of Andrew Jackson **ACREE**, who died in this place September 13th, 1841. She lived beloved and respected and died lamented, leaving an only infant son aged 4 months. American Eagle, 5/27/1842.

Married, At Macon, Tennessee, on the 4th instant by Rev. J. W. **KNOTT**, Dr. G. W. **ACREE** and Mrs. L. E. **SHARPE**. Memphis Daily Appeal, 3/5/1857.

Died, On the 5th inst., of Cholera Infantum, Josephine Adelia, daughter of George W. and the late Mrs. Martha L. M. **ACREE**. Memphis Daily Appeal, 11/6/1852.

Married, On the 2d inst., at the residence of the bride's father, W. H. **ALLEN**, Esq., of Montgomery county, Tennessee, by Rev. J. W. **HANNAH**, Dr. H. M. **ACREE**, late of this city, to Miss Carrie Allen. Memphis Daily Appeal, 9/23/1857.

Mr. David **ADAMS**, of the firm of E. M. Apperson & Co., who had returned from New Orleans on the packet Ben Franklin, too feeble to be removed to his home, died on board that steamer this morning, at a quarter to four o'clock. His funeral will take place from his late residence on Adams street, at 2 o'clock to-morrow afternoon. Memphis Evening Ledger, 2/13/1858. The friends and acquaintances of the late David Adams and family are respectfully invited to attend his funeral This Afternoon....from his residence on Court street. Services by Rev. Mr. Steadman. Memphis Daily Appeal, 2/14/1858.

Died, In this city on the evening of the 24th instant, of cholera morbus, Lester A. Adams, son of H. T. and Rebecca G. **ADAMS**, aged __ years, four months and five days....Memphis Daily Appeal, 1/27/1859.

Married, Near Cockrum, Miss., March 2d, by Rev. Wm. Cary **CRANE**, Mr. John D. **ADAMS**, late of Charlotte, N.C., and Miss Mary N. **PRYOR**, of DeSoto county, Miss. Memphis Daily Appeal, 3/15/1857.

It becomes our painful duty to announce the death of our distinguished citizen, the Hon. Stephen **ADAMS**. He died at his residence in the vicinity of this city yesterday morning, after an illness of only a few days....Judge Adams was, we believe, a native of Tennessee, but removed to Mississippi about twenty-five years ago, and there resided until a few months since. During a long period he held high public positions in that State, filling successively a seat in the Legislature, upon the Bench, in the Lower House of Congress, and more recently in the United States Senate....Memphis Daily Appeal, 5/12/1857.

Married. At Purdy, Tenn., on the 5th of September by S. D. **PACE**, Esq., Mr. Thad L. **ADAMS** to Miss Martha E. **RANDOLPH**, all of McNairy county. Christian Advocate copy. Memphis Daily Appeal, 10/18/1853.

I am prepared to receive propositions for contracts to supply the volunteer troops with such articles of subsistence etc., as will be necessary while in camp near Memphis...W. A. **ADAMS**, Ast. Q.M.U.S.A. Daily Enquirer, 10/2/1847.

Married—On Friday the 18th inst., by the Rev. Jeptha **HARRISON** at the residence of Mr. A. **KERNAHAN**, Mr. W. G. **ADAMS**, merchant, to Miss Alison E. **SCOTT**, both of this city. Memphis Enquirer, 1/25/1839.

A man by the name of William or Bill **ADAMS**, grocery keeper in Grand Junction, was killed by the cars just as they were entering that place night before last. The cars were passing the switch on their way up, and it is not known whether he stepped or fell off. He was, however, run over and killed instantly.... Memphis Daily Appeal, 10/8/1858.

Married, On the 5th May, by Woodson **VADEN**, Esq., Wm. C. **ADAMS** to Miss Eliz W. **NEWLAND**. Weekly Appeal, 6/12/1846.

Married, In Tipton county on the 6th inst., by Rev. D. H. **CUMMINS**, Mr. William H. **ADAMS**, of Pulaski county, Ark., and Miss Fanny **CALHOUN**, of Tipton county. Memphis Daily Appeal, 1/10/1857.

Coroner Horne yesterday held an inquest on the body of H. **AHREN**, who was found at nearly midnight on Saturday, in the house of Stephen **SULLIVAN**, on the Bayou, near DeSoto and Union streets, lying dead, with five stabs in the abdomen. It appeared Ahren had retired as if to go to bed, but marks showed that he had been attacked in the yard, and some articles found there, as well as a knife that was identified, showed that he was killed by a man named Edward **MITCHELL**, who escaped....Memphis Daily Appeal, 11/2/1858.

.....Late on the afternoon mentioned (Tuesday), one of the returned volunteers named **URSERY** (Nat. Ursery, we believe he is named), of Capt. Cook's company, drove up in a buggy in front of Whitsitt's Grocery on Market Square, and used obscene language. Mr. Joseph **AIKEN**, whose family, with other ladies, were on the portice of Mr. Whitsitt's family residence immediately adjoining, standing at the door, rebuked him for his obscenity, telling him that there were respectable females within hearing. Ursery then got down and went into the Grocery with Aiken towards the counter. Some further altercation ensued, and a slight blow or blows were given by Aiken in resentment of the continued obscenity of Ursery, when the latter drew a large Bowie-knife and stabbed Aiken through the heart, killing him instantly. He fell and expired without uttering a word. Ursery attempted to make his escape, but was arrested and lodged in the Calaboose....Mr. Aiken has left a wife and a large family behind him, among whom are several children and a mother-in-law, who depended upon him for their support......Daily Enquirer, Thurs., 6/17/1847.

Died – In this city on Wednesday 2d inst., Josephine Frances, infant daughter of Frederic and Louisa **ALBERT**. Weekly Appeal, Fri., 9/4/1846.

Married, On Wednesday evening, 13th inst., at the residence of the bride's mother, by Rev. John **BATEMAN**, Mr. John H. **ALBRECHT** to Miss Mary C. **WEAVER**, all of this city. Memphis Daily Appeal, 10/14/1858.

Married, On the 23d ult. at the bride's house, by Esq. S. J. **McELWEE**, George W. **ALBRIGHT** to Miss N. Caroline Vick, daughter of R. **VICK**, of Marshall county, Miss. Memphis Daily Appeal, 3/13/1859.

Died, At North Mt. Pleasant, Miss., on the 6th of February, Cornelia Carolina, daughter of John and Frances J. **ALBRIGHT**, disease scarlet fever, age four years, eleven months and twenty-three days. Memphis Daily Appeal, 2/19/1857.

We are authorized to announce Col. Adam R. **ALEXANDER**, a candidate for Brigadier General of the counties of McNairy, Hardeman, Fayette and Shelby. Memphis Enquirer, 3/21/1836.

Died. In this vicinity, on Wednesday last, after a short illness, Mr. Henry **ALEXANDER**, formerly of Plymouth, N.C., aged 59 years. He was one of "God's noblest works," and before he emigrated to this State, had served as sheriff of Terrill county, N.C., more than twenty years. His two sons who emigrated with him in the early bloom of manhood, preceded their father to the world of spirits, much beloved and mourned. Raleigh papers, N.C., will please copy. Memphis Daily Eagle, Tues., 1/4/1848.

Married, At the residence of the bride's father in Tipton county, Tenn., on the night of the 8th inst., by Rev. Mr. Evans, Mr. J. _. **ALEXANDER**, of Marshall county, Miss., to Miss Fanny **SANFORD**. Memphis Weekly Appeal, 12/15/1858.

Married, On the 1st inst., at the residence of A. **HOLLOWAY**, Esq., near Somerville, Tenn., by Rev. F. **BYNUM**, Mr. J. M. **ALEXANDER** and Mrs. S. J. **BAUGH**, all of Fayette county, Tenn. Memphis Daily Appeal, 10/10/1857.

Died—In this vicinity on the 21st (or 31st) Ann Carr, infant daughter of James W. and Mary Jane **ALEXANDER**, aged 9 months and 10 days. American Eagle Weekly, 8/1/1845. Died, In this vicinity on the 13th instant, Mary Virginia, infant daughter of James W. and Mary Jane Alexander, aged 3 months and 23 days. American Eagle, 10/20/1843.

Married, On the 15th instant by Esquire Waldran, Mr. John **ALEXANDER** and Miss Julia A. **DINSMORE**, all of this city. Memphis Daily Appeal, 4/17/1857.

Died, On Sunday morning, June 29th, Mrs. Cynthia D., wife of John M. **ALEXANDER**, of Macon, Tenn., aged forty years. Charlotte (N.C.) papers please copy. Memphis Daily Appeal, 7/3/1856.

Married. In this city, on Tuesday last, Dr. L. M. **ALEXANDER**, of Bayou Sara, La., to Miss Margaret **RUDISILL**, of this city. The Daily Eagle, Fri., 2/25/1848.

Married: In this city, on the 13th inst., by Rev. J. H. **GRAY**, Mr. P. H. **ALEXANDER**, to Miss E. E. **LECOQ**, both of this place. Weekly Memphis Eagle, 3/22/1849. Died, On Monday evening, the 17th inst., at the residence of Mr. J. P. **BENTON**, in Tuscumbia, Ala., Mr. P. H. Alexander, a native of Pennsylvania, but formerly a resident of Memphis, Tenn. Memphis Daily Eagle & Enquirer, 5/27/1852.

Died, At his residence near New Castle, in Hardeman county, Tenn. on Wednesday, 30th March, 1853, Rankin **ALEXANDER**, in the 65th year of his age.....He had been for a long period of years a consistent member of the Presbyterian church, and in all the relations of life, as husband, father, master, neighbor and friend, he had been a pattern worthy of imitation to his numerous family.....The deceased had resided in Hardeman county for the last 17 years, but was a native of Mecklenburgh county, North Carolina. His ancestors were among the signers of the famous "Mecklenburgh Declaration of Independence," and in the great struggle which followed for the liberties of the country they bore ample testimony to the truth of their convictions as expressed in that document.....Memphis Daily Eagle & Enquirer, 4/7/1853.

Married, By Rev. N. P. **MOORE**, near Macon, Tenn., Samuel J. **ALEXANDER** to Miss Mollie W. Towles, daughter of John N. **TOWLES**, Esq, all of Macon, Tenn. Memphis Daily Appeal, 10/26/1858.

Z. C. **ALEXANDER**, we are requested to state, is a Candidate for the Office of Sheriff of Shelby county at the ensuing March election. The Appeal, 8/25/1843. Died. On the 3d inst. at the residence of Mrs. A. M. **RUDISILL**, Henrietta Clay, only daughter of the late Z. C. Alexander, aged 5 years, 3 months, and 12 days. Weekly American Eagle, 5/6/1847.

Married, On the 3rd inst. by U. **HENDRICKS**, Esq., Dr. J. F. **ALGEA**, of Portersville, Tenn., to Miss Sarah E. **McCORKLE**, of Dyer county, Tenn. Memphis Daily Eagle & Enquirer, 5/24/1853.

Married, On Tuesday evening, the 18 th inst., by the Rev. W. A. **PASAVANT**, John **ALGEO**, Esq., of Memphis, Tenn., to Miss Amanda, daughter of Capt. Robt. **GREERILLE**, of Manchester.—*Pittsburg Com. Journal*, Dec. 21st. Memphis Daily Eagle, 1/3/1850.

Died, In this city on the 5th inst., of abscess of the liver, Mr. John **ALGEO**, (brother of W. J. **ALGEO**, of the firm of Duval, Algeo & Co.,) in the 30th year of his age. Mr. Algeo came here a few weeks ago from Pittsburg, of which place he was a native, and at the time of his death a citizen, to make arrangements to become a permanent resident of this place. He resided here a greater portion of the time since 1846....He leaves a wife and three children to mourn....His remains were deposited in Morris Cemetery, to await their removal to Pittsburg. Memphis Daily Appeal, 8/8/1856.

Died: In this city on the 28th inst. of congestion of the lungs, Margaret W., consort of William J. **ALGEO**, aged 28 years. Memphis Whig, 10/31/1855.

Married, On the 15th inst., at the residence of Mr. H. T. **WILLIAMS**, near Fisherville, by Dr. W. G. **LANCASTER**, Mr. __. N. **ALLEN** and Miss Mary J. **WILLIAMS**, of Independence county, Ark. Memphis Daily Appeal, 10/20/1857.

We are authorized to announce Alexander **ALLEN**, of Germantown, a candidate for the office of County Trustee for Shelby county. American Eagle Weekly, 9/12/1845.

Married. On Wednesday the 25th inst. by Rev. G. W. **COONS**, at the house of W. S. **WELLS** in this County, Mr. Charles **ALLEN**, to Miss Rebecca **REINHARDT**, all of this city. Memphis Daily Eagle, 1/29/1848. Died, on the 8th inst., Mrs. Rebecca, wife of Charles Allen, in the 22d year of her age. The deceased formerly from Norwalk, Con., had resided among us two or three years.....After calling to her bedside her afflicted companion and infant child, she bade them an affectionate farewell, charging him with the responsibility and care of the little pledge she was about to leave...She was buried from the Presbyterian church, and the large concourse of citizens, together with the fraternity of Odd Fellows, who followed her remains to their last resting place, testify the deep respect for the departed, while such spontaneous sympathy is well calculated to console the desolate husband and her distant relatives. The Tri-Weekly Memphis Enquirer, 3/10/1846.

Married, At the Gayoso House, on the morning of the 7th, by the Rev. W. C. **ROBB**, Mr. David A. **ALLEN**, of Mississippi, to Miss Elmira C. **JONES**, of this city. Memphis Eagle, 10/11/1849.

Married—On the 27th ult., by the Rev. David J. **ALLEN**, Mr. Nath'l. G. **ALLEN**, of Haywood county, to Miss Caroline M. **MOSBY**, of this city. Daily Enquirer, 2/14/1847.

Notice. To George G. **ALLEN**, Morning **ALLEN**, Tennessee **ALLEN**, heirs at law of Elizabeth **ALLEN**, deceased, and all others concerned or interested in the premises. I will petition the next Circuit Court to be held for the county of Shelby, at the court house in Raleigh, on the first Monday in May next, to appoint commissioners to divide and set off to me and my heirs in severnalty, my interest or shares in the following tract of land, lying in said county, to wit: section eleven, in township one, range eight, west of the basis meridian in the late Chickasaw cession—my portion of the said tract being six-ninths of the same. John D. **BRADFORD**. Weekly Appeal, 2/12/1847.

The subscriber would dispose of on accommodating terms his tract of land, containing 320 acres, in township 1, range 8, north half of section 18. The above land is well watered and desirable in all respects, and lies in 6 miles of the Mississippi River, and in three miles of Horn Lake. George G. **ALLEN**. Memphis Enquirer, 7/21/1838.

Died—In this city on the 7th inst., at the residence of his brother, Mr. J. D. ALLEN, Alderman of the 3d Ward, Mr. Morris S. ALLEN, aged about 26 years. The deceased came to this city a few months ago from the city of New York, with the view of becoming a permanent resident...He was a member of the order of "United Americans." Daily Memphis Enquirer, 7/10/1849.

Died, At the residence of her father, James D. ALLEN, in Hardeman co., August 15, 1848, Miss Martha Virginia Allen, in the eighth year of her age...She would affectionately and earnestly ask her dear sister Mary...to teach her to pray...Memphis Daily Appeal, 9/16/1848.

Died, In Hernando, on the 20th of February, Miss Sarah F. Allen, daughter of Col. James D. & Martha ALLEN, aged 23 years. Memphis Daily Eagle & Enquirer, 3/6/1853.

Died, In Sandusky, Ohio, on the 18th inst., Mr. John F. ALLEN, Merchant, of Memphis, a gentleman much esteemed. Memphis Daily Eagle, 7/24/1850.

Married, At the house of Aaron ASKEN, Esq., of Panola county, Miss., on the 16th instant, by Rev. J. R. HAMILTON, President of the C.W. Baptist Female Institute, John J. ALLEN of Rutherford county, Tenn., and Miss Mary A. ASKEN. Memphis Daily Appeal, 4/24/1856.

Died, in Memphis, on Saturday 21st inst., of Hydrocephalus, John Cage, only child of Joseph C. and Susan ALLEN, aged one year, nine months and one day. Memphis Daily Appeal, 2/27/1852. Died, in St. Augustine, Florida, on the 28th ult., of pulmonory consumption, Capt. Joseph C. Allen, Naval Storekeeper at the Memphis Navy Yard. Capt. Allen served as a Lieutenant in Col. (now Governor) Campbell's Regiment of Tennessee Volunteers, which regiment, by superior gallantry, daring and discipline, won the highest credit at the battle of Monterey. Among the scores which were mown down by the well-directed and destructive batteries of the enemy, Capt. Allen fell severly wounded and disabled for life. He was then only in his 23rd year.—The disability produced by his wounds _____ him to resign his commission, but he was immediately appointed by President Polk an assistant Commissary...at New Orleans, then the principal depot of supplies for the army, until the close of the war. He received the appointment of Naval Storekeeper at Memphis in 1849, from President Taylor...As a husband, father, brother, master and citizen, the sincere grief with which his loss is lamented is the best testimony...In his last moments he received every attention and kindness, from the strangers around his bed; his attending physician, Dr. Peck, and the proprietor of the Florida House, which even long and well-tried friendship could have secured. By order of Maj. Allen LOWD, Commandant of the U.S. Garrison at St. Augustine, his mortal remains were interred with military honors in the military cemetery, attached to the Barracks...Capt. Allen was born in Sumner county, Tenn., on the 8th of January, 1824, and was in his 29th year at the time of his decease...Nashville and Gallatin papers please copy. Memphis Daily Appeal, 2/27/1852.

The undersigned having been qualified as administrator of the Estate of Jos. D. ALLEN, dec'd. and Morris S. ALLEN (with the will annexed) requests all those owing either estates to come forward.....R. L. KAY. Weekly Memphis Eagle, 10/18/1849.

Died, in this city, on Monday night, the 24th August, Lewis ALLEN, in the 38th year of his age. The deceased was born in Mason county, Eastern Virginia, and had recently moved to this place, together with an aged mother, who with all his acquaintances mourn her irreparable loss. The Tri-Weekly Memphis Enquirer, 9/1/1846.

All persons indebted to the estate of Michael ALLEN, deceased, are requested to come forward...Wm. ENGLISH, Adm'r. Memphis Daily Appeal, 7/18/1851.

Died, at the residence of R. A. ALLEN in this City, on the morning of the 24th inst., with inflamation of the lungs – after an illness of five days, Celeste C., daughter of R. A. and Maria D. Allen, aged two years and three months. The Appeal, 4/26/1844. Died—In this city on the 27th ult. Mrs. Maria Dudley Allen, consort of Capt. Robert A. ALLEN, in the twenty-fifth year of her age.....Weekly Appeal, 4/4/1845.

Married, On the 1st inst., at the residence of the bride's brother near Germantown, by Rev. L. D. **MULLINS**, Mr. T. Wade **ALLEN** to Miss Mattie **ANDERSON**, all of Shelby county. Memphis Daily Appeal, 12/24/1859.

Died, On Wednesday, 18 inst., Mr. Thomas **ALLEN**, aged 61 years, formerly of Beaufort co., N.C., and for the last ten years a resident of Shelby county. Memphis Daily Appeal, 2/27/1848.

Married, In Lafayette county, Miss., on the 9th of April, by Rev. D. G. **BURNEY**, D.D., Col. Thos. B. **ALLEN** and Miss Martha T. **HARRIS**, all of Lafayette county. Memphis Daily Appeal, 5/7/1856.

Died—In Memphis on Saturday the 9th inst. of tetanus, William, infant son of W. F. (?) and M. C. **ALLEN**, aged 10 days. The Appeal, 11/17/1843.

Married. On the 23d ult. at the residence of Wm. J. **BONNER** by Rev. Saml. **WATSON**, Mr. W. H. **ALLEN** to Miss Lucy T. **BONNER**, all of Desoto Miss. Memphis Daily Appeal, 12/3/1854.

Married, On the 22d inst. by Rev. Jno. **WILSON**, Mr. William **ALLEN**, of Fayette county, to Miss Jane, daughter of N. H. **NELSON**, of Tipton county. Memphis Weekly Appeal, 12/29/1858.

Died—In this city on Saturday, 29th ultimo, William S., infant son of William F. and Mary C. **ALLEN**. Weekly Appeal, 9/4/1846.

Married, On the evening of the 30th ult., at the Second Presbyterian Church by Rev. Dr. Grundy, Mr. Wm. H. **ALLEN**, of Grenada, Miss., to Miss Kate **BLEDSOE**, of Memphis. Memphis Daily Appeal, 1/1/1858.

Died. In this city, on Tuesday the 15th inst., Mr. Thomas **ALLISON**, in the 68th year of his age.....He emigrated some years since from South Carolina to Alabama, and from thence to this place in 1844...He had for many years been a professed follower of Christ and a member of the Presbyterian church, and at the time of his death was in communion with the 1st Presbyterian church in this city...He has left an affectionate family who mourn his departure...Weekly American Eagle, 12/24/1846.

Died, at the residence of her brother, John D. **ALSTON**, in DeSoto county, Miss., on the 6th inst., in the fifteenth year of her age, Miss Nancy W. **ALSTON**, (familiarly known by the pet name of Mitty)....Memphis Daily Appeal, 11/11/1856. Departed this life, on the 13th inst., at the residence of Colonel Finly **HOLMES**, DeSoto county, Mississippi, John D. Alston....Memphis Daily Appeal, 8/16/1857.

Married, On the 30th of December by the Rev. S. J. **REID**, Mr. Phillip S. **ALSTON** to Mary Ann **POTTOK**, all of Panola county, Miss. Memphis Daily Eagle & Enquirer, 1/12/1853.

Married—At "Carysbrook", Miss., on Tuesday evening, 18th inst., by the Rev. Samuel G. **LITTON**, Rev. Philip W. **ALSTON**, of Memphis, to Miss Elizabeth **CARY**, of Desoto county, Miss. Memphis Enquirer, 2/28/1840. Death of Rev. Philip W. Alston.—The painful and unexpected intelligence of the death of the excellent and beloved minister of the Episcopal Church of this city, reached us yesterday. He left this city in ill health some ten or twelve days since, and arrived in Columbia on the morning of the 17th, on a visit to the family of Bishop Otey, where he expired of a congestive chill, on the morning of the 18th....Mr. Alston graduated at Chapel Hill College, North Carolina, in 1835 we believe, prepared himself for the Christian Ministry under the roof of the good and holy bishop where he returned to die, and his first ministerial charge after he had fitted himself for the holy orders, was over the church in this city, which he organized in 1839, and whose devoted and affectionate minister he continued to his death...The body of the lamented deceased reached Randolph on board the steamboat Empire, on Tuesday evening. American Eagle, 6/24/1847.

Married, On the evening of the 8th inst., at the house of Dr. Jameson, by Rev. Joseph R. **HAMILTON**, President of the Cold Water Baptist Female Seminary, Mr. Wm. J. **ALSTON**, of Houston county, Texas, and Miss Elizabeth M. **JAMESON**, of Marshall county, Miss. Memphis Daily Appeal, 10/14/1856.

Married. At Arkansas Post on the 14th ult. by the Rev. B. L. **HALLER**, Mr. Zerah S. **ALTON** to Miss Fannie E. Hamilton, daughter of Hon. John T. **HAMILTON**, all of Arkansas county. Memphis Daily Appeal, 3/24/1854.

A young Spaniard by the name of Octavio **ALVAREZ** who had been in the employ of the firm of Fernandez & Cardonna, put a period to his existence yesterday morning by placing a pistol to his right temple and blowing out his brains. He bid the family where he was boarding a farewell forever, remarking that he was going to New Orleans, never to return. When he got on the pavement by Mr. Lehman's store he met one of the gentlemen connected with the establishment in which he had been employer, and bidding him farewell forever, committed the fatal deed. No reason is assigned for the act. He had no relatives this side of Cuba. Memphis Daily Appeal, 7/7/1854.

Died, At his residence near Aberdeen, Ark., on the morning of the 22d of January, 1858, of pneumonia, Rev. Lewis **AMES**, in the 71st year of his age. Raleigh, N.C., papers please copy. Memphis Daily Appeal, 2/91858.

Married, In Carroll county, Missouri, on Thursday, -- instant, General James J. **AMONET**(?), of this vicinity, to Miss Kate **HUDSON**, of the first-named county. Memphis Daily Appeal, 11/22/1857.

Died, In Pontotoc, Miss., on the 16th ult., in the 37th year of her age, Mrs. Sarah W., wife of Benj. D. **ANDERSON**, and daughter of Rev. J. **LINDLEY**, for many years President of the Ohio University. The deceased professed religion early in life and united with the Cumberland Presbyterian Church....May her children and relatives love the Saviour in whom she rejoiced ....Memphis Daily Appeal, 10/4/1856.

Died, yesterday, at seven o'clock A.M., at the residence of R. J. **JENNINGS**, Esq., two and a half miles north of town, Mr. Charles C. **ANDERSON**, in the 35th year of his age. He was an old and esteemed citizen of Memphis. The funeral will take place at two o'clock to-day, from Capt. Jennings' residence....Memphis Daily Avalanche, 2/16/1859.

Died. On Sunday 19th inst. at the residence of her husband, Mrs. Eliza G., wife of G. M. **ANDERSON**, in the 27th year of her age. Memphis Daily Appeal, 3/24/1854. Married. On the 3rd(?) instant by Rev. Mr. _____, Mr. G. M. Anderson, of Memphis, to Miss Rachael T. **BARKER**(?), of Tipton county, Ten. Memphis Appeal, 1/13/1855.

Report of the Board of Health, For the last 24 Hours, to 12 M., June 21...H. W. **ANDERSON**, cholera; Franklin **MADDING**, cholera...Daily Memphis Enquirer, 6/22/1849.

Married, In this city on the 30th ult. by Rev. Dr. Gray, Col. J. P. **ANDERSON**, Marshall of Washington Territory, to Miss Etta **ADAIR**. Memphis Daily Appeal, 5/3/1853.

Married, In this city on Saturday last, the 30th April, by the Rev. D. L. **GRAY**, Col. J. Patton **ANDERSON**, of Mississippi, to Miss Etta Adair, daughter of the late Gov. **ADAIR**, of Kentucky. Memphis Daily Eagle & Enquirer, 5/2/1853.

Married, In Immanuel Church at LaGrange, Tennessee, on the 14th inst., by Rev. Mr. Page, Mr. James H. **ANDERSON**, Esq., of Holly Springs, Miss., and Miss Lide G. **SMITH**. Memphis Daily Appeal, 9/23/1857.

The friends and acquaintances of the family of the late John **ANDERSON**, are requested to attend the Funeral of their mother, Mrs. Anderson, this evening at 4 o'clock, from her residence on Alabama street. Services by Rev. Mr. Thomas. Memphis Whig, 7/1/1856.

Died. In this city at half-past 5 o'clock on the evening of the 9th inst., of Billious Congestive Fever, John **ANDERSON**, Sr., aged 65 years. The deceased was a native of Maryland, whence he emigrated to Monticello, Ky., where he married the estimable lady who has survived him and is left to mourn his death.

In the year 1826, he settled in Memphis, then a mere village, where he has ever since lived....Memphis Daily Appeal, 6/14/1854.

Died, At the Worsham House in this city, on Sunday night last, 2nd inst., John A. ANDERSON, of Helena, Ark., aged 33 years and 2 months. The deceased was the step-son of the late Dr. BYBEE, of this city, and brother of the late Representative in Congress from Washington Territory, J. Patton ANDERSON....He leaves an afflicted wife and troops of friends to mourn his untimely demise. Memphis Weekly Appeal, 5/12/1858.

Married, On Tuesday evening of the 4th inst. by the Rev. John SHERALD, Col. John H. ANDERSON to Miss Virginia A., daughter of Dr. John J. BURNETT—all of Carthage, Tenn. Memphis Daily Eagle & Enquirer, 1/15/1853.

Died, On the 12th of August, in DeSoto county, Miss., Mrs. Isabella M., wife of Mr. John M. ANDERSON, in the 24th year of her age. Memphis Daily Appeal, 9/11/1856.

Married: In this city, on the 16th inst., by the Rev. Mr. Page, R. M. ANDERSON, Esq., to Miss Lucy A., daughter of Geo. H. WYATT, Esq., of Donaldsonville, La. Weekly Memphis Eagle, 8/23/1849. Died, In Placerville, California, on the 18th September, 1858, Mrs. Lucy A. Anderson, consort of Hon. Robt. M. Anderson, aged about 27 years, leaving a disconsolate husband and three dear little children, two daughters and one son, to mourn their irreparable loss. Mrs. A. was the daughter of Maj. Geo. H. Wyatt, formerly a citizen of Memphis, and was married to Robert M. Anderson, son of Col. N. ANDERSON, in Memphis, in August, 1849....Memphis Daily Appeal, 10/26/1858.

Died, On the 16th instant, Nelson Anderson, son of Nathaniel ANDERSON, in the 17th year of his age. His death was caused by the falling of a horse he was riding, on the evening of the 15th....Although he lived some eight hours, he never spoke after the accident. Memphis Weekly Appeal, 11/24/1858.

At a meeting of a portion of the young men of this city, held at O'Hanlon's Exchange, on Thursday evening last, a Military Company was organized under the name of "Nelson Guards," in honor of the gallant Lieutenant Fred B. NELSON, who fell upon the heights of Cerro Gordo. The following named young gentlemen were chosen as officers: Robert M. ANDERSON, Captain; Wm. A. PORTER, 1st Lieutenant; Robt. T. O'HANLON, 2nd Lieutenant; John W. CAMP, Brevet 2nd Lieutenant; John M. WILLIAMS, Orderly Sergeant. Weekly Memphis Eagle, 5/31/1849. We are authorized to announce Robt. M. Anderson a candidate for the office of Register of Shelby County, at the March election. Daily Enquirer, 7/3/1847. Robert M. Anderson, formerly of this city, is the newly elected Lieutenant Govenor of California....So says the *Bulletin* of yesterday morning....It will be remembered that Mr. Anderson was formerly associated with the late Henry VAN PELT, as co-editor of the *Appeal*, and was for some years a practicing lawyer in this city. He is the son of our old and respected friend, Col. Nat. ANDERSON...Memphis Daily Appeal, 10/19/1855.

Married, At the residence of Leonidas TROUSDALE, in this city, by Rev. J. H. GRAY, on Wednesday evening, 13th inst., Gen. Samuel R. ANDERSON, Postmaster of Nashville, to Mrs. Susan ALLEN, daughter of B. B. TROUSDALE, Esq., of this city. After receiving the congratulations of their friends, the newly wedded pair took passage on the Huntsville, for the city of Nashville. Memphis Daily Appeal, 2/14/1856.

Died, At his residence on Wolf river, two miles north of Memphis, of typhoid fever, Shelley C. ANDERSON, aged twenty-three years. Funeral to take place at 10 o'clock A.M., September 25, from the residence of his brother-in-law, R. J. JENNINGS, on Commerce street, over the Bayou. Services by Rev. A. M. BRYAN. Memphis Daily Appeal, 9/25/1857.

Married, On Monday evening, the 19th inst., by Rt. Rev. Bishop Otey, T. Carey ANDERSON, Esq., to Miss Bettie Otey, daughter of Col. W. L. OTEY, all of Phillips county, Ark. Memphis Daily Appeal, 7/21/1858.

Married, In Austin, Texas, on the 30th ult., by Rev. Wm. M. **BAKER**, T. Scott **ANDERSON**, Esq., to Mrs. M. McNeil **HARPER**, all of that city. Memphis Daily Appeal, 2/23/1858.

On Tuesday the 3d of March next I will sell at the late residence of Thomas **ANDERSON** deceased, on the Stage Road, 3 miles east of Raleigh, all the stock, farming utensils…belonging to said Estate…Memphis Daily Eagle & Enquirer, 2/8/1852.

Died, On Tuesday, July 5th, at his residence near Cold Water Depot, in DeSoto county, Miss., after a short but painful illness, William Henry **ANDERSON**, in the 23d year of his age. Memphis Daily Appeal, 7/10/1859.

Died—On Wednesday evening last, at the residence of his father, in Memphis, after a short illness, William N. **ANDERSON**, of the firm of Anderson & Davis, of this town, in the 23d year of his age….At a called meeting of the Members of the Memphis Fire Company No. 7, the following preamble and resolutions, being offered by a member, were unanimously adopted: Whereas, the sad intelligence of the death of our much esteemed ex-member Mr. Wm. N. Anderson, having been received…..American Eagle, 2/14/1842.

On yesterday, Mr. O. P. **NEWBY**, having a difficulty with Mr. Jim **ANDREWS**, who had been in his employ, shot Mr. Andrews, and inflicted what is supposed to be a mortal wound. Mr. Andrews was not dead at sunset yesterday, but he was considered hopelessly wounded. Mr. Newby received two severe cuts with a knife, but they were not considered dangerous. We cannot obtain the particulars, and would not probably be justified in stating them, as the matter will no doubt be judicially investigated. Daily Memphis Enquirer, 9/16/1849.

The subscriber having determined to retire from business, will dispose of his present stock of Goods at New York prices…The stock consists of Dry Goods, Hardware, Hats, Boots, Shoes, Etc. Jos. J. **ANDREWS**. Daily Enquirer, 4/1/1847.

Died—In this city, on Monday evening, Capt. Samuel E. **ANDREWS**, aged 28 years. Capt. A. was a native of Philadelphia, and brother of our enterprising merchants, Messrs. Jos. I. and S. **ANDREWS**. Tri-Weekly Memphis Enquirer, Thurs., 11/26/1846.

The friends and acquaintances of Mrs. Sarah **ANDREWS** are respectfully invited to attend her funeral, from the residence of Chas. **RICHMOND** on Alabama street, this morning…. Memphis Daily Appeal, 5/5/1859.

Married, In this city on the 30th ult., by Rev. J. T. C. **COLLINS**, Mr. Wm. H. **ANDREWS** to Miss Julia A. **GRACE**. Memphis Weekly Appeal, 5/5/1858.

Married, In this city on the 12th inst., by Rev. A. **THOMAS**, Mr. John W. **APPLEBEE**, of Baltimore, Md., to Miss Maggie A. **DECKER**, of this city. Memphis Daily Appeal, 10/13/1859.

Married, On the 4th inst. by the Rev. W. H. **CRAWFORD**, Dr. D. __. **ARBUCKLE** and Miss Marion H. **LAKE**, all of Hardeman county, Tenn. Memphis Daily Eagle & Enquirer, 1/26/1853.

J. B. **ARCHER**—The name of this gentleman is widely and favorably known, as the ever-obliging clerk of the steamboat *Southerner*. We have the pleasure of introducing him to our readers in another character, as Capt. J. B. Archer, in command of the good steamboat *John Bell*. The *Bell* will leave our landing on Monday evening next at 4 o'clock for Louisville. She is a light boat, built expressly for low water and will be found just the boat to ascend the Ohio in. Memphis Daily Appeal, 9/11/1858. Married, In New Orleans, on the evening of the 22d inst., at the First Presbyterian Church, by the bride's father, Rev. Edson **HART**, Capt. J. B. Archer, of the steamer Southerner, to Miss Helen D. Hart, of Louisiana. Memphis Daily Appeal, 6/28/1859.

A poor fellow named Hugh **ARCHIBALD**, who has for sometime been suffering with chronic diarrhea, was yesterday so overcome with sickness that he lay down near a board pile in the Navy Yard, and there died....Memphis Daily Appeal, 9/21/1858.

S. S. **ARMISTEAD**, Sign and Fancy Painter, Leaf's Row, opposite Front Row. Memphis Daily Appeal, 10/13/1847.

Died, At the residence of her father, on the 1st inst., Ann C. S. **ARMOUR**, aged 20 years and 10 months. Her funeral will take place this morning at 11 o'clock, from St. Mary's Church....Memphis Weekly Appeal, 12/8/1858.

Died, On Sunday morning, November 9th, Mrs. Eliza G. Armour, wife of Mr. David **ARMOUR**, of this vicinity. The deceased was proverbial for her many virtues, but for none was she more esteemed, than for those social and Christian virtues which adorn the family circle—make home the abode of peace and the joy of her husband, the child and the friend. Weekly Appeal, 11/14/1845. Died, At his residence in this city, yesterday evening, October 29th, David Armour, aged 56 years. His friends and those of the family, are requested to attend his funeral, from his residence on Hernando street...Divine service by Rev. Mr. Coons. Memphis Daily Appeal, 10/30/1851.

We regret to state that at the fire last night, one of the Engines ran over a little boy and killed him almost instantly. The wheels passed over his abdomen. He was a son of Mr. Armour, of North Memphis, called Hillen **ARMOUR** – a fine youth of some sixteen summers. We never saw a more harrowing scene than was presented by the spectacle of the father over his dead son. Memphis Daily Eagle, 5/1/1850.

Married: At the Crutcher House, Nashville, on the 24th inst. by Rev. J. T. **EDGAR**, D.D., James **ARMOUR**, Esq., of Memphis, to Miss Emily S. Bowdoin, daughter of the Hon. Walter **BOWDOIN**, of Springfield, Mass. Memphis Whig, 10/29/1855.

Died, At noon, on the 14th inst., Lizzie Lee, daughter of Jno. D. and Achsah G. **ARMOUR**, aged one year, ten months and twenty-five days. The funeral will take place this evening (Wednesday) at 6 o'clock from the residence of Mr. W. **ARMOUR**.....Memphis Daily Eagle & Enquirer, 6/15/1853. Died, in Memphis, August 21st, 1855, Mrs. Achse Armour, consort of J. D. Armour, Esq., aged 26 years....The deceased leaves a bereaved husband and child and numerous relatives and friends to mourn her departure....Memphis Daily Appeal, 8/26/1855.

Married, At the residence of the bride's parents, near Rienzi, Tishomingo county, Miss., on the 14th January, 1858, by Rev. P. **HOYLE**, Mr. M. B. **ARMOUR** to Miss M. A. **MOORE**. Memphis Daily Appeal, 1/22/1858.

Died, On the 5th instant at the residence of Henry **LAKE**, in this vicinity, Mrs. Mary **ARMOUR**, in the eighty-first year of her age. Baltimore papers copy. Memphis Daily Appeal, 10/10/1856.

Died, At Jones' Bar, on the South Yuba river, California, on the 18th of February, Richard C. **ARMOUR**, son of David **ARMOUR**, formerly of Memphis, aged 25 years....Memphis Daily Appeal, 4/22/1857.

Died, On Friday, December 5th, Mrs. Elizabeth C., consort of Wm. **ARMOUR**, aged 50 years. Memphis Daily Appeal, 12/8/1851.

....Proceedings had in the Clerk's Office, Chancery side of the Common Law and Chancery Court of the city of Memphis, Monday, October the 17th, 1859. William **ARMOUR**, Jr., executor of David **ARMOUR**, deceased, Complainant, vs. Janette **ARMOUR**, and her guardian John H. **SNEED**, Defendants. *Bill suggesting insolvency of Estate.* In this cause, it is ordered that all persons interested or claiming to be creditors of the estate of David Armour, deceased, do come forward, exhibit their demands....Memphis Daily Appeal, 11/8/1859.

Died, At the residence of J. S. **CLAYTON**, Esq., near this city, on the 5ᵗʰ instant, Abraham W., infant son of B. L. and Mary **ARMSTRONG**, of Panola, Miss., aged 19 months. Memphis Appeal, 7/7/1855.

Married, In Hernando, Miss., on the 27th ult. by Rev. Wm. Carey **CRANE**, Mr. James **ARMSTRONG**, of Moulton, Ala., to Miss Lucy J. **McKISSACK**, of Desoto county. Memphis Daily Eagle & Enquirer, 1/12/1853.

Died, At the residence of Col. J. 1. **FOREMAN**, Arkansas, on Tuesday, the 20ᵗʰ inst., Mrs. Jennie ARMSTRONG **BARTLETT**. Her friends and those of her brother, J. W. **ARMSTRONG**, are invited to attend her funeral from Calvary Church, on To-Morrow Morning...Memphis Daily Appeal, 9/22/1859.

The friends and acquaintances of Mrs. M. A. **ARMSTRONG** are invited to attend the funeral of her daughter, Miss Alice E., this evening at 4 o'clock from the Episcopal Church. Died, Yesterday, July 29ᵗʰ, about the hour of twelve M., Miss Alice Elizabeth, eldest daughter of Mrs. Mary E. Armstrong of this city....Miss Armstrong was born the 8ᵗʰ day of December, 1830, and was, consequently, in the 26ᵗʰ year of her age....Her widowed mother and bereaved sisters and brother have all the sympathy and consolation which a sorrowing community can afford to them....Memphis Daily Appeal, 7/30/1856.

Married, On Tuesday evening, the 15ᵗʰ inst., at the residence of the bride's father on Union street, by Rev. R. C. **GRUNDY**, D.D., Mr. Martin J. **ARMSTRONG** to Miss Fredonia O. **PATRICK**, all of Memphis. Also, on the same evening, by the same, at the residence of the bride's mother on Beal street, Mr. Douglas **CALDWELL** to Miss Fannie **PIERCE**. Memphis Daily Appeal, 12/17/1857.

Married—On Sunday 14th inst., by N. G. **CURTIS**, Esq., Mr. Wm. **ARRINGTON** to Miss Caroline **NEVILLS**, all of Memphis. Daily Enquirer, 3/16/1847,

We mentioned on Wednesday that David T. **ASH**, proprietor of the Washington Street Theatre, had on the previous evening been severely wounded by the accidental discharge of a pistol....about ten o'clock yesterday morning....his pulse commenced sinking and he fell into a state of physical exhaustion. From this time he drooped rapidly, and at half past five o'clock last evening he breathed his last....Mr. Ash was an old citizen, widely known and highly esteemed....As he was unmarried, he had not assumed domestic relations....Saturday, 12/25/1858, Memphis Weekly Appeal, 12/29/1858. A gentleman of this city who was intimate with the late David T. Ash in his life time, received a letter yesterday from a sister of the deceased, who resides in Chester county, Pennsylvania, giving directions for the removal of the body to that locality. Mr. Ash, we believe, was a native of Chester county....Memphis Daily Appeal, 4/12/1859.

On Tuesday of last week, Mr. **ASHBRIDGE**, an attache of the Memphis and Ohio Railroad, met with an accident of so serious a nature that he died night before last from the effects of his wounds. He was sitting on the edge of a car, as the train passed over a bridge near the depot, and his back was injured by coming in contact with the timbers of it. A splinter from a stick of wood, which became displaced by his moving, passed through the fleshy part of his leg....Memphis Daily Appeal, 2/19/1857.

Died—At the Richmond House in this city on Monday the 7th inst., Dr. N. H. **ASHE**, a surgeon in the U.S. Army. We learn the deceased was a citizen of Ky., and was on his return home from the army in Mexico. His remains are deposited in the cenotaph, to await the arrival of friends. Louisville papers copy. Daily Memphis Enquirer, 2/8/1848.

The cheapest Clothing ever offered in the south and west is now to be found at the Old Kentuck Clothing Store, Exchange Square, facing the river, (new store.)—Boots, Shoes, Hats, Etc. Thos. P. **ASHE**. Daily Enquirer, 4/2/1847.

Married, On Wednesday, 2d inst., at the residence of G. **SMITHER**, Esq., by Rev. G. P. **SCHETKY**, Mr. W. J. **ASHFORD** to Miss Mary E. **SMITHER**, all of this city. Memphis Daily Appeal, 6/5/1858.

Married—By William **LAWRENCE** Esq. on Friday, the 26ᵗʰ ult. Mr. James L. **ATCHESON** to Miss Levina **STANLEY**,--both of this county. Memphis Advocate, 11/3/1827.

Married, In this city on the evening of the 30th ult., at the Cumberland Presbyterian Church by Rev. J. W. KNOTT, Mr. Benjamin H. ATKINSON to Miss Jennie A. Robinson, eldest daughter of Captain J. J. ROBINSON, all of this city. Memphis Daily Avalanche, 4/1/1859.

Died, In this city on the 5th inst., Alice Harvey, only daughter of J. H. and M. A. ATKINSON, aged one year and eleven months. Memphis Daily Appeal, 1/6/1857.

Died, At the residence of Dr. Davis G. TUCK, Christian county, Ky., on Friday, March 23d, 1849, Thomas T., infant son of Q. C. and Sarah E. ATKINSON, of Memphis, aged 14 months and 22 days. Weekly Memphis Eagle, 4/5/1849. Died, At the residence of Dr. Davis G. Tuck, Christian county, Ky., on Thursday, June 7th, 1849, Arabella West, infant daughter of Q. C. and Sarah E. Atkinson, of Memphis, aged 2 months and 10 days. Weekly Memphis Eagle, 6/21/1849.

Married. On the evening of April 18th by the Rev. D. C. PAGE, Mr. F. J. ATWOOD and Miss Rebecca WINDIATE—both of this place. Memphis Daily Appeal, 4/21/1854.

New Establishment. Franklin Book Bindery. The subscribers would respectfully inform the citizens of Memphis and the adjacent country that they are now prepared to execute all orders in their line...J. A. AUER & Co. Daily Memphis Enquirer, 5/21/1848.

A young lady, a native of Germany, who has resided in this city about one year, whose name was Teresa V. D. AUER, fell from the second story window of the Philadelphia House, at the corner of Front Row and Market alley, about 12 o'clock Thursday night, and sustained injuries which caused her death in a few minutes after the accident occurred....Memphis Daily Appeal, Sat., 9/10/1859.

Many of our readers, says the *Evening News* of yesterday, will be pained to learn the death of the amiable and accomplished wife of our esteemed fellow-citizen, Col. H. R. AUSTEN. Her melancholy decease occurred a few days ago, at Bailey's Springs, near Florence, Ala., whither the family had gone with the hope of benefitting her health....The mortal remains of Mrs. A. were brought to this city by railroad on Wednesday evening, and shortly after transferred to a boat bound to Vicksburg, where they will be interred....Memphis Daily Appeal, Sun., 9/20/1857.

House and Lot, For Sale. A comfortable frame dwelling with all the necessary outhouses, on the corner of Poplar and Third streets, near the Presbyterian Church, Memphis. Lem AUSTIN. The Appeal, 1/5/1844.

It having been resolved by the Democrats to celebrate the victory achieved in the election of Buchanan and Breckinridge, by the firing of cannon, Mr. Valentine AUSTIN was deputed to take charge of the cannon. Four discharges took place, when, owing to negligence not satisfactorily explained to us, Mr. Austin met with an accident which deprived him of life. We arrived on the ground a few minutes after the occurrence and found Mr. A. writhing in the agonies of death. His right arm was shot off near the elbow and his lungs were destroyed....He has left a family in indigent circumstances....The funeral of the late Brother Valentine Austin will be attended at Morris Cemetery on Sunday evening next....Memphis Daily Appeal, Wed., 11/12/1856.

Married, At the residence of Col. John C. BRAHAN in Panola county, Miss., on Wednesday morning, June 16, 1858, by Rev. Mr. Fagg, Col. James L. AUTREY, of Marshal county, to Miss Jennie C. VALLIANT. Memphis Daily Appeal, 6/17/1858.

Married, Near Lagrange, Fayette co., on Wednesday, the 12th inst., by Rev. D. C. PAGE, Mr. A. H. AVERY of Memphis, to Miss Henrietta S. POLK, of Fayette county. Memphis Daily Appeal, 4/22/1848. Died, In the vicinity of La Grange on Tuesday evening, the 17th inst., Herbert, infant son of A. H. and H. S. Avery, aged nine months and sixteen days. The friends and acquaintances of the family are invited to attend his funeral at 11 o'clock this morning from their residence on Main street, below Linden. Memphis Whig, 6/19/1856. Death of A. H. Avery, Esq.—It is with a melancholy regret....that we are called upon, this morning, to record the death of the above named gentleman. This sad event occurred yesterday afternoon, at the residence of Henry B. **CHILES**, in this city, where he was temporarily resting, after having sought in vain, in a more genial climate, during the past winter, some shadow of relief from that great enemy of mankind—consumption!....Mr. Avery was a native of Buffalo, N.Y., and at the time of his death, was in his thirty-seventh year. Since 1850, with only short intervals of relaxation, he has been engaged as reporter and associate editor of several journals of this city....Funeral invitation....Services by Rev. Geo. P. **SHETKY**, at Grace Church. Hacks will be in attendance to convey friends to Winchester Cemetery, where the remains will be deposited. Memphis Daily Avalanche, 5/9/1859.

Died, In this city on Saturday last, Charles Polk, infant son of Hamilton and Henrietta **AVERY**—aged nine months and twenty-one days. Memphis Daily Appeal, Mon., 11/10/1851.

Died—On the 6th inst. in this City, Dr. Nathan **AVERY**, 54 years of age. The Tri-Weekly Memphis Enquirer, 3/10/1846.

We are authorized to announce Wm. T. **AVERY** Esq., a candidate to represent Hardeman, Fayette and Shelby, in the State Legislature. American Eagle, 4/21/1843. Married, On the 16th inst., at Athenia, the residence of Mrs. Lumpkin, in Mississippi, by the Rev. W. C. **ROBB**, Wm. T. Avery, of this city, to Miss Chastilette (?) **JONES**, of Mississippi. Memphis Daily Appeal, 12/23/1852.

A large deputation from the fire department attended funerals of the late Capt. Wm. H. **AXTEL** and Martin **GLANCEY**. The deceased were both members of Fire Company No. 6, the former having served as commander of the company. Memphis Daily Appeal, 9/13/1859.

Married: On Thursday evening Dec. 10th, 1857, at the residence of Samuel **MENDENHALL**, by Rev. L. D. **MULLINS**, Mr. W. H. **AXTELL**, of this city, to Miss Sarah A. Mendenhall, of Shelby county. Memphis Evening Ledger, 12/17/1857. Died, Near White's Station in this county, on the 6th inst., Mrs. Sarah Mendenhall, consort of W. _. Axtell, aged 26 years. Memphis Daily Appeal, 4/10/1859.

Married, On Wednesday evening, the 12th inst., at the residence of James **ROBINSON**, Esq., by Rev. G. W. **COONS**, Mr. T. P. **AYDLETT**, of this city, to Miss Susan M. **HUTCHINGS**, of this vicinity. Memphis Daily Eagle, 6/14/1850. Died, On the morning of the 3rd inst., Percy, infant son of Thos. P. and Sue Aydlett. The friends of the family are respectfully invited to attend the funeral This Day (Friday) at 2 o'clock P.M. from their residence on Adams street. Divine services by the Rt. Rev. J. H. **OTEY**. Memphis Daily Appeal, 12/4/1857.

Married, on Saturday last, at the residence of Dr. E. F. **WATKINS**, by the Rev. P. **ALSTON**, Joseph **AYRES**, Esq., late of New Orleans, to Miss Mary G. **WYATT**. Weekly American Eagle, Thurs., 8/14/1846.

Died, At Green Plains, Ark., on Thursday the 29th, Mr. Joseph F. **AYRES**, brother of T. S. **AYRES**, of this city. Memphis Daily Eagle, 9/3/1850.

Died. Yesterday, June 27th, at the Richmond House, after a long and painful illness, Dr. K. H. **AYRES**, formerly of Greene county, East Tennessee, in the 35th year of his age...East Tennessee papers please copy. Memphis Whig, 6/28/1856.

Married, On Thursday evening, the 3d inst., at the residence of R. **TOPP**, Esq., by Rev. Geo. W. **COONS**, Samuel W. **AYRES**, of this city, to Miss Elizabeth L. Cook, daughter of Judge Wm. A. **COOK**, dec'd., formerly of Nashville, Tenn. Memphis Daily Eagle, 1/4/1850. Died, Of congestion of the brain, in the afternoon of Friday, the 22d inst., at half past 6 o'clock, Samuel W., Jr., son of Samuel W. and E. L. Ayres, aged 8 years, 8 months and 8 days....Memphis Daily Appeal, 7/31/1859.

Died, At the St. Nicholas Hotel, New York, while on a visit to that city, on Sunday, September 28th, 1856, Treadwell S. Ayres, Jr., only son of Treadwell S. and C. M. **AYRES**, aged 13 years and 28 days. The friends and acquaintances of the family are invited to attend his funeral from the residence of his father, on

Second street, east of Court square, on Wednesday, October 29th at 10 o'clock A.M. Funeral services by Rev. J. W. **KNOTT**. Memphis Daily Appeal, 10/29/1856.

Died, Yesterday morning, the 20th inst., Nannie, youngest child of Mrs. M. F. **BACCHUS**. The funeral will take place this morning at 10 o'clock from the family residence on the corner of Third and Madison streets. Memphis Daily Avalanche, 1/21/1859.

Married, On Wednesday evening, the 24th inst., by Rev. Coons, Mr. William **BADGER** to Miss Harriett, eldest daughter of Mr. Charles **MILLER**, all of this city. Weekly Memphis Eagle, 12/31/1849.

We regret to learn that Mr. Mathew D. **BAIL** died suddenly of appoplexy in this city Wednesday evening. Memphis Daily Appeal, Fri., 9/30/1859.

The friends and acquaintances of Sylvester **BAILEY** are requested to attend the funeral of his son Robert B., this (Wednesday) Morning at 10 o'clock, from his residence below Fort Pickering, to Morris' Cemetery. Memphis Daily Eagle & Enquirer, Wed., 5/18/1853.

We invite the attention of our community to the professional card of Dr. W. T. **BAILEY**, who has chosen our growing and thriving city for his future home. The Doctor comes among us from old South Carolina, with a high reputation as a skillful and experienced physician....Memphis Daily Appeal, 1/12/1858.

Married, On Friday, the 27th of November, 1857, by Rev. Thomas **TAYLOR**, Dr. B. F. **BAIRD** to Miss Julia P. **MITCHELL**, all of Fayette county, Tenn. Memphis Daily Appeal, 12/4/1857.

Died. At his residence near Lafayette Depot, Fayette county, Ten., at 6 o'clock on the evening of February 20th, after a painful illness of twelve months, Anne Baird, consort of John L. **BAIRD**, and sister of our townsman Edward **DASHIELL**....As a wife, a christian, sister, friend and neighbor, she harmoniously blended the virtues which most strikingly exalt and embellish the character of the true woman....Maryland papers please copy. Memphis Daily Appeal, 3/4/1855.

A man by the name of Frederick **BAIRN** went to the bayou yesterday morning for the purpose of drowning a dog, when taking a fit, he fell forward with his face in the water and was drowned. Memphis Daily Appeal, 4/21/1854.

Married, On the 20th inst., in St. Francis county, Ark., by Rev. Jacob **HARE**, E. M. **BAKER**, Esq., to Miss Fanny **BOONE**, all of that county. Memphis Daily Appeal, 7/22/1859.

Married. In Shelby County on Thursday evening last, at the residence of Col. Edward **WARD**, by the Right Rev. Bishop Otey, John W. **BAKER** Esq. of Virginia, to Miss Mary Lang Florida **JONES**, daughter of the late Col. Benjamin B. **JONES**, of Alabama. Randolph Recorder, Fri., 6/5/1835.

Married, On the 18th inst., Mr. John W. **BAKER**, of this city, to Miss Annie E. **JONES**, of Middleton, Ky. Friend John has left us and taken to himself a lovely bride, from her "old Kentucky home." May unalloyed happiness and prosperity attend him whereever he may go. Memphis Daily Avalanche, 8/20/1858.

Married—On the 24th(?) December, '45, by Rev. N. M. **GAYFORD**, Mr. Peter **BAKER** to Miss Rebecca **WILEY**, all of Memphis, Tenn. Memphis Enquirer, 1/1/1846.

Married, On the 16th instant in St. Francis county, Ark., by Hon. J. M. **GRIGSBY**, Mr. W. R. **BAKER** to Mrs. S. N. **PURYEAR**, all of St. Francis county. Memphis Daily Appeal, 10/22/1859.

Married. In Somerville at the residence of Dr. Maury by Rev. Dr. Page of our city, Mr. W. Rufus **BAKER**, of Shelby county, to Miss Lucy **MAURY**, of Somerville. Memphis Daily Appeal, 4/1/1855. Died. In Somerville on Monday morning, the 18th inst., at 1 o'clock, at the residence of her father, Dr. H. W. **MAURY**, Mrs. Lucy Jane, consort of Mr. Rufus Baker. The subject of the above notice was born in Fayette county, Tenn., on the 1st of August, 1834.... Tenderly reared by fond and affectionate parents and surrounded not only by deeply devoted brothers and sister....But the blow falls heaviest and with most insupportable severity upon the torn and anguished heart of him who, but a few short weeks ago, claimed her at the bridal altar....Memphis Whig, 6/20/1855.

Died, At his residence in this county, ten miles from Memphis, on Saturday evening last, Mr. Wm. F. **BAKER**, one of our most valuable and highly esteemed citizens. Memphis Eagle & Enquirer, 3/3/1852. I offer for sale a most valuable plantation eight miles Southeast from Memphis and one mile from the Pigeon Roost Plank Road, containing about eight hundred Acres....Geo. L. **HOLMES**, Administrator of Wm. F. Baker, dec'd. nov18. Memphis Appeal, 1854.

We are pained to learn that Hugh **BALCH**, an interesting son of C. **BALCH**, Esq., of Raleigh, accidentally killed himself while hunting yesterday near his home. Memphis Appeal, 10/5/1852.

Died, At his residence near Raleigh, on the 21st inst., John K. **BALCH**, former Sheriff of this county, in the 31st year of his age. Memphis Enquirer, 3/25/1837.

Arkansas Land Agency. The undersigned will attend to the payment of taxes, location of land claims, investigation of land titles, purchasing, selling or examination of land in any part of the State, with quickness and fidelity, and on reasonable terms. The surveys and other field operations will be under the immediate eye of one of the undersigned, a practical surveyor, who has traversed every portion of the State...D. J. **BALDWIN**, H. B. **ALLIS**. Memphis Eagle, 6/22/1848.

Married, On the 10th inst., at the residence of the bride's father near Macon, Fayette county, Tenn., by Rev. Geo. W. **PLATTENBURG**, Mr. Gaston **BALDWIN**, of Arkansas, to Miss Samuella **SWIFT**. Memphis Daily Appeal, 2/16/1858.

Memphis & Charleston Railroad. The friends of this enterprise will be gratified to hear that Mr. Wm. **BALDWIN**, the track layer, has arrived in our city and will proceed immediately upon the discharge of his duties in laying down the rails eastwardly from La Grange, completing two miles per week for the distance of twenty-seven miles....Memphis Daily Appeal, 3/6/1855.

On the morning of October 15, Martha Jane, consort of B. P.(?) **BALL**, left the earth form and passed from our sight to the glorious realms of eternal light....Memphis Daily Appeal, 10/20/1858.

Married—By Rev. J. E. **DOUGLAS**, May 31st, in Marshall county, Miss., Mr. Carroll F. **BALLARD** and Miss Martha A. **MOORE**. Memphis Daily Avalanche, 6/4/1859. (Author's Note: Name **BULLARD** in the Memphis Daily Appeal, 6/8/1859.)

Tribute of Respect. Odd Fellows Hall, Collierville, May 1, 1857. Whereas, In the All-wise dispensation of the Creator of the Universe, we have been called to pay the last tribute of respect to our beloved Brother, Dr. H. G. **BALLARD**, who departed this life on yesterday, at his residence in Fayette county....Resolved, That we deeply sympathize with the disconsolate widow and children....Memphis Daily Appeal, 5/20/1857.

Died, In this city on the morning of the 20th instant, after a protracted illness, Samuel O. **BALLARD**, aged forty-one years. The remains of the deceased will be removed to Somerville this morning, there to be interred by those of his wife. The deceased, we believe, was a native of Baltimore, but from early manhood has been a citizen of West Tennessee, and was, at the time of his death, Collector of Customs at this port....Memphis Daily Appeal, 4/21/1857.

Married, On yesterday morning at the residence of John B. **CONNONALLY**, in Marshall county, Miss., by Rev. Mr. Rodgers, Col. David W. **BALLEW**, Senator in the Tennessee Legislature, from the counties of McMinn, Polk, Meigs and Monroe, to Miss Mattie A. **LOW**. Memphis Daily Appeal, 1/2/1856.

Died: In Baltimore, Maryland, on the 8th inst., James Monroe Bankhead, eldest son of Gen. Jas. **BANKHEAD**, U.S.A. Memphis Whig, 8/20/1855.

Smith P. **BANKHEAD**, Attorney At Law, Memphis, Tenn....Memphis Daily Appeal, 4/8/1856.

Whereas the Governor of Tennessee, has heretofore issued his proclamation setting apart Thursday the 25 inst. to be kept as a day of thanksgiving and prayer throughout this commonwealth: Therefore, I Enoch **BANKS**, Mayor of the Town of Memphis, recommend to the good people of our town its observance as a day of thanksgiving and praise...Daily Enquirer, 11/24/1847. Died, At Bailey's Springs, Ala., on Saturday, 24th inst., Hon. Enoch Banks, of this city, in the 60th year of his age. Memphis Appeal, 7/31/1852. The friends and acquaintances of the late Enoch Banks, Esq., are invited to attend his funeral, from his late residence on the corner of Second and Poplar streets, this evening...Memphis Appeal, 8/12/1852.

Died—On Wednesday the 9th inst. at the residence of his Son, in the vicinity of this place, Gen. James **BANKS**, a native of Pennsylvania, and lately an emigrant to this county....Memphis Advocate, 7/12/1828.

Died. At his residence in De Soto county, Miss., on Saturday last, Mr. Lemuel **BANKS**, an old and much esteemed citizen of that county. Memphis Appeal, Wed., 9/13/1854.

Died, At the residence of his father in Panola county, Miss., on the 28th ult., James F. Banks, son of Wm. C. and Rebecca **BANKS**, aged 10 years, 1 month and 9 days. Memphis Daily Appeal, 9/27/1855.

Married, On the 20th inst., by Rev. T. C. **COLLINS**, Mr. Joseph **BANNER**, of Des Arc, Ark., to Miss Rachel _ove, of this city. Memphis Weekly Appeal, 3/31/1858.

Died—In this place on Sunday the 4th inst., after an illness of a few hours John Mortimer, son of Jesse and Margaret **BANVARD** (?), aged 10 years, 9 months and 2 days. Louisville and New York papers please copy. Weekly Appeal, 10/9/1846.

Married: On the 30th ult. at the Second Presbyterian Church by Rev. J. H. **GRAY**, Mr. Joseph **BARBIERE**, Jr., to Miss Mary G. Levett, eldest daughter of Joseph S. **LEVETT**, Esq., all of this city. Memphis Whig, 11/1/1855.

Married, On the 22nd December at Council Bend, Ark. By Joseph D. **WILCOMB**, Esq., Mr. G. N. **BARBOUR**, late of New Madrid, Mo., to Mrs. Mary Anna **WILLIAMS** of the former place. Memphis Appeal, 1/2/1854.

Dr. J. M. **BARCLAY**, Having located permanently in Memphis, respectfully offers his professional services to the public. Office near the Gayoso House. Weekly Appeal, 4/11/1845.

Petition for Divorce. James **BARDING** vs. Pamly V. **BARDING**. Ref. Docket, Circuit Court, February Term, 1844. On motion, and for satisfactory reasons shown to the Court, it is ordered that publication be made in some public newspaper printed in the town of Memphis for three successive weeks, the first insertion to be made two months before the next term of this court, commanding the said Pamly Barding to cause her personal appearance in this cause to be entered in this cause, on or before the first day of the next term of this court, and plead, answer, or demur to the said petition plea in this cause for divorce, or the same will be taken as confessed and set for hearing ex parte at the next ensuing term of this Court. Sam'l R. **BROWN**, Cl'k. The petition charges a willful and malicious desertion on the part of the defendant without any cause, for two years previous to filing said petition, and prays that complainant may be divorced from the bonds of matrimony. R. A. **ANDERSON**, Sam F. **MOSELEY**, Solicitors for comp'nt. The Appeal, 3/8/1844.

All persons having claims against the estate of the late A. P. **BARDON** will present them as per law to me. Chas. M. **DENIE**, Adm'r. Memphis Appeal, 1/4/1854.

Married, On the evening of the 20th instant, at her father's residence, by Rev. A. **COWAN**, Mr. J. **BARKER** to Miss J. **CLAY**, all of Tippah county, Miss. Memphis Weekly Appeal, 6/2/1858.

Died, At the residence of her son, David W. **MUNROE**, at Hickory Wythe, Fayette county, Tenn., on the 25th ultimo, Mrs. Mary **BARNARD**, in the 76th year of her age. She was born in the city of Richmond, Va., November 25th, 1776, but has been a resident of Hickory Wythe for the last fifteen years...The papers of Richmond, Va., and Boston, Mass., are requested to copy. Memphis Eagle & Enquirer, 2/24/1852.

Married, On Sunday evening the 13th inst. by Rev. J. E. **DOUGLASS**, Dr. J. J. **BARNETT** to Mrs. Minerva B. **BLOUNT**, both of Rossville, Fayette county. Memphis Daily Appeal, 12/22/1857.

Died, On the 23d inst. at the residence of his son-in-law, Dr. Murphy, in Desoto county, Miss., Rev. John **BARNETT**, of Henderson, Ky., in the 70th year of his age. Memphis Eagle & Enquirer, 2/26/1853.

Departed this life on the 2d inst., on board the steamboat Saladin, Mrs. Emily Barns, in the 34th year of her age, of Yallabusha county, Miss., and consort of S. **BARNS**. She labored under a most excruciating disease for about four months, all of which she bore with Christian fortitude. She was a member of the Primitive Baptist church....She has left a husband and five children and a numerous circle of acquaintances to mourn her loss..... Memphis Enquirer, 6/4/1848.

We understand that Capt. Wm. D. **BARRETT** has purchased the steamer Duroc, for the St. Louis and Memphis trade...Having become a resident of our city, and having an extensive acquaintance in St. Louis...Memphis Appeal, 1/28/1852.

Died, On the 19th August, 1856, in Fayette county, Tenn., near Oakland, Wm. McNeil, son of W. B. and A. H. **BARROW**, aged two years and seven months. Memphis Daily Appeal, 10/8/1856.

Married, On Sunday last, at the residence of Mr. M. I. **MILLER**, by the Rev. T. L. **GRACE**, pastor of the Catholic Church, Dr. Daniel **BARRY**, to Miss Eliza J. **MOORE**, all of this city. Memphis Appeal, Fri., 6/4/1852.

Departed this life, at Raleigh, on the 21st inst., Martha Ann, infant daughter of Henry A. and N. L. **BARRY**. Weekly Appeal, 6/26/1846.

We are authorized to announce V. D. **BARRY** as a candidate for Alderman of 3d Ward.... Memphis Appeal, 2/18/1848. Hon. V. D. Barry died at his residence in this city yesterday evening of apoplexy. He was fifty-seven years of age. Judge Barry was a prominent lawyer, a thorough classical scholar, and had occupied the circuit bench in this State for several years. His death will be very much regretted in the circle of his numerous friends. The friends and acquaintances of the late V. D. Barry are invited to attend his funeral this morning at 10:00 o'clock, from his residence on Market St. Memphis Appeal, 4/29/1853. (Author's Note: Name given as Valentine D. in another notice.)

Died—at Purdy on the 17th ult., after a protracted illness which she bore with Christian fortitude, Mrs. Frances A. Barry, consort of Dr. Wm. **BARRY**, in the 26th year of her age. For 13 years has the deceased been a worthy and exemplary member of the Presbyterian Church...She was a most excellent and devoted wife, a kind mother and sincere friend...We would for the sake of a fond father and devoted husband, that our sad chronicle could end here; but on the 27th ult., it pleased an all wise Providence to visit again that afflicted circle, and restore to a lost mother's arms her infant son, Wm. Henry Barry, aged 3 months and 18 days. Thus robbed of a partner and child, may the bereaved husband find consolation in the soothing balm, that his loss is their eternal gain. Weekly Appeal, 6/6/1845.

Married, On Tuesday, the 1st inst., at the residence of the bride's father, in Crittenden county, Ark., Mr. F. H. **BARTON** to Miss Alice E. **FOGLEMAN**, all of Crittenden county. Memphis Daily Appeal, 2/2/1859.

Died, In Crittenden county, Arkansas, July 19, Richard Hardin Barton, son of Jas. F. and Frances **BARTON**, aged two years and two days. Louisville *Journal* please copy. Memphis Daily Appeal, 7/22/1857.

An Extra from the office of the Empire *Democrat* announces the mournful fact that Roger **BARTON** is no more. He expired at his residence 5 miles north of Holly Springs, on Sunday last, 4th inst. His disease was acute rheumatism of the stomach which he suffered with great fortitude for more than two weeks....As a politician he ranked first in consistent _____ to Democratic principles and to Southern rights. He has been for many years the known favorite of a large portion of the Democracy of North Mississippi for U.S. Senator. It was but recently that the President voluntarily tendered to him the position of Consul to Havana, which he declined. In all the social relations of life, Maj. Barton was genial....Maj. Barton was a native of Tennessee and pursued a long and useful career as a practitioner of law in West Tennessee....Memphis Appeal, 3/6/1855.

Died, On the 14th of November, 1857, at Kickapoo, Texas, J. Quitman Barton, son of Thomas M. and Harriet A. **BARTON**. Huntsville Democrat please copy. Memphis Weekly Appeal, 1/6/1858.

Married, At Collierville, on the 8th instant by Rev. S. **WATSON**, Dr. John T. **BASKERVILLE**, of Memphis Conference, and Mrs. A. T. J. **HARE**. Memphis Daily Appeal, 1/18/1857.

Died. In Lagrange, Ten. April 27th, Joseph B., son of R. J. and Eliza **BASS**. Memphis Daily Appeal, 5/2/1855.

......This truth was painfully impressed upon our minds as we stood by the bedside of our friend, Mrs. Martha Bass, wife of Dr. Thomas C. **BASS**, and daughter of James **WILLIAMS**, formerly of Sumner county, Tenn...Could the skill of her physicians, the attention of her friends, or the intense anxiety of her husband have prevailed, she would not now be numbered with the dead...on Friday evening, between four and five o'clock, she breathed her last, in the 38th year of her age, having her husband and 3 small children to mourn her loss. Being affected with congestion of the brain, she spoke but few words during her illness, yet we have hope in her death. The Petersburg papers will please copy. Weekly Appeal, Fri., 11/6/1846. The subscriber offers for sale, his tract of land containing 300 acres. 75 of which are in cultivation and under good fence, with good comfortable buildings and every necessary out-house, first rate stables, etc. It is one of the best stands in the county for a tavern, having the advantage of the roads leading from Memphis to La Grange and to Holly Springs, also on the road leading from Somerville to Hernando.....T. C. Bass, Shelby county, Oct. 25,1839. Memphis Enquirer.

Miles **KERR**, who killed Green B. **BATEMAN**, at the mouth of Old River on the 10th inst., was examined yesterday before his Hon. Judge King. The witnesses were examined on the part of the State by J. P. **CARUTHERS**, Attorney General, and D. M. **CURRIN** Esq., and for the defendant by Messrs. Cox and Brown. Kerr was held to bail in the sum of $8,000 to appear at the first term of the Circuit Court in Tipton County. Mr. K. at once offered such bail as was accepted, and set at liberty. Kerr had voluntarily placed himself in the custody of the Sheriff of this County. Memphis Enquirer, 4/20/1848.

Married. On the 11th instant by the Rev. Dr. J. H. **GRAY** at "Old Homestead," Captain Morgan **BATEMAN**, of the Julia Dean, to Miss Annie E. **EDWARDS**, of this city....Memphis Appeal, 5/12/1854.

Married—On the 4th inst., by the Rev. Mr. Cowen, Mr. W. H. **BATEMAN**, of this city, to Miss Sarah Elizabeth, daughter of Calvin **GOODMAN**, Esq., of DeSoto county, Mi. Daily Enquirer, 2/6/1847.

Married. At Elm Wood, near Jackson, Tenn., on Wednesday evening, 11th instant, by the Rev. J. W. **RODGERS**, Dr. Lucius L. **BATTLE**, of Arkansas, to Miss Martha B., second daughter of Col. Robert I. **CHESTER**, Marshal of West Tennessee. Memphis Appeal, 10/17/1854.

Report of the Board of Health. For the last 24 hours, ending 12 o'clock, M, July 24.....Mrs. Alice **BATTON**, age 20.....Memphis Enquirer, 7/25/1849.

We are authorized to announce John V. **BAUGH** as the Democratic candidate for the Office of Sheriff of Shelby County at the ensuing March election. Memphis Appeal, 2/20/1852. The friends and acquaintances of R. D. and John V. Baugh are requested to attend the funeral of their late brother, A. B. **BAUGH**, from the residence of O. H. **LYTLE** (or **LYDE**), on Second street, this Thursday evening at four o'clock. Memphis Daily Appeal, Thurs., 4/17/1856.

Married, On Wednesday evening, January 14th, 1852, by the Rev. Joseph E. **DOUGLASS**, Mr. Wm. A. **BAUGH** to Miss Julina P. **STONE** – all of Fayette county, Tenn. Memphis Eagle & Enquirer, 1/22/1852.

Died, On the 3rd of April, 1859, at her residence in Marshall county, Miss., Mrs. Mary Ann, wife of W. P. **BAUGHMAN**, and daughter of Ephraim and Christiana **HOOVER**, in the 24th year of her age. Memphis Daily Appeal, 4/14/1859.

Conrad **BAUMGARTNER**, Architect, Draftsman & Surveyor, Respectfully informs the public that he has opened an office at his residence at the corner of Second and Jackson streets, Fort Pickering. American Eagle, 4/21/1843.

Notice is hereby given to all persons having claims against the Estate of Abraham **BAYLISS**, dec'd, that the insolvency of said estate has been duly suggested to the Clerk of the county court of Shelby county, Ten......Memphis Enquirer, 5/13/1837.

Married, in this city, on Friday evening last, by the Rev. G. W. **COONS**, Mr. Brunson **BAYLISS**, to Mrs. Maria L. **LEWIS**, all of Memphis. American Eagle, Thurs., 10/21/1847.

John Y. **BAYLISS**, Cotton Factor. American Eagle, 9/29/1843.

Married, On the 2nd inst., at the residence of Col. John **McKINNON**, of Marshall county, Miss., Mr. Wm. **BAYLISS**, of this city, to Miss Sarah B. **McINTYRE**. Memphis Eagle, 9/5/1850.

Married, At the residence of Dr. A. B. C. **DUBOSE**, on the 15th instant, by Rev. J. E. **DOUGLASS**, President of the M.F. Institute, George W. **BAYNE**, Esq., of Memphis, to Miss Lizzie R. **DUBOSE**, of the county. Memphis Daily Appeal, 1/17/1856.

Married, Near Raleigh, on Sunday, the 4th instant, by Rev. Mr. Dewoody, John **BEAMISH** to Miss E. **MURRAY**, all of this city. Memphis Weekly Appeal, 4/14/1858.

Married, At the Whitmore House on the 30th of July, at five o'clock in the morning, by Rev. Z. H. **WHITEMORE**, Mr. R. C. **BEARD**, of Holly Springs, and Miss J. G. **BLEDSOE** of DeSoto county, Miss. Memphis Daily Appeal, 8/9/1856.

Married, On the 13th Instant by the Rev. Jeremiah **WILLIAMS**, Rev. T. L. **BEARD**, of the Memphis Conference, to Mrs. Elizabeth **WILEY**, of Shelby county, Tenn. Memphis Daily Appeal, 11/15/1855.

Married—On Tuesday the 19th inst. by the Rev. Mr. Johnson, Mr. Robt. E. **BEASELEY** of Holmes county, Miss., to Miss Mary Jane, eldest daughter of Maj. **BARTON** of Shelby county, Tenn. Memphis Enquirer, 2/22/1839.

The friends and acquaintances of the late Thos. B. **BEATTIE** are requested to attend his funeral at 3 ½ o'clock this afternoon from the residence of Mr. Pugh on Madison street. Services by the Rev. Dr. Gray. Memphis Appeal, 10/12/1854. The remains of our townsman Dr. T. B. Beattie were attended to the grave yesterday....where he was buried by the City Guards with military honors. Memphis Appeal, 10/14/1854.

Died—On the morning of Wednesday the 22d, in the eighth year of his age, James Marye, son of Thomas B. **BEATTY**, Esq. Memphis Enquirer, 5/24/1839. Died, in this vicinity, on the 25th inst., of a chronic affection of the liver, Thomas B. Beatty, formerly of Boling Green, Caroline County, Va. He emigrated to this place in the fall of 1839.......American Eagle, 9/30/1842.

Married, On the 13th day of May, 1856, by Rev. J.S. **WINFORD**, Dr. A. **BEATY** and Miss Mary L., daughter of William and Ann M. **BOND**, (the latter deceased,) all of Shelby county, Tenn. Memphis Daily Appeal, 5/22/1856.

Died. In this city, on the 11th inst., George Coons, infant son of Arthur and Lucilla M. **BEATY**, aged 14 months. Weekly American Eagle, 9/17/1846.

Died—On the steamer Albatross on her passage from Newport Barracks, Ky. to this city, John T. **BEAVERS**, a native of Prince William county, Va., and a member of Capt. Walker's company in the new Rifle Regiment. His remains were yesterday interred in this city, attended by his late comrades. Daily Enquirer, 4/6/1847.

Having obtained letters of Administration on the estate of John **BECHTOLD**, deceased, at the October Term, 1855, of the County Court of Shelby county, all persons having claims....John **BAUM**, Adm'r....Memphis Daily Appeal, 10/11/1855.

Having sold out my entire stock of Medicines, etc. to Dr. Jas. **BECK**, I return my thanks to my former patrons and customers. S. T. **TONCRAY**. Oct. 11/1839. Memphis Enquirer.

Married. On Tuesday, July 20th, 1855, Mr. Joshua E. **BECK** to Miss Lucy A. **NOONER**, of the county of Tipton and vicinity of Salem. Memphis Daily Appeal, 8/9/1855.

I have a comfortable Dwelling House in South Memphis for rent, formerly occupied by W. S. **BOLING**, with all necessary conveniences. William C. **BECK**. Memphis Enquirer, 1/27/1846. Yesterday evening an altercation took place in this city, between Mr. Wm. C. Beck and Mr. J. M. **WILSON**, partners in business, which resulted in a recontre, in which Mr. Beck received several stabs with a knife. The wounds are not deemed fatal. We cannot say how the difficulty originated. Memphis Enquirer, 10/25/1848. Died. In this City on the evening of the 11th inst., in the 39th year of her age, Mrs. Delia Beck, consort of Mr. William C. Beck of this place. She has left an afflicted husband and eight little children to mourn their irreparable loss. The deceased was a worthy and consistent member of the Baptist Church...Memphis Enquirer, 10/15/1848.

Died on Thursday morning last, at 6 o'clock, Mr. Henry **BECKEL**, of the firm of J. & H. Beckel, Fort Smith, Ark. I.O.O.F.—The members of Memphis Lodge No. 6 and Chickasaw Lodge No. 8, are requested to meet at their hall at 4 o'clock P.M., Sunday, May 1st, for the purpose of escorting the remains of our late Brother, Henry Beckel, of Frontier Lodge No. 3, I.O.O.F., Fort Smith, Ark., from Morris Cemetery to steamer Jennie Whipple. Memphis Daily Appeal, 5/1/1859.

Died, at the residence of her father, B. W. **BEDFORD**, Sr., in Panola county, Miss., on Friday, August 31st, at 4 o'clock, P.M., Miss Martha Bedford, aged about 15 years. An only daughter—an only sister— gone!....A pupil both of the Memphis Female College and the Cumberland Presbyterian Sabbath School but a few short months....Memphis Daily Appeal, 9/4/1855.

Messrs. H. H. and H. L. **BEDFORD**, Attorneys at Law.—Attention is called to the card of these gentlemen in this morning's paper. These young gentlemen have recently removed from Panola county, Miss., with the view of making Memphis the theatre for their professional ambition. They graduated with high honor at the Lebanon Law School....Memphis Daily Appeal, 6/2/1858.

Delta Kappa Epsilon Hall. Cumberland University, October 20, 1858. Whereas, it has pleased the Supreme Ruler of the Universe....to remove by death....our much beloved and highly esteemed brother, H. H. **BEDFORD**, of Memphis, Tenn....Memphis Weekly Appeal, 11/10/1858.

Died, On the 12[th](?) inst. of cholera, Robert Emmet Bedford, youngest son of James and Mary **BEDFORD**, aged two years and eight months. New Orleans Picayune and Delta please copy. Memphis Daily Appeal, 5/15/1855.

Died: In this city, on Sunday last, Mr. Jabez **BEHARREL**, in the 26th year of his age. The deceased was for many years a merchant of this place, and had by his amiable disposition, his strict integrity and general deportment, endeared himself to a large circle of friends who will long hold him in pleasing remembrance and lament his untimely end. Memphis Eagle, Wed., 8/30/1848.

Married, In this city on the 28th inst., by J. **WALDRAN**, Esq., Mr. H. D. **BELL** to Miss Susan **BONDURANCE**, all of this city. Memphis Daily Appeal, 9/30/1858.

Died, At the house of Thomas **CHAMBLISS**, near Memphis, Tenn., Mr. James G. **BELL**, in the fiftieth year of his age. Petersburg, Va. Papers please copy. Memphis Eagle & Enquirer, 4/16/1852.

The friends and acquaintances of John and Margaret **BELL**, are invited to attend the Funeral of their infant daughter, Mary Emma, this morning, at 9 o'clock, from their residence on Pontotoc street, between Main and Shelby. Memphis Appeal, 7/17/1851. The friends and acquaintances of John and Margaret Bell are invited to attend the funeral of their son, John C., this afternoon…Memphis Appeal, 5/14/1852.

The Jackson, Miss., papers contain the announcement of the death of Joseph E. **BELL**, a teacher in the public schools of that city, who died on the 30th ult., in the 25th year of his age. Mr. Bell resided for a short time in this city in 1857, and was for a brief period connected with the press in this city. Memphis Daily Avalanche, 5/9/1859.

Married, on the 6th inst., at 5 o'clock P.M. by the Rev. S. **DENNIS**, Mr. Thomas W. **BELL** to Mrs. Mary M. **WILLIS**, all of South Memphis. Memphis Enquirer, 12/13/1848.

Died, In Haywood county, Tenn., at Bell's Station, on the Memphis and Charleston Railroad, on Saturday, December 4, at 1 o'clock P.M., Walter **BELL**, aged 81 years, 3 months and 9 days. The deceased was _____ by weeping friends to the grave on the Sunday evening following….Memphis Weekly Appeal, 12/29/1858.

Married—On the 24th inst. by Joseph **LOCKE**, Esq., Mr. Wm. Hacket **BELL**, late of Hide County, North Carolina, to Miss Susan **WILLIAMS**, of this county. Memphis Enquirer, 5/11/1836.

Departed this life in Berlin, Hardeman county, 2d of February, 1855, Mrs. Pheby R. Bellote, consort of Clement **BELLOTE**, of a painful disease of the nervous system….leaving an affectionate husband and many kind children to mourn her irreparable loss. The deceased was born in Dinwiddy county, Va., on the 6th of December, 1805. In the thirteenth year of her age she….attached herself to the M.E. Church….On the 22d of December, 1825, she was married to C. Bellote….Memphis & Arkansas Christian Advocate please copy. Memphis Daily Appeal, 2/23/1855.

Married—on Wednesday, 2nd Sept. in the vicinity of "Lenow's Springs," by the Rev. Reuben **BURROW**, Mr. Brown **BELOAT**, to Miss Tennessee **WILLIAMS**. Weekly Appeal, 9/11/1846.

Mr. Brown **BELOATE**, who resides near Hickory Wythe, in Fayette county, was instantly killed on last Tuesday by falling from the stairway of a gin and sticking a knife, which he held in his hand, through his heart. He leaves a wife and six children to mourn his loss. Memphis Daily Appeal, Fri., 1/29/1858.

The widow of the deceased Mr. John **BENDER**, returns thanks to the numerous friends and the members of the Fire Department, and of "Washington Rifle Company" for their attendance on her husband's funeral. Memphis Daily Appeal, 5/25/1856.

To the Ladies of Memphis and vicinity, Feeling it a duty that I owe to my sex, I offer them my services in the practice of Obstetrics. To inspire them with confidence I wish to state that I have spent a great part of my time for last 15 years in the study of this useful science under the directions of my own husband, who is himself a physician. That I have for several years been extensively and successfully engaged in practice, and that I have obtained Prof. H. Quinn's certificate as an accomplished Obstetrician…I can at all times be found, unless professionally employed at my residence on the corner of Vance and Hernando Streets, South Memphis.... Clemancy **BENHAM**. Memphis Appeal, 8/5/1848.

On yesterday about twelve o'clock, a promising son of Mr. H. **BENHAM**, aged four years, was instantly killed by the falling of two heavy pieces of scantling in the lumber yard of Mr. Cennell, at the foot of Jefferson street....Memphis Daily Appeal, 10/11/1856.

Died, On Sunday, January 30th, Ada, daughter of Virginia and E. A. **BENSEN**—aged six years, eight months and twenty-six days. On Monday, January 31st, Frank, son of Virginia and E. A. Bensen—aged four years four months and seven days. Funeral services at 3 o'clock P.M. by Rev. A. H. **THOMAS**, of the First Methodist Church, at their residence on Court street. Memphis Daily Appeal, 2/1/1859.

On Friday the 27th ult., Mr. Henry **BENSON**, who lived near Concordia, Tenn., was instantly killed by the discharge of a pistol in his own hands. Mr. B.'s mind was somewhat deranged in consequence of unfortunate pecuniary affairs, and he had previously expressed a wish to die and threatened to take his life. The face of the deceased was horribly mutilaten, and the fore part of his skull blown away. One ball passed entirely through his head, scattering brains and hair in every direction, and another went through the roof of the house. He had just eaten a hearty breakfast, and before going to work took the pistol and appeared to be loading it, just before the report was heard. Mr. Benson leaves a wife and several children....Memphis Daily Appeal, 4/10/1856.

Taken up by David H. **BENTLEY**, living about five miles north east of Raleigh, one clay bank horse....The Appeal, 10/27/1843.

Notice—By virtue of a fi. fa. Issued from the circuit court of Shelby county, and to me directed, I will expose to public sale, at the court house in the town of Raleigh, on the 20th day of March next, all the right, title, claim and interest that Jesse **BENTON** has of, in and to a certain parcel or tract of Land, containing thirteen hundred and ninety two acres, being part of a 1500 acre grant in the name of Jesse **STEED**; granted to said Steed by the state of North Carolina, lying on the waters of Loosahatchie, in the 11th District, range 7, section 4, adjoining the lands of John **RALSTON** on the east, and the heirs of _____ **GOODLOE** on the north.—Also, seven hundred and forty nine acres, being part of a 1650 acre tract, No. of entry 964, ranges 3 & 4, sections 2 & 3, same district, adjoining Thomas **OWEN's** 5000 acre entry. Also, as the property of John **BOULTON**, the following tracts of Land, to wit: one hundred and eight acres, being part of said 1500 acre grant to Jesse **STEED**, in the south east corner of said grant described above. One hundred acres situated on the waters of Loosahatchie river, being part of Samuel **HARRIS's** 5000 acre grant, and conveyed from Wm. **HARRIS** to said Boulton by deed bearing date 20th November, 1825; one hundred acres part of said grant conveyed by deed bearing date 14th June, 1827, from Andrew S. **HARRIS** to said Boulton; two hundred and eight acres, part of said grant, conveyed by deed bearing date 8th May, 1826, from Zeno T. **HARRIS** to said Boulton. Taken at the suit of James **KIMBROUGH** and Buckly **KIMBROUGH**, administrators of the estate of John **KIMBROUGH**, dec'd.; the two first tracts as the property of said Jesse **BENTON**, the others as the property of Jno. **BOULTON**, one of his securities, to satisfy a judgement obtained by the said Kimbroughs, adm'rs as aforesaid, against the said Jesse Benton, and John Boulton and Samuel R. **BROWN**, his securities. Sale within the hours prescribed by law. A. B. **CARR**, Coroner of Shelby county. Memphis Advocate, 2/23/1828.

Married, In Philadelphia, on the evening of August 21st, at the Synagogue, "House of Israel," Crown street, by Rev. Gabriel Papa, Julius J. **BERLIN**, Esq., of Memphis, Tenn., to Miss Bertha **POTSDAMER**, of Philadelphia. Memphis Daily Appeal, 8/30/1859.

Married, On the 26th inst. by Rev. J. T. C. **COLLINS**, Mr. C. L. **BERNARD** to Mrs. Eliza **STANBACK**, of this city. Memphis Daily Appeal, 11/28/1857.

Mr. A. H. **BERRY**, editor and proprietor of the Fayetteville Journal, died at his residence in Fayetteville, Tenn. on Saturday last. It will be remembered that Mr. Berry was severely injured in the great storm which occurred in Fayetteville in 1851. It is supposed his death was caused by injuries then received. Mr. Berry formerly resided in Memphis. Memphis Eagle & Enquirer, Tues., 4/5/1853.

Departed this life on the 4th inst., Mrs. Mary E. Berry, daughter of the late John **MARKHAM** and grand-daughter of Justice **FLEMING**, of Virginia, and consort of Dr. Reuben B. **BERRY**, of this city.....sincerely devout and strictly conscientious in the performance of all the duties of wife, mother, mistress.....Memphis Eagle & Enquirer, 2/9/1853. Dr. Reuben **BERRY**, Jr., of our city, whom we noticed some time since as having been appointed as Surgeon in the Russian army, left last Saturday for the purpose of taking the next steamer for his place of destination. He is a young man of much promise and we....wish him health and prosperity in his new field of labor. Memphis Daily Appeal, 8/21/1855. Death of Dr. Reuben B. Berry.—The Richmond *Enquirer* brings us the melancholy tidings of the death of this young physician. He was, we believe, the eldest son of Dr. R. B. Berry of this city, had resided here some time, and was engaged in the medical profession, in connection with his worthy father. He died at Portsmouth, Va., on the 21st September, a victim to his sympathy for the distresses of others. Memphis Daily Appeal, 10/3/1855. Memphis, Tuesday, Nov. 18, 1855.—At a meeting of the physicians of this city according to previous public notice, Dr. Wm. V. **TAYLOR** was called to the Chair and Dr. A. P. **MERRILL** appointed Secretary....Whereas, It hath pleased an over-ruling and all wise Providence to remove, by the hand of Death, Dr. Reuben B. Berry....Resolved, That to the orphan children of the deceased, who have lost by a father's death, their last and for some time past their only parental guide, we offer our heart-felt sympathies....Resolved, That the Secretary of this meeting furnish to the children of the deceased a copy of these resolutions....Memphis Whig, 11/14/1855. We regret to learn that Dr. R. B. Berry departed this life yesterday evening. He was first attacked by the late prevailing fever and has been lying for many days....Memphis Daily Appeal, 11/11/1855. State of Tennessee.—Proceedings had in the Clerk's office, Chancery Side of the Common Law and Chancery Court of the City of Memphis, Friday, October 10th, 1856, Henry C. **BERRY**, Mary H. **BERRY**, James J. **BERRY**, Fanny B. **BERRY** and others, heirs at law of Reuben B. Berry, dec'd., and James **LENOW**, Administrator, etc., Complainants vs. Theophelus **SANDERS**, James E. **MERRIMAN**, Mary H. Berry and others, creditors of Reuben B. Berry, dec'd., Defendants. Bill suggesting Insolvency of Estate, etc....Memphis Daily Appeal, 10/12/1856.

Married, at Oak Grove, Fayette county, on the 26th inst., by the Rev. Sam'l **NEAL**, Mr. Henry **BESTWICK**, of Memphis, to Miss Martha A. **FALWELL**, of the former place. Daily Enquirer, 10/1/1847.

Yesterday evening a little girl, two years of age, daughter of Mr. Phil **BETHA**, residing on Court street, fell into an open cistern, and was drowned. Memphis Eagle, 3/1/1850.

Married, On Wednesday, the 26th instant, at the First Methodist Church by Rev. J. W. **KNOTT**, Mr. Anderson C. **BETTIS** and Miss Fanny **PRIOR**, of this vicinity. Memphis Daily Appeal, 11/29/1856.

I offer for sale, upon the best terms ever offered in this country, my farm, known as the Bettis place, on the State Line road, two miles from Memphis. The place contains 128 acres...Apply on the premises to Wm. D. **MAYS**, in Memphis. D. **BETTIS**. Memphis Eagle, 8/13/1847.

Married, In this county, on the 13th inst., by Rev. Dr. Wilkerson, Maj. Shelby A. **BETTIS** to Miss Fady A. **WOMACK**. Memphis Eagle, 2/16/1850.

A funeral sermon occasioned by the death of Mr. T. **BETTIS**, will be preached in the first Presbyterian Church on to-morrow morning by the Rev. J. A. **GRAY**, D.D. Memphis Appeal, 9/2/1854.

To Travellers. The subscriber living four miles from Memphis, will take Horses at Livery....Tillman **BETTIS**. Memphis Advocate, 4/28/1827. Died, In this vicinity on the 14th inst., Thomas Anderson, infant son and only child of Tilman C. and Elizabeth Jane Bettis, aged 13 months. Weekly American Eagle, 8/7/1846. Taken up by Tilman Bettis, living 3 miles east of Memphis, on the State Line Road, one black Horse......The Appeal, 10/27/1843.

Married. In Maysville, Ky. by the Rev. Hugh **THOMPSON**, Mr. M. S. **BETTS**, editor of the Detroit Times, Michigan, to Miss M. E. **WILSON**, of Maysville. Memphis Appeal, 7/19/1854.

Married, On Wednesday the 9th inst., by the Rev. Dinn C. **PHARR**, C. **BIAS**, Esq., late of Memphis, Tenn., to Miss Mary C. **GATEWOOD**, of Bath co., Va. Memphis Eagle & Enquirer, 6/22/1852.

Married, on the evening of the 22d inst., at Richland, in this county, by the Rev. Samuel **HODGE**, Cesario **BIAS**, Esq. of this city, to Mrs. Mary Jane **KENNEDY**, formerly of Bath county, Va. The Tri-Weekly Memphis Enquirer, 6/25/1846. Died—In this county, yesterday morning, at the residence of her husband, Mrs. Mary Jane Bias, wife of C. Bias, Esq.....Weekly Memphis Eagle, 5/3/1849.

Died—In this city, on the morning of the 1st February, Mr. Albert **BICKFORD**, in the 21st year of his age. Mr. Bickford was a volunteer in a company from Worford Bennington county, Vermont, and was engaged in three of the last battles of his country. His disease was Chronic Diarrhea. Vermont papers please copy. Memphis Enquirer, 2/2/1848.

Died—July 28th, 1843, at Charlestown, Mass., William A., only child of W. A. and Louisa **BICKFORD** of this city, aged six months. American Eagle, 8/25/1843.

By virtue of a Decree of the Common Law and Chancery Court of the city of Memphis, made at the July Term, 1851, on the Law aide thereof in the case of the administrators of Benjamin **BIGGS**, Dec'd., vs. the Heirs of Benjamin Biggs, I shall, on Wednesday the 1st day of October, 1851...proceed to sell...twelve acres of Land belonging to the estate of the said Benj. Biggs...Memphis Appeal, 8/27/1851.

Married. At Fisherville, Tenn. on the 4th instant by Dr. Wm. G. **LANCASTER**, Dr. R. H. **BIGGS** to Miss Tennessee, daughter of Ezekiel **SANDERLIN**. Memphis Appeal, 1/16/1855.

Died. At Columbia, Tenn., on Saturday, 14th inst., Isaac Newton **BILLS**, Esq., Merchant of Woodville, Jackson Parish, Louisiana, late of Columbia, Tenn. Mr. Bills was a Professor of Mathematics in the Columbia Female Institute during the palmiest days of that Institution....for the sudden bereavement which has deprived a large family connection of one upon whom they doted. Mr. Bills emigrated to Louisiana about two or three years since and launched into a successful mercantile business. He was on a visit to his relatives near Columbia at the time of his death. He was about 45 years of age. Memphis Appeal, 10/28/1854.

Married, On the evening of the 18th inst., Mr. Leonidas **BILLS** and Miss Mary M. Miller, daughter of Pitsor **MILLER**, all of Bolivar, Tenn. Memphis Daily Appeal, 5/23/1857.

Married, At the residence of the bride's father in Bolivar, on Wednesday evening, December 2d, by Rev. Mr. Thompson, Mr. Wilson T. **BILLS** to Miss Lucy Wood, eldest daughter of Dr. Geo. **WOOD**. Memphis Daily Appeal, 12/8/1857. Died, At the residence of Dr. Geo. Wood, in Bolivar, on last Saturday, 13th inst., Mr. Wilson T. Bills, in the 27th year of his age. The deceased was a native of Bolivar, being the son of one of its oldest and most respected citizens, but had resided at Woodville, La., for several years past. He had just returned to his native State and town, and married the lady of his early affection....Memphis Daily Appeal, 2/20/1858.

Died, At Duck Hill, Carroll county, Miss., on the morning of the 6th(?) inst., Mrs. Priscilla P. Binford, wife of Capt. John A. **BINFORD**. Memphis Daily Appeal, 2/25/1858.

Married, At the residence of Mr. Dean, on Sunday 5th instant by the Rev. Mr. Madden, Mr. Frank G. **BINGHAM** of Nashville, and Miss Lizzie J. **DEAN**, of Clarksville. Memphis Appeal, 6/26/1853. The friends and acquaintances of F. G. and L. J. Bingham are respectfully invited to attend the funeral of their infant daughter, Theresa, this morning at 10 o'clock from their residence on St. Nicholas street. Services by Elder J. E. **MERRIMAN**. Memphis Daily Appeal, 10/1/1856.

Married, On the 12th of February, 1857, by Rev. J. L. **CROSS**, Mr. Wm. **BINGHAM**, of Mississippi, and Mrs. Mary **MATTHEWS**, of Shelby county, Tennessee, at the residence of her father, Benj. Y. **WINSTON**, near Memphis. Memphis Daily Appeal, 2/20/1857.

Our police succeeded in arresting a man named *Evans STEVENS*, on yesterday, who is charged with killing a citizen of Obion county, in this State, named John **BIRD**. The murder was committed sometime since, and *Stevens* has kept himself out of the reach of his pursuers until now. Memphis Daily Appeal, 4/25/1856.

Cincinnati Matches, Fancy Soaps, Inks and Perfumery. The Subscriber having purchased the Steam-Match Machine and Factory of Birney, Winans & Co....William **BIRNEY**. Daily Enquirer, 6/29/1847.

Died. On the 8th inst. at Cincinnati, after a protracted illness of bronchitis, Miss Josephine Maria **BISHOP**, in the 19th year of her age....Memphis Appeal, 2/3/1855.

Died, At the Commercial Hotel on the 10th inst. of Pneumonia, George W. **BLACK**, of Jacksonport, Arkansas. His remains were interred by the Masonic Fraternity in due form. Memphis Eagle & Enquirer, 1/13/1853.

Died, In Marshall county, Miss., Mrs. Mary Almira, wife of M. M. **BLACK**. St. Louis papers please copy. Memphis Daily Appeal, 1/31/1856.

Died, In Madison County, Tenn., on the 29th of July last, Mrs. Maville (?) Amanda, wife of Wm. G. **BLACK**, aged 20 years. Weekly American Eagle, 9/10/1846.

Gideon **BLACKBURN**, jr and John **HOWERTON** took into their heads on Tuesday to cut up a "shindy" with some German butchers living out on the Raleigh road, and "carried on" in so outrageous a manner as to require the interposition of the beat constable, who brought them to town. Arrived in town, in charge of the officer, they again became rebellious to legal authority, in such a manner as to make it necessary for the police to administer a little wholesome discipline. Finally they were taken to the magistrate's office from whence one of the parties (Blackburn) "vamossed" while some formalities were being attended to, across the river. The other was let off, on the ground, we believe, of his being in the service of the United States as a teamster, and was yesterday shipped off to Mexico....Daily Enquirer, 4/8/1847.

I wish to sell 320 acres of Lane, lying immediately on the road leading from Memphis to Hernando, three or four miles from Memphis, a fine stand for a house of entertainment—about 100 acres improved; a good double log house...Any person wishing to purchase, can see me on the premises, and examine for themselves. Wesley **BLACKMORE**. Weekly Appeal, 12/4/1846.

Departed this life suddenly on the evening of the 12th instant, Miss Jane C. **BLAKE**, in the 60th year of her age; and for the last 40 years a consistent member of the Presbyterian Church.... Weekly Appeal, 4/17/1846.

Married, On Tuesday the 27th inst., by Jessee **WALDRAN**, Esq. Geo. L. **BLAND** Esq., of South Carolina, to Miss Margaret **JOHNSON** of Memphis, Tenn. Memphis Daily Appeal, 6/30/1848.

Law Side of Common Law and Chancery Courts. City of Memphis. Nancy A. J. Blankenship vs. C. Colbert **BLANKENSHIP**. Petition for Divorce. In this cause, it appearing to the Clerk and Master that the defendant, C. Colbert Blankenship, is a non-resident of the State of Tennessee, it is therefore ordered that publication be made....requiring the said defendant to appear at the July term of this Court, commencing on the first Monday in July, 1859, and plead, answer or demur to plaintiff's petition or the same will be taken for confessed, and set for hearing *ex parte*. Memphis Daily Avalanche, 4/4/1859.

Died—At Olive Branch, Miss., on Saturday last, Mr. T. W. **BLANKENSHIP**. Tri-Weekly Memphis Enquirer, Tues., 12/1/1846.

Our old democratic friend, Mr. B. **BLEDSOE**, who has a neat farm on the Chulahoma road, about 15 miles from the city, stocked with the finest fruits in the country, offers it for sale...Memphis Appeal, 10/20/1852.

I offer for sale the plantation on which I now reside in De Soto county, Miss., thirteen miles from Memphis and adjoining Finley **HOLMES** on the south. The tract contains 1052 acres....Benjamin **BLEDSOE**. Memphis Appeal, 11/2/1855.

By virtue of a Deed of Trust executed to me by Job **BLEDSOE**, which is duly recorded in the Register's office of Shelby County, in Book H, pages 518 and 519, I will offer at public sale...on the 12th day of May, 1847, the following described Property, lying and being in the County of Shelby...Richard A. **BLOUNT**. Daily Enquirer, 4/20/1847.

Taken up by P. R. **BLEDSOE**, living in district No. 1, at Covington, a Bay Roan Horse...S. **HULL**, Ranger, T.C. Weekly American Eagle, 6/26/1846.

We are authorized to announce Watts **BLEDSOE**, a candidate for the office of Constable of the District including Memphis. American Eagle, 2/21/1842.

Married, In Fayette County, on the 8th inst., Mr. Wm. J. **BLEDSOE**, of La Grange, to Miss Juliana, daughter of Doct. A. **GOODE**. Memphis Enquirer, 2/25/1837.

Died, At the residence of Dr. Augustus **ROWLETT**, in Marshall county, Miss., on the 18th instant, Mrs. Eliza **BLOCKER**, aged 68 years. New Orleans papers please copy. Memphis Daily Appeal, 10/23/1855.

On Wednesday, near Dr. Williams', five or six miles from the city, A. P. **BLOOD**, conductor of the freight train on the Memphis and Charleston Railroad, accidentally fell from the platform of the car while the train was in rapid motion. The left shoulder blade was splintered to pieces by the fall and injuries so serious sustained, that after an hour and a half's suffering he expired....Memphis Daily Appeal, Sat., 11/28/1857.

The subscriber having qualified as Administrator on the estate of Jesse **BLOODWORTH**, late of Shelby County, deceased, notifies all persons indebted to the estate...Joseph **CARL**, Admn'r. Weekly American Eagle, 3/18/1847.

Died, On Thursday, June 26th, of congestive chill, Fanny, aged eight years, only child of Soloman and Rebecca **BLOOM**, of Pine Bluff, Ark. Pine Bluff *Republican* please copy. Memphis Daily Appeal, 7/1/1856.

Mr. John **BLOUNT**, who fell from the balcony of a hotel in Holly Springs on Friday last, has since died from his wounds. Memphis Daily Appeal, Tues., 9/1/1857.

Died, On the 10th instant, Thomas Winborn, only child of the late John **BLOUNT**, of Rossville, Tenn., aged one year and nine months. Helena Shield will please copy. Memphis Daily Appeal, 6/22/1858.

Married, at Sunny Lawn, Hertford County, North Carolina, on the 22d ult., by the Rev. Mr. Li___, Mr. Richard A. **BLOUNT**, of Memphis, Tenn., to Miss Barsha E. **SAUNDERS**, daughter of the late Thomas **SAUNDERS**, of Gates Co. Memphis Enquirer, 4/6/1848.

The funeral of Elizabeth Sears, the wife of Benjamin B. **BLUME**, is appointed at 11 o'clock, A.M. Service at the residence of the family, on Union street...Daily Enquirer, 1/12/1847.

Married, On Wednesday morning, 25th inst., near Shelby Depot, by Rev. Thomas **BONE**, Mr. Henry **BOARDMAN**, of Germantown, to Miss Cordelia M. **GRIFFIN**, both of this county. Memphis Daily Appeal, 11/26/1857.

Mrs. Frances W. **BOBO**, who died in Panola county, Mississippi, last week, bequeathed the sum of one thousand dollars to an aged female servant. Died, In Panola county, Miss., on Thursday evening, the 28th ult., in the 78th year of her age, Mrs. Francis W. Bobo. South Carolina papers please copy. Memphis Daily Appeal, 11/3/1857.

We learn that a Frenchman named **BOCHER** put an end to his life yesterday, in this city, by taking a portion of arsonic. He died in a short time. We cannot obtain further particulars. He left a wife and son. Memphis Enquirer, 8/20/1848.

Married, At Lauderdale Factory, near Florence, Ala., on Tuesday evening, the 25th inst., Mr. James S. **BODDIE** and Miss Julia T. **CASSITY**. Memphis Daily Avalanche, 1/27/1859.

Dr. Joseph L. **BOHANNAN** departed this life on Tuesday evening the 6th inst. The subject of this obituary emigrated from Richmond, Va., some eight years since, and has resided in our town from the period of his emigration, with but a short intermission...Deeply as his loss will be deplored by his relations and a widowed wife, with an only child, a lovely daughter...The "Memphis Blues" after paying the last tribute of respect to the memory of their late fellow citizen, and honorary member, Dr. Joseph Bohannon......The Appeal, 8/16/1844.

We learn, with painful regret, that R. L. **BOHANNON**, one of the volunteers from this city, has died of his wounds received in the Battle of Cerro Gordo. Poor Dick! He was a kindly, true hearted man, who whatever may have been at times his faults towards himself, was as true as the needle to the pole in obeying the dictates of honor, justice and philanthropy, in his intercourse with his fellows. Poor Dick! Light be the turf above his head—Enquirer. Weekly American Eagle, 5/13/1847.

Married, On the 20th instant in this city, by Esq. Horne, Mr. F. **BOIE** to Miss Bettie **EYRICH**(?), all of this city. Memphis Daily Appeal, 7/22/1859.

Married: On Tuesday the 21st inst. near Henderson, Ky., by Rev. Mr. Hays, Mr. Daniel E. **BOISSEAU**, of this city, to Miss Sallie B. **BORUM**, of Henderson county, Ky. The happy groom returned to the city yesterday....Memphis Whig, 8/25/1855.

Shelby County, Tenn. Circuit Court, October Term, 1844. Petition For Divorce. George **BOLISKY** vs. Margaret **BOLISKY**. It appearing to the Circuit Court at the last term, that the defendant resides beyond the limits of the State of Tennessee, and out of the jurisdiction of the said Court, it is ordered that publication be made in the Memphis Appeal, for three successive months, for the defendant to appear and plead, answer or demur, or that the said petition will be taken pro. confesso. The bill charges willful abandonment and adultery. E. W. M. **KING**, Sol. The Appeal, 12/6/1844.

Trust Sale of Real Property. By virtue of a deed of Trust to me executed by William S. **BOLLING**, to secure a debt therein specified which the said Bolling owes to David **WILLS**, bearing date July the 22d, 1845, and registered in the county of Shelby, in book S, page 263, 264 and 265, which said deed conveys to me in trust, to provide for the payment of the said debt, sundry town lots with the improvements and appurtenances thereunto belonging and therein described, situated in South Memphis, near the Gayoso House...I will, on Thursday, the 1st day of January, 1846, as Trustee, sell at public sale...J. E. **TEMPLE**. Memphis Enquirer, 1/3/1846.

Married, On the 29th(?) ult., at the residence of Col. C. A. **BLACKMAN**, by Rev. W. C. **CRANE**, Mr. Charles **BOLTON** to Miss Sallie **JETER**. Memphis Daily Appeal, 1/20/1859.

Died—On Saturday evening the 27th ult., at 3 o'clock, in Randolph, Tenn., John **BOLTON** of Big Creek, Shelby county, Ten., after a short and painful illness of about 48 hours, occasioned by swallowing a fish bone, aged 56 years 4 months and 19 days. Mr. Bolton was one of the first settlers of this county; he emigrated as early as 1822, and settled on Big Creek to seek his fortune in agricultural pursuits....and left a widow and six children to bemoan his unfortunate death. Memphis Enquirer, 11/3/1838.

Married, At White Sulphur Springs, Tenn., April 24th, 1859, by David A. **ROBERTS**, Esq., Mr. John **BOLTON** to Miss Parthena **ROBERTSON**, all of Hardin county, Tenn. Memphis Daily Appeal, 4/30/1859.

Married, On the 26th ult., at the residence of R. **BOND**, Esq. by Thomas J. **ROSS**, Esq., Dr. W. B. **CRENSHAW**, of Avoyelies parish, Louisiana, to Mrs. Pheraby G. **ROSS**, eldest daughter of R. W. **BOND**, Esq., of Shelby county. Memphis Daily Appeal, 2/1/1853.

The funeral of the late Rice **BOND**, Esq., was largely attended yesterday by his friends and the members of the Masonic fraternity. His remains were deposited, we understand, at his father's residence, about fifteen miles in the country. Mr. Bond died recently at Lake Providence, La., of consumption. He was a young man of talent and highly esteemed by all who knew him. Memphis Avalanche, 4/11/1859. The death of our late esteemed fellow-citizen, Rice Bond, Esq., is announced. The sad event occurred on his brother's plantation, in the State of Louisiana. The deceased was for many years a useful member of the Shelby County Agricultural Association, and at one time the Secretary of that organization. His remains will be interred at Raleigh tomorrow....Memphis Daily Appeal, 4/9/1859.

We had three fires last evening in the course of a couple of hours. The first occurred about sunset, in a small frame building on the northeast corner of Second and Adams streets, occupied by Mr. Stephen **BOND**, which was consumed...Weekly Memphis Eagle, 10/25/1849.

Married, In this county, on the 28th ult., at the residence of E. S. **GILES**, Esq., by the Rev. D. P. **COFFEY**, Mr. T. G. **BOND**, to Mrs. Margaret M. **GILES**. The Appeal, 4/5/1844.

Hall Of Morning Star Lodge, No. 186. The following preamble and resolutions were adopted, to-wit: Whereas, It has been the order of divine Providence to take from our Lodge our much-esteemed friend and worthy brother, Tallas_ee G. **BOND**, who departed this life November 14, 1857....Resolved, That we request the Rev. R. **BURROW** to preach the funeral sermon of the departed brother at New Salem Church, on the third Sabbath in December....Memphis Daily Appeal, 11/25/1857.

Married, On the 30th inst. at Somerville, Tennessee, by Bishop Noland, J. W. **BONDURANT** to Rebecca R., second daughter of Henderson **OWEN**, Esq. Memphis Daily Appeal, 9/1/1857.

Taken up by B. A. **BONGUS**, living 18 miles from Memphis, on the State Line road, one black horse.....Memphis Enquirer, 1/14/1837.

Died—At the residence of his father, Col. Robert H. **BONNER**, Marshall county, Miss., Robert Hubbard Bonner. He was born on the 6th April, 1855, and died on the 21st of October, 1858. He had had scarlet fever some weeks previously....Memphis Weekly Appeal, 11/10/1858.

Married, On the 20th inst. by Elder N. P. **MOORE**, Mr. Wm. H. **BONNER** to Miss Mattie E. **THOMAS**, all of Fayette county, Tenn. Memphis Daily Appeal, 10/24/1857.

Died—In Somerville on the 29th ult., Edmund **BOOKER**, Jun'r. of Randolph, in the 26th year of his age.....Memphis Enquirer, 8/11/1838. Died: In this city, on the 26th, Josiah E. **BOOKER**, son of Edmund Booker. Weekly Memphis Eagle, 8/30/1849.

The Luella, a new boat brought into the trade by Captain Jim **BOOKER**, left last evening for Louisville ....Memphis Appeal, 8/8/1854.

Died. On the 16th inst. at his residence near Marion, Crittendon county, Ark., Mr. Joseph P. **BOOKER**, aged 58 years. The deceased was the father of our fellow-townsman, Capt. Ed. **BOOKER**. Memphis Whig, 12/20/1855.

For Sale, The place where I now reside, 4 miles south of Covington, Tipton county—known by the name of the Mountain. The tract contains 203 ¾ acres of rich land—the improvements consist of a large and convenient frame dwelling house, kitchen, smoke-house, etc...The Mountain Academy, now in successful operation, is within 200 yards of the dwelling, and the Mount Carmel Church within a quarter of a mile...J. G. **BOON**. Memphis Enquirer, 1/14/1837.

Died—At his residence near Covington, on Saturday last, of congestive fever, Robert G. **BOON**, aged 28 years, formerly of Johnston County, North Carolina.—An amiable and excellent man, his death is sincerely lamented by all who knew his virtues. Memphis Enquirer, Sat., 8/5/1837.

Died, On the 10th inst., at the residence of her mother, Mrs. E. A. **BOOTH**, in the town of Sommerville, Miss Anna E. **BOOTH**...Weekly Memphis Eagle, 8/16/1849.

Died, In Sommerville, on the 8th inst., at 8 o'clock P.M., in the 18th year of her age, Miss Elizabeth Carey **BOOTH**...To know the deceased was to love her; a dutiful daughter, an affectionate sister, and kind friend...Memphis Enquirer, 9/15/1848.

Died—At La Grange, at the residence of his brother, Dr. John **BOOTH**, formerly a resident of Memphis. American Eagle, 9/9/1842.

Married. On Tuesday, August 7th, by Rev. R. L. **ANDREWS**, Mr. R. G. **BOOTH** to Miss Adine M., daughter of Maj. W. S. **RANDOLPH**, of Panola county, Miss. Memphis Daily Appeal, 8/18/1855.

Died—On Wednesday last, at his residence, near this place, Capt. Thomas **BOOTH**, an aged and highly respectable citizen. Capt. B. was a native of Virginia, resided several years in North Carolina, but was for the last fifteen years a resident of this State.....He will long be lamented and his memory cherished by an extended circle of friends and acquaintances. Daily Memphis Enquirer, Sat., 4/7/1849.

We learned yesterday that a son of Dr. **BORDLEY** of this city, died recently in Nicaragua, of chills and fever. Memphis Daily Appeal, 3/24/1857.

Died—At her residence in this county, on Friday the 24th inst., Mrs. Ann Boren, consort of Col. James F. **BOREN**, in the 21st year of her age; leaving a disconsolate husband and infant daughter to mourn their irreparable loss...Mrs. Boren has been a consistent member of the Baptist church for many years...Weekly Appeal, 7/31/1846.

Married, On the 9th inst. at the residence of Mr. Thomas **SCRUGGS**, in DeSoto county, Miss., by W. D. **WALDROSS**, Esq., Mr. W. A. **BOREN**, attorney at law, Hernando, Miss., to Miss M. E. Wright, daughter of M. D. **WRIGHT**, Esq., of Franklin, Tenn. Memphis Daily Appeal, 2/11/1858.

Died—In this place on the 25th ult. in the 28th year of her age, Mrs. Huldah (?) G., late consort of Dr. Solon **BORLAND**, after an illness of several months. Mrs. B. with her husband, removed from Nansemond County, Va., to this place early last winter. Her health had been in a delicate state several months previous to her death, though she was not thought to be in danger until a short time before that event....She had received an education superior to what falls to the lot of most females....She has left two interesting children to the care of their surviving parent. Memphis Enquirer, 9/2/1837. Married—On Tuesday evening last by the Rev. Philip W. **ALSTON**, Dr. Solon Borland, editor of the "Western World", to Miss Eliza B. **HART**—all of this place. Memphis Enquirer, Fri., 7/26/1839.

Married, On Saturday afternoon by the Rev. Father Grace, at the Catholic Church, Mr. James **BORO**, merchant, to Miss Sarah **WEIBEL**, both of this city. Memphis Appeal, Mon., 7/28/1851. Died, In this city on Tuesday, November 4th, 1856, Mrs. Sarah Ann Boro, wife of James Boro, Esq. Pennsylvania, Louisville, Ky. and New Albany, Indiana papers please copy. Memphis Daily Appeal, 11/19/1856.

The funeral of Joseph Boro, infant son of James **BORO**, will take place from his residence at 3 o'clock P.M., Sunday, March 8th, 1857. Memphis Daily Appeal, 3/8/1857.

Died, In Bolivar, Hardeman county, on Saturday last, 4th instant, Luan Borum, wife of Joseph B. **BORUM**, Esq., of Henderson, Kentucky, of consumption. Her remains were deposited in the cenotaph of Elmwood Cemetery for interment when her husband arrives....Memphis Daily Appeal, 10/9/1856.

Married—On the evening of the 30th ult. by Rev. Dr. Edgar, Mr. Charles **BOSLEY**, Jr. to Miss Martha A., daughter of Mr. A. D. **CARDEN**, of Nashville. American Eagle, 4/21/1842.

Died, At Oxford, Miss., on the 23d inst., of inflammation of the bowels, James David **BOST**, son of Alfred and Elizabeth **BOST**, of Panola county, aged 21 years and 8 months....around him were clustered the hopes of a fond father, a devoted mother, and of affectionate brothers and sisters.... He was and had been for five years, a consistent and devoted member of the Methodist Church.... The deceased, a few days before his death, left the bosom of his family to attend the Commence- ment Exercises of the University at which he had formerly been a student, when he was seized with the malady that terminated his earthly existence....Memphis Daily Appeal, 7/30/1856.

Richmond House. The undersigned, and late proprietor of the "Exchange Hotel," Memphis, has taken the above house, and is now ready to accommodate those who may give him a call. His house is in the centre of business, on Front Row, just below Madison street...John G. **BOSTICK**, Proprietor. Daily Enquirer, 4/8/1847. On Sunday last, Major John G. Bostick, an old citizen of Shelby county and a soldier of the war of 1812, died at his residence seven miles from the city, in the 73d year of his age. Memphis Daily Appeal, Tues., 3/31/1857.

The subscriber would respectfully announce to the citizens of Memphis and its vicinity, that having purchased and taken possession of the "Central Landing Coffee House," formerly occupied by P. **VEVIER**, he intends keeping the best of Liquors, Cigars and Oysters, which he will sell at reduced prices...John H. R. **BOSTICK**. Memphis Enquirer, 12/3/1847. Died, On Sunday, the 24th of April, 1859, Albert, youngest son of J. H. R. and J. E. Bostick, aged 14 months. Memphis Daily Appeal, 5/1/1859.

Died, July 19, at the residence of H. E. **MORGAN**, in Shelby county, Tennessee, Mr. Marcus A. **BOTELER**, aged 23 years and 3 months. Papers at Decatur and Talladega, Alabama, please copy. Memphis Daily Appeal, 7/21/1857.

Married, On the 1st instant, Mr. Gilbert B.(?) **BOUCHER** to Miss P. A. **HANKLEY**, of Hardeman. Memphis Weekly Appeal, 12/15/1858.

Married, In LaGrange, on the 12th inst., by Rev. J. T. C. **COLLINS**, Mr. W. R. **BOUGH** to Mrs. S. A. **McREE**, both of LaGrange, Tenn. Memphis Daily Appeal, 1/15/1858.

Mr. James T. **BOURNE**, collector and surveyor of this port, received news from Louisville of the death of his brother yesterday, and left for that place last evening on the *Express*. Memphis Eagle & Enquirer, 6/27/1852.

Married, In Henry county, Tenn., on the 25th ultimo, by __. T. L. **DANIEL**, Mr. B. T. **BOWDEN** and Miss Drusilla **PRICE**. Memphis Daily Appeal, 1/18/1857.

We learn from a communication from D. **SLEDGE**, Esq., that Mr. Gideon **BOWDEN**, who was killed on Nonconnah Creek by negroes, was overseer for Col. F. R. **SLEDGE**. He was sent for by Mack and Hogan, to pursue the negroes with dogs, when he met with his death. Mr. Sledge states he was a highly respected gentleman, and he leaves a widow and three little children....Memphis Daily Appeal, 9/8/1858.

State of Tennessee—Shelby County; ____ Term, 1825. Whereas, Samuel R. **BROWN**, Sheriff and collector of the public taxes for said county, for the year 1824, reported to court the following tracts of land as having been given in for the taxes of said year....Heirs of Epaphroditus **BOWEN** 640 acres range 4 section 2; James **CATTERAN** 240 acres part grant No 21; Tilman **DIXON** 199 acres range 8 section 5 No 415; Dvs of Geo **DOUGHERTY** 500 acres ranges 7 & 8, section 1; Arther **HENLY** 512 acres range 4 section 5 No 162; John **JONES** 800 acres range 7 section 3 No 614; Edward **PIOTTE** 640 acres range 4 section 3 No 362; Wm **POLK** 4750 acres part of grant 387; Polk & Deaveraux 500 acres range 4 section 6 No 144; E **ROBESON** 100 acres No 356; John **TERRELL** 1000 acres range 9 section 4 No 819; Samuel H. **WILLIAMS** 260 acres range 6 section 4, No. 46; Willoughby **WILLIAMS** 1000 acres range 4 & 5 section 5....Where- upon it is considered by the court, that said several tracts of land, or so much thereof as shall be sufficient, of each of them, to satisfy the taxes....Memphis Advocate, 11/3/1827.

Married. On the 20th February by Rev. W. Parker **SCOTT**, at the residence of Arthur **RUCKS**, Esq., on Deer Creek, Miss., G. A. **BOWEN**, Esq., to Miss Amanda V., daughter of John K. **YERGER**. Memphis Daily Appeal, 3/17/1855.

Married, On Wednesday evening last, by Rev. P. W. **ALSTON**, Mr. John H. **BOWEN**, Merchant, to Miss Mary C., daughter of Mr. Wm. **ARMOUR**, all of this city. American Eagle, Fri., 5/2/1845.

Died. In this city on the morning of the 21st instant of Scarlet Fever, Poston, son of W. P. and Elizabeth **BOWEN**. Memphis Whig, 5/22/1855.

Married, By Rev. Thomas **TAYLOR** on the 1st inst., at the residence of Capt. John **TATE**, near Macon, Fayette county, Major B. **BOWERS**, of Hardeman county, to Mrs. S. H. **CANLIFFE**. Memphis Daily Appeal, 11/3/1859.

Married, In LaGrange, Tenn., on the 20th inst., Mr. James __. **BOWERS** and Miss Lucy **LANDRUM**. Memphis Daily Appeal, 8/23/1856.

Departed this life on the 10th of December last, at the residence of his father, Maj. B. **BOWERS**, in Hardeman county, Ten., Mr. Thomas Caswell **BOWERS**, in the 22d year of his age. Mr. Bowers was born in Edgecombe county, N. Carolina, and emigrated with his parents to this county almost in his infancy. Under the withering effects of "Hepatitus Chronica" he lingered some six weeks ere his death...In the hearts of his fond and affectionate parents, brothers and an only sister, and of devoted friends, his memory will never die. Middleburg, Hardeman county, Tenn. 2/13/1847. Raleigh, (N.C.) papers will please copy. Weekly Appeal, 2/19/1847.

Died, On the 14th October, at his residence near Sommerville, Maj. Geo. **BOWERS**, aged 58 years. Memphis Daily Eagle, 11/6/1850.

Died, on the 26th day of July, 1859, in Monroe county, Ark., Mrs. Henrietta L. Bowers, wife of Sutherland **BOWERS**, and daughter of Dr. Wm. C. **BRYAN**, of this city. The deceased was in her twenty-first year. She left two young children....Memphis Daily Appeal, 8/2/1859.

Married: On the evening of the 9th inst., by Rev. Samuel **WATSON**, at the residence of the bride's mother, on Union street, Mr. William P. **BOWERS**, of the Avalanche Office, and Miss Catharine Jane **SPICKERNAGLE**. Memphis Evening Ledger, 2/10/1858. ....The friend, whose death we are now constrained to record, is William P. Bowers....He was a printer by occupation and learned his trade in the Appeal office, and never have we seen Billy Bowers away from his post....At the time of his death, Mr. Bowers was President of the Typographical Union of this city....He had gone on a tour of health to the Hot Springs in Arkansas, and died in Little Rock last Saturday, the 24th inst. He was married only a few months ago to a lovely young lady of this city, and was stricken down with disease the day after his marriage. Our warmest sympathies are extended to his weeping young widow and his attached relatives. Never was there a truer or a nobler man. Memphis Weekly Appeal, 5/5/1858. At a regular meeting of the Memphis Typographical Union No. 11, held on the evening of May 5, 1858....received with much pain the intelligence of the death at Little Rock, Ark., on Friday, the 23d April, 1858, of our esteemed fellow-craftsman—William Priddy Bowers....Memphis Weekly Appeal, 5/12/1858.

Married, In Jackson, Tenn., on Thursday, 13th inst., by Rev. Dr. McCullough, Mr. William **BOWLES**, of the firm of Bowles & Smither of this city, to Miss Caroline **HASKELL**, of the former place. Memphis Appeal, 11/18/1851.

Married, yesterday morning, at 8 o'clock by the Rev. Mr. Stark, Mr. Z. P. **BOWLES** of Randolph, to Miss Elvira W. **MONTAGUE** of this city. American Eagle Weekly, 2/28/1845.

Married, On Wednesday the 5ᵗʰ inst. by J. **WALDRAN**, Esq., Mr. J. C. **BOWLIN** to Miss Elizabeth **HARRIS** daughter of Sneed **HARRIS**, all of Shelby county. Memphis Eagle & Enquirer, 1/7/1853.

Mrs. Elizabeth C. Bowling, daughter of George and Rebecca **WALTON**, was born in Lawrence county, Ala., August 29ᵗʰ, 1819; was married to Mr. Geo. W. **BOWLING** October 25ᵗʰ, 1837;....joined the Methodist Episcopal Church South in 1855, and died in Marshall county, Miss., November 3d, 1856. By the death of this excellent woman a devoted husband, two affectionate children and the church and the community in which she lived have been severely bereaved....Memphis Daily Appeal, 12/11/1856.

Died, On Deer Creek, In Issequence county, Mississippi, on the 21st of February last, Mr. Richard **BOWLS**, in the 46th year of his age, formerly of Halifax county, North Carolina...His remains were brought to Memphis to-day on the Western World, to be conveyed to LaGrange, Tenn., where the last tribute of respect will be paid by his numerous friends and much bereaved family, to whom he was all affection. Raleigh (N.C.) papers please copy. Memphis Eagle & Enquirer, 4/21/1852.

Died, On the 12ᵗʰ of October, 1855, Milton Fairchild Bownds, youngest child of Thomas and Margret **BOWNDS** of Independence county, Arkansas, aged 10 months. Little Rock papers please copy. Memphis Daily Appeal, 11/6/1855.

Died, On the 25th inst. Mr. Edward **BOYCE**, at the residence of his brother, in Fayette county, Tenn. Memphis Eagle & Enquirer, 1/27/1852.

Died: In this city, yesterday, James J., infant son of James and Susan Ann **BOYD**. Funeral at ½ past 4 o'clock this evening, from No. 72 Front Row. Memphis Eagle, 10/24/1848.

Married, On Wednesday, the 30ᵗʰ ult., by Rev. J. T. **PICKETT**, at St. James' church, Bolivar, Tenn., Mr. John C. **BOYD** to Miss Sarah **MYRICK**, of Hardeman county. Memphis Daily Appeal, 12/4/1859.

Married, On the 11ᵗʰ inst. at the residence of J. L. **BAGLEY**, Esq., Whiteville, Tenn., Mr. Robert _. **BOYD** to Miss Emily G. **BAGLEY**. Memphis Weekly Appeal, 12/15/1858.

Shortly after six o'clock last evening, a difficulty arose on board the Daniel Boone, between Robert M. **BOYD**, the third cook, and Robert **CASEY**, second pastry cook of the steamer, both free men of color, which resulted in the death of the former. A quarrel arose between the two, and after some sharp words, Boyd picked up a hot gridiron from the stove, with which he inflicted several blows upon the head and face of Casey. The latter seized a large carving knife, and rushed upon Boyd....stabbing him in the left breast, inflicting a wound which produced death in a few moments....Memphis Daily Avalanche, 5/17/1859.

Died, on Thursday, 11th inst., at the residence of Mrs. Tarleton in this city, Mr. William **BOYD**, late of Paris. It may be agreeable to the friends of the deceased to learn that he received the kindest attention during his illness, and that the last offices were performed in a becoming manner by the Masonic Fraternity, of which he was a member. Memphis Enquirer, 1/21/1848.

S. W. **BOYER** of Memphis was killed by Andrew J. **DONALDSON** (nephew of Hon. A. J. **DONALDSON**) at Clarendon, Monroe county, Ark., on Tuesday night last. The weapon used was a double-barrelled shot gun, the load entering the heart, and producing instantaneous death. They were brothers-in-law, and the unfortunate occurrence was the result of a family difficulty. We understand the deceased was at Clarendon attending to a suit instituted against him in that court. Boyer had married Donaldson's sister, and the affray grew out of Boyer's ill-treatment of his wife....Boyer had been married a second time, and it is a remarkable fact that he had an affray with his former brother-in-law, which grew out of his ill-treatment of his first wife, in which he killed his wife's brother, a gentleman named Wilburn. Memphis Daily Appeal, Sat., 9/17/1859.

Died, at the Phoenix Hotel on the 28ᵗʰ ult., Mr. Bartley **BOYET**, stranger. His remains were incased in a metalic coffin and deposited in one of the cemeteries of our city, to await the orders of his relatives. Memphis Daily Appeal, 4/3/1856.

A fatal accident occurred on the Memphis and Ohio Railroad at Gasden Station, a short distance from Humboldt, on Monday evening. A young man named Charles E. **BOYKIN**, a son of the gentleman who keeps the station, and a switch-tender, by accident became entangled between the freight cars and locomotive, and was killed almost instantly. By the accident his head and face were horribly crushed and mangled. The deceased had a wife and two children. Memphis Daily Appeal, Wed., 7/13/1859.

Col. George W. **BRADBURY** expired a quarter past nine o'clock, last evening, after an illness of five days…He had not yet attained to the prime of manhood, yet he had acquired for himself a high reputation as one of the most original and sprightly writers of the day, and from his literary labors he had but just begun to reap the reward. He has left a young wife and child to mourn his early death. His funeral will take place this afternoon, at two o'clock, from his late residence, on Third street, between Sycamore and Broadway…Many of our citizens will remember him as a delegate to the great Southwestern Convention in this city…Daily Enquirer, 11/11/1847.

Married, On the 19th inst. by Rev. C. R. **HENDRICKSON**, Mr. Gabriel **BRADEN** to Miss Sarah Ann **BENNETT**, all of Memphis. Memphis Appeal, 4/23/1853.

Died, On the 20th inst. in Fayette county at the residence of J. P. **BRADEN**, Esq., Miss Frances P. **WILSON**, in the eighteenth year of her age. Memphis Appeal, 6/28/1853.

Died, On the 21st instant, in Fayette, at the residence of her father, Miss Martha E. **BRADEN**, in the fourteenth year of her age. Memphis Appeal, 6/28/1853.

Died, On Thursday night the 11th inst., J. W., son of J. W. and Annelijah **BRADFORD**, aged three years two months and twenty-seven days. Memphis Appeal, 7/22/1851.

We tender our thanks to Mr. J. W. **BRADFORD**, clerk of the fine steamer Saxon, for full files of late St. Louis papers. Memphis Appeal, 3/26/1853.

Coroner Waldran held an inquest over the body of King **BRADFORD**, who was shot last Friday by John **LUNSFORD** and died on Friday night at 10 o'clock. Verdict—"Came to his death from wounds inflicted by having been shot with a double barreled gun, held in the hands of John Lunsford." Memphis Appeal, Mon., 1/23/1854.

Married, At the residence of W. C. **BRADFORD**, on the evening of the 25th, by Rev. J. O. **STEADMAN**, Mr. Robert P. **BRADFORD** to Miss Mary **BRADFORD**, both of this city. Memphis Weekly Appeal, 3/31/1858.

Married—On Thursday evening, in this county, by Rev. John H. **GRAY**, Mr. Wm. T. **BRADLEY** to Miss Susan S. **FEATHERSTON**. American Eagle Weekly, Friday, 7/4/1845. Died: On the 30th of July last, Mrs. Susan S. Bradley, daughter of the late Lewis Featherston ….As a wife, a sister, a friend, in each and every relation of life, she displayed those qualities which elicited and secured the heart's warmest devotion….Weekly Memphis Eagle, 9/6/1849.

Died. In this city on Friday morning, April 20th, Joseph J. Francis, son of Richard F. and Sarah F.(?) **BRADSHAW**, aged one year. Richmond, Va. papers please copy. Memphis Daily Appeal, 4/21/1855.

An inquest was held yesterday morning in South Memphis at the house of Jas. K. **MURRAH**, Esq., over the body of Thomas **BRADSHAW**. The deceased and his brother went to bed together about 11 o'clock on Saturday night: Thomas being in the enjoyment of his usual good health. In the morning when his brother got up to breakfast he left Thomas, as he thought, asleep, but after awhile wondering why he did not get up, he went upstairs to call him, and to his astonishment and grief, found that he was a corpse. Thomas was a carpenter by trade, sober and industrious, and about 22 years of age. The jury of inquest brought in a verdict of "death by the visitation of God." Memphis Appeal, 9/13/1852.

McMackin House Restaurant – Silas **BRAHAN** & Co., would inform the public that they have opened a Restaurateur in the house recently known as the McMackin House…American Eagle, 3/3/1843.

State of Tennessee, Shelby County—April term, 1826.—Whereas, Samuel R. **BROWN**, sheriff and collector of the public taxes for said county of Shelby, for the year 1825, reported to court the following tracts of land as having been given in for the taxes for said year…to wit; Wm. **BRANDON**, 75 acres, range 7, section 2; Wm. **BRANDON**, 445 acres, range 7, section 2; J G & T **BLOUNT**, 1836 acres, grant 81; Same 1062 acres, grant 242; Same 1062 acres, grant 181; Same 200 acres, entry 562, range 5, section 5; Wm. **BRADSHAW**, 130 acres part of 576 acres, range 8 section 1; Robert **BROOKS** 160 acres, entry 50 range 7 section 4; Wm. **BRADSHAW** 2500 acres, entry 127 ranges 4 & 5 section 1; Rep. of John **CHILDRESS**, 223 ¼ acres, entry 244 range 8 section 3; Clingman & Poindexter, 1666 2/3 acres entry 550 range 6 section 7; Jas. **CATTERAN** 240 acres, part of grant 21; George **GILLESPIE**, 181 acres, entry 606 range 1 section 5; Gooch & Strother, 5000 acres; Cairo **HARRIS** 208 1/3 acres part of grant 17; Zeno **HARRIS**, 208 1/3 acres part grant 17; Sydney **HARRIS** 208 1/3 acres part grant 17; Thomas **HENDERSON**, 1000 acres No 803; Thomas **HENDERSON** 640 acres, No 739 range 3 section 5; Allen **JONES** 379 acres, entry 619 range 4 section 3; John **JONES** 800 acres, entry 614, range 7 section 3; J & J **IRVIN** 640 acres entry 577, range 4 section 1; Wm T **LEWIS** 243 ½ acres part entry 897; Heirs John **LAWS** 1000 acres entry 789 range 4 section 3; John J **LONG** 304 acres ranges 7 & 8 section 1; Archibald W. **OVERTON** 80 acres part of entry 490; Nimrod **PICKENS** 640 acres entry 767 range 6 section 2; Edward **PIOTTE** 650 acres entry 862 range 4 section 3; Larkin **PRICE** 625 part of J **M'DOWELL's** 5000 acre entry; Abner **PILLOW** 500 acres entry 624 range 7 section 4; Caleb **PORTOCK** 67, entry 660 range 7 section 3; Wm **RUSSELL** 640 acres; Tyre **RHODES** 640 acres entry 603 range 5 section 6; Elijah **ROBERTSON** 100 acres No 338; Shaw & Craig 640 acres entry 602 range 6 section 2; Abner **SHARP** 2000 acres grant 19; Richard **SMITH** 2500 acres entry 387 range 6 section 3; Wm **SHARP** 400 acres grant 1538; Wm **SHEPHERD** 1028 acres, grant 174; Same 1128 acres, grant 245; Same 1252 entry 387 range 4 section 1; John **TERREL** 1000 acres entry 819 range 9 section 4; James **TREMBLE** 1250 part of grant 469; Willoughby **WILLIAMS** 800 acres part of 1000 acre entry ranges 4 & 5 section 5; Solomon **WATERS** 640 acres entry 92 range 6 section 4….it is ordered by the court that said several tracts of land or so much thereof as shall be sufficient of each of them, to satisfy the taxes….be sold as the law directs. Memphis Advocate, 11/3/1827.

We are glad to welcome to our city Dr. S. E. **BRATTON**, late of South Carolina, who has determined to cast his lot with us, in the prosperous and growing fortunes of Memphis….Memphis Daily Avalanche, 4/29/1859.

I offer for sale my beautiful and desirable residence, in the vicinity of Memphis, about half a mile from the south-east corner of the Corporation, containing 26 ½ acres…E. D. **BRAY**. Memphis Daily Eagle, 12/5/1850.

The remains of Mrs. Mary P., relict of the late Dr. Edward **BREATHITT**, will be attended from the Gayoso House this morning at 11 o'clock, and deposited in the Cenotaph of Butler Cemetery, South Memphis…Sunday morning, February 7th, 1847. Daily Enquirer. It is with painful regret that we announce the demise of Mrs. Mary P., relict of the late Dr. Edward Breathitt, of Nashville. She departed this life yesterday morning at the Gayoso House, about 5 o'clock, amidst the tears of several members of her family who were in attendance during her illness…Daily Enquirer, 2/7/1847.

Died, at the residence of his brother, Edward **BREATHITT**, in Coahoma county, Miss., on the 18th of October, John Eaton **BREATHITT**, in the 31st year of his age. Daily Enquirer, 11/12/1847.

We learn with regret that Mr. Robert **BRECKINRIDGE** was shot in the head and instantly killed in Jackson, Tennessee, on Saturday last, by Mr. Samuel W. **ELROD**. We have learned no particulars. Memphis Daily Appeal, Tues., 7/7/1857.

Married, In St. Francis county by Rev. A. M. **BRYAN**, of Memphis, Mr. James **BRETT**, Jr., to Miss Sue **PATTON**. Memphis Daily Appeal, 2/13/1859.

Mr. Herring **BREWER**, of Dyer County, committed suicide on Thursday night last by hanging himself with the reins of a bridle to the joist in the room where he was sleeping. Mr. Brewer has been for a number of years a very good citizen and in prosperous circumstances but for the few months past has appeared to be in a deranged state of mine—Trenton American 16 ult. Memphis Eagle, Thurs., 3/23/1848.

Married, In this city on Thursday evening, December 24th, by Rev. Mr. Schetsky, Moreau **BREWER**, Esq., of Cairo, Illinois, to M'lle Sophie Louise **TRUMPY**, of Switzerland, Europe. Memphis Daily Appeal, 12/27/1857.

Middleburg, Tenn., Oct. 20th, 1851. At a called meeting of Hatchie Lodge, No. 1151, of Free and Accepted Masons, the following preamble and resolutions were unanimously adopted: Whereas, It hath pleased an all wise Providence…to remove from the circle of our earthly fellowship our brother, Dr. Martin C. **BRIAN**…Resolved, That as a further mark of our high esteem for departed worth, we send a copy of our proceedings on this sad occasion…to the truly bereaved parents and family of our deceased brother …Memphis Appeal, 11/18/1851.

From Our Volunteers.—Several of the Volunteers from this place have returned, under furlough, either sick themselves, or in attendance on the sick. They describe "sojering" on the Rio Grande as a slightly different piece of business from mustering for the "Halls of the Montezumas" in Memphis…We learn from one of the returned volunteers that only four of these who went from this place have died, viz: Geo. W. P. **MOORE** and Dennis **BRICK** of Capt. Ruth's company; S. H. **JOHNSON** (of South Memphis) and P. A. **BLYTHE** of Capt. Cook's; Wm. **GOODRICH**, _____ Massey, _____ Kelly and J. M. **THEIRS**, of Capt. Jones' company, Madison county; E. Crowder, A. **WEBB** and Yancy **WICKS** of Capt. Murray's company, Carroll county. The Tri-Weekly Memphis Enquirer, 9/29/1846.

Died, At the Sewanee House in Nashville, on the 25th inst., Mrs. Bridges, consort of B. H. **BRIDGES**, aged about 50 years. Memphis Daily Appeal, 9/28/1855.

The friends of Elizabeth and Egbert **WOOLDRIDGE** are invited to attend the Funeral of their Nephew, Thomas **BRIDGES**, at their residence this evening at 4 o'clock. Memphis Daily Appeal, 4/28/1857.

Married, In this city on the evening of October 20th, 1857, at the residence of the bride's father, by Rev. J. W. **KNOTT**, Mr. Wm. H. **BRIDGES** and Miss Kate E., daughter of L. R. **RICHARDS**, Esq. Memphis Daily Appeal, 10/22/1857.

Died, At the residence of her husband, near Memphis, on the 31st May, Mrs. Ann C. **BRINKLEY**, in the 22d year of her age…American Eagle Weekly, 6/6/1845.

Memphis and Arkansas Packet. The regular Steam packet Ferry Boat, Captain Brinkley, has recently undergone an entire and thorough overhauling, from keel to hurricane, and from stern to stern, and is now in complete order for the accommodation of the travelling public…the subscriber will promptly attend to passengers on board, at the foot of Union street. G. A. **BRINKLEY**. Memphis Eagle, 10/11/1847.

A most unfortunate affair took place yesterday morning about 8 o'clock, resulting in the probable death of one of our most popular steamboat captains and most estimable citizens. It appears that Captain George **BRINKLEY**, of the James Laughlin, and Mr. Charles **MAY**, of the firm of Newby & May, had passed a few words the previous evening relative to the hiring of a hack, after which Captain Brinkley made some threats, which being conveyed to Mr. May, caused him to arm himself for an attack. Yesterday morning, as Dr. Creighton and Captain Brinkley were passing up Main street and in the direction of Mr. May's stable, that gentleman, apprehending an attack, fired upon Captain Brinkley, one ball taking effect in the abdomen, one in the right hip and one under the cap of the right knee. It is feared his wounds will prove mortal. The circumstance is to be regretted for both are well known citizens and are highly esteemed as high toned and honorable men. Memphis Appeal, 8/3/1854. It is our painful duty to announce the death of Captain George Brinkley, who died at Dr. Creighton's office yesterday morning at a quarter before six o'clock….He leaves an affectionate family and a numerous circle of relatives and warm friends….His remains were taken to Winchester Cenotaph yesterday evening. Memphis Appeal, 8/4/1854.

Mr. John **BRINKLEY**, of this city, has been appointed a Conductor on the Charleston Railroad…Memphis Appeal, 9/17/1852.

Married. On the 24th ult. by Rev. Justinean **WILLIAMS**, Sr., R. C. **BRINKLEY**, Esq., of Memphis, Tenn., and Miss Elizabeth M., daughter of the late Col. James G. **MHOON**, of this county. [North Alabamian, Nov. 3rd] Memphis Appeal, 11/7/1854.

Married, In Fayette Co., on the 6th inst., by the Rev. B. W. **WILLIAMS**, B. W. **BRITT** Esq., late of Virginia, to Miss Mary S., daughter of James B. **EWELL**, Esq. American Eagle, 8/14/1846.

Died, At the residence of her Father, in Memphis, Ten., on Saturday morning, the 10th inst., Mary E. **BRITTINGHAM**—aged 19 years and 7 months. Memphis Appeal, 1/13/1852.

Died, At Baltimore, Maryland, of consumption, Edwin R. **BROADERS**, in the 24th year of his age. Memphis and New Orleans papers please copy. Memphis Whig, 7/1/1856.

Married—In Vicksburg, Miss., on Thursday 27 ult., by Rev. Dr. Weller, Mr. S. A. **BRODHEAD** of Memphis, to Miss Mary W. **CLARK**, late of Richmond, Va. Memphis Enquirer, 1/12/1839.

Land For Sale. 480 acres of land being on both sides of the Pidgeon Roost road, 12 miles south east of Memphis, in Shelby county…Anyone wishing to see the land and learn the terms, will please call on the subscriber who lives adjoining. Jeremiah **BRONAUGH**. Memphis Daily Eagle, 8/13/1847. Married, In this county, on the 4th instant, by the Rev. A. W. **YOUNG**, Dr. J. S. **POINDEXTER**, of Christian co., Ky., to Miss Anna Louisa Bronaugh, daughter of Jeremiah Bronaugh, Esq., of this vicinity. Memphis Eagle & Enquirer, 2/7/1852.

The remains of the distinguished artist, David **BRONSON**, late of Memphis, were brought to this city Wednesday evening by the steamer *Jennie Whipple*, in charge of Capt. C. C. **GRAY**, who was on terms of intimacy with the deceased. The remains will be taken to New York for interment. Mr. Bronson, it will be remembered, died at Little Rock , about six months since. Memphis Daily Appeal, Fri., 12/30/1859.

Married. On the 14th instant by the Rev. J. H. **GRAY**, D.D., Dr. B. F. C. **BROOKS**, of Yazoo City, to Mrs. E. E. **ALEXANDER**, of Memphis. Memphis Appeal, 2/16/1855. Died, On Tuesday morning, the 9th inst., after a short illness, Mrs. Evelina E. Brooks, wife of Dr. B. F. C. Brooks, aged thirty years and nine months. Her parents became permanent residents of Memphis in 1846, where she was married to Dr. Brooks the 14th of February, 1855….She leaves a bereaved and disconsolate husband, two infant children— one a babe of only a few days….Memphis Daily Appeal, 6/13/1857. Married, On Monday, 8th instant, by Rev. Dr. Bryan, Dr. B. F. C. Brooks, of this city, to Miss Mary _. **STEEL**, of Grand Junction. Memphis Weekly Appeal, 3/17/1858.

Married, In Brownsville, Tenn., on the 26th inst., by Rev. John **BATEMAN**, Mr. Benjamin W. **BROOKS** to Miss L. V. **OWEN**. The Franklin Examiner will please copy. Memphis Daily Appeal, 1/30/1859.

Married, On the 9th inst. by Rev. James **YOUNG**, Mr. E. W. **BROOKS**, of this city, to Miss Eliza **RALSTON**, of Big Creek, Shelby county, Tenn. Memphis Weekly Appeal, 11/17/1858.

Having suggested to the clerk of the County Court the insolvency of the estate of F. W. **BROOKS**, deceased, I hereby notify all the creditors of said estate, and all persons interested to file their claims…J. A. **LEWIS**, Administrator. Memphis Appeal, 7/26/1848.

Married, At the residence of Mrs. Scott, near Raleigh, on the 16th instant, by Rev. J. H. **GRAY**, D.D., Mr. Hugh M. **BROOKS** to Miss M. J. **SCOTT**. Memphis Daily Appeal, 1/19/1856.

Last Monday evening a fight occurred near Raleigh between Isaac **BROOKS** and Thornton **ANDERSON**, in which Mr. Brooks was stabbed in the breast, arm and shoulder. Mr. Anderson had married and separated from Mr. Brooks' daughter and the difficulty grew out of this unfortunate circumstance. Anderson is under arrest and awaits his trial. Memphis Appeal, Thurs., 10/12/1854.

Departed this life on Friday night, 11th inst., at his residence on Big Creek, Mr. Lewis **BROOKS**, of Billous Pleurisy, after 11 days illness; his sufferings were very severe. His walk was always upright, and he was resigned to his death. Memphis Enquirer, 5/26/1838.

Married, At the Baptist Church in this city, on Wednesday evening, the 3d inst., by Rev'd Dr. Finley, W. J. **BROOKS**, of Memphis, to Miss Lizzie B. **HILL**, of Jackson, Tenn. Memphis Eagle, 4/8/1850.

Married: In Dangerfield, Texas, on the 20th June, Wm. **BROOKS**, Esq., formerly of Shelby co., Tenn., to Miss Matilda **HUGHES**, of Cass co., Texas. Weekly Memphis Eagle, 7/26/1849.

Married. On Tuesday, August 1st by H. F. **HILL**, Esq., Mr. Jacob **BROT_EPE** to Miss Rosina **DEFELI**. Memphis Appeal, 8/2/1854.

Mr. A. H. **BROWN** (long known as the proprietor of the Maltbie House,) departed this life at Clinton, Louisiana, April 2d, leaving a widow and three orphan children together with a numerous circle of acquaintances to mourn his loss. Memphis Enquirer, 4/18/1848.

Died – In Raleigh, on Saturday last, of congestive fever, Miss Alethea **BROWN**, of Covington, aged 18 years. Memphis Enquirer, Thurs., 9/8/1836.

There was a very good attendance at Odd Fellows' Hall on Saturday night, to witness the presentation of diplomas to the graduates of the Memphis Medical College. The following gentlemen were granted diplomas: B. H. **BROWN**, J. J. **CARLTON**, J. J. **CRISP**, J. M. **GADDIS**, O. P. **GREENWOOD**, G. P. **MATTHEWSON**, J. L. **NOEL**, C. B. **VAN SPIEGEL**, B. J. **THIGPEN**, A. J. **THOMPSON** and A. J. **SIMMONS**....Memphis Daily Appeal, Tues., 3/2/1856.

Married, On the 9 th instant, at Eureika, near Sledgeville, Miss., by the Rev. David O. **ANDREWS**, Bedford **BROWN**, Esq., of this city, to Miss S. R. A. **STOKES** of Panola. Richmond Enquirer and Whig will please copy. Memphis Appeal, 9/12/1851. For Sale—A valuable Farm lying on the Mississippi river, 20 miles from Memphis, in the county of Tipton, Tenn., containing 600 acres....Bedford Brown. Memphis Appeal, 10/1/1853.

Married, On Thursday evening, the 29th instant, by Esquire Horne, Mr. David S. **BROWN**, of New York, and Miss Mary Jane **POLK**, of Memphis, Tenn. Memphis Daily Appeal, 1/31/1857.

A Cold-Blooded Murder—We learn that on Tuesday morning a Mr. E. M. **BROWN** was shot by one Thomas **HOFTER**, at Bloomington, Tipton county, on account of an old grudge between the two. Mr. B. had started to Memphis in company with some five or six of his neighbors, and was overtaken at Bloomington by Hofter, and while talking he was asked by some one of the party what he was going to do with his double-barreled shotgun, to which Mr. Brown replied that he thought he was hunting squirrels, and then Hofter, stepping back, said, "No, I hae this gun for such rascals as you," and shot him down. He then made his escape. Memphis Daily Appeal, 10/9/1856.

All persons indebted to the estate of Honor **BROWN**, deceased, will make immediate payment...Dan **VAUGHT**, Ex'r. Memphis Enquirer, 9/2/1837.

Married: In this city, on the 11th inst., by the Rev. G. W. **COONS**, Dr. J. N. **BROWN**, to Miss Mary B., daughter of Major James **PENN**, both of this city. Memphis Eagle, 10/12/1848.

Lieut. J. N. **BROWN**, U.S.N., recently attached to the Memphis Navy Yard, one of the most gallant and accomplished officers of the Navy was in the city yesterday from his plantation in Coahoma county, Mississippi. Memphis Daily Appeal, 9/11/1855.

Married, On the 16th of April by A. L. **McCAIN**, Esq., in the village of Potersville, Tipton county, Tenn., Mr. J. Turner **BROWN** and Miss Susan **WHITLOCK**, both of that vicinity. Memphis Daily Appeal, 4/30/1857.

Married, On the 19th November, 1857, in Lauren's District, South Carolina, by Rev. J. T. **PEARCE**, Dr. J. W. **BROWN**, of Lafayette, Miss., to Miss Rachel **BELL**, of the former place. Memphis Daily Appeal, 12/4/1857.

Died, Of measles, in Grenada, Miss., on Thursday last, Miss Jennett T. **BROWN**, in the 18th year of her age. Memphis Daily Appeal, Sun., 6/7/1857.

Married, In this county on the 5th(?) day of April last by W. G. **ROBERTS**, Esq., Mr. John **BROWN** to Mrs. Mariah **LOVING**. Memphis Appeal, 6/26/1855.

Died, on Tuesday the 24th February, Mrs. Jane B. Brown, consort of Col. John L. **BROWN**, formerly of Memphis.—Nash. Union. Weekly Appeal, 3/6/1846.

Died, At Memphis, Tenn., August 14th, 1852, Dr. John T. **BROWN**, of Lancaster county, Pennsylvania. Lancaster City and Intercourse papers please copy. Memphis Appeal, 8/17/1852.

Died on the morning of the 17th inst., at the residence of her father, Capt. C. B. N. **RICE** in Copiah county, Mississippi, Mrs. Elizabeth Brown, widow of the late Joseph **BROWN**, and mother of Hon. A. G. **BROWN**, Senator to Congress from Mississippi. This venerable lady was nearly seventy-five years of age....She was raised in South Carolina and emigrated to Mississippi with her husband more than thirty years ago, and settled in Copiah county, then a frontier country....The deceased had followed her husband and four children to the grave, leaving three sons and one daughter to mourn her loss....Memphis Daily Appeal, 11/27/1855.

Married, On the 25th ult. at the residence of F. W. **GOODRICH**, Esq., of Shelby county, Tenn., by Rev. Wm. Carey **CRANE**, Dr. L. M.(?) **BROWN**, of Georgia, to Miss Georgiana **MALONE**, of Shelby county, Tenn. Memphis Weekly Appeal, 3/17/1858.

Married, On the 19th inst. by Rev. Philip **TUGGLE**, Mr. R. B. **BROWN** to Miss Mary A. Harrison, eldest daughter of Capt. C. **HARRISON**, all of this county. Memphis Daily Appeal, 12/23/1855.

We have lately fallen into possession of the facts connected with a remarkable surgical operation for strangulated inguinal hernia, performed by Dr. R. F. **BROWN**, of our city, in the immediate vicinity of Memphis, upon a Negro man, belonging to a gentleman known to many of our citizens. The disease had been of five days existence before the operation, and the bowels which had been all this time in the left groin, had adherred both to the rupture and the misentery. The Negro has now recovered and is doing well. A report of this unusally successful and highly creditable operation in surgery is in process of publication in the New Orleans Medical Journal, and will soon be given to the public. Memphis Eagle, 12/20/1850.

We are pained to learn of the death of Dr. R. H. **BROWN**, of Macon, Fayette county, Tennessee, which occurred on Wednesday, the 4th inst. He was an old and esteemed citizen of Fayette county....His disease was pneumonia. Memphis Daily Appeal, 11/8/1857.

Died, at Mason, Tenn., Monday evening the 27th December, Robert A., son of Dr. Robert A. and Lucy Ann **BROWN** in the tenth year of his age. Memphis Appeal, 1/25/1848.

Married: On the 15th inst., by the Rev. Mr. Dennis, Mr. S. B. **BROWN**, to Miss Minerva L. **MONTAGUE**, both of this city. Memphis Eagle, 11/18/1848.

Departed this life on Thursday the 8th inst., after a protracted and painful illness, Charles Emmerson, infant son of Col. S. R. **BROWN**. Memphis Enquirer, 11/17/1838. Died. Near Raleigh, Ten. on Wednesday morning the 9th inst. Mrs. Nancy Brown, consort of Col. S. R. Brown. Memphis Enquirer, 8/19/1837.

Died. On Wednesday, December 6th, Anna Herschell, daughter of S. R. and S. A. **BROWN**, aged two years....Services by Rev. H. S. **PORTER**. Memphis Appeal, 12/7/1854.

Married. At the residence of Col. Sam **WINSTON** on the 1_th instant, by Rev. Joseph **EATON**, Mr. W. D. **BROWN**, of Memphis, and Miss Mu_adora **RUCKER**, of Rutherford county, Tenn. Memphis Whig, 5/16/1855.

Died, in this city on the 15th instant, Mrs. America E., wife of Mr. W.N. **BROWN**, (firm of Jones, Brown & Co.,) and daughter of Mrs. S.R. **FORREST**, of DeSoto county, Miss....She was born July 7th, 1837, at Tuscaloosa, Alabama and was, therefore, when she died, eighteen years, nine months and eight days old. On the 7th of July, an equal, in a class of ten young ladies....she graduated at the Mississippi Female College....and left a devoted husband, a doting mother, affectionate brothers and sisters, warm hearted friends, and an innocent but unconscious infant, two months old, to mourn....Her remains were interred at her mother's residence, near Hernando....Memphis Daily Appeal, 4/26/1856.

Married, In this city on Wednesday the 7th instant, by Rev. Thos. **JOYNER**, Mr. W. N. **BROWN**, of this city, to Miss Helen **ALLEN**, of Shelby county. Memphis Daily Appeal, 12/8/1859.

Masonic Tribute of Respect. Whereas, It has pleased an all-wise Providence to remove from our midst our esteemed brother and friend, William D. **BROWN**, we therefore offer (as members of South Memphis Lodge No. 118, A.Y.M.) our sincere condolence to his bereaved family....Memphis Daily Appeal, 5/27/1857.

Married, At the residence of Mrs. Anne M. **BROWN** on Sunday morning, 13th inst. by the Rev. Dr. Edgar, Wm. L. **BROWN**, Esq., and Miss Mary **McNEIL**, all of Nashville. Memphis Eagle & Enquirer, 3/23/1853.

Married. In Hernando, on the 2d inst. by the Rev. L. C. **TAYLOR**, Mr. Wm. N. **BROWN**, of the firm of Brown, Jones & Co., to Miss America Forrest, daughter of the late Jonathan **FORREST** of Desoto County, Mississippi. Memphis Appeal, 1/9/1855. Died, On Sunday morning, the 21st of December, A.D. 1856, in DeSoto county, Miss., of scarlet fever, America C., only child and infant daughter of Wm. N. Brown (of the firm of Jones, Brown & Co.) and his late wife, America Forrest, aged nine months. Memphis Daily Appeal, 12/23/1856.

We were pained yesterday to learn of the death of our fellow-citizen, Wm. R. **BROWN**....He was a week ago stricken down by paralysis while performing his duties as a mail agent on the Mississippi river. He came to Memphis some years ago from Giles county, Tennessee, which county he had formerly represented in the Legislature of the State. For some years he held a prominent position in the Navy Yard of this city, a position conferred by President Polk. He leaves a widow and a large family of children to mourn his death. They have the sympathy of a large circle of friends, both in Middle and West Tennessee. Memphis Daily Appeal, 11/18/1856.

William T. **BROWN**, jr., died of his wounds early yesterday morning and was buried last evening. Memphis Whig, 5/22/1855.

Died. In this city on Monday morning last at three o'clock, Mr. Wm. T. **BROWN**, jr., son of the Hon. W. T. **BROWN** of this city, after a short but painful illness....Memphis Appeal, Tues., 5/22/1855.

Married—On Monday the 1st inst. by the Rev. Wm. **HYER**, Mr. William W. **BROWN**, to Miss Serelda **FRAIM** (?) all of this vicinity. The Appeal, 1/5/1844.

Died, On Friday, February 16th, at half-past 4 A.M., of whooping-cough, Royal Weidler, son of J. W. S. and Samantha C. **BROWNE**, aged 10 weeks and 5 days. Memphis Weekly Appeal, 3/3/1858.

Married, At Aurora, Indiana, on Wednesday the 16th inst. by Rev. Mr. Sullivan, Mr. Joseph **BRUCE**, of Memphis, to Miss America, Daughter of Capt. James **WEAVER**, of the former place. Memphis Eagle & Enquirer, 2/23/1853.

Married, On Thursday, the 27th, by Rev. P. S. **GAYLE**, Mr. William S. **BRUCE**, V.G. of Memphis Lodge No. 6, I.O.O.F., to Miss Elizabeth **WORLAND**. Memphis Enquirer, 1/29/1848.

Married, On the 27th ult., at the residence of the bride's father, at Canton, Ohio, by Rev. Mr. E. **BIRKETT**, Mr. Samuel **BRUCH**, of this city, and Miss Kate Patterson, daughter of Rev. _. C. **PATTERSON**. Memphis Daily Avalanche, 2/10/1859.

Married, On Monday Evening, the 10th inst., in Calvary Church, by the Rev. Dr. Page, Mr. Elias E. **BRUNNER**, of Vicksburg, Miss., to Miss Susan W. **GLADDING**, of this city. Memphis Eagle, 6/12/1850.

The friends and acquaintances of A. C. **RUSSELL** are invited to attend the funeral of the late Mrs. Elizabeth **BRUNS**, from his residence on Shelby street, at 9 o'clock this morning. Memphis Daily Appeal, 7/20/1856.

The body of Frederick **BRUNS**, who was drowned on Monday last while on a hunting excursion, was found and brought in on yesterday. A duck and a squirrel were found in his game bag. Memphis Appeal, Sat., 11/15/1851.

Rev. Alfred M.. **BRYAN**, who has been on a visit to our city for the last ten days in obedience to the request and call of the Cumberland Presbyterian Church, leaves this evening on the packet *Memphis* for Pittsburg, his former residence. Having accepted the call made upon him by the Church, he will return accompanied by his family, about the 1st of January. Mr. Bryan is a native of Logan county, Ky., was licensed by Father Harris in the year 1820, and ordained to the whole work of the ministry in 1824—was commissioned...to respond to the call from Pennsylvania. After laboring some years in the field, he established the church in the city of Pittsburg to which congregation he has preached for the last twenty-three years....Memphis Daily Appeal, 11/27/1855. We deeply regret to learn by a dispatch received here, that a son of the Rev. Mr. Bryan was killed by the explosion of the boilers of the steamer Metropolis, on the Ohio river, above Cincinnati, a few days since. Mr. Bryan, with his family, was on board the ill-fated steamer en route to this city, to assume the pastoral charge of the Cumberland Presbyterian Church. Mr. B. is now on the steamer Delta, and will arrive in the city about Wednesday next. Memphis Daily Appeal, Tuesday, 4/1/1856. Died, On the evening of the 6th(?) instant, in the 7th year of her age, Louisa Rahm, daughter of Rev. A. M. and Ann Eliza Bryan. The friends and acquaintances of the family are invited to attend her funeral This Evening at 3 o'clock, from the residence of her father, on Market street, second door East of Third street....Memphis Daily Appeal, 4/7/1857. We regret to learn that our esteemed friend, Rev. Dr. Bryan, of the Cumberland Presbyterian Church, yesterday resigned the pastoral care of that church, having accepted a call from the Cumberland Presbyterian Church in Pittsburg. Memphis Daily Avalanche, 2/28/1859.

Married, On the 13th instant by Rev. Mr. Thomas, Mr. S. L. **BRYAN** to Miss Mary L. **WAYNSBURG**—all of this city. Memphis Daily Appeal, 10/16/1859.

Died, of billious fever at the residence of her grandson, Richard **CLARK**, in South Memphis on Friday, September 28th, Mrs. Sally Ann **BRYAN**, aged 66 years....We feel that words are empty and powerless to depict the loss of the idolized mother to her beloved and only daughter, to her devoted grand daughter, whom she reared, and from whom death alone could separate her—these, and the absent grandchildren and the little children to the third generation....Memphis Whig, 10/2/1855.

W. C. **BRYAN**, Resident Dentist, Memphis, Tenn. Office on Shelby Street...Daily Enquirer, 6/4/1847. Died, On the 10th inst., Emma, youngest daughter of W. C. and Clara E. Bryan. Memphis Whig, 6/12/1856.

I will sell on the premises to the highest bidder at public outcry, on Monday, December 10, 1855, at 12 o'clock, M., a farm consisting of 320 Acres, lying 7 miles east of Cockrum's ___ Roads, near the Chulahoma and Memphis Roads, belonging to the estate of Thomas **BRYANT**, deceased....A. A. **BRYANT**, Adm'r. Memphis Daily Appeal, 9/14/1855.

Died, At 3 o'clock, A.M., January 31st, 1853, Mrs. Mary Bryce, widow and relict of the late Archibald **BRYCE**, of Goochland county, Va. The friends and acquaintances of the family are requested to attend her funeral.....from her late residence, corner of Monroe and Third streets. Richmond, Va. papers please copy. Memphis Eagle & Enquirer, 2/1/1853.

The subscriber offers his present residence for sale, on the Pigeon Roost Road, 21 miles from Memphis...B. B. **BUCHANAN**. Memphis Eagle & Enquirer, 4/27/1852.

From the Eagle – Departed this life, yesterday morning, at the residence of W. W. **HART**, Miss Emily **BUCK**, sister of Mr. Silas **BUCK**. This bereavement is peculiarly distressing and melancholy, and should call for the sympathies of the friends of this worthy gentleman, as it has pleased a Wise Providence to take from him, within a few weeks, a beloved wife, a mother, and sister. The Appeal, 11/10/1843.

The Ripley *Advertiser* of the 10th inst. contains the following paragraph, from which it appears that the body of the man which drifted on the shore five miles below Randolph with his skull fractured and a wound in his breast, is supposed from the circumstances detailed, to have committed suicide: Our Community was painfully shocked and surprised at the intelligence brought by last Tuesday evening's mail of the almost certain suicide of our fellow townsman J. H. **BUCK**, by drowning himself in the Mississippi River.— Letters have been received from him stating such to have been his intention on the 31st ult., and giving directions about his affairs here....Memphis Appeal, 8/18/1854.

Married, In this vicinity, this morning, by the Rev. Mr. Hyer, Henry G. **BUCKINGHAM** (of the firm of G. N. Candee & Co.) to Miss Eliza **McINTOSH**. American Eagle, 10/20/1843.

Married, On the 17th inst., by J. **WALDRAN**, Esq., Mr. W. A. **BUFFALOE**, to Mrs. Mary Jane **HOWELL**, all of this city, formerly of Holly Springs, Miss. Memphis Daily Eagle, 12/19/1850.

It becomes our painful duty to record the death of our esteemed friend and fellow citizen: Abraham C. **BUFORD**, Esq., late of the firm of Woodward & Buford, Commission Merchants, New Orleans, who departed this life on the morning of the 27th ult., at the residence of James F. **LAUDERDALE**, Esq., near this place. Mr. Buford, with his family, was just returning from New Orleans, to spend the summer with their relations near Germantown.....Mr. Buford was in the 33d year of his age.....He has left a wife and child to mourn his untimely loss. Several years ago he became a member of the Presbyterian Church.....He was buried near Germantown...American Eagle, 5/6/1842.

Married, On the 22d inst., by the Rev. Dr. H. S. **PORTER**, Mr. Abram I. **BUFORD** to Miss E. Ida **BRYAN**. Memphis Appeal, 12/23/1852.

Capt. **BUGHER** – John we mean – is here, on hand with the fast running packet *John Swasey*, ready to accommodate those of the good citizens of Memphis who may wish to travel towards a more northern clime—leaving at 5 o'clock this evening for Louisville and Cincinnati...Memphis Eagle & Enquirer, 6/22/1852.

Died—In this city, of scarlet fever, at the residence of Mrs. Ann **GRAHAM**, on Friday evening the 28th ultimo, Margaret Madora, aged six years—also on the evening of Saturday, the 29th ult., Sarah E., aged 8 years, both little daughters of Mrs. Mary E. **BULLARD**, late of Fayette county. These little girls were the only children of their afflicted mother, who is now left alone a disconsolate widow and mother.....Weekly Appeal, 12/12/1845.

Married, On the 4th inst. by Rev. Robert **FRAZIER**, Mr. Albert **BULLINGTON** to Miss Fanny **REASONOVER**, both of Desoto county, Miss. Memphis Eagle & Enquirer, 5/7/1853.

Died, In this city on the evening of the 10th inst., Mrs. Susan Bullock, consort of Major M. **BULLOCK**, joint Representative from Madison county....She was long a member of the Methodist Church....— *Jackson (Tenn.) Whig.* Memphis Daily Appeal, 10/18/1857.

Married, In St. Francis county, Ark., on Tuesday, April 23d, by Rev. T. S. N. **KING**, Mr. Creed M. **BUMPASS**, of Memphis, to Miss Mary Virginia **HICKS**, daughter of John H. **HICKS**, Esq. Memphis Eagle, 5/1/1850.

Maj. Jno. L. **BUNCH**, late of Alabama, has become connected with the editorial *corps* of the *Avalanche*, succeeding Mr. Franc M. **PAUL** as local editor, who retires....Memphis Daily Appeal, 10/1/1859.

M. J. **BUNCH**, Attorney At Law. Office on Main street...Memphis Appeal, 12/15/1852.

Married, On the evening of the 2d instant, by Rev. T. A. **WARE**, at the residence of Rev. J. W. **KNOTT**, in Memphis, Mr. Sam. I. **BUNCH** to Miss Sallie, daughter of the late Gen. Levin H. **COE**. Memphis Daily Appeal, 12/5/1855.

Died, in La Grange, Texas, August 5th, 1854, Mrs. Nina E. Bunting, wife of Rev. R. F. **BUNTING**, Pastor of the Presbyterian Church of that place and daughter of Dr. S. H. **DOXEY**, late of Hardeman county, Tenn. She was in the 18th year of her age....Memphis Appeal, 9/5/1854.

Married, Near Hernando, Miss., on the 20th inst. by Rev. Wm. Carey **CRANE**, Dr. G. Oscar **BUNTYN**, of Shelby county, Ten., to Miss Adeline C. **ODOM**, of De Soto county, Miss. Memphis Appeal, 4/23/1853.

Having obtained letters of administration on the estate of Spencer C. **BUNTYN**, at the April term, 1859, of the County Court of Shelby county, the undersigned gives notice to all persons having claims....G. **BUNTYN**. Memphis Daily Appeal, 4/12/1859.

Married, On Wednesday evening, the 14th inst., at the residence of Col. J. _. **WILKINS**, by Elder Wm. J. **BARBEE**, Mr. E. L. **BURFORD** to Miss M. E. **PRITCHARD**, all of DeSoto county, Miss. Memphis Daily Appeal, 12/18/1859.

Married, At the residence of C. H. **BENNETT**, Cedar Lake, Texas, by Rev. Mr. Dashiell, Mr. S. R. **BURFORD**, of DeSoto county, Miss., and Miss Kate C. **BENNETT**. Memphis Daily Appeal, 9/19/1856.

Died, At his residence on Water Seca(?) Bayou, Jefferson county, Ark., on the 16th instant, Zadock H. **BURFORD**, in the 47th year of his age. Moulton Democrat please copy. Memphis Daily Appeal, 7/26/1859.

Died. In Louisville, Ky., on the 10th December last, Mr. Wm. H. **BURGESS**, of Madison county, Tenn. Memphis Appeal, 1/9/1854.

Report of the Board of Health. For the last 24 hours ending 12 M., July 14. Mr. Patrick **BURK**, (Irish) aged 45, Appoplexy.....Memphis Enquirer, 7/15/1849.

A frame building, occupied as a boarding house by Patrick **BURKE**, near the corner of Beal and Shelby streets, was consumed by fire about half past 1 o'clock this morning...Memphis Appeal, 7/28/1851.

Died, In Tipton county, Tenn., of Typhoid Fever, on the 30th of March last, Mr. Anderson **BURKHART**. He was a member of the Cumberland Presbyterian Church and has left a large circle of friends to mourn his loss. Memphis Weekly Appeal, 4/21/1858.

We regret to be informed that the Rev. Mr. **BURNS** is shortly to leave our city, where, as Pastor of the Second Baptist Church he has made himself so universally respected and useful as a clergyman and so beloved by all classes as a man. Mr. Burns has accepted a call for a congregation at Jackson,

Mississippi...Memphis Appeal, 4/16/1852. Married. At the Mansion House, Jackson, Miss., on Tuesday evening, 15th inst., by Rev. Mr. Pomeroy, Rev. D. E. **BURNS**, Pastor of the Baptist Church, to Miss Tellula **SLAUGHTER**. Memphis Appeal, 8/25/1854.

James **BURNS**, an Irishman, fell overboard from the steamer Honduras, at the landing on Saturday and was drowned. Memphis Appeal, Tues., 10/5/1852.

Died, At Commerce, Miss., on the 23d of February, 1858, Wm. Henry, son of R. H. and Mary A. **BURNS**, aged 7 years, 8 months and 4 days. Memphis Weekly Appeal, 3/3/1858.

Died, In this city on the 11th inst., Flora, only child of Lutha S. and Jane C. **BURR**, aged 1 year, 2 months and 11 days. Memphis Eagle, 8/14/1850.

James A. **BURRELL** & Co. Beg leave to inform the inhabitants of Memphis, its vicinity and the surrounding country, that they have commenced the Saddle, Harness and Trunk Manufacturing ...Memphis Appeal, 1/13/1848. Married, on the 18th inst., by the Rev. James **ROBINSON** Mr. Jas. A. **BURRELL**, of this city, to Miss Jane, daughter of Wm. **FITZSIMMOUS**, Esq., of Alleghany City, Pa. Memphis Enquirer, 4/26/1848.

A difficulty occurred on last Thursday evening, in Whiteville, Tenn., in which, it is stated, a Mr. Montgomery killed John **BURTON**; both were residents of that place. Memphis Appeal, 12/13/1854.

Married.—in the vicinity of Sommerville, on the 23d of August, by the Rev. H. **CHAMBERLAIN**, Maj. William **BURTON**, Esq., Circuit Court Clerk, to Mrs. Sarah C. **WATSON**, all of this town. Memphis Enquirer, 9/5/1848.

Mr. J. **BUSSEY**, of Collierville, in this county, was shot in this place on Wednesday last about 2 o'clock, by Albert G. **MOON**, who immediately made his escape. Mr. Bussey's recovery is thought, by the physicians, to be extremely doubtful. Memphis Enquirer, Fri., 5/1/1840.

Died, In Madison county, on Saturday, 9th inst., of inflammation of the brain, Birwell **BUTLER**. Memphis Appeal, 8/18/1851.

Mr. E. C. **BUTLER**, late of Nashville, has located his interest in Memphis and is now opening a most superb stock of Dry Goods...Memphis Appeal, 1/23/1851.

The undersigned having been qualified at the April term, 1849, of the County Court of Shelby County, as Administrator of the estate of R. M. **BUTLER**, dec'd., hereby notifies all persons having claim...J. M. **PATRICK**. Memphis Eagle, 5/3/1849.

Died, In Jackson, Tenn., on the morning of Saturday last, after a lingering illness of two years, Mrs. Martha __., consort of Dr. Wm. E. **BUTLER**, of Jackson, in the 66th year of her age. The family of Mrs. Butler were among the pioneers of West Tennessee, having settled in Madison county at an early period when the county was a wilderness. She was for forty-five years an exemplary member of the Presbyterian Church....winning the love and affection of all who surrounded her in the relations of husband, child, friend and neighbor....Memphis Daily Appeal, 9/9/1857.

Married, On the 6th inst. at Grenada, Miss., by Rev. Wm. Carey **CRANE**, President of Semple Broaddus College, Wm. R. **BUTLER**, Esq., to Miss Penelope V. H. **TALBERT**, of the first named place. Memphis Daily Appeal, 12/10/1859.

Died, At Friar's Point on the 10th inst., of Cholera Morbus, Wm. T. **BUTLER**, aged 32 years, a native of Ireland. He has been a very respectable citizen of this city for the last seven years. His remains were interred in the Catholic graveyard on Monday morning. Being a member of the Hibernian Society, the members of that body attended his funeral in a procession...Memphis Appeal, 12/14/1852.

The friends and acquaintances of Mr. Z. **BUTLER** are requested to attend the funeral of his wife at 3 o'clock This Evening from the corner of Madison and Fourth streets. Services by Rev. Mr. Drane. Memphis Daily Appeal, 6/15/1858.

Dr. Joseph Norman **BYBEE**, Offers his services in the various branches of The Medical profession to the people of Memphis....The Appeal, 10/4/1844.

Ethan E. **BYRON** was yesterday arraigned and brought before Justice Curtis on a charge of having obtained money under false pretences from Messrs. Bond and Odell, and in default of bail was committed to jail to await his trial at the next term of the Criminal and Commercial Court of Memphis. Memphis Enquirer, 4/20/1848.

Mr. and Mrs. **CADWALLADER**, residing on the corner of Main and Pontotoc streets, were taken down with the fever last week and are now both dead, leaving no children to inherit their name and hard earned property. Memphis Whig, 10/2/1855.

Married, In this city on Thursday evening, September 2d, by Rev. J. H. **GRAY**, D.D., Mr. E. **CADWALLADER** to Mrs. Isabella **ROBINSON**, all of this city. Memphis Appeal, 9/4/1852.

Miss Harriet **CAIN**—We are gratified to learn that this accomplished young lady-artist has taken up her residence in this city with a view of practising here permanently her beautiful art of portrait painting. Memphis Daily Avalanche, 6/20/1859.

An affray occurred in Eaton, Gibson county, Tenn., on the 30th ult., in which two men were killed, one by the name of J. P. **CALAHAN** and the other W. **BUCHANAN**. Calahan, it seems, had posted Buchanan, using approbrious epithets, which resulted in an interview and demand for retraction. Calahan refused to retract. Shots were exchanged, Calahan being killed upon the spot, and Buchanan died the following Tuesday. Memphis Appeal, Tues., 10/9/1854.

Married, On the 20th inst., at the residence of Mrs. Crenshaw, by Rev. J. T. C. **COLLINS**, Mr. E. W. **CALDWELL**, of the firm of Copeland, Edmonds & Co., to Mrs. Lucy _. **CRENSHAW**, of Shelby county, Tenn. Memphis Daily Appeal, 1/21/1859.

Married, On the 22d inst., by Rev. Dr. Grundy, Jas. C. **CALHOUN**, Esq., of South Carolina, to Miss Blandina M., second daughter of _____ **KIRTLAND**, Esq., of this city. Memphis Weekly Appeal, 12/29/1858.

Jeremiah **CALLAHAN**, a native of Ireland and a man of family, fell from the second story window of the Mississippi House, on Shelby street, Monday night, and died from injuries received by the fall a few hours afterwards....Memphis Daily Appeal, Wed., 5/4/1859.

A man named William **CALLAHAN** died very suddenly in the city calaboose Wednesday night, under such circumstances as to warrant the belief that his death was caused by the rupture of a blood-vessel. The deceased was confined on a charge of vagrancy, and it is a melancholy fact that his wife was incarcerated with him at the time of his death....Memphis Daily Appeal, 11/18/1859.

The members of the Typographical Union of this city yesterday attended the funeral of ED. T. **CALLAN**, a respected member of that body, who was from St. Albans, Vermont. Mr. Callan had been employed at the Appeals office....His complaint was consumption. The Typographical Union attended to him with the kindest care during his sickness, and buried him in their lot in Elmwood Cemetery....Memphis Daily Appeal, 7/9/1858.

Married, On the morning of the 12th instant, at the residence of Mrs. J. W. **HARRIS**, by the Rev. Joseph R. **HAMILTON**, Mr. Jackson C. **CALLICOTT** and Miss Fannie W. **HARRIS**, both of DeSoto county, Miss. Memphis Daily Appeal, 8/21/1856.

Died. In this city, on Monday last, of paralysis, Mrs. Mary A. **CALMESE**, recently of Covington, in the 65th year of her age. The deceased was suddenly attacked while riding in a carriage, and died in a few hours. Memphis Eagle, Thurs., 6/7/1849.

Married, In this city on Thursday 11th inst., by Justice Rose, Mr. B. F. **CAMP** to Miss Margaret **JACKSON**—all of Memphis. Memphis Appeal, 3/13/1852.

W. M. F. **CAMP**. Having located in Memphis, tenders his professional services, to the public. Memphis Appeal, 10/14/1847.

Married, In Northampton Co., North Carolina, on the 19th Sept., by Rev. Mr. Wilson, Dr. William F. **CAMP**, of Memphis, to Miss Sarah **RIVES**, of the former place. Memphis Daily Eagle, 10/16/1850.

Married, on Thursday evening, 13th inst., by Rev. Dr. Warner, Mr. David G. **CAMPBELL** to Miss Levina **BURNS**, all of this city. Memphis Enquirer, 8/15/1846.

Married, At the residence of the bride's father in Choctaw county, on Thursday, the __ last, by Rev. J. F. **GOLDING**, Mr. J. L. **CAMPBELL** to Miss Eliza F. **McCAUGHEY**, all of Choctaw county, Miss. Memphis Daily Appeal, 12/16/1857.

Married—At Calvary Church, in Memphis, on the 4th inst., by Rev. Geo. **WHITE**, Mr. B. C. **CANDEE** to Miss Mary **MOSIER**, all of this city. Memphis Daily Avalanche, 5/7/1859.

We understand that Prof. B. H. **CAPERS**, of this city, has accepted a liberal offer, the Presidency of the "Southern Female College," near Rockey Springs, Miss., in connection with Dr. T. H. **CAPERS**....Prof. Capers will move to the scene of his labors in September....Memphis Daily Avalanche, 6/10/1859.

Married, At the residence of O. C. **WOODWARD**, Esq., in this city, on the evening of the 16th instant, by Rev. A. M. **BRYAN**, Frank G. **CAPERS**, Esq., to Miss Victoria **WOODWARD**, all of Memphis. Memphis Weekly Appeal, 3/24/1858.

Died, on 20th September last, John **CAREY**, a resident of Shelby co, Tenn. Memphis Enquirer, 3/25/1837.

Died, in this vicinity, on the 4th, Mrs. Mary **CAREY**, aged 57 years. American Eagle, 7/14/1843.

Married, In South Memphis, on the 8th inst., by Rev. J. H. **GRAY**, Mr. D. **CARLISLE**, of Memphis, to Miss Jane **EDWARDS**, of the former place. Memphis Enquirer, 8/10/1848.

Petition for Divorce. Harriet J. **CARLISLE**, versus Daniel **CARLISLE**. In the Law Side of the Common Law and Chancery Court of the city of Memphis. It appearing to the undersigned, Clerk and Master in vacation, from the Complainant's petition that the Defendant, Daniel Carlisle, is a non-resident of the State of Tennessee....commanding him to appear before the Judge of said Court, at the court house in Memphis, on the First Monday in November Next, and plead, answer or demur the Plaintiff's petition, or it will be taken for confessed and set for hearing *exparte*....Memphis Daily Appeal, 10/7/1858.

Gov. Andrew Johnson has re-appointed John M. **CARMACK**, Esq., of Shelby county, one of the Directors, on the part of the State, in the Memphis and Charleston Railroad Company. Memphis Daily Appeal, 10/10/1857.

Died, On Saturday evening the 27th inst., of Croup, David Brown, infant son of James A. and Elizabeth M. **CARNES**, of this city. Memphis Appeal, 11/29/1852.

Married, By the Rev. Mr. Tomes on the evening of the 5th inst., Dr. Henry **CAROW** to Miss Catherine, daughter of the late David **SAFFARANS**, Esq., all of Nashville. Memphis Eagle & Enquirer, 1/15/1853.

Married, In Jackson, Tenn., on the evening of the 24th December last, at the residence of the bride's father, by Rev. Aaron V. **JONES**, Mr. John C. **CARPENTER**, late of Eaton(?), N. Y., to Miss Mariah **TAYLOR**. Memphis Daily Appeal, 1/13/1858.

Died, Suddenly, at his plantation, fourteen miles above this place, on the night of the 3rd instant, Capt. Gideon **CARR**, aged about 55 years. He was an old and respectable settler, having been a resident of this vicinity for the last nine years. Memphis Advocate, 3/8/1828.

Died. In this city, on Saturday, the 7th inst., Capt. James C. **CARR**, in the 51st year of his age. The subject of this notice was born in Sumner co., in this State, and removed to Memphis in 1844. He leaves an interesting family...Memphis Appeal, 6/14/1851.

Married—On Wednesday, 24th inst., at the residence of James **WOODS**, Esq., by the Rev. S. S. **MOODY**, Mr. Jesse D. **CARR**, merchant, of this place, to Miss Elizabeth **WOODS**, formerly of Philadelphia. American Eagle, 5/25/1843. Jesse D. Carr, Receiving, Forwarding and Commission Merchant, and Dealer in Groceries and Produce, Memphis, Ten. The Appeal, 7/7/1843.

Married, On Thursday, 18th January, by the Rev. Dr. Page, Mr. John Hudson **CARR**, to Miss Sallie C. **ANDERSON**, daughter of Maj. Nath'l **ANDERSON**, U.S.A. all of this city. Memphis Eagle, 1/25/1849. All persons having claims against the Estate of John Hudson Carr, dec'd., are requested to present the same for payment.....E. M. **YERGER**, Adm'r., Sallie C. Carr, Adm'x. of the late J. H. Carr. Memphis Eagle, 10/18/1849. It has become the painful duty of this Lodge again to consign to their final resting place the remains of a worthy member of their mystic order.—Brother John Hudson Carr is no more. He died at the residence of his father-in-law, Col. N. **ANDERSON**, of this city, on the morning of the 19th instant. He was a native of Virginia. Brother Carr was a gentleman in easy circumstances, of extensive connexions, of a disposition mild, amiable, social and conciliatory; and but recently married.....The several Lodges of the Masonic brother-hood, in this city, united in paying the last sad homage to the memory of departed worth. The Rev. Dr. Page officiated according to the rites of the Episcopal Church.....The city papers, and the "Reveille," at Glasgow, Ky., will please copy. Memphis Enquirer, 7/24/1849.

Died, On the 2d inst., in Yalobusha county, Miss., of inflammation of the bowels, aged seventeen months, John Oates, infant son of Louis _. And Lucy J. **CARR**, of this city. Memphis Daily Appeal, 8/5/1859.

Whereas, It has pleased the Great Master of the Universe, on Wednesday, the 20th inst., to call from labor to refreshment, our late brother, Wm. **CARR**, in the __th year of his age....Resolved, That we sincerely sympathize with his bereaved family, who have been deprived of an affectionate husband and a kind and indulgent father....South Memphis Lodge, No. 118. Memphis Daily Appeal, 5/26/1857.

Married. At the residence of R. T. **KENNEDY**, in Pittsburg, on the 29th ult. by Rev. Mr. Howard, Wm. C. **CARR**, Esq., of Memphis, Ten., to Miss Margie E. **KENNEDY**, of Pittsburg. Memphis Appeal, 12/14/1854.

Married, At Centre Hill, Miss., on Tuesday evening, the 17th instant, by Rev. J. M. **ROGERS**, Mr. Wm. C. **CARR**, of Prairie county, Ark., to Miss Lucie W. **PERRY**, of DeSoto county, Miss. Memphis Daily Appeal, 7/24/1855.

We regret to see announced in the St. Louis papers of the 17th, the death of Mrs. **CARRELL**, mother of the Assistant Editor of this paper. Mr. C. received information of his mother's dangerous illness on Saturday last, and immediately left for St. Louis. He did not, however, arrive in time again to look upon her, and to receive a mother's dying blessing... Memphis Eagle, 9/30/1848.

We regret to announce the death, in New Orleans, of our former fellow-citizen and confrere of the Eagle, E. J. **CARRELL**, Esq. We find the following notice of his death in the Picayune of the 29th ultimo: Yesterday evening we were pained to hear of the death of E. J. Carrell, recently editor of the Crescent newspaper and formerly engaged in the editorial profession at Memphis, in Tennessee. Mr. Carrell had lately devoted himself to the practice of the law.....Memphis Appeal, 12/5/1853.

Married. At the residence of ex-Govenor J. W. **MATTHEWS**, Marshall county, Miss., R. H. L. **CARROLL** to Miss Margaret **HOLLOWAY**, of Hopefield, Ark., on the 31st of July, 1855. Memphis Daily Appeal, 8/9/1855. Died, In Hopefield on the morning of the 1st of January, 1858, Mrs. Margaret A., wife of R. H. L. Carroll. Memphis Daily Appeal, 1/8/1858.

Our whole community have been affected painfully at the sudden death of Hon. Thomas B. **CARROLL**, Mayor of the City, which melancholy event occurred at his residence on Hernando street on Sunday evening at 10 minutes to 4 o'clock. The disease which terminated so fatally to one who had hitherto been considered in the most robust health, was inflammation of the bowels....Col. Carroll was the second son of the late Hon. Wm. **CARROLL**, Governor of Tennessee during several successive terms, and chief *aide de camp* to Gen. Jackson at the battle of New Orleans. He received his collegiate education at the University of Nashville and soon after he entered upon manhood's estate, removed to Panola county, Mississippi, where he successfully engaged in mercantile pursuits....From that county he removed to Helena, Ark., and from the latter place to this city, about twelve years since....Memphis Daily Appeal, 4/28/1857.

For Sale. A large and commodious dwelling house, Office, Kitchen, Smoke house, Stable, etc., will be disposed of at private sale on accommodating terms. It is situated on the corner of Beale and Second st., Memphis...Apply to Col. Wm. H. **CARROLL**. Memphis Appeal, 1/3/1851. .....Col. Wm. H. Carroll, the new Postmaster who will succeed Mr. Latham the present incumbent in this city.....Memphis Appeal, 4/20/1853. There was a meeting of the members of the Memphis Battalion, comprising the one hundred and fifty-fourth regiment Tennessee Volunteers....last evening, for the organization of the regiment by the election of officers....The following officers were elected by acclamation: Wm. H. Carroll, Colonel; Preston **SMITH**, Lieutenant Colonel; A. H. **DOUGLASS**, Major; Marcus J. **WRIGHT**, Second Major; G. H. **MONSARRAT**, Adjutant; J. H. **EDMONDSON**, Quartermaster; H. H. **PAYNTER**, Commissary; Gustave **WAGNER**, Sergeant Major; Dr. A. **THUMEL**, Surgeon; Dr. Frederick **H_CKE**, Assistant Surgeon....Memphis Daily Appeal, 11/17/1859. The friends of Col. Wm. H. Carroll and lady are invited to attend the funeral of their daughter, Ellen W. Carroll, from their residence This Day....Services by Rev. Bishop Otey. Memphis Daily Appeal, 12/20/1859.

Married, On the 23d inst., at 9 o'clock, A.M., by Rev. B. F. **GRIFFIN**, Mr. J. S. **CARROTHERS** to Miss Fannie **HILL**, all of Shelby county, Tenn. Memphis Weekly Appeal, 12/1/1858.

Married, On the morning of the 10th instant by Rev. J. _. **DOUGLASS**, at the residence of the bride's father, in Pocahontas, Tenn., Mr. J. J. **CARRUTH**, of Rossville, Tenn., to Miss Mary Jane **CLARK**. Memphis Daily Appeal, 8/14/1858.

$50 Reward! On Saturday, the 18th of July last, a fellow calling himself W. D. **WINCHESTER**, called at my stable and hired a mule, with the promise to return the same day, since when neither man nor mule has been heard from Winchester, from appearance, is a man about 22 years old, sandy complected, five feet 7 or 8 inches high, and would weigh 135 lbs...S. M. **CARSON**, Memphis. Daily Enquirer, 8/5/1847.

A citizen named D. F. **CARTEL**, who lived near the Bayou, was drowned in the river at the foot of Beal street, while bathing Sunday evening. Memphis Daily Appeal, Tues., 8/30/1859.

Married, On the evening of the 30th of December, by Rev. H. B. **RAMSEY**, Mr. Braxton **CARTER** and Mrs. Martha **YATES**, all of Shelby county, Tenn. Memphis Daily Appeal, 1/8/1857.

Married, On the 16th of December by the Rev. S. J. **REID**, Mr. W. B. **CARTER** to Miss Rebecca E. **BROWN**, all of Panola county, Miss. Memphis Eagle & Enquirer, 1/12/1853.

The subscriber offers for sale one of the most valuable Plantations in the county of Shelby. It lies on the Plank and Railroads, one half mile of Germantown, fronting a half mile on said Roads and extends back South to Non Conner bottom...This tract contains 665 acres...Wm. **CARTER**. Memphis Appeal, 9/30/1852.

Shelbyville, Tenn., January 6th, 1836. Awful Occurrence—By Fire! On Tuesday night last, the 3d instant, the dwelling-house of William **CARTER**, Esq. in this vicinity, took fire…The fire broke out at a late hour in the night, and before its progress was discovered, it succeeded in effecting the entire destruction of the dwelling-house…Esq. C. and his wife, together with three of their children between the ages of one and seven years, likewise perished amidst the devouring flames. The evidence that all the above parties were consumed by the fire, exists in the fact that their bones were to be seen bleaching upon the ruins the next morning…The balance of this unfortunate family, consisting of some five or six other children, together with some servants, succeeded in making their escape. It is said that Mrs. C. at one time effected an escape from the burning ruins, but on recollecting that her children were sleeping amidst the flames, she instantly yielded to the impulse of woman's generous nature, and in the plentitude of maternal affection rushed to the relief of her dying children; but alas! Unfortunate woman, her strength was too weak—the fire overtook her and she perished in the midst of its piercing flames. Squire Carter was an old and respected citizen of this county…Memphis Enquirer, Sat., 1/14/1837.

Died, At his residence in Gibson county, Tenn., on the morning of the 4th of August, Maj. Joseph M. **CARTHEL**, in the 56th year of his age. The deceased was a native of Georgia, but emigrated in early life to Maury county, Tenn., whence he removed in 1829 to Gibson county, in the Western District…he united with the Presbyterian church…Memphis Eagle, 9/6/1849.

The last number of the Holly Springs Empire Democrat comes to us shrouded in mourning for the death of Alexander T. **CARUTHERS**, who breathed his last at Holly Springs on the evening of the 31st ult. Mr. Caruthers was a native of Virginia, was for some years a citizen of Tennessee, whence he removed to Mississippi in 1835, and for fourteen years held the office of Circuit Court Clerk of Marshall county. Memphis Daily Appeal, 1/9/1855.

Died, On the 20th December, 1852, in the town of Hernando; at the residence of Mrs. E. **ORNE**, Franklin L. **CARUTHERS**, son of John P. and Ann R. **CARUTHERS**, of Tunica county, Miss. The deceased was born in the county of Rockbridge, Virginia, on the 13th day of December, 1833. Memphis Eagle & Enquirer, 1/1/1853.

Married, On Tuesday last, by Rev. B. F. **GRIFFIN**, Mr. J. Slaught **CARUTHERS** to Miss S. Frank **HILL**, both of Hazel Flat, Tenn. Memphis Weekly Appeal, 11/24/1858.

Died—in Jackson, Tenn., in the 51st year of her age, after a protracted illness, Mrs. Frances E. Caruthers, wife of James **CARUTHERS**, Esq., for many years a citizen of that place….She was the daughter of Thomas and S. **McCORRY** and was born in Knoxville, Tenn., in the year 1808….She became a member of the Protestant Episcopal Church in the year 1843….Memphis Daily Appeal, 3/13/1859.

Married, At Columbus, Miss., on the 10th March, 1853, by the Rev. Thos. W. **DORMAN**, James H. **CARUTHERS**, Esq. of Lafayette county, Ark., to Miss Sarah E. **HUMPHREYS**. Memphis Eagle & Enquirer, 3/27/1853.

The friends and acquaintances of Judge **CARUTHERS** are invited to attend the funeral of his brother, James H. **CARUTHERS**, from the Gayoso House, to-day at three o'clock P.M. Memphis Daily Appeal, 1/11/1856.

Married, On the 6th instant at the residence of M. B. Bry_es, in Prairie county, Ark., Col. Walter J. **CARUTHERS**, of Madison county, Tenn., to Miss S. E. **BLAIN**, of Fayette county, Tenn. Memphis Weekly Appeal, 5/5/1858.

Died, At the residence of Mr. McLamee, in Fort Pickering, on October 2nd, George **CARVELLE**, in the 52nd year of his age. St. Louis Republican and Milwaukee Sentinel please copy. Memphis Daily Appeal, 10/4/1857.

Married, At the residence of the bride's mother near Holly Springs, Miss., on the 24th inst., by Rev. J. W. KNOTT, Mr. Ma_ville M. CARVOOTH(?) and Miss Rachel T. JEFFERIES, all of Marshall county. Memphis Daily Appeal, 11/29/1857.

Died: In Covington, Tenn. on Monday, September 22d, Octavius CARY, in the 25th year of his age. Memphis Appeal, 10/7/1851. To the Creditors of Octavius Cary, deceased. Having suggested the insolvency of said Cary's estate to the Clerk of Tipton County Court...Henry SANFORD, Adm'r. Memphis Eagle & Enquirer, 1/15/1852.

Married, On the 28th ult., in White county, Arkansas, Mr. S. S. CARY, of Memphis, to Miss M. E. MARTIN, of Jacksonport, Ark. Memphis Daily Appeal, 9/8/1855.

Died, At the residence of her father, Aulsey DEAN, Esq., in Hardeman county, Tenn., on the 21st inst., Mrs. Gilla CASEY, aged forty-nine years, four months and seventeen days. She was an exemplary member of the Baptist Church. Memphis Daily Appeal, 11/25/1857.

Married, At the residence of the bride in Hardeman county, Tenn., January 5th, 1858, by Rev. A. S. DORRIS, Col. R. D. CASEY, of Rapp's Barring, Marion county, Ark., to Mrs. Cynthia G. JOYNER, of the former place. Memphis Evening Ledger, 1/12/1858.

Married, On Thursday evening, the 1st inst., at the residence of Col. S. R. BROWN, by Rev. Samuel DENNIS, Mr. F. M. CASH, to Miss E. H. DRAKE, all of this city. Memphis Daily Eagle, 8/3/1850. Died, In this city on the 17th instant, William Drake, son of Francis M. and Elizabeth H. Cash, aged 19 months. Memphis Daily Appeal, 7/18/1856.

Married, Last evening at the Second Presbyterian Church, by Rev. Dr. Grundy, Mr. J. H. CASH to Miss Italia A. Walsh, daughter of Dr. B. WALSH. Memphis Daily Appeal, 5/13/1859.

Thos. COSTULOW, an old and peaceable Irish laborer, who has been employed for the last five or six years in levelling the gravel on our streets, was wantonly murdered on last Saturday in the upper part of the city, by another Irishman, named Dan'l DORSEY. He was first knocked down with what is called a sling shot, and then his head was violently struck against the pavement so that death instantly ensued. The murderer has escaped. Memphis Appeal, Mon., 4/25/1853. (Author's Note: Spelled CASTILLO and CASTELLO also.)

Departed this life August 7th, 1855, at 8 o'clock A.M., Mrs. Mary, consort of J. G. CATHEY, of Marshall county, Mississippi, in the 46th year of her age. She was born in Maury county, Tennessee, June the 22d, 1809; married in the eighteenth year of her age, and emigrated to Mississippi in the year 1834. She joined the Christian Church in 1836(?)....Memphis Daily Appeal, 8/16/1855.

Although but a new comer in the trade, Capt. Sol CATTERLIN, with his fine, fast running packet *Sam Cloon* has already proved himself a trump among the traveling community. The *Cloon* will leave this evening at 5 o'clock, for Louisville and Cincinnati...Memphis Eagle & Enquirer, 6/22/1852.

Married, On yesterday evening at the residence of James PYE, Esq. by the Rev. W. C. ROBB, Mr. Nicholas CAVELINE to Mrs. Sabina DOEBLER, all of this city. Mr. & Mrs. Caveline left yesterday evening on the Memphis, to spend the honey-moon in Louisville. Memphis Eagle & Enquirer, 5/12/1853.

M. C. CAYCE, Mammoth Livery Stable....Main street, opposite the Gayoso, Memphis, Ten. Memphis Appeal, 4/21/1853.

Married. On the 7th inst. at the residence of her father, Mr. Wm. T. ARTHUR, by Rev. D. C. PAGE, James Ronald CHALMERS, Esq. to Miss Rebecca ARTHUR, all of Holly Springs, Miss. Memphis Appeal, 6/14/1854.

Died, In Coahoma county, Mississippi, on the 6th instant, Eliza ___th Chambers, daughter of Henry and Virginia **CHAMBERS**, aged five years, one month and three days. Memphis Daily Appeal, 9/11/1857.

Married, On the evening of the 28th ult., by the Rev. R. **McCOY**, at Hickory Grove, the residence of her father, J. W. **ROYSTER**, Miss Mary Heath, to Dr. W. H. **CHAMBERS**, formerly of Buckingham county, Va. Richmond (Va.) papers please copy. Memphis Eagle, 12/6/1849.

Died, on the morning of the 17th instant, at his residence near Memphis, after a painful illness of two months, Thomas **CHAMBLISS**, in the 44th year of his age. The subject of this brief notice was a native of Sussex county, Va., whence, in his early years, he removed to the Western Division of this State.... Memphis Appeal, 11/25/1854

Married, On the evening of the 6th inst., at Mason's Depot, by Rev. J. J. Somerv___, Mr. W. A. **CHANCY** to Miss Ann **VERSER**. Memphis Daily Appeal, 12/10/1857.

At a called meeting of the Independent Order of Odd Fellows of Memphis, held in their Hall on the 9th of July, on motion: Resolved, That we sincerely regret the untimely death of our beloved brother, Wm. H. **CHAPLAIN**, whose kindness and urbanity had much endeared him to us all...Resolved, That we tender to the bereaved relations and friends of our deceased brother our heartfelt sympathies over the unfortunate loss which they, in common with ourselves, have sustained in the death of our lamented brother.... Memphis Eagle, 7/11/1848.

The writer of this simple notice was greatly pained....to find....in the Pittsburg Post, the death of the daughter of one of his most valued friends, Amelia Neville **CHAPLIN**. This young and lovely dower perished in the 18th year of her age....To her parents and the other members of her immediate family she will be remembered....Memphis Daily Appeal, 1/11/1855.

Married, On the 29th instant by Rev. Dr. A. M. **BRYAN**, at the residence of David M. **CURRIN**, of this city, Mr. Geo. **CHAPMAN**, of this city, formerly of Liverpool, England, and Miss Laura A. **CURRIN**, of Memphis, Tenn. Memphis Daily Appeal, 11/30/1856.

The friends and acquaintances of the late Dr. J. M. **CHASE** are requested to attend his Funeral from the residence of William **CHASE**, on Second street, This Afternoon....Services by Rev. T. J. **DRANE**. Memphis Avalanche, 2/9/1859. Died, At Mayatee, Florida, on the 21st December last, Dr. J. M. Chase, of this city. Dr. Chase had been for many years a citizen of Memphis....He was a young man of much promise....Memphis Daily Appeal, 1/6/1859.

Married, on the 3rd inst. by the Rev. Jeptha **HARRISON**, Mr. William **CHASE** to Miss Mary Ann **JOINER**, both of Memphis. Memphis Enquirer, 10/4/1839. Tailoring, William Chase. Weekly Appeal, 11/28/1845. We are authorized to announce William Chase, Esq., as a candidate for re-election to the office of Justice of the Peace, in the 5th Civil District. The Daily Eagle, 2/16/1848.

For Sale Cheap. 1500 Acres of Best Cotton Land. Having engaged in the Memphis and St. Francis Plank Road Co., I have determined to sell the valuable Plantation, which lies 40 miles below Memphis, on the east side of the Mississippi river...G. W. **CHEEK**. Memphis Appeal, 1/17/1852. Mr. G. W. Cheek has bought the new and elegant steamboat Falcon, to run as a packet from Mound City, in Arkansas, to Memphis, Tenn....J. G. **BERRY**, Master. Memphis Appeal, 2/17/1854.

Married, On Thursday evening, the 8th inst., by the Rev. D. E. **BURNS**, Mr. John A. **CHEEK** and Harriett **CARR**, all of this city. Memphis Appeal, 1/10/1852.

To Planters. The Sampson Portable Lever Cotton Press. Patented to the Inventor, M. D. **CHEEK**, Memphis, Tenn...Weekly Memphis Eagle, 5/24/1849.

Married, On the morning of Tuesday, 12th inst., at the residence of the bride's father, by Rev. Mr. Boswell, C. W. **CHERRY**, Esq., to Miss Sallie R. **WILLIAMSON**, all of Memphis. Memphis Daily Appeal, 5/13/1857.

Died, At Elmwood, near Jackson, on the evening of the 9th inst., Andrew Jackson **CHESTER**, in the 20th year of his age, son of Col. Robert J. **CHESTER**....Although he was deprived in infancy of the care and training of his excellent mother, his father reared him so as to give promise of usefulness in manhood. He was well known to the writer of this notice, who witnessed with pleasure the warm affection of his heart for his *new* mother....Memphis Daily Appeal, 10/16/1856.

The funeral _____ _____endent upon the death of our _____ citizens, Jno. K. **CHESTER**, were performed yesterday evening...The corpse was conducted to its last resting place by the brotherhood of Free Masons, and buried with Masonic honors...The ceremonies at the Episcopal Church and at the grave, administered by the Rev. Dr. Page...Memphis Appeal, 1/3/1851. Tribute of Respect. Memphis, Jan. 1st, 1851. At a call meeting of the Board of Mayor and Aldermen of the city of Memphis, E. H. **PORTER**, Esq., as Chairman, announced the death of Col. John K. Chester, late City Recorder...Memphis Appeal, 1/3/1851. Whereas, The great Architect of the Universe, in his divine Providence, has seen fit to remove from our midst, brother John K. Chester...a sincere friend, a devoted husband, and an affectionate father...To his widow and orphan children we offer our consolations...Memphis Appeal, 1/13/1851. We learn from the Coffeeville (Miss.,) Appeal, that the negro who was executed at this place for the murder of Col. J. K. Chester, was the property of D. L. **HERRON** of Coffeeville...Memphis Appeal, 1/15/1851. The Gazette learned the following facts from a passenger of the steamer Winfield Scott, late from below. A few weeks since a white man and a negro, both of them claiming residence in Cincinnati, arrived at Memphis. Some persons there suspecting that the negro was a slave, and attempting his arrest, the white man placed in the hands of the negro a revolver, with which he shot John K. Chester, who died immediately...These murders occurred on New Year's Day. Mr. Chester is well known here, having at one time been in the grocery trade on Front street, and afterwards clerk on the steamer E. W. Stephens...Memphis Appeal, 1/21/1851.

Married. At Inglewood, Shelby county, Tenn. on Monday, the 22d inst. by Rev. D. L. **GRAY**, Col. Robt. 1. **CHESTER**, U.S. Marshall for the District of West Tennessee, to Mrs. Jane P. **DONELSON**. Memphis Daily Appeal, 1/26/1855.

The friends and acquaintances of the late Thomas B. **CHESTER** are respectfully invited to attend his funeral at 3 o'clock P.M., October 15, 1858. Divine services by Rev. J. P. **SCHETKY** at Grace Church....Memphis Daily Appeal, 10/15/1858.

Married, On Wednesday evening, May 25th by Rev. T. L. **GRACE**, Mr. Antonio **CHIARELLA** to Mrs. Mary **BRUNS**, all of this city. Memphis Appeal, 5/26/1853.

Died, At his residence on Spring Creek, Madison county, Tenn., on the 13th ult., after an illness of several months, Nelson **CHILDRESS**, in the sixty first year of his age. He was a native of Virginia, --removed to Williamson county in 1815—of which he was elected high sheriff—and removed to Madison in the year 1830...Weekly Appeal, 6/5/1846.

William **CHILDRESS**, formerly of Louisville and for some time past a resident of Memphis, shot himself dead at the United States Hotel yesterday about noon....the wants of his small though dependent family, which were only relieved now and then by the generosity of friends, pressed heavily on his sensitive nature....Memphis Appeal, 11/18/1854.

Married, On the 18th ult., by His Honor G. B. **LOCKE**, Mr. Wm. K. **CHILDRESS**, to Miss Mary Jane **THOMPSON**, all of this city. Memphis Eagle, 2/9/1849.

Married, On the 6th inst., by Rev. J. W. **PENDER**, Mr. Henry B. **CHILES**, of Memphis, to Miss Arabella E. **MITCHELL**. Memphis Appeal, 1/8/1851.

Married, At the Cumberland Presbyterian Church by Rev. Dr. Bryan, on Thursday evening, 13th inst., Mr. J. S. **CHILES** to Mrs. Annie **VAN WAGENEN**, all of this city....That these and all other desirable blessings attend both Sam and Annie, is the sincere wish of their friend, A. Memphis Weekly Appeal, 5/19/1858.

We are authorized to announce S. B. **CHOTE** a candidate for Lieut. Colonel of 128th Regiment of T. M. Memphis Enquirer, 4/12/1836.

Died, In Lebanon, Tennessee, on Saturday the 12th inst., Kate Safford, infant daughter of Wm. B. and Marie __. **CHRISP**, aged fifteen months and fourteen days. Memphis Daily Appeal, 9/20/1857. Died, On Tuesday, the 28th inst., Marie Rebecca, consort of W. B. Chrisp, Esq. The friends and acquaintances of the family are respectfully invited to attend her funeral from Wesley Chapel. Memphis Daily Appeal, 9/29/1858.

Died at his residence in Shelby county, on the 17th instant, Frederic **CHRISTIAN**, in the forty first year of his age, after a short and painful illness of five days. He was a native of Charles City county, Virginia, and was amongst the earliest settlers of this county, having emigrated to it twenty years ago. In the selection of a victim, the hand of death could not, perhaps, have fallen upon a citizen more universally respected, esteemed and beloved than was Frederic Christian. It was his unhappy lot more than ten years ago, to be left by the death of his most amiable and affectionate wife, with two infant children, the satisfaction of whose presence at his dying bedside was denied him, they being absent at distant schools.....American Eagle Weekly, 6/27/1845.

Died.—At the residence of her husband in the parish of Iberville, Louisiana, on the 28th ultimo, Mrs. Mary, consort of Dr. James C. **CHRISTIAN**, formerly of Memphis, in the 22d year of her age. Weekly Memphis Eagle, 4/19/1849.

Married—On Monday evening, 20th inst., by Rev. Mr. Gray, Mr. John B. **WELD**, of New Orleans, to Miss Mary C., daughter of Wyatt **CHRISTIAN**, M.D., of this city. The Tri-Weekly Memphis Enquirer, 7/23/1846. It is with the most poignant regret that we announce the death of our esteemed fellow citizen, Dr. Wyatt Christian. He died on Tuesday evening last, at his residence in this city, after a short illness, and was interred yesterday...The Tri-Weekly Memphis Enquirer, Thursday, 9/17/1846. Obituary...Dr. Christian was a native of Charles City county, Virginia and emigrated to this place in 1825. H was in his 48th year at the period of his death. His long residence and eminent skill in the practice of medicine had put him at the head of his profession...The Tri-Weekly Memphis Enquirer, 9/19/1846. Died in this city on the 17th inst., Mrs. Mary B. **CHRISTIAN**, consort of the late Dr. Wyatt Christian, aged 48 years. Mrs. C. survived her lamented husband but twelve months....Though surrounded by her affectionate children who were melting into tears as she bade them all farewell.....American Eagle, 9/23/1847.

Married, At the Worsham House on the 4th inst., by Josiah **HORNE**, Esq., Mr. L. **CHRISTY**, of Holly Springs, Miss., and Mrs. Elizabeth **NELINES**, of DeSoto county, Miss. Memphis Daily Appeal, 10/5/1856.

Thanks to Capt. Church: At a meeting of our citizens last evening at the City Reading Room, John **KIRK**, Esq., was called to the chair and J. Knox **WALKER**, Esq. was appointed as secretary....Resolutions were adopted rendering a just tribute to Capt. C. B. **CHURCH**, of Steamer Bulletin, for his noble and heroic conduct in rescuing his passengers from destruction by his cool, prompt and courageous measures, and a committee of 50 persons were appointed to wait upon Capt. C. and express to him the high appreciation of the citizens of Memphis of his conduct in this regard. Memphis Daily Appeal, 4/4/1855.

The friends of Paul **CICALLA** are invited to attend the Funeral of his late wife, Helena Cicalla, from his residence on Shelby street, This Morning, at 9 o'clock. Memphis Daily Appeal, 1/28/1858.

Died—At the residence of Mr. Wm. **SOMERVILLE**, in Tipton county, Tenn., on Saturday the 2d of August, 1851, of Typhoid Fever, Benjamin Watkins Leigh **CLAIBORNE**, in the 22d year of his age. The deceased, after an absence of three years, had just returned from the University of N. Carolina, where he graduated, in June last, with distinction...He had barely time to meet the affectionate welcome of his aged mother, before he was prostrated by the disease...Richmond (Va.) Enquirer and Raleigh (N.C.) Standard, will please copy. Memphis Appeal, 8/21/1851. Tribute of Respect. Philanthropic Hall, Chapel Hill, Sept. 5th, 1851. Whereas, We have heard the sad intelligence respecting the death of our late and much beloved fellow-member, Benjamin W. L. Claiborne, of Tipton county, Tenn...Memphis Appeal, 9/22/1851.

Married, On the 4th of May, at the residence of the bride's mother, by Rev. John A. **WHEELOCK**, Mr. Jessie M. **CLAIBORNE** to Miss Eleanor _. **MARKHAM**, all of Tipton county, Tenn. Memphis Daily Appeal, 5/13/1859.

Died, at his residence at Sledgeville, Panola county, Mississippi, Friday morning about thirty minutes before one o'clock, A.M., May 9th(?), Col. Robert **CLANTON**, aged 68 years, 11 months and 11 days....The deceased was born in Sussex county, Virginia, May 28th, 1787, where he joined the Baptist Church in early manhood....Memphis Daily Appeal, 5/30/1856.

The subscriber tenders his hearty thanks to the citizens of Memphis and its vicinity for their liberal patronage during his six years residence in Memphis...Fred'k. H. **CLARK**. Daily Enquirer, 7/29/1847.

Married, In Victoris, Texas, on the 25th inst., at the residence of Dr. H. R. **HOPSON**, by Rev. John M. **COCHRAN**, Mr. H. A. **CLARK**, of New Orleans, to Miss Maggie E. **WARE**, formerly of Memphis, Tenn. Memphis Daily Appeal, 7/18/1857.

Married, On Wednesday, June 10th, by Rev. C. R. **HENDRICKSON**, Mr. Henry J. **CLARK** and Miss Virginia J. **GWYNN**, all of this city. Memphis Daily Appeal, 6/11/1857.

Died: On the morning of the 15th in this city, Mrs. Virginia Clark, wife of James **CLARK**. The friends and acquaintances of the family are invited to attend the funeral this morning the 16th, at 9 o'clock, at the residence of her husband on Beale street. Services by Rev. Dr. Page. Danville Register please notice. Memphis Whig, 8/16/1855.

Married, At the Central Hotel on the 31st January, by Rev. J. H. **GRAY**, D.D., Mr. James **CLARK** to Mrs. Anna D. **ROYSTER**. Memphis Daily Appeal, 2/2/1856.

Yesterday morning an Irishman named James **CLARK**, who boarded at the house of Mr. Foley, at the corner of Commerce and Main streets, was found lying dead on a box in his room. He had been at work as usual the day before and showed no signs of sickness....Memphis Daily Appeal, 2/12/1858.

Died—In this town, on Thursday evening last Mr. James H. **CLARK**, late of Bolivar. Memphis Enquirer, Sat., 5/5/1838.

Married, In Coahoma county, Miss., at the residence of Capt. James **ALCORN** by the Hon. G. R. **MORTON**, on the 30th ultimo, John **CLARK**, Esq., to Miss Eliza Jane **ALCORN**; all of Coahoma county. Memphis Appeal, 6/13/1854.

Mr. Jno. C. **CLARK**, one of our most worthy and enterprising citizens, died on yesterday from the effects of a burn received while waiting on a sick brother. He was in the act of mixing a preparation of turpentine, when it accidentally took fire, and his clothes becoming saturated with it, he was burned so seriously that he lingered only some twelve days...Memphis Appeal, 9/30/1851.

Died—In this City on Wednesday last, after an illness of only a few days, Mr. Peter **CLARK**, formerly of the firm of Messrs. John Williams & Co., Nashville. Mr. Clark removed to Nashville some few years since from Petersburg, Virginia, of which State he was a native. The Appeal, Fri., 5/2/1844.

All persons are notified, that I will pay no debt heretofore contracted by Kenedy **LONERGAN**, except what was directly used and expended in the business of Lonergan & Clark or myself...William **CLARK**. Daily Enquirer, 11/4/1847.

Married, In this city on the evening of the 26th inst., at the residence of the bride's father, by Rev. Dr. Bryan, Mr. D. A. **CLARKE** to Miss Mollie R. **WOLFE**, both of Memphis. Memphis Daily Appeal, 10/28/1858.

Married, On the 24th inst. by Rev. J. H. **GRAY**, D.D., Mr. James R. **CLARKE**, of the steamer St. Francis, to Miss Elizabeth **LOVIN**, of this city. Memphis Daily Appeal, 6/26/1856.

John C. **CLARKE**, Boot Maker and Leather Dealer, Late of Louisville, Has opened a Boot Manufactory and Leather and Binding Store, on Front Row...American Eagle, 9/23/1847.

Married, In this vicinity, on the evening of Tuesday last, by the Rev. Mr. Coons, Mr. Richard G. **CLARKE**, to Miss Mary H., daughter of Dr. Jesse **ISLER**. Weekly Appeal, Fri., 7/4/1845.

Died—At the Richmond House, on the 3d inst., John G. Bostick, infant son of William B. and Eliza **CLARKE**, aged five months and two days. Daily Enquirer, 3/5/1847.

Died: In this city, on the morning of Saturday, August 25th, in the 38th year of his age Rev. James H. **CLARKSON**, a native of Kentucky. Rev. Mr. C. was a member of the order of St. Dominic, but for some time past had been associated in the pastoral charge of the Catholic Church of this city....Weekly Memphis Eagle, 8/30/1849.

Married, In Fayette county, on the 4th instant, by Rev. J. D. **METCALF**, Dr. I. **CLARY**, of Somerville, to Miss Annette **THOMPSON**, of Hickory Wythe. Memphis Daily Appeal, 9/13/1857.

We are much pained to record the demist of Rev. James **CLARY**, priest of the Catholic Church of this city. He died yesterday of bilious fever, after an illness of four days....Memphis Whig, 9/19/1855. (Author's Note: Spelled **CLEARY** in another paper and listed cause of death as yellow fever.)

Death of Col. Joseph W. **CLAY**. The announcement of Col. Clay's death will be received with sincere regret by all of his friends and acquaintances. He died at his residence at South Bend, Arkansas last Thursday and was in the 49th year of his age. The cause of his death was a violent attack of Pneumonia, originating from a cold contracted on a recent visit to New Orleans. Mr. Clay was a very wealthy planter.....The deceased formerly resided in the neighborhood of Nashville. Memphis Eagle & Enquirer, Tues., 3/15/1853.

We learn that Hon. A. M. **CLAYTON**, of Mississippi, has formed a partnership for the practice of the law in this city with one of our most prominent and successful lawyers, and will soon remove here as a permanent citizen....Memphis Appeal, 8/12/1854.

Married, In this county, at the residence of John W. **CLAYTON**, Esq., on Monday, the 10th instant, at 8 o'clock, A.M., by Rev. Samuel **DENNIS**, Geo. W. **LUKE**, Esq., of Pontotoc, Miss., to Miss Louisiana C., daughter of Maj. John B. **RODGERS**, of Walnut Bend, Arks. Memphis Eagle, 12/13/1849.

We are pained to learn that a child of Mr. C. C. **CLEAVES** was severely burned yesterday.... Memphis Daily Appeal, 11/7/1856. The child of Mr. Cleaves, burned so severely on Thursday evening, died early yesterday morning. His clothes caught fire from a stove in the kitchen, and before the flames were subdued, portions of the little fellow's body were burnt to a crisp.... Memphis Daily Appeal, 11/8/1856.

Died, Near Oakland on Friday morning, 20th inst., at 6 o'clock, after an illness of only thirty hours, Mr. W. H. **CLEAVES**, of Fayette county, Tenn. Memphis Daily Appeal, 8/21/1859.

Married, On the 15th inst., at the residence of Wm. **CLEAVES**, Sr., Fayette county, Tenn., by the Rev. Jno. F. **BAKER**, Mr. John D. **CLEAVES** to Miss T. D. H. E. **MASON**. Memphis Eagle & Enquirer, 6/19/1852. Died. At his residence near Oakland, Fayette county, Tenn., on the 21st instant, William Cleaves, senior, aged 70 years. Memphis Appeal, 7/23/1853.

Married, At the residence of Mr. Pleasant **WORD**, near Oakland, Fayette county, Tenn., on May 1st by Rev. Moses **GREEN**, Dr. Thomas E. **CLEERE** and Miss Lucy F. **WORD**. Memphis Daily Appeal, 5/10/1856.

The friends and acquaintances of Mr. **VAN TASSEL** are invited to attend the funeral of Mrs. Sophia **CLEMENT**, from the residence of Col. Sullivan, on Poplar street at __ o'clock this morning. Memphis Whig, 6/25/1856.

Married, On the 15th instant at the residence of Mr. Henry **FERGUSON**, by Rev. Jas. O. **STEADMAN**, Mr. Wm. James **CLEMENTS** to Miss Mariah **COX**, all of this city. New York Sun and Tyrone Constitution, Ireland, please copy. Memphis Weekly Appeal, 4/28/1858.

On Thursday evening last a difficulty occurred in this place between John R. **NIEL** and Walter G. **CLEVELAND**, constable of this township, which resulted in the death of the latter from a pistol shot—and the wounding, perhaps mortally, of Niel, by stabs with a bowie knife. Cleveland lived until yesterday about 10 o'clock. We are not fully advised of the cause of the difficulty. Cleveland leaves a family. Niel is unmarried....*Helena Shield*, Aug. 15th. Since the above was received we learn that Mr. Niel died of his wounds. Memphis Daily Appeal, 8/21/1855.

We are authorized to announce Wm. T. **CLIFTON** as a candidate for Beat Constable of the 14th Civil District, (including South Memphis) at the ensuing March election. Memphis Eagle, 12/23/1847.

We have already announced the fact that William A. **CLINE**, of Mt. Pleasant, Miss., had attempted to destroy his life in this city by taking strychnine, in Court Square, Friday morning....He lingered however, in great suffering until yesterday afternoon, when he died the death of a suicide. The unfortunate man was induced to commit the rash act, he said, through the conviction of the infidelity of his wife, who resides in this city. Memphis Daily Appeal, Sunday, 10/16/1859. ....He was a native of New Orleans, was a painter by profession and had resided in Mt. Pleasant, Miss., but about four months, having been married there within that time. His mother resides at present in New Orleans. Cline came to this city on Saturday last, in company with his bride's father....He was connected with General Walker's expedition to Nicaragua and spent nine months in that country, being attached to Company C. Memphis Daily Appeal, 10/18/1859.

Died, On the 9th of May, 1856, at his residence in Panola county, Miss., after a long illness, Col. Robert **CLINTON**, in his 69th year. Memphis Daily Appeal, 5/20/1856.

Mr. W. H. **CLOWES**, formerly an assistant editor of the *Bulletin*, committed suicide by taking laudanum, at Richmond, Va., on the 6th inst. He was driven to despair and suicide by indiscretions and follies working upon a supersensitive mind and determining him to put an end to his career. Mr. Clowes possessed a brilliant talent, the refinement and gentleness of the old school in all his intercourse with man, and a warm and trusting heart. Peace to his ashes! Memphis Daily Appeal, 1/12/1858.

Married, on the 20th inst., in the Parish of Iberville, La., by the Rev. Dr. Burke, at the residence of R. **McGAVOCK** Esq., Mr. D. **CLOYD** of Va., to Miss E. **McGAVOCK**. Memphis Eagle, 1/4/1849.

The name of the young man drowned at the landing on Wednesday evening, we have ascertained to be C. R. **COBB**, son of Dr. T. B. **COBB**, of Henderson county, Tennessee. His body has not yet been recovered. Memphis Daily Appeal, Tues., 11/4/1856.

The subscriber keeps constantly on hand a large assortment of Dry Lumber, suitable for building and fencing...Yard opposite Exchange Square, on the Batture. Marcus E. **COCHRAN**. Memphis Eagle, 5/17/1848. Married, On the 25th inst., by the Rev. L. D. **MULLINS**, at the residence of Richard **LEAKE**, Mr. Marcus E. **COCHRAN**, to Miss Sophia E. **LEAKE**; both formerly from Virginia. Weekly Memphis Eagle, 10/4/1849.

Departed this life, on Friday morning, the 10th inst., Mrs. Mary E. Cocke, consort of Boler **COCKE**, in the 21st year of her age...The Tri-Weekly Memphis Enquirer, 7/16/1846.

Married, On the 9th inst., in Copiah county, Miss., Ex-Chancellor Stephen **COCKE** to Miss **WILING**, of that county. Memphis Weekly Appeal, 12/22/1858.

Died, At the residence of her husband near the town of Panola, Miss., on Saturday the 7th inst., Mrs. Jane Sanderson, wife of Mr. Wm.(?) **COCKE**, in the 67th year of her age. The deceased was a native of Buckingham county, Va., but the last forty odd years of her life were spent in Tennessee and Mississippi. Panola, Miss., July 10th, 1855. Clarksville, Tenn. and Arkadelphia, Ark. papers please copy. Memphis Appeal, 7/13/1855.

D. **COCKERELL** has removed his Livery Stable to the building recently occupied by D. A. **FAUCETT**, on Main street, corner of Monroe...Daily Enquirer, 8/6/1847.

The friends and acquaintances of the late W. S. **COCKERELL** are respectfully invited to attend his funeral this morning at 9 o'clock, from his late residence on Union street. Memphis Appeal, 8/31/1852.

Died, On the morning of the 26th inst., of Bilious Pleurisy, at his residence in South Memphis, Mr. S. W. **COCKRELL**, in the 33d year of his age. Memphis Eagle, 1/28/1850.

Married, On Thursday evening, the 1st inst., at the residence of L. **WEBB**, Esq., W. S. **COCKRELL**, Esq., of this city, to Miss M. E. **BOSLEY**, of this county. Memphis Eagle, 8/3/1850.

Married, On the 16th inst., by Rev. Mr. Thomas, at the residence of the bride's mother, near this city, Col. Jessee **COE**, of Florida, to Miss Alice E. **COE**. Memphis Daily Avalanche, 2/17/1859.

Your last week's paper contained an announcement of the death of Major Joseph **COE**, who died at his residence in Fayette county, on the 25th of April, and was buried in Somerville with Masonic honors....Major Coe was born near Baltimore, Maryland, in the year 1783. He moved thence to Guilford county, North Carolina, in which place he remained until about the year 1808, when he came to Tennessee, and settled in Maury county. Upon the breaking out of the War of 1812 he entered the army, and was present at the battles of Taledega and Horse Shoe. After peace was restored he continued to live many years in Maury, but moved thence to Molton, Alabama, where he first began to take an active part in politics. He was twice sent to the Legislature by the Democracy of that District. Returning to Tennessee, he moved from place to place until he finally settled in Somerville. Here, also, he was honored with the confidence and suffrages of his party, and was elected to the Legislature....The subject of this notice had reached the advanced age of seventy-four years....But one tie bound him to life—the aged partner of his joys and sorrows. She who through fifty-two years had borne with him the burden of life....The old man died childless, though he had had two noble sons, grown to man's estate....Both sons met with untimely deaths. The younger perished with Fanning's regiment in Texas. The elder, Levin H. **COE**, fell a victim in a conspiracy brought about by his active zeal and bold endeavors in promoting the interests of Memphis and her citizens....Memphis Daily Appeal, 6/9/1857. Died, At her residence in Fayette county, on the 29th ult., Mrs. Margaret **COE**, aged 76 years. [Only a few months ago the aged consort of the deceased was borne to the tomb, and now she follows close behind to join him in another and a better world. Mrs. Coe was the mother of our late lamented fellow-citizen, Gen. Levin H. **COE**, and also of Green **COE**, who fell at the Alamo by the side of David Crockett. These were her only children. But her childrens' children survive to mourn her loss and follow her to the tomb.] Memphis Weekly Appeal, 3/17/1858.

Death of Gen. Levin H. **COE**. After suffering terribly for sixty-three days, from the wound inflicted on him by Jos. **WILLIAMS**, Gen. Coe was released from his agony on last Saturday, at 2 P.M. He died aged 43 years...Memphis Eagle, Monday, 8/12/1850. Gen. Coe occupied a very prominent position as a citizen, lawyer, and politician, in this State. There was probably no office in the gift of the Democratic party of Tennessee, which he could not have commanded.—In 1848 it recommended him to the national convention of the Democratic party as a suitable candidate for the Vice-Presidency; and shortly after, it unsuccessfully solicited him to accept a gubernatorial nomination...He has passed from earth; and today's bright, cheerful sun looks down upon the dead, a darkened and desolated household, upon fatherless children and a widowed wife, mourning the loss of that which the earth cannot give again. Even as we write, the sorrowing escort which bore him back for burial to the quiet scenes of his early boyhood, has reached its destination…Perhaps ere now, the falling dirt has rattled harshly upon his coffin, and his parents, made desolate and childless in their extreme old age, have cast the last look of agony upon their dead…The remains of Gen. Coe were taken to Sommerville for interment…Memphis Daily Eagle, 8/13/1850.

Married, In this city on the 12th inst., at the residence of the bride's father, by Rev. Dr. Barbee, A. B. **COFFEE**, Esq., of Jackson, Miss., and Miss Anne **WILLIS**, of this city. Memphis Avalanche, 2/15/1859. Married, On the 12th inst. at the residence of the bride's parents….Mr. A. B. Coffee, of New Orleans, eldest son of the late Gen. Washington **COFFEE**, of Mississippi, to Miss Ann Amelia, youngest daughter of Jos. and Maria **WILLIS**, late of Jackson, Miss. Memphis Daily Appeal, 2/15/1859.

The subscriber tenders his services to the citizens of Memphis and its vicinity, as a new and fashionable shoe and boot maker, living on Chickasaw Street….Elijah **COFFEE**. Memphis Advocate, 11/3/1827. We were yesterday shown the first receipt ever given for a subscription to a Memphis newspaper. The receipt was given to Rev. Elijah Coffee, who is still living, and is, we believe, the oldest resident of Memphis in her limits. The paper is in the following words: Rec'd (by the hands of Maj. M. B. **WINCHESTER**, three dollars,) from E. Coffee, for the *Memphis Advocate* for one year, commencing on the 10th of January, 1827. Memphis Daily Avalanche, 4/29/1859.

Married. In this city on the 27th instant by Rev. H. S. **PORTER**, D.D., Mr. F. M. **COGSWELL** to Miss Celia V. **BOND**. Memphis Appeal, 9/29/1854. The friends and acquaintances of F. M. and T. J. **COGSWELL** are invited to attend the funeral of their father, from the Christian Church, corner Linden and St. Martins street, at 2 o'clock, P.M. This Day. Services by Rev. J. D. **MERRIMAN**. Memphis Daily Appeal, 8/5/1857.

Esquire Horne was called upon yesterday to inquire into the causes incident to the sudden disolution of two individuals. In one instance a man named Conrad **COLDERBACK**, who was found dead at the residence of Mr. Weigle, in the upper part of the city, had died during the previous night from the effects of intemperance….Memphis Daily Avalanche, 1/19/1859.

On Friday evening Thomas, son of widow **COLE**, residing on the Horne Lake road, eight miles from the city, sportively raised a gun against his twin sister Jane; without intention on his part, the gun went off. It was loaded with small shot, and the whole load lodged in her neck, severing the jugular vein. The poor girl died in a few minutes, but before expiring she assured her mother that Thomas had fired by accident…. Memphis Daily Appeal, 12/18/1859.

Married, On the 3d instant at the residence of the bride's father, near Rosstown, by Rev. N. **SULLIVAN**, Mr. E. M. **COLE** and Miss F. A. **ROSS**, all of Shelby county. Memphis Daily Appeal, 12/9/1856.

Married—On Thursday the 1st inst. by Rev. L. D. **MULLINS**, Mr. Thomas W. **COLE** to Miss Eliza J. **CHOATE**, all of this County. Tri-Weekly Memphis Enquirer, 10/8/1846.

Married, In Fayette county on the 10th instant, by Rev. M. **ZELLNER**, Mr. W. L. **COLE** and Miss Mary J. **PARKER**. Memphis Daily Appeal, 8/23/1856.

The new road leading from Raleigh to Memphis being abandoned for want of funds to complete it, and no more could be obtained by subscription…I have built and repaired bridges, and opened the road the greater part of the way to Memphis and my charge for labor on said road is two hundred dollars, which imposes the necessity of establishing a toll-gate until I am reimbursed in that amount…Daniel **COLEMAN**. Memphis Daily Eagle, 10/19/1848.

Married—At Hazel Dell, Hardeman county, on Wednesday morning, January the 5th by the Rev. Mr. Jansen, Mr. James **COLEMAN**, of Memphis, to Miss Ellen **DAVID**, of Hardeman county, Tenn…..Memphis Eagle & Enquirer, 1/6/1853. The friends and acquaintances of James Coleman are requested to attend the funeral of Mrs. Ellen E., his wife, from the residence of N. C. **DAVID**, at 10 o'clock This Morning. Services by Rev. Dr. Grundy. Memphis Daily Appeal, 12/29/1859.

Married, On the 16th instant at LaGrange, Tenn., by Rev. R. C. **GRUNDY**, Col. John **COLEMAN**, of Memphis, to Miss Bettie Blair **SPEER**. Memphis Weekly Appeal, 12/22/1858.

Married. At Woodland Place, in DeSoto county, Miss., on the 2nd day of November, 1854, by the Rev. Jas. N. **TEMPLE**, Col. John F. **COLEMAN**, of Columbus, Ga., to Miss Fanny S., daughter of the Rev. Wm. **McMAHAN**. Memphis Appeal, 11/18/1854.

Married, On the 29th inst. by Rev. A. T. **SCRUGGS**, Mr. S. T. **COLEMAN** to Miss Elizabeth **MCRAE**, niece of Gov. **MCRAE**, both of Marshall county, Miss. Memphis Daily Appeal, 2/3/1856.

Married, In this city on the 12th inst., by Rev. John H. **GRAY**, D.D., Col. Walter **COLEMAN** to Mrs. M. A. **KEELING**, all of this city. Memphis Appeal, 8/13/1852.

Died, On Tuesday, December 21, Amelia Ann, wife of J. S. **COLLIER**, of this city. She had been a member of the First Baptist Church in this city during the last fourteen years. Metropolis, Illinois, papers please copy. Memphis Weekly Appeal, 12/29/1858.

Died, on the 3d ult., near Richmond, Louisiana, Dr. Abram N. **COLLINS**, son of Maj. E. T. **COLLINS**, of Randolph.....He was noble, generous, and kind—unwavering as a friend, dutiful as a son, and devoted as a brother....But lately affianced to a beautiful and lovely girl.....Weekly Memphis Eagle, 4/12/1849. Died, At Randolph, on the 7th July, Marine Webster Collins, son of Maj. E. T. Collins, aged 11 years and ___ months. Weekly Memphis Eagle, 7/12/1849.

Married—In this city, on Monday Evening last, by Hon. E. W. M. **KING**, Mr. Brice A. **COLLINS**, to Mrs. Priscilla **COLLINS**. Daily Memphis Enquirer, Thurs., 9/28/1848.

Obituary. On the morning of the 13th ult., at St. Agnes Academy of this city, in the 14th year of her age, Frances Hulbert Collins, eldest daughter of Thomas M. and Virginia W. **COLLINS**. Memphis Eagle & Enquirer, 6/5/1853.

Notice is hereby given to all whom at may concern, that at the October Term of the County Court of Shelby county, I shall apply to the Court for the privilege of erecting a Dry and a Floating Dock at Memphis or South Memphis. James **COLLINSWORTH**. Daily Memphis Enquirer, 7/8/1848.

Married, On the 29th December, at the residence of G. **PAYELLE** in this city, by Hume F. **HILL**, Esq., Mr. Peter **COMAS** to Miss Alice **ROLAND**. Memphis Eagle & Enquirer, 2/1/1853.

On Tuesday night, station house keeper Copeland found Robert **COMPERRY**, who is well known in the city, lying on the pavement on Front Row. As he had often seen him in similar situations, from the effects of liquor, he took him into the station house and locked him up. He was taken sick soon afterward, and early in the morning he breathed his last....The deceased appeared to be about fifty-five years of age. Mr. Comperry was formerly of Clarksville, in this State; he was a respected merchant, dealing in corn and wheat. He removed to Nashville, where he became wealthy....He had, unfortunately, no family ties, not having married....He came to this city some three years ago....Memphis Daily Appeal, Thurs., 2/3/1859.

Common Law and Chancery Court of the City of Memphis. David **FAUCETT**, adm'r. of E. R. **COMPTON**, dec'd., et als. Vs. O. Bill, filed Feb. 21st, 1852. All persons claiming to be creditors of E. R. Compton...Memphis Eagle & Enquirer, 2/25/1852.

Married, On Tuesday evening, the 25th inst., by Rev. Dr. B. F. **HALL**, at Mrs. M. **PAYNE's**, in South Memphis, Mr. R. F. **COMPTON** to Miss Mary **PAYNE**—all of this city. Memphis Appeal, 11/27/1851.

E. L. **CONANT**, Exchange Broker, Memphis, Tenn. Weekly Appeal, 4/11/1845.

Married. On the 4th instant by the Rev. S. **WATSON**, Mr. John **CONAWAY** to Miss Parmelia **HARRIS**, all of this county. Memphis Appeal, 9/6/1854.

Theodore C. **CONE**, Esq., Attorney At Law.—Attention is invited to the card of this gentleman, who has recently removed from the State of Georgia to this city, for the purpose of practicing his profession. Mr. Cone is the son of Hon. F. H. **CONE**, one of the very ablest jurists in that State....Memphis Daily Appeal, 11/3/1857.

We stated Saturday that a man named Martin **CONLEY** had been run over by the train at the Memphis and Charleston Railroad depot, in this city on Friday evening, by which accident his leg was so horribly crushed that amputation was rendered necessary. The unfortunate man failed to rally from the horrible shock of amputation, and died Saturday evening. Memphis Daily Appeal, Tues., 10/4/1859.

At the southeast corner of Main and Commerce streets stands a gloomy looking, dilapidated house, above the level of the street. The front apartment is of the sort of half grocery that is generally denominated a doggery. The rear is used as a boarding house by a number of Irish laborers. The house is kept by a tall stout Irish woman, who is known by the name of "Big Mary"....Big Mary....is living with her seventh husband. Three of her husbands have met with violent deaths, being killed in or near the "dark house of blood." A son met with the same sanguinary fate, also near his mother's gloomy habitation. The other three husbands died of cholera or other diseases. A week ago a nephew of Mary's, a fine looking young Irishman of twenty-one, came up from Dean's Landing, where he had been working as a laborer....Last night, soon after dark, just as some dozen boarders had concluded supper, a crash was heard in the grocery and the upper part of the door was split and partly forced in. The whole party, with one exception, remained seated, without any curiosity as to the cause of the attack, or any desire to protect the property of their hostess. One man looked out, but he could see nobody, and all concluded that "somebody" had been throwing bricks. Twenty minutes after this, Peter **CONMAGHER**, Big Mary's nephew, went out at the side door; he soon came in again, exclaiming: "I am shot;" fell into one of the boarder's arms and instantly died. Examination showed that a pistol ball had penetrated the right side just below the breast....Memphis Daily Appeal, 12/18/1857.

Married—On yesterday by the Rev. Mr. Coons, Mr. H. D. **CONNELL**, to Miss Ann **LAWRENCE**, daughter of Jas. **LAWRENCE**, Esq. dec'd, all of this city. Memphis Appeal, 8/22/1848.

Died, At his residence in Montgomery county, Tenn., on the 12th inst., John **CONNELL**, Sen. In the 70th year of his age. He was born in Spartenburg District, South Carolina and removed to Robertson county in 1810. Memphis Eagle & Enquirer, 2/2/1853.

Died, In this city, of consumption, on the 31st December, at the residence of John **MAGIVNEY**, Mr. John W. **CONNELL**, aged 34 years. Mr. Connell was a native of Dublin, Ireland, and has for the last three and a half years been employed in the capacity of clerk in the post office in this city. Cape Girardeau Eagle please copy. Memphis Eagle & Enquirer, 1/1/1852.

Married, In Brownsville, Haywood county, Tenn., on the 24th ult. by Rev. J. E. **BRIGHT**, Mr. Charles **CONNER**, late of Memphis, to Miss Eloise **COLMAN**, daughter of the late Dr. **COLMAN**, formerly of Virginia. The Richmond Whig and Culpepper Observer please copy. Memphis Appeal, 11/1/1853.

On Thursday evening last, a girl of about seven years old, who says her name is Sarah **CONNOLLY**, was found weeping near Court Square. On questioning her, she said her mother, who was a widow, died a few days ago, and she was driven from the place where they had resided. The child was kindly taken in by Mrs. Tippett, on Second, near Jefferson, where the girl's friends, if she has any, may find her. Memphis Daily Appeal, Sun., 12/13/1857.

Esq. Horne held an inquest yesterday on the body of Mary **CONNOR**, a widow woman about thirty-five years of age, who died very suddenly of apoplexy....Thursday night....Memphis Daily Appeal, Sat., 10/29/1859.

Married—On Wednesday, 2nd inst. by James **ROSE**, Esq., Mr. **BIRCHARD**, of Massachusetts, to Miss Margaret C. **CONRAD**, of this city. Memphis Enquirer, 8/6/1848.

Thomas **CONVERSE**, an unfortunate man who has been indulging in dissipated habits, and consequently was reduced to privations and exposure, died on Wednesday evening....Memphis Daily Appeal, Fri., 2/11/1859.

Died. At the residence of hs son, Owen, in this city, on yesterday morning at 7 o'clock, Mr. Thomas **CONWAY**, sen., at the advanced age of eighty-two years. His funeral will take place to-day at 10 o'clock A.M. from the residence of Mr. Owen **CONWAY**, opposite the City Hotel....Memphis Appeal, 9/23/1854. Having taken out letters of Administration on the estate of Thomas Conway, deceased, at the Nov. Term of the County Court of Shelby county....Margaret **CONWAY**, Administratrix of Thos. Conway, dec'd. Memphis Daily Appeal, 11/8/1855.

At the residence of Thos. **CONWAY** nearly opposite the Navy Yard gate, seven persons died from Saturday night to Sunday night, and were, we understood yesterday morning, all lying dead in the house. There are various conjectures about this strange and sudden fatality, the most probable one being that they were poisoned...Memphis Appeal, Tues., 11/28/1854.

The friends and acquaintances of Thomas **CONWAY** are respectfully invited to attend his funeral, from his residence on Jackson street, this evening at 2 o'clock. Memphis Daily Appeal, 10/5/1855.

Married, On the 27th ult., at the residence of the bride's father, by Rev. J. H. **CLARK**, Mr. C. S. **COOK**, of Memphis, Tenn., to Miss Harriet J. **COLLINS**, OF Freedom, Ohio. Memphis Daily Appeal, 10/8/1858.

At the March Term, 1850, of the County Court of Shelby county, Tenn., the undersigned was appointed Administrator of Mrs. Catharine S. **COOK**, deceased...Sam W. **AYRES**, Adm'r. Memphis Daily Eagle, 4/17/1850.

Married, On Wednesday evening last by Rev. J. O. **STEADMAN**, at the residence of Col. C. D. **MCLEAN**, Mr. Geo. W. **COOK** and Miss Sallie J. **LOVE**. Memphis Daily Appeal, 7/18/1856.

Died, In this vicinity on Monday last, Richard Swanson, oldest child of Marcus and Amelia **COOK**, in the ninth year of his age....The Appeal, Fri., 12/13/1844.

Died, In this city, on the 15th inst., Capt. Morgan B. **COOK**, long a resident of this city. Capt. Cook was about thirty-two years of age, and formerly an officer in the Mexican War. Memphis Eagle & Enquirer, 6/17/1852.

Married, At the residence of S. W. **AYRES**, Esq., on the 12th instant, by Rev. Mr. Robb, W. L. B. **COOK**, Esq., and Miss Jennie, daughter of Mr. Isaac **AYRES**, all of this city. Memphis Daily Appeal, 2/14/1856. Died, On the 16th December, 1857, William L. B., son of W. L. B. and Jennie Cook, aged six months and three days. Memphis Daily Appeal, 12/20/1857.

Departed this life at 10 o'clock, the 20th instant, in DeSoto county, Miss., Rebecca D. Cooke, consort of F. L. **COOKE**, Esq. She was born in North Carolina, Penson county, in the year 1815 the 20th (or 26th) of November, and joined the Methodist Church at an early day when very young. After many years she joined the Missionary Baptist Church, of which she lived a most exemplary life....She left behind her six children—four by her first husband and two by her second. Memphis Daily Appeal, 11/27/1856.

Died, In this city, on Saturday morning, at the residence of her son-in-law, Seth **WHEATLEY**, Esq., Mrs. Catharine S. Cooke, relict of the late Judge Wm. L. **COOKE**, of Nashville, in the 47th year of her age.....Weekly Memphis Eagle, Thurs., 12/20/1849.

Married, In Louisville, on the 18th inst., by the Rev. Edward P. **HUMPHREY**, Mr. John **COONEY**, Jr. of Ten., to Miss Jennie C. **LOUGEE**, of Louisville, daughter of the late Mr. Noah **LOUGEE**. Memphis Eagle, 10/1/1850.

First Presbyterian Church, Poplar Street, east of Second...Rev. G. W. **COONS**. Daily Enquirer, 2/28/1847. We regret to learn that the Reverend Geo. W. Coons, for so long the beloved Pastor of the First Presbyterian Church of this city, feels compelled to resign his charge in consequence of ill health.... Memphis Appeal, 10/7/1852.

Married, At Bolivar on the 22d (?) ult. by the Rev. Daniel **STEPHENS**, E. C. **COOPER** Esq. of Shelbyville, to Miss Mary E. **STEPHENS** of the former place. The Appeal, 11/1/1844.

Married, On the 26th of April, by Esquire Waldran, George **COOPER** to Miss Matilda **BR_MATIN**, all of this city. Memphis Eagle & Enquirer, 4/28/1852.

Married, In Hickman, Ky., on the 16th inst., by Rev. Mr. Cowgill, Mr. H. H. **COOPER**, of Memphis, to Miss Delia M., daughter of our former townsman, Geo. R. **REDFORD**. Memphis Daily Appeal, 12/25/1857.

Married, In Panola county on Thursday, 14th instant, by Rev. W. **DUPUY**, Mr. John A. **COOPER** and Miss Caroline **FINCH**. Memphis Daily Appeal, 2/22/1856.

Died, At his residence on Shelby street in this city, of paralysis, Mr. Joseph **COOPER**, in the fifty-sixth year of his age. Memphis Appeal, 3/29/1853.

Married, By Rev. John **RHYME** on Wednesday, the 8th inst., at the residence of the bride's father, Col. Robinson, Dr. Joseph H. **COOPER**, late of Memphis, to Miss Amanda **ROBINSON**, all of Jacksonport. Memphis Daily Appeal, 7/18/1857.

Married, By Rev. C. **HENDRICKSON**, Mr. Mathew J. **COOPER** and Miss Mary E. **OWEN**, of Shelby County. Memphis Whig, 4/19/1856. Married, On the evening of the 17th instant at the residence of Henry Owen, Esq., in this county, by the Rev. C. R. Hendrickson, Mr. M. T.(?) Cooper, of the firm of Stockley, Cooper & Co., of this city, and Miss Mollie E. Owen. Friend Mat, we congratulate you in the choice of so excellent a wife....Memphis Daily Appeal, 4/19/1856.

Married, On Tuesday evening, 17th instant, by Rev. J. H. **GRAY**, Mr. J. **COPELAND** to Miss Lou. C. **BUTLER**, all of this city. Memphis Daily Appeal, 12/20/1855.

Died, At Macon on the 6th inst., Ida Clay, infant daughter of (N. W. and Isabella **COPELAND**). American Eagle Weekly, 10/31/1845. Died—At Raleigh on the 26th September last, Isabella, wife of N. W. Copeland. American Eagle Weekly, 10/31/1845. Died—In this vicinity, yesterday morning, Newton W. **COPELAND** aged 34 years. Mr. Copeland was a native of Middle Tenn., and has resided in Raleigh, in this county, for the last several years, whence he removed to this city a few weeks since to engage in our employ as clerk and bookkeeper. His death was most sudden and unexpected.....He was a consistent member of the Presbyterian church.....His remains were conveyed to Raleigh to be placed by the side of his consort, who departed on her pilgrimage to Heaven about a year ago.....The Tri-Weekly Memphis Enquirer, 9/29/1846.

All persons indebted to the Estate of William **COOPWOOD**, deceased, are requested to come forward...C. P. **STRICKLAND**, Administrator. Memphis Appeal, 9/3/1851.

Married, On Thursday evening, 24th inst. by J. **WALDRAN**, Esq., Mr. Daniel W. **CORBITT** to Miss Mahala W. **LELDAN**, all of this city. Memphis Appeal, 2/26/1853.

Married, On Thursday evening last, by the Rev. G. W. **COONS**, Mr. Geo. **CORNELL**, to Miss Mary N., daughter of Ira **ROBINSON**, all of this city. American Eagle, Thurs., 12/2/1847.

Died, In this city yesterday evening at the residence of her father-in-law, Mr. J. J. **ROBINSON**, Miss Bettie **CORNWELL**, aged 18 years and 2 months. Memphis Daily Appeal, 1/11/1856.

Joseph F. **CORNWELL**, Draper and Tailor, Has just opened a shop on Front Row...Memphis Eagle, 10/6/1848. Joseph Cornwell, formerly of this city, and well known here, was found dead in the street at Troy, Tenn., a few days since. His death was caused by intemperance. Memphis Appeal, 7/19/1852.

Married, At Calvary Church, on the 29th inst., by Right Rev. Jas. H. **OTEY**, Dr. James **CORREY**, of Chattanooga, and Miss Kate, daughter of Samuel P. **WALKER**, Esq., of this city. Nashville, Chattanooga and Pittsburgh papers please copy. Memphis Daily Appeal, 1/30/1857.

Married, On yesterday evening in this vicinity by the Rev. Mr. Robb, Mr. Patrick **COSGROVE** to Miss Elizabeth **LYNES**(?). Memphis Appeal, 4/21/1853.

Wrapping Paper on Consignment. 800 Reams small, medium and large size Wrapping Paper...F. H. **COSSITT** & Co. Memphis Eagle, 6/22/1848.

Married, At the residence of Wm. A. **JONES**, Green Plains, Ark., on the 22d inst. by Rev. J. E. **DOUGLASS**, Mr. E. H. **COTTON**, of LaGrange, Ten. to Miss Fannie M. **LOGWOOD**, of Green Plains. Memphis Appeal, 6/25/1853.

Died, at his plantation four miles east of Raleigh, on Wednesday last, of an inflamation of the lungs, Major Joseph **COTTON**, aged 50 years......American Eagle, 1/31/1842.

Chancery Sale. Charles W. **HUNT**, Executor, and others vs. Alice Cotton and others, heirs of Leonidas **COTTON**, deceased, and Joel L. **JONES**, Administrator of Leonidas Cotton, deceased. In pursuance to an order made, at the May Term, 1848, by the Chancery Court, at Sommerville in this cause, I shall proceed to sell, in the town of Lagrange, Fayette county, Tennessee, on Saturday the second day of September next...the following described tract of land, it being the tract of land purchased by Leonidas Cotton of John **HUNT**, now deceased, lying and being in the county of Fayet and State of Tennessee, containing 722 ¼ acres, and consisting of the following two tracts or parcels adjoining each other, to wit: One tract or parcel containing 640 acres, in District 10, range 5, and Section 1, granted to Thomas **HENDERSON** by grant No. 18,372...The other tract or parcel containing 82 ¼ acres, be the same more or less, being part of a tract granted to Thomas **POLK**, by Grant No. 19,990...1. B. **McCLELLAN**, C. & M. June 24, 1848. Memphis Appeal, 7/15/1848.

Thomas **COULEHAN**, Blacksmith, Main street, South Memphis. Weekly Appeal, 10/3/1845.

Esquire Horne held an inquest yesterday upon the body of Thomas **COUSINS**, who died suddenly in this city Wednesday night. The deceased had been engaged as a laborer at one of the cotton sheds and died, it is presumed, of dissipation and exposure....Memphis Daily Avalanche, Fri., 2/11/1859.

Married—At 9 o'clock yesterday morning at the Second Presbyterian Church by Rev. Dr. Gray, Mr. John **COWAN** to Miss Ann M. **BROWN**, all of Memphis. Memphis Appeal, 11/4/1853.

Pursuant to a Decree of the Chancery Court at Memphis, made at the May term, 1848, thereof, in the case of Thomas L. **COWAN** and others, complainants, against Theophilus **STARKE** and others, defendants, I shall sell in front of the Commercial Hotel, in the city of Memphis, on the 7th of August, 1848...Section Seven, and __ of Section Eighteen, in township one, Range five, West, lying in Shelby county, Tenn...J. H. **TALBOT**, C. & M. By his Deputy, Thomas M. **EAST**. Memphis Daily Eagle, 6/22/1848.

All those indebted to the firm of Wm. and Jos. **COWAN** for 1835 will please come forward immediately and make payment, as I am determined not to give longer indulgence. Wm. **COWAN**, Surviving partner of Wm. & Jos. Cowan. Memphis Enquirer, 1/7/1837.

We regret to learn from yesterday's *News* that Mr. Wm. F. **COWAN**, an old and highly esteemed citizen of this place, died recently at St. Louis, of consumption. He was in the 53d year of his age. Memphis Daily Appeal, 9/23/1855.

Died. In Portersville, of congestive fever, Mrs. Sarah M. Cowan, consort of Mr. Wm. H. **COWAN**, aged 21 years.....Memphis Enquirer, 9/16/1837.

Taken up by E. **COWGILL**, living about 4 miles northwest of Raleigh, one small brown mare mule...Weekly Appeal, 9/25/1846.

Died—Near Memphis, on the 1st inst., in the twentieth year of her age, Mrs. Euphemia Theresa, consort of Edward **COX**, and eldest daughter of Horace N. **WARD**, of Georgia. American Eagle, 4/7/1843.

Married, At 3 o'clock on Sunday evening last, by Rev. D. E. **BURNS**, Mr. Wm. **COX** to Miss Mary **BAIN**, all of this city. Memphis Appeal, Wed., 3/24/1852.

Married, On the 24th inst., by the Rev. H. L. **GRAY**, Dr. William S. **COX**, of Louisiana, to Miss Emma **McKNIGHT**, of Shelby co., Tenn. Memphis Eagle & Enquirer, 2/25/1852.

Official Report of Deaths. From the 1st August, to 11 o'clock on the 5th, 2 deaths have occurred within the limits of the Corporation, - viz: Sarah **CRABTREE**, (transient) aged 24 years, died of chronic affection. John C. **MINOTT**, (arrived, sick, from Arkansas, some six or eight weeks since,) died of liver complaint. The Appeal, 8/9/1844.

Married, In Danville, Kentucky, on the morning of the 19th inst., by Rev. __. J. **BULLOCK**, of Walnut Hill, Mr. Addison **CRAFT**, of Holly Springs, Mississippi, to Miss Frances Breckinridge Young, daughter of the late Dr. John C. **YOUNG**, of Centre Hill. Memphis Daily Appeal, 11/29/1857.

Married: In this city, on the 11th inst., at Calvary Church, by Rev. Dr. Page, Mr. J. N. **CRAFT**, to Miss Jessie **OLMSTED**, all of this city. Weekly Memphis Eagle, 7/19/1849.

Died—in this city on the 18th inst., Virginia M., daughter of Mrs. Maria A. **CRAFT**, aged 7 years and 11 months. American Eagle Weekly, 12/26/1845.

Died, At his mother's residence in Limestone county, Ala., September 6, 1855, W. A. **CRAIG**, of Dallas county, Ark. Little Rock, Ark. papers please copy. Memphis Daily Appeal, 9/20/1855.

Married, On the 18th at Brownsville, Tenn., by Rev. E. J. **WILLIAMS**, Mr. Thos. **CRANDELL** and Miss Ann R. **LEWIS**, late of New Albany, Indiana. Memphis Daily Appeal, 4/20/1856.

The friends and acquaintances of Wm. **CRANE** are invited to attend the funeral of his wife, from the Second Presbyterian Church, this evening....Memphis Daily Appeal, 9/27/1859.

We learned yesterday a few particulars from Capt. McDonough, of a melancholy and fatal accident which occurred in the Mississippi river, opposite Helena, on Saturday last. It seems that a party consisting of six persons was out in a small sail boat, when they were accidentally run over by the steamer *Robert J. Ward*, and three of the party drowned. The names of those drowned are Col. J. T. **CRARY**, a promising young lawyer of Helena, formerly of Middle Tennessee, but more recently of Bolivar, in this State; Mr. Carrell, and a mail carrier by the name of Brown. The three persons rescued are Mr. **CLEBORNE**, of Helena, Mr. **HUMPHREYS**, Sheriff of Tunica county, Miss....Memphis Daily Appeal, Tues., 4/29/1856.

Died, near Whiteville, Hardeman county, Tenn., on the 17th ult., infant child of W. W. and A. M. **CRAWFORD**, aged 11 months, 5 days. Weekly Appeal, 12/12/1845.

Capt. Jas. A. **CREIGHTON**, of this city, takes command of the fine little steamer Obion, and will start for Helena and the St. Francis river this morning...The most of our city readers will remember Capt. Creighton as the gentlemanly and highly popular commander of the fast little steamer Countess,--Engaged a year or fifteen months ago in the White river trade...Memphis Appeal, 9/25/1852. The friends and acquaintances of the late James A. Creighton are invited to attend his funeral at 10 o'clock this morning from the residence of his father, corner of St. Patrick and Pontotoc Sts., South Memphis. Memphis Appeal,

3/17/1854. Judge Hill, accompanied by Mr. Elliott and the ____ of the party who accompanied them to the wreck of the Caroline, on White river, returned on the T. P. Leathers yesterday morning. They camped near the scene of the disaster and remained three days using every effort, with partial success, to recover the bodies of those who were lost. They succeeded in recovering the bodies of Capt. Jas. A. Creighton, Mr. **AYDLOTT**, Mrs. **HAILEY**, of Tippah co., Miss., and those of two deck hands, unknown....The remains of Mrs. Hailey were buried some three miles below the wreck and those of Capt. Creighton and Mr. Aydlott were brought to this place night before last, on the steamer Naomi.... The remains of Mr. Aydlott we presume will be cared for by the public authorities until a claimant comes for them. Some papers found upon him are in the possession of Mr. Elliott, and it would seem that he had lived near Sulphur Well or Sulphur Springs....He is the son-in-law of a Mr. **WORTHAM**....The following bodies were rescued from the wreck of the Caroline by Mr. Hill and the gentlemen who accompanied him: Mrs. Haley, whose residence is unknown; John **WARNER**, deck hand, St. Louis; Mr. Jackson **AYDELLOTTE**, Shelby county, Tenn.; Henry **CRAWFORD**, near Milwaukee, Wisconsin; Capt. James Creighton, Memphis....Memphis Appeal, 3/17/1854.

Died, On the night of Friday last, of cholera, Mrs. Mary **CREIGHTON**, relict of the late Dr. Creighton, of Jackson, Tenn. Memphis Appeal, Mon., 7/7/1851.

R. W. **CREIGHTON**, M.D., Respectfully offers his services, professionally, to the citizens of Memphis and vicinity. N.B. Diseases of the Eye and Lungs will receive special attention. Office on Main street...between Madison and Monroe streets. Memphis Appeal, 9/1/1851.

Died, On the 22d inst. at the residence of his Uncle, Henry **LAKE**, Samuel Barnes **CREIGHTON**, in the 14th year of his age. Baltimore papers please copy. Memphis Appeal, 8/30/1852.

A Mr. Thomas **CREMER**, living in the neighborhood of Raytown, Tenn. was instantly killed on the 25th ult., by the accidental falling of a saw-log from a wagon which he was driving.....Memphis Eagle & Enquirer, 5/13/1853.

I offer for sale my Residence, called "Mount Airy," in Shelby county, 23 miles from Memphis. The tract contains 1378 acres...Those wishing to purchase will call on me on the premises, two miles south of Wash's store, on the road leading from Memphis to Sommerville. Asbury **CRENSHAW**. Weekly Memphis Eagle, 10/18/1849.

Married, On the 10th instant by Rev. Frank _. **HOUSE**, Mr. C. Lum **CRENSHAW** to Miss Rachael L. _odson, all of Big Creek, Shelby county, Tenn. Memphis Weekly Appeal, 12/29/1858.

Married. On the 29th ult. by J. N. **RALSTON**, Esq., Mr. Charles **CRENSHAW** to Miss Juliana S. **WAMMACK**, both of this county. Memphis Daily Appeal, 11/10/1855.

Died, at one o'clock yesterday, the 17th of June, at the residence of her son-in-law, (Major James H. **CRENSHAW**, of this place,) Mrs. Dorothea S. **WINSTON**, eldest child, by the second marriage, of Hon. Patrick **HENRY**, of Virginia, in the year 1777. The deceased had as few of the frailties of human nature as any woman that ever lived. She was a woman of strong mind and retained her faculties to the last hour of her life....The funeral of the late Mrs. Winston will take place at the "Bluff City Manufacturing Mills," this afternoon at four o'clock. Religious services by Rev. Dr. Page....Richmond papers copy. Memphis Appeal, 6/18/1854.

I offer for sale the tract of Land on which I now reside, containing 1252 ½ acres, 800 acres cleared, the balance woodland, thirteen miles from Memphis and lying on both sides of the Memphis and Ohio Railroad. The improvements are a good dwelling, with eight rooms, good gin house, and mill....Thos. C. **CRENSHAW**. Memphis Daily Appeal, 11/23/1856.

Died. In Paris, Henry county, on the 20th ult., Mr. Smith **CRIDDLE**. American Eagle Weekly, 12/5/1845.

Married, In Pontotoc, Miss., on Tuesday morning, December 2_th by Rev. W. L. **SLACK**, D.D., Mr. James W. **CROCKER**, of Memphis, to Miss Mollie A., daughter of Dr. J. A. **WARE**, of the former place. Memphis Weekly Appeal, 1/13/1858.

One of the most painful and distressing incidents that we have ever been called on to record occurred near this city about a half mile west of the Raleigh road and 1 ½ miles from town on Tuesday afternoon the 9th inst. Mr. David F. **CROCKETT**, a young man of high respectability and of worthy family, wandered out to a forest a few hundred yards from the residence of Esquire Chace, and deliberately put an end to his existence by hanging himself with his black silk cravat and silk handkerchief to the _____ of a sapling. When accidentally found on the succeeding evening (Wednesday) by a boy who went out to chop wood in the forest, he was still hanging on the limb, his clothes saturated with water from the rains of the night previous and all the evidence about him of a deliberate design to terminate his existence. Mr. C. had been confined to his room for several days by a violent attack of sickness and appeared to be convalascing. He had determined to leave on the cars the next morning for his home in Middleburg, Hardeman county, and left his room about 4 o'clock on Tuesday evening, announcing that he had important business in town requiring his attention before his departure ....He had been engaged in the mercantile business for several years at Middleburg....His funeral took place yesterday morning at Morris Cemetery, to which his remains were attended by a large procession of his friends and acquaintances. Memphis Appeal, 1/13/1855.

On Thursday the 25th inst., the members of the Memphis Bar convened at the office of the Chancery Clerk, to pay the proper respect to the memory of their deceased professional brother, John W. **CROCKETT**...Whereas, The Hon. John W. Crockett, one of the members of this Bar, departed this life at his residence on the evening of the 24th inst...Memphis Appeal, 11/27/1852. The remains of our late townsman and much esteemed fellow-citizen, John W. Crockett, were intered in the cemetery at Paris in this State on the 12th ult. They were attended to their last resting place by the Independent Order of Odd Fellows and Masons, both of which fraternities he was an old and worthy member. Memphis Appeal, 1/7/1853.

We learn that our young friend and townsman, Robert W. **CROCKETT**, has taken an interest in the Brownsville *Eagle*, of which paper he will in future be the associate editor of Mr. Battle....Memphis Daily Appeal, 11/11/1855.

Died. On the 8th inst., Mrs. Mary **CROFFORD**, at the residence of her son-in-law, W. **CRANE**, on Union st.....Services by Rev. Dr. Gray. Memphis Appeal, 7/9/1854.

Died, At the residence of her son-in-law, J. K. **BRANCH**, in this county, of congestive chill, Mrs. S. H. Croom, wife of Wm. **CROOM**, Esq., formerly of Jackson, Tenn., in the 59th year of her age. North Carolina papers will please copy. Memphis Daily Appeal, 3/23/1859.

Memphis Medical College. The first course of Lectures in this Institution will open on the first Monday in November next, in the city of Memphis, and continue four months. Faculty: James Conquist **CROSS**, M.D., Professor of Institutes and Medical Jurisprudence. Abner **HOPTON**, M.D., Professor of Chemistry and Pharmacy. Joseph Norman **BYBEE**, M.D., Professor of General and Special Anatomy. George R. **GRANT**, M.D., Professor of Theory and Practice of Medicine. D. J. M. **DOYLE**, M.D., Professor of Surgery. H. V. M. **MILLER**, M.D., Professor of Obstetrics and Diseases of Women and Children. Francis A. **RAMSEY**, M.D., Professor of Materia Medica and Therapeutics.....A. **HOPTON**, Dean of the Faculty. The Tri-Weekly Memphis Enquirer, 7/9/1846. A Former Resident Gone.—The Maysville (Ky.) papers chronicle the death of Dr. J. Conquest Cross, in that city on Monday week last, from a complication of disease. He was an accomplished scholar and eminent physician and had filled with much success professorships in the medical colleges at Cincinnati, Lexington and this city. Memphis Whig, Wed., 9/12/1855.

Died, On the 15th of March, 1857, after a short illness, Mrs. Mary C., wife of John H. **CROSS**, aged 27 years and 20 (or 29) days. Norfolk (Va.) papers please copy. Memphis Daily Appeal, 4/5/1857.

Married, In this city on the 25th inst., at the residence of Mrs. Crossland, by Rev. W. H. **LEIGH**, Mr. F. W. **CROSSLAND** to Mrs. Ann **DOUGLASS**, all of this city. Memphis Weekly Appeal, 3/3/1858.

Rev. B. T. **CROUCH**, formerly of the Memphis Conference, has been appointed on the Benicia and Martinez Circuit, by the Pacific Conference of the Methodist Episcopal Church, in California, San Francisco District.....Memphis Eagle & Enquirer, 6/3/1853.

Died. In Covington, Thomas **CRUTCHER** Esq., aged 28 years, formerly of Nashville. His friends, and all were such, passed the customary obituary resolutions of sorrow and tribute to his living excellence. Memphis Enquirer, 8/19/1837.

A difficulty has for sometime existed between Mr. Samuel S. **CRUTE**, who resides near Byhalia, Marshall county, Miss., and Mr. Jones, the husband of his daughter. In consequence of family troubles, Mrs. Jones, with her child, had been living with her father, apart from her husband. On Sunday, Jones entered the grounds of Mr. Crute....With a threat that if certain papers were not given up to him he would take them at any risk....Crute presented a shot gun. Jones still came on, when Crute fired, killing him immediately.... Mr. Crute was not arrested. Memphis Daily Appeal, Thurs., 2/17/1859.

Died, near Brownsville, Tenn., on the 10th inst., Robert B., son of Thomas and Elizabeth **CUBBINS**, aged three years, one month and five days....Memphis Appeal, 7/14/1855.

Married. On Thursday evening, the 17th inst., by Rev. Mr. Bright, Rev'd David H. **CUMMINGS**, to Miss Emma **HOLMES**, all of Tipton county. American Eagle, 8/25/1843.

I will sell the tract of Land, 620 acres, on which I reside....The above land lies one mile north of North Mount Pleasant, Marshall county, Miss....Also a tract containing 624 acres, lying on Chuwalla(?), 8 miles southeast of Holly Springs....Levi **CUMMINGS**. Memphis Daily Appeal, 11/2/1855.

Married. On the 25th inst. by Rev. John R. **CLEARY**, Mr. William **CUMMINS** to Miss Bridget **QUINLAN**, all of this city. Memphis Daily Appeal, 4/29/1855.

Married, In Aberdeen on Tuesday evening, the 15th inst., by Rev. Bishop Paine, Miss Pauline Sykes, daughter of Dr. W. A. **SYKES**, and Mr. Early **CUNNINGHAM**. Memphis Daily Avalanche, 2/23/1859.

Married, by Rev. T. A. **WARE**, on the 28th, at the Whitemore House in this city, Mr. F. M. **CUNNINGHAM** and Miss Elizabeth E. **HYSLOP**. Memphis Daily Appeal, 5/29/1856.

Married, On the 13th instant by Rev. Mr. Pickens, Miss S. __. **GWYN**, of Fayette county, Tenn., and Mr. R. H. **CUNNINGHAM**, of Kossuth, Tishomingo county, Miss. Memphis Daily Appeal, 5/21/1856.

Died. On Friday morning, 25th ult., at the residence of H. D. **SMALL**, near Memphis, Mrs. Lockey **CURLE**, aged about 90 years. Mrs. C. was a native Virginian, and long a resident of that state. She lived a widow for 68 years—a Christian of the Episcopal church...Richmond (Va.) papers please copy. Weekly Memphis Eagle, 6/7/1849.

Died, On Sunday morning last, Col. Z. H. **CURLIN**, aged 56 years, a highly respectable citizen of this vicinity, formerly of Hickman county, Kentucky. Hickman papers please copy. Memphis Daily Appeal, 7/30/1858.

One of the Irish laborers engaged on the steamer, Evansville, in rolling Cotton last evening, accidentally fell from the staging leading from the wharf to the boat, and was drowned. He was rolling a bale of Cotton at the time, and fell backward into the stream, sinking immediately, under the guard of the Rescue. He was not seen to rise after he fell, and his body has not yet been found. The name of the unfortunate man was Wm. **CURRIE**. Memphis Daily Appeal, 2/21/1856.

David M. **CURRIN**, the Democratic Electoral Candidate for this District, will speak at Court Square, on Tuesday evening next, (Aug. 1st,) at 8 o'clock, P.M. Memphis Appeal, 7/30/1848. David M. Currin, Attorney At Law, Memphis, Tenn. Office South side of Court Square.... Memphis Appeal, 9/23/1852. Col. David M. Currin, of Memphis, has been sojourning with his friends in this neighborhood, for a week past. After a hard race for Congress, in which he was defeated, he looks well and seems cheerful.—*Franklin Review, Aug. 17.* Memphis Daily Appeal, 8/22/1855.

Died, on the 5th ult., at his residence near Sommerville, Fayette county, Tennessee, Col. James **CURRIN**, aged 73 years, formerly of Fluvanna county, Virginia...In his death his neighbors have lost a valuable citizen and his family a kind and devoted parent. Memphis Enquirer, 4/14/1848.

Died, At the residence of his father, R. P. **CURRIN**, in Lauderdale county, Tenn., on the 9th inst. at 9 o'clock, A.M., Mr. William James **CURRIN**, aged 25 years. Memphis Appeal, 5/18/1853. Died, At his residence in Lauderdale county, on the 27th of July last, Mr. R. P. Currin, late a citizen of Franklin, Tenn. Memphis Daily Appeal, 11/3/1857.

Died—At Spring Mill, Lauderdale county, Tenn., on the 5th inst., Francis Elisha Currin, son of Robert P. **CURRIN**, Esq., of this place, in the twenty-first year of his age......The Appeal, 7/26/1844.

A laborer on a coal-boat, named Chas. **CURTAIN**, fell overboard near the old wharfboat, about ten o'clock yesterday morning, and was drowned. After a diligent search the body was found a few hours afterward....Memphis Daily Appeal, 9/9/1859.

The friends and acquaintances of Theodore **CURTIS** are invited to attend his funeral from the residence of his father, S. B. **CURTIS**, on Second street, between Exchange and Market, at 10 o'clock this morning. Memphis Daily Appeal, 8/7/1858.

Died: On the 13th July, at the residence of B. R. **TREZEVANT**, near Germantown, Tenn., Mrs. Ameliora G. Cutchin, relict of the late Capt. Robt. **CUTCHIN**, of Nansemond county, Va., aged 60 years. Norfolk papers will please copy. Memphis Eagle, 7/20/1848.

Married. In Tipton county, on the 15th ult., Mr. Alexander **DACUS**, aged 83 years, to Miss Rebecca **STARNES**, aged 27 years. Memphis Eagle, 9/5/1850.

Married, On Tuesday evening, 19th inst., by Rev. Geo. W. **COONS**, Mr. Wesley C. **DADSON**, of Alabama, to Miss Sarah A. **MOFFITT**, of this vicinity. Memphis Eagle & Enquirer, 4/21/1853.

Died, At the Gayoso House, July 23d, Frances Plummer, daughter of Ed. W. and Annie B. **DALE**—aged twenty-two months. Memphis Daily Appeal, 7/24/1858.

Compliments to Mr. and Mrs. Dalton.—The bridal party given to Mr. C. R. **DALTON** and his interesting Lady at the Commercial on Tuesday evening last was a most tasteful and agreeable affair....Memphis Daily Appeal, Thurs., 2/5/1857.

Married. In Fayette county on the 9th inst., Mr. J. Calvin **DALTON** to Miss D. **BRYANT**. Memphis Appeal, 10/21/1853.

Married: On Sunday evening by Thos. B. **FIRTH**, Esq., Mr. J. T. **DALTON** to Miss Lettie **TISDEL**, all of La Grange, Tenn. Memphis Evening Ledger, Thurs., 12/31/1857.

Died, At his residence in Macon, Fayette county, Tenn., after a short illness, on the 28th November, 1857, William E. **DALY**, Esq., a highly esteemed citizen. Memphis Daily Appeal, 12/4/1857. Died, In Collierville, Tenn., on the 29th ult., W. E. Daly, Esq., of Macon, Tenn., in the _4th year of his age. The deceased left his home and family on Monday previous to his death for Memphis, whither he was called on business; was taken ill the following night, and started for his home next day, but so violent was the attack that he was unable to proceed further than Colliersville, where he breathed his last. His remains were on the following day....taken charge of by the Masonic Fraternity and carried to Mt. Pleasant burying ground....Thus has passed away a most inestimable citizen, a loving husband, a kind parent and a good Mason....Memphis Daily Appeal, 12/5/1857.

Married—in this city on the 24th inst., by the Rev. W. WARREN, Mr. J. D. DANBURY to Miss Emma FRAIM. Tri-Weekly Memphis Enquirer, 10/31/1846.

Married. In this city on Thursday evening, the 3d instant, by Rev. T. T. C. COLLINS, John D. DANBURY, Esq., Alderman of the Fourth Ward, to Miss Sallie G. LONG, of Columbus, Ohio.... Memphis Whig, 5/4/1855.

Married, On the 1st instant by Rev. J. W. KNOTT, Mr. G. W. DANDRIDGE, of Boston, Texas, and Miss P. C. SMITH, of this city. Memphis Daily Appeal, 1/3/1857.

Died, In Monroe county, Ark., on the 30th day of August last, Reuben Bates, infant son of G. W. and M. V. DANFORTH, aged two months two days. Memphis Daily Appeal, 9/23/1859.

Henry M. DANIEL, Receiving & Forwarding Merchant, Randolph, Tenn. Weekly Appeal, 7/11/1845. Died, On Tuesday morning, October 16, Col. Henry M. Daniel, aged 67 years. The friends and acquaintances of the family are requested to attend his funeral This Evening at 3 o'clock on Germantown Plank Road. Memphis Daily Appeal, 10/27/1858.

Married, On Tuesday last, 17th inst., by Elder J. P. KERN, Mr. John W. DANIEL and Miss Joanna C. TARKINTON, all of Des Arc. Memphis Whig, 6/26/1856.

Lewis W. DANIEL, Attorney at Law, Office on Main, between Poplar and Washington sts., Memphis. Memphis Appeal, 12/13/1847.

Married, On the 23d ult. by H. T. THOMPSON, Esq., Mr. Thomas M. DANIEL, of Tipton county, to Mrs. Sarah Jane LAMBERT, daughter of Zachary and Sarah HARRISON, of this county. Memphis Eagle & Enquirer, 3/11/1853.

Married—In Tippah County, Miss., on the 25th of March, at the residence of the bride's father, by Rev. R. NULL, Mr. Wm. A. DANIEL to Miss Cattie CRAWFORD. Memphis Daily Avalanche, 4/27/1859.

The following report gives the verdicts of the Coroner's Jury from January 9 to the present—seven months: G. W. DANIELS, an American, from a blow over the head by a chair in the hands of a Mr. Wright; Lewis, a slave of Sam YATES, found dead in his bed; an Irishman, name unknown, by accidentally falling into a well; Col. R. N. WILLIAMSON, by accidentally coming in contact with a bridge on the Memphis & Ohio Railroad; Antonio, an Italian, by intemperance; Wm. KEMPLAN, by accidentally shooting himself with a pistol; F. BOWEN, a child two years old, by falling into a pool of water; an Irishman by the name of Taylor, from intemperance; Peter MALONEY, an Irishman, by railroad cars running over his body; W. C. MATHEWS, an American, and Jas. WILLIAMS, an Englishman, shot by Benj. CONNOR; M. MADDON, an Irishman, by being struck over the head with an axe-handle in the hands of M. Fitzgerald; Jno. GRIFFING, an Irishman, by being stabbed by some one unknown to the jury; Thos. S. LAWLIS, an American, came to his death by being drowned in Wolf river; T. WILLIAMS, an American, (convict,) by being drowned in the river, in attempting to escape; J. C. HOWARD, an American, by being drowned in Wolf river; C. RYAN, an Irishman, by falling from an upper porch; Geo. SMITH, by accidentally falling between two plum trees....J. WALDRAN, Coroner. Memphis Daily Appeal, 8/7/1856.

Official Report of Deaths. Four deaths have occurred within the limits of the Corporation during the past week – viz: Child of Zachius DANIELS, here but a short time from Arkansas, aged two years. John KELTNEY (?), a native of Ireland, of congestive chill. Child of Mr. LYLE, citizen, age 13 years. Negro man of Durant HATCH, citizen, of congestive chill. The Appeal, 9/6/1844.

Married, On the evening of the 1st of February by Rev. T. L. **GRACE**, John **DANNAVAN**(?) to Mary Anne **DOYLE**. Memphis Daily Appeal, 2/28/1858.

American Hotel. The subscriber respectfully informs his friends that he has this day opened the new and splendid Hotel at the corner of Main and Adams street in this city…E. H. **DASHIELL**, Memphis, Nov. 2, 1847. Daily Enquirer, 11/4/1847.

Married, On the 17th instant at the residence of the bride's father, Capt. A. J. **EDMONDSON**, Blithwood, Marshall county, Miss., by Rev. J. H. **GRAY**, Geo. **DASHIELL** and Miss Tate Edmondson. Memphis Daily Appeal, 9/18/1856. Died, Of croup, on the morning of the 10th inst., at the residence of Captain A. J. Edmondson, in Marshall county, Mississippi, Andrew Edmondson, infant son of George and Sarah R. Dashiell, aged five months and four days…. Memphis Daily Appeal, 12/13/1857.

Died, In Stephenson, Ala., on the 6th inst., of Congestive Chill, Robert N. **DASHIELL**, aged 34(?) years, 10 months and 26 days. Memphis Weekly Appeal, 12/15/1858.

Married, On the 27th instant at the residence of the bride's father at Oxford, Miss., by Rev. Mr. Birney, Thos. R. **DASHILL**, of Memphis, to Miss Fannie, daughter of the Hon. J. M. **MOWRY**. (Author's Note: could be **HOWRY**.) Memphis Daily Appeal, 10/30/1859.

Jeremiah Lodge No. 158. Whereas information has been received of the death of Jas. **DAUGHTY**, a member of this Lodge, who departed this life sometime since….Memphis Daily Appeal, 5/26/1859.

Married, In Hanover county, Virginia, on the 29th of October, 1855, by Rev. Mr. Atkinson, Mr. Isaac **DAVENPORT** and Miss Susan **WINGFIELD**. Memphis Daily Appeal, 2/14/1856.

John C. **DAVENPORT**, a member of the Day Police, and a resident of this city the past twenty years, died on Sunday night at his residence, corner of Main and Linden street, of yellow fever. Memphis Whig, Tues., 11/27/1855. Tribute of Respect. South Memphis Lodge No. 118, Mon., 12/10/1855. After having paid Masonic honors to the remains of brother John C. Davenport….Resolved, That we hereby tender the sincere sympathy of this Lodge to the bereaved widow, family and friends….Memphis Appeal, 12/13/1855.

Married, At the residence of the bride's father, by Rev. J. H. **GRAY**, D.D., on the 22d instant, Mr. E. G. **DAVIDSON** and Miss Mary Winchester, eldest daughter of James **ARMOUR**, Esq., all of this city. Memphis Daily Appeal, 11/23/1856.

Died, In the city of Memphis, Tenn., on the 12th day of March, 1857, in her 20th year, Mrs. Sarah Jane **DAVIDSON**, daughter of Obed and Elizabeth **NICHOLSON**….Her sudden death is a sore bereavement to her husband and an irreparable loss to her dear little babe….Memphis Daily Appeal, 3/14/1857.

Married. On the 8th instant by Rev. J. T. C. **COLLINS**, Rev. T. P. **DAVIDSON**, of this city, to Mrs. Sallie L. **CHAMBERLAIN**, of this county. Memphis Daily Appeal, 11/9/1855.

Died—….on the night of the 2d inst., Mrs. Sarah A., wife of W. J. **DAVIE**, Esq., of this city, aged 31 years and 8 months. Memphis Avalanche, 6/4/1859. The second day of June, 1859….closed the earthly career of Mrs. Sarah Ann Davie, wife of Col. Winston J. Davie, at Memphis, Tenn. She was born October 8, 1827; was the daughter of the late Gen. Charles **PHILLIPS**, of Harris county, Ga., and married in Kentucky in August, 1845….As a mother, a sister, a daughter, a wife, no one was ever more affectionate or devoted….Her gentle form now reposes, in company with her little children who have preceded her, in the family cemetery in Kentucky….Memphis Daily Appeal, 6/14/1859.

Married, In Tallahatchie county, Miss., at the residence of Walter A. **MANGUM**, Esq., by Rev. A. H. **BROOM_**, Col. A. W. **DAVIS** and Miss Catharine Eaton **MANGUM**. Memphis Daily Appeal, 3/1/1857.

Rev. C. A. **DAVIS**, of Lexington, Mo., having accepted a call to the pastoral charge of the First Cumberland Presbyterian Church in this city, has arrived here with his family....Memphis Daily Appeal, 5/7/1859.

Married, On the 25th instant by Rev. Mr. Webber, Mr. Chas. R. **DAVIS**, of the firm of R. A. Parker & Co., and Miss Laura, daughter of Mr. Andrew **TAYLOR**, near Collierville, Tenn. Memphis Daily Appeal, 3/27/1856.

A man named Henry **DAVIS**, a tailor by trade, formerly of this city, lost his life in Cincinnati on Tuesday last, by falling to the floor from a chair in which he was standing. His skull was fractured, and he died a short time after the accident occurred. Memphis Daily Appeal, Fri., 9/2/1859.

Married, On the 1st instant by Rev. J. W. **KNOTT**, at the residence of her father in Marshall county, Mississippi, Miss Mary _. **BENTON** and Mr. Henry C. **DAVIS**, of the firm of Jones, Brown & Co., of this city. Memphis Daily Appeal, 7/2/1856.

The Carthage Casket contains an account of a shocking murder committed on the body of Holland **DAVIS**, a worthy and respectable citizen of Smith county, in the public highway, on the 30th ult., by a man named William D. **HALE**. The arm of the deceased was found broken, and on his body the Coroner counted thirty-four stabs, inflicted with a large knife. Hale has fled. American Eagle, 10/21/1847.

Married, At Collierville, on Thursday, the 4th inst., by Rev. A. M. **BRYAN**, Mr. J. Carson **DAVIS**, of this city, and Miss Mollie **DUNN**. Memphis Daily Appeal, 6/14/1857.

Died, in Spring Hill, Miss., on Thursday, the 13th inst., of inflammation of the brain, Martha Nelson, daughter of Dr. J. S. and N. E. **DAVIS**, aged 12 years and 3 months....Athens (Ala.) papers please copy. Memphis Daily Appeal, 1/18/1859.

By virtue of an execution to me directed from the Worshipful Court of Pleas & Quarter Sessions for Shelby County, I shall expose to Public sale at the Court-House in the Town of Memphis on the 14th day of October next, all the right, title & interest that John **DAVIS** has in & to 1,012 Acres of Land, lying in Shelby county, & being part of 3000 acres, by grant No. --- taken in execution to satisfy a judgement that John **RALLSTON**, John **BROWN**, William **LAWRENCE**, James **KIMBROUGH** & Samuel R. **BROWN** recovered against the said John Davis unless the same be previously paid. Joseph **JAMES**, Coroner of Shelby county. By virtue of an execution to me directed from the Worshipful court of Pleas & Quarter sessions for Shelby county, I will expose at public sale at the court-house in the Town of Memphis on the 14th day of October next, all the right title & interest that John Davis has to 733 & a third Acres of Land, being part of 2000 acres, granted to Alexander **M'CULLOCH** by grant No. 42 dated 10th July 1788 adjoining a 1000 acre Tract in the name of J. G. and Thomas **BLOUNT** taken in execution to satisfy a judgement...Sam'l. R. **BROWN**, Sheriff Shelby county. The Pioneer, 9/9/1823

The friends and acquaintances of John **DAVIS** are requested to attend the funeral of his late wife, Julia D., from his residence, corner of Shelby and Gayoso streets, This Evening....Memphis Daily Appeal, 9/9/1859

Died, In this city February 9th, 1857, Fieldon H., daughter of John H. and Sarah **DAVIS**. Memphis Daily Appeal, 2/11/1857.

At about 12 o'clock Richard **SMITH** was brought before Justice Ross, charged with a deadly assault upon Mr. L. W. **DAVIS** on Wednesday forenoon.....Memphis Appeal, Friday, 6/24/1853. .....We learn with profound regret that Mr. Davis breathed his last at about half-past eight on Saturday morning.....The funeral of Mr. Davis took place on Saturday afternoon, at 5 o'clock. His remains were followed to the grave by his pupils and a very large concourse of ladies and gentlemen.....Before his death Mr. Davis bequeathed the property of which he died possessed to one of his little pupils. Thus has passed from earth at the early age of thirty years a useful, good and an honorable man.....Memphis Appeal, Mon., 6/26/1853.

Died—In this city, of consumption, on Tuesday evening last, 14th inst., after a lingering and painful illness, Miss Lucy M., daughter of the late Mr. **DAVIS**, of Batavia, N.Y...The Tri-Weekly Memphis Enquirer, 9/19/1846.

Died, At his residence, in Shelby county, Tenn., on the 31st ultimo, in the sixty-third year of his age, Tinsley **DAVIS**, a native of Hanover county, Va. Early in life he emigrated to Fayette county, Ky., and settled amongst his relations in the Spring of 1817; in company with his brother and other relatives he removed to Jackson's Purchase, Mississippi, near North Alabama, and in 1839 he removed to his present location...The writer of these lines has known him intimately in all the locations, and sympathizes with his orphan children, kindred and friends, wherever he was know. Huntsville (Ala) and Richmond (Va.) papers will please copy. Memphis Eagle, 2/8/1850.

Raleigh Hotel – The subscriber having purchased the hotel premises of Mr. J. C. **RUDISILL**, in Raleigh, Tenn., informs the public and customers of the stand, that he is prepared to accommodate travellers with every convenience and fare possible to be attained...William D. **DAVIS**. Memphis Enquirer, 11/4/1837.

Deaths – On the 18th inst. John D. Martin, aged 17 months – only son of Rufus K. **DAWSON**. Memphis Enquirer, 6/23/1838.

Died, In Haywood county, on the 12th instant, Mrs. Day, wife of the Rev. George W. **DAY**. American Eagle Weekly, 9/26/1845.

John H. **DAY**, Esq., one of the oldest and most respectable citizens of this city, after a protracted illness, died at his residence on the 15th instant, in the 59th(?) year of his age. The subject of this notice was born in Hanover county, Virginia, and moved to Madison county in 1881. For many years he was engaged in the occupation of an instructor of youth....Memphis Daily Appeal, 8/27/1856.

Married, At the residence of the bride's father, on the 28th ult., by Rev. L. D. **MULLINS**, Mr. W. P. **DAY** and Miss Sarilda, daughter of Thomas **GILES**, Esq. Memphis Daily Appeal, 10/1/1856.

We are authorized to announce Wm. P. **DAY** as a candidate for Trustee of Shelby county at the ensuing March election. Memphis Appeal, 8/1/1853.

Married, At "Park Place," on Tuesday evening, 19th inst., by Rev. J. O. **STEADMAN**, M. D. **DEADERICK**, Esq., to Miss Jennie R. **PARK**, all of this city. Memphis Daily Appeal, 5/21/1857.

Married, On Saturday evening by Rev. Father Daley, at the residence of Mrs. **HOURCEIGT**, on Court street, Manuel **DE ARAGON**, of Havana, Island of Cuba, and Miss Octavia **HOURCEIGT**, of Bordeaux, France. Memphis Daily Appeal, Tues., 3/24/1857.

Married, On the evening of the 7th inst., in Tipton county, by Judge Humphries, Capt. John **DEARING**, of the steamer *Joan of Arc*, and Miss Sarah Eliza, daughter of Isaac **CLARK**, Esq. Memphis Daily Appeal, 1/10/1857.

Married, On the 13th inst. by Rev. R. R. **EVANS**, at the residence of Mrs. Yates, Mr. W. W. **DEARMOND** and Mrs. Elizabeth **GREISHABER**, all of Shelby county. Memphis Daily Appeal, 11/18/1856.

Married, At the residence of Wm. **ROOK**, Esq. on the 19th by Judge B. G. **LAWRENCE**, Mr. C. A. **DEAVER** to Miss Nancy L. **ROOK**, all of Marshall county, Mississippi. Memphis Eagle & Enquirer, 1/29/1853.

Married. On the 5th inst. by Rev. C. M. **BUTLER**, D.D., J. D. B. **DeBOW**, of Louisiana, and Caroline, daughter of Geo. **POE**, Esq., of Georgetown, D.C. Memphis Appeal, 8/25/1854.

The body of a drowned man was found in the river, in the vicinity of Fort Pickering, on Sunday, which had evidently been in the water for some time. A subsequent examination satisfied the friends of the deceased that the remains were those of Thos. **DEERY**, who came to this city from Vicksburg about six weeks since, and who drowned himself about that time in a fit of mental derangement....Memphis Daily Appeal, Wed., 6/14/1859.

Died, On Monday, 12th inst., Mr. **DE LA MONEY**, of Memphis, Tenn., aged 42 years. Memphis Weekly Appeal, 7/14/1858.

Died. Yesterday evening of Congestive Fever, Mary Delannay, daughter of James L. **DELANNAY**, aged about 10 years. The friends and acquaintances of the family are invited to attend the funeral of the deceased at 3 o'clock this evening, from the residence of his son, on Linden street. Divine service by Rev. Dr. Gray. Memphis Appeal, 9/19/1854.

Died: On Saturday, 13th inst., of the prevailing fever, Eleanor, wife of W. J. **DELANO**, late of Dayton, Ohio, aged 32 years. Also, at the residence of W. J. Delano, the same evening—one hour after—of the prevailing fever, Miss Emily **STEWART**, (late of Dayton, Ohio) aged about 22 years. Memphis Whig, 10/15/1855. In our last issue we announced the death of Mrs. W. J. Delano and Miss Emily Stewart, late of Dayton, Ohio. They left earth's troubles at the same hour;--the wife leaving a noble and devoted husband and children, the sister a good brother and many distant friends and relatives. The two have been in our city but a short time, but their noble spirits would not allow them to remain inert in the time of sickness; they went to the beds of the husband's sick friends and at last fell martyrs to their own goodness....Memphis Daily Appeal, 10/16/1855. The following just tribute of respect to the excellence of the wife of our friend, W. J. Delano....we find in the Dayton, Ohio *Journal*, the place of Mrs. D.'s nativity: Died.—At Memphis, Tenn. on the 14th of October, of yellow fever, Mrs. Eleanor Odlin Delano, aged thirty-three years, wife of Wm. J. Delano, and daughter of P. **ODLIN**, Esq., of this city. Mrs. Delano was educated at the Steubenville Female Seminary....and graduated in that institution in the class of 1839. In the spring of 1855, she removed from this city with her husband to Memphis....Memphis Daily Appeal, 10/26/1855.

Died, Near this city on the 17th inst., in the 28th year of her age, Mrs. Sarah C. DeLaunay, wife of Maj. J. L. **DeLAUNAY**...The Columbia (Tenn.) papers will please copy. Memphis Eagle, 1/23/1850.

Died. On the 6th instant near Oxford, Miss., Mrs. Maranda C., consort of Capt. Wm. **DELAY**, late editor of the Democratic Flag. Memphis Appeal, 8/1/1854.

Married, On Tuesday evening the 27th inst., by Rev. J. B. **FERGUSON**, Claiborne **DELOACH**, Esq., of Memphis, Tenn., to Miss Imogene A., daughter of Moses **NORVELL**, Esq. of this city.—*Nashville Gazette*30th ult. Memphis Eagle & Enquirer, 2/6/1852.

The friends and acquaintances of Josiah **DELOACH** are requested to attend the funeral of his wife, Mahulda, on this (Tuesday) morning, at 10 o'clock, from his residence 3-4 of a mile south of the Gayoso House. Funeral services by Rev. J. H. **GRAY**. Monday, 30th March, 1847. Daily Enquirer, 3/30/1847. It has become our melancholy duty to record the death of Mahulda, consort of Josiah Deloach, Esq., of this vicinity. She departed this life, after a short but painful illness, on the 29th ultimo, in the 34th year of her age.....And in the hour of death she gave to her afflicted husband and children a touching assurance of the efficiency of her faith....Daily Enquirer, 4/2/1847.

Married—Near Somerville on the 1st ult., by Rev. J. **McFERRAN**, Mr. Lloyd W. **DELOACH** of Tipton County, to Miss Harriet **ALLEN**, daughter of Col. Jesse **ALLEN**. We noticed the above marriage in our last, but unfortunately tied Mr. Deloach to a wrong lady. Memphis Enquirer, 4/5/1836. (Author's note: the last edition mentioned here was 3/29/1836.) Died—On the first instant, at the residence of her father, Col. Jesse **ALLEN**, near Memphis, Mrs. Harriet Deloach, consort of L. W. Deloach aged 30 years. In all the endearing relations of life, as a wife, mother, daughter, sister, she was a pattern worthy of imitation...Memphis Enquirer, 7/15/1845. We are pained to learn of the demise of Lloyd W. Deloach, formerly a much esteemed citizen of this county, and brother of our friend, Josiah **DELOACH**, Esq., at Grand Junction. Many of our old citizens recollect and still have in remembrance that good old genial companion whose society they were wont to delight. It will be a sad feeling to them to hear the announcement of his death, occurring beyond the reach of their sympathy, far away among the wilds of

Texas. He died near Carthage, in that State, on the 4t^{h} inst., and but this consolation is left to his old friends, that he died surrounded by his own immediate family....Memphis Daily Appeal, 9/22/1858.

Died. On the 5th of June at the residence of her husband, near Germantown, after a short illness, Mrs. Elizabeth Deloach, consort of William **DELOACH**, Esq., aged about 63 years. The deceased was an affectionate wife, a devoted mother and a kind and charitable friend. She had been for many years an exemplary member of the Baptist Church.....American Eagle, 6/24/1847.

A telegraphic dispatch to a brother in this city conveys the melancholy intelligence that Charles M. **DENIE** died in New Orleans on Saturday last, of an affection of the brain. Mr. Denie had only been residing in New Orleans about three months, and was, we believe, a reporter for one of the morning journals....Mr. Denie was at one time connected with the *Evening Express* as editor, and subsequently as editor of the *Sunday Whig*....Memphis Daily Appeal, Tuesday, 2/3/1857. The friends and acquaintances of Charles M. Denie are respectfully invited to attend his funeral, from the residence of his brother, John A. **DENIE**, on Union street, east of the bayou, this afternoon....Memphis Daily Appeal, 2/10/1857.

The friends and acquaintances of Mrs. Felicity **DENIE** are respectfully invited to attend her funeral from the residence of Mr. A. **WALLACE**, on Union street, This Afternoon at 3 o'clock. Memphis Daily Appeal, 10/20/1858.

Married, On the 6th inst., by Rev. J. **ROGERS**, Mr. John A. **DENIE**, of the firm of Wallace & Denie, Memphis, to Miss Mary E. **WALKER**, of Brownsville. Memphis Appeal, 11/10/1852.

Cumberland Presbyterian Church, Court st., east of Court Square, Rev. Samuel **DENNIS**. The Daily Enquirer, 2/28/1847. Married, In Holmes county, Miss., on Wednesday, 26th March, by Rev. S. G. **BURNEY**, Rev. Samuel Dennis, of this city, to Mrs. Z. V. **HALE**, of the former place. Memphis Daily Appeal, 4/2/1851. The Rev. Mr. Dennis will preach at the Cumberland Presbyterian Church on Sabbath next...He leaves us next week to enter his new field of labour in the South. Memphis Appeal, 4/18/1851.

Married, Up stairs, over the City Ice House, on Saturday night last, by Hume F. **HILL**, Esq., Mr. Mitchell **DENO**, of this city to Miss Nancy **HICKS**, formerly of Cincinnati...Mr. Mitchell _____ is a very clever gentleman, of about 50 years of age, while Miss Nancy Hicks is just about "sweet-seventeen"...Memphis Appeal, Tues., 9/21/1852.

Died, In the town of Randolph, Tipton county, Tenn., on Thursday the 19th of June, 1856, of Malignant Scarlet Fever, Ann Eliza, the eldest daughter of James and Harriett A. **DENSFORD**, aged sixteen years, four months and twenty-five days. The deceased was born in Jefferson county, Ky., on the 25th day of January, 1840. Louisville *Democrat* please copy. Memphis Daily Appeal, 6/26/1856.

Married, In Tipton county on Thursday the 18th inst., Mr. John T. **DENSFORD** to Miss Amanda **LAMB**. Memphis Weekly Appeal, 3/3/1858.

Married, In Memphis on Thursday, 30th ult., by the Rev. D. E. **BURNS**, Mr. H. G. **DENT**, to Miss Sarah L. G., daughter of the Rev. P. S. **GALE**—all of this city. Rutherford Telegraph copy. Memphis Appeal, 11/1/1851.

Died, At the residence of her son-in-law, John **NASH**, Chestnut Bluff, Tenn., November 22, 1858, of typhoid fever, Mrs. Hepy **DENT**, after an illness of twelve days, in the sixty-first year of her age. Mrs. Dent held no fellowship with any branch of the Christian Church since her residence in Tennessee, some thirty odd years, but was baptized into the Lutheran Church in South Carolina....Memphis Weekly Appeal, 12/8/1858.

Married, On the 24th instant at the Gayoso House, Mr. L. **DESOBRY** to Miss Talbot, both of La. Memphis Daily Appeal, 7/26/1859.

Information wanted of Michael **DEVIRE**, a bricklayer by trade, who left Memphis some two months since for Paducah or St. Louis. His wife arrived here a few days since in search of him, from Ireland, and would thankfully receive any information as to his whereabouts...Memphis Eagle & Enquirer, 5/23/1852.

The subscriber, grateful for past favors, and solicitous of future patronage, would respectfully announce to the public, that he has permanently located himself in the new buildings, corner of Adams street and the Batture square, where, in connection with his boats, he will transact a general Produce, Grocery, Feed, Forwarding and Storage Business...W. M. **DEVOE**. Daily Enquirer, 11/4/1847.

Des Arc, August 8th, 1854. The Lodge of the I.O.O.F. was called together this evening at 5 o'clock. The N.G. announced the painful intelligence of the death of our much beloved and esteemed brother, Robert D. **DEWOODY**, who departed this life at his father's residence, near Raleigh, Tenn., on the 31st of July....Memphis Appeal, 8/17/1854.

We are authorized to announce Wm. L. **DEWOODY**, a candidate for Clerk of the County Court of Shelby County, at the ensuing election. Daily Enquirer, 7/3/1847. Married, On the 27th inst., by the Rev. David L. **GRAY**, Wm. L. Dewoody, Esq., of Raleigh, to Miss Jane M. **PHARR**.—all of Shelby county. Memphis Appeal, 8/30/1851.

Married, On the 27th January in the town of Bloomington, by J. S. **HILL**, Esq., Col. William **DICKERSON** to Miss Lotte **HENLEY**, all of Tipton county, Tenn. Memphis Daily Appeal, 2/11/1858.

Married, On the 16th instant by Rev. John **WILSON**, Mr. Joseph **DICKEY** to Mrs. Mary E. **BROWN**, daughter of the late Henry **MOORE**, all of Tipton county, Tenn. Memphis Weekly Appeal, 3/3/1858.

Married. In the city of New York on the 25th ult. by the Rev. Wm. R. **YORDON**, of the Dutch Reformed Church, Mr. Christian **DICKINSON**, of the Island of St. Thomas, and Rosa O. **CLARK**, of Memphis, Tenn. Memphis Whig, 5/9/1855.

Married, On Thursday morning, February 3d by the Rev. Mr. Robb, Mr. John **DICKSON**, of Hernando, Miss., to Miss Sarah **BROWN**, daughter of Col. Brown, of this city.....Nashville papers please copy. Memphis Appeal, 2/4/1853.

Married. At the residence of Mr. Griffith on the evening of the 16th instant by Rev. J. W. **KNOTT**, Mr. W. H. **DICKSON**, of Helena, Arkansas, and Miss E. **THORNTON**, of this city. Helena papers please copy. Memphis Whig, 7/17/1855.

Married, in this city, on Tuesday last, by Rev. Dr. Page, Mr. William T. **DIEMER**, of Mississippi, to Mrs. Pauline **LEFORT**, of this place. Memphis Enquirer, Thursday, 6/7/1849. Paris House Confectionery. The subscriber informs the customers of the above House and the public generally, that he has taken possession of this well-known Establishment, and that he is the Proprietor of the same...William T. Diemer. Memphis Enquirer, 6/7/1849.

By a dispatch from our Mr. B. F. **DILL**, received last night, we learn that his brother, Mr. R. S. **DILL**, died at Catoosa Springs, Ga., on the 14th inst....Memphis Daily Appeal, 8/21/1856. Since we received the telegraphic announcement of the death of R. S. Dill, Esq., we have seen a letter from his brother, Mr. B. F. Dill, one of the editors of this paper, to a friend in this city. From it we learn that Mr. Dill died at Catoosa Springs, in the State of Georgia, on the 14th inst., whither he had gone to recruit his health which had been suffering for some weeks. It will be gratifying to Mr. Dill's numerous friends to learn that he received the most brotherly kindness and attention during his last illness from old friends in Georgia....Mr. Dill was very much respected in this city, where he had resided since 1851....Memphis Daily Appeal, 8/24/1856.

Benjamin F. **DILL** has removed his law office to the house occupied by the editor of the Enquirer—where he may be found at all hours. Memphis Enquirer, 2/25/1837.

Died in this city yesterday evening at 7 o'clock, Capt. D. W. **DILL**. Capt. Dill served with honorable distinction in the Seminole campaign in Florida in 1836 and also as Captain of the Augusta Blues in Col. Jackson's Georgia Regiment of Volunteers in Mexico in 1846 '7....His friends and acquaintances and those of his brothers, B. F. **DILL**, Esq., (one of the Editors of this paper) and R. S. **DILL**, are invited to attend his funeral from his lodgings on Main street, between Adams and Washington, this afternoon at 4 o'clock. Memphis Daily Appeal, 4/14/1855.

At a regular meeting of Morning Sun Lodge, No. 144, of Free and Accepted Masons, at their Hall, on the 14th of February, A.D. 1852, the special committee...offered the following preamble and resolutions.... Whereas, In the Providence of God, our highly esteemed brother, Past Grand Master, Edmund **DILLAHUNTY**, has been removed from our midst, by the unsparing hand of death...Memphis Eagle & Enquirer, 3/17/1852.

H. **DILLAHUNTY**, Attorney at Law. (Late of Florence, Alabama) Has settled in Memphis and will attend the Common Law and Chancery Court of the city, and the Circuit and Chancery Courts of the adjacent counties...Office on Madison st. Memphis Appeal, 3/27/1851.

Married, On Sunday last, the 6th inst., by Rev. Father Grace, Mr. John **DIVINE** to Miss Ellen **O'BRIEN**, all of this city. Memphis Eagle & Enquirer, 2/8/1853.

Married—In Desoto county, Miss., at the Baptist Church South of Cold Water, on Sunday the 18th inst., Mr. B. H. **DOCKERY**, late Merchant of this place, to Miss Emily, daughter of Maj. James A. **MORTON**. Memphis Enquirer, 3/25/1849.

Married, At the residence of A. W. **STOKES**, Esq., in Hernando, Miss., on Thursday the 14th, by Rev. Jas. **DENNIS**, Prof. James O. **DOCKERY**, of Hernando, to Miss Annie D. **McKENZIE**, of Brooklyn, New York. Richmond Enquirer and Baltimore Patriot please copy. Memphis Daily Appeal, 1/21/1858.

Died, In DeSoto county, Miss., on the 27th of November, Mrs. Elizabeth A., wife of Thomas C. **DOCKERY**, in the 24th year of her age. Memphis Daily Appeal, 12/9/1857.

The friends and acquaintances of Capt. James **DODDS** are respectfully invited to attend his Funeral, at 10 o'clock this morning, from his residence on Commerce street. The Tri-Weekly Memphis Enquirer, 4/28/1846.

Married, on the 7th inst., by Rev. J. H. **GRAY**, Mr. Cyrus A. **DOEBLER** to Miss Salina **DOEBLER**, all of this city. Memphis Enquirer, 6/9/1849.

Mrs. Martha Eliza Doggett, wife of Mr. Asa **DOGGETT**, and daughter of James D. and Philicity __. **NICHOLS**, was born November 29th, 1837....She became a pupil in the Mississippi Female College, under the care of Rev. W. C. **CRANE**, in 1850 and continued the greater part of the time a faithful scholar in that institution until the summer of 1856. In the spring of that year she professed religion, was baptized, and united with the Hernando Baptist Church, Mississippi.... She was married November 29th, 1855 and died at her husband's residence, in DeSoto county, on the morning of October 7th, 1856....Memphis Daily Appeal, 11/2/1856.

Married—In Marshall county, Miss., on the 13th inst., Mr. Wm. **DOHERTY** of Collierville, Tenn., to Miss Elizabeth **FOSTER**. Memphis Enquirer, 9/22/1838.

The insolvency of the estate of Joshua **DONALDSON**, dec'd, having been suggested to me by the administrator thereof...Memphis Eagle & Enquirer, 1/13/1852.

Married. On Tuesday morning the 6th instant, at the residence of Gary **WILLIAMS**, Esq., by Rev. Thomas P. **STONE**, Mr. Marshall H. **DONALDSON** to Miss Harriet **WILLIAMS**, all of Desoto county and vicinity of Florence. Memphis Appeal, 2/16/1855.

Married: On Wednesday evening, January 24th, at the residence of her father, by the Rev. P. S. **GAYLE**, Mr. W. J. **DONALDSON**, of Memphis, to Miss Sallie E., daughter of Turner **PERSON**, of Shelby county. Memphis Eagle, 2/8/1849.

Pursuant to a decree made at the November term, A.D. 1851, of the Common Law and Chancery Court of the city of Memphis, in the case of Wm. B. **HILL**, Adm'r. of Wm. J. **DONALDSON**, dec'd...Memphis Eagle & Enquirer, 4/8/1852.

The friends and acquaintances of Maj. Andrew J. **DONELSON** are invited to attend the funeral of his son, Lieut. A. J. **DONELSON** from the Second Presbyterian Church....to-day. Memphis Daily Appeal, 10/21/1859.

Died—On the 4th instant, at the residence of John **DONELSON** of Shelby county, his Wife, Laura M., daughter of Doctor William P. **LAWRENCE** of Nashville. The Appeal, 4/26/1844.

Died, At his residence in Shelby county, Tenn., on the evening of the 23d April, 1851, aged about 40 years, Doct. Samuel **DONELSON**. His little daughter, Mary, died on the 6th(?). Thus, father and child, passed away at so short an interval. Memphis Appeal, 5/8/1851. Died, At Inglewood, the residence of Mrs. Jane P. **DONELSON**, in this vicinity, on the 29th of June, after a brief but severe illness, Samuella, aged two years and seven months, youngest child of Dr. Samuel Donelson, deceased. Memphis Appeal, 7/7/1853.

We are sorry to be called upon to publish the death of P. K. **DONNELLY**, of the firm of Smith & Donnelly, builders of levees in Arkansas. Mr. Donnelly was in the act of passing into the *New Uncle Sam*, at Cairo, on Thursday, when the board upon which he stepped turned and precipitated him into the river where he was drowned. Memphis Daily Appeal, 9/25/1858. The friends and acquaintances of Patrick Donnelly are invited to attend his funeral from the residence of Phillip **GARVIN**, on Alabama street, This Afternoon. Memphis Daily Appeal, 9/26/1858.

Married—On the 1st inst. at 4 o'clock A.M., Mr. William B. **DONOHO**, to Miss Maria J. **SHOEMAKE**, all of Holly Springs, Miss. Memphis Appeal, 6/7/1848. The friends and acquaintances of W. B. and Maria Donoho are requested to attend the funeral of their son, Shoemake, from the residence of his grandfather, F. **SHOEMAKE**, Shelby street, this afternoon....Memphis Daily Appeal, 11/30/1859.

Married—In Eaton, Ohio, on Thursday the 10th inst., by Rev. Mr. Mitchell, Mr. D. O. **DOOLEY**, of Memphis, to Mrs. Jane B. **HALDERMAN**. The Tri-Weekly Memphis Enquirer, 9/22/1846. Died. In this city on Monday morning, March 5th of pneumonia, Maggie C., youngest daughter of D. O. and Jane B. Dooley, aged 2 years and 8 months....The friends and acquaintances of the family are invited to attend the Funeral This (Tuesday) Morning at 10 o'clock, from their residence on the corner of Shelby and Butler streets....Memphis Whig, 5/6/1855.

Married—On Tuesday the 16th inst., by Rev. W. D. F. **SAWRIE**, Mr. Felix G. **DOOLEY**, to Miss Mary Eliza **WHITSITT**, both of Memphis. Memphis Enquirer, 5/20/1837. Died—In this city on Monday the 14th inst., Mary Elizabeth, infant daughter of F. G. and Mary E. Dooley, aged 4 years...The friends and acquaintances of the parents are invited to attend its funeral, at half past 10 o'clock this morning, from their residence on Exchange Street. Memphis Enquirer, 7/15/1845. Died, On the 2d inst., Margaret Catherine, only daughter of F. G. & Mary Eliza Dooley, aged four years and three months. Memphis Eagle & Enquirer, 1/5/1853.

Married, At the Second Presbyterian Church in this city, Thursday evening, 9th instant....Mr. Chas. H. **DORION**, Jr., and Miss Ellen C. Morrison, eldest daughter of John **MORRISON**, Esq., all of this city. Memphis Daily Appeal, 4/11/1857.

The undersigned offers for sale his valuable tract of land, lying three miles north of La Grange, containing about eight hundred acres....Robert **DORTCH**, La Grange, Tenn. Memphis Daily Appeal, 9/5/1855.

The subscriber having obtained letters of administration on the estate of Jno. R. **DOUGHERTY** dec'd requests all those indebted to said estate to come forward....S. R. **BROWN**, Adm. Memphis Advocate, 2/23/1828.

....A. H. **DOUGLASS**, Mayor. Memphis Whig, 8/2/1855.

Married, On the 14th January by Rev. T. **JOYNER**, Mr. W. B. **DOUGLASS** and Miss Henrietta **HARE**, all of Fayette county, Tenn. Memphis Daily Appeal, 2/6/1857.

Dr. A. **DOWELL**, Having permanently settled himself in Memphis, respectfully tenders his services to the citizens of the town...Office west side of Main, five doors north of Jefferson street—residence on Union, east of the Bayou. Daily Enquirer, 7/13/1847.

B. F. **DOWELL**, Attorney and Counsellor at Law, West side of Main, and five doors North of Jefferson street, Memphis, Tenn. Daily Enquirer, 6/22/1847.

Died, in Angelina county, Texas, Dr. John L. **DOXEY**, son of Col. John S. **DOXEY**, of Pontotoc county, Miss. The circumstances under which the deceased came to his death are of a very painful character. He, in trying to relieve his negro man from the suffocating gas, carbonic acid, that had collected in a well he was digging, unfortunately fell from the top, a distance of forty feet; and afterwards he and the boy were taken from the fatal hole, both dead. Dr. Doxey was about 28 years old....Angelina Co., Texas, June 18, 1855. Memphis Appeal, 7/7/1855.

The remains of Dr. **DOYLE**, a surgeon of superior abilities and great reputation, recently a professor in the Memphis Medical College, were yesterday brought to his family in this city, from Helena, Arks., at which place he died suddenly. Memphis Eagle, 8/12/1850.

The friends and acquaintances of Edward **DOYLE** are requested to attend his funeral this Evening at 3 o'clock, from his late residence in this city. Memphis Enquirer, 4/23/1848.

We are pained to learn, as we did yesterday by the telegraph, that our former townsman, Mr. John **DOYLE**, is among the killed in the battle of Rivas. It is only a month or two since he left our city with letters to Gen. Walker, from whom he at once received a Lieutenant's commission. He was a young man....He had previously gone through a campaign in Mexico and was injured to the service. He was a native of Ireland, but had been for many years a citizen of Memphis, where he has troops of friends....Memphis Daily Appeal, 5/4/1856.

Married, On the 17th of July by Rev. J. **WILSON**, Mr. Hervy **DRAFFIN** and Miss Elizabeth, daughter of James **WRIGHT**, Sr., all of Tipton county, Tenn. On the same evening, by Rev. Mr. McPhadden, Rev. Edwin **LUCADO** and Miss Margaret, daughter of Mr. Robert **LEMONTON**, all of Tipton county, Tenn. Memphis Daily Appeal, 8/30/1856.

Married, In this city on Saturday, the 28th ult., by Rev. C. T. **QUINTARD**, Mr. J. R. **DRAKE**, formerly of Boston, to Miss Sarah H.(?), youngest daughter of the late Henry **INMAN**, of New York. [Mr. Drake is the Telegraphic agent of the New York Associated Press in this city....] Memphis Daily Appeal, 12/1/1857. Mr. J. R. Drake, the late well-known telegraphic agent of the Associated Press in this city, left here yesterday for Louisville, having resigned the position which he has filled here during the past two years....Mr. Drake will be succeeded by Mr. W. H. **CODY**, late of Columbus, Miss. Memphis Daily Appeal, 4/10/1859.

Ohio Papers Please Copy. Died, in Memphis, on the 14th February, Mr. Orren **DRAKE** of Ohio, aged some 25 years—he had just arrived from New Orleans, and been trading on the river, and said he was from Ohio; his trunk contained land tax receipts paid in Iowa. He left effects to amount of some $150, which his relatives can have by applying to J. P. **WORTHAM**, Memphis. Memphis Eagle, 2/22/1849.

Elder T. J. **DRANE** has arrived in our City, and will enter on his services as Pastor of the First Baptist Church next Sunday. Memphis Daily Appeal, 10/3/1857.

Died, On the 24th of July last, at Horne Lake, Miss., Edwin P. **DRAPER**, a native of Virginia. The Tri-Weekly Memphis Enquirer, 8/13/1846.

Married, On the 25th inst., by the Rev. Geo. W. **COONS**, Andrew W. **DREW**, Esq., to Miss Rebecca J. **MILLER**, all of this city. Memphis Eagle & Enquirer, 3/27/1852.

Married, On the 15th inst., by Rev. H. **PORTER**, D.D., John O. **DREW** and Rosanna **LEACE**—all of this city. Memphis Appeal, 1/17/1852.

Married, On Tuesday Evening, the 12th inst., by the Rev. J. D. **HENDERSON**, Miss Sarah E., daughter of E. M. **DRIVER**, Esq., of this place, to Mr. W. R. **HUNT**, of Panola, Miss. Memphis Eagle, 2/19/1850. Died, At St. Augustine, Florida on the 9th February last, Mrs. Julia S. Driver, formerly of this city and consort of the late E. M. Driver. Memphis Eagle & Enquirer, 3/2/1853.

The undersigned having duly qualified as executors of the last will and testament of Eli M. **DRIVER**, late of Memphis, deceased, all persons having claims against the estate...W. R. **HUNT**, Giles L. **DRIVER**, Executors. Memphis Appeal, 11/5/1851. One Hundred and Twenty Thousand acres of choice land for sale, belonging to the estate of Eli Driver late of Memphis, Tenn. Lying in the counties of DeSoto, Tunica, Panola, Tallahatchie, Yallobusha, Lafayette, Marshall, Tippah, Pontotoc, Chickasaw, Ittawamba, Monroe and Tishomingo, Mississippi and the counties of Hardin, McNairy, Fayette and Shelby, Tenn...Wm. R. **HUNT**, Giles M. Driver, Executors. Memphis Eagle & Enquirer, 2/17/1852.

Married, At the Planters House in this City, on Sunday the 20th inst., by the Rev. Mr. **HIER**, Mr. Andrew **DRUMMOND** of Edinburg, Scotland, to Miss Jane C. **SCALES**, of Shelby county. Weekly Appeal, 4/25/1845. Died, In Shelby County, of consumption, on the 5th instant, Andrew Drummond, a native of Edinburg, Scotland, aged 32 years 7 months. Memphis Appeal, 12/8/1851.

Died, On the 28th instant, at the residence of John H. **JONES**, Esq., of Consumption, Mrs. Jane C. **DRUMMOND**, in the 32d year of her age....The only child left by this lady will be adopted into the family of her sister, whose kind and motherly regard will ever make for it a more than good home. Memphis Daily Appeal, 1/29/1856.

Died, On the evening of the 9th inst., in Hopefield, in the 18th year of her age, Miss Sarah Elizabeth, daughter of Sarah and Joseph E. **D'SPAIN**. Death has entered the family circle and borne their only daughter....Arkansas papers please copy. Memphis Daily Appeal, 2/26/1859.

Married, On the 15th of April, 1858, in Washington City, at the residence of the bride's father, by Bishop Pierce, Mr. D. M. **DuBOSE**, of Memphis, to Miss Sallie Toombs, daughter of Senator **TOOMBS**. Memphis Weekly Appeal, 5/12/1858.

Died, In Franklin, Tenn. on Saturday the 12th inst. Miss Helen **DUDLEY**. The Appeal, 8/25/1843.

Died—On the 2d inst. Mrs. Juliet **DUDLEY**, consort of Doctor Dudley, late of Petit Gulf, Mis. who was....landed from the "Car of Commerce"....Memphis Advocate, 10/6/1827.

The Coroner was called upon yesterday to hold an inquest on the body of Mary **DUFFY**, who resided on Winchester street, and who died while laboring over the wash-tub yesterday morning. The verdict of the jury was to the effect that the deceased died from natural causes. Memphis Daily Appeal, 12/31/1859.

Married, At Hazel Dell, near Bolivar, Hardeman county, on the morning of the 2d inst., by Rev. R. V. **TAYLOR**, Mr. G. M. **DUGAN** and Miss Mollie A. **DAVID**(?). Memphis Daily Appeal, 2/5/1857.

Mr. Ned **DUGAN**, an attache of J. C. Holland & Co., who was shot on the 12th inst., in an affray in front of the Merchants Hotel, by Mr. Nelson **WOODS**, a hack driver of the aforesaid firm, died yesterday from the effects of his wounds. Mr. Woods is in custody and will be tried soon. Memphis Daily Appeal, 5/26/1857.

The friends and acquaintances of George W. **DUKE** are invited to attend his funeral at the residence of Mr. J. S. **CLAYTON** on Germantown road, on Monday 31st inst....Memphis Daily Appeal, 10/30/1859.

A young man by the name of John M. **DUKE**, a printer by profession, who arrived in this city a short time ago, died early yesterday morning of the flux, after a very brief but painful illness.... He was the son of Simeon **DUKE**, of Paulding, Miss. Memphis Daily Appeal, 9/15/1857.

Married, At the residence of John E. **VAN PELT**, on the 22d inst., by Rev. Thomas **JOINER**, Mr. Robert **DUKE** and Miss Rebecca Isabella **MASON**, all of Fayette county, Tenn. Memphis Daily Appeal, 1/27/1857.

Tribute of Respect. At a stated meeting of Oakland Lodge No. 8__, State of Mississippi, held on Saturday, December 27th, 1856, A.L. 5856, the following preamble and resolutions were presented and adopted: Whereas, An All-wise Providence in the inscrutable dispensations of His wisdom, has removed by death from our midst our cherished and esteemed brother, Thomas W. **DUKE**, who departed this life at his residence on the 16[th](?) instant....Memphis Daily Appeal, 1/3/1857.

We learn from the officers of the Daniel Boone that David **DUNBAR**, (brother of Hugh **DUNBAR**, of this city,) who keeps a trading boat at or near Beulah, on the river, has been missing for two or three days past, and fears are entertained that he has been murdered.... Memphis Avalanche, 5/17/1859. Mr. Hugh Dunbar....returned to the city yesterday, bringing with him the remains of his brother. The funeral of the deceased will take place to-day from the residence of his mother near the Charleston Railroad depot. Memphis Daily Avalanche, 5/20/1859.

In Circuit Court of Shelby County, Tennessee. Elizabeth J. Duncan vs. Abram W. **DUNCAN**. Petition for Divorce. On application and it appearing to the Clerk from affidavit filed in this _____, that the defendant is a non-resident of the State of Tennessee, Ordered that publication be made for three successive weeks....requiring the defendant to appear at next term of said Court to be held on the third Monday in September next, at Raleigh....to plead, answer....or the same will be taken for confessed and set for hearing ex parte. Robert L. **SMITH**, Clerk. Memphis Daily Appeal, 8/21/1855.

Married, At the Christian Church Thursday night, January 1st, by Rev. Dr. W. J. **BARBEE**, Mr. E. D. **DUNCAN** and Mrs. Marie M. **GABBERT**, all of this city. Memphis Daily Appeal, 1/3/1857.

Married, On Thursday evening, October 16, 1856, in Washington City, D.C., at the residence of the bride's uncle, (Hon. Robert J. **WALKER**,) by Rev. Smith **PYNE**, D.D., John **DUNCAN**, of Yalobusha, and Lucy Duncan **HOWELL**, of Natchez, Mississippi. Memphis Daily Appeal, 10/26/1856.

Married, On the 24th instant at the residence of her father, in Maury county, Tenn., R. A. F. **DUNCAN**, Esq., of Memphis, and Miss Martha L. **GRAMBERY**. Memphis Daily Appeal, 7/29/1856. At a meeting of the members of the Memphis Bar held in Memphis on the first day of April, 1857, the following proceedings were had in relation to the death of R. A. F. Duncan. Hon. John P. **CARUTHERS** was called to the chair....Your committee has heard with feelings of deep regret of the death of our promising brother in the profession, R. A. F. Duncan....Memphis Daily Appeal, 4/2/1857. Administrator's Notice. All persons having claims against the estate of R. A. F. Duncan, deceased, are hereby notified to file the same within four months from this date with the Clerk of the County Court at Raleigh....B. B. **WADDELL**. Memphis Weekly Appeal, 5/12/1858.

Died—On the 27th ult., Thomas **DUNCAN**, who had been landed on the 25th from the "Car of Commerce," for the purpose of procuring medical attendance. He was on his way to Pittsburg. Memphis Advocate, 10/6/1827.

Married, On Thursday evening 29th August by the Rev. Samuel **DENNIS**, Mr. Wm. R. **DUNCAN** to Miss Mary A. **BROWN**, daughter of S. R. **BROWN**, Esq., all of Raleigh, Shelby county, Tenn. The Appeal, 9/6/1844.

Died—At the house of Col. F. **McWEATHERHEAD**, near Fort Jesup, on the 26th of December last, Daniel A. **DUNHAM**, Esq., of Covington, Tenn. Memphis Enquirer, 2/4/1837.

Died, At the residence of her son-in-law, David S. **GREER**, near this city, at 1 o'clock on yesterday morning, Mrs. Susannah H. Dunlap, relict of the late Hugh **DUNLAP**, of Henry county, and mother of Hon. W.(?) **DUNLAP**, of this county, in the 84th year of her age....Memphis Daily Appeal, 1/7/1859.

Married, On Wednesday evening the 17th inst. by the Rev. Wesley **WARREN**, Capt. A. J. **DUNN** to Miss Mary Ann, daughter of Bailey **ANDERSON**, Esq. of this county. Weekly Appeal, 6/26/1846.

Married, At Belle Air, in Davidson county, on the 26th inst., by Rev. Dr. Edgar, D. L. **DUNN**, Esq., of Memphis, to Miss Annie Nichol, daughter of William **NICHOL**, Esq. Memphis Daily Appeal, 8/1/1858.

Died—In Shelby County, Mrs. Mary Dunn, aged 55 years, consort of Major David **DUNN**. Southern Statesman, 3/16/1833

Died—In this vicinity, on Friday last, Doctor Dudly **DUNN**, aged 73 years. The deceased was one of our oldest citizens—a gentleman of high standing in his profession; the practice of which he had for many years declined; plain and unpretending in his manners, kind and charitable to the poor, an affectionate husband and father, a humane master, and for many years a devout member of the Methodist Episcopal Church...Memphis Appeal, Thurs., 1/20/1848.

Died, At the residence of her mother, Mrs. Emily H. **DUNN**, on Wednesday, 17th inst., Mollie C. **DUNN**, aged 15(?) years, 4(?) months and 9 days. Memphis Daily Appeal, 8/18/1859.

We regret to learn that on Monday last, Mr. Issiah **DUNN**, manager for Mr. Ira **GREEN**, living in the Southern part of this county, was killed by a negro man belonging to the plantation, named Roberson...Mr. Dunn was a respectable young man. His relations we are informed reside in some of the upper counties of the District...Memphis Enquirer, Tues., 7/11/1848.

Died, In Huntsville, Alabama, on the 27th inst., of apoplexy, Mrs. P. A. **DUNN**. Memphis Daily Appeal, 8/28/1857.

Died, On Wednesday, the 29th of December, 1858, at the residence of his mother, near Memphis, Perry A. **DUNN**, aged 19 years and 9 months. Memphis Daily Appeal, 1/8/1859.

Executor's Notice. The undersigned having duly qualified as Executor of the last will of Samuel G. **DUNN**, dec'd., all persons having claims against the estate are hereby notified to present them...for settlement ...W. M. **DUNN**. Weekly Appeal, 10/9/1846.

Married—On Tuesday evening, the 26th ult., by the Rev. H. S. **MORGAN**, Mr. Samuel J. **DUNN**, of Shelby county, to Miss Mary M., daughter of Mr. William **VADEN**, late of Chesterfield, Va. Memphis Enquirer, 1/6/1838. Died, In Fayette county, on the 4th inst., Mrs. Mary M., wife of Samuel J. Dunn, in the 42d year of her age. Memphis Daily Appeal, 10/11/1856.

Died, On the 27th instant, in this vicinity, at 2 o'clock P.M., of apoplexy, Mr. Wm. M. **DUNN**. Memphis Daily Appeal, 2/28/1857.

Died, On Monday morning, December 22d, Lizzie Walthall, daughter of L. J. and Amelia M. **DUPREE**, aged five months. Memphis Daily Appeal, 12/23/1856.

Married, At the residence of Dr. J. J. **WILLIAMS**, near this city, on Tuesday, 18th inst., by Rev. J. O. **STEADMAN**, Mr. A. P. **DUPUY**, of Fayette county, Tenn., and Miss Julia M. **WILLIAMS**, of Shelby. Memphis Daily Appeal, 11/19/1856.

Starke **DUPUY**, M.D. Botanic Physician, Cures all he can, but poisons nobody—Office at his residence on Union street East from Howard's Row...Memphis Appeal, 11/14/1847.

Mr. F. A. **DUVAL**, for some time past connected with the Commercial Department of the *Bulletin*, leaves on the cars this morning for Grenada, Mississippi, for the purpose of taking up his abode there. The columns of that paper will attest his energy and ability. Memphis Daily Appeal, 4/17/1856. Died, In Panola, Miss., on Saturday afternoon, 6th instant, Mrs. Mary _. A. Duval, wife of F. A. Duval, and daughter of Arthur and Rachel **MABSON**(?) of Memphis. The remains of the deceased were brought to this city by yesterday morning's train from Panola, and have been placed in the vault of Elmwood Cemetery, for interment this morning. Memphis Weekly Appeal, 3/17/1858.

Married, In this city on Thursday, 5th inst., by the Rev. G. W. **COONS**, at the residence of his brother, Geo. W. **DUVAL**, Esq., Mr. F. A. **DUVAL**, Editor of the "Southerner," Claiborne, Ala., to Miss Mary H., daughter of Dr. Cyrus **SPOOHER**, of Lowell, Ohio. Memphis Appeal, 5/7/1853. We were pleased to meet last evening our old friend, Frank A. Duval, Esq., formerly of the press of this city, and recently one of the editors of the Claiborne (Ala.) *Champion*, who came up on the steamer Imperial from New Orleans. We understand that he is on his way to Panola, Miss., where he goes to take charge of the publishing department of the Panola *Star,* a position formerly held by him....Memphis Daily Avalanche, 6/17/1859.

The County Jailor, W. H. **EAMES**, Esq., called on us yesterday and exhibited a certificate from a number of respectable gentlemen, entirely exonerating him from all blame in the matter of the escape of Edgar, Keisacker, and others...Weekly Memphis Eagle, 3/1/1849.

Died. At Raleigh, Shelby county, Tenn., on February 1st, 1855, after a short illness, Wm. H. **EANES**, Esq., a native of Chesterfield county, Va., but for the last ___ years a resident of the above county. Petersburg, Va. papers please copy. Memphis Daily Appeal, 2/3/1855. The funeral sermon of Wm. H. Eanes, Esq., who died at Raleigh on Wednesday night last, will be preached at the Cumberland Presbyterian church next Sabbath morning by Rev. Dr. Porter. Memphis Daily Appeal, 2/4/1855.

G. **EARLE**, formerly a clerk in the American Hotel, committed suicide yesterday, by hanging himslef from a bed post. Sickness and poverty were the cause. Memphis Eagle, 3/30/1850.

Died, At his residence in DeSoto county, Miss., on the morning of the 29th ult., of typhoid pneumonia, Mr. H. H. **EASON**, fifty-five years of age. The deceased was a native of North Carolina, from which State he emigrated in the year 1852....North Carolina papers please copy. Memphis Daily Appeal, 5/3/1859.

Died—At his residence, on the 14th inst., 18 miles east of Memphis, Mr. Howell D. **EASON**. Memphis Enquirer, 2/18/1837.

Lieut. **RANDOLPH**, of the United States Navy, returned from a long cruise and died not long afterwards, and last week his wife died in Washington. She was the daughter of General John H. **EATON**, of Tennessee. Memphis Daily Appeal, 4/24/1855.

Shelby County Court, Oct. Term, 1855, R. V. **RICHARDSON**, Adm'r of Richard **ECHOLS**, dec'd. vs. Robert W. **ECHOLS**, Martha A. **ECHOLS**, and David E. **LOWRANCE**, Ann _. **LOWRANCE**, James _. P. **LOWRANCE**, Joel **LOWRANCE**, who are minor children of Levi **LOWRANCE** and Sarah **LOWRANCE**, dec'd., and Rob't. C. **LOWRANCE**, minor child of L. W. **LOWRANCE** and Elizabeth **LOWRANCE**, deceased. It appearing to the court from affidavit filed in this cause that defendants are heirs and distributees at law of Richard Echols, deceased, and are non-residents of the State of Tennessee ....Memphis Daily Appeal, 10/11/1855.

Died. On the 12th inst. in Shelby county, Ten., at the residence of his father, Dr. Edward W. **ECKLES**, of Hinds county, in the 42d year of his age. He was born in Sussex county, Virginia, and has left a wife and six children to mourn his loss. Vicksburg papers please copy. Memphis Appeal, 6/16/1854.

I will sell to the highest bidder on Thursday, the 30th day of November, at the late residence of William **ECKLES**, dec'd., in Shelby county, Tenn., one mile east of Buntyn's Station, on the Memphis & Charleston Railroad....D. J. **ECKLES**, Adm'r. with the will annexed. Nov 19. Memphis Appeal, 1854.

Died, in this county, on the 6th inst., at the residence of John **HILL**, Esq., Mr. John C. **EDDINS**, in the 69th year of his age. Mr. Eddins was a native of Edgecombe district, South Carolina, where he remained up to middle age, when he removed to Madison county, Tenn. He resided in that county til 1835, when he changed his place of abode to Marshal county, Miss., where he remained till 1848, when he took up his residence in this county, 9 miles south of Memphis...For many years a member of the Baptist Church...Memphis Eagle & Enquirer, 5/10/1852.

Died, at Gallatin, Tenn., on the evening of the 31st ult., Henry, infant son of Mr. Andrew Henry **EDGAR**, of this city, in his third year. Daily Enquirer, 9/8/1847. Mr. Editor -- I noticed a few days ago in your paper, that Andrew H. Edgar, Esq., had accepted the professorship of languages in the Memphis University...Daily Enquirer, 9/14/1847.

Married, In Toronto, C.W., on the 12th inst., at the church of the Holy Trinity, by Rev. Dr. Darling, Mr. Wm. **EDGAR**, of Memphis, to Margaret Ann **JONES**, of the former place. Nashville papers please copy. Memphis Daily Appeal, 7/24/1859.

Married, In Macon, on the 29th ult., by the Rev. R. **HOLOWAY**, Mr. Israel **EDINGS** to Miss Rebecca **BROWN**. Also, Mr. Jordan **GARRETT**, to Miss Harriet **BROWN**. Memphis Eagle, 5/6/1848.

Died, On Wednesday, the 22d September at the residence of his son, H. B. **EDMONDSON**, Andrew **EDMONDSON**, in the 69th year of his age. Memphis Appeal, 10/1/1852.

Married, On Wednesday evening the 9th inst. by Rev. G. W. **COONS**, Mr. James H. **EDMONDSON**, to Miss Mary C., daughter of F. **TITUS**, Esq., all of this city. Memphis Appeal, 2/11/1853. Died, Yesterday morning at 8 ½ o'clock of typhoid fever, at the residence of her father F. Titus, Esq., Mrs. Mary _., wife of James _. Edmondson, of this city, in her 22d year....Memphis Daily Appeal, 6/7/1855.

Married—In Hardeman county, on the 30th ult. by Rev. Mr. Peck, Mr. James B. **EDWARDS** to Miss Eliza V. **WILKERSON**, daughter of Dr. Wilkerson, of said county. Memphis Advocate, 11/10/1827.

At daylight yesterday morning the body of a man of about twenty-five years of age was found on the bluff nearly opposite Madison street. In one of the pockets was a bottle that had contained whisky, in another pocket was a two ounce phial in which a little laudanum remained. It appears by his trunk that his name was Jo **EDWARDS**. He had been staying at the Tennessee House about three weeks. A verdict was returned in accordance with the evidence. Memphis Daily Appeal, 10/28/1857. Another inquest was held by the Coroner this morning, upon the body of a man found on the bluff in front of Monroe street. As near as could be ascertained at the time, it was thought to be a gas-fitter by the name of John Edwards, who has been here some time....Memphis Evening Ledger, 10/27/1857.

Mr. S. T. **PEOPLES**, the mate of the steamer *Julia Dean*, informs us that Mr. Ranson **EDWARDS**, one of his crew, met with an accident early on Wednesday morning last, which resulted in his death twenty-four hours afterward. In taking on lumber at Aberdeen, Arkansas, a heavy piece of scantling slipped from the hands of those having it in their charge, and struck Mr. E. in the abdomen....he died on Thursday morning in great agony. His remains were brought to this city and it may be some consolation to his friends to know that he has been buried in one of our grave-yards....Mr. E. is from Obion county, Tenn., where his relations and friends now reside. Memphis Daily Appeal, Sat., 4/19/1856.

Married, At her residence, in this county, on the 24th inst., by G. **BARTLETT**, Esq., Mr. W. N. **EDWARDS** to Mrs. Jane **JONES**. Memphis Appeal, 8/30/1852.

Married, On the 10th inst. by the Rev. Mr. Tomes, Mr. Frederick **EICHBAUM** to Miss Josephine, eldest daughter of William **PRICHARD**, Esq., all of Nashville. Memphis Eagle & Enquirer, 3/17/1853.

Died—At his residence in Fayette County, Ten., on the 20th December last, after a short but severe illness....Col. Geo. H. **ELCAN**, leaving a disconsolate widow and a large family of children to deplore their irreparable loss. The deceased, son of Leon and Elizabeth **ELCAN**, was born in Buckingham county, Va., on the 28th February, 1800. When quite a young man he emigrated to North Alabama and settled near Huntsvile. After a residence of some years in Alabama he removed to Tennessee and settled in Fayette county, where the major part of his life was spent....Huntsville, Ala. and Richmond, Va. papers please copy. Memphis Daily Appeal, 2/3/1855.

Died, On the 12th inst. at his residence in Shelby county, Tenn., Dr. Alfred **ELDRIDGE**, in the sixty-first year of his age, formerly a resident of North Carolina. Raleigh papers, North Carolina, and Richmond Enquirer, Virginia, will please copy. Memphis Weekly Appeal, 11/24/1858.

Died, On the 22d inst. at the residence of her brother, Thomas **CHAMBLISS**, near Memphis, Mrs. Mary G. Eldridge, consort of Richard K. **ELDRIDGE**, in the forty-fifth year of her age. The deceased was a native of Sussex county, Va., and had resided with her family in this section of country during the past 16 years. She had been a consistent member of the Methodist Episcopal Church for a number of years prior to her death.....Petersburg, Va. papers please copy. Memphis Appeal, 2/23/1853.

Dr. W. H. **ELDRIDGE**, Having permanently settled in Memphis, respectfully offers his services to the inhabitants of the city and country. Residence at Fletcher's Central Hotel.....Weekly Appeal, 10/9/1846.

Memphis Classical and Commercial Academy: Louis **ELKIN**, A. B. principal ...Memphis Enquirer, 5/13/1837.

We learn that Capt. Elliott, the former respected captain of the steamboat *Shotwell*, died on Wednesday on board the steamboat *Uncle Sam*. This will be sad news to the wide circle that took a pride in numbering Capt. Elliott among their friends. Memphis Daily Appeal, Thursday, 10/8/1858. Some of the papers at a distance state that they are informed by telegraph, that Capt. B. L. **ELLIOTT** died in Memphis of yellow fever. We wish to inform these papers that we have had no yellow fever in this city, and consequently Capt. Elliott did not die of that disease in this place; he died on board the *New Uncle Sam*, when that boat was on its way up the river. Memphis Daily Appeal, 10/15/1858.

Died, In this city on Saturday night last, Mr. James **ELLIOTT**. Memphis Appeal, Mon., 8/18/1851.

Married, By Rev. J. W. **KNOTT** at the South Memphis Methodist Church, on the 10th instant, Mr. John D. **ELLIOTT** and Miss C. C. **TURNER**, all of this city. Memphis Daily Appeal, 9/12/1856.

State of Tenn. Shelby County, Circuit Court, Sept. Term, 1846. William **ELLIOTT** vs Abigail Elliott. On motion and it appearing to the court from the return of the Sheriff on the subpoena issued in the premises, that the defendant is not an inhabitant of this State, it is ordered that publication be made three successive weeks, in some newspaper published in the city of Memphis, requiring defendant to make her appearance at the next term of this court at the court house in Raleigh on the 1st Monday in January next, and plead, answer or demur to the complainant's petition, filed for a divorce, or the same will be taken for confessed, and heard ex parte. Sam. __ **BROWN**, Clerk. American Eagle, 10/15/1846.

Married. On Tuesday evening, January 23d by the Rev. J. W. **KNOTT**, Mr. Wm. **ELLIOTT** to Miss Hannah _. **MILLER**. Cincinnati and Hamilton, Ohio papers please copy. Memphis Daily Appeal, 1/25/1855.

Circuit Court Sale. A. Dowell, Administrator of Wright W. **ELLIOTT**, deceased, versus Mississippi **ELLIOTT** and Leonidas **ELLIOTT**, heirs of the said Wright W. Elliott. In pursuance of the order made in this cause at the January term, 1847, of the Circuit Court of Shelby County, Tenn., I will sell, on Saturday, the 3d day of April, 1847, ...a Tract of Land, it being entry No. 169, in said county and grant No. 4265, containing 140 (?) acres, situated on an island above the mouth of Wolf River, in sight of Memphis.....Sam. R. **BROWN**, Clerk. Daily Enquirer, 3/21/1847.

Married, By J. **HORNE**, Esq., at the Worsham House, on the morning of the 27th inst., Mr. John **ELLIS** and Miss Julie **NOLAN**, of Holly Springs, Miss. Memphis Daily Appeal, 3/28/1857.

Died, In Jackson, Tenn., on Wednesday evening, 15th instant, at the residence of her father, Wm. H. **LONG**, Mrs. Caroline V., consort of Mr. James **ELROD**. Memphis Daily Appeal, 1/22/1856.

Married, On Sunday evening, 8th inst., by James **ROSE**, Esq., Benj. **EMANUEL**, to Miss Juliana Marks, daughter of Alexander **MARKS**, all of this place. Memphis Enquirer, 11/10/1846.

We are authorized to announce Jos. **EMERSON**, a candidate for the office of Justice of the Peace, for the 14th Civil District, at the approaching March election. Memphis Eagle, 2/4/1848.

Died of Smallpox in this city on the 3d inst., Mrs. Mary **EMERSON**, in the 57th year of her age. She had been a member for several years of the Presbyterian church...Those who feel her departure most sensibly, are her afflicted husband and children...Memphis Eagle, 4/8/1850.

First Launch at Old Fort Pickering. Permit me through the columns of your worthy journal, to mention the launch to be made from the above yard, of Primus **EMERSON**,--the most distinguished and noted boat builder of the West. Mr. E. located here some months since, having left St. Louis owing to a scarcity of timber and space sufficient for a yard there...Memphis Appeal, 7/17/1851.

At a late hour Wednesday evening, the clothing upon Mrs. Engel, the wife of Mr. Frederick **ENGEL**, who resides on Talbot street, caught fire by accident, and there being no person in the room at the time to render her assistance, the unfortunate woman was so badly burned that she died at an early hour yesterday morning. A little child in the room at the time was also badly burned by the accident. Memphis Daily Appeal, Fri., 12/23/1859.

Married, on the 26th inst., at the residence of Mrs. Matilda **JAMES**, by the Rev. F. P. **DAVIDSON**, Mr. Wm. E. **EPPES**, of Holly Springs, to Miss Elizabeth R. **JAMES**, of this city. Memphis Enquirer, 11/29/1848.

Died—In this city, yesterday morning, Mr. Thomas W. **ERSKINE**. The friends and acquaintances of the deceased are requested to attend his funeral, from the residence of David **PARK**, on Second street, this morning, at 10 o'clock. Divine service by Rev. Mr. Coons. Memphis Eagle, 5/21/1849.

Married. On Thursday evening the 1st of February, 1855, by J. Madison **KIRK**, Esq., Mr. A. M. **ERWIN** to Mrs. Elizabeth S. **HARRIS**, daughter of David **TURNER**, all in the vicinity of Bone Yard, Tishomingo co., Miss. Memphis Daily Appeal, 2/6/1855.

Died: In this city, on Sunday morning, the 28th day of July, Mrs. Elizabeth A. **ERWIN**, in the 23d year of her age. She was an acceptable member of the M.E. Church South.....She faded in the morning of life, under the ravages of consumption, leaving an affectionate husband and a large circle of friends.... Cincinnati papers please copy. Memphis Eagle, 8/9/1849.

The subscriber has at his yard, opposite Washington street, near the river, a large assortment of Dry White Pine, and worked Flooring, which he offers cheap for cash or approved paper. John T. **ERWIN**. Memphis Eagle, 6/14/1849.

Married, November 8th at the Church of the Holy Trinity, by Dr. R. T. **QUINTARD**, Mr. Thos. J. **ERWIN**, of Mobile, Ala., to Miss Valerico **WINCHESTER**, of this city. Memphis Daily Appeal, 11/15/1859.

Died, At his residence in Madison county, Tenn., on the 23rd January, Mr. John **ESTES**, an old and highly esteemed citizen. Memphis Eagle & Enquirer, 2/2/1853.

The body of Mr. Enoch B. **ETHRIDGE**, of the late firm of Woolsay & Ethridge, of New Orleans, arrived here last evening by the steamer New Falls City. Mr. E. was the brother of the Hon. Emerson **ETHRIDGE**, and his remains were received here by his brother-in-law, Mr. J. G. **PARKER**, and will be forwarded to the residence of the father of the deceased in Weakly county for interment. Memphis Daily Avalanche, 6/6/1859.

Died. In this city on Sunday night last, of Consumption, at the residence of Wm. **PARK**, Gordius(?) F. **ETHRIDGE**, aged 35 years. Mr. Ethridge had for many years been a citizen of Memphis, where, by his many good qualities, both of head and heart, he had drawn around him a large circle of warm and devoted friends, who are left to mourn his untimely demise....His remains were accompanied to their last resting place yesterday evening by a large concourse of relatives and friends. Memphis Appeal, Tues., 2/21/1854.

Married, On Wednesday, 2_th January, 1851, in the vicinity of Oakland, Tenn., by the Rev. T. H. **BAYLISS**, Mr. Jas. S. **EVANS** to Miss Cornelia F. **TROTTER**, all of Fayette County. Nashville and Louisville Advocates please copy. Memphis Appeal, 2/11/1851.

Died, In Shelby county, at the residence of Dr. John R. **EVANS** – John Milton **EVANS**, of Congestive fever; aged 14 years 6 months. The Appeal, 9/27/1844.

Married, On Thursday evening, May 15th, 1851, by Rev. S. J. **HENDERSON**, Mr. Wm. J. **EVENS** to Miss Sarah H. **VAUGHN**, all of this city. Memphis Appeal, 5/17/1851.

Married, On Tuesday evening, 3d inst., by Rev. W. M. **EWING**, Mr. L. G. **EWING** to Miss Iantha V. **GRIFFIN**, all of Shelby county, Tenn. Memphis Daily Appeal, 5/7/1859.

Married, On Wednesday evening, the 12th inst., by the Rev. Dr. Page, Mr. C. M. **FACKLER** to Miss Anna Kirk, eldest daughter of John **KIRK**, Esq.—all of this city. Memphis Eagle & Enquirer, 1/14/1853.

Married, May 4th at Bridgeport, Conn., by Rev. George Thrall, at Christian Church, Mr. J. B. **FAIRCHILD**, of the firm of Fairchild & Morris, to Miss Jennie M. **WADE**, of Bridgeport, Conn. Memphis Daily Appeal, 5/19/1859.

We learn from the *W. T. Whig* of the 16th inst., that an affray took place in Jackson on the preceding Wednesday, between John **FAIRLESS**, of Shelby County, and Jas. **SOWELL**, jr. of Madison county, in which the former was killed by the contents of a shot gun fired by Sowell. The whole load entered the head just above the temple, shockingly scattering the brains of the deceased, who only survived the shot a few hours. Memphis Eagle, Tues., 2/20/1849.

Died, of consumption, on the 12th instant, in the vicinity of Memphis, Mrs. Frances D., wife of Mr. G. **FALLS**, of the firm of Falls & Cash, of this city, and daughter of Mrs. E. M. Ma____. The deceased was born in Rutherford county, Tennessee, May 9th, 1821; professed religion and became a member of the Cumberland Presbyterian Church in 1840....A more devoted wife, or dutiful daughter, or affectionate sister....In the death of Mrs. Falls, not only a loving mother, a doting husband, affectionate children and admiring friends, but a church community and society are called upon to deplore their irreparable loss....Memphis Daily Appeal, 8/16/1855.

Married, At the residence of the bride's father, on the fourth inst., by Rev. S. **WATSON**, Mr. G. **FALLS** and Miss Lavonia, daughter of J. F. **McKINNEY**, Esq. Memphis Daily Avalanche, 2/10/1859.

On Sunday night, about 12 o'clock, Michael **FANNING** was knocked down, near the South Memphis Market House, and his pockets rifled of $5 (?), and a Gold Watch...Memphis Appeal, 9/5/1848.

Married, On the 8th inst., by the Rev. S. G. **STARKES**, Rev. P. S. **FANT**, to Miss Elizabeth W. **HARDIN**, of Marshall county, Miss. Memphis Appeal, 10/17/1851.

Married, At the Gayoso House last evening, by A. M. **BRYAN**, D.D., Mr. John R. **FARABEE** to Miss Carie L. **MARSHALL**, of Marshall county, Miss. Also, at the same time and place, and by the same, Mr. R. H. M. **COCKRELL** to Miss Maggie W. **STARK**. Memphis Weekly Appeal, 12/29/1858.

Married, On the night of September 1st, 1859, by Elder C. B. **YOUNG**, Mr. Jas. D. **FARLEY** to Miss Maggie A. **KUYHARDALL**, all of Panola county, Miss. Memphis Daily Appeal, 9/6/1859.

Married. At the residence of Brantly **SUGG**, Esq., of Marshall County, Miss., at 8 o'clock, A.M., on the 20th inst. by Rev. Joseph R. **HAMILTON**, Principal of C. W. Baptist Female Seminary, Dr. William S. **FARLEY**, of Panola, to Miss Sallie A. **SUGG**, of Marshall. Memphis Appeal, 12/24/1854.

Married, In this city on yesterday evening, April 16th, by Rev. Mr. Ware, Mr. C. M. **FARMER** and Mrs. S. F. **ETHRIDGE**, daughter of the late Dr. **CHRISTIAN**. Memphis Daily Appeal, 4/17/1856.

Died, In this city, on the 19th inst., Mrs. Eleanor M. **FARMER**, in the 50th year of her age. Somerville Star please copy. Memphis Daily Appeal, 10/21/1857.

Married: On the 17th inst., near Macon, Tenn., by the Rev. R. L. **WALLER**, Mr. H. M. **FARMER**, of Macon, to Miss Ann E. **HESTER**, of Memphis. Memphis Daily Eagle, 7/30/1849.

The friends of H. F. and C. M. **FARNSWORTH** are invited to attend the funeral of their infant daughter, Charlotte Mary, at their residence on Second Street, near Beal, at 4 o'clock this afternoon. Memphis Eagle & Enquirer, 6/26/1852.

Married: At Christ's Church, Nashville, on the 24th inst. at 12 o'clock by Rev. Charles **TOMES**, Dr. Robert J. **FARQUHARSON**, late of the U.S. Army, to Miss Mary Lydia **SMITH**, all of that city. Memphis Whig, 10/29/1855.

Report of the Board of Health. For the last 24 hours ending 12 o'clock M, July 5th Michael **FARRAL**, aged 40, cholera...Memphis Enquirer, 7/6/1849.

Married, On the 22d instant at the residence of Wm. **DUNN**, Esq. by Rev. Robert **FRAZIER**, Mr. J. M. **FARRAR** to Miss Elizabeth S. **RODGERS**, all of Shelby county, Tenn. Memphis Appeal, 3/24/1853.

From the law-card of our friend, Jno. P. **FARRELLY**, Esq., late of St. Louis, it will be seen that he has selected our city as his future place of residence....Mr. Farrelly removed from Arkansas to St. Louis about three years since....Memphis Daily Appeal, 11/11/1855.

Elizabeth **FARRINGTON**, Administratrix of all and singular the goods and chattles, rights and credits of the late Rufus M. **FARRINGTON**, having suggested to me, Wm. L. **DEWOODY**, Clerk of said court, the insolvency of said estate...Memphis Appeal, 5/12/1851.

Married, On the 22d instant, by the Rev. Mr. McMahan, Gen. J. F. **FARRINGTON** of this city, to Miss Mary Pope, daughter of John S. **McGEHEE**, Esq., of Panola county, Miss. The Appeal, 11/1/1844. Died, On the 28th(?) ult., at Pensacola, Florida, wither he had repaired of regaining his health, our fellow-citizen Gen. Jacob F. Farrington...His remains reached our city on the morning of yesterday, and were interred at 11 o'clock. Memphis Appeal, 2/7/1851.

John C. **FARRINGTON**, Attorney at Law, Memphis, Tenn.—Office on Main street, second door north of Washington. The Memphis Enquirer, 6/18/1846.

The friends of Col. Joshua P. **FARRINGTON** are requested to attend his burial this morning, from his residence, three quarters of a mile north-east of the city...Memphis Eagle, 2/7/1850.

The friends and acquaintances of Wm. and Emeline **FARRIS** are invited to attend the funeral of their eldest Son, Cincinatus, this morning at 10 o'clock from their residence on Elliot st., three doors West of Hernando. Memphis Whig, 6/21/1856.

Married in this county on the 7th inst., by the Rev. Isaac H. **FOSTER**, Mr. D. A. **FAUCETT**, of Memphis, to Miss Mary Ann Elizabeth, daughter of H. G. **BARBEE**, Esq. The Appeal, 11/15/1844. Died—On Thursday 11th inst., of bilious pleurisy, Mrs. Mary Ann Faucett, aged 31(?) years, and consort of D. A. Faucett, Inn keeper near this City. This lady was a pious member of the Reformed Baptist Church.....The Appeal, 4/19/1844.

It is with feelings of deep regret, that we attempt to record the death of our worthy, and much beloved citizen, brother David A., son of James and Elizabeth **FAUCETT**, born in Orange County, North Carolina, Nov. 8th, 1811, and departed this life, March 14th 1847, at his residence in Memphis, in the 36th year of his age, leaving a bereaved consort and three children, together with other relatives and numerous friends to mourn their loss. He made a profession of religion at a Methodist Camp-meeting in the fall of 1838 or 1839, and united himself the same fall to the Baptist Church at Shiloh, Fayette County, and after having removed to this place two or three years subsequent to that time he attached himself to a church of the same order.....American Eagle, 4/8/1847.

Died, Near Portersville, Tipton county, Tenn., on the 14th instant, Mrs. Mary **FAULKER**, late of Lancaster District, South Carolina. Also, about six hours afterwards, her son William, aged about 23 years. Disease of both Flux. Memphis Daily Appeal, 7/26/1856.

Married, On the 18th instant by Rev. Mr. Thomas, Dr. A. N. **FAUSETT** to Miss Martha Jane **MORTON**, all of Fayette county. Memphis Weekly Appeal, 5/26/1858.

Married, On the 14th instant by Rev. A. H. **THOMAS**, Mr. Wm. **FAYE_S** to Miss Mena **D'LIFNE**, both of Memphis. Memphis Daily Appeal, 12/17/1859.

Died, In this city on the 2d inst., of consumption, Mr. Robert A. **FEENEY**, in the 24th year of his age. The deceased was raised here, and no one ever enjoyed more fully the confidence and esteem of his acquaintances than he did. He was deprived at an early age of his father, (who died at this place of cholera in '32,) and was separated from his mother about the same time, yet without the guidance or counsel of either he formed for himself a character that was without a blemish....The day before his death he made his will and gave directions for his funeral with as much composure as he would have attended to ordinary business when in good health. City and Huntsville, Ala. papers will please copy. Daily Enquirer, 8/4/1847.

Married, October 28th at Greenwood, near this city, by Rev. J. O. **STEADMAN**, R. S. **FEILD**, M.D., to Miss Annie, daughter of J. S. **LeMASTER**, Esq., all of this county. Memphis Daily Appeal, 10/30/1857.

Notice is hereby given to _____ **FELBZ**, a cabinet maker, who left his two sons Christopher and Thornam_, in a destitute situation, that unless he comes forward and makes provision for their support, they will be presented to the County Court to be bound out as the law directs. L. **VOLMER**. Daily Enquirer, 2/1/1847.

C. S. **FENNER**, M.D., General & Ophthalmic Surgeon, Memphis, Tenn. Dr. Fenner has permanently located at Memphis....Residence & Office on Shelby street....Memphis Appeal, 8/6/1854. Died, At the residence of her son, Dr. C. S. Fenner, on Court street, yesterday morning, Mrs. Mary W. **FENNER**, in the 67th year of her age. Memphis Daily Appeal, 5/3/1857.

Married, On Tuesday evening, December 29th, by Rev. Dr. Grundy, Mr. John H. **FENTEM** to Mrs. Mary Ann **HIGGINS**, all of this city. Memphis Daily Appeal, 12/31/1857.

Died, in the vicinity of Memphis, on Wednesday, 17th inst., Willie Shepherd, infant daughter of Susan and Wm. W. **FERGERSON**, aged sixteen months. Memphis Daily Appeal, 8/19/1859.

Died—At Greeneck, Ark., on the 16th ult., Mrs. Betsey **FERGUSON**, formerly of Fayetteville, Ten., aged 66 years. Memphis Enquirer, 10/4/1839.

Died, In Tippah county, Miss., on Saturday, 27th of March, Daniel **FERGUSON**, Esq., in the 26th year of his age. Dyersburg, Tenn., and Lynchburg, Va., papers please copy. Memphis Weekly Appeal, 4/7/1858.

John G. **FERGUSON**, (Late of Nashville,) Attorney at Law, Memphis, Tenn. will practice in the Courts of Shelby and the adjoining counties. Office on Court Square…Memphis Appeal, 8/15/1851. The Nashville *Patriot* contains the following just, truthful and touching obituary of John G. Ferguson, Esq., a prominent young lawyer of that city, and who formerly resided in Memphis, where he has many warm and devoted friends, and where his mother and several of his brothers and sisters reside….Died—In this city, July 11th inst., John G., eldest son of James B. **FERGUSON**, deceased….Memphis Daily Appeal, 8/5/1859.

Married. On the evening of the 21st inst., at the residence of Mrs. Judge Betts, by the Rev. Dr. Watson, Mr. W. W. **FERGUSON** to Miss Susan C. **LOCKE**. Memphis Appeal, 12/24/1854.

Tribute of Respect. The following Preamble and Resolutions in reference to the death of Wm. O. **FERGUSON**, Esq., were introduced by Doct. Thos. T. **REEVES**, before the quarterly term of our County Court, on Monday last, and unanimously adopted. Whereas, it has pleased the all wise Ruler of the Universe, by an inscrutable dispensation of his Providence, to remove from our midst the late W. O. Ferguson, Esq., Chairman and Presiding Justice of this Court….Memphis Daily Appeal, Wed., 4/11/1855.

Married, At Wyalusing, the residence of Col. B. L. **HOLCOMB** in Marshall, Texas, on Wednesday evening April 14th, by the Rev. M. W. **STAPLES**, Capt. Drury **FIELD** of that place, to Miss Fannie I. **POLK**, of LaGrange, Fayette county, Tenn. Memphis Eagle & Enquirer, 5/12/1852.

Died. In Dyersburg, Dyer county, Tenn., on the 9th inst., Jas. H. **FIELD**….He was about 65 years of age and was one of the oldest citizens of Dyer. Mr. F. was a member of the Baptist Church….Memphis Daily Appeal, 4/1/1855.

Married, On the 8th instant at the residence of the bride's father, near College Hill, Lafayette county, Miss., by Rev. E. J. **WILLIAMS**, Mr. M. S. **FIELDER**, of Memphis, to Miss Jeannie **MAY**. Memphis Daily Appeal, 3/10/1859.

Married, On the 16th inst., by Rev. E. H. **GREEN**, Mr. David **FIGHT** and Miss Ellen **BANKS**, both of Tipton county, Tenn. Memphis Daily Appeal, 10/23/1857.

Died, Suddenly, on the 11th inst., at Lebanon, Ohio, Mrs. H. M. Finlay, wife of the Rev. John **FINLAY**, formerly of this place. Memphis Daily Appeal, 3/26/1857.

Died, At Paola(?), Kansas Territory, on the 17th November last, Mr. William H. **FINLAY**, second son of the late John **FINLAY**, of this city, in the 31st year of his age. Memphis Daily Appeal, 1/9/1859.

Married, At Holly Springs, Miss., on Thursday 2__ th inst., by Rev. Dr. Page, Hon. J. J. **FINLEY**, Mayor of Memphis, to Miss Margaret H., daughter of Col. Jno. B. **MARTIN**, of Marshall county, Miss. Weekly Appeal, Fri., 11/28/1845.

James **FINLEY**, Esq., of Dickson county, committed suicide a few days since, by blowing his brains out with a pistol. Mr. F. was a lawyer, an amiable and generous man…No cause is assigned for his self-destruction.Daily Enquirer, 11/3/1847.

Married, On Sunday the 2d inst., by the Rev. P. W. **ALSTON**, Maj. John B. **FINLEY**, attorney at law, of Osceola, Ark., to Miss Elizabeth **LAMB**, of this city. Weekly Appeal, 11/7/1845.

Married, In Fayette county, Tenn., on the 14th inst. by Rev. Mr. W. **WEBBER**, Mr. G. G. **FINNEY**, of Memphis, to Miss E. B. **DAVIS**, of the former place. Memphis Whig, 2/16/1856.

J. G. **FINNIE**, Esq., has purchased the interest of Mr. Jno. C. **LANIER** in the Eagle & Enquirer printing establishment and has become an equal Proprietor and partner in the same.....Memphis Appeal, 3/24/1853.

Thomas James **FINNIE**, Esq.—*Dear Sir:* We herewith present you a cane of the finest material and most exquisite finish, as a manisfestation of our personal regard and esteem....Your efforts and those of your co-laborers in behalf of the sick of our city during the prevalence of the late epidemic, cannot be too highly appreciated....Mr. F. will of course preserve the token....and hand it down to his children, (alas! he has none now!) as an invaluable heirloom....Memphis Daily Appeal, 11/1/1855.

William **TAYLOR** and Augustus **FINNING** were yesterday brought before Esquire Curtis on a charge of arson—the burning (of) the cotton shed of W. **HOWARD**...They were convicted on the testimony of Mr. Griffin, who turned State's evidence, and in default of bail were committed to prison. Memphis Appeal, 10/26/1848.

Died, in this city, yesterday morning (23d inst.) John B. **FINNY**, aged about 50 years. He was one of our oldest citizens and was a benevolent, kind-hearted man. Daily Enquirer, 7/25/1847.

As a son of Mrs. Doyle was shooting at a mark yesterday, James K. P. (or R. P.) Fisher, son of our Recorder, happened to be passing on the opposite side of the fence, when a ball passed through the plank and entered his body, from which he died during the day. Memphis Daily Appeal, 7/20/1855. The friends and acquaintances of Major G. W. and Mrs. Elmira **FISHER** are invited to attend the funeral of their son, James K. P., this afternoon at 4 o'clock, from their residence on Madison street, to proceed to Elmwood Cemetery. Services by Rev. Dr. Porter. Memphis Daily Appeal, 7/20/1855.....On Thursday morning last little "Jimmy K. P." a little son of our worthy Recorder, Maj. George W. Fisher, about 12 years of age....Memphis Daily Appeal, 7/21/1855.

Married, In this city on Wednesday, the 14th instant, by Rev. A. M. **BRYAN**, Mr. T. A. **FISHER** to Miss Annie M., daughter of the officiating minister. At the same time, Mr. J. R. **GARRISON** to Miss A. B., daughter of Major Geo. W. **FISHER**, all of this city. The happy quartette left on the Ingomar the same evening for the Crescent City. Memphis Weekly Appeal, 4/21/1858.

Married—On the 17th inst. by the Rev. Jeptha **HARRISON**, Mr. Wm. P. **FISHER**, merchant of this place, to Mrs. Maria B. **PEACOCK**, late of Fredericksburgh, Va. Memphis Enquirer, 4/19/1839.

Married, Yesterday morning, May 27th, at the residence of the bride's mother, by Rev. Mr. Steadman, Mr. F. B. **FISK** to Miss Lucy Jane, daughter of the late Col. Sam'l. **LEAKE**, of Shelby county. Memphis Daily Appeal, 5/28/1857.

Died, in this city on the 1st instant, Mrs. Mary R., wife of Wm. H. **FITCH**, Jr., after a lingering illness....Although she had resided but a comparatively short time in this city, she had endeared herself to those who made her acquaintance....Springfield, Illinois and Youngston, Ohio papers please copy. Memphis Daily Appeal, 4/6/1856.

Married, On the 20th instant at Corinth, Miss., by Rev. M. **HOWELL**, Mr. J. D. **FITZ**, of Boston, to Miss Fannie A. **PEAK**, of the Peak Family. Memphis Daily Appeal, 3/22/1859.

Married, On Tuesday evening, the 23d inst., by Rev. Geo. W. **COONS**, Mr. Henry **FITZGERALD**, to Miss Sarah W. **BELL**, all of this city. Memphis Eagle, 7/29/1850. Died, In this city on Sunday morning, 3d inst., Emma B., youngest daughter of Henry and Sarah W. Fitzgerald, aged 2 years and 4 months. Memphis Daily Appeal, 5/5/1857.

Patrick **FITZGERALD**, formerly a deck hand on the *Nebraska*, got off a flat-boat at the mouth of Wolf river yesterday to bathe. Soon after leaving the boat he was seen to strangle, after which he sunk and was drowned. It is supposed that he got into a gully that was covered with water. The body was recovered. Memphis Daily Appeal, 8/6/1858.

Married, On the evening of the 30th December, ult., by Geo. J. **BIBB**, Esq., Mr. Peter B. **FITZPATRICK**, to Miss Susan **COOK**, all of Lauderdale county, Tenn. Memphis Appeal, 1/11/1851.

Geo. **FLAHERTY**, Respectfully informs the citizens of Memphis, that having resumed business at his old stand, on Court street, east of Court Square, near the Cumberland Presbyterian Church, he will attend punctually to all orders of Interments in the North or South Memphis Cemeteries...Memphis Eagle, 8/9/1847.

The friends and acquaintances of Geo. **FLAHERTY** are respectfully invited to attend his funeral from his late residence, corner of Court and Second streets. Services at the Catholic Church at 3 o'clock P.M. to-day. Memphis Daily Appeal, 9/5/1858. We have through inadvertance heretofore omitted to notice the death of Mr. George Flaherty, which occurred at his residence in this city, on the 5th inst. At the time of his death he was in the 47th year of his age, had been a resident of this city about fifteen years....Memphis Daily Appeal, 9/16/1858.

One of the contractors, Jno. **FLAHERTY**, on the levee near Helena, is said to have suddenly disappeared, having some $1500 in his possession. He was a young man of dark complexion, slim and about five feet ten inches in height. Any information concerning him will be thankfully received by his brother, Patrick **FLAHERTY**, of our city. Memphis Daily Appeal, 12/5/1855.

New Music Store. P. **FLAVIO** has the honor to inform the Ladies and Gentlemen of Memphis, that he will open on the 14th inst., a Music Store on Madison street...Memphis Enquirer, 11/26/1846.

Death of Philip **FLAVIO**—We sincerely regret to record the death of this old and well-known citizen, which occurred on Thursday night last. His death was very sudden, having been caused by a fit of apoplexy. Mr. Flavio....was a native of France, and closely allied to a noble family there, and would have inherited a title and estates had he not been forced to leave the country before reaching his majority during the pendency of one of the numerous revolutions which formerly distracted it. He came to America and settled in New Orleans, where he resided for some years. During his residence there he received an appointment from the French Government which attached him to the embassy from that country to the then Republic of Texas. Memphis Avalanche, Sat., 6/11/1859. ....The deceased was a native of France, and it is known that he belonged to a branch of the family of Louis Phillipe....Memphis Daily Appeal, 6/11/1859.

Married, On the 5th instant by Rev. W. Carey **CRANE**, Mr. Jas. Madison **FLEINE** to Miss Rebecca Jane **MOODY**, all of DeSoto county, Miss. Memphis Daily Appeal, 10/14/1859.

At a meeting of Mechanics' Fire Company No. 4, of the city of Memphis, held on the 8th inst...Whereas, It has been deemed proper by the great Ruler of the universe to take from us our brother A. T. **FLEMING**, who was always ready to do his duty as a man and as a citizen—an affectionate husband and a confiding friend...Memphis Appeal, 8/12/1852.

The members of Fire Co. No. 4 were out in full regalis yesterday to attend the funeral of Mr. Alex. **FLEMING**, one of their members, who died on Wednesday. Memphis Daily Appeal, Fri., 9/21/1855.

Departed this life, at his residence in Memphis, on the 2d instant, 1855, E. B. **FLEMING**, in the 42d year of his age, of bilious fever. The deceased leaves a wife and five children and a large circle of friends to mourn his loss. At the residence of the late E. B. and C. A. Fleming, Knox Fleming, aged ten months, disease congestive chill. Memphis Daily Appeal, 9/12/1855.

Married, On last evening, Mr. Benjamin F. **FLEMMING** to Miss Augusta **STRATTON**, both of Memphis. Memphis Appeal, 11/3/1853.

Frank **FLESHART**, a youth of 16 or 17 years of age, was killed by an accidental discharge of his gun, whilst hunting with a companion, in the neighborhood of this city, yesterday. The entire load passed into and about his heart. Memphis Eagle, 2/27/1850.

Married—On the 7th inst., by Rev. Geo. W. **COONS**, Mr. J. M. **FLETCHER**, to Mrs. Elizabeth **HENDERSON**, all of this place. American Eagle, 10/15/1846.

Died, On the morning of the 25th instant, Charlotte May, infant daughter of Robert and Jennie **FLETCHER**, aged one year, two months and sixteen days. Memphis Daily Appeal, 7/27/1859.

A very superior article of Premium Pumps, suitable for Wells or Cisterns, and at about half the price of the metal pump, for sale by Thos. M. **FLETCHER** & Co. Daily Enquirer, 5/7/1847.

Tribute of Respect. At a called meeting of DeSoto Lodge No. 100, held at Cockrum on Tuesday, the 22d day of July, A.D. 1856, A.L. 5856, the following preamble and resolutions were adopted. Whereas, the Supreme Grand Master has seen fit to remove from us Brother Shadrick **FLEWELLEN**, who died on Sunday, the 2_th inst.....Memphis Daily Appeal, Fri., 8/15/1856.

Married, On the 13th of March, near Centre Hill, DeSoto county, Miss., by Rev. Wm. Carey **CRANE**, Mr. James **FLEWELLEN** and Miss Martha Fredonia **BRIGANCE**, all of that county. Memphis Daily Appeal, 4/1/1856.

City Baths & Barber Shop, Jefferson street, one door East Commercial Hotel. George **FLIEDNER**, Barber & Fashionable Hair Dresser. Memphis Appeal, 11/25/1852.

Died, At her residence on the 15th inst., Mrs. Mary Flinn, consort of Mr. Wm. W. **FLINN**, and daughter of Benjamin and Permelia **BLEDSOE**, all of Desoto county, Mississippi. Lexington (Ky.) papers please copy. Memphis Eagle & Enquirer, 6/21/1853.

Married, On Sunday morning, the 6th inst., by the Rev. P. A. **WALKER**, at Mount Comfort Church, Major R. **FLINT** to Miss Nancy **McKINNEY**, all of Hardeman county, Tennessee. Memphis Eagle & Enquirer, 3/17/1853.

The undersigned respectfully announces to the citizens of Memphis and vicinity, that he will on Monday next, open an English, Classical and Mathematical School on Court street...He has in his possession recommendations from gentlemen of high standing at Somerville, at which place, for the last two months, he was the assistant of Mr. Blake.....Wm. S. **FLIPPIN**. Memphis Eagle, 1/8/1846.

Died, Of Congestive Fever, at his residence, near Mount Comfort, in Hardeman County, Tenn., on Saturday the 4th Inst., (September) Joseph B. **FLYNT**, in the 26th year of his age. He was born in Lincoln County, Tenn., where he was raised until he was eleven years old. His parents then removed to the place of his latter residence and death...He left behind him three brothers and four sisters...Memphis Appeal, 9/28/1847.

Died, In DeSoto county, Mississippi, on the 18th February, 1854, James C., son of Martin and Esther **FLYNT**, aged one year, three months and nineteen days. On the 9th of September, 1856, Jefferson Davis, son of Martin and Esther Flynt, aged one year, ten months and eighteen days. Huntsville *Democrat* and Lincoln *Journal* copy. Memphis Daily Appeal, 9/18/1856.

Married, On the 30th ult., by the Rev. Mr. Burns, Mr. Shad R. **FO_ERS** of this city, to Miss Sarah A. W. **SEAY**, of Tippah county, Miss. Weekly Appeal, 8/28/1846.

Died, Sunday evening last, in Jackson, Mr. Francis A. **FOGG**. Memphis Appeal, Thurs., 5/5/1853.

Married, In this city on the 1st inst., by Rev. J. T. C. **COLLINS**, Mr. B. F. **FOLGER** to Miss S. C. **TARPLEY**, all of Memphis, Tenn. Memphis Daily Appeal, 1/15/1858.

We have here in Memphis a man who without pretension or presumption, or ostentation of any kind, possesses as many of the elements of true artistic genius as any man we ever knew. We have seen several crayon sketches, original and copies from his pencil and we do not exaggerate when we say that for delicacy of touch, perspective, and accuracy and shading, they are equal to any steel engravings we have seen.....Mr. T. B. **FOLGER** is the gentleman we allude to.....Memphis Appeal, 10/12/1853.

The friends and acquaintances of Wm. M. and Nannie **FOLWELL** are invited to attend the funeral of their infant daughter, Katie, from their residence on Beale street at 4 o'clock. Services by Rev. J. H. **OTEY**. Memphis Daily Appeal, 8/7/1856.

Hon. H. S. **FOOTE** is now in the city, having come here to practice his profession and reside permanently. Chancellor Charles **SCOTT**, of Mississippi, we see it announced in the Mississippi papers, has made final arrangements to remove his family to this city in a few days....Memphis Daily Appeal, 12/20/1857.

Married, On the 10th instant by the Hon. George W. **BEAZLEY**, at the residence of the bride's father in St. Francis county, Ark., Alexander **FORBES**, Esq., to Miss Francis E., daughter of Lewis R. **HINTON**, all of said county. Memphis Daily Appeal, 1/23/1856.

Rev. Benj. **FORBES**, residing in the vicinity of Hickory With, Fayette county, Tenn., was killed on the 26th ult., by his son, with a billet of wood...Memphis Appeal, 3/3/1851.

Died, On the 12th instant, James **FORBES**, aged 25 years. Cincinnati papers please copy. Memphis Daily Appeal, 9/14/1855.

Died—In this city, on Wednesday, 29th inst., J. (?) N. **FORD**, of Louisville, Ky., a volunteer, private of Capt. Heady's Company, Kentucky Calvary. Louisville papers please notice. Weekly Appeal, 8/7/1846.

Married, By Rev. Samuel **WATSON** on the evening of the 15th instant, in the vicinity of Memphis, at the residence of Newton **FORD**, Esq., his two daughters; Miss Mary Ford and Mr. Samuel M. **RAINS**, of DeSoto county, Miss., and Miss Betty Ford and Dr. D. W. **BYNUM**, of DeSoto county, Miss. Memphis Daily Appeal, 1/21/1857.

Married, In this city, on the 23d inst., by the Rev. Mr. Robb, Mr. Robert P. **FORD**, of Memphis, to Miss Martha A., daughter of John H. **DAY**, Esq.—*Jackson W.T. Whig.* Memphis Eagle, 2/1/1850.

Married: In Lexington, Ky., on the 6th inst., by the Rev. J. H. **BROWN**, Mr. W. G. **FORD**, of this city, to Miss Mary S. **SANDERS**, of the former place. Memphis Eagle, 3/1/1849.

Died, In this city, September 12th, of typhoid fever, Wm. M. **FORD**, aged 26 years....Memphis Daily Appeal, 9/13/1857.

A young man named Wm. **FORSYTH** fell from the third story window of the Commercial Hotel last evening, about 8 o'clock, and was instantly killed. The deceased was a saddler by trade, and had been in the city but a short time. His relatives live in Macon, Ga. Memphis Daily Appeal, 9/22/1859.

Died. At his late residence near Potersville, Tipton county, Tenn., on the 2d instant, Mr. E. **FOSTER**. City and Nashville papers please copy. Memphis Appeal, 12/19/1854.

Died, at the residence of her father, Robert **HILL**, in Tipton county, Mrs. L. W. P. Foster, consort of R. T. **FOSTER**, on the morning of the 10th inst., at half past 12 o'clock, in the 21st year of her age, leaving an affectionate husband, one child and numerous friends to mourn her loss. Memphis Appeal, 5/20/1851.

Married, On Wednesday, the 18th ult., by the Rev. Robert **PAYNE**, Turner **FOSTER**, Esq., of Memphis to Ann Eliza, daughter of Col. John S. **WILSON**, of this county.—Florence Gaz. Weekly Appeal, 3/13/1846.

Died on the 17th June last, at the residence of his son Doctor W. N. **FOSTER**, Salem Miss., Anthony D. **FOSTER**, Esq. of Hardeman county, Tenn., in the 63d year of his age. Mr. Foster was formerly a resident of Wilkes co. N.C. emigrated to Tennessee in 1819 and to this county in 1827...Middleburg, Tenn., July 24, '48. Memphis Appeal, 7/26/1848.

Many of our readers, and particularly our brother firemen will regret to hear that Charles **FOULK**, or more familearly known as Charley Mason, was drowned from the steamer Europa while descending White river, about one hundred miles from the mouth, last week. He attempted to pass around the guards of the boat, which were crowded with cattle, and was gored in the side by one of them, and knocked into the river. The engines were stopped immediately, but efforts to save him were unavailing. He was a member of Invincible Fire Company of this city. He had but recently removed to New Orleans with a sister and four female children, who have thus suddenly been deprived of their dependence and protection. Memphis Evening Ledger, 2/1/1858.

Died, On the 28th inst., Marcellus A., son of G. P. **FOUTE**, Esq. The friends of the family are invited to attend the funeral of the deceased at 3 ½ o'clock P.M., To-Day, from Grace Church. Memphis Daily Appeal, 9/30/1859. Died, On the 11th instant, Hazelhurst, son of G. P. and J. C. Foute, in the 5th year of his age....Memphis Daily Appeal, 10/12/1859.

Married, On the 13th instant at the residence of the bride's father, by Rev. P. L. **HENDERSON**, Mr. F. G. **FOWLER**, of South Carolina, to Miss Lou A. **MURDAUGH**, of Kossuth, Miss. Memphis Daily Appeal, 3/18/1859.

I intend to move south; I therefore offer for sale that beautiful cottage residence on the Pigeon Roost Road, in the suburbs of Memphis, one mile from the Mississippi river. It contains eight and seven on hundredth acres, subdivided into five lots...Reference is made to T. S. **AYRES**, Esq., my near neighbor....Also one lot 70 by 165 feet, in South Memphis, on Shelby street, about two squares north of F. P. **STANTON's** residence. J. W. **FOWLER**. American Eagle Weekly, 12/26/1845.

Married—On Tuesday evening last, by Rev. Philip **ALSTON**, John W. **FOWLER**, Esq., Sheriff of Shelby County, to Miss Caroline, daughter of W. J. **OLDHAM** Esq., of Coahoma county, Miss. Memphis Enquirer, Friday, 5/17/1839. Died—In this place on Friday evening last of billious fever, Mrs. Caroline Fowler, consort of Jno. W. Fowler, Esq., and second daughter of Col. W. J. **OLDHAM**, of Coahoma county, Miss., in the 18th year of her age. Memphis Enquirer, Fri., 8/9/1839.

Died, On Wednesday morning, March 20th, of Bronchitis, Willie O., only son of John W. and Louise **FOWLER**. Aged 3 years, 6 months and 27 days. Memphis Eagle, 3/21/1850.

Married, On Wednesday, the 6th inst., by Rt. Rev. J. H. **OTEY** at the residence of R. A. **PARKER**, Esq., Col. John W. **FOWLER** to Mrs. Rosa **EAGLE**, of this city. Memphis Daily Appeal, 1/7/1858.

Died—On Sunday morning, 9th inst., of congestive fever, Lawrence Decatur, aged seven years; only son of Austin and Amelia **FOWLKES**. American Eagle, Fri., 11/14/1845.

Married, In Davidson county, on the 24th ult., Dr. Jeptha **FOWLKES** of this city, to Mrs. Maria J. **WARD**. Weekly Appeal, 2/13/1846. Died: In this city, of consumption, yesterday morning, Mrs. Maria Fowlkes, wife of Dr. J. Fowlkes, in the 34th year of her age. She was highly esteemed by all who knew her.— *Enquirer* of yesterday. Weekly Memphis Eagle, 2/8/1849. Married, On Tuesday evening the 26th inst., by the Rev. G. W. **COONS**, Dr. Jeptha Fowlkes, Editor of the Express, to Mrs. Sarah **LAMB**, all of this city. Memphis Appeal, 10/28/1852. Dr. Jeptha Fowlkes has been elected President of the Farmers' & Merchants' Bank of this city, and James T. **LEATH** Cashier, by the new directory.....Memphis Appeal, 3/24/1853. Died. On the morning of the 26th, an infant daughter of Jeptha L. and Mary C. Fowlkes, aged about two years. Memphis Appeal, 7/28/1854.

Married, In Somerville, Tennessee, July 16(?), 1857, by Rev. Mr. Wilson, Mr. Thos. Jefferson **FOWLKES**(?), of Memphis, to Miss Julia A., daughter of Mr. Wm. **BURTON**, of Somerville. Memphis Daily Appeal, 7/18/1857. The friends and acquaintances of T. _. Fowlkes are requested to attend the funeral of his wife, Julia A. Fowlkes....This Morning....from the residence of S. **FOWLKES** on Adams street....Memphis Daily Appeal, 2/18/1859.

Report of the Board of Health. For the last 24 hours so far as Reported, June 26th...John **FRANK**, aged 37, Inflammation of Bowels...Memphis Enquirer, 6/27/1849.

Married, On the 13th January, by Rev. Dr. Haasel (?), Mr. T. F. **FRANK**, of Memphis, Tenn., to Miss Emily **DIETZ**, of this city.—*Chillicothe Ohio Correspondent*, Jan. 17th. Memphis Eagle & Enquirer, 2/7/1852.

Died, Of congestive chill, on the 11th of July, at 8 o'clock A.M., near her residence at Early Grove, Miss., Mrs. A. A. Franklin, wife of C. B. **FRANKLIN**. Memphis Daily Appeal, 7/16/1859.

Isaac **FRANKLIN** late of Sumner county, Tenn., died on the 24th of April last. He began life as a boatman, and in that capacity commenced the acquisition of a fortune which, at the time of his death exceeded a million of dollars. He had large estates in the Parish of West Feliciana, La., independent of an immense estate in Tenn...he so disposed of his property in this State, as that one-third of it should, whatever might be the number of his children at his death, go to the Seminary in Sumner county.... Moreover, the will provides, that it shall be built on his plantation in Sumner county, the selected retreat of his declining years...The revenues arising from the property, says the will, are to laid out in building proper and suitable edifices on my Fairvue Plantation, in the county of Sumner...American Eagle, 10/15/1846.

Drs. J. H. & J. W. **FRANKLIN**, Having permanently located in Memphis, offer their professional services to the citizens thereof, and its vicinity. Office in Chase & Gibbs' new building, South East corner of Exchange Square. Residence on Poplar street, near the Presbyterian Church. The Appeal, 7/7/1843.

Died—On Sunday the 5th inst., near Lagrange, Ten., Mr. James H. **FRANKLIN**, (son of Peachy **FRANKLIN**, dec'd, formerly of New Glasgow, Va.) aged about 26 years. The Appeal, 5/24/1844.

Died, On yesterday, August 26th, Mary, beloved daughter of Joseph and Sophia **FRANKLIN**. Memphis Daily Appeal, 8/27/1856.

Died, In La Grange, Tenn., May 18th, Martha G., infant daughter of Thomas D. and M. L. **FRANKLIN**, aged eight months and thirteen days. Memphis Eagle & Enquirer, 5/22/1852.

Married—By Rev. J. E. **DOUGLAS**, May 30, in Fayette county, Tenn., Mr. William H. **FRANKS** and Miss F. J. **ROBERTSON**. Memphis Daily Avalanche, 6/4/1859.

It will be remembered that some days ago Gasper **FRANSIOLA**, who with his brother keeps a saloon on Front Row, below Madison street, was stabbed in a difficulty with a man from East Tennessee. The wound was in the back, and Fransiola lingered until Monday morning, when he died....Memphis Daily Appeal, Wed., 3/30/1859.

J. A. **FRANSIOLI** & Co., Importers & General Dealers in China & Glass Ware, Memphis, Tenn. Weekly Appeal, 9/5/1845.

Upon the death of Gertrude Frayser, eldest daughter of Dr. John R. **FRAYSER**...Although scarce twelve years of age, she possessed all the attributes, both in mind and manner, of a girl far more advanced in years...Memphis Eagle, 11/26/1850.

We have inadvertently omitted to make editorial mention of the appointment of our esteemed fellow-citizen, Ceylon B. **FRAZER**, Esq., Inspector-General, with the rank of Brigadier-General...Memphis Appeal, 11/18/1851. It becomes our painful duty to record the death of a prominent member of the Memphis bar—a warm-hearted gentleman, a zealous and devoted friend, an affectionate husband, and an exemplary citizen—Gen. Ceylon B. Frazer. Gen. Frazer died on Sunday night last, at his residence in this city, of inflammatory sore throat, after a severe season of suffering, lasting about one week. He leaves a wife and four children to mourn his sudden and premature loss....His funeral will take place this morning at 10 o'clock from his residence on the Hernando road. Memphis Weekly Appeal, Wed., 3/24/1858.

Married, On Thursday evening, the 13th inst., by the Rev. W. B. **BEAVER**, Jeremiah **FRAZER**, Esq., to Miss Emily Wall, daughter of Frederick **WALL**, Esq., all of Fayette county, Tenn. Memphis Appeal, 11/21/1851.

Died, At Mount Ancient, Jackson county, Ala., on the 5th day of May, 1856, Abner **FRAZIER**, aged about fifty-five years. Memphis Daily Appeal, 6/4/1856.

Died, On the 30th ult., Abner Sanford, son of Rev. Robt. And Isabella C. **FRAZIER**, aged one month. Memphis Daily Appeal, 7/1/1856.

Married, by the Rev. Amos **CLEAVER**, on Thursday, 20th inst., at the residence of her father, in Madison county, Miss Virginia, eldest daughter of Col. Jesse **PERKINS**, to T. A. **FREELAND**, Esq., of Claiborne county. Memphis Eagle & Enquirer, 6/1/1852.

Married, On Tuesday evening, the 26th ult., by Rev. B.(?) S. **GILL**, Mr. Thos. J. **FREEMAN** to Miss Josephine R. Williamson, daughter of Mr. Jas. S. **WILLIAMSON**, all of Panola county, Miss. Memphis Daily Appeal, 11/2/1858.

Died, In Hardeman county, Tenn., Mr. Martin **FREWITT**, on the 16th February, 1858, aged about 73 years. Columbia (_.C.) papers please copy. Memphis Daily Appeal, 2/19/1858.

Married, On the 12th inst., at the residence of Gardiner **FRIERSON**, Esq., by the Rev. J. H. **GRAY**, Thomas H. **JACKSON**, Esq., of New Orleans, to Miss Seraphina R. D. **FRIERSON**, of this city. Memphis Appeal, 8/14/1851.

M. B. **FRIERSON**, Sec. Board of Health. Memphis Daily Appeal, 6/27/1848. Married: In this city, on Thursday evening, by Rev. Dr. Page, Milton B. Frierson, M.D., to Miss Cassia P., daughter of Dr. L. **SHANKS**, both of this city. Memphis Eagle, Saturday, 9/30/1848. The friends and acquaintances of Dr. M. B. Frierson and lady are invited to attend the burial of their son, James W. S. Frierson, this (Sunday) evening, at 3 o'clock, from their residence on Market street. March 13, 1853. Memphis Eagle & Enquirer.

Died, In this city on the evening of the 25th inst., of congestive chill, Mr. Geo. _. **FROST**, aged twenty-four years and eight months. Cincinnati papers please copy. Memphis Daily Appeal, 6/28/1859.

Married, On the 11th inst. at the residence of Mr. Hawthorne, by Rev. John **BATEMAN**, Mr. J. E. **FROST** to Miss Tennessee **OLIVER**. Memphis Weekly Appeal, 11/24/1858.

Married, in Georgetown, Ohio, on the 20th ult., by the Rev. J. R. **GIBSON**, Mr. J. T. **FULFORD**, of Memphis, Tenn. to Miss Mary Ann **KING**, of the former place. Memphis Enquirer, 8/5/1848.

Married, On the morning of the 24th inst., by Rev. Dr. Glover, at the residence of Major Duncan, near Raleigh, Tenn., Mr. Henry H. **FULLER** and Miss Kate **DUNCAN**. Memphis Daily Avalanche, 1/25/1859.

Married, On the 27th inst., at Hickory Wythe Springs, Fayette county, Mr. James T. **FULLER**, of New Orleans, to Miss Lucy A. Trezevant, daughter of L. C. **TREZEVANT**, Esq. Memphis Enquirer, 7/30/1848.

The friends and acquaintances of Mr. and Mrs. W. S. **FULTON** are requested to attend the funeral of their daughter, Flora, from their residence on Mosby street This Day at 2 o'clock P.M. Memphis Daily Appeal, 11/24/1857. The friends and acquaintances of Mr. and Mrs. W. S. Fulton are invited to attend the funeral of their son, George Philler, from their residence on Mosby street, This (Thursday) Morning, at 9 A.M. Memphis Daily Appeal, 12/3/1857.

Married, On Thursday evening, the 16th instant, at the residence of Capt. A. B. **SHAW**, in this city, by Rev. Geo. W. **COONS**, Dr. Danl. W. **FUNK** to Miss Ann E. **McLANE**. Memphis Eagle, 5/18/1850.

George C. **FURBER**, Attorney and Counsellor at Law, Germantown, Tenn. The Appeal, 10/4/1844. Married, on this morning, the 14th instant, by Friends ceremony before E. **HARRISON**, Esq., Geo. G. Furber, Esq. of Memphis, Tenn., to Sarah H. Jones, daughter of Aquila **JONES**, of this city…Cin. Times…Memphis Appeal, 10/3/1848.

Joseph W. **FURBER**, formerly of Germantown in this county, and the author of a work on the Mexican War, has been appointed and confirmed Marshal of Minnesota, vice H. L. **TILDEN**, removed. Memphis Eagle & Enquirer, 2/27/1852.

All persons indebted to the Estate of Martin **FURLONG**, dec'd. are requested to make payment…Wm. **CARSON**, Ad'mr. Memphis Appeal, 11/19/1851.

We take pleasure in calling attention to the card of James V. **FUSSELL**, who has established himself in this city, in the commission business….Memphis Daily Appeal, 7/18/1856.

We are pained to learn that Mr. L. W. **FUSSELL** died suddenly at the residence of his brother in this city. Mr. F. served through the Mexican war with credit to himself; at the hard fought battle of Cerro Gordo, he was severely wounded. He was formerly Sheriff of Davidson county in this State….At the time of his decease he was in the prime of life, being only thirty-eight years of age….His remains were deposited in a cenotaph, and a dispatch sent to his family….Memphis Daily Appeal, 1/27/1857.

Married, On the 12th inst., DeSoto county, Miss., by Rev. Wm. **WELCH**, Lafayette **GABBERT**, M.D., of Arkansas, to Miss Mary Jane **McCORKLE**. Memphis Daily Appeal, 1/16/1858.

The members of the Temperance Legion are requested to meet at the Cumberland Church to-night…. Lycurgus **GABBERT**, Sec'y. Daily Enquirer, 6/22/1847.

The friends and acquaintances of Dr. M. **GABBERT** and family are requested to attend the Funeral of his wife, Elizabeth Gabbert, this evening at 3 o'clock, from his residence on Vance street. Memphis Appeal, 10/26/1852. It is with sincere regret that we have to announce the death of one of our oldest and most esteemed citizens, Dr. Gabbert. He breathed his last on Wednesday evening last, and was attended to his grave yesterday by a large circle of friends….In connection with his profession, Dr. Gabbert has filled several chairs in our Medical Colleges…Memphis Daily Appeal, Fri., 10/12/1855.

Married. On the evening of the 6th inst. at Cynthiana, Harrison County, Ky., by Rev. Samuel **RODGERS**, A. Jackson **GAINES**, of Batesville, to Miss Mary E. **REDMON**. The parties arrived on the A. L. Shotwell and have taken residence at the Gayoso, en route for their home on the beautiful White, of Arkansas…. Batesville Standard and Little Rock Democrat please copy. Memphis Daily Appeal, 3/21/1855.

We feel authorized to call a meeting of the people of Memphis, to meet at 4 o'clock, This Evening, at Hightower Hall, to make arrangements to pay the respect due to the memory of Maj. Gen. Edmund Pendleton **GAINES**, recently deceased….Memphis owes more to Gen. Gaines, as a valuable citizen for several years, as a good man, and as the projector of the great works of improvement proposed to centre here, than any other man on the globe….Memphis Enquirer, 6/13/1849.

Died, At his daughter's residence in DeSoto county, Miss., on the 9th day of November, 1856, in the ninety-second year of his age, Henry **GAINES**….Memphis Daily Appeal, 12/11/1856.

Major J. P. **GAINES** has sold his farm and negroes, and intends taking his family to Oregon, with a view of locating there permanently. Memphis Eagle, 11/22/1849.

We are authorized to announce P. G. **GAINES**, Esq., as a candidate for the office of Brigadier General, for the 23d Brigade of Tennessee Militia, composed of the counties of Shelby and Fayette. Memphis Enquirer, 11/14/1846. Died, On Thursday morning (14th inst.) in this city, Gen. P. G. **GAINS**, in the 60th year of his age. The subject of this notice was born in Robertson county, in this State, and removed to the Western District in 1829. For the past 20 years, he has been a resident of Memphis. As a member of the legal profession...In 1839 he was elected a member of the Legislature from Shelby county...Denied the enjoyment arising out of the ties of a domestic relation, all the purer feelings of his soul seemed merged in sentiments of general benevolence and sympathetic charity...O'er his dying couch bent no relation to soothe the mortal anguish...Memphis Appeal, 8/18/1851.

Married, By the Rev. R. A. **FEE**, Dr. B. R. **GAITHER**, of Tipton, Tenn., to Miss Mary J. **GRAVES**, of Tippah, Miss. Memphis Eagle & Enquirer, 6/5/1853.

Married, On Thursday afternoon at the residence of the bride's father, by Rev. R. C. **GRUNDY**, D.D., Mr. Duncan **GALBREATH**, of the firm of Meacham & Galbreath, to Miss Haddie Orne, youngest daughter of Capt. R. H. **ORNE**, all of this city. Memphis Daily Appeal, Sat., 7/10/1858.

Having disposed of my entire interest in the concern of Williams & Gale to J. D. **WILLIAMS**, I would respectfully solicit for him a continuance of the patronage so liberally bestowed on us. In withdrawing from trade in Memphis, I have many regrets, and but one consideration could induce me to do so, the restoration of my health. I came to Memphis when it was but a village, and have seen it prosper and grow into a flourishing city...Tom **GALE**. Memphis Eagle, 10/16/1848.

Died, in this city, on Thursday, the 27th inst., Mr. Michael **GALLAGHER**, in the 77th year of his age. The deceased was born in the county of Tyrone, Ireland, but has been for a period of many years a citizen of the United States...Uniformly an edifying member of the Catholic church, he died regretted by a large number of relations and friends, in the brightest hope of a happy immortality. Tri-Weekly Memphis Enquirer, 8/29/1846.

Married, In this city on the 1st December, inst. by the Rev. Michael **McALEAR**, P.C. **GALLAHER**, attorney at law, to Mary W., daughter of the late John **GALLAGHER**, Esq. of Moulton, Ala. The Appeal, 12/6/1844. The friends and acquaintances of P. C. Gallagher, Esq. are requested to attend his funeral from his late residence on Adams Street, over the Bayou, this morning at 10 ½ o'clock. Daily Enquirer, 10/28/1847. Died, on the 27th ultimo, at his residence in this city, Patrick C. Gallagher, Esq., a native of county Donnagal Ireland—aged 40 years. The deceased had been for the last few years a respected citizen of this place. As a member of the bar he was an ornament to his profession.....He has left among others to mourn his untimely loss, a young and devoted wife, whose only consolation under so heart-breaking a bereavement was, that she received his last sigh, breathing a lively hope of a blessed immortality. Daily Enquirer, 11/7/1847.

Married, On the 15th ult., by Rev. Mr. Eakin, W. T. **GALLAWAY**, of Fayette county, Tenn., to Miss Elizabeth **WALL**, of Marshall county, Miss. Memphis Daily Appeal, 1/19/1859.

Having been duly qualified as Administrator of John **GALLOWAY**, deceased, all persons having claims against his estate are hereby notified to present them....O. M. **ALSUP**, Administrator, with will annexed. Memphis Daily Appeal, 1/27/1859.

Hall of Morning Sun Lodge No. 144, April 11, 1856} Whereas, Information having reached us of the death of our beloved brother, R. E.(?) **GALLOWAY**....Resolved, That Woodlawn Lodge No. 211 has our thanks for the part it took in the funeral obsequies of our departed brother. Resolved, That a copy of these resolutions be sent to his bereaved family....Memphis Daily Appeal, 4/24/1856.

Married, On Wednesday evening, 2d inst., by Rev. Mr. Starks, Mr. Thomas W. **GAMEWELL**, of Jackson, Tenn., to Miss Mary Ann **PARKER**, of this city. American Eagle, 4/4/1845.

On Monday evening a sad accident occurred at the levee near the foot of Beale street, which resulted in the death of a man named John **GANAN**....It seems that Ganan and his companions were working on the sand privilege of Mr. Leake and others, and had made an excavation into the side of the bluff some four or five yards deep, when suddenly the overhanging portions gave way and fell with great force upon the three men. Ganan's head was badly mashed, his skull being broken and his brain exposed....Memphis Daily Avalanche, Wed., 4/20/1859.

Married, On the evening of the 10th instant by James **ROSE**, Justice of the Peace, Mr. Christian **GANTENLINE** to Miss Rebecca **McKONLEY**. Memphis Eagle & Enquirer, 2/13/1853.

Married, On Sunday evening by Rev. R. C. **GRUNDY**, at the residence of Mr. Starks, in the vicinity of North Memphis, Mr. John **GARCELON**, of Boston, to Miss R. **WHITAKER**, of Charleston, Va. Memphis Daily Appeal, Tues., 5/31/1859.

Married, At the Gayoso House, on the 19th inst., by Rev. Samuel **WATSON**, of this city, Mr. Ed. A. **GARLAND**, of Rome, Ga., to Mrs. Nannie I. **WILLIAMS**, of Sardis, Miss. Augusta, Ga., papers please copy. Memphis Daily Appeal, 10/20/1859.

Married, On the 25th ultimo by Rev. J. W. **KNOTT**, Mr. B. G. **GARRETT** and Miss M. A. **COLLINS**, all of this city. Memphis Daily Appeal, 1/1/1857.

Married, In New York, September 20th by Rev. Mr. Clapp, Miss Augusta **BROWNE**, the well-known and distinguished musical composer and authoress, of this city, and Mr. J. W. B. **GARRETT**, a distinguished young artist, of Memphis, Tenn.—Home Journal. Memphis Daily Appeal, 10/14/1855. Our friend, the celebrated *artiste*, Mr. J.W.B. Garrett, Esq., will leave this or tomorrow morning for the East, for the purpose of soon locating in Louisville, Ky....Memphis Daily Appeal, 1/12/1856.

Land For Sale. The subscriber now offers for sale the valuable tract of land on which he now lives, in Haywood county, near the Big Hatchie turnpike, and within one mile and a half of steam-boat navigation...There is 935 acres in the tract...There is a good comfortable dwelling-house...Kenneth **GARRETT**. Memphis Enquirer, 1/14/1837. Died, At his residence four miles east of Memphis, on Wednesday night last, of consumption, Kenneth Garrett, in the 52d year of his age. Memphis Appeal, Friday, 11/12/1852. On tomorrow, the 17th, Mr. H. G. **SPRUILL**, Executor of Kenneth Garrett, will sell a large quanity of valuable lands, located about four miles from the city and fronting on the Raleigh and State Line Plank Roads.....Memphis Eagle & Enquirer, 1/16/1853.

Married—At Raleigh, Shelby County, on the second inst., by the Rev. William **WHITSITT**, Mr. B. S. **GARRISON**, to Miss Sarah C. **BRYAN**. Memphis Enquirer, 3/21/1836. Died—On the 29th (?) ult., William Loudon, infant son of W. B. S. and Sophia E. Garrison. American Eagle, 7/4/1845. All persons having claims against the estate of W. B. S. Garrison dec'd., are required by this notice, to present them to W. B. **WALDRAN**.....Sophiah E. **GARRISON**, W. B. **WALDRAN**, Executors. Memphis Eagle, 5/3/1849.

Tribute Of Respect. Chickasaw Lodge, No. 8, I.O.O.F. Whereas, It has pleased Divine Providence, in his wisdom to take from our midst our friend and brother, John A. **GARRISON** ....Memphis Daily Appeal, 2/4/1857.

The Rev. Samuel **DENNIS**, of Mississippi, will preach the funeral sermon of the late Mrs. S. E. **GARRISON**, at the Cumberland Presbyterian Church in this city on to-morrow at 10 ½ o'clock. Memphis Daily Appeal, 5/24/1856.

Died, On the 4th inst., Mrs. Rosannah, consort of Thos. S. **GARRISON**, near Hickory With, in the 51st year of her age. Memphis Daily Appeal, 12/9/1856.

Married, On Tuesday evening, 26th instant, by Rev. R. C. **GRUNDY**, D.D., at the residence of the bride's mother, in the vicinity of Memphis, Horace _. **GARTH**, of Paducah, Ky., to Miss Alice D., eldest daughter of the late William L. **JONES**. Memphis Daily Appeal, 4/28/1859.

Died, On the 1st of August, Elvira Ann, daughter of F. C. and Mary A. R. **GARTRELL**, aged one year. Memphis Daily Appeal, 9/14/1856. Died, On the 13th of April, 1858, in Desoto county, Miss., Mrs. _. C. Gartrell, consort of Dr. F. C. Gartrell. Memphis Weekly Appeal, 4/21/1858.

Married, In DeSoto county, Miss., on the 12th inst., Dr. J. C. **GARTRELL** to Mrs. Louisa **HARMAN**. Memphis Daily Appeal, 2/18/1859.

Died, of Pneumonia, at his residence in DeSoto county, Miss., on the 27th of December, 1858, William C. **GARTRELL**, aged 35 years, 4 months and 27 days. The deceased was born in Abbeville District, S. C., July 29th, 1822....He professed religion in 1841, and united with the Baptist Church....In his untimely demise, his heartbroken wife has lost an affectionate husband, his two orphan children, who are too young to realize their irreparable loss, have been deprived of the wholesome admonition and instruction of an indulgent father....Memphis Daily Avalanche, 1/25/1859.

Coroner Waldran held an inquest over the body of a man found in the river yesterday, whose name is supposed to be Michael **GARVIN**, from a letter found on his person. He appeared to have been but a short time in the water. Memphis Evening Ledger, 10/27/1857.

The friends and acquaintances of Philip **GARVIN** are respectfully requested to attend the funeral of his infant son, from his residence on Alabama street, at 3 o'clock this evening. Memphis Daily Appeal, 7/30/1856.

The friends of Mr. Phillip and Catherine **GARVIN** are invited to attend the funeral of their son John R., on Sunday the 3d at 2 o'clock, from their residence on Thornton Avenue. Memphis Daily Appeal, 5/2/1857.

A German named Jacob **GATEKURST** died yesterday morning from the effects of drinking too much water after being much heated. He was a blacksmith by trade and was in employ at Wedgwood's shop on Main street. Memphis Daily Appeal, 9/23/1855.

Died, On Monday morning, 29th inst., at her father's residence, of disease of the bowels, Sarah Elizabeth, infant daughter of Saml. M. and Lucy L. **GATES**, aged 8 months and 8 days. Memphis Eagle, 7/30/1850.

Died, At the residence of his father, Maj. William A. **GATES**, Fayette county, Tenn., on the 21st instant, Lafayette A. J. J. **GATES**, in the 14th year of his age. Memphis Eagle, 5/3/1850.

Died, On Sabbath morning, Richard Samuel, infant son of R. B. and Elizabeth **GATLING**. The funeral will take place at 10 o'clock this morning from their residence on Vance street, South Memphis.... Memphis Eagle, Mon., 12/25/1848.

Married, On the 11th inst. in this city, at the Synagogue, by Rev. J. J. **PERES**, Dr. J. M. **GAUS** and Miss Charlotte **MARCUSE**....Memphis Daily Appeal, 10/12/1859.

Mr. Chas. **GAY** has opened a new French restaurant on Washington street, between Main and First alley....Memphis Daily Appeal, 12/22/1859.

Died, Yesterday, of congestion of the lungs, George W. **GAY**, Clerk of the steamer St. Francis No. 3, aged about 30 years. The friends and acquaintances of the deceased are invited to attend his funeral, from the residence of S. M. **PICKERELL**, on Exchange street at 10 o'clock this morning. Memphis Daily Appeal, 8/16/1859.

Married. At the residence of H. G. **DENT** on Thursday morning, May 3, by Rev. Mr. **WILLIAMSON**, Mr. Samuel M. Jo_ _ and Miss Fannie J. **GAYLE**, all of this city. Memphis Whig, 5/4/1855.

Baptist Church, Second, between Adams and Washington, Rev. P S. **GAYLE**. Daily Enquirer, 2/28/1847. Died, Suddenly on Wednesday, June the 8th, at Clinton, Miss., Rev. Peter S. Gayle. Mr. Gayle was for some years pastor of one of the Baptist Churches in this city and enjoyed an extensive acquaintance throughout West Tennessee.....Memphis Appeal, 6/15/1853.

Married, On the evening of the 5th instant at the residence of T. B. **NORMEN_**, Esq., by Rev. C. C. **CONNER**, Dr. Thos. C. **GAYLE**, of Memphis, and Miss M. A. **ECKFORD**, of Aberdeen, Miss. Memphis Daily Appeal, 3/7/1857.

Married, at Bolivar, on the 29th November by Rev'd Mr. Peck, Mr. Charles W. **GAZZAM**, of Cincinnati, to Miss Clementina Lea, daughter of Mr. John **LEA**, merchant, of Bolivar. Memphis Advocate, 12/8/1827.

Died. At the residence of her husband, Bedford county, on the 3d inst., Mrs. Merideth P. **GENTRY**. Memphis Appeal, 3/17/1854.

The Post Master at Purdy writes us that J. E. **GEORGE** has left the State, and requests us to stop his paper. Memphis Enquirer, 2/15/1839.

Information Wanted. The undersigned having just arrived in Memphis from Germany, desires to meet with Miss Lucia **KINN**, a German lady and a resident of Memphis some three months.... Joseph **GERINGER**. Memphis Appeal, 11/3/1854.

Died, on Wednesday evening last, Ella Catherine, infant daughter of Thomas and Catherine D. **GHOLSON**, aged 1 year and 9 months. Memphis Appeal, Fri., 2/11/1848.

Notice. In consequence of the death of Wm. T. **GHOLSON**, a member of the firm of Bayliss, Hart & Co., notice is hereby given that the firm of Bayliss, Hart & Co., is consequently dissolved. Memphis Enquirer, 8/26/1837.

The undersigned has just received his stock of Rich Cloths, Cassimers and Vestings ...A. F. **GIBBS**, Merchant Tailor, Madison st. Daily Enquirer, 11/4/1847. Married, On Tuesday, the 8th inst., by the Rev. Dr. Grey, Mr. A. F. Gibbs, to Miss E. J. **WARD**; all of this city. Memphis Eagle, 1/11/1850.

Married. In this city on Thursday 8th inst. by the Rev. Mullen, Geo. Cooper **GIBBS** of New Orleans, to Elizabeth A., second daughter of the late Spencer W. **ELCAN**. American Eagle, 4/15/1847. Died. At the residence of her mother, in this city, on Tuesday, the 23d May, in the 20th year of her age, Elizabeth Elcan, consort of Geo. C. Gibbs, of N. Orleans. Memphis Eagle, 5/27/1848.

Died, On the 9th inst. in this city, Dr. Thomas F. **GIBBS**, late of Georgia, aged sixty-three years. His friends and acquaintances, and those of R. F. and Frank Y. **GIBBS**, P. W. **HARRIS** and C. M. **VERNON**, are invited to attend his funeral to-day at eleven o'clock A.M., from his residence, No. 115 Main street, near Poplar street. Memphis Daily Appeal, 12/10/1859. Departed this life in the city of Memphis on the morning of the 9th inst....Dr. Thomas Fortson Gibbs, in the 64th year of his age. Dr. Gibbs was a native of Eibert county, Ga., and the grandson of Thomas **FORTSON**, one of the earliest and most venerated settlers of Northern Georgia....He was the son of the Rev. William **GIBBS**, and descended from a very ancient English family who settled in Virginia long before the Revolution. This family came into England with William the Conqueror, from Normandy, and intermarried with that daring clan in Scotland....Nor was the subject of this notice a degenerate representative of this time-honored race....measuring six feet six inches in hight....William Gibbs, the father of Dr. Gibbs, enlisted as a soldier at the age of 16 under his relative Capt. Churchill **GIBBS**; was actively engaged in several of the hardest fought battles, and was present at the surrender of Cornwallis....Memphis Daily Appeal, 12/25/1859.

Died. In this city on Wednesday, the 4th instant, Mrs. H. P. Gibson. The friends and acquaintances of Arthur D. **GIBSON** and the family are requested to attend the funeral....Memphis Whig, 5/5/1855.

Married, On Thursday, the 22d inst., at the residence of S. F. **HALLMAN**, by Rev. Dr. White, Mr. David **GIBSON** to Miss Annie **DUNBAR**—all of this city. Louisville papers copy. Memphis Daily Appeal, 12/25/1859.

Married—On Wednesday evening last by Rev. M. Gray, Mr. 1. Y. **GIBSON** to Miss Catherine, daughter of H. **VAN PELT**, Esq. all of this city. The Tri-Weekly Memphis Enquirer, Saturday, 6/13/1846. Died in this city on the forenoon of Tuesday last, Mrs. Catharine J. Gibson, late consort of Mr. Isaac Y. Gibson, and daughter of the senior editor of this paper—aged twenty three years. She had been slightly indisposed for several days, but no serious apprehensions were entertained either by her physicians or her friends, until a few hours before her dissolution. Less than half a year has passed since we took up our pen to record the demise of our eldest daughter, and now we are called up to discharge a like painful and heart-rending duty to our next. The bridal garments in which she was arrayed a little less than three brief months since, have been exchanged for the habitments of the grave. The fond anticipation of a devoted husband of many coming years of wedded happiness have been suddenly crushed, and his hearth made desolate, the young sisters feel that they have lost a second mother, and the fond father that he is almost left alone. Yes, of seven children presented us by a devoted and deeply lamented wife, there are now but two. Two were cut off in their infancy; then followed their angel-mother—a third was called away in the innocent and beautiful girlhood......--Appeal. The Tri-Weekly Memphis Enquirer, Saturday, 9/5/1846. Married, At the residence of Judge Barry, on Tuesday evening, 9th September, by the Rev. T. L. **GRACE**, Mr. I. Y. Gibson, to Miss Rebecca **MOORE**, all of the city of Memphis. Memphis Appeal, 9/11/1851.

Married. On Wednesday evening, the 6th inst., by the Rev. Dr. Warren, Mr. J.(?) Y. **GIBSON**, to Miss M. A. W. **ABELL**, all of this city. American Eagle, 10/14/1847.

Mrs. Mary A. Gibson, consort of L.(?) Y. **GIBSON**, is no more! The subject of this memoir ceased to live and suffer on earth this morning at sunrise...The balmy influence which this whole death-bed scene had over the by-standers, and the aching heart of her husband can never be forgotten...Memphis, Tenn., April 30, '50. Memphis Eagle, 5/1/1850.

We are authorized to announce Jas. **GIFT** as a candidate for 2nd Major in the 128th Regiment Tennessee Militia. Memphis Enquirer, 4/20/1836. Died, At his residence in Shelby county, Ten., on the 17th inst. of Pleuro-Pneumonia, Mr. James Gift, aged 50 years and 2 days. The deceased was born in Montgomery county, Tenn., February 15th, 1803. He leaves a wife and nine children and many friends to mourn his irreparable loss. Eagle & Enquirer and San Francisco (Cal.) papers please copy. Memphis Appeal, 2/21/1853.

The following letter from our esteemed fellow-countryman, Col. W. W. **GIFT**, to the senior editor of the *Appeal*, will be read with much interest, especially by those of our citizens feeling an interest in the fortunes of many who have left our city and vicinity in search of the New Eldorado. San Francisco, Dec. 14th, 1850. My Dear Van Pelt.—The pleasant recollections of old Tennessee and very many kind friends, prompts me to address you a few lines...Our worthy friend and fellow-townsman, Wm. H. **LAUDERDALE**, died here on the 3rd inst., of Typhoid Fever. His father was up in the mines and as yet, is not apprised of the death of his son. Dr. **WHEATON** is here, also Chas. **STEWART** and Son, Jno. **McKEON** and Mr. **HOUSTON**. Robt. **ANDERSON** and young Wyatt have left for Stockton, where they will meet Maj. **WYATT**. H. H. **MEANS** is at Stockton...Wm. M. **PERKINS** is here, well, with a dairy, making money. Jo. **DUN** (?) is here with **MORAN** in the auction business, and it promises well. James **RICE** jr., is here in a good practice. Jesse D. **CARR** is here, and has made a large fortune—some say $200,000....Benj. **DOWEL** has been here but left; Dr. **CURTIS** and Brother are at Sacramento City, both well. Maj. **GILLIS** is in the mines doing very well, better than any of his Tennessee friends...Memphis Appeal, 1/28/1851. We find the following flattering notice of our former friend and fellow citizen, Col. W. W. Gift in the San Jose correspondence of the Alta Californian. Col. Gift we believe is Seargent at Arms in the California House of Assembly...Memphis Appeal, 5/13/1851. We learn that our former fellow-citizen, Col. Wm. Gift, of California, arrived in our city yesterday. Memphis Appeal, 4/12/1853. We were yesterday visited by two distinguished citizens of California, Col. W. W. Gift and Mr. G. P. **JOHNSON**, of San Francisco, late deputy Marshall of that State. Col. Gift.....has been appointed Register of the Land Office by the President, a position for which he is well fitted. Memphis Appeal, 4/14/1853. Married, At the residence of Col. Wm. W. Gift, near Martinez, California, October 15th, 1856, by Rev. S. Woodbridge, Miss Rachel J. **GIFT**, formerly of this county, and Mr. William F. **WOOD**, of Shasta, California, formerly of Saline county, Missouri. Memphis Daily Appeal, 11/21/1856.

Died, At his residence in Smithville, Tenn., on the 19th inst., Joseph **GILBERT**, father of our fellow-citizen, John V. **GILBERT**, and officer in the war of 1812 with Great Britain. He was in the 68th year of his age. Nashville papers copy. Memphis Daily Appeal, 12/25/1859.

Dr. S. **GILBERT** & Son, Have opened an office on Howard's Row, and are now prepared to prescribe for all persons who cannot visit their Infirmary. Wm. P. **GILBERT**, M.D., offers his services to the citizens of Memphis and the surrounding country in the practice of medicine generally...Daily Enquirer, 11/4/1847. We had the pleasure on yesterday of a visit from our old friend and former fellow-citizen, Dr. Gilbert. The Doctor is in most excellent health, and we presume will spend a few days among us, previous to his departure for New York, which, we are informed by him, is the point of his destination. Memphis Daily Appeal, 7/29/1851.

Married—In Issaquena county, Miss., on the 20th inst. by the Rev. Dr. Dunn, Dr. Wm. P. **GILBERT**, of Memphis, to Miss Emily C., daughter of Ambrose **GIBSON**, Esq. Tri-Weekly Memphis Enquirer, 10/31/1846.

Married, On the 7th day of January, 1858, in Panola county, Miss., by Rev. R. L. **ANDREWS**, Mr. John A. **GILCHRIST**, of North Alabama, to Miss Texana A. **JONES**. Memphis Daily Appeal, 1/9/1858.

Married, By Rev. L. B. **GASTON** in Tishomingo county, Mississippi, on Wednesday, 25th inst., Mr. R. M. **GILES**, of our city to Miss Sue F. **PHILLIPS**, of Tishomingo. Memphis Daily Appeal, 11/29/1857.

The undersigned offers his splendid Tract of Lane for sale, containing 850 acres, situated on the road leading from Memphis to Raleigh, 4 miles from the city of Memphis; upon which there is a comfortable dwelling house, gin house and other necessary and comfortable buildings...For further particulars call and see me at the Gayoso...C. K. **GILLESPIE**. American Eagle, 12/16/1847.

Died, In this city yesterday afternoon, Eliza Gillis, wife of Maj. Charles **GILLIS**. Memphis Daily Appeal, 5/21/1857.

We are authorized to announce Wm. D. **GILMORE** as a candidate for the office of Constable of the Memphis district. Mr. Gilmore being a Printer...American Eagle, 2/21/1842.

Some four or five of our city hunters went out deer hunting yesterday morning, and returned home to dinner, having killed four deer and wounded the fifth, and all done within four miles of Memphis, south. Dr. Bryan killed two fawns with one barrel of his gun, and with the other, killed the mother—a fine fat doe. Jake **GILTNER** killed a doe at a hundred yards with one of his barrels, and wheeling, broke anothers leg with the other...Memphis Daily Eagle, 10/4/1848.

Died. In this city on Monday the 19th inst., of inflammation of the lungs, Mrs. Eliza Carson, wife of Mr. James **GILZEAN** (?), aged 29 years. American Eagle, 4/29/1847.

Died, In this city, on Tuesday Mr. Thomas **GINN**, merchant, after a short illness. The Appeal, Fri., 12/13/1844.

The First Piano Manufactured in Memphis. We dropped into Mons. L. **GITTER**'s Piano Rooms on Second street, south of Union, on Thursday evening last and witnessed the performance of the two little Misses Gitter upon a new seven-octave, iron frame, piano forte just finished by Mons. G. out of Tennessee oak and white walnut, which abounds in our immediate vicinity....Mons. G. built pianos in Paris for many years....He left there on account of the political revolutions and came to this country in 1848, and has been erecting pianos in New Orleans and Nashville, and for the last two years in Memphis....Memphis Daily Appeal, 9/1/1855.

Married, On the 18th inst., by J. **WALDRAN**, Esq., Mr. H__ry **GLASS** to Miss Minnie **GABBART**, all of this city. Memphis Daily Appeal, 8/21/1858.

Married. In Panola county, Miss., by Rev. Mr. Young, on the 15th inst., Col. P. T. **GLASS**, of Ripley, Ten., to Miss Maria **PARTEE**, of said county. Memphis Daily Appeal, 8/21/1855.

An old gentleman named John **GLEASON** died very suddenly at his residence on Poplar street yesterday....the deceased had died of disease of the heart. Memphis Daily Appeal, 11/23/1859.

A cabin passenger by the steamer *St. Francis No. 3*, named John **GLEASON**, died very suddenly of pneumonia on board that boat, on the St. Francis river, on Friday last, and was buried at Ashport, at the head of navigation on the L'Anguille river. The deceased was from this city, and left a family and other relatives here, who received his effects yesterday. Memphis Daily Appeal, Tues., 12/20/1859.

A deck passenger named Lawrence **GLEASON**, who came up to this city yesterday morning from Council Bend on the *Kate Frisbee*, was suffering from some complaint, supposed to be the flux. On reaching here he was placed on a dray to be taken to the hospital, but soon after being placed on the vehicle he died.... Memphis Daily Appeal, 11/6/1857.

Married, On the 20th instant by Rev. J. T. **MERRIWETHER**, at the residence of the bride's father, Mr. Walter S. **GLEEN** to Miss Fannie **JOHNSON**, all of this city. Memphis Daily Appeal, 10/21/1859.

Patience Wilkinson Glenn, the daughter of Dr. Cary **WILKINSON**, of Virginia, and wife of Col. D. C. **GLENN**, of Mississippi, was born in Charles City county, Virginia, October 23d, 1826; was married in Holly Springs, Mississippi, in November, 1846, and died on Friday, the 20th June, 1856, at her residence in Jackson, Mississippi, after a painful illness of fifty days, in full communion with the Catholic church, the church of her adoption and choice, leaving a husband and four children to weep her loss.—*Holly Springs Democrat, June 27*. Memphis Daily Appeal, 7/8/1856.

Died, In this city, on Wednesday, December 4th, Dr. Jas. H. **GLIDDEN**. His funeral will come off to-day, at 10 o'clock a.m., from the residence of J. S. **LEAVITT**, South Memphis, Vance street, between Shelby and Main. Memphis Daily Eagle, 12/5/1850.

Death of Geo. R. **GLIDDON**, Esq.—We are pained to hear of the death of G. R. Gliddon, Esq., formerly Consul of the United States for Cairo, Egypt, but better known as the author of a very learned work entitled, "Types Of Mankind and Indigenous Races." He died at Panama, where he had been residing for some months past. His brother, Mr. W. A. **GLIDDON**, of this city, left yesterday for New York to settle up his affairs. Memphis Daily Appeal, 12/2/1857.

Married, On the evening of the 12th(?) instant, by Rev. J. W. **KNOTT**, Mr. J. H. **GLIDEWELL** and Miss Catharine **BENDER**, all of this city. Memphis Daily Appeal, 11/11/1855.

Died, Of Consumption at his residence in this city, this morning, Mr. John H. **GLIDEWELL**. His friends and those of his family, are invited to attend his funeral from his late residence on St. Patrick street, second house below Vance, to-morrow evening at 3 o'clock. Memphis Evening Ledger, 1/29/1858.

....Capt. Ben. V. **GLIME**, the clerk of the ill-fated steamer, died in this city yesterday from injuries received by the explosion of the *St. Nicholas*. The deceased was a native of Virginia, and his father yet lives at Parkersburg, in that State....Capt. G. had been a boatman from manhood.... The deceased was in the flush of manhood, having but just attained the age of thirty-five, and having been united to his now sainted wife but ten months ago....Memphis Daily Appeal, 4/27/1859.

Died, At LaGrange, Tenn., yesterday morning, Thomas B. **GLOSTER**, postmaster at that place, aged about 33 years, after a week's illness of pneumonia....Memphis Daily Appeal, 1/5/1859.

Married—On Thursday evening, the 21st of March, Mr. Jess(?) M. **GLOVER** to Miss Casandra H. **COWGER**. American Eagle, 4/14/1842.

Married, On Wednesday, the 28th inst., by the Rev. Mr. Dennis, Mr. Daniel **GOBER**, Jr., of Fayette county, to Rosella C., daughter of Mr. E. **McDAVITT**, of this city. Weekly Memphis Eagle, 4/5/1849.

Died. On 2nd September, at the residence of Thomas **REED**, near Denmark, Franklin, infant son of Jas. D. and Pheraby **GOFF**, of Memphis, age 11 months. This dispensation of Providence is peculiarly afflictive to the parents, as their child had been endeared to them by long affliction, and the father was absent at the time....Memphis Eagle, 9/20/1849. Died, In this city on Wednesday, 1st inst., Mrs. Pheraby W. Goff, wife of Mr. J. D. Goff, Merchant of Memphis. Memphis Daily Appeal, 12/3/1852.

Died: In the city of Baltimore, Md., on the 27th of August, 1848, John W. **GOFF**, of Memphis, Tenn. The deceased, for several years past, had been engaged in the mercantile business in this city, and we feel that we express but a common sentiment, when we say that Death has deprived us of one of our most estimable citizens.....Peace be unto his ashes. Memphis Eagle, 9/5/1848.

Taken up by M. W. **GOLDESBEY**, living about 8 miles north of Raleigh, one chestnut sorrel horse.... Weekly Appeal, 9/25/1846.

Murder—A young man named Wilson **GOLDSBY**, was killed at a Camp-meeting in the northern part of this county, by a man named Forbus.—Goldsby was seated near the altar—at which the congregation were engaged in religious services—when Forbus is said to have approached and inflicted a fatal stab without giving notice of his purpose. Goldsby was the son of Miles **GOLDSBY**, a respectable citizen of this county, and was about 21 years old. It is said there was an old grudge between him and Forbus. The Tri-Weekly Memphis Enquirer, 9/10/1846.

The funeral procession of Mrs. Geraldine Gonder, wife of Mark F. **GONDER**, and daughter of Rev. P. H. **LUNDY**, will take place from the residence of J. M. **GONDER** on Kerr's avenue to the Memphis and Charleston Railroad Depot, to-day....Memphis Daily Appeal, 10/26/1859.

We are indebted to the courtesy of Mr. John **GOODBRAD**, the keeper of an A No. 1 bar on board the fine steamer C. E. Watkins, for a can of fresh oysters...Memphis Daily Appeal, 11/20/1851.

From the Pulaski Gazette....It is our painful duty to record the death of John W. **GOODE**, Esq., who departed this life, on the 15th inst., at the residence of his father-in-law, Spencer **CLARK**, Esq., in this town. Mr. Goode was for many years one of the brightest ornaments of Pulaski's social circle—a prominent member of the legal profession—at one time a Representative in the Legislature from this county...A few years since, he removed to Aberdeen, Miss., and more recently to the city of Memphis...A week or two since he came on a visit to his friends in this place, the picture of fine health...he was suddenly cut down in the midst of fondly affectionate relatives and doting friends, in the prime of manhood and usefulness. Memphis Daily Appeal, 9/3/1851.

Died.—In Covington, Tenn., on Sunday morning the 20th of December, in the 87th year of his age, Col. Thomas **GOODE**. He was born in Mecklenburg County, Virginia, on the 12th of February, 1760, and in his 16th year, when the bugle of war first sounded our Revolutionary struggle, he joined the first Virginia Regiment, and spent five years as a soldier in the service of his country, during most of which time he was with Gen. Washington and shared in the hardships and glories of the times; he was at the battles of Trenton, Princeton, the surrender of Cornwallis etc., and wore through life marks of his sufferings. On the 15th of March last, he was separated by death from the companion of his youth and old age with whom he had lived 67 years; after which time his decline seemed more rapid. For 55 years Col. Goode was a consistent member of the Methodist Episcopal Church…The "South Western Christian Advocate" will please copy. Weekly American Eagle, 1/7/1847.

Married, On the 25th instant by Rev. J. W. **KNOTT**, Mr. Wm. **GOODE** to Miss Elizabeth **SIBLEY**, all of this city. Memphis Daily Appeal, 9/26/1855.

Married, In Nashville at the residence of the bride's father, on the morning of the 21st inst., by Rev. Dr. A. G. **GOODLET**, Mr. E. E. **GOODLET**, of the firm of E. E. Goodlet & Co., Nashville, and Miss Josephine **BROWN**. It is with the above brief notice that we chronicle the departure from the ranks of single blessedness of our friend and former townsman….Memphis Daily Appeal, 9/23/1859.

New Firm. J. H. **GOODLETT**, (Late of the firm of Stratton, Goodlett & Co.) R. D. **GOODLETT**, W. W. **MILAM**, W. H. **GOODLETT**, ag't. J. H. & R. D. Goodlett & Co., Cotton Factors and Commission Merchants. Office over 45 Front Row, Memphis, Tenn. Memphis Daily Appeal, 8/29/1855.

Died, At the residence of James C. **BUTLER**, Madison county, Tenn., little Rocind, daughter of J. H. and R. S. **GOODLETT**, near Memphis, being 3 years, 7 months and 11 days old….Too lovely and pure for earth, the angels claimed the prize, and on the 11th day of August, 1856, bore it home, where with a sainted mother, she sings the wonders of redeeming grace….Oh, how unbounded was the affection of her dear aunt, with whom her mother had left her….Memphis Daily Appeal, 9/3/1856.

Died in this vicinity, of Puerperal Fever, on the 18th instant, Mrs. Eliza Jane Huston, consort of R. D. **GOODLETT**, Esq., commission merchant of this city, but recently of Mansker's Creek, Davidson county, in this State, leaving four children and an infant but ten days old, a disconsolate husband and many relatives and friends to mourn and bewail her sudden death….Her corpse is deposited in the Cemetery, to be buried by the side of her father, according to her request. Nashville Christian Advocate and Nashville Banner of Peace will please copy. Memphis Daily Appeal, 4/20/1856.

Married. Last evening at the Episcopal Church by Bishop Otey, Dr. J. C. **GOODMAN**, formerly of Va., to Miss Nina C. **WHITE** of this city. Memphis Appeal, 12/15/1854.

We have been shown a private letter dated West Point, Ark., March 30, 1852, which gives an account of a terrible murder supposed to have been recently committed near Augusta, Ark. The body of Mr. Solomon K. **GOODMAN** was picked up in White river a few days since, with his throat cut from ear to ear. When last seen he was ascending the river in a skiff with a man named Crosby. Crosby stated that the boat had capsized and that Goodman was drowned…Mr. Goodman was well known in Memphis, where he has relatives. Memphis Daily Appeal, 4/10/1852.

Married. On the 20th inst., in the Parish of Iberville, La., by the Rev. Dr. Burke, at the residence of R. **McGAVROCK** Esq., Mr. W. A. **GOODMAN** of Memphis, to Miss Harriet R., daughter of R. McGavrock Esq. Memphis Eagle, 1/4/1849.

Married—At Huntsville, Ala., on the evening of the 18th inst., Walter A. **GOODMAN**, Esq., of Holly Springs, Miss., and Miss Corinne Acklin, daughter of Col. Wm. **ACKLIN**, of the former place. Memphis Daily Avalanche, 5/23/1859.

Married: On Tuesday evening, 11th inst., at the residence of Mr. F. A. **LUCAS**, by Rev. Geo. W. **COONS**, Mr. John C. **GOODRICH**, of New Orleans, to Miss Eliza **WALKER**, of this city. Memphis Eagle, 7/13/1848.

Died—On Saturday the 7th inst., at the residence of her husband, in Shelby county, Mrs. Cleora (?) M., consort of Mr. T. W. **GOODRICH**.—the dec'd was in the 18th year of her age….Weekly Appeal, 2/20/1846.

Married, On the 15th instant at the residence of the bride's father, by Rev. J. E. **DOUGLASS**, Mr. J. R. **GOODWIN**, of Batesville, Miss., to Miss Mollie **MULLINS**, of Shelby county, Tenn. Memphis Daily Appeal, 11/19/1859.

The friends and acquaintances of Mr. and Mrs. W. A. **GOODWIN** are invited to attend the funeral of their infant son, Randolph McGavock, at their residence on Court street This Morning....Memphis Daily Appeal, 8/18/1859.

P. H. **GOODWYN**, Has associated with him, from and after this date, his son, Wm. A. **GOODWYN**. The business of General Agents will be conducted by them under the firm of P. H. Goodwyn & Son. Office, Front Row, just above Adams street. American Eagle, 10/15/1846. Died. Yesterday morning about 9 o'clock, Clara Leslie, only daughter of P. H. and Martha Goodwyn, aged 2 years, 1 month and 18 days. The friends of the family are invited to attend her funeral this morning at 10 o'clock, from their residence on Main st. American Eagle, 5/6/1847.

Married. On the 5th inst. by Rev. C. R. **HENDRICKSON**, Mr. R. D. **GOODWYN** and Miss Sallie A., daughter of Geraldus **BUNTYN**, Esq., near this city. Memphis Daily Appeal, 1/7/1854.

Died: Yesterday afternoon, at 4 o'clock of Pneumonia, Mr. Samuel S. **GOOKIN**. Memphis Eagle, 2/8/1849.

Married, On Thursday, the 6th instant, by Elder C. B. **YOUNG**, Mr. John **GORDEN** and Miss Masuha H. **ARMS**, all of Panola county, Miss. Memphis Daily Appeal, 11/15/1856.

Married, On Thursday, 7th instant, at the residence of Yancey **WILEY**, Esq., in the vicinity of Oxford, by Rev. L. B. **GASTON**, Mr. James **GORDON**, of Pontotoc county, and Miss C. Virginia **WILEY**, of Lafayette county, Miss. Memphis Daily Appeal, 2/19/1856.

Zebulon **GOSS**, who was shot on Monday night by one Joe **FRAINE**, an account of which we gave in our issue of yesterday, died yesterday about 10 o'clock. He worked for some time here at the Memphis and Charleston Depot. His antecedents connect him with Chattanooga and vicinity, though his father and mother lived over the river, and were with him at his death. Memphis Daily Avalanche, Wed., 4/6/1859.

Married, On Wednesday evening, 4th inst., by Rev. Wm. **HYER**, Mr. C. Wesley **GOYER**, and Miss Laura A., eldest daughter of Wm. **HARSSON**, Esq., all of this city. Memphis Enquirer, 7/7/1849.

Roman Catholic Church, Corner of Adams and Third Sts., Rev. Jos. T. **ALEMANY**, Rev. Thos. L. **GRACE**. Daily Enquirer, 2/28/1847....The N.Y. Truth Teller, a Roman Catholic journal, has the following announcement. The Reverend Thomas L. Grace, of Memphis, Tennessee, to be Bishop of the Diocese of California. This gentleman is a member of the Order of St. Dominick, and a brother of Pierce C. **GRACE**, Esq., of St. Louis. He studied in Rome at the College of Minerva, and is an eloquent and feeling orator...Memphis Eagle, 9/3/1850. Rev. Father T. L. Grace, of this city, has been created a Bishop by the powers at Rome, and assigned to the Bishopric of St. Pauls, Minnesota, and we learn that he has accepted the appointment.... Memphis Daily Avalanche, 3/25/1859.

Married, In this city on Wednesday evening, November 12th, by Rev. A. M. **BRYAN**, Mr. George W. **GRADER**, of Boston, Mass., and Miss Mary E. Klinck, daughter of J. G. **KLINCK**, Esq. Memphis Daily Appeal, 11/14/1856.

Married, Last evening, by the Rev. Mr. Gray, Mr. Barnet **GRAHAM**, merchant, to Mrs. Sallie C. **CARR**, daughter of Maj. Nat. **ANDERSON**. Memphis Daily Eagle, 10/11/1850.

Married, On the morning of the 29th inst. at the residence of the bride's father, Mr. Wm. **PROUDFIT**, Mrs. Jane **PERKINS**, of Brownsville, Tenn., and Mr. George C. **GRAHAM**, of Shelby county. Memphis Daily Appeal, 7/31/1856.

Died—Of bilious fever on the 27th ult., Dr. George F. **GRAHAM**, about 30 years of age, formerly of Lincoln county, N.C. practising physician of this town for the last eight years, with the exception of one summer, leaving a widow with one child to mourn his untimely fate. Memphis Advocate, 10/6/1827. Will be sold at his late dwelling house, in the town of Memphis, at public auction, commencing on Thursday, the 15th day of November next....Joseph **GRAHAM**, Adm'r. Memphis Advocate, 10/27/1827.

Married, On the 17th inst. by Rev. Dr. Page, Mr. James **GRAHAM** to Miss Octeve S. **PATTERSON**, both of this city. Memphis Daily Appeal, 7/20/1855.

In the Circuit Court for Hardeman County, Tenn. John **GRAHAM** (vs) Elizabeth Graham, Divorce. January Rules, 1851. In this case it is ordered that publication be made in the Memphis Appeal for three successive weeks, requiring the defendant, Elizabeth Graham, to appear at the next term of said court, to be held at the court House in Bolivar, on the 4th Monday in February next, and plead, answer or demur to Plaintiff's petition, or the same will be taken for confessed and heard *ex parte*. E. C. **CRISP**, Clerk. Memphis Daily Appeal, 1/14/1851.

As Trustees in a Deed of Trust, executed by John D. **GRAHAM**, bearing date the fifth day of August 1843, and registered in the office of Shelby County, Tenn., in Book O, pages 280, 281 and 282, conveying to us the undersigned the following described tract of land, to secure the payment of a sum of money therein specified, we shall expose to public sale...on Saturday, the 26th day of September 1846....situated in said County of Shelby, about 4 miles south, of the south boundary line of the Corporation of Memphis, on the east bank of the Mississippi river, containing about 60 acres...J. T. **TREZEVANT**, Chas. **LOFLAND**, Trustees. Weekly American Eagle, 9/17/1846.

Married, On Monday morning, the 26th inst., at the residence of W. C. **MAXWELL**, Esq., in Panola county, Miss., by Rev. Mr. Acton, Mr. H. W. **GRANADE**, of Green county, Ark., to Mrs. Susan **BARTLETT**, of Panola. Memphis Daily Appeal, 12/28/1859.

Married, On the 6th inst., by Rev. J. W. **PENDER**, Mr. J. F. **GRANBERY** to Miss Mary C. **MITCHELL**—all of Fayette county. Also, at the same time, place and by the same, Mr. Henry B. **CHILES**, of Memphis, to Miss Arabella E. **MITCHELL**. Memphis Daily Appeal, 1/8/1851.

Married, On the 19th inst. by J. **WALDRAN**, Esq., Jerome **GRANDOLPHO** to Ellen **CARNES**, all of this city. Memphis Eagle & Enquirer, 1/21/1853.

Married, On the 3d inst. by Elder T. J. **DRANE**, Mr. Lewis **GRANT** to Miss Mary E. **JONES**, both of this city. Memphis Weekly Appeal, 3/17/1858.

Died, In Covington, Tipton county, Tenn., on the 19th instant, Miss Emaline Grant, the daughter of William and Martha **GRANT**, late of Wilson county. Middle Tennessee papers copy. Memphis Daily Appeal, 10/25/1856.

Married, On Wednesday evening the 11th inst., by Hume F. **HILL**, Esq., Mr. Wm. M. **GRANT**, to Miss L. **NOEL**, all of this city. Memphis Appeal, 2/13/1852.

Married. On the 15th September, 1853, at the residence of R. C. **PERKINS**, Esq., Fayette county, Ten., by the Rev. Samuel **LAMBERT**, Mr. John O. **GRAVES** to Miss Bettie **PERKINS**. Memphis Appeal, 9/22/1853.

Married, In this city on the evening of the 3d April, by Rev. Mr. Henderson, Mr. Jno. M. **GRAVES**, to Miss Sophia C. **MADDOX**—all of this city. Memphis Appeal, 4/7/1851.

Died—In De Soto county, Miss., about three weeks since, Dr. Benjamin F. **GRAY**, after a few hours illness. American Eagle, 2/14/1842.

The friends and acquaintances of Geo. W. **GRAY** are invited to attend the funeral of his late brother, William F., from the Cumberland Presbyterian Church, Court street, at 3 o'clock P.M. Memphis Daily Appeal, 11/15/1857.

Second Presbyterian, South Memphis, Beal Street, Rev. J. H. **GRAY**. Daily Enquirer, 2/28/1847. Married, On the morning of the 7th by the Rev. J. N. **WADDELL**, Mr. John O. **HARDIMAN**, of Noxubee county, Mississippi, to Miss Jane H. Gray, daughter of the Rev. John H. **GRAY**, of this city. Memphis Daily Appeal, 9/9/1853.

Married, On June 3d by Rev. Mr. Allen, Dr. James W. **GRAY** and Miss Cordelia L. **DABNEY**, all of Marshall county. Memphis Daily Appeal, 7/19/1856.

Married, At Cold Water Depot on the 8th day of January, 1857, by M. D. **WALDROP**, Esq., Jeremiah **GRAY**, of Tishomingo county, and Miss Melinda **SMITH**, of DeSoto county, Miss. Memphis Daily Appeal, 1/11/1857.

Married, On the 11th inst., by Rev. Wm. Carey **CRANE**, Mr. Washington L. **GRAY** to Miss M. Amanda Johnston, (of the class of 1856, of Mississippi Female College,) eldest daughter of Stephen D. **JOHNSTON**, Esq., all of DeSoto county, Miss. Memphis Daily Appeal, 11/26/1857.

The undersigned, a member of the 1st Pennsylvania Regiment, discharged on account of sickness, desires before leaving Memphis to tender his heartfelt thanks to Mr. Wesley and Henry **TEST** and their ladies, Joseph **UNDEGRAFF**, Henry and Jacob **GARTMAN**, William **GRAY**, and other natives of York county, Pa., residing in Memphis, as also to Dr. Shanks, for their attention and kindness...Peter **AHER**, Jr. of Company C. Daily Enquirer, 1/23/1847.

Married, On Tuesday, the 5th inst., by the Rev. William **HENDERSON**, Wm. **GREATHOUSE**, Esq., of Kentucky, to Miss Mary A., daughter of Rev. B. W. **JOHNSON**, of this city. Louisville Journal please copy. Memphis Eagle, 2/19/1850. Died, Very suddenly, on the 27th ult., at the residence of Rev. B. W. **JOHNSTON** in this city, George Walker, aged three years and six months, only child of William and Mary A. Greathouse, of Crittendon county, Arkansas....Memphis Appeal, 8/1/1855.

Married. On Thursday, January 18th, by the Rev. William **CRAWFORD**, Mr. A. H. **GREEN** to Miss Nancy J. **ATKERSON**, all of Hardeman county, Ten. Memphis Daily Appeal, 1/31/1855.

Tribute Of Respect. At a called meeting of the Trustees of Covington Female Seminary, held on the 19th of March, 1857, the following preamble and resolutions were unanimously adopted: Whereas, It has pleased Divine Providence to remove from us by death our highly esteemed friend, Mr. F. M. **GREEN**....Memphis Daily Appeal, 3/24/1857.

Married, On Thursday, the 22d inst. by Rev. Mr. McCoy, Dr. H. D. **GREEN**, of Monroe county, Ark., to Miss Minnie J. **SWIFT**, of Fayette county, Tenn. Memphis Daily Appeal, 12/25/1859.

Married, At the residence of the bride's father, on Wednesday, the 20th inst., by Rev. T. A. **PIERCE**, Dr. J. Lewis **GREEN**, of Jackson, Tenn., to Miss Jennie A. **CABINESS**, of Brunswick county, Va. Memphis Daily Appeal, 7/26/1859.

Married, In Jackson, Miss., on the 27th ult., by Rt. Rev. Bishop Green, Dr. J. S. **GREEN** and Ella P., daughter of Col. J. J. **WILLIAMS**, all of Mississippi. Memphis Daily Appeal, 2/10/1858.

Married. At Bending Oak, Tippah county, Miss., on the evening of the 14th instant, by Rev. A. H. **THOMAS**, James A. **GREEN**, Esq., to Miss Mollie L. Stricklin, daughter of Hardy W. **STRICKLIN**, Esq. Memphis Daily Appeal, 8/28/1855.

Departed this life, on Tuesday the 25th inst., at the residence of his brother Dr. John A. **GREEN**, Covington, Tenn., James W. **GREEN**, aged about 58 years. Weekly American Eagle, 6/3/1847.

Married, By the Rev. D. H. **CUMMINS**, at the residence of R. W. **SANFORD** on Thursday, April 7th, John Uriah **GREEN** to Miss Mary Jane **SANFORD**, all of Tipton county, Tenn. Memphis Eagle & Enquirer, 4/12/1853.

Married, In Randolph on the evening of the 4th inst. by the Rev. P. W. **ALSTON**, Mr. Joseph A. **GREEN**, to Miss Elizabeth Frances **NEWMAN**. American Eagle Weekly, 3/14/1845. The friends and acquaintances of Joseph A. and Elizabeth Green are requested to attend the funeral of their daughter, Lizzie Bird, at the residence of B. **BAYLESS**, This Morning....Services by Rev. Mr. Wheelock. Memphis Daily Appeal, 1/25/1859.

Married. On Thursday, 23d inst., by Rev. David H. **CUMMINGS**, Mr. Marcus C. T. **GREEN**, to Miss Sarah Ann Sanford, eldest daughter of R. W. **SANFORD**, Esq., all of Tipton county. Memphis Eagle, 3/29/1848.

The latest and best variety of hibred Roses and Green-house plants...for sale at my Green-house adjoining the Corporation Bayou, on the old State Line road, immediately East of the Raleigh road...Paul **GREEN**. Memphis Appeal, 2/1/1848. The Estate of Paul Green, Deceased. The undersigned having obtained letters of Administration from the County Court of Shelby county, Tennessee, on the above estate, hereby notifies all creditors of the same to present their claims....Maria **GREEN**. Memphis Daily Appeal, 6/2/1858.

Married, On the 31st ult., by the Rev. P. R. **BLAND**, Dr. S. **GREEN**, of Fayette county, to Miss Sallie B., daughter of B. B. **DeGRAFFENREID**, of the same co. Daily Memphis Enquirer, 11/1/1848.

Died, On Saturday morning, after protracted illness, Wm. B. **GREEN**, in the 70th year of his age. The friends of the deceased, together with those of his son, W. F. **GREEN**, are respectfully invited to attend the funeral from the First Methodist Church this evening. Memphis Daily Appeal, Sun., 9/25/1859.

Died, In Jackson, Miss., on the 17th instant, Mrs. Sallie S. Greene, wife of B. H. **GREENE**, Esq. Nashville and Savannah (Ga.) papers please notice. Memphis Daily Appeal, 1/27/1859.

State of Tenn., Shelby County, Sep. Term, 1846. Joseph **GREENE** vs Mary W. Greene. Petition for Divorce. On motion, and it appearing to the court from the return of the Sheriff on the subpeona issued in this State: It is ordered by the court that publication be made in some newspaper published in the city of Memphis for three successive weeks, requiring defendant to appear at the court house in the town of Raleigh before the Judge of our next circuit, on the 1st Monday in January next, plead, answer or demur to complainant's petition in this behalf, or the same will be taken for confessed and set for hearing ex parte. Sam. R. **BROWN**, Clerk. Weekly American Eagle, 10/15/1846.

The friends and acquaintances of L. S. and Sarah R. **GREENE** are requested to attend the funeral of their little daughter, Mary Josephine, from their residence on Madison street, this (Thursday) morning...Services by the Rev. Dr. Page. Memphis Daily Eagle, 5/15/1851.

Taken up by John O. **GREENLAW**, living two miles west of Raleigh, on the Stage Road, one Roan mare.....The Appeal, 10/27/1843.

Died. Of Pneumonia, at Raleigh, January the 2d, 1847, Mrs. Narcissa I., consort of W. B. **GREENLAW**, Esq., in the 25th year of her age. The subject of this notice was a pious and devoted Christian.—She made profession of religion in the fall of 1841, and connected herself with the Cumberland Presbyterian Church....Sister Greenlaw was a most estimable woman. As a companion she was devoted, a tender and affectionate mother, an indulgent mistress, a true friend....Just before she expired, a most touching scene transpired.—She called for her little daughter about seven years old, and conferred on her a mother's last blessing. She then requested that her sister-in-law, Mrs. Tate, should take her and be a mother in her place.—She called for her younger children—two precious little boys—told them their mother was going to leave them to return no more, and with the utmost feeling, committed them to God, and the care and protection of her deeply afflicted husband....Weekly American Eagle, 1/14/1847.

Married, On the 8ᵗʰ inst. by Rev. Allen S. **WYNNE**, Col. Robert **GREER** to Mrs. Marie **TAYLOR**, all of Big Creek, Shelby county, Tenn. Memphis Daily Appeal, 3/13/1859.

Married, In this city by Jas. **ROSE**, Esq., on Tuesday, September 7, 1852, Mr. Andrew **GRIDER** to Miss Christiana **FRITZ**, all of this city. Memphis Daily Appeal, 9/9/1852.

Masonic Tribute. Departed this life, very suddenly, at his residence near this city, on the morning of the 29ᵗʰ instant, our brother, John H. **GRIDER**, in his fifty-second year. Having been a resident of this vicinity for seventeen years....Committee South Memphis Lodge No. 118. Memphis Daily Appeal, 4/1/1857.

Married—On the 15ᵗʰ inst. at the residence of the bride's father, Franklin, Tenn., by Rev. M. L. **ANDREWS**, Mr. Wm. H. **GRIDER**, of this city, and Miss M. M. **HORTON**. Memphis Daily Avalanche, 6/20/1859.

Mrs. Sarah C. Gridley, consort of Martin **GRIDLEY**, Esq., was followed to her last resting-place by a long funeral procession yesterday. Memphis Daily Appeal, 7/30/1856.

Died, In Shelby county, Tenn., on the 7ᵗʰ of August, Mr. G. A. **GRIFFIN**, aged 59 years. Memphis Daily Appeal, 9/11/1856.

Married, On the 2th instant, at the residence of the bride's mother, by Hume F. **HILL**, Esq., Mr. Lewis **GRIFFIN** to Miss Eliza **CHILDERS**, all of Fort Pickering. Memphis Daily Appeal, 7/28/1859. (Author's note: date is newspaper error.)

Died, In Shelby county, August 7ᵗʰ, 1856, Mrs. Mary S. **GRIFFIN**, aged fifty-two years. Memphis Daily Appeal, 8/30/1856.

Married, At the residence of Mrs. M. **HART**, on Thursday, the 14th inst., by the Rev. J. H. **GRAY**, Mr. J. C. **GRIFFING** of this city, to Miss M. L. **HART**, of Shelby Co. Nashville and Louisville and Frankfort (Ky.) papers please copy. Memphis Daily Eagle, 11/18/1850.

Married, On the evening of the 5th(?) inst., by Rev. Mr. Coons, Mr. James B. (?) **GRIFFING**, Merchant, to Miss Fanny M. Grant, eldest daughter of G. M. **GRANT**, M.D., all of this city. Memphis Appeal, 2/7/1851.

Married. On Wednesday evening, 17ᵗʰ instant, at the residence of Mrs. Lucretia **BAKER**, by Rev. C. K. **HENDRICKSON**, Dr. W. A. **GRIFFING**, of Memphis, to Miss Aurelia W. **BAKER**, of Shelby county. Memphis Daily Appeal, 1/19/1855.

Married, On the 27ᵗʰ January in the town of Portersville, by A. W. **SMITH**, Esq., Lieut. J. L. **GRIGGS** to Miss M. C., daughter of J. B. **WALD**, Esq., all of Tipton county, Tenn. Memphis Daily Appeal, 2/11/1858.

Married, On Monday evening, November 22d, by Rev. Dr. _____, Mr. Chas. A. **GRISWOLD**, of New York, to Miss Mary A. Grant, daughter of Mr. George **GRANT**. On Monday evening, November 22d, at the residence of George Grant, in this city, Mr. E. F. **BROCCHUS**, of this city, to Miss Mary **ALLEN**, of Chester, Illinois. Memphis Weekly Appeal, 12/1/1858.

N. L. and George **GRISWOLD**, 71 & 72 South street, Sole Agents for the Sale of Colt's Standard Cotton Duck...Memphis Eagle & Enquirer, 4/27/1852.

State of Tennessee Shelby County, Circuit Court, May Term A.D. 1847. Wilson **SANDERLIN**, Administrator of Jas. **GROOMS**, deceased, Joshua **GIST** and his wife, Susanna, Thomas H. RICHARDSON and his wife Elizabeth, and Ann **GROOMS**, now Ann **ROBERTSON**. Vs. Edward

GROOMS, John GROOMS and wife, Mary, Isaac and Henry GROOMS. Petition to Sell Slaves. This cause came on this day for hearing before the Hon. E. W. M. KING, Judge, etc., upon the petition, and it appearing to the Court that the defendants, Edw'd Grooms, Jno. Grooms and wife, Mary Grooms, Isaac Grooms, and Henry Grooms, are not inhabitants of this State: It is therefore ordered, adjudged and decreed, that publication be made in the Appeal..... for two successive months requiring the defendants to appear at the next term of this court at the Court House in Raleigh on the 1st Monday in September next, to plead, answer or deliver to the petition in this behalf, or the same will be taken for confessed, and set for hearing exparte. Memphis Appeal, 7/29/1847.

In Chancery, Common Law and Chancery Court at the city of Memphis.—May Rules, 1851. Moses GROOMS, jr., as Administrator de benis non of Isaac GROOMS, dec'd., vs. Thomas GROOMS, Hannah SWEAT, et. al. It appearing from affidavit of complt. that said defendants are non residents of Tennessee, it is therefore ordered that they enter their appearance herein, on or before the 4th Monday of May, 1851, and defend the same...Memphis Daily Appeal, 5/5/1851.

The undersigned would call the attention of the citizens of Memphis, and the surrounding country, to his extensive assortment of Furniture...Madison st. H. M. GROSVENER. Memphis Daily Eagle, 11/4/1847. Married, On the evening of the 16th, at Holly Springs, by the Rev. Mr. Dodd, H. M. Grosvener, of Memphis, to Martha NILES, of Holly Springs. Memphis Daily Eagle, 7/22/1850.

Died, In Brownsville on Saturday, the 4th inst., Mrs. Emma C., wife of Wm. Barry GROVE and daughter of the late Rev. Robert RIVERS. Memphis Daily Appeal, 6/14/1853.

Died, At Paducah, Ky., Thursday, 9th instant, of cholera infantum, Rebecca Nellie, infant daughter of Rev. R. C. and Ellen S. GRUNDY, in the 15th month of her age. Memphis Daily Appeal, 9/16/1858.

Died, At his residence in Fayette county, Tenn., on the 24th August last, of billious fever, Col. Wm. GUERRANT, aged 52 years. The deceased was a native of the county of Goochland, Va., but had been a resident of Fayette for the last ten years—during which time he had secured to himself the enviable reputation of an honest man, a good citizen, a kind neighbor and an affectionate husband and parent...The Appeal, 10/13/1843.

Died, At Baltimore, on the evening of the 18th ultimo, after a short but painful illness, in the thirty-seventh year of her age, Honora S., wife of George GUEST, and daughter of Gen. James BANKHEAD, of the United States Army. Memphis Daily Appeal, 5/1/1856.

Married: On the 19th inst., at Greenwood, the residence of her father, in Shelby county, by the Rev. W. A. YOUNG, Henry L. GUION, Esq., of this city, to Miss Margaret J., daughter of James LEMASTER, Esq. Memphis Daily Eagle, 10/21/1848. Died, on Tuesday the 14th inst., at Greenwood, the residence of James LEMASTER, Esq., John, infant son of H. L. and Margaret Guion, aged 11 months and 1 day. Memphis Appeal, 9/17/1852. The remains of Mrs. Margaret J., wife of H. L. Guion, having arrived from Cleveland, Ohio, where she died on the 8th instant, the friends and acquaintances of the family are invited to attend her funeral from their residence on Union street, this Friday afternoon at 3 o'clock. Services by Rev. O. STEADMAN. Interment at Elmwood Cemetery. Memphis Whig, 9/28/1855.

Died, On the 11th of July, 1856, of Congestion of the Brain, Mrs. Martha L., consort of Soloman GULLETT, Esq., of Germantown, Tenn. Nashville *Banner of Peace* please copy. Memphis Daily Appeal, 9/20/1856.

Died, In Brooklyn, New York, on Friday, September 26th, Georgie, second son of Dr. C. B. and Jenny M. GUTHRIE, late of Memphis, aged five years and eight months. Memphis Daily Appeal, 10/7/1856.

Married. On the 4th ult. by Rev. R. H. BUNTING, Dr. Jos. H. GUY to Miss Roan, daughter of James CARLTON, Esq., of Colorado county, Texas. Memphis Daily Appeal, 5/2/1855.

Died, On the 13th day of October, near Byhalia, Miss., Robert A., eldest son of John A. and Margaret **GWIN**. He was in his seventh year. His death was produced by disease of the throat....Memphis Daily Appeal, 11/3/1858.

Died in this city on the 20th of March last, Parmelia A. R. **GWYN**, of typhoid fever. She was an amiable and interesting girl, an obedient, dutiful daughter, a kind and affectionate sister. She has left a mother, a brother and sisters, relations and many friends to mourn her early departure. Hopkinsville Ky and Yancyville N.C. papers will please copy the above. Memphis Daily Appeal, 4/18/1851.

Married, At the residence of the bride's mother, on Wednesday evening, 7th instant, by Rev. R. C. **GRUNDY**, D.D., W. A. D. **GWYNN** to Miss Eliza A. **HENDERSON**, all of this city. Memphis Daily Appeal, 9/10/1859.

Pontotoc House, Memphis, Tenn. This establishment, on the North-East corner of Maine and Winchester streets and opposite the City Hotel, is now open by the subscriber for the reception of travellers and boarders....This establishment will be superintended by Gen. T. C. **McMACKIN**, so extensively and favorably known by the travelling community.....William **HACK**. The Appeal, 12/22/1843.

Married, At Immanuel Church, LaGrange, Tenn., by Rev. William **FAGG**, Prof. James H. **HACKLETON**, late of Holly Springs, Miss., to Miss Minnie W. **NASH**, late of Fayette county. Memphis Daily Appeal, 9/25/1857.

Died—In this city on Monday morning last, at the residence of his father-in-law, Samuel **McMANUS**, Esq., Mr. Fielding **HACKNEY**, a native of Todd county, Ky., in the 29th year of his age. While quite a youth the deceased settled in Lagrange, Ten., where he subsequently became actively engaged in mercantile operations, until the year 1839; when, in common with thousands of others, he fell a victim to those calamitous convulsions in commerce, the history of which is familiar to all....his remains were attended to the grave by a large number of our citizens, and interred with masonic honors by the brethren of the masonic fraternity, of which he was an upright and honored member.—Enquirer. The Appeal, Fri., 2/16/1844.

Married, On the morning of the 26th April, at Bowling Green, Ky., by Rev. Mr. Baugher, Jas. F. **HACKNEY**, of Memphis, to Miss Alice J. **HERDMAN**, of the former place. Memphis Daily Appeal, 5/3/1859.

The undersigned, living at New Albany, Indiana, wishes information of the present place of residence of his sister, Mrs. Mary **HAGMAN**, who formerly lived at Yazoo City, Miss., and about two months ago lived with a family about four miles from Memphis. He is very anxious that she should come to New Albany and make his house her permanent home....John **TRUNK**. Memphis Daily Appeal, 12/15/1859.

Died, On the 3d ult., at Ciego de Avilla, Island of Cuba, Wm. F. **HAILE**, Jr., of the firm of Foster & Haile, of this city. Memphis Daily Avalanche, 2/1/1859.

Coroner Horne yesterday held an inquest over the body of Conrad **HALDERBACH**, who died suddenly, in a home where he was staying; the jury brought in a verdict of death from intemperance and exposure. Memphis Daily Appeal, 1/19/1859.

Died—In this place, at Johnson's Hotel, on the 16th inst., Col. Thos. **HALE**, of Jackson, and a native of Va. The deceased was returning home from N. Orleans, at which place he contracted the disease, billious fever, which terminated his life....Memphis Enquirer, 5/19/1838.

We regret to learn that Mr. W. H. **HALE**, the late popular local agent of the Overland Mail company, has resigned the position which he has held in this city for some time....Mr. B. F. **KANDY**, of New York, has been appointed to fill the vacancy. Memphis Daily Appeal, 12/30/1859.

An Irishman by the name of Wm. **HALE**, was found dead near Hickory Withe, on Wednesday evening, the 18th inst. He was very dissapated, having been drunk for several days previous to his death. He was on the chain gang in this city three weeks during last fall or winter, but was released on account of sickness....He was decently interred by the citizens, in the public burying ground near that place....Memphis Daily Appeal, 7/23/1857.

Married, In Jackson, Tenn., on the 12th instant, by Rev. Jas. **HOLMES**, Mr. Claudius B. **HALL**, of Covington, Tipton county, to Miss Mary Eliza **FLOWERS**, of Jackson. Memphis Daily Appeal, 4/17/1859.

Died, In Somerville, on the 6th inst., Geo. W. **HALL**, son of W. E. **HALL** at the age of 21 years and 8 months. Memphis Daily Appeal, 4/15/1856.

Married, In Tipton county, December 27th, by the Rev. D. H. **CUMMINGS**, James **HALL**, Esq., to Miss Sarah, daughter of Dr. S. **LEMMONS**. Memphis Daily Eagle, 1/3/1850.

Died—In this county on Monday last, Mrs. Martha C. Hall, wife of Joel **HALL**, late of Sussex Co., Va., aged 30 years. Memphis Enquirer, Saturday, 12/2/1837. Died—On the 26th April, in the 58th year of her age, Mrs. Nancy **TOSER**, at her son-in-law's, Mr. Joel Hall, in Shelby county, Tenn. She came to this county about two years ago from Sussex county, Virginia.... Memphis Enquirer, 5/11/1838.

The subscriber proposes to sell a fine tract of land, containing 332 acres; lying two miles southeast of Germantown, Tenn...Joel H. **HALL**. Memphis Daily Appeal, 9/25/1851.

Died, In Hernando, Miss. on the 6th inst., Mrs. Ann W. Hall, wife of Dr. Jos. G. **HALL**, aged 56 years. Memphis Daily Appeal, 6/26/1853.

Died, In Hernando, Mississippi, at the residence of Judge Foote, on Wednesday morning, the 4th inst., Joseph Troy, infant son of Lemuel H. and Helen M. **HALL**, aged fourteen months and six days. Memphis Daily Appeal, 11/6/1857.

Married, On the 10th of November by Rev. D. H. **CUMMINGS**, and near Covington, Tipton county, Tenn., Mr. Robert **HALL** to Miss **STILL**, both of that county. Memphis Weekly Appeal, 12/8/1858.

The Athens *Herald* of Saturday last says: "On Tuesday evening last Mr. Samuel **HALL**, a conductor on one of the freight trains on the Memphis and Charleston Railroad, was accidentally knocked off the cars at the Decatur Bridge, and almost instantly killed. The wheels of several cars passed over him, cutting off both legs and mangling the body in the most horrible manner." Tuesday, 11/9/1858. Memphis Weekly Appeal, 11/10/1858.

P. C. **HALLEY**, having qualified as Executor of the estate of Francis **HALLEY**, dec'd., hereby notifies all persons indebted to the said estate, to come forward and make immediate payment .....Weekly Appeal, 12/25/1846.

We learn from the officers of the James Laughlin that young Gideon **BLACKBURN**, formerly of this city, shot forty-eight buckshot through Isaac **HALSTEAD** on last Friday night, about 7 o'clock, in front of Mr. Anderson's residence at Island 64, on the Arkansas side. From what we can learn, the parties had a difficulty before the shooting occurred, in which Halstead, being a stout athletic man, got the better of the fight over Blackburn, who was the smallest and more weakly of the two. At the time of the shooting however, Halstead stepped out in front of the house and told Blackburn to come out, attempting, as Blackburn says, to draw a pistol. At this moment Blackburn fired both barrels of a double barreled gun, the contents of both of which entered the body of Halstead, who dropped dead.—This side of the story is from Blackburn, who has thus far made good his escape....Memphis Appeal, Tues., 10/31/1854.

The subscriber would respectfully inform the citizens of Memphis, and vicinity, that he has permanently established himself here, for the purpose of making Gold and Silver Ware to order, setting of precious stones, all kinds of repairs, engravings, etc…His shop is on Court street near Main. Jos. **HALTER**. Memphis Daily Eagle, 3/6/1848.

We are pained to learn that on Friday last Mr. Yancey **HAM**, a citizen of this county and at the time overseeing for the Hon. John C. **THOMPSON**, near this place, was instantly killed by the accidental discharge of his gun, the contents entering near the region of the heart. The deceased was a good citizen and has left several brothers and near relatives in this county…. [Hernando (Miss.) Press] Memphis Appeal, 11/25/1854.

James P. **HAMBLETON**, M.D. Physician and Surgeon. (Formerly of Virginia.) After an experience of two years in Hospital and private Practice, offers his services to the citizens of Memphis and vicinity. References. – Universities of Virginia and Pennsylvania. Medical Department of Hampden Sydney College…Office on Court street, between Main and Second streets. Memphis Eagle & Enquirer, 2/17/1852.

Married: In peace, love and unity on the 6th inst. by Rev. C. C. **GLOVER**, M.D., Mr. Joseph S. **HAMER** to Miss Mary O. Wilcox, eldest daughter of C. G. **WILCOX**, all of Tippah county, Miss. Memphis Whig, 11/9/1855.

Married, On Saturday the 2d inst., by the Rev. Stephen **HAMER**, Henry **HAMER** Esq., to Miss Diana **HARDISON**, all of this county. The Tri-Weekly Memphis Enquirer, 5/9/1846.

Married, On the 4th instant by Rev. H. G. **SPENCER**, at the residence of Thomas **HAMERS**, Mr. W. T. **HAMER** and Miss Sallie J. **MASK**, all of the vicinity of Salem, Miss. Memphis Daily Appeal, 3/11/1857.

Died, In this city on the morning of the 22d inst., Mrs. Mary E., wife of James **HAMILTON**, Esq. Charleston (S.C.) and Georgia papers please copy. The funeral will take place from the Methodist Church, corner of Second and Poplar streets. Memphis Daily Appeal, 9/23/1859.

Married, In Mississippi county, Ark., on the 18th inst. by Sam'l. B. **LANIER**, Justice of the Peace, Pitts **HAMILTON**, Esq., of James' Bayou, Mo.(?), to Miss Lou., daughter of Rev. Johnson **TURNER**. Memphis Daily Appeal, 1/23/1859.

Married, On Monday, May 18th, at the residence of Mrs. Sarah E. **MONTGOMERY**, by Rev. D. H. **CUMMINGS**, Thomas **HAMILTON** and Miss Battie S. **MONTGOMERY**, both of Tipton county, Tenn. Memphis Daily Appeal, 5/20/1857.

Married, On the 13th inst. in this city, by Elder T. J. **DRANE**, Mr. James N. **HAMLET**, of Arkansas, to Miss Laura G. **CAMPBELL**, of this city. Memphis Daily Appeal, 1/15/1858.

The friends and acquaintances of Mr. J. F. **HAMLIN** are invited to attend the funeral of his late wife, Judith A. R. Hamlin, from his residence at Norwood at 10 o'clock this morning…Burial services will take place at Elmwood Cemetery…Memphis Daily Appeal, 4/23/1856.

On a stormy night in the month of December, 1855, the writer of this article wended his way to the cotton factory in the environs of this city….He found a man named John **HAMMERSTEIN** lying on the floor in the agonies of death. He heard some twenty women detail the cause of his death, and found two sons mourning the loss of a parent. He also saw the pane of glass which was perforated with the discharge of John **BOWLES'** gun—the murderer of John Hammerstein…. When John Bowles is tried by a jury of his countrymen, we will be satisfied with their verdict ….Memphis Daily Appeal, 12/13/1856. A man by the name of John **BOWLES** shot a man last evening at the Bluff City Mills, by the name of John **HAMERSTON**. He shot him with a gun, killing him almost instantly. The evidence was very contradictory and it is thought by some that Bowles did not kill the man he intended to. He was examined before Esq. Horne and bound over for trial at the Criminal Court in the sum of $3,000. Mr. B., we learn, was engineer on a White River packet. Memphis Daily Appeal, 12/9/1855.

Died, In this city on the 9th inst. of Pleurisy, Dr. A. D. **HAMMOND**, of St. Louis, in the 53d year of his age. St. Louis papers please copy. Memphis Eagle & Enquirer, 2/11/1853.

Died, on Friday 7th inst., of scarlet fever, near Collierville, Tenn., three children of Dr. J. C. P. **HAMMOND**—Lee, aged five years; Harry, aged two and a half or three years, and little Fanny, about three months old....Memphis Daily Appeal, 11/12/1856.

Married, On the 10th September, at the residence of the bride's father, near Fisherville, by Dr. W. G. **LANCASTER**, Mr. A. B. **HAMNER** and Miss M. A. V. **HOOKER**, all of Shelby county, Tenn. Memphis Daily Appeal, 10/13/1857.

Married. Near Fisherville, Tenn. by Rev. M. W. **WEBBER**, Mr. A. W. **HAMNER** to Miss M. E. **WEBBER**, all of Shelby co., Tenn. Memphis Appeal, 11/23/1854.

Married, On the morning of the 19th inst. by Rev. A. W. **JONES**, Mr. C. S. **HAMNER**, editor of the Dyersburg *Recorder* to Miss Martha J. **COCKRILL**, of Jackson, Tennessee. Memphis Daily Appeal, 8/23/1857.

Died—In this city on Monday evening, the 8th inst., Henry R. **HAMPTON**, a Printer, in his 19th year, and for some months past employed in this office....Weekly Appeal, 6/12/1846.

Married, In Sommerville, on the 30th ult., by the Rev. Jos. T. **ALEMANY**, Mr. Jas. W. **HAMPTON** of Memphis, to Miss Henrietta **McEVOY** of the former place. Daily Enquirer, 10/3/1847. A tribute to the memory of James W. Hampton, who died at Cooper's Well, November 30th, in the 31st year of his age. On last Sabbath morning we were called to assemble around the couch of the dying...Mr. J. W. Hampton, from Memphis, Tenn., having been deeply afflicted for more than twelve months with chronic diarrhea...he contracted a violent cold, which resulted in acute Pneumonia, brought on by exposure; he having been so tenderly watched in his own cherished home by a doting wife...Franklin, Ten., papers please copy. Memphis Appeal, 12/11/1851.

I offer for sale my lands in Shelby County, 15 miles from Memphis, near Cuba post office, containing about 800 acres....For terms apply to Col. G. B. **LOCKE**, of Memphis, or to the subscriber, residing at Raleigh, Tenn....John W. **HAMSON**. Memphis Appeal, 6/6/1854.

We are pained to announce the accidental drowning of a son of Mr. A.(?) S. **HANCOCK**, merchant of this city, which sad event occurred about five o'clock last evening, while the lad was bathing in the Mississippi river, below the foot of Beal street....up to eight o'clock last night the body had not been found. The name of the deceased is John Hancock, and he was between twelve and thirteen years of age....Memphis Daily Appeal, 7/18/1857.

Married, On 28th instant by Rev. J. W. **BATES**, Mr. Cal. **HANCOCK**, of Marshall county, Miss., to Miss M. A. **GALLAWAY**, of Lafayette. Memphis Daily Appeal, 3/30/1859.

Married, at the residence of her father in Marshal county, Miss., on the 28th inst., by the Rev. J. H. **GRAY**, Mr. John A. G. **HANCOCK** to Miss Mary E. **DELOACH**. Memphis Enquirer, 3/31/1848. Died, In DeSoto county, Miss., on Saturday, the 30th day of August, of congestive chill, John W., son of John A. G. and Mary E. Hancock, aged 2 years, 4 months and 21 days. Memphis Daily Appeal, 9/4/1856. Died, On Tuesday, the 15th inst., in DeSoto county, Mississippi, Kate, youngest daughter of John A. G. and Mary E. Hancock, aged one year, one month and twenty-four days. Memphis Daily Appeal, 9/17/1857.

Married, At the residence of her father, Wm. A. **MASK**, Esq., of Hardeman county, by Rev. Thos. **TAYLOR**, Miss Kate M. Mask to Wm. F. **HANCOCK**, of New Castle, Hardeman county. Memphis Daily Appeal, 9/18/1855.

The firemen on Sunday, in their uniforms, attended to their last resting place, at Winchester Cemetery, the remains of Elisha **HANLAN**, a respected member of Company No. 4. Memphis Daily Appeal, 10/6/1857.

Married, On Tuesday night, 10th inst., by Rev. R. C. **GRUNDY**, D.D., at the residence of Mr. G. **WORLEY**, Mr. James **HANNAH**, Jr., of the firm of Hannah & Shanks, to Mattie W. **THOMPSON**. Memphis Daily Appeal, 11/12/1857.

Died, In this city on Saturday evening, 5th inst., after a brief illness, Col. Robert **HANNAH**, an old resident of Memphis.....He had resided in Memphis for many years.....Memphis Daily Appeal, 3/7/1853.

The friends and acquaintances of the late Thomas **HANNEGAN** are respectfully invited to attend his funeral....This Evening, from his late residence, No. 8 Exchange Building. Memphis Daily Appeal, 8/27/1859. Having taken out letters of administration on the estate of the late Thomas Hannegan, deceased, notice is hereby given to all persons indebted to said estate....Ann **HANNEGAN**, Administratrix. Memphis Daily Appeal, 9/8/1859.

Married, On Tuesday evening the 17th inst., by Rev. Father Grace, Miss Mollie A. **MAGIVENY** and Gustavus A. **HANSON**, both of this city. Memphis Whig, 6/19/1856.

Mr. Jas. **HARBACH**, late steward of the Worsham House, has taken the Wharf-boat Hotel, recently kept by Mr. _adleman, and it is now fitted up in fine style....Memphis Daily Appeal, 5/16/1857.

The undersigned offers for sale his Plantation near the Pigeon Roost Plank Road, in Shelby county, ten miles from Memphis. The tract of land contains about 700 acres....William **HARBERT**. Memphis Daily Appeal, 11/2/1855.

Married, In this city on Wednesday the 18 inst. by the Rev. G. W. **COONS**, Mr. George C. **HARDIN** to Miss Juliet M., daughter of Dr. Geo. R. **GRANT**, all of this city. Memphis Eagle & Enquirer, 5/20/1853.

Married, In Little Rock at the residence of Gen. Samuel **MITCHELL**, on Wednesday evening the 14th inst., by Rev. Mr. Morgan, John E. **HARDING**, of Arkansas, late of Nashville, Tenn., to Miss Bettie Mitchell, daughter of Gen. Saml. Mitchell. Memphis Whig, 5/29/1856.

Died, At his residence in Mississippi county, Arkansas, on the morning of the 13th, Hon. Thomas M. **HARDING**, in the thirty-third year of his age....Mr. Harding was a native of Davidson county, Tennessee, from whence he removed to Arkansas in 1846. He was chosen to represent his county in the last General Assembly.....Memphis Daily Appeal, 3/24/1857. Died, On the morning of the 13th instant, at his residence in Social Bend, Mississippi county, Arkansas, Thomas M. Harding....Nashville and Little Rock papers will please copy. Memphis Daily Appeal, 3/15/1857.

Died. On the 27th instant, in this city, at the residence of her brother Lemuel P., Miss Catharine J. **HARDAWAY**...The Appeal, 1/31/1845.

Died—Yesterday, August 13th, Charles L. **HARDAWAY**, of this city, about 38 years of age, of Jaundice. The funeral will take place to-day, at 10 o'clock, A.M., from the corner of Washington street and Front Row.....Memphis Daily Appeal, 8/14/1847.

Died—in this city on the morning of Thursday last, after a short illness, Mr. James P. **HARDAWAY**, aged about 5__ years. The deceased became a citizen of this place at an early period; and was much esteemed for the sterling integrity of his character. Weekly Appeal, Fri., 7/24/1846.

Died, At Full Accord, Marshall county, Miss. on the 24th instant, James Peterson, son of Dr. John P. and Alice **HARDAWAY**, aged 18 months. Memphis Appeal, 6/26/1855.

We are authorized to announce Lemuel P. **HARDAWAY** a candidate for re-election as Sheriff of Shelby county at the ensuing March election. American Eagle, 6/30/1843. A letter from our fellow citizen Maj. Nath **ANDERSON**, conveys the painful intelligence of the decease of Mr. Lemuel P. Hardaway, for many years a citizen of Memphis, and much respected by its citizens. He expired at the mouth of the Rio Grande on the 26th ult. after ten days illness of dysentary. Major Anderson says, "I am having his remains put in a leaden coffin, and shall send them to Memphis, or bring them with me when I return, (which will be in some two or three weeks) in order that they may receive the last sad rites from his Masonic brethren." Memphis Appeal, 11/7/1848.

On yesterday morning....a man named Michael **HARDIGAN**, who was at work on the new house in course of construction near the corner of Main and Washington streets, met with an accident which caused his death in a short time.——hile arranging some planks on the joists of the second floor, he missed his footing and fell, striking his right side with great force against one of the joists....before he could be placed on a bed at his boarding-house....he expired....The deceased, we learn, leaves a wife and several children in England. Memphis Daily Avalanche, 7/14/1859.

Died. In Sommerville, Tenn., on the 29th September, 1853, Miss Leannah Hardwick, daughter of Mr. L. C. **HARDWICK**, aged 13 years and 11 days....Memphis Daily Appeal, 10/4/1853.

Died—On the 6th instant, Mrs. Martha Hardy, the amiable consort of Rufus S. **HARDY**, and daughter of the late Levi **JOY**, Esq. As a wife, mother and christian, Mrs. Hardy was all that her bereaved friends could have wished her. Weekly Appeal, 7/24/1846.

Married—In Shelby county, on the 19th inst., by the Rev. Mr. McFerran, Mr. Jno. A. **HARE**, of Fayette co., to Miss Mary B. **WARE**. Memphis Enquirer, 1/10/1840.

Died, At the Prentiss House, in Vicksburg, on his way to Cooper's Well, at half past 10 P.M., on Sunday night, Sept. 30th, of chronic dyspepsia, Col. Starkie **HARE**, of Shelby co., Tenn., aged about 45. Memphis Daily Eagle, 10/7/1850.

Married, By Jesse **WALDRAN**, Esq. on the 12th inst., Mr. Wm. **HARE** to Miss Mary **HENRY**, all of this city. Memphis Eagle & Enquirer, 6/14/1853.

Died, in Memphis, on Wednesday evening, June 2, 1859, of acute inflammatory rheumatism, Charles **HARPER**, Esq. The deceased was born on the 3d day of January, 1824, in Worcester county, Maryland. When quite a boy, his active and enterprising disposition induced him to move westward. He located in Lexington, Ky., where he resided several years, engaged in the mercantile business....From thence he removed to our city, where he was engaged several years in the wholesale grocery business; from here he went to New Orleans, where he still followed the same line of business....New Orleans, Baltimore and Lexington, Ky., papers please copy. Memphis Daily Appeal, 6/28/1859.

Died, on the evening of the 13th, after a short and painfull illness, which she bore with the fortitude and resignation of a true christian, Eleanor White **HARPER**, wife of Capt. Harper, of this city. The sudden demise of this truly good and amiable lady, has plunged an affectionate husband and a large interesting family into the deepest affliction.....As a devoted daughter, her last fond wishes were breathed for her venerable mother, still living....As a christian, she was a strict and faithful member of the Methodist Episcopal Church for a period of twenty years up to her death.....She was born March 14th, 1801, was a native of North Carolina, and educated in the city of Raleigh, of the same State....Raleigh (N.C.) and Nashville (Tenn.) papers please copy. Weekly Memphis Eagle, 6/21/1849.

Married—In Tipton co., Tenn., on Wednesday, the 16th of September, by the Rev. Jno. **WILSON**, Dr. R. B. **HARPER**, to Miss Martha, daughter of Andrew **McQUISTON**. Memphis Appeal, 10/2/1847.

Married. On the 14th instant near Fisherville, Tenn., by Wm. G. **LANCASTER**, Esq., Mr. A. **HARRELL** to Miss S. Fannie, daughter of Mr. B. W. **WEBBER**, all of Shelby county. Memphis Daily Appeal, 3/21/1855.

The Carrollton (Miss.) Democrat learns that an accident happened, a few days since, in the neighborhood of Shongalo, which resulted in the death of Mr. J. J. **HARRELL**, a well-known citizen of this county, by the accidental discharge of a gun in the hands of a Mr. Bowes. It appears that they were in pursuit of a runaway negro at the time, and had just come in sight of him, when they came to a fence. Mr. Harrell was behind the other, and within a few steps of him, when the gun went off, and the whole contents passed through Mr. Harrell. He fell dead on the spot. Memphis Daily Avalanche, 4/11/1859.

Died, At his residence near Elba, in Fayette county, on the 10th instant, Wm. **HARRELL**, Esq., in the fifty-third year of his age. The deceased leaves an interesting family. Memphis Daily Appeal, 10/21/1856.

Died at her residence in LaGrange, on Thursday the 7th instant, Mrs. Bttie Harrington, wife of Samuel J. **HARRINGTON**, and daughter of Stephen and Eliza H. **JARMON**, formerly of Hardeman county, Tenn. The deceased was aged 29 years 3 months and 19(?) days. Early in life she made a profession of religion and united with the Presbyterian church….Her husband and children were called to her and she calmly gave to each a farewell kiss. Father, mother and brothers, with a large circle of friends, mourn her loss….Memphis Daily Appeal, 4/19/1859.

Died, in this city, yesterday morning, in the 14th year of her age, Malvina Bass, daughter of Mr. A. O. **HARRIS**. The friends and acquaintances of the family are respectfully invited to attend the funeral services at 10 o'clock this morning, from the Episcopal church. Memphis Daily Eagle, 4/19/1848. Died— In this City on Wednesday last, Miss Maria Harris, daughter of A. O. Harris, Esq…..Memphis Enquirer, Wednesday, 12/13/1848. Married, In Calvary Church, Memphis, last evening at 8 o'clock by Rev. D. C. **PAGE**, D.D., Mr. William **PROUDFIT**, of Brownsville, to Miss Laura Harris, daughter of A. O. Harris, Esq., of this city. Memphis Daily Appeal, 11/25/1852.

Died, In this city, last evening, at the residence of his brother, E. O. **HARRIS**, Esq., Mr. W. T. **HARRIS**, for many years a resident and Merchant at Randolph, Tennessee. The friends and acquaintances of the deceased are requested to attend his funeral this morning at 10 o'clock, from the Episcopal Church. Memphis Daily Eagle, 11/5/1850.

Married, On the 14th December, 1859, by Rev. L. Hensley **GRUBB**, Mr. Geo. W. **HARRIS**, of Shelby county, near Germantown, Tenn., to Miss Beatrice E. Harris, at her father's, Franklin **HARRIS**, of Jackson county, near Larkinsville, Ala. Memphis Daily Appeal, 12/18/1859.

Married, At the Presbyterian church in Raleigh on Wednesday evening, the 1st inst. by the Rev. D. L. **GRAY**, Howell **HARRIS**, Esq., to Nancy P. **BOSHER**, all of Raleigh. Memphis Eagle & Enquirer, 6/4/1853.

Married, In this city at the residence of Thos. J. **TURLEY**, Esq. on Thursday evening, the 2d inst. by Rev. Mr. Robb, Mr. Isaac W. **HARRIS** to Miss Sarah A. **La BONE** (**BOWE**?), all of this city. Memphis Eagle & Enquirer, 6/4/1853.

Gen. Isham G. **HARRIS**. Gen. Harris, the gallant, eloquent and distinguished champion of the Democracy of Tennessee, arrived at his home, near this city, yesterday morning on the Eastern cars….Democratic Nominations. For Governor, Isham G. Harris, of Shelby. For Congress, William T. **AVERY**; For County Representatives, William C. **DUNLAP**, E. W. M. **KING**. Memphis Daily Appeal, 7/30/1857. County Representatives.—Dunlap and King are certainly elected, the latter by 23 votes over his next highest competitor, and the former by a much larger majority….The Governor elect is also a citizen of Shelby….Memphis Daily Appeal, 8/8/1857.

Married, On the 21st instant by Rev. Reubin **BURROW**, J. S. **HARRIS**, Esq., and Sarah, daughter of Scott **BAYNE**, Esq., all of Shelby county. Memphis Daily Appeal, 8/23/1856.

Married, on the 29th inst., by N. G. **CURTIS**, Esq., Mr. James B. **HARRIS** to Mrs. Matilda **THOMPSON**, all of Memphis. Daily Enquirer, 7/31/1847.

Married, In Calvary Church, Memphis, on Wednesday evening, 29th September by Rev. D. C. **PAGE**, D.D., Mr. Jas. B. **HARRIS**, of this city, to Miss Martha J. **ARNOLD**, of Crittenden county, Ark. Memphis Appeal, 10/1/1852.

Died, At Grand Lake, Ark., on Saturday, the 23d day of January, Mr. James B. **HARRIS**, in the 28th year of his age. The Florence (Alabama) papers will please copy. Memphis Daily Appeal, 2/12/1858.

Married, At the residence of Mr. John **MARTIN**, Memphis, by Rev. Mr. Collins, Col. James T. **HARRIS**, of Memphis, and Mrs. Maria L. **MARTIN**, of Ark. Memphis Whig, 4/18/1856.

Died—Suddenly, in this county on the 22d ult., Mrs. Nancy Harris, aged 70 years, consort of Capt. Matthew **HARRIS**, dec'd., who emigrated from Nelson county, Va. She was enjoying her usual health at dinner, and lay down to rest as she was in the habit of doing after dinner, and soon died without a struggle. The Appeal, 5/2/1844.

An inquest was holden on Monday last, upon the dead body of a man of the name of Nehemiah **HARRIS**, found lying in a decayed condition, in the woods, near the place of Stephen R. **MORRIS**, in the vicinity of the city. Verdict of the jury, that he came to his death "by shooting himself while in a state of derangement." The deceased came to the house of W. Morris some ten days before, in a gloomy and unhappy state of mind, and on Thursday morning last, took a gun and went out as he said to kill squirrels. As he did not return during the day, some apprehensions were entertained concerning his fate, and search made for him in the neighborhood. On Monday last he was found in a dreadfully putrid situation, the gun lying by his side, having evidently been discharged by himself, the muzzle placed at his chin, and the whole contents lodged in his head, producing instant death. There were certain papers found in his possession, one of which from its singular character may be of use to his surviving relatives, who are said to reside in Mississippi. Memphis Appeal, Fri., 6/23/1848.

Lieut. Reuben **HARRIS**, U.S.N. We regret most sincerely to learn that Lieut. R. Harris, U.S.N., who has been connected with the Memphis Navy Yard for 3 years, as acting Master, has been detached from theYard, at his own request, on account of ill health.....He takes his departure for Vicksburg this evening on the fine steamer Bulletin.....Memphis Appeal, 1/12/1853. A most genial and delightful festival was given at the United States Hotel on Monday evening last, in honor of Passed Midshipman Reuben Harris, of the Navy, by a number of his friends, on the occasion of his final departure from this city....Memphis Eagle & Enquirer, Thurs., 3/17/1853.

Died, On the 4th instant, seven miles below Memphis, Mrs. Sneed **HARRIS**, of disease of the lungs; aged 43 years. Memphis Daily Appeal, 9/6/1856.

Wm. **HARRIS**, a preacher, dentist, etc., was convicted by our criminal court last evening for kidnapping a slave boy from Mr. Bowles, and sentenced to the Penitentiary for five years—the jury recommending him to the mercy of the court—the only contingency by which we presume they were enabled to agree upon a verdict, after being out six days. The general opinion is that Harris deserves no further mercy than the jury awarded him in the leniency of their verdict. The defence set up was insanity—which unfortunately for Harris, burst out all of a sudden after his arrest for the crime. We hear great praise awarded to Edwin **YERGER** (?) Esq., for the distinguished legal ability and eloquence displayed by him in the prosecution. Harris was defended by Judge Wm. T. **BROWN** and J. **DELAFIELD** Esq...American Eagle, 7/24/1846.

Gov. Trousdale has appointed Hon. Wm. R. **HARRIS**, Judge of the Common Law and Chancery Court at Memphis, in the place of Hon. Wm. B. **TURLEY**, deceased. Memphis Daily Appeal, 6/13/1851. The terrible casualty which befel Hon. Wm. R. Harris, on the steamer *Pennsylvania*, in common with hundreds of other devoted fellow creatures, terminated in his death yesterday morning at 6 o'clock....He leaves behind him a devoted family....He was the elder brother of the Governor of Tennessee, who has been at his bedside from the moment of his arrival from the scene of the disaster that caused his death....Memphis Daily Appeal, 6/20/1858.

We regret to learn that Dr. Zeno **HARRIS** was lying in a very critical condition last evening with yellow fever. He lives in South Memphis, where he had exhausted himself before his attack by visiting the sick around him. Since writing the above, we learn that Dr. Harris died last night. Memphis Daily Appeal, 9/28/1855. We were in error yesterday morning in announcing the death of Dr. Zeno Harris. We are happy to state that he was still living last night, though, we regret to say, with little hope of recovery. Memphis Daily Appeal, 9/29/1855. We weep while we record the sad and untimely death of one of the noblest of the medical fraternity of our city. Dr. Zeno Harris....departed this life last night, in the 26th year of his age....During the illness of Dr. H. his lovely infant was seized and carried off by the same malignant disease....He leaves a deeply afflicted widow to mourn....Memphis, Saturday, Sept. 29, 1855. Memphis Daily Appeal, 9/30/1855.

I offer for sale the plantation on which I now reside, 15 miles from Memphis on the Pigeon Roost Plank Road, in De Soto county, Miss., containing 400 acres....D. W. **HARRISON**. Memphis Appeal, 7/28/1854.

Died, At his residence in Shelby county, on the 4th day of April, 1857, Mr. Henry **HARRISON**, in the sixty-second year of his age. Memphis Daily Appeal, 4/12/1857.

Married. Last evening, 19th inst., by Hume F. **HILL**, Esq., Mr. Henry T. **HARRISON** to Miss Emma F. **BARKER**, both of Memphis Theatre. Memphis Appeal, 3/21/1855.

Married, On the 20th inst. at Mrs. Logan's in this city, by Rev. J. T. C. **COLLINS**, Mr. James C. **HARRISON** to Miss Virginia **ST. JOHNS**, both of Memphis, Tenn. Memphis Daily Appeal, 12/22/1859.

Died—On the 31st ult. Rebecca Thompson, aged nine months, daughter of the Rev. Jeptha **HARRISON**, of this city. Memphis Enquirer, 9/7/1839.

I offer at private sale my Lands, north of Hatchie river, in Shelby co., 18 miles from Memphis, containing 797 ½ acres....The improvements are good Frame Houses and have been erected within the last two years. Also the Negroes on the place....John W. **HARRISON**. Memphis Appeal, 2/17/1854. Died, At his residence in the county of Shelby, Tenn., of pulmonary consumption, on the evening of the 15th of February, 1859, Mr. John W. Harrison, in the 48th year of his age, leaving a disconsolate wife and seven children to mourn....Mr. Harrison was a native of Brunswick county, Va. He removed to Shelby county, Tenn., in the fall of 1847, where he continued to live till called hence by death....Richmond and Petersburg, Va., papers will please copy. Memphis Daily Appeal, 3/3/1859.

On Saturday morning the 3rd instant, Mrs. Sophia Harrison, relict of Joshua **HARRISON**, deceased, terminated her earthly existence at the house of her son-in-law, Dr. R. B. **RUCHER**, in the vicinity of Middleton, a few miles south of this place, by hanging herself. [Murfreesboro News, 7th. Memphis Daily Appeal, 3/15/1855.

Married, At Covington on the 5th instant by Rev. Mr. McFadden, R. H. **HARRISON**, M.D., and Miss Mattie V., daughter of Dr. Isaac **TOWEL**. Memphis Daily Appeal, 5/9/1856.

Married, By the Rev. Dr. Page, on Thursday evening, 27th June, Mr. James **HART** to Miss Mary Batte Locke, daughter of Jos. **LOCKE**, of Shelby county. Memphis Daily Eagle, 7/2/1850.

Died—In this town, on Thursday morning last, Arthur, infant son of Col. Jas. A. **HART**. Memphis Enquirer, Sat., 7/1/1837.

Died, On the 28th ult. in Shelby county, in the vicinity of Memphis, Mrs. Martha Hart, relict of the late Robert W. **HART**, in her 66th year. The deceased was born in Guilford county, North Carolina and subsequently resided for many years near Nashville, in Middle Tenn. She was a devoted member of the Presbyterian church for about 27 years previous to her death, and has left to her children and posterity a rich legacy in a life of almost unexampled purity and goodness.... Nashville papers please copy. Memphis Daily Appeal, 4/4/1853.

Died, On Tuesday evening, July 1st, Miss Rody **HART**, after a long and painful illness of paralytic affection. The deceased was one of the first inhabitants of Memphis….Memphis Daily Appeal, 7/3/1856.

Died. At Fort Pickering, on Thursday last, Mrs. Aurelia, consort of Capt. W. W. **HART**, aged 38 years…..May a kind Providence provide for the lambs of the fold made so desolate and temper the winds, that they breathe kindly upon the shorn and motherless little ones….Memphis Eagle, 5/27/1848. Died—At Fort Pickering, on the 15th inst., Com___ Woolcott, only son of W. W. Hart. American Eagle, 1/17/1845. It is with deep regret that we announce to our readers, the death of one of our oldest and most highly respected citizens, Capt. W. W. Hart. But a few weeks since, it was our melancholy duty, as a journalist, to announce the demise of his estimable lady, Mrs. Aurelia Hart. The eyes of the unfortunate orphans are still damp with the tears of affection, in memory of a most beloved mother….Memphis Appeal, 6/27/1848.

Married, On Wednesday evening, December 10th, by Rev. Dr. Gray, A. 1. **HARTLEY**, Local Editor of the *Eagle & Enquirer,* and Miss Margaret **COOK**, all of Memphis. Memphis Daily Appeal, 12/12/1856.

The insolvency of the Estate of Nathan **HARTSFIELD** having been suggested before the Clerk of the County Court of Tipton county, Tenn…Memphis Daily Appeal, 10/26/1852.

Died—In Memphis, Tenn., on Tuesday morning the 22d inst., James **HARTWELL**, aged about 19 years. The Appeal, 8/25/1843.

Report of the Board of Health. For the last 24 hours, ending 12 o'clock M, June 30….N. W. **HARTWELL**, aged 86, Cholera…..Daily Memphis Enquirer, 7/1/1849.

Married, Near Colliersville, Shelby county, April 4th, by the Rev. Mr. Halley, Mr. Wilkinson **HARTWELL** to Miss Sarah **SNOW**. The Appeal, 4/19/1844.

Administrator's Notice – Being duly qualified by the Honorable County Court of Shelby, administrator of the estate of Madison P. **HARVEL**, deceased, notice is hereby given to all those indebted to said estate to make payment…..J. W. **TYUS**, Adm'r. Memphis Enquirer, 10/27/1838.

A large portion of the populace were astonished yesterday afternoon by the report that a man had been shot on Main street….It seems that a difficulty occurred in Mr. Holland's stable on yesterday afternoon between a young man named N. W. **NORFLEET**, from Chulahoma, Miss., and Mr. **HARVER** and his son William, which resulted in the shooting of the latter by Mr. Norfleet….We neglected stating that the wound received was from a pistol in the hands of Mr. Norfleet and that the ball entered between the second and third ribs, and is supposedly by his physician to have lodged in his back….the parents of William Harver have the sympathy of the community in their affliction. Memphis Daily Appeal, 10/28/1856. We were pained to learn last evening that Wm. Harver….died at 12 o'clock yesterday. Memphis Daily Appeal, 10/29/1856.

Pursuant to a decretal order of the Circuit Court of Shelby County, at the January term, 1848, I will on the 1st day of April, 1848, proceed to sell on the premises to the highest bidder for cash, the entire interest of the heirs of Wm. **HARVEY** dec'd., in and to a certain twenty-Five or six, acre tract of Land, situated on the State Line Road about 2 ½ miles from Memphis, saving and reserving to Lucy Ann **HARVEY** the widow of said Wm. Harvey, her dower interest in the same. Memphis Eagle, 3/11/1848.

Gen. Wm. T. **HASKELL**.—We are pleased to learn that this distinguished gentleman has become a citizen of Memphis. He has located here for the purpose of devoting himself unreservedly to the practice of his profession. Memphis Eagle & Enquirer, 3/20/1853. We regret to announce the death of Gen. Wm. T. Haskell, late of this city. The sad occurrence took place at Hopkinsville, Ky., on Monday last. Gen. H. was a brilliant orator and a gallant soldier. Memphis Daily Avalanche, Fri., 3/18/1859.

Married. On the 18th inst. by the Rev. N. **SULLIVAN**, Mr. D. M. B. **HASSLER** to Miss Jennie R., eldest daughter of Robert **LOCKE**, Esq., all of LaGrange, Tenn. Memphis Daily Appeal, 10/20/1854.

123

Died, On the 14th of November, 1857, at Kickapoo, Texas, J. Quitman Haston, son of Thomas M. and Harriet A. **HASTON**. Huntsville Democrat please copy. Memphis Daily Appeal, 1/5/1858.

Died—In this place on Friday last, in the 21st year of his age, Robert Henry, eldest son of the late Durant **HATCH**. Weekly Appeal, Fri., 9/11/1846.

Married, On Thursday the 7th inst. in Madrid Bend, Tenn., by the Rev. Geo W. **BUSHY**, Mr. Richard H. **HATCHER**, of New Madrid, Mo., to Miss Harriet H. **MARR**, of the former place. Memphis Eagle & Enquirer, 4/19/1853.

Died, At Brownsville, Tenn. on the 26th inst., Mr. W. F. **HATSELL**, aged 22 years. Memphis Eagle & Enquirer, 2/2/1853.

Married, On the 18th January by the Rev. R. **DAY**, Mr. L. B. **HAUGHTON** to Miss Margaret E. **ASKEW**, both of Madison county, Tenn. Memphis Eagle & Enquirer, 2/2/1853.

On Monday morning last, Dr. W. P. **HAUGHTON**, of this city, was killed by his horse running away with his buggy, some thirteen miles from here, in the neighborhood of Quincy....When found, his foot was hung in the fore spring of the buggy and his head was lying nearly under the hinder-wheel. His neck was broken in two places and his back and both legs were also broken. He had his little son with him at the time, who was knocked senseless and very severely injured, but who, it is thought, will probably recover....Aberdeen (Miss.) Democrat. Memphis Appeal, 7/16/1854.

Died, On Wednesday the 9th inst. at the residence of his father Mr. Wm. **HAUSON**, on Linden street, South Memphis, Edward **HAUSON**, aged 21 years and 7 days....Memphis Eagle & Enquirer, 2/10/1853.

Married, In this city on the 23d inst., by G. P. **SCHETKY**, Mr. _. W. **HAVENS** to Miss Cornelia **ULMO**. Memphis Weekly Appeal, 12/1/1858.

Married—On Wednesday evening, 5th inst., by the Rev. Samuel **DENNIS**, Dr. B. H. **HAWKINS**, of Raleigh, to Miss Lucy E. **VAUGHAN**, of this county. Memphis Enquirer, 2/7/1840.

Married—On the 21st instant, by Rev. M. E_____, Mr. Jas. L. **HAWKINS** to Miss Sarah, daughter of Edm'd H. **VAUGHAN**, Esq. of Shelby county. Memphis Enquirer, 12/30/1837.

Married, In this city on the 4th inst., at the residence of Mr. Samuel M. **JOBE**, by Elder T. J. **DRANE**, Dr. W. S. **HAWKINS**, of Jackson, Tenn., to Miss Susan M. **JOBE**, of Memphis. Memphis Weekly Appeal, 3/17/1858.

Died, At 6 o'clock P.M., on the 10th inst., of scarlet fever, Avis Chapman, youngest daughter of M. and S. A. **HAWKS**. Funeral services from their residence, Pontotoc street, between Shelby and Main....Memphis Daily Appeal, 2/11/1858.

We regret to learn, from the California papers, that W. W. **HAWKS**, son of Dr. F. **HAWKS**, died in San Francisco, Calif., last month. He had just returned from one of the Sandwich Islands, where he had gone with the vain hope that the mild climate of Tahiti would restore his declining health. Mr. Hawks lived for some years in Marshall county, and emigrated to California in 1850. When he reached that State, he located at San Francisco, where he soon became a prominent man, having frequently represented that city in the Legislature of the State....Memphis Daily Appeal, 4/30/1859.

Died....on Wednesday morning, March 2, at the residence of A. **WOODWARD** on Adams street, Judge H. **HAWLEY**, aged 77 years....Memphis Daily Appeal, 3/2/1859.

Married, on Thursday evening last, by the Rev. Samuel **WATSON**, Mr. Joseph H. **HAWLEY** to Miss Susan C. **BROWN**, all of Memphis. The Appeal, Fri., 10/6/1843.

Died, In this city, on the 25th of May, Mary Rose, infant daughter of R. B. and M. V. **HAWLEY**, aged four months and five days. Memphis Eagle & Enquirer, 5/28/1852. The friends and acquaintances of the families of J. H. and R. B. Hawley are invited to attend the funeral of J. Henry **HAWLEY**, from his late residence on the new Raleigh road This (Wednesday) Evening at 3 o'clock. Memphis Daily Appeal, 8/5/1857.

We are authorized to announce John W. **HAWTHORN**, as a Candidate for Beat Constable in the 13th Civil District, at the ensuing March election. Memphis Daily Appeal, 12/19/1847.

We part this morning with one of the oldest employees in our office, Mr. John J. **HAY**, who leaves us with the view of going through a course of studies in the Virginia University.... Memphis Daily Appeal, 4/28/1857.

Notice. Law Side Common Law and Chancery Court of the City of Memphis, September 7th, 1859. George **HAYDEN**, exparte petition. Petitioner, a free man of color, has this day filed in said Court, his application to voluntarily convey himself into slavery and choose a master, and said petitioner and D. R. **COOK**, his desired owner, are hereby required to appear at the next November term of said Court....Memphis Daily Appeal, 9/8/1859.

Married. On Wednesday evening the 2d inst. by Esq. Parker, Major J. **HAYDEN**, to Mrs. Elizabeth **BORLAND**, all of South Memphis. Weekly American Eagle, 9/10/1846.

Died, at the Gayoso House on the 5th inst., Mrs. Elizabeth B. Hayden, wife of J. A. **HAYDEN**, Esq., of St. Louis, in the 20th year of her age. During the brief residence of the departed in this city, she had won the esteem of a large number of sincere friends, who deeply sympathise with her relatives abroad in the melancholy loss they have sustained in the untimely decease.... American Eagle Weekly, 3/7/1845.

Married. On the 18th instant at the residence of her father, Dr. J. M. **WALKER**, by the Right Rev. Bishop Otey, Mr. A. J. **HAYES**, of Jackson, Tenn., and Miss Elizabeth M. Walker, of this city. Memphis Whig, 4/20/1855.

Died, in this city on the 26th inst., G. W. **HAYES**, son of Mrs. Eliza **CARROLL**, in the fourteenth year of his age. St. Louis papers please copy. The friends and acquaintances of Mrs. Eliza Carroll are invited to attend the funeral of her son, George Wesley Hayes....Memphis Daily Appeal, 10/27/1859.

Married, In this city on the evening of the 3d inst., by Rev. Mr. Steadman, Mr. John **HAYNE**, of New York, to Miss Margaret **MILLER**, of this city. Memphis Daily Appeal, 8/5/1858.

Col. W. Scott **HAYNES** died at New Orleans on the evening of the 4th inst. Col. Haynes was attached to the Liberating Army invading Cuba under Lopez, was taken prisoner and released by the Captain General. Col. H. formerly edited a paper at Shelbyville, in this State. Memphis Eagle & Enquirer, 5/10/1853.

Married, On the 17th inst., near Germantown, by the Rev. L. D. **MULLENS**, Mr. D. L. **HAYNIE**, to Miss M. L. **SUGGS**, all of this county. Memphis Eagle & Enquirer, 3/25/1852.

Memphis Wharf Company. A payment of Ten Dollars upon each share of the capital stock of this Company is required to be made on the 25th inst. by order. Jno. W. **HAYNIE**, Treas. Memphis Enquirer, 8/5/1837.

Land For Sale. A First Rate Farm, containing 260 acres...lying seven miles South of Memphis, on the Horn Lake Road...Thornton **HAYNIE**. Daily Enquirer, 7/28/1847.

Married. On the evening of the 18th at "Villa Rose," by Rev. Bishop Otey, Andrew J. **HAYS** to Miss Elizabeth M., only daughter of Dr. J. M. **WALKER**. Memphis Daily Appeal, 4/21/1855.

Married, On the 10th of December, 1856, by Rev. J. S. **WINFORD**, Mr. Henry M. **HAYS** and Miss Nancy C. **KOONCE**, both of Shelby county, Tenn. Memphis Daily Appeal, 12/17/1856.

Died, In Jackson, Tennessee, on the 14th inst., Sarah Rebecca, youngest child of General and Mrs. S. J. **HAYS**, aged five years, six months and seventeen days. Memphis Daily Appeal, 8/23/1857. Died, In this city on the morning of the 25th, Martha Narcissa, daughter of Gen. S. J. Hays, aged nine years and seven months. Thus, in less than two weeks, has death visited the family of our neighbor and taken two bright jewels of the family household....—*Jackson Whig*. Memphis Daily Appeal, 8/30/1857.

Married, On the 6th January at Oakland Springs, Decatur county, Tenn. by the Rev. John **FISHER**, Rev. Isham G. **HEARN**, of the Memphis Conference, to Miss Anna K., daughter of Col. Wallace **DIXON**. Memphis Eagle & Enquirer, 2/2/1853.

Married, In New Albany, Miss., on Sunday, the 2nd instant, by Rev. Williams S. **SMITH**, Joel A. **HEARN** to Mrs. Ellen C. **ALLMON**. Memphis Weekly Appeal, 5/26/1858.

Died, In this city yesterday evening, Peter **HEIN**, aged 38 years. The friends of his family and brother, Adam **HEIN**, are requested to attend his funeral This Morning, from his residence, corner of Main and Winchester streets, at 8 o'clock. Memphis Daily Appeal, 7/3/1856.

A German named George **HEISER**, was brought before Judge Hill yesterday for Organ Grinding. His Honor having no ear for that particular kind of music fined Heiser $5 and costs. The Mayor, being more susceptible to the influence of the concord of sweet sounds, remitted the fine...Memphis Daily Appeal, 1/8/1852.

George **HELM**, Esq., a talented and highly respected gentleman, and son of ex-Governor Helm, of Kentucky, died in this city at the residence of George W. **DIXON**, on Tuesday night. The deceased had but recently removed to this place, and was engaged in the practice of Law. His remains will be taken to his former home, in Kentucky, for interment. Memphis Evening Ledger, Thursday, 1/28/1858. We regret to learn that George Helm, Esq., late of Kentucky, died at the residence of his uncle, Geo. Dixon, Esq., in this city, on Tuesday night last, in the twenty-fifth year of his age....The deceased was a son of ex-Governor Helm, of Kentucky, and a grandson of the late Hon. Ben. **HARDIN**, who, next to Mr. Clay, was the most remarkable man Kentucky ever produced....Memphis Weekly Appeal, 2/3/1858.

Married, On the 25th inst. by Rev. I. Z. **STERNHEIMER**, Mr. I. **HELMAN** to Miss R. **APPENHEIMER**, all of this city. Memphis Weekly Appeal, 6/2/1858.

A little boy by the name of Wm. **HEMPLE** whose parents reside on the Corner of Center Alley and Exchange Streets, while playing with an old pistol yesterday, by some means discharged it and the ball passed directly through his heart and came out of his back, entering the hand of his sister and inflicting a severe wound. The little fellow tried to reach his mother, but fell dead before he had advanced half a dozen steps. He was twelve years of age. This is another warning to parents how they allow children to play with fire arms. Memphis Whig, 2/19/1856.

The friends of the late Anderson **HENDERSON** are requested to attend his funeral This Afternoon at 2 o'clock from the First Presbyterian Church. Memphis Daily Appeal, 10/26/1858.

Married, On the 21st, at the residence of John D. **FENNELL**, by Rev. James L. **CHAPMAN**, Mr. Connally F. **HENDERSON**, of Memphis, Tenn. to Miss Sarah Eliza **FENNELL**, of Desoto county, Miss. Memphis Daily Appeal, 10/23/1852.

Died, On the 17th inst., at the residence of W. S. **BENSON**(?), Esq., in Marshall county, Miss., Isabella, infant daughter of Mr. J. M. **HENDERSON**, aged one year and five months. Memphis Daily Appeal, 10/21/1857.

Died, On yesterday morning, Ledwell Dawson, aged 4 ½ years, son of Jackson Reed and Ann Eliza **HENDERSON**, of Memphis. Memphis Daily Appeal, 10/31/1851.

Died, On the 18th October, 1852, at the residence of Wm. E. **BOWERS**, Esq., James **HENDERSON**, aged 16 years, 7 months. Memphis Daily Appeal, 11/30/1852.

Married—On Tuesday evening Inst., by Rev. Jeptha **HARRISON**, at the residence of Dr. Wyatt **CHRISTIAN**, Mr. Joseph **HENDERSON**, Merchant of this place, to Miss Elizabeth **COCKE**. Memphis Enquirer, Fri., 6/14/1839.

Died – In this city, at an early hour yesterday morning, Joseph **HENDERSON**, Esq. aged 32 years; a native of Donegall, Ireland, but for many years a resident of Memphis, and one among her early and enterprizing merchants.....--Enquirer of the 2d. The Appeal, 2/9/1844.

Land For Sale – As Trustees of the Presbyterian and Methodist Churches of Memphis, we offer the Camp Ground containing 14 acres. It has a good spring on it, and is situated about 4 miles from Memphis, near the stage road. For particulars, apply to either of us, or to C. **BIAS**, Memphis. Littleton **HENDERSON**, Dudly **DUNN**, Trustees. P.S. I have 10 acres adjoining the above land which is also offered for sale. Littleton Henderson. Memphis Enquirer, 4/26/1839. Departed this life on the 9th inst. Miss Eliza Henderson, daughter of Littleton Henderson, Esq. The deceased died from the effect of a fall from a horse... Memphis Enquirer, 3/18/1847. The friends and acquaintances of Mrs. Mary King, consort of Littleton Henderson, are invited to attend her funeral, at Wesley Chapel, at 10 o'clock in the morning. Services by Rev. J. W. **KNOTT**. Memphis Appeal, 11/21/1854. We were pained yesterday to hear of the death of one of our oldest and most respected citizens, Mr. Littleton Henderson, who departed this life last Sunday evening. Mr. Henderson's citizenship in Memphis dates back to its earliest settlement. He was regarded as the father of the First Presbyterian Church in this city....Memphis Daily Appeal, Tues., 4/7/1857.

Died, At Raleigh, Tenn., June 4th, 1852, in the 27th year of her age, Mrs. Sarah W. **HENDERSON**.... Memphis Eagle & Enquirer, 6/9/1852.

Married, In Christian county, Ky., on the 6th instant, by Rev. Mr. White, Col. Wm. T. **HENDERSON**, of Corsicans, Texas, and Miss Martha Louisa **EDWARDS**, of Kentucky. Memphis Daily Appeal, 10/25/1856.

Died....on the 25th ult., John Arthur, son of Dr. W. J. and L. T. **HENDRICK**, aged six years and nearly six months. The Richmond (Va.) Christian Advocate and Richmond Enquirer copy. Memphis Daily Appeal, 12/3/1859.

Married—On Wednesday evening, 9th inst., in this vicinity, by Rev. A. G. **McNUTT**, Mr. J. E. **HENDRICKS** to Miss Jane R. **McMILLAN**, all of this county. American Eagle Weekly, 7/11/1845.

Died. On the morning of the 24th, in the 2__ th year of her age, Mrs. Ellen F. Hendrickson, consort of the Rev. C. R. **HENDRICKSON**, pastor of the 1st Baptist Church of this city. Memphis Eagle & Enquirer, 5/31/1854.

Died—In this town on Sunday morning last, of congestive fever, Mr. Turner B. **HENLEY**, aged 37 years, formerly of McMinnville, this state. Memphis Enquirer, Thurs., 9/1/1836.

A Mrs. **HENLY**, living on Wolf river, was killed on Monday last from the discharge of a gun. Report says that Mrs. H. and her husband were scuffling for the possession of the gun, when it went off, killing the woman immediately. No legal investigation has, as yet, taken place. Memphis Daily Appeal, Sat., 8/7/1852.

The friends and acquaintances of Maj. A. H. **HENRY** are requested to attend his Funeral from the First Baptist Church, this evening....Memphis Daily Appeal, 1/12/1859.

Departed this life, at the residence of his parents, in the city of Memphis, on the 10th of July last, Lewis Henry, in the sixth year of his age. The deceased was the youngest child of A. J. and M. M. **HENRY**....His disease, which was cholera....Memphis Daily Appeal, 9/11/1855. The recent death of the late lovely, loving and beloved Mary E. Henry....third daughter of A. J. Henry, Esq., and the late lamented M. M. Henry, departed this life at the residence of her father, in this city, on the 6th of April last, in the 16th year of her age, after a short but painful attack of quick consumption....Her love for her parents and brothers and sisters was second only to her love of God and truth....Memphis Daily Appeal, 5/17/1857.

Died—in this city on the 11th of January, ult., after a brief but severe attack of pneumonia, in the 52d year of his age, Major Andrew Jackson **HENRY**. Mr. Henry was a native of Kentucky, but moved to Alabama when quite a boy, and thence to Somerville, Tenn., with his bride, in the year 1828, where he remained until he came to this place....He came to this city in the fall of 1841 and engaged in the cotton and commission business, in which, like many others, he was unfortunate, and a few brief years reduced him from comparative wealth to the necessity of taking a clerkship....One after another, five lovely children, some of them just budding in the charms of infant innocence, and others rich in the flush of mature youth and virtues, were borne to the grave; while the wife and mother, who had been the center of the home scene, also slept in the center of that scene which is the final home of us all....The mortal remains of Major Henry were buried in the Morris Cemetery, attended by the Hon. Fraternity of Free and Accepted Masons, of which he was an honorable and worthy member....Memphis Daily Appeal, 3/18/1859.

Died, in Marion, Ark., on the 2d instant, James A. **HENRY**, eldest son of Wm. **HENRY**, of Shelby co., Tenn. Memphis Enquirer, 2/21/1840.

An Irishman named John **HENRY** committed suicide yesterday morning about six o'clock in front of Claney's boarding house, on Winchester street below Main, by cutting his throat from ear to ear with a razor....Mr. Henry had been a laborer on the railroad until a short time since. He was about twenty-seven years of age. He had only been known in this city two months....Memphis Daily Appeal, 5/10/1857.

Died: In De Soto Co., Miss., on the 13th ult., Mrs. Rebecca J. Henry, consort of Col. John S. **HENRY**. Weekly Memphis Eagle, 2/8/1849.

Died, In this city on the 11th inst., at the residence of J. A. **McCALL**, Miss Mary E. **HENRY**, of this county. Memphis Eagle, 5/22/1850.

Married, On the 26th inst., by J. **WALDRAN**, Esq., Mr. P. **HENRY** to Mrs. Phoebe **ROARK**, all of this county. Memphis Eagle, 5/28/1850.

Married, on the 13th inst., by the Hon. E. W. M. **KING**, at the office of E. O. **PERRIN**, Mr. Robert **HENRY** to Miss Elizabeth **ANDERSON**, all of this city. Mr. Editor.—There are some peculiar incidents connected with the above singular match which may not prove wholly uninteresting, and perhaps as an example it may prove profitable. The parties came to this city a short time since from New Orleans as husband and wife, but the nuptials never having been celebrated, the grand jury returned bills of indictment against both parties "for offending against the peace and dignity of the State." The parties, before appearing at the Commercial and Criminal Court, took advice of counsel as to the best plan of defence; whereupon, finding them devotedly attached to each other, their lawyer advised an immediate solemnization of the rights of matrimony, and that the ceremony be performed by his Honor the presiding Judge, to which they readily assented, and a "nol. pros." was entered in both cases...Daily Memphis Enquirer, 5/11/1848.

Married. In Lafayette county, Miss. on the 6th inst. at the residence of Dr. John H. **CRISP**, by Rev. Dr. **COTTON**, D. C. **HERNDON**, Esq. to Miss Timaxena **BOWLES**.—Also at the same time and place, by the same, W. D. **HOLDER**, Esq. to Miss Therese C. **BOWLES**. Memphis Appeal, 6/18/1854.

Died, On yesterday morning at his residence in this county, Col. A. Hamilton **HERRON**, formerly of Madison county. Memphis Daily Appeal, 1/10/1857.

Herron House, at the West end of Howard's Row, Memphis, Tenn. – This house is now open for the reception of travellers and boarders. Tho's R. **HERRON**. The Appeal, 9/22/1843.

Married, At the residence of the bride's father, Mr. Kelsey, near Tyr__ (Miss.) on the 17th of August, by Rev. Mr. Meeks, R. __. **HIBLER**, of Panola county, and Miss Ann **KELSEY**, of Marshall county. Memphis Daily Appeal, 9/6/1856.

Died, On Saturday morning at half-past 1 o'clock, Mrs. Elizabeth F. S. **HICKEY**, a native of Flemingham, Massachusetts, aged 68 years. Her death was sudden, from an affection of the heart. Memphis Daily Appeal, 1/19/1858.

A delegation from the fire department attended the funeral of the late John **HICKEY**, who was a member of Relief Fire Co. No. 7. Memphis Daily Appeal, 11/29/1859.

Died, At his residence in Hickman's Bend, Ark., on the 10th instant, Dr. Elliott **HICKMAN**, in the seventy-seventh year of his age. Memphis Weekly Appeal, 12/22/1858.

Died, In Paris, Henry co., Tenn., on 29th Sept., Miss Susan **HICKMAN**, aged 17 years. The deceased was a member of the Methodist Church in this city. Memphis Daily Eagle, 10/4/1850.

Died, On Saturday evening of inflammation of the bowels, Frank, infant son of Capt. Frank and Sarah C. **HICKS**. Memphis Whig, Monday, 6/9/1856. Capt. Frank Hicks, the late popular commander of the sunken steamer Daniel Boone, arrived in this city. He has been detained at his plantation, a short distance below this city, by the severe illness of two members of his family. Memphis Daily Appeal, 12/20/1859.

Married: In this city, on Thursday evening, by the Rev. Mr. Mullins, Mr. J. F. **HICKS**, to Miss Sarah C. **CARTER**, of Germantown. Memphis Daily Eagle, Sat., 9/30/1848.

Married, On the 17th instant by Rev. R. D. **SHINDLER**, Will **HICKS**, Esq., editor of the Searcy (Ark.) Eagle, to Miss Mattie **LIGHTLE**, of Fayette county, Tenn. Memphis Daily Appeal, 3/20/1859.

The Funeral Discourse of the late John B. **HIESTAN**, will be delivered in the Cumberland Presbyterian Church on Sabbath Morning next, at 11 o'clock A.M. by the Rev. R. **FRAZIER**. Memphis Appeal, Sat., 5/31/1851.

Tribute to Prof. Robert A. **HIGGINS**. At a meeting of the students of Semple Broaddus College held in the Chapel on Wednesday, March 23, 1859....announced....the decease of the Professor of Mathmetics and Natural Science....Resolved, That the untimely decease of Professor Robert A. Higgins, who departed this life this day....Memphis Daily Appeal, 4/5/1859.

Died, On Sunday last, of Paralysis, Capt. Wm. T. **HIGGINS**, in the 27th year of his age. Memphis Daily Appeal, Sun., 2/27/1848.

Married, On the 31st January, 1856, by David B. **CHAIRS**, Esq., Theopholis **HIGGS** and Miss Margaret B. Chairs, all of Hardeman county, Tenn. Memphis Daily Appeal, 2/24/1856. Died, of Scarlet Fever, on Wednesday, the 29th day of December, 1858, at the residence of his uncle, Theophilus Higgs, in Hardeman county, Tenn., Marcus L. **HIGGS**, in the 18th year of his age.... He made a profession of religion in August last and attached himself to the Missionary Baptist Church at Pleasant Grove, Tenn....Halifax, N.C., papers copy. Memphis Daily Appeal, 1/4/1859.

Elizabeth J. **HIGHTOWER**, by her next friend, Robert I. **NELSON**, vs. James **PENN**, Planters Bank of Tennessee, W. W. **HART**, Farmers' & Merchants' Bank of Memphis, Seth **WHEATLY**, Charles **LOFLAND**, J. N. **MOON**, D. **HIGHTOWER**, Peter G. **REEVES** and Nathaniel **ANDERSON**. Office of the Clerk and Master of the Chancery Court at Memphis, Tenn. December Rules, 1847. Injunction Bill. It appearing to the Clerk and Master from affidavit that the defendants, Peter G. Reeves and Nathaniel Anderson are non-residents of the State of Tennessee: It is therefore ordered, that publication be made in the Appeal…for three successive weeks, requiring them to appear at the next term of said Chancery court…on the 4 h Monday in May next…J. H. **TALBOT**, Cl'k & Master, By Wm. L. **DEWOODY**, Dept'y Cl'k. Dec. 11, 1847. Memphis Daily Appeal, 12/15/1847.

Married, On the 3rd instant in Giles county, Tenn., Mr. John D. **HIGHTOWER**, of Panola county, Miss., to Miss Sallie Adell, daughter of Giles A. **REYNOLDS**, Esq. Memphis Daily Appeal, 10/16/1855. Died, At Sardis, Miss., on the 15th instant, at 7 o'clock A.M., of scarlet fever, Stephen G., infant son of J. D. and Adelle Hightower, aged four months and fifteen days. Nashville papers please copy. Memphis Daily Appeal, 4/21/1857.

Married, On the 15th instant, by Rev. Mr. Estill, Rev. A. J. **McG_WN**, editor of the Texas Presbyterian, to Miss Martha **HIGHTOWER**, of Walker county….[Texas Presbyterian, Aug. 18. Memphis Daily Appeal, 9/12/1855.

Married, on the 17th inst., by the Rev. W. **BRYANT**, Mr. Charles **HILL**, of Franklin County, N.C., to Miss Ann, daughter of J. B. **PERSON**, of this county. Daily Memphis Enquirer, 5/21/1848.

The friends and acquaintances of Chas. H. **HILL** are respectfully invited to attend his funeral, from his residence on Adams street extended on This (Friday) Afternoon, the 28th inst., at 2 o'clock. Memphis Daily Appeal, 8/28/1857.

Left His Mother—A lad of about 11 years of age named Edward **HILL**, son of a widow lady of this place, secreted himself on the *Monarch* on her last trip to New Orleans, and when the boat arrived there managed to elude the vigilance of the officers. He is supposed to be at large in that city. Edward has light, sandy hair, dark hazel, nearly black eyes, and is marked with a boil on the right portion of his forehead in the edge of his hair. He is sprightly and talkative and would probably be called a "bad" boy. The only clothing he had on when he eloped, was blue cottonade pants, and a coarse domestic shirt. By representing himself as an orphan, he won upon the kind feelings of a French passenger whose little son was also on board. This gentleman left the boat at night, on its arrival in the city, and it is supposed that Edward slipped off about the same time with the purpose of rejoining him. Any person who will give information in regard to him, or place him in charge of the officers of either of our Memphis packets, will confer a lasting debt of gratitude upon a bereaved and distressed mother….Memphis Enquirer, 10/8/1846.

Died, On the 22d inst., Evelina B., daughter of H. F. and E. C. **HILL**, aged 3 years and ten days; their friends are invited to attend the burial to-day at 9 o'clock A.M., at the Butler Cemetery—service by the Rev. J. L. **GRAY**. American Eagle Weekly, 5/23/1845.

Died, In New Orleans on the 11th inst. at 5 A.M., after a protracted illness, Mrs. Hill, wife of H. R. W. **HILL**. Memphis Eagle & Enquirer, 4/19/1853.

Hume F. **HILL**, Esq., received his commission on Monday last, to act as Notary Public for Shelby county. He has also been commissioned to take testimony, etc., in all the U.S. Courts. And last, though not least, he has the appointment of Commissioner for the probate of Deeds, Records, etc., from every State in the Union. Memphis Daily Appeal, 11/6/1851.

Died, Friday, August 1st, Emma, infant daughter of Ira and Mary T. **HILL**. The friends and acquaintances are invited to attend the funeral this evening at 4 o'clock, from their residence on Third street, near Court. Services by Bishop Otey. Memphis Daily Appeal, 8/2/1856.

Died, near the _____, Tipton County, Tenn. on the 27th of May, Samuel, son of John and Henrietta **HILL**, aged one year and four months….Memphis Daily Appeal, 6/29/1854.

John B. **HILL** has removed down opposite the Lower Steamboat Landing, between Monroe and Union streets, Front Row, where he is opening a splendid stock of new Goods, direct from the eastern cities…Daily Enquirer, 11/14/1847.

Died, On Wednesday the 11th inst., at the residence of Mr. William **DODSON**, in De Soto County, Miss., where she was at school, Eliza, eldest daughter of John C. and Sarah Ann **HILL**, of this city. Daily Enquirer, 8/19/1847.

Married, By Rev. Wm. **NOLAN**, on the 12th inst., at 11 o'clock, at the residence of the bride's father, in Haywood county, Mr. John P. **HILL** (from Hill & Hayley), of Memphis, to Miss Eliza P. **SHORT**, of the former place. Memphis Daily Appeal, 5/13/1857.

Married, At Covington, Tipton county, Tenn., on Thursday, the 15th November, by Rev. C. T. **QUINTARD**, Lafayette **HILL**, M.D., and Miss S. C. Tipton, daughter of the late Gen. Jacob **TIPTON**. Memphis Daily Appeal, 11/21/1855.

Died, at Grand Junction, on Tuesday, 9th inst., Lucien W. **HILL**, second son of the late Dr. Duncan **HILL**, of Marshall county, Miss., aged twenty-one years, five months and eighteen days....Memphis Daily Appeal, 8/20/1859.

Married, On the 8th instant by Rev. W. H. **THOMPSON**, at the residence of the bride's father, Hardeman county, Tenn., Mr. Napoleon **HILL**, of Memphis, to Miss Mary Morton Wood, daughter of Capt. Wm. H. **WOOD**. Charlottsville (Va.) and Columbia (Tenn.) papers please copy. Memphis Daily Appeal, 7/13/1858.

Col. **HASKELL**, with 170 sick and wounded of the 2d Tennessee Regiment (his own) reached New Orleans on Wednesday evening last on the ship *Eudora*. The remainder of the regiment were speedily to follow; and we may confidently expect them all at home now in a few days...Officers Returned—The following officers came over with Col. Haskell on the *Eudora*:--Lieut. Col. **CUMMINGS**, Surgeon T. B. **HILL**, Capt. G. W. **McGOWN**, Capt. H. F. **MURRAY**, Capt. H. J. **RICHARDSON**, Lieut. G. W. **BOUNDS**, Lt. J. W. **CHAMBERS**, Lieut. Wm. G. **McADOO**, Lieut. A. J. **ELLIS**, Lieut. E. **SULLIVAN**, D. F. **DOUGLASS**, sutler, and 170 wounded and sick privates of the 2d Regiment, Tennessee Volunteers. Daily Enquirer, 5/25/1847.

Died, On the 20th of April, at the residence of T. **PERSON**, in Shelby county, Mrs. Matilda W. Hill, consort of W. B. **HILL**. Memphis Eagle, 5/14/1850.

Taken up by Wm. **HILL**, living 6 miles east of Raleigh, one bay filly....Memphis Enquirer, 1/14/1837.

Died—At the residence of her father, in this county, on Saturday, 7th July, Alpine E., daughter of Matilda W. and Wm. B. **HILL**; aged one year and five months—died of Pneumonia. Memphis Enquirer, 7/31/1849.

Wm. Kenan **HILL**, Cotton Factor & Commission Merchant, No. 4 Front Row, Memphis. Memphis Daily Appeal, 9/10/1853. Married. In this city on the evening of the 12th instant at the residence of A. M. **HOPKINS**, Esq., by Rev. J. O. **STEADMAN**, Mr. Wm. Kenan Hill, of Memphis, and Miss Emily Bibb Pleasants, daughter of the late Col. J. J. **PLEASANTS**, of Huntsville, Ala. Memphis Whig, 6/14/1855. (Author's note: Name given as A. M. **HOPSON** in another paper.)

Law Side Common Law & Chancery Court of the City of Memphis. Sarah Isabel Hill vs. William S. **HILL**, Petition for Divorce. It appearing to the Clerk and Master, from complainant's petition herein filed, that the defendant, William S. Hill, is confined in the Jail and Penitentiary House of this State, so that process cannot be served upon him, it is ordered that publication be made for three successive weeks in the Memphis Appeal....Requiring him to plead, answer or demur, to complainant's petition by or on the first Monday in November next, or the same will be taken for confessed and set for hearing ex-parte. Wm. T. **AVERY**, Clerk. By Marcus J. **WRIGHT**, D.C. Memphis Daily Appeal, 8/27/1854.

Married, On the morning of the 2d inst., by Rev. Lorenzo D. **MULLINS**, at the residence of A. **MUNSEN**, Esq., Mr. Jos. B. **HILLIS**, of Arkansas, to Miss Mollie _. **ALLISON**, of Shelby, Tenn. Memphis Daily Appeal, 2/3/1858.

Taken up by Ward H. **HILTON**, living 6 miles south of Raleigh, one grey mare......Memphis Enquirer, 1/14/1837.

Married, On the evening of the 2d of February by Rev. Jno. **WILSON**, Mr. James **HINDMAN** to Miss Sarah **LYNN**, all of Tipton county, Tenn. Memphis Daily Appeal, 2/11/1858.

Married, In the vicinity of Helena, Ark., on Tuesday evening, November 11th inst., Col. T. C. **HINDMAN** and Miss Mollie W. **BISCOE**. Memphis Daily Appeal, 11/14/1856.

Married, By Rev. A. D. **METCALFE** on the 10th inst., at the residence of the bride's mother, near Macon, Mr. D. G. **HINEMAN** to Miss Mary A. **STOCKINGER**. Memphis Daily Appeal, 2/17/1859.

Whereas, letters of administration on the estate of Stephen **HINNANT**; decd. were granted to the undersigned by the county court of Fayette county, at its April term, therefore all persons indebted....Nancy **HINNANT**, Adm'x. Robt. C. **M'ALPIN**, Adm'r. Memphis Advocate, 5/3/1828.

Married, At Judge Walker's in Savannah, Tenn., on the afternoon of the 21st, by the Rev. D. **MERRIMAN**, Gen. Eugene J. **HINTON**, of Madison county, Miss., to Miss Anastasia **JONES** of Maury county, Tenn. Memphis Eagle & Enquirer, 3/2/1853.

Married, On Saturday, October 11th, by Esq. Horne, Mr. Saml. **HIRCH**, of Batesville, Ark., and Miss Rosalie **ELY**, of Hopkinsville, Ky. Memphis Daily Appeal, 10/12/1856.

Married, On the 17th inst., at the residence of J. S. **LANDEKER**, by James **ROSE**, Esq., Mr. Aaron **HIRSCH** to Miss Amelia **BLACKMAN**, all of this city. Memphis Eagle & Enquirer, 6/20/1852.

Died. On Thursday morning at half past 10 o'clock of dysentery, Walter, infant son of William and Sophia **HITCHCOCK**, aged one year and six months. Memphis Appeal, Sun., 7/2/1854.

Eagle & Enquirer Job Office. Having secured the services of Mr. John **HITCHLER**, late foreman of the St. Louis Union Job Office, well known throughout the West for his skill and experience...Memphis Eagle & Enquirer, 5/29/1852. We regret to learn that Mr. John Hitchler, the superintendant of the job department of the *Bulletin* office, was attacked yesterday afternoon, while he was engaged with his duties in the office, with an affliction which bore some resemblance to apoplexy....Mr. H. is very generally esteemed for his amiable qualities and is one of the most accomplished job printers in the South or West. Memphis Avalanche, 1/26/1859. The friends and acquaintances of Mr. John Hitchler are respectfully invited to attend his funeral This Morning....from his late residence on Linden street. Services at St. Peter and St. Paul's Church. Memphis Daily Avalanche, 1/27/1859. ....He was removed to his house and soon after midnight was no more—a blood vessel was ruptured and he died from effusion of blood on the brain. We had known Mr. Hitchler many years; and in Cincinnati, in St. Louis, as well as in Memphis, he always sustained the character of a preeminently honest....man. Mr. Hitchler leaves a widow and five very young children....He was a consistent and unprejudiced member of the Roman Catholic Church, and his remains will be conveyed to the cemetery belonging to that denomination....Memphis Daily Appeal, 1/27/1859.

Died, on the 20th inst., Mary Eliza, infant daughter of Wm. H. and Mary S. **HITE**, Jr., aged 16 months. Daily Memphis Enquirer, 7/22/1848.

Married, On Tuesday morning, the 24th inst., at 4 o'clock at the residence of Dr. Henry **LAIRD**, in this city, by Rev. H. C. **MORTON**, Mr. Joseph F. **HOBGOOD**, of Sardis, Miss., to Miss Virginia **LAIRD**, of Giles county, Tenn. Memphis Daily Appeal, 11/25/1857.

Married, In this city on Thursday evening the 20th inst., by Rev. Dr. Grundy, W. W. **HODGE** and Miss Emily F. **RODGERS**. Memphis Daily Appeal, 1/22/1858.

Died, Of apoplexy on the 19th instant, at the residence of John T. **HODGES**, Walnut Bend, Ark., John W. **HODGES**, formerly of Van Buren, Hardeman county, Tenn. Memphis Daily Appeal, 2/23/1859.

The friends of Mr. J. P. **HOFFMAN** are respectfully invited to attend the funeral of his wife, from their residence on Causey street this afternoon at 4 o'clock. Memphis Daily Appeal, 7/30/1857.

Died, On the 27th instant, Elizabeth D., eldest child of the late Jno. H. **HOFFMAN**, aged _0 years. The funeral will take place from Grace Church to-day....Philadelphia papers please copy. Memphis Daily Appeal, 8/28/1858.

Died—In this place, on Tuesday, the 7th inst., Jane M., aged about three years, and on Thursday the 9th, John M., aged about five years, children of Geo. B. and Lucy **HOLLAND**. American Eagle, 6/10/1842.

John **HOLLAND**, Labourer, was found dead yesterday morning on the flateau near the Bayou in the upper end of the city. No clue to the cause of his death has been obtained. Memphis Appeal, 6/4/1851.

Married, On the 7th inst. by Rev. J. T. C. **COLLINS**, Mr. John H. **HOLLENBECK**, of New York, to Miss Maggy **SMITH**, all of this city. Memphis Daily Appeal, 12/3/1857.

We are pleased to quote the first sale of new Cotton, from the plantation of Findley **HOLMES** and Mr. Shackleworth, 8 bales, at 97-16 and 12 ½ cents. Sold at auction.....Memphis Enquirer, 9/8/1846. Died, at the residence of Col. Finley Holmes in Desoto county, Miss., on the 13th inst., Mary Emily, infant daughter of Dr. L. and Sallie _. **HOMES**, in the 11th day of her age. Memphis Weekly Appeal, 12/1/1858.

Married, In this city on the 27th instant by the Rev. J. H. **GRAY**, Mr. George C. **HOLMES** to Miss A. Fannie Jones, daughter of Hon. James C. **JONES**. Nashville papers please copy. Memphis Appeal, 11/28/1853.

Isaac **HOLMES**, an employee of the Gayoso Stables, Main street, about 10 o'clock last night, while intoxicated, fell into a well attached to the house of J. and M. **FLAHERTY**, on Union street, and was drowned....Memphis Daily Appeal, 10/24/1858.

Died. In Covington, on Monday morning, the 10th inst., Elizabeth Martha, youngest daughter of James D. and Elizabeth P. **HOLMES,** aged four years and five months. Memphis Eagle, 9/27/1849.

Died, At the residence of James **HADLY**, Esq., in Union county, Arkansas, on the 1st instant, James **HOLMES**, Esq., formerly of North Carolina and late of Tipton county, Tenn., in his 86th year. Memphis Daily Appeal, 9/27/1855.

Married—At Calvary Church on Tuesday evening, 22d inst., by the Rev. Mr. Wheelock, Mr. Wm. **HOLMES**, to Miss Mary E. H. **TEMPLE**, all of this city. Memphis Eagle, 5/31/1849. Died, On Wednesday, 2d inst., Lucy Anna, daughter of William and Mary E. Holmes, aged 2 years and 2 months. Memphis Eagle & Enquirer, 6/6/1852.

Died. In this city, on Tuesday last, Mary Ann, infant daughter of C. K. **HOLST** Esq. Memphis Eagle, Tuesday, 5/30/1848. Died, In this city, February 18th, of brain fever, Charles H., son of C. K. Holst, aged 10 years, 1 month and 10 days. Memphis Eagle & Enquirer, 2/22/1852.

By virtue of a trust deed to me executed by Neil B. **HOLT**, on the 23d day of November, 1837, and recorded in the Register's office at Raleigh, in book G, pages 54 and 55, I will, on Saturday the 18th inst., sell to the highest bidder for cash, all of the lots of ground in said deed described, owned by said Holt, and upon one of which he now resides. John T. **TREZEVANT**, Trustee, Jan. 3, 1840. Memphis Enquirer.

Married, In New York, on Tuesday morning, April 14th, by Rev. G. N. **HOUGHTON**, in the Church of the Transfiguration, Thomas **HOLYOAKE**, formerly of Memphis, and Ellen Mary, daughter of the late Thomas **HISSKELL**, of Philadelphia, Pennsylvania. Memphis Daily Appeal, 5/8/1857.

Married, On the 22d of October, 1857, at the residence of the bride's father, by Rev. _. W. **EPPES**, Mr. A. C. **HOMES** to Miss Jane J. **CARR**, all of Desha County, Arkansas. Memphis Daily Appeal, 11/12/1857.

Notice is hereby given to all persons having claims against the estate of James H. **HOOD**, deceased, to file them with the Clerk of the County Court of Fayette County, Tenn…William **CLAMPITT**, Administrator. Daily Memphis Enquirer, 3/21/1849.

Died, On the 27th inst., at the residence of B. C. **BROWN**, Esq., in this city, John R. **HOOKER**, Esq., in the thirtieth year of his age. Memphis Daily Appeal, 1/30/1858.

Died.—At the residence of his father, in Shelby county, on Wednesday, the 1st day of September, of Typhus fever, R. B. **HOOKER**, aged 20 years and 22 days. The deceased was a young man of sterling integrity, modest and retiring in his manners, and warm in his attachments to his friends; a dutiful son and an affectionate brother….Nashville papers please note. American Eagle, 9/16/1847.

Married, At the residence of the bride's father, Esquire Bonds, of Shelby county, Tenn., by ------ on the 25th of November, Mr. Malcus **HOOKS**, of Tipton county, Tenn., to Miss ----- **BONDS**. Memphis Weekly Appeal, 12/8/1858.

Strayed or Stolen From the subscriber on the night of the 22d inst., a large sorrel Horse…I will pay five dollars to any person returning said horse to me on the State Line Road, one mile from Memphis. Nicholas **HOOPER**. Daily Enquirer, 3/28/1847.

A dreadful affair transpired recently in Gibson county, in this State, resulting in the death of two brothers named Hopper. A bitter feud existed between them growing out of the division of some property, left by a deceased uncle. The younger brother, who appears to have been a prodigate character, came from Kentucky, and was lurking about the premises of the other with the design of assassinating him. This being known, the elder brother went with a party of friends in pursuit. They found him in his camp, and a fight with firearms ensued between the two brothers, in which both were mortally wounded. The younger, who commenced the attack, died instantly; the other in a few hours. The elder brother, A. C. **HOPPER**, is spoken of as a good citizen, and leaves a wife and children. [Enquirer. Memphis Daily Appeal, 10/8/1851.

We neglected yesterday to record the destruction by fire on Sunday night of the new dwelling house of Prof. Abner **HOPTON**, on Union street, east of the bayou. The building has just been completed, but had not been moved into. We understand there was no insurance, and that incendiarism must have been the cause of the loss. Memphis Eagle, Wed., 7/24/1850.

Married, At the court house in Holly Springs, on the morning of the 29th May, Mr. Jesse **HORN** to Miss Mary **COX**. Memphis Appeal, 6/7/1848.

Married, On the 5th inst. at the residence of the bride's mother, in this city, by Rev. Z. H. **WHITEMORE**, Mr. J. G. **HORNE** and Miss Elizabeth **FISHER**, all of Memphis. Memphis Daily Appeal, 6/14/1857.

Married: On the 18th inst., by the Rev. M. J. **BLACKWELL**, Josiah **HORNE** Esq., of this city to Mrs. Susan M. **THOMAS**, of Tipton county. Memphis Daily Eagle, 10/23/1848.

Yesterday about eleven o'clock a brutal murder was committed in the yard attached to Waggener & Co.'s Mill, on Poplar street above the Bayou. The victim was R. M. **HORSELEY**, a man about 35 years of age, and the murderer, a young man named Charles **WELLS**, a nephew of Mr. H. He deliberately pulled out a pistol, and presenting it to the left side of Mr. H.'s head, fired, inflicting a terrible wound. Mr. H. hallooed murder, when Wells drew a bowie knife and stabbed him to the heart. Horseley never spoke after he was stabbed, but walking a few steps fell to the ground, where his body was lying at one o'clock yesterday, the Coroner having just concluded holding an inquest. After committing the deed, Wells fled down Poplar street, with the weapons in his hand, pursued by a son of Mr. H….Mr. Horseley….leaves a wife and three children to mourn his death….Memphis Daily Appeal, 3/10/1857.

134

Married, In this city at the residence of Mr. R. B. **MITCHELL**, on the 16th instant, by Rev. _. C. Horton, Mr. E. B. **HOTCHKISS**, editor of the Somerville Star, to Miss Mildred M. **COBBS**. Memphis Weekly Appeal, 12/22/1858.

Married. On Wednesday evening last by J. **WALDRAN**, Esq., Mr. J. **HOTTER** to Miss Catharine **HENIGER**, all of this city. Memphis Appeal, Fri., 9/22/1854.

Married, On the 1st inst. at the residence of Mr. B.(?) R. **LOTHLAND**, of Fayette county, Tenn., Mr. H. **HOUSE**, Esq., of DeSoto county, Miss., to Miss Lena **BLANCH**, of New York. Memphis Daily Appeal, 11/17/1858.

Married, On the 14th instant at the residence of the bride's father, near Fisherville, by Dr. W. G. **LANCASTER**, Mr. Henderson **HOUSE**, of Mississippi, to Miss Hessie **MUNCRIEF**, of Fayette county, Tenn. Memphis Weekly Appeal, 12/29/1858.

Died—on the 22d inst., at the residence of her husband, in South Memphis, Mrs. Eliza L. **HOUSTON**, after a severe illness of seven days...was one of the little band that constituted the 2nd Presbyterian Church in this city on the last Sabbath in 1844. She has left a devoted but disconsolate Husband—and three affectionate children...Weekly Appeal, 4/25/1845.

Married, On the 29th ult., by the Rev. Mr. Dennis, Mr. Jno. **HOUSTON** of South Memphis, to Mrs. Isabella **SPICKERNAGLE**, consort of the late William **SPICKERNAGLE**. Weekly Appeal, 2/20/1846.

Maj. Wm. **HOUSTON** was, on Friday last, elected to the office of City Recorder, which was vacated by the death of our lamented fellow-citizen, Jno. K. **CHESTER**...Memphis Daily Appeal, 1/7/1851.

About six o'clock last evening as a party of young men were returning from a fishing expedition, one of the number, Mr. Alexander **HOWARD**, was drowned....Having become muddy while drawing their seine, Mr. Howard expressed a determination to wash off his pants. Just as the skiff was entering Wolf river from Loosa Hatchie, he jumped over the side of the skiff, intending, no doubt, to hold on to the sides, but by some means missed his hold and sunk to rise no more....Mr. Howard was a brother of the senior partner of the old firm of Howard & Laird of this city.... Memphis Whig, 7/10/1856.

Married, On Sunday evening, 3d instant, by Rev. Dr. Glover, Mr. Daniel J. **HOWARD** and Miss M. Rebecca **SHELTON**, all of LaGrange, Tenn. Christian Advocate copy. Memphis Daily Appeal, 2/5/1856.

Married, On Tuesday, the 4th inst., by the Rev. F. A. **OWEN**, Mr. Jas. M. **HOWARD**, of the firm of F. H. Cossitt & Co., to Miss Roberta F., daughter of Mrs. Mary T. **WILKINSON**—all of this city. The Appeal, 2/7/1845.

Died. At his residence in this city at 9 o'clock A.M. yesterday, James M. **HOWARD**, Esq., in his 41st year. Memphis Daily Appeal, 4/13/1855. ....Mr. Howard was a native of Sumner county, Tenn. Having passed some years of his early manhood in Mississippi, he removed to Memphis in 1840 or 1841....Memphis Daily Appeal, 4/14/1855.

Died, On the 24th instant, of inflammation of the brain, at the residence of his uncle, Robert **WILKINSON**, in DeSoto county, Miss., Freak C. Howard, eldest son of Mr. James M. **HOWARD**, of Memphis, aged 13 years. Memphis Daily Appeal, 7/28/1859.

Married, On the 15th of December, at the residence of J. M. **VEITCH**, by Mr. D. **WALDROP**, Esq., Joseph J. **HOWARD** to Miss M. E. **VEITCH**, all of DeSoto county, Miss. Memphis Daily Appeal, 12/18/1857.

Married, At the residence of the bride's father, on Monday, 12th instant, by Rev. R. C. **GRUNDY**, D.D., Mr. W. T. **HOWARD**, of the firm of W. Howard & Co., to Miss Amelia J., second daughter of F. **HUNGERFORD**, Esq., all of this city. Memphis Daily Appeal, 7/15/1858.

The friends and acquaintances of Mr. and Mrs. Wardlow **HOWARD** are respectfully invited to attend the funeral of their late nephew W. R. **HOWARD**, from their residence on Shelby street, at half past 2 o'clock this evening. Divine Services by Rev. Mr. Collins. Memphis Daily Appeal, 11/27/1855.

Died, In this city on Tuesday evening, March 31st, Mrs. A. **HOWCOTT**, aged forty-six years. The friends and acquaintances of the family are invited to attend her funeral this evening at 4 o'clock, from the South Memphis Methodist Church, Hernando street. Memphis Daily Appeal, 4/1/1857.

Died, In this city on Monday evening at 5 o'clock, Hon. John **HOWCOTT**, late of Canton, Miss. Memphis Appeal, Wed., 11/24/1852.

N. **HOWCOTT**, Surgeon Dentist, Memphis, Tenn. Office on Main, between Washington and Poplar Streets. Memphis Appeal, 2/6/1848. The friends and acquaintances of the late Dr. N. Howcott are invited to attend his funeral This (Sunday) Evening at 3 o'clock, from his residence on Beal street. Memphis Daily Appeal, 11/9/1856.

Married, At the residence of Mr. John A. **SCOTT**, in Haywood county, on the 3d inst., by the Rev. J. E. **BRIGHT**, Dr. Junius H. **HOWELL**, of Brownsville, to Miss Virginia L., daughter of the late Robert **SCOTT**. American Eagle Weekly, 12/19/1845.

Married, In Fayette county, Tenn., on the 13th instant, at the residence of L. **TODD**, Esq., by Rev. Thomas **TAYLOR**, Mr. W. E. **HOWELL** to Miss Harriet **TODD**. Memphis Daily Appeal, 10/23/1858.

Died, On the 22d ult. of congestive fever, Mrs. Allen **HOYLE**, in the 35th year of her age. Died, On the 20th ult., of congestive chill, Alexander Creighton, son of Mr. and Mrs. Allen Hoyle, aged 3 years and 10 months. Memphis Whig, 3/6/1856.

Married, In this city on Thursday evening, by Rev. Dr. J. H. **GRAY**, at the residence of the bride's sister, Wm. Allen **HOYLE** and Miss Fanny V. **KEEFE**, all of this city. Memphis Daily Appeal, 12/20/1856.

Married. On the 27th of March by Rev. R. H. **BUNTING**, Mr. Dave A. **HUBBARD**, of Fayette county, Texas, to Miss M. A. **STUART**, of Columbus, Texas. Memphis Daily Appeal, 5/2/1855.

Died, In Jackson, Tenn., on Sunday night last, of Pneumonia, Rev. E. H. **HUBBARD**, pastor of the Methodist Church and Professor in the Female Institute. Memphis Daily Appeal, Thurs., 5/5/1853.

Married, In this city on the 22d inst., by Esquire Horne, Mr. John **HUBER** to Miss Mary E. **COX**, all of this city. Memphis Daily Appeal, 6/24/1859.

On Saturday evening last, a most brutal murder was committed in Lauderdale county.—Mr. **HUCKELBY**, an old Revolutionary soldier, was returning from Brownsville, when a negro fellow, belonging to a gentleman by the name of Coggshall, attacked him with a billet of wood, completely beating in the back part of the old soldier's head…Mr. Huckelby was 86 years old. American Eagle, Thurs., 7/15/1847.

Died—In this place on Wednesday night last, on board the wharf boat of W. W. Hart & Co., of billious pneumonia, Capt. **HUDSON** of the steamboat Logansport. Memphis Enquirer, Fri., 3/15/1839.

Died, On the 26th(?) November, 1858, at his father's residence in Panola county, Miss., of consumption, Hall **HUDSON**, aged 31 years and 11 months. Memphis Weekly Appeal, 12/1/1858.

Married, by Woodrow **VADEN**, Esq., on the 7th May, Tho's. W. **HUDSON** to Mrs. E. C. **McKENNIE**. Weekly Appeal, 6/12/1846.

Married, in Fayette County, on the 18th inst., by W. **CAMPBELL**, Esq., Col. Seaton **HUDSPETH** to Miss **WINN**. Memphis Enquirer, 10/24/1848.

Married. On the 5th inst. at Monterey, McNairy co., Ten., by John **HAM**, Esq., L. M. **HUGGINS**, of Gravel Hill, Tenn., to Miss S. E. Sheffield, daughter of Major E. **SHEFFIELD**. Memphis Appeal, 12/12/1854.

Pursuant to the provisions of a deed in trust executed to me for the benefit of A. J. **ROWAN**, by Thos. A. **SHELTON**, dated July 3, 1847. 1 shall proceed and sell 1280 acres of land in Crittenden county, Arkansas, and the house and lot in Shelby county, described in said deed of trust…on Monday, the 17th day of July instant…Daniel **HUGHES**, Trustee. Memphis Enquirer, 7/6/1848.

Married, On January 1st, 1850, at the residence of Judge Morgan, DeSoto county, Miss., by the Rev. A. W. **YOUNG**, Mr. James B. **HUIE** to Miss Sarah Edmonson, daughter of Capt. Wm. **EDMONSON**, of Shelby county, Tenn. Memphis Eagle, 1/10/1850.

Married, on the 30th ult., at the residence of Thomas M. **COLLINS**, Esq., Arkansas, by the Rev. Dr. Page, Henry T. **HULBERT**, Esq. of this city, to Miss Valeria, daughter of Maj. E. P. **COLLINS** of Randolph, Tenn. Memphis Enquirer, 6/7/1848. Henry T. Hulbert, Attorney at Law—Memphis, Tenn. Memphis Daily Appeal, 5/25/1848. The friends and acquaintances of Henry T. and Valeria Hulbert are invited to attend the funeral of their infant son Joseph Pickett, from their residence on Poplar street….Services by Rev. Dr. Page. Nov. 8th, 1854. Memphis Appeal. Died. On Tuesday, the 7th inst., Joseph Pickett, infant son of Henry T. and Valeria Hulbert, aged 18 months. Memphis Appeal, 11/10/1854. Died, On the 26th instant, Henry T., infant son of Henry _. And Valeria Hulbert, aged 22 months. Memphis Daily Appeal, 7/28/1857. The friends and acquaintances of H. T. and Valeria Hulbert are invited to attend the funeral of their infant daughter, Lizzie Collins, from their residence on Poplar street this morning….Services by Rev. Dr. White. Memphis Daily Avalanche, 6/25/1859.

We regret to learn that a difficulty occurred Thursday between George **HULBURT**, brother of Henry T. **HULBURT**, Esq., of this city, and another young man named Henry **BURGETT**, both of whom are well known in Memphis, which resulted in the death of Mr. Hulburt. The brother of the deceased left this city yesterday to take charge of the remains of the deceased. The affray occurred about fifteen miles below the city, in Arkansas. Memphis Daily Appeal, 9/17/1859.

Married, In Marion county, Ark., on Thursday, 3d inst., John E. **HULL** to Miss Matilda A. **KILLOUGH**. Memphis Whig, 4/24/1856.

Died on Wednesday, 30th inst., at the residence of William **CRUMP**, Esq., in Marshall county, Miss., Miss Lucy M. **HULL**, in the 21st year of her age. The National Intelligencer will please copy. Daily Enquirer, 11/7/1847.

Married: In this city on Thursday evening the 23d inst. by Rev. J. H. Gray, Mr. Garrett **HULS**(?) and Miss Lydia **PIERCE**, all of this city. Memphis Whig, 8/24/1855.

Died, At his residence in Monroe county, Ten., on the 25th ult., Andrew Russell **HUMES**, in the 31st year of his age. Daily Enquirer, 10/8/1847.

Died, On the eve of the 19th inst. at his residence near Saulsbury, Tenn., Maj. B. B. **HUMPHREY**, leaving many friends and relatives to mourn his irreparable loss. The deceased had long been an invaluable and well beloved citizen of that vicinity. Memphis Daily Appeal, 11/25/1857.

Married, At the Cumberland Presbyterian Church in this city, October 7th, by Rev. A. M. **BRYAN**, Mr. J. H. **HUMPHREYS** and Miss Annie Eliza **WARD**, all of this city. Memphis Daily Appeal, 10/9/1857.

The friends and acquaintances of P. W. **HUMPHREYS** are invited to attend his funeral to-day (Wednesday) at 10 o'clock A.M., from his late residence on Market street….In the announcement of the death of Perry W. Humphreys, many a bitter regret will visit the hearts of a numerous and deeply attached circle of acquaintances and friends….Memphis Daily Appeal, 4/8/1857.

Died. Near Nashville, on Saturday the 4th instant, Mrs. Amanda Pillow, wife of the Hon. West H. **HUMPHREYS**. Memphis Appeal, 3/17/1854.

Married—On the 1st July, by the Rev. Mr. Crawford, Mr. Isaac T. **HUMPHRIES**, of Shelby, to Miss Jane **TILSON**, of the same county. Weekly Appeal, 7/18/1845.

HUNT – Married, On the 21st ult., near Bellemont, Fayette county, Dr. A. D. **HUNT** to Miss Sallie M. **NELSON**, all of said county. Memphis Eagle, 1/4/1849.

Married, On the 10th instant by Rev. Dr. Gray, Geo. E. **HUNT**, Esq., of Panola county, Miss., to Miss Eliza M. **HANNAH**, of this city. Memphis Daily Appeal, 4/11/1856.

Died, In Hardeman county, on the 8th of October, Miss Mary A. Hunt, daughter of the late John **HUNT**, in the 21st year of her age. Memphis Daily Eagle, 10/21/1848.

Death of Gen. Memucan **HUNT**.—We regret to learn that Gen. Hunt departed this life at the residence of Mr. John C. **NELSON**, in Haywood county, Tenn., on the 26th inst. He was distinguished as a General in the Texas Revolution and was the first Minister sent from the Republic to the United States....The intelligence of his death will be received with deep sorrow by a large circle of warm friends, particularly in the Southern States. Memphis Daily Appeal, 6/27/1856. Tribute of Respect. At a regular meeting of Wesley Lodge No. 104, of Free and Accepted Masons, convened at their Hall in Wesley, Tenn., on Saturday, July 5th, A.L. 5856, A.D. 1856, the following resolutions were unanimously adopted, to-wit: Whereas, in the inscrutable dispensation of an all-wise Providence, our distinguished friend and brother, General Mumucan Hunt, of Texas, was called from time to eternity, on the morning of the 26th ultimo, in the vicinity of our Lodge, at the residence of our brother, J. C. Nelson, of Haywood, Tennessee, and was, at the request of said deceased, buried with Masonic Honors, at the burial-ground of his brother, Maj. T. T. **HUNT**....Memphis Daily Appeal, 8/24/1856.

Died, In the town of Randolph, Tipton county, Tenn., on the 13th June, 1856, of Malignant Scarlet Fever, Neadis Isis, aged two years, one month and twenty-four days. Also on the morning of the 14th following, of the same disease, Henry Anderson, aged four years, two months and one day—youngest son and daughter of Milton and Neadis Isis **HUNT**. Memphis Daily Appeal, 6/26/1856.

Died. In the neighborhood of Wesley, Tenn., on the 10th of August, Mary Hilliard, consort of Nathaniel **HUNT**, Esq., aged 58 years. American Eagle, 8/26/1847.

Taken up by Thomas W. **HUNT**, living in Memphis, one chestnut sorrel mare......The Appeal, 10/27/1843.

Married, On the 25th(?) February, by Rev. B. **MEDLIN**, Mr. A. J. **HUNTER** to Miss Bettie L. **MITCHELL**, all of Fayette county, Tenn. Memphis Weekly Appeal, 3/17/1858.

Died, Near Macon, Fayette county, Tenn., on Saturday, July 26th, Augustus H., son of Dr. George T. and Ann E. **HUNTER**, aged 4 months. Memphis Daily Appeal, 7/29/1856. Died, Near Macon, Fayette county, Tenn., on Tuesday, 2d of September, John W., son of Geo. T. and Ann E. Hunter, aged 18 months and 9 days. Memphis Daily Appeal, 9/6/1856.

The friends and acquaintances of J. R. and P. W. **HUNTER** are requested to attend the funeral of their son, Joseph, at the First Baptist Church....February 8th. Memphis Daily Avalanche, 2/8/1859.

Died, in this city at 2 o'clock Wednesday morning, of inflammation of the brain, Thos. W. **HUNTER**, of the firm of Horton & Hunter, in the twenty-fourth year of his age. Mr. Hunter was a graduate of the State University of Mississippi, at Oxford....He was a bright, consistent and exemplary Mason....In him society has lost much; his parents a noble son....Memphis Daily Appeal, 8/5/1856.

Married, In this city on the evening of the 17th inst. at the residence of the bride's father, by Rev. J. L. **ROBINSON**, Mr. Geo. T. **HUNTSMAN** to Miss Anna M. **HENRY**, all of this city. Memphis Daily Appeal, 12/19/1857. The friends and acquaintances of the late George T. Huntsman are respectfully invited to attend his funeral This Day….from the First Baptist Church….Memphis Daily Appeal, 4/2/1859.

Married. In this City on Thursday, March 1st by the Rev. H. V. **PORTER**, D.D., Thomas W. **HURLEY**, Student of the Memphis Medical College, to Miss Mariah D. **NEAL**. Memphis Daily Appeal, 3/6/1855.

Died—Of a liver complaint near Covington, at 3 o'clock on the morning of the 2d ult. Robert Dannel **HURST**, aged 27 years. Mr. Hurst was a native of North Carolina, born in Lenoir, but principally raised in Dublin county, and moved to this county about two years since….left many friends and acquaintances, and one Brother, in this county, to deplore his untimely loss. Memphis Advocate, 7/19/1828.

Death has been again in our midst and the loved and kind hearted Angie **HUTCHESON** is no more. Scarce two short years have passed since she came among us a perfect stranger, to visit a loved sister, and although she expected to remain but a short time, she met with so many kind friends and became such a favorite, that she had been persuaded to linger until snatched from among us by the last destroyer, Death. In a few short weeks she would have been the bride of one to whom she had given her heart's warmest and purest affection….Memphis Whig, 9/19/1855. At a meeting of the teachers and scholars of the "First Baptist Sabbath School" of Memphis, the following preamble and resolutions were unanimously adopted: Whereas our Heavenly Father, in the dispensation of Providence, hath removed from among us our beloved associate and teacher, Miss Angeline **HUTCHESSON**….Memphis Daily Appeal, 9/26/1855.

A man named **HYNSON** was killed on the Pigeon Roost Road by the breaking of the shaft of a stump puller last Wednesday. The fragment struck him killing him instantly. Memphis Daily Appeal, Fri., 6/18/1852.

Married, In this city on the 11th inst. by the Rev. Dr. Porter, Augustus R. **HYNSON**, of St. Louis, to Miss Nanie **FLEMING**, of this place. St. Louis papers please copy. Memphis Appeal, 10/13/1853.

Married. On the 4th of July by Rev. Dr. Page, at the residence of John **POPE**, Esq., his daughter Judith to Frederick **INGATE**, Esq., of the firm of C. C. Ingate & Son, of London, residing at Patras, Greece. Memphis Daily Appeal, 7/6/1855.

Married, At Kingston, Ulster county, New York, on the 29th of April, by Rev. George **WATERS**, Duncan **INGRAHAM**, of Memphis, Tenn., and Miss Julia, youngest daughter of the late Hon. John **SUDAM**. Memphis Daily Appeal, 5/11/1856.

Died; in this city, yesterday at 12 o'clock, after a severe illness of four weeks, Charles Sidney, infant son of Francis and Elcee Ann **INGRAHAM**, aged 11 months and 8 days. New York and Boston papers please notice. Daily Enquirer, 6/29/1847. Died, On Monday, at 12 o'clock, Henry Laughton, youngest son of Fra. and Elcee Ann Ingraham, aged 14 months. Weekly Memphis Eagle, 6/21/1849.

We are pained to learn that Dr. John A. **INGRAM**, a well known physician of Madison county, Tennessee, died on Tuesday last, the 5th inst. of pneumonia. Memphis Eagle & Enquirer, 4/10/1853.

Died. In Bloomington, Illinois, on the 25th of May, of Consumption, Mrs. Rhoda Jane Ingle, wife of James **INGLE**, formerly of Memphis, in the thirty-fifth year of her age. She had been a consistent member of the Presbyterian Church for fifteen years….She leaves her husband and four little boys to mourn their loss. Memphis Whig, 6/20/1855.

Died, On Friday evening at 6 o'clock, Mr. Francis **INGLING**, cabinet maker, of erysypelas(?). His funeral will take place at 9 o'clock a.m. this day, from his residence, nearly opposite the Gayoso House. His friends and acquaintances are respectfully requested to attend. Memphis Appeal, Saturday, 9/3/1853. At the August term of the County Court of Shelby county, just passed, the insolvency of the estate of the late Francis Ingling was only suggested….F. **REICHENBACHER**, Adm'r. Memphis Appeal, 8/11/1854.

A plasterer named Edward **INWOOD**, who was at work in front of the third story of the Gayoso House yesterday, fell from the scaffolding to the ground, receiving such serious injuries that after a short period of suffering he ceased to exist. He was a fireman belonging to the No. 5 company, of which he was First Engineer....Memphis Daily Appeal, 11/14/1857.

Married, At the first Presbyterian Church by the Rev. Mr. Kay, Mr. Henry **IRBY**, of Mississippi, to Miss Virginia A., daughter of Col. Isham G. **LUNDY** of this vicinity. Richmond Va. papers please copy. Memphis Daily Appeal, 5/27/1853.

Married, At the residence of Col. Cullen **BARRON**, on the 8th May, by Rev. Thomas **TAYLOR**, Mr. Thomas **IRION** to Miss Delilah **BALDWIN**, all of Hardeman county, Tenn. Memphis Eagle, 5/15/1851.

Married. On the 20th inst., at the residence of Maj. G. **BARTLETT** in this County, by the Rev. Thomas **TAYLOR**, Mr. Wm. M. **IRION** to Miss Mary A. Glasgow, youngest daughter of the late Capt. John **GLASGOW**—both of Hardeman county. Memphis Daily Appeal, 3/25/1851.

Death beheld in any position, is solemn and impressive, but when contemplated in connection with a long life of piety, and a triumph in the last struggle of mortality, it seems disarmed of half its terrors. Such was the life and death of Mrs. Amelia Irons, consort of Mr. Wm. **IRONS**, who departed this life on the 18th of July, A.D., 1849; born in Wilkes county, Georgia, and died in Hardeman county, Tenn...Memphis Eagle, 9/20/1849.

Mr. Henry **IRVINE** met with a sudden death on Saturday night, by falling or jumping out of the second story window of a house on Second street. The deceased had been sick for some time, and it is supposed that he was laboring under a fit of delirium when the above occurrence took place. Memphis Daily Appeal, 8/23/1852.

During the noon adjournment of the Memphis Commercial and Criminal Court, yesterday, Judge E. W. M. **KING**, its presiding Judge, furiously assaulted, with a pistol and cane, C. **IRVING**, Esq., junior editor of the Enquirer, for an article published in the Enquirer of that morning, censuring Judge King's conduct and interference at the corporation and county election polls, on Saturday last...Judge King it is said discharged three barrels of a revolving pistol, one of which lodged in the surface of Mr. Irving's wrist, and another striking the hand of Mr. Dashiell, the hotel-keeper; he also used his cane, and severely beat Mr. I. over the head and face with his pistol. Mr. I. had his pistol to drop from his hand at the time his wrist was shot; he knocked the Judge down it is said with his own cane, which he had thrown down after first striking Irving; they were finally parted while closely clinched and both down upon the floor. Mr. Irving is a small, weakly man, and the Judge a stout six-footer and over...Memphis Eagle, 3/10/1848.

Charles **IRVING**, Esq.—We have seldom been more gratified than on Sunday evening last by greeting this gentleman on his return "from the wars" in Mexico. Our readers will at once recognize in him the talented pro. tem. Occupant of our chair in '45, and the writer of the sprightly letters from the Army signed "C. I., Eagle Guards." He returns in fine health, and with a flow of spirits amply abundant for a very lively description of "the elephant." The arrival of "Charley," with his old store of piquant good humor largely increased by his military observation and experience, is and will be hailed by his acquaintances with as much joy and satisfaction as if he had enjoyed an hundred opportunities of acquiring over so much glory. In the name of all our readers, we bid him welcome home. Daily Enquirer, 4/27/1847. Charles Irving, Esq., formerly of this city, has been engaged to assist in the editorial department of the Nashville Union. Memphis Eagle & Enquirer, 2/22/1852.

Married. On Thursday evening, 16th inst., by Rev. Dr. Porter, R. McGavock **IRWIN** to Mrs. Augusta B. **TRICE**. Memphis Daily Appeal, 11/18/1854.

Dr. Wm. T. **IRWIN** left this city with his family, yesterday, by the steamer John Simonds, for Havana, whither he goes with the hope of improving the health of an interesting little boy. Memphis Daily Avalanche, 2/10/1859.

Married, In Searcy, Ark., on the 9th inst., Mr. Benjamin **ISBELL** to Miss Mattie C. **BURROW**. Memphis Daily Appeal, 2/20/1858.

The Rev. E. D. **ISBELL** has delivered up his charge in this place and has removed with his family to Kentucky. They left on the Cumberland Valley on Saturday last....Memphis Daily Appeal, Tues., 7/18/1854.

Died—On the 22nd ult. Jesse M. **ISBELL**, Esq., aged 43 years, a highly respected citizen of this county, leaving an amiable wife and seven children to lament his death. He was for many years a professor of religion, and a consistent and worthy member of the Baptist Church. The Appeal, 10/6/1843.

We learn from Capt. Barnett, of the packet Editor, that on Tuesday morning about 2 o'clock, Mr. John P. **ISLER** was killed by being shot in the head with a rifle ball from his own rifle. It appears that a party, the deceased being one of the number, were out on a camp hunt and during the night Mr. Isler and one or two others left the camp for a hunt. After being out some time, the deceased's gun was heard and upon going to him, he was found mortally wounded, speechless and dying. He died before his friends could get him back to camp. Mr. Isler was a son of Dr. Isler and brother-in-law of _. G. **CLARK**, Esq., of this city, as also Capt. Barnett (Burnett(?), of the Editor. He was raised and educated in this city and removed from here some four or five years since to his late residence, about 100 miles above here, on the river. He was a man of excellent qualities and leaves a large circle of relatives and friends to mourn his early and untimely death. Memphis Whig, Fri., 11/9/1855.

Married. On the evening of the 16 inst. by Rev. J. W. **KNOTT**, Mr. Wm. **JACK** to Miss Eugenie **BUSTER**, all of this City. Memphis Appeal, 2/17/1854. A little boy, about 18 months old, son of Mr. Wm. Jack, of this city, was drowned on Saturday last in a tub of water, owing to the carelessness or design of his nurse. The nurse fled. Memphis Daily Appeal, Tues., 8/12/1856.

During the last trip of the *Evansville*, a gentleman named Andrew **JACKSON**, who was unwell when he got on board the boat at Memphis, died of pneumonia. His death occurred on the 8[th](?) inst. Mr. Jackson resided twelve miles from Grand Glaize, Ark., where his wife and five children reside. He was recently from Kentucky, where a brother named Henry **JACKSON** is still living. Memphis Daily Appeal, 2/12/1857.

It being my fixed intention to remove West this Fall, I am determined to dispose of my valuable Plantation lying on the waters of the North Fork of Wolf River, one mile from the Memphis and Charleston Railroad and four miles northwest of Lagrange, Tenn. This farm contains 1257 acres ....I will also sell a very superior farm in Monroe City, Arkansas within two miles of White River and just 28 miles west of Helena. Prairie Place is at present occupied by Judge Jones, and contains 1,000 acres....H. G. **JACKSON**. Memphis Daily Appeal, 7/29/1854. Desirous of being with my relatives in the West, I am resolved to dispose of my valuable Plantation....H. G. Jackson. Memphis Daily Appeal, 9/14/1855.

Died, On the 29th inst., in this city, Henry **JACKSON**, in the 48th year of his age; the friends and acquaintances of the family are invited to attend his funeral from his residence on Court Square this evening (Sunday) at 3 P.M.—Services by the Rev. Geo. W. **COONS**. Memphis Appeal, 4/30/1848. Died, in this city, on Thursday night, 18th inst., of Scarlet fever, Martha Olivia, youngest daughter of the late Henry Jackson, in the 7th year of her age. She was a sweet intelligent child, justly dear to all who knew her. Daily Memphis Enquirer, 5/26/1848.

Married, In this city on the evening of the 31st ult., at the residence of the bride's father, by Rev. R. C. **GRUNDY**, D.D., Mr. Howell E. **JACKSON**, of Jackson, Tenn., and Miss Sophia **MOLLOY**. Memphis Daily Appeal, 6/2/1859.

The friends and acquaintances of Mr. Hugh **JACKSON** are invited to attend his funeral this morning at 10 o'clock from the 1st Presbyterian Church. Services by the Rev. Geo. W. **COONS**. The Daily Eagle, 11/9/1846. Odd Fellows Hall, Memphis, Tenn., Nov. 9, 1846—Upon the return of the members of the

Order to their Hall, from paying the last tribute of respect to the remains of brother Hugh Jackson, who departed this life on Sabbath the 8th inst......The Daily Eagle, 11/10/1846.

The friends and acquaintances of J. A. **JACKSON**, are invited to attend the funeral of his wife, Mary Elvira, this afternoon, at half past 3 o'clock, from his residence on Adams street. Daily Enquirer, Sunday, 8/29/1847. Died, on Saturday, the 28th inst., Mrs. Mary Elvira Jackson, at the age of eighteen years, nine months and eight days....She became early attached to the form of worship of the Episcopal Church.... Daily Enquirer, 8/31/1847.

Died—At his residence in this place on Wednesday morning, the 22d instant, after a short illness, John **JACKSON**, Esq., aged 47 years, formerly of Creine, County Monaghan, Ireland. Memphis Enquirer, 5/24/1839.

Died—In Shelby county, Tenn., on the 15th day of April, 1849, at the residence of her father—Miss Margaret **JACKSON**, aged 20 years....Weekly Memphis Eagle, 4/26/1849.

Married, On the 26th ult., by Rev. Alex. **STEVENSON**, Mr. Robt. E. **JACKSON**, of Monroe county, Ark., and Miss Laura A. **ELDRIDGE**, of Jackson county, Ark. Memphis Daily Appeal, 9/5/1856.

Married, on Wednesday, 19th of April, near Germantown, by the Rev. P. S. **GAYLE**, Wm. **JACKSON**, M.D., to Miss Mary Jane Morgan, daughter of John **MORGAN**, Esq. Daily Memphis Enquirer, 5/4/1848.

Married. On Thursday evening, the 11th inst., by Hume F. **HILL**, Mr. J. C. **JACOBS** to Miss Amanda **POLLOCK**, all of this city. Memphis Daily Appeal, 1/13/1855.

Married, On the 9th instant by Elder T. J. **DRANE**, Mr. T. W. **JACOBS** to Miss B. C. **JONES**, all of this city. Memphis Daily Appeal, 3/12/1859.

Married. At the Cumberland Presbyterian Church on the 18th instant by the Rev. Dr. Porter, Mr. D. G. **JAMES** and Miss Louisa H. **BALL**, all of this city. At the same time and place, by the Rev. Dr. Porter, Mr. W. W. **DAVIDSON** and Miss Kate G. (note: middle initial J. in another paper.) **JAMES**, all of this city. Memphis Whig, 4/20/1855. Died, Near this city, of consumption, on Tuesday evening, 18th inst., Louisa H., consort of D. G. James, of this city, and daughter of Capt. Henry **BALL**, of Erie county, Pa., in the 28th year of her age. Pittsburgh and Erie papers please copy. Memphis Daily Appeal, 1/21/1859.

Died: At Briar's Point, Miss., on the 30th ult. of yellow fever, Mr. G. W. **JAMES**, formerly of this city, in the 34th year of his age. Memphis Whig, 11/3/1855.

Died, On the 1st inst., of scarlet fever, George Mitchell, youngest son of the late George W. and Matilda **JAMES**, aged 18 months. Memphis Whig, 3/6/1856.

Lafayette Tavern. Henry F. **JAMES**, Has the pleasure to inform the public, that his buildings, on Mississippi Row, in Memphis, are now in complete order for the accommodation of travellers....Memphis Advocate, 3/22/1828.

Commercial Hotel, Jefferson Street, Memphis, Tenn. Joshua F. **JAMES** begs leave respectfully to announce to the public that he has leased the above spacious and elegant Hotel...J. F. James. Memphis Enquirer, 6/13/1849.

The friends and acquaintances of Mrs. Matilda **JAMES** are respectfully invited to attend her funeral on to-morrow Evening....from her late residence on the Horn Lake road, Fort Pickering. Services by Rev. A. M. **BRYAN**. Memphis Daily Appeal, 1/1/1859. Died—In Memphis, Tenn., on the last day of December, 1858, in the sixty-first year of her age, Mrs. Matilda James. Sister James was born in the State of Georgia, on the 14th of May, 1798. Emigrated to the southwestern part of the State of Kentucky about the year 1818. Professed religion at the old Salem Campground, Livingston county, and soon after united with the Cumberland Presbyterian Church ....Sister James was one of the first white settlers in Memphis and was the First Cumberland Presbyterian....known to have settled in the place....Memphis Daily Appeal, 2/17/1859.

Married, Near Germantown on Wednesday, the 19th inst. by Rev. R. R. EVANS, Mr. Thomas JAMES, of Memphis, to Mrs. Louisa A. A. MILLER. Memphis Daily Appeal, 9/23/1855.

Married, On the 4th instant by Rev. J. T. C. COLLINS, Judge Thomas JAMES to Mrs. M. L. KRAFFT, both of this city. Memphis Weekly Appeal, 3/17/1858.

We regret to learn that Mr. W. R. JAMES, a highly respectable merchant of this city, died at Jacksonport, a few days since. Memphis Enquirer, 6/22/1849.

We are pained to record the death from drowning of Mr. William JAMES, of this city, a brother of Thomas JAMES, the well-known coal dealer, which occurred yesterday about noon. Mr. James was upon the wharfboat superintending the working of several coat barges at the stern of the boat, when, in attempting to spring from the wharfboat upon one of the barges, he missed his aim and fell into the river. He doubtless came up from under one of the coat boats, which rendered it impossible for him to extricate himself, as he was not seen after his body struck the water....Mr. James was a widower, and resided on Linden street near the river. He leaves three children to mourn....Memphis Daily Avalanche, 5/12/1859. The friends and acquaintances of the late William R. James are invited to attend his Funeral this morning....from the residence of Thos. James, on Tennessee street, below Linden. Services by Dr. Grundy. Memphis Avalanche, 5/16/1859. ....It is proper to state that at the time of his death, Mr. James was not a married man, his wife and child having died some time ago. It is painful to record, however, that he left five orphan children to mourn....Memphis Daily Appeal, 5/14/1859.

Married, On Wednesday evening, 29th inst., at Raleigh, Ten., by the Rev. D. E. BURNS, Mr. Wm. M. JAMES to Miss F. C., daughter of Wm. UNDERWOOD, Esq.—all of Memphis. Memphis Appeal, 10/31/1851.

The fine low-water steamer, Belle of Hatchie, will leave Memphis for Jacksonport, and all intermediate landings, on Saturday, July 8, at 4 P.M., and will run as a regular packet from Memphis in the above trade throughout the season. For freight or passage, apply on board, Wm. R. JAMES, Agent. Madison Street. Memphis Eagle, 7/6/1848. Letters of administration having been granted to the undersigned by the County Court at the July term, instant, on the Estate of the late William R. James, deceased ...J. S. CURTIS, Administrator, and Frances JAMES, Administratrix...Memphis Enquirer, 7/11/1849.

We are authorized to announce James JAMESON a candidate for County Trustee at the approaching March election. Daily Enquirer, 11/5/1847.

Married, In Fayette county on the 24th inst., by Rev. H. R. EVANS, Dr. Wm. H. JAMESON, of Collierville, and Mrs. Mildred W. MEBANE, of said county. Memphis Whig, 6/26/1856.

We are authorized to announce Col. Richard B. JARMON, of Fayette, a candidate for Brigadier General of 22nd Brigade of Tennessee Militia, composed of the counties of McNairy, Hardeman, Fayette and Shelby. Memphis Enquirer, 3/21/1836.

Died, Near Lebanon, Tenn. on the night of the 25th of June last, of Cholera, Theodore C. JARMON, son of Stephen and Eliza H. JARMON, of Hardeman Tenn., aged twenty-two years, five months and sixteen days. The deceased was a student at Lebanon Law School....It will be gratifying to his friends and relatives to know that he had recently made a profession of religion and attached himself to the Cumberland Presbyterian Church....Memphis Appeal, 7/8/1854.

We announce with deep regret the death of Hon. Spencer JARNAGIN. He died of Cholera on Tuesday evening...Mr. Jarnagin was for several years a Senator in Congress from this state...As a politician, a lawyer, a companion, relative and friend, his memory is surrounded with bright associations...Memphis Daily Appeal, Thurs., 6/26/1851.

Red River Hotel. Corner of Main and Winchester Streets, F. **JAUS**, Proprietor. The Appeal, 12/13/1844.

Married, December 19, by Rev. A. H. **THOMAS**, Mr. J. Manly **JEFFERDS**, of St. Louis, Mo., to Miss Mary J. **LARRISON**, of Memphis, Tenn. Memphis Daily Appeal, 12/20/1859.

Died—In the vicinity of Memphis, on Monday, the 11th (?) inst., Mr. Joshua T. **JEFFERSON**, aged about 26. Mr. Jefferson was a native of Delaware, but for the last five years has been engaged as a tradesman on the river.....American Eagle, 4/14/1842.

Married, At the First Methodist Church on the morning of the 12th inst., by Rev. J. W. **KNOTT**, Mr. Francis W. **JEGGETTS** and Mrs. A. **CARR**, all of this city. Memphis Daily Appeal, 9/13/1855.

Died, In Hernando, Mississippi, at the residence of Dr. Joseph __. **HALL** Mr. Barton W. **JENKINS**, formerly of Columbia, Tenn. Memphis Daily Eagle, 8/15/1848.

Died, In Cuba, Shelby County, Tenn., on the 12th of January, 1859, Dr. G. P. **JENKINS**, aged 29 years. He was born in Maury county, Tenn. When but a youth he moved with his parents to Marshall county, Miss. He graduated with high honors in Medicine at the Memphis Medical School, in the year 1852. He was for many years a devoted and consistent member of the Presbyterian Church....He was far, far away from his near relatives, yet he was nursed and cared for by warm and devoted friends. His great wish and desire was that his brother might visit him ere he left earth. His prayer was granted. The writer of this, with a younger brother, having received from his attending physician, notice of his critical situation, had the good fortune to arrive in time to be with him two days before his death....P.H.J. Memphis Daily Avalanche, 1/22/1859.

Married, In Covington, Ky., June 26, by S. G. **ARNOLD**, Esq., Mr. James **JENKINS**, of the firm of Shaw & Co., Memphis, Tenn., to Miss Mary Louisa **LITTLEFIELD**, of the former place. American Eagle Weekly, 7/18/1845.

Died, near Chulahoma, Miss., October 26th, 1855, Walter S. **JENKINS**, aged 71 years and one month. He was born in Pittssylvania county, Virginia. At an early age he emigrated to the wilds of Middle Tennessee, settled in Maury county and lived there till the year 1840. He then removed to Marshall county, Miss., where he lived up to the day of his death. At the age of seventeen he joined the Presbyterian Church....He leaves a wife and seven children to mourn his loss.... Memphis Daily Appeal, 11/17/1855.

Died—On Saturday last, of a protracted diarrhea, Amanda Lenora, infant daughter and only child of Miles G. and Elizabeth F. **JENNINGS**. The Appeal, Fri., 6/21/1844.

Married—On Thursday evening, by Rev. J. **HARRISON**, Mr. Robert J. **JENNINGS** to Miss Harriet, only daughter of Mr. John **ANDERSON**. American Eagle, Fri., 5/25/1843.

On Friday morning last, says our evening contemporary, Wm. **JESTES** left his boarding house, in the upper part of the city, to go to his work—he being employed in a blacksmith shop—since which time he has not been seen or heard from by his wife....Jestes is about six feet high, spare made, has black hair and eyes, dark side whiskers, a crooked finger on each hand, and is about 26 years of age....He had been in the city with his wife about two weeks—coming from Napoleon, Ark. Any information as to his whereabouts will be thankfully received by his wife, Margaret Jestes....Memphis Daily Appeal, 9/1/1857.

Died, on the night of the 27th February last, at 11 o'clock, at her father's residence, Gen. D. **BOON** of De Soto County, Miss., Mrs. Evelina Virginia **JETER**, aged 34 years 4 months and 11 days. She had been a strict and exemplary member of the Baptist Church for the last sixteen years.....She has left a husband and four children.....Memphis Eagle, 3/22/1849.

Died, On Tuesday, January 20th, at her residence in Lauderdale county, Tenn., Mrs. Elizabeth D. **JETT**, mother of Col. J. F. **JETT** of this city. Mrs. Jett died after a very short illness, in the 62d year of her age...Memphis Eagle & Enquirer, 1/25/1852.

A young lad by the name of Brad **JEWELL** was drowned while bathing near the wharf boat yesterday evening. Memphis Appeal, 8/6/1854. The Whig of yesterday contradicts our statement in regard to the drowning of Brad Jewell. We are glad if such is the case, but we got our information from the lads in the telegraph office, and they were confident that was his name. Memphis Daily Appeal, 8/8/1854.

Died, Yesterday evening at 8 ½ o'clock, after an illness of two weeks, Oscar D. **JOHNS**, in the 22d year of his age. The friends and acquaintances of the deceased are invited to attend the funeral This Afternoon at 3 ½ o'clock, from the residence of J. S. **LOGAN**, on DeSoto street, between Vance and Linden. Memphis Daily Appeal, 4/21/1857.

Married—On the 25th of November, by O. **GRIFFIN**, Esq., Mr. B. **JOHNSON** to Miss Eliza B. **HAMPTON**, of Fayette county, Tenn. Tri-Weekly Memphis Enquirer, 12/3/1846.

Married, Monday evening, the 5th inst., by Rev. Dr. Stedman, Mr. Charles W. **JOHNSON** to Miss Mollie E. **FOWLKES**, all of this city. We announce....this morning the marriage of our young friend, Mr. Charles W. **JOHNSTON**, the accomplished deputy in the clerk's office of the criminal and common law courts....Memphis Daily Appeal, 12/6/1859.

The friends and acquaintances of Cyrus **JOHNSON** are requested to attend the funeral of his mother, Mrs. Susanna **JOHNSON**, from his residence, corner of Third and Jefferson streets, This Afternoon....Services by Rev. J. O. **STEADMAN**. Memphis Daily Appeal, 8/20/1859.

Married. On the 3rd instant by Rev. Dr. Porter, Mr. D. B. **JOHNSON**, of Holly Springs, to Miss Margaret E. **WHITE**, of this vicinity. Memphis Daily Appeal, 1/9/1855.

Married. On the evening of the 22d instant, by the Rev. Dr. Page, at the residence of Mr. John B. **HOLMES**, D. T. **JOHNSON**, Esq., of this city, to Miss Sallie A., only daughter of the late Frederick **CHRISTIAN**. Weekly Memphis Eagle, 11/1/1849.

We are pained to learn that Mr. David B. **JOHNSON**, the worthy and accomplished President of LaGrange Female College, died on Thursday evening last....Memphis Daily Appeal, Sat., 1/31/1857.

Died, On the 27th of August, 1857, Walter D., infant son of G. D. and Mary M. **JOHNSON**, aged four months....Services by Rev. J. N. **TEMPLE**. Memphis Daily Appeal, 8/28/1857.

The friends and acquaintances of G. D. and Nancy M. **JOHNSON** are respectfully requested to attend the funeral of their daughter, Adelaide Maria, from their residence on Poplar street, below Third, this afternoon at 4 o'clock. Services by Rev. J. W. **TEMPLE**. Memphis Daily Appeal, 9/25/1857.

Married, In this county on Thursday evening, the 23d ult., by the Rev. Mr. McLellin, Mr. Giles **JOHNSON**, formerly of Madison county, to the amiable and beautiful Miss Ann **YORK**, all of this county. West Tennessee Whig please copy. Memphis Eagle & Enquirer, 1/7/1853.

Married, On the 11th inst. at the Cumberland Presbyterian Church by Rev. A. M. **BRYAN**, Mr. J. Cumming **JOHNSON** and Miss Lizzie, daughter of G. W. **FISHER**, Esq., both of this city. Memphis Daily Appeal, 6/12/1856.

Died, In this place on the 31st of January, 1853, Jackson L. **JOHNSON**, aged 26 years, 3 months and 26 days. He was the son of Gideon H. and Bithlin **JOHNSON** and was born in Abberville District, South Carolina, and raised in Florence, Alabama and left for California 30th day of April, 1848; and died within a few days after his arrival in this place, and was interred decently by his friends. He was a dutiful child and an affectionate brother....Memphis Eagle & Enquirer, 2/4/1853.

Married, On the evening of the 27th ult., at the residence of John **NEWSOM**, Esq., by Rev. J. W. **KNOTT**, of the Methodist Episcopal Church, Mr. John **JOHNSON**, of the firm of Keller & Johnson, to Miss Amanda **AKIN**, all of this city. Memphis Daily Appeal, 1/1/1856.

Died, At the residence of her husband in DeSoto county, Mississippi, on Sunday evening, the 19th of July, at 4 ½ o'clock, after a brief but painful illness, Mrs. Rosannah T., consort of M. D. **JOHNSON**, in the 26th year of her age. Her remains were removed to Marshall county, Mississippi, and interred in the burying ground near the residence of her parents and where repose several members of her family....She leaves two little children, an afflicted husband and a large number of relatives and friends to mourn her irreparable loss....The deceased was a native of Mississippi. Holly Springs, Hernando, Lexington and Jackson papers please copy. Memphis Daily Appeal, 7/31/1857.

Married, On the 28th inst., at Happy Hill, the residence of the bride's father, by Rev. John T. **MERIWETHER**, Rev. W. C. **JOHNSON**, of the Tennessee Conference, to Miss Hettie(?), daughter of R. B. **ALEXANDER**, of the vicinity of Holly Springs, Miss. Memphis Weekly Appeal, 5/5/1858.

Died—At Randolph on the 20th ult., Mrs. Malvina Johnson, wife of Dr. Wm. F. **JOHNSON**, in the 43 year of her age....Mrs. J. spent the earlier portion of her life in Kentucky, where she married, and then removed with her husband to Brownsville in this State.—After spending a number of years in Brownsville, she removed to Randolph...Weekly Appeal, 10/10/1845.

Married—On Tuesday the 10th inst. by the Rev. W. **HYER**, J. G. **FINNIE**, Esq., of Morganfield, Ky., to Miss Susan T., daughter of the Rev. B. W. **JOHNSTON**, of this city. Louisville Journal will please copy. Daily Memphis Enquirer, 4/13/1849. The friends and acquaintances of Rev. Benj. W. Johnston are invited to attend the funeral of his wife, Mrs. Eliza Johnston from his residence on Vance Street this evening at 3 o'clock. Memphis Daily Appeal, 3/18/1855.

Died, Friday, July 31st, 1857, of Consumption, Clarkson **JOHNSTON**, in the 22d year of his age. Memphis Daily Appeal, 8/4/1857.

Died, on the Humboldt river, (California,) ten miles from its head, on the 19th of July, of _____ Cholera, W. W. M. **JOHNSTON**, formerly of this city. Memphis Daily Appeal, 10/6/1852.

Died, In Hernando, Miss., on the morning of the 14th inst., Henrietta, daughter of Wm. H. and Annie P. **JOHNSTON**, aged two years, two months and eleven days. New Orleans and Louisville papers please copy. Memphis Daily Appeal, 8/19/1857.

Died, In Germantown on the 14th instant, at the residence of Dr. W. N. **MORGAN**, Miss E. **JOINER**. Miss Joiner was a native of North Carolina, and has long lived in this neighborhood, and much beloved by all who knew her. Memphis Daily Appeal, 1/21/1857.

We are authorized to announce Henry B. **JOINER** as a candidate for Alderman of the 4th Ward, at the ensuing election. Memphis Daily Appeal, 2/23/1848.

Married, On Tuesday evening the 15th inst., by the Rev. M. T. **ALLEN**, Rufus S. **JOINER**, Esq., to Miss Sarithina, daughter of P. H. **BAIRD**, Esq., of Shelby county. Weekly Appeal, 4/18/1845.

Died, at 5 P.M. on yesterday at his residence, Mr. Z. **JOINER**. He was one of the oldest citizens of Memphis, having resided here near thirty years, and was distinguished for his industry and integrity. We are requested to invite his friends and acquaintances to attend his funeral at 4 o'clock P.M., this evening, June 6th, 1848. Memphis Enquirer, 6/6/1848.

Married—On Tuesday evening last, by Rev. Jeptha **HARRISON**, Mr. A. B. **JONES** to Miss Louisiana I. **ANDERSON**, both of this county. Memphis Enquirer, Fri., 3/8/1839.

The Chancery Court commences its session on tomorrow. We hear that it will be holden in the Banking house of the Farmers' & Merchants Bank. Hon. Calvin **JONES** is the Judge. Memphis Enquirer, 5/21/1848.

...It is with the most poignant regret that we announce the decease of Gen. Calvin **JONES**, at his residence in the vicinity of Bolivar, on the evening of the 20th inst. in the 73d year of his age...A notice of the deceased in the Bolivar "New Era" locates the nativity of Gen. Jones in Connecticut, where he received a liberal education. In early life he emigrated to Raleigh, N.C. and entered the practice of medicine and attained high distinction. For several years he edited a public journal with signal ability. He was there promoted by the Legislature to the office of Major General and accomplished much in elevating (as a disciplinarian) the militia of that state...Fourteen years since he emigrated to the county of Hardeman and quietly pursued the cultivation of the soil, happy and contented in the midst of his family...The Raleigh, N.C. papers will please copy. Memphis Enquirer, 9/29/1846.

Died, In Crittenden county, Ark., on the 10th ultimo, at the residence of her daughter, Mrs. J. **GREER**, Mrs. Catharine M. **JONES**, of pneumonia, aged 61 years. Memphis Daily Appeal, 2/1/1856.

1,600 Acres of Land For Sale—The subscriber offers for sale the tract of land, known as the Solitude tract, lying on the North Fork of Big Creek, in Shelby county, Tenn. There are 700 acres of the land well cleared and in a fine state of cultivation...The improvements are a comfortable dwelling house, Gin house and Mill, Ice house, negro cabins, etc. Chamberlayne **JONES**. The Appeal, 11/3/1843.

Married, At the Presbyterian church in Vicksburg, on Tuesday evening, 29th November, by Rev. E. H. **RUTHERFORD**, Chamberlayne **JONES**, Jr., Esq., of Shelby county, Tenn., to Miss Carrie Thompson, eldest daughter of the Hon. Alexander H. **ARTHUR**, of Vicksburg. The local readers will find a marriage announcement....which will interest them. The groom is a gentleman well known in this city, and the fair bride is no less a personage than the grand-daughter of Judge Wm. **THOMPSON**, of this city. Memphis Daily Appeal, 12/7/1859.

Charles C. **JONES** informs the public generally, that he has just finished the Ball-Room Building at the Commercial Hotel, and is now prepared to execute all kinds of Carpentering in the latest style; he having carried on the Carpentering business for six years in one of the principal eastern cities...His place of business is on Court street, between 2nd and 3d. The Daily Eagle, 2/28/1848.

Married, On the evening of the 30th ultimo by the Rev. Dr. Kay, Mr. George W. **JONES**, to Miss Martha C. Means, daughter of W. B. **MEANS**, Esq., all of this city. Memphis Daily Appeal, 7/2/1853. Died, July 21, Willis, infant son of Geo. W. and M. C. Jones, aged seven months and seven days. Memphis Daily Appeal, 7/23/1859.

Married, On the 1st instant at the residence of the bride's father, by Rev. J. W. **STRANTHER**, Mr. Henry A. **JONES**, of this city, to Miss Mary Lee, daughter of Edmond **FITZPATRICK**, of Lauderdale county, Tenn. Memphis Daily Appeal, 11/4/1859.

Married, At Calvary Church, on Wednesday, the 21st inst., by Rev. Bishop Otey, J. Calvin **JONES**, Esq., to Miss Mary L. **KIRK**, all of this city. Memphis Daily Appeal, 7/23/1858.

The friends and acquaintances of Capt. J. R. **JONES** are requested to attend the funeral of his wife, Mrs. Sarah Jones, from his residence, corner of St. Patrick and Huling streets, this (Saturday) afternoon at 2 o'clock. Memphis Daily Appeal, 10/3/1857.

Died, In this city at about 8 o'clock this morning, of Typhoid Fever, J. Seawell **JONES**. [Columbus Eagle. The deceased is better known to the world as "Shocco Jones," whose financial exploits some fifteen years ago became famous through the columns of Hagans Sentinel. He was a man of remarkable genius. [Mississippian. Memphis Daily Appeal, 3/6/1855.

Jas. Calvin **JONES**, (late of Pontotoc, Miss.,) Attorney at Law, Memphis, Ten.....Memphis Appeal, 4/18/1853. Died, In this city on yesterday evening, Richard, infant son of Jas. Calvin and Rhoda V. Jones, aged eleven months and 17 days....Memphis Eagle & Enquirer, 5/27/1853.

Married, On the 14th inst., by Rev. James **HOLMES**, Mr. Jasper N. **JONES**, of Memphis, to Miss Mary J. Claridge, only daughter of Dr. H. **CLARIDGE**, of Cageville, Haywood county, Tennessee. Memphis Daily Appeal, 5/22/1857.

Departed this life on Sunday evening, the 6th instant, at his residence in this county, of congestive fever, La Fayette **JONES**, aged about 38 years, leaving a wife and child and numerous relatives and friends....The Appeal, 9/15/1843. Died—On Friday morning the 10th inst., at her residence near her father's Mrs. Susan A. Jones, relict of Lafayette Jones dec'd., and daughter of Dr. Dudley **DUNN** in the 31st year of her age. Weekly Appeal, 7/17/1846.

Married—on the 21st inst., by Rev. G. W. **COONS**, Mr. Marcus **JONES**, to Miss Mary E. **PORTER**, all of this city. Memphis Enquirer, 11/23/1848.

Married, On the 26th inst., near Germantown, by A. L. **YANCEY**, Esq., Col. Norman N. **JONES** to Miss Susan **RIVES**. Memphis Appeal, 7/30/1848.

The friends and acquaintances of O. C. **JONES** are requested to attend the funeral of his late wife, Mrs. M. H. Jones, from his residence on Vance street, this morning at 10 o'clock....Memphis Whig, 8/20/1855.

Married. At Hamilton Place, Tenn., on Tuesday the 24th ult. by Right Rev. J. H. **OTEY**, R_ap C. **JONES**, of N. Carolina, and Sarah R., eldest daughter of Gen. L___ J. **POLK**. Memphis Whig, 5/15/1855.

Married, In Hardeman County, on Thursday evening last, Mr. Thomas C. **JONES** of Bolivar, to Miss Mary, daughter of Wm. **IRIONS**, Esq. Memphis Enquirer, Sat., 5/27/1837.

Died, on Monday, 15th instant, at the house of Bolton, Dickins & Co., in this city, of congestive fever, Thomas C. **JONES**, of Weakly county, Tenn...He has left an affectionate wife and three small children to mourn his loss. Daily Enquirer, 11/16/1847.

Married, On Tuesday evening, the 23d ultimo, by Rev. J. **BOONE**, Mr. Vinkler H. **JONES**, of Bastrop county, Texas, and Miss Laura J., daughter of Dr. S. H. **DOXEY**, of LaGrange, formerly of Hardeman county, Tenn. Memphis Daily Appeal, 1/18/1857.

Died, In St. Francis county, Ark., on the 5th inst., of typhoid fever, Lucy J., daughter of Hon. W. A. and Mary J. **JONES**, aged 12 years. Memphis Daily Appeal, 11/11/1859.

Married, on the 9th inst., by Rev. J. H. **GRAY**, Mr. W. M. **JONES** to Miss M. A. **WOOD**, of this city. Daily Memphis Enquirer, 8/12/1848.

We regret to learn that W. S. **JONES**, who was injured sixteen days ago by a cart passing over his back, on Vance street, died on Sunday. He leaves a wife and family. The deceased was a man of estimable character and was much respected. His remains were yesterday forwarded to Henderson, Ky., by the *Alvin Adams*. Memphis Daily Appeal, Tues., 2/16/1858.

Married, At Hernando, Miss., on Wednesday evening, the 9th inst., by Rev. C. C. **CONNER**, Mr. H. F. **JORDAN** and Miss Laura J. **DOCKERY**, daughter of Dr. Dockery, of Hernando, Miss. Memphis Daily Avalanche, 2/10/1859.

Died, In Bolivar, Tenn. on the 21st inst., Lillian, daughter of Levy and Mary F. **JOY**, aged one year eleven months and fifteen days. Columbia, Tenn. & Petersburg, Va., papers will please copy. Memphis Eagle & Enquirer, 6/24/1853.

Died, At her residence in Bolivar, yesterday morning, 30th inst., at 4 o'clock, Mrs. Martha A. Joy, widow of the late Levi **JOY**, Sr. She was an exemplary member of the Baptist Church.... Memphis Daily Appeal, 12/31/1857.

Died, on the 7th instant, at the residence of her father, Major J. W. **ROYSTER**, of Shelby county, Mrs. Bettie S., consort of Jonathan **JOYNER**, late of Hardeman county, in the 24th year of her age....She was a kind and cheerful friend, an obedient and confiding daughter, a devoted wife, and a tenderly affectionate mother....Memphis Daily Appeal, 9/11/1855.

Died, in this city, April 23d, Mrs. Mary E. Joyner, in the 20th year of her age, consort of Mr. W. **JOYNER**. In the death of this truly interesting lady, her friends, the church of Christ, and society at large, have sustained a very severe loss.....She was a consistent member of the First Presbyterian church in this city.....May her affectionate and bereaved husband and mother and friends, in the midst of their affliction....[Richmond, Va. Papers please copy] Memphis Enquirer, 5/30/1846.

Married, on the 27th ult., by the Rev. Geo. W. **COONS**, in Panola county, Miss., Mr. Wm. **JOYNER** of this city, to Miss Maria L., eldest daughter of the late Dr. Elijah **HUNT** of Panola county, Mississippi. Daily Memphis Enquirer, 5/2/1848.

Married, On the 8th inst., at the Gayoso House, in this city, by the Rev. Mr. Gray, Mr. Simon **KAHN**, of Bolivar, to Miss Sarah **KAHN**, of Cincinnati, Ohio. Memphis Daily Eagle, 1/9/1850.

....It falls to our lot to announce the death of a *confrere* and associate—Maj. Hiram **KAINE**, City and Commercial Editor of the Memphis Appeal. This melancholy event occurred on Monday night last, the 26th ult. at 12 o'clock. Maj. Kaine emigrated to Memphis in the spring of 1851 and forthwith became city Editor of the Memphis *Enquirer*, where he remained for several months. On quitting that establishment he became associated with us in the same capacity until the fall of that year, when he connected himself with the proprietor and Editor associate in the Evening *Express*. He returned to this office in May last and resumed his former post as city editor and remained with us until his death....Maj. Kaine was connected at various times with several newspapers of Pittsburgh and with one or two of the country papers of Pennsylvania. He has left a helpless and most interesting family to mourn their bereavement....Memphis Appeal, 1/2/1854.

Married. In Holly Springs, Miss. on Wednesday morning the 10th inst. by Rev. Dr. Reaves, Mr. Joseph K. **KANE**, of Nashville, Tenn., to Miss Susan A. C. **LOVING**, of the former place. Memphis Appeal, 5/12/1854.

Yesterday morning about eight o'clock, a deck-hand on the steamer *Kate Frisbee*, named Martin **KANE**, fell overboard from the guards and was drowned....Mr. Kane was born in Ireland and was about twenty-five years of age. He was an unmarried man, but leaves relatives and friends in this city to mourn his sudden death. Memphis Daily Appeal, 2/13/1857.

Died—In Clinton, Ark., on the 5th of May, 1859, Mr. Theodore B. **KANE**, in the forty-third year of his age. He had been for the last ten years a minister of the Baptist Church. Memphis Daily Avalanche, 5/31/1859.

Died, Near Des Arc, Arkansas, on Thursday morning last, Mr. William A. **KARR**, in the 76th year of his age. The deceased was born near Charlotte, N.C., and emigrated to West Tennessee, where he had resided—except the past six months—for twenty-seven years. He had been a member of the Presbyterian Church near forty-three years. Thus has passed away another of "the men of the olden time." Memphis Daily Appeal, Wed., 11/18/1857.

The friends and acquaintances of Mrs. Caroline **KATTMAN** are invited to attend her funeral from her late residence on Shelby street, this afternoon at 2 ½ o'clock. Memphis Daily Appeal, 2/11/1857.

Mr. Ernst **KATTMANN** of the Germania House, died yesterday of dropsy. We believe that he was at one time editor of the German paper in this city. His funeral takes place at 9 o'clock this morning from his residence near the Gayoso. Memphis Whig, 7/27/1855.

D. **KAUFMANN** having this day associated himself with his brother, Adolph **KAUFMANN**, the Clothing and Gent's General Furnishing Business....oct3. Memphis Daily Appeal, 11/7/1854.

Married, On Monday evening the 13th inst., by the Rev. Thos. G. **DAVIDSON**, Paul C. **KAY**, to Elenor F. S. **PEACE**, all of this city. Weekly Appeal, 7/24/1846.

Mrs. Susan **KERLEY**, wife of Mr. Wm. G. Kerley, of Shreveport, La., and sister of our esteemed fellow-citizen, R. L. **KAY**, after a brief visit to her brother's, left here two weeks ago, in good health, with her three children. She reached the residence of her brother, in Todd co., Ky., on Saturday evening, 20th ult., and on Sunday, 21st ult., the mother and two children were attacked by cholera, and in a few brief hours put off mortality to put on immortality...Memphis Daily Eagle, 7/31/1850.

We omitted to notice the departure for Cuba about a week since, of Captain A. C. **KEATON**, of Memphis, with a company of about thirty. Capt. Keaton, we understand, commanded a company in the Cardenas affair. Memphis Daily Appeal, 8/23/1851.

Died. At his residence in Benton county, Tennessee, on the 18th day of July, 1855, Holloway **KEE**, an old and highly esteemed citizen of this county. He was a native of Wake county, N.C. Raleigh Register and North Carolina papers copy. Memphis Daily Appeal, 8/9/1855.

It is with deep pain that we announce the death of Dr. Thos. **KEEFE**, who breathed his last at his residence in this city yesterday evening. His disease was congestion of the brain; and his sudden and unexpected demise wil cast a gloom upon the hearts of many who esteemed him for his many good qualities. Peace to his ashes.—*Evening News of yesterday*. Memphis Daily Appeal, 10/9/1855. We understand that the preparations and medicines of the late Dr. T. Keefe are now in the possession of his brother, M. **KEEFE**....Memphis Daily Appeal, 10/12/1855.

We learn that Messrs. David H. **KEELING**, Frederick **GULL**, and Maj. **WYATT**, well known citizens of this place, will leave for California, on next Thursday. They will select such a route as will give speed and economy of travel...Memphis Eagle, Tuesday, 8/14/1849. Married, On the evening of the 4th inst., by the Rev. Thos. L. **GRACE**, at the residence of E. M. **YERGER**, Esq., Mr. David H. Keeling, to Miss Nannie **HOSKINS**, all of Memphis. Memphis Eagle & Enquirer, 5/8/1852.

Died, In this city yesterday morning, of Consumption, David S. **KEELING**. Memphis Daily Appeal, 10/23/1856.

The Store House on Main street, opposite Odd Fellows' Hall, lately occupied by E. A. **KEELING**, deceased...Subject to the widow's dower. Also, two brick tenements on Madison street, belonging to said E. A. Keeling's Estate. Sale to take place on Saturday, Sept. 20, 1851...W. F. **MASON**, A. **WRIGHT**, Executors of E. A. Keeling. Memphis Appeal, 9/1/1851.

Edward A. **KEELING**, Receiving, Forwarding & Commission Merchant, Madison street.... Memphis Daily Eagle, 8/2/1847.

Married, At LaGrange, Tenn., on the morning of the 1st inst., by Rev. G. G. B. **FREEMAN**, Mr. T. G. **KEEN** to Miss Emeline M. **HAWLEY**, both of Aberdeen, Miss. Memphis Daily Appeal, 10/3/1857.

Memphis Daguerrean Gallery...The undersigned is prepared to execute the finest specimens in his art...N. E. **KEENAN**. Memphis Appeal, 2/23/1848.

Married, On the 1st inst. by Rev. C. R. **HENDRICKSON**, Mr. F. T. **KEESACKER** to Miss Margaret A. **SEVIER**, all of this city. Memphis Eagle & Enquirer, 3/2/1853.

Funeral Notice. I.O.O.F. The members of the order in good standing are invited to meet at the Hall at 2 o'clock, p.m., this day (Sunday) to attend the funeral of our late brother, John **KEHOE**, of San Francisco Lodge, No. 3, California....Memphis Daily Appeal, 11/19/1854.

We are authorized to announce Capt. Joseph **KEISER**, as a candidate for Alderman of the 1st Ward, at the ensuing election. Memphis Daily Appeal, 2/23/1848.

Col. W. B. **KEITH** of Jacksonport, Arkansas, died at Memphis at about half past eight o'clock A.M., Wednesday, October the 28th, 1857, of Laryngitis. His remains will be taken to Panola, Mississippi, where his funeral will take place at eleven o'clock A.M., Friday, October __th, 1857....Memphis Daily Appeal, 10/29/1857.

Married, On the 15th instant at the residence of Mr. Appleby, by Rev. A. H. **THOMAS**, Mr. H. M. **KELLER** to Miss Hellen M. **DECKER**, both of Memphis. Memphis Daily Appeal, 12/17/1859.

Married, At Fort Pickering, on the 22nd inst., by the Rev. Michael **McALEER**, Mr. Joseph **KELLER**, of Memphis, to Mrs. Elizabeth **BAUMGARTNER**, of the former place. American Eagle Weekly, 5/30/1845.

The friends and acquaintances of Joseph **KELLER** are invited to attend the funeral of his daughter, Georgiana, from his residence on Adams street this morning at 9 o'clock. Memphis Daily Appeal, 4/1/1857.

The friends and acquaintances of Mr. Joseph **KELLER** are invited to attend the funeral of his son, John, at half past 2 o'clock This Evening. Memphis Daily Appeal, 4/7/1857.

Dr. Thos. F. **KELLER**, late of Tuscumbia, Ala., has taken the office recently occupied by Dr. Bryan, on the corner of Shelby and Union streets....Memphis Daily Appeal, 5/9/1856.

Married, In St. Louis, on Monday, 27th inst., at the residence of Mr. C. **McSORLY**, by Rev. A. **DAMON**, Mr. M. R. **KELLEY**, of Memphis, and Miss Kate **McSORLY**, of St. Louis. Memphis Daily Appeal, 11/1/1856.

Esquire Horne was called upon yesterday to hold an inquest on the body of Patrick **KELLEY**, who died the previous night at a boarding house on Poplar street. The deceased came up on the steamer *Nebraska* Saturday....stating that he had received a slight injury on the boat by the fall of a box....Memphis Daily Appeal, Thurs., 10/20/1859.

A Good Farm for Sale. Two and a half miles south-east of Germantown and within one mile of the Memphis and Charleston Railroad, containing 220 acres of land....I will sell a bargain in the above farm... as I wish to go West. A. J. **KELLY**. Memphis Daily Appeal, 11/9/1854.

In relation to an unfortunate affair which occurred in Germantown, on Thursday afternoon last, by which a gentleman by the name of James **KELLY** was accidentally seriously injured by the explosion of a pistol which I held in my hand, I submit the following certificate...P. A. **LEWELLIN**. We, the undersigned, believing P. A. Lewellin to have accidentally, though unfortunately, shot James Kelly...exculpate him from blame, all of us being the relatives or friends of the sufferer: James M. **KELLY**, Jr., James M. **KELLY**, Sr., (father,) Elizabeth **CLARK**, (grandmother,) Wm. **CLARK**, A. J. **MATLOCK**, Elizabeth **KELLY**, (mother,) Pauline **SANDERS**, (aunt,) J. A. **CLARK**, (uncle.) Memphis Eagle & Enquirer, 3/28/1852.

Married, In this city, on Tuesday evening, 24th inst., by Rev. R. C. **GRUNDY**, Thos. **KELSALL** to Miss Belvadora **WILSON**. Memphis Daily Appeal, 5/26/1859.

Married, On the 29th inst., by Rev. Dr. Henderson, Mr. Thomas F. **KELSEY** to Miss Emily J. **GILL**, both of Shelby county, Tenn. Memphis Daily Eagle, 5/31/1850.

Died, On the 30th of August, at the residence of his father-in-Law, Mr. Thomas S. **KELSEY**, aged 26 years. Memphis Eagle, 9/6/1850.

Trust Sale. In pursuance to the terms and conditions of a Deed of Trust made by Wing W. **KENCHELOE** to me, as trustee, and registered in the office of Register of Shelby County, Tenn., on the second day of June, 1845, in Book S, pages 63 and 64, I shall proceed to sell...on the 4th day of August, 1847...One lot of Ground lying in Shelby County, Tenn., East of and near to the Town of Memphis, containing one acre...Daily Enquirer, 7/17/1847.

Common Law & Chancery Court at Memphis. Petition for Divorce, filed in the Law Side of said Court the 25th of August, 1852. Eliza J. **KENDALL** vs. Geo. W. **KENDALL**. It appearing to the Clerk, from the affidavit of the complainant's made in this cause, that the defendant is a non-resident of the State of Tennessee...Memphis Daily Appeal, 8/31/1852.

Mr. Jas. G. **KENDALL**, well known as an expert electrician, and long connected with the Western Union Telegraph Company at Cincinnati, has become connected with the telegraph office in this city. Memphis Daily Appeal, 8/17/1859.

Married, In this city, on the 1st inst., by Rev. Dr. Gray, Jacob L. **KENNEDY**, Esq., of this city, to Miss Ellen H., daughter of Dr. S. **GILBERT**, of New Orleans. Memphis Daily Eagle, 10/3/1850.

Died—In South Memphis, on Saturday, very suddenly, Mr. Jas. **KENNEDY**, a native of Ireland, but for many years an honest, kind-Hearted and excellent citizen of this place, highly esteemed, and whose death is much regretted. At his death he was a member of the Board of Aldermen of South Memphis. Daily Enquirer, Tues., 6/22/1847.

Died, Of consumption yesterday morning, Mr. Martin **KENNEDY**, aged 29 years...The deceased was an exemplary citizen, husband and friend....He leaves a youthful widow and infant child to mourn his premature loss. The friends and acquaintances of Martin Kennedy are invited to attend his funeral, from his residence, corner of Main and Huling streets, This Morning, at 10 o'clock. Services at the Catholic Church by Rev. T. L. **GRACE**. Memphis Daily Appeal, 2/9/1856.

Coroner Waldran held an inquest yesterday over the body of R. **KENNEDY**, found on the Raleigh road. The deceased had been sick for some time and had wandered by the road side where he died. Verdict in accordance with the above facts. Twenty dollars were found on his person. Memphis Daily Appeal, 10/21/1852.

Died—Of congestive fever, on the 4th inst., at his residence, 10 miles from Memphis, Mr. Wm. H. **KENNEDY**, formerly of Stanton, Va., aged 29 years. Surrounded with the comforts and elegancies of life, blest with the love of an affectionate companion, possessing the esteem of a large circle of acquaintances, he was cut down and laid low in the grave in a most unexpected hour. His disease ran its course in three days. American Eagle, 9/9/1842.

Married, At the residence of the bride's father, on the 4th inst., by Rev. J. W. **KNOTT**, Mr. L. G. **KENNETT**, of the steamer St. Francis, and Miss L. R. **RICHARDS**, of this city. Memphis Evening Ledger, 1/8/1858.

Masonic Tribute. South Memphis Lodge, No. 118, Memphis, Sept. 29, 1857. Departed this life September 25, 1857, Brother E. W. **KENNEY**, at his residence, near Germantown, Tenn....Memphis Daily Appeal, 9/30/1857.

Married, On Thursday evening the 12th inst., by Dr. B. F. **HALL**, Mr. Michael W. **KENNEY**, to Miss Caroline **KLINCK**, all of this city. Memphis Daily Appeal, 2/14/1852. Died, In this city on the 17th instant, of inflammation of the brain, Robert Emmett, infant son of M. W. and Carolina Kenney, aged one year and five months. Memphis Daily Appeal, 3/20/1856

The firm of Hunt & Kennon is this day dissolved. The claims and accounts of the firm are in the hands of J. T. **SWAYNE**, Esq., Howard's Row, Memphis, who is alone authorized to collect and settle the same by suit or otherwise...Memucan **HUNT**, Richard **KENNON**. Memphis Enquirer, 7/11/1848.

I offer for sale the tract of land on which I now reside. It is distant from Memphis about 19 miles and on the line of the Memphis and Charleston Railroad and the Plank road. The tract contains 954 acres and is divided by the Memphis and Charleston Railroad into two tracts; one-third on the south of said Road and the balance on the north....Edward W. **KENNY**, Germantown P.O., Shelby county. Memphis Daily Appeal, 8/28/1855.

Died, In this city on yesterday, Barbara Ann, infant daughter of Michael W. and Carolina **KENNY**, aged one year four months and twenty-one days. Memphis Daily Appeal, 8/14/1858.

Died, On the 11th inst., at the residence of Mr. A. **TRIGG**, Mrs. Lucy Jane **KENT**. American Eagle, 8/18/1843.

Don't fail to attend to-day the sale of personal property at the late residence of Mr. N. H. **KERCHEVAL**, deceased, South of the first gate on Hernando Plank Road....See advertisement of W. D. **DUNN**, Esq., Administrator....Memphis Daily Appeal, 9/28/1855.

Married, By the Rev. J. H. **GRAY**, on the 3d inst., at the residence of Mrs. S. **WARD**, on Big Creek, in this county, the Rev. A. H. **KERR** to Miss M. J. C. **WARD**. Weekly American Eagle, 3/6/1846.

...We also learn of the death of Col. Andrew **KERR**, an elderly gentleman, well known in this city from his long residence near it, and his wealthy landed interest adjoining it; he resided on the river below, in Tunica county, Miss. He died at Augusta, Geo., at the residence of his brother. Memphis Eagle, 7/27/1850. The tract of land adjoining the city of Memphis on the South, which belongs to the heirs of Andrew Kerr deceased, will be offered at public sale in 10 and 20 acre lots on the 1st of May next. This sale is made under a decree of the Chancery Court authorising it, and appointing me trustee to carry it into effect. The tract extends from the river three miles East and contains 1254 acres...Sam'l **KERR**, Trustee. Memphis Appeal, 4/5/1851.

Died, In this city yesterday morning Mr. James D. **KERR**, for the last year a citizen of this place...He died of bilious fever after an illness of a few days. Memphis Appeal, 7/10/1852. At a meeting of the City Guards, held at their drill room the 9th day of July, 1852, called to pay a last tribute of respect to the memory of Jas. D. Kerr, late a member of the Guards...He died on Friday, the 9th inst., at 9 o'clock, at the residence of Capt. **FRELEIGH**, on Linden street, leaving a wife to mourn for an estimable husband...Memphis Daily Appeal, 7/15/1852.

Died, On the 10th inst. at the residence of his father, near Memphis, Edmond Burke Kerr, son of John **KERR**, in the 22d year of his age. Augusta (Ga.) papers please copy. The friends of the family are requested to attend his funeral from the family residence on Kerr avenue, To-Day at 4 o'clock P.M. Memphis Weekly Appeal, 4/14/1858.

Joseph **KERR**'s Inn & Boarding House, Sign of the *Cross Keys*, near the landing at the mouth of Wolf river, Memphis, Tennessee, is continued open as a house of *Public Entertainment*. Memphis Advocate, 3/22/1828.

Died—At Greeneck, Ark., on the 22d ult., Wm. D. **KERR**, aged 16 years. Memphis Enquirer, 10/4/1839.

Married, On Tuesday evening, 18th inst., in the Second Presbyterian Church by Rev. R. C. **GRUNDY**, D.D., William Henry **KERR**, Esq., to Miss Julia Gordan **LAW**, all of Memphis. Memphis Daily Appeal, 10/20/1859.

The members of Gayoso Division No. 60, Sons of Temperance, will meet at their Hall at 3 ½ o'clock, this evening, for the purpose of attending the burial of our deceased Brother, Zenas H. **KERR**...A. M. **HOPKINS**, R.S. Memphis Enquirer, 4/6/1848. (Spelled Zenos H. **KARR** in Memphis Eagle, 4/6/1848.)

Married—On yesterday morning at the residence of Judge Bailey, in this city, at 8 o'clock in the morning, by Rev. Wm. **HYER**, Rev. Mr. **KESTERSON** of the Memphis Conference, to Miss Ann **HARDAWAY**. Daily Enquirer, 5/14/1847.

Married, On Thursday, the 15th instant, by Rev. George **WHITE**, assistant Rector of Calvary Church, Leonidas **KETCHUM** to Anne Chambers **BRADFORD**, both of this city. Memphis Weekly Appeal, 4/28/1858.

Died, At his residence in Coahoma county, Mississippi, on the 19th inst., James S. **KILLEBREW**, in the fifty-ninth year of his age. Clarksville *Jeffersonian* please copy. Memphis Daily Appeal, 7/31/1857.

Notice is hereby given to the heirs of James **KIMBELL**, deceased late of Murry county Tennessee, and to all others concerned that, at the next October sessions, of the county Court, for the county of Shelby and state aforesaid, I shall petition the court to appoint commissioners to lay off to me one equal fifth part of a 2560 acre tract of land, lying on Nonconner creek, and entered in the name of said James Kimbell by entry No. 806, in the eleventh surveyors district range seven, section one.—Said fifth part being the locative interest. Tho. H. **PERSON**, Locator. Memphis Advocate, 2/23/1828.

Married—In this place, on Thursday the 11th inst., by the Rev. Mr. Davidson, Mr. John **KIMBLE**, to Miss Nancy **WHORTON**. Memphis Enquirer, 8/18/1836.

The subscribers having taken out Letters of Administration upon the estate of John **KIMBROUGH** dec'd. at May term 1823 Shelby Tenn.—Hereby gives notice to all having claims against said estate to present them...B. **KIMBROUGH**, Jas. **KIMBROUGH**, Administrators. Aug. 1, 1823. The Pioneer, 9/9/1823

Departed this life on the fifteenth inst. at the residence of his mother, six miles east of Memphis, Nathaniel **KIMBROUGH**... Memphis Enquirer, 4/20/1836.

Died, At his father's residence in Carroll county, Miss., on the 28th ult., Adolph, infant son of Mr. O. L. **KIMBROUGH**, aged two years and five months. Memphis Daily Appeal, 9/2/1856.

Taken up by C. F. **KING**, living two miles from Memphis on the State Line road, one black mare....The Appeal, 10/27/1843.

Married, On Thursday evening, the 15th instant, at the residence of Mr. J. W. **JONES**, by Rev. Mr. Welch, Mr. Chas. C. **KING**, of Helena, to Miss Annie M. Taylor; youngest daughter of the late Col. John K. **TAYLOR**, of Little Rock, Ark. Memphis Daily Appeal, 11/17/1855.

Died, Thursday noon, 5th June, 1856, Harry Byrd, son of Henry S. and Lelia R. **KING**, aged three years and two months. The funeral will take place from the residence of his parents, Jefferson street, East of Third....to the Winchester Cemetery. Memphis Daily Appeal, 6/6/1856.

Married, In this city on the 13th inst., at the First Methodist Church, by Rev. L. D. **MULLINS**, Mr. M. C. **KING**, of the firm of Stewart, King, & Co., and Miss Mattie **McMURRY**. Memphis Daily Appeal, 10/14/1856.

Thomas Benton **KING**, a son of Judge E. W. M. **KING**, of this city, returned home yesterday from Nicaragua, by way of New York, at which place he arrived some few weeks ago, on board the Cyenne. He is in robust health, and though bearing evidence of the hardships incident to the life of a soldier, he is otherwise unchanged. Memphis Daily Appeal, 8/25/1857.

By virtue of a Decree of the Circuit Court of Shelby county, Tennessee, at January term, 1856, on the petition exparte of Thomas J. L. **KING**, et. al, heirs and distributees of Thomas **KING**, dec'd., I will, on Monday, 5th of May next, at the residence of E. M. **BELL**, _ miles southeast of Raleigh, on the LaGrange road.... sell at auction one hundred and seventy acres of land....being the same tract on which said Bell now lives, after laying off widow's dower.... Memphis Daily Appeal, 3/30/1856.

Died, near this city, July 18th, William Marion **KING**, aged about 25 years....Memphis Daily Appeal, 7/19/1855.

Died, In Tishomingo county, Miss., on the 8th inst., Thos. B., aged three years, only son of T. D. and M. A. **KINGSBURY**, of Arkadelphia, Clark county, Ark. His remains were brought to this city and buried in Elmwood Cemetery. Memphis Daily Appeal, 10/14/1856.

The subscribers have good Dry Wood, below Island No. 75, on the Mississippi side, in boats, at Two Dollars Per Cord...John **PATTERSON**, Ozzin **KINGSBY**. Memphis Daily Eagle, 7/6/1848.

Married, On the 7th instant by Rev. B. W. **JOHNSON**, Captain Riley **KINMAN**, of this city, and Miss Mattie **HOOKER**, late of Aberdeen, Ark. Memphis Daily Appeal, 10/10/1856.

Died, In Tipton county, Tennessee, on the morning of the 17th of February last, Mrs. Lucy Kinney, wife of Mr. Jesse **KINNEY**, in the forty-second year of her age. The deceased was the mother of a large family and has left a disconsolate husband and ten children to mourn her loss....Memphis Daily Appeal, 4/18/1856.

Died, At the residence of Dr. A. **DAVIS**, in Sommerville, Tenn., on the evening of the 29th June, 1851, of typhus fever, Miss Jane **KIRK**, aged 18 years. The deceased had just returned from Sommerville, some weeks since, whither she had been for the last twelve months, like a ministering angel, endeavoring to relieve the wants and smoothe the dying pillow of her aged and afflicted Grand Father, to her relatives and friends in Memphis...After remaining a short time with her sister, she again determined to visit Sommerville, for the purpose of being present at the last sad ceremonies occasioned by the decease of her aged relative, but ere she reached her destination, death had laid his iron grasp upon her blooming form...Memphis Daily Appeal, 7/3/1851.

Died, On the 17th inst., Virginia, daughter of John and Mary **KIRK**, aged 13 years. American Eagle Weekly, 5/23/1845.

The Somerville Reporter of Saturday announces another probably fatal accident by the careless trifling with fire-arms...On Saturday last, two highly respectable young men (brothers) named Alexander and Robert **KIRKPATRICK**, were trifling with a pistol, in a room at La Grange, they believing it to be without a charge.—The result was that the pistol was discharged by Alexander, and the greater portion of the contents lodged in the left breast of his brother Robert. Medical aid was immediately procured, and the wound examined—It appeared that five buck-shot had taken effect, causing a very dangerous wound, though hopes were entertained that it would not prove fatal...American Eagle, Fri., 8/8/1845.

We see announced the death of Mr. Plummer **KIRKPATRICK**, a California emigrant from La Grange, in this State. He died at Sacramento City, about the first of last November, of Cholera. Memphis Daily Appeal, 1/11/1851.

Died. Suddenly of Cholera Infantum, on the 2d inst., at Hickory Wythe Springs, Isaac, only son of I. B. and L. S. **KIRTLAND** of this city, aged 11 months and 4 days. American Eagle, 8/12/1847. Choctaw Land Scrip. The subscriber has the above Scrip for sale, which pays for any Lands subject to entry in the States of Mississippi, Louisiana, Alabama and Arkansas. I. B. Kirtland. Daily Enquirer, 5/21/1847.

Married, On January 21st by Esquire Waldran, Mr. James H. **KIRTLAND** and Miss Mary **DAVIS**. Memphis Daily Appeal, 1/23/1857.

Died, In this city at half-past 3 o'clock on Thursday morning last, after a brief illness, of Congestion, Mr. Richard **KIRTLAND**, in the 33d year of his age. The deceased was a native of Virginia, where his parents and family connexions still live, but for some years he had been a citizen of Memphis, where by his urbanity and gentlemanly bearing, he had drawn around him a large circle of warm and devoted friends....His remains were borne to their last resting place yesterday evening by a large cortege of sorrowing friends. May they rest in peace. Richmond (Va.) papers will please notice. Memphis Daily Appeal, Fri., 4/1/1853

Married, On Thursday evening last by Rev. Mr. Whitemore, Mr. Hayne I. **KLINCK** and Miss Margaret Anna Robertson, second daughter of Col. J. F. **ROBERTSON**, all of this city. Memphis Daily Appeal, Sat., 8/16/1856.

Married, On Tuesday evening, July 20th, at the residence of the bride's father, by Rev. J. T. C. **COLLINS**, Mr. J. F. **KNAPP**, of the firm of Goodyear, Knapp & Co., to Miss Mollie C. Bradford, only daughter of Watt C. **BRADFORD**—all of this city. Holly Springs, Miss., and Cincinnati papers please copy. Memphis Daily Appeal, 7/21/1858.

Married, On the 17th instant at the residence of the bride's father, by Rev. W. A. **COTHRAN**, Dr. W. **KNIGHT**, of Fayette county, Tenn., to Miss Minerva V. **KELLY**, of Shelby county, Tenn. Memphis Daily Appeal, 11/19/1859.

Married, On the 20th ult., by the Rev. J. **BURNS** Mr. R. J. **KOONCE** to Miss M. A., second daughter of Dr. W. M. **WARNER**—all of Shelby county, Tenn. Memphis Daily Appeal, 10/3/1851.

C. **KORTRECHT**, Attorney At Law, Raleigh, Tenn. Daily Memphis Enquirer, 11/15/1848.

Married, On Wednesday the 26th instant by Rev. J. M. **ROBINSON**, Charles **KORTRECHT**, Esq., of this city, to Miss Augusta A. **BETTS**, near Huntsville, Madison county, Ala. Memphis Daily Appeal, 9/29/1855.

Philadelphia Carriage Warehouse. A fresh supply of every description of Carriages, just received and for sale very low at the above establishment back to Front Row...J. H. **KRAFFT**. Memphis Eagle, 8/13/1847.

Married, On the 27th inst. at the residence of J. W. S. **BROWN**, in this city, by Rev. Mr. Meriweather, Mr. Benjamin **KRUSE**, of Cincinnati, to Miss Margaret **GREEN**, of Peoria, Illinois. Memphis Daily Appeal, 3/30/1859.

Dr. F. A. **KUEFFNER**, Homeopathic Physician, Offers his services to the citizens of Memphis and the vicinity, in the various branches of the Medical Profession...at his office, corner of Adams and Second streets...Daily Memphis Enquirer, 6/1/1848.

Married, On Thursday the 20th ult. by Rev. F. D. **PINER**, Mr. Samuel **KUYKENDALL** to Miss Martha **KEITH**, all of Panola county, Miss. Memphis Eagle & Enquirer, 2/10/1853.

Died. On the 30th inst., at the hospital in this city, Mr. Granville **LACEY**, ship carpenter, supposed, from papers in his possession, to be from Baltimore. Weekly Memphis Eagle, 6/7/1849.

We learn that a fatal street recontre took place about noon on Wednesday last, in Somerville, between Wm. A. **LACY** and J. A. **WILSON**, Esqs., both young gentlemen of the bar, in which Mr. Wilson was killed from a pistol shot by Mr. Lacy. The cause of this bloody interview, was a publication made in the newspapers by Mr. Wilson, on the 1st of September last, after Mr. Lacy had departed for the Rio Grande, a member of Capt. Lenow's company of Fayette Cavalry, denouncing Mr. Lacy as having been guilty of crimes the most dishonest, infamous and penal; and alleging as his excuse for making said publication, that since the departure of Mr. Lacy, he had learned that Mr. L. had circulated reports that he had been guilty of infamous and dishonest acts...when he arrived in Somerville, we learn, a hostile meeting was generally expected and on their getting a sight of one another, both drew their pistols, (revolvers) and exchanged two shots, the first from Mr. Lacy piercing Mr. W.'s arm, and the second his vitals, neither of Mr. W's taking effect...American Eagle, Thurs., 10/29/1846.

On Friday night a number of persons assembled at the house of Mr. D. **DERN**, on Auction street, on the west side of the bayou, for a dance....Between ten and eleven o'clock, another difficulty occurred, in the course of which Andrew **LAHIFF** was stabbed in the middle of the breast, over the pit of the stomach. The knife reached his heart and almost immediate death ensued....The commission of the act was attributed to a grudge somebody held toward the deceased....Memphis Daily Avalanche, 4/4/1859.

Married, On the 17th inst., near Hickory Wythe, by the Rev. M. T. **ALLEN**, Mr. James M. **LAIN** to Miss Jane **KARR**. Weekly Appeal, 2/20/1846.

Died, On June 7th, 1853, James H. Laird, only son of Dr. H. & M. **LAIRD**, at Middletown, Ky., in the 23d year of his age. His disease was chronic diarrhea, with which he had been afflicted two years....The corpse was conveyed to Belmont, Miss., where the bereaved parents now deeply mourn over their irreparable loss. Nashville papers please copy. Memphis Eagle & Enquirer, 6/14/1853.

Rialto Restaurant, Immediately under Hightower Hall. The subscribers are now prepared for the Fall and Winter campaign, and respectfully invite their friends and the public generally to call on them whenever the inner man requires refreshing, either in the way of substantials, delicacies, or the purest of Wines, Liquors and Cigars...Joshua F. **JAMES**, Luther **LAIRD**. Daily Enquirer, 11/4/1847. Married, On Thursday 20th inst., by the Rev. Mr. Gray, Mr. Luther Laird to Mrs. Jane M. **OSWALD**; both of this city. Memphis Daily Appeal, 11/22/1851.

Died, On the evening of the 12th of July, 1858, at the residence of Henry **LAKE**, Esq., in the vicinity of Memphis, Henry, son of Wm. H. and Kate M. **LAKE**, aged 13 months and five days. Baltimore papers please copy. Memphis Daily Appeal, 7/16/1858.

Married, On the evening of the 23d inst. at the First Baptist Church by the Rev. D. **ISABEL**, William H. **LAKE**, Esq. to Miss Catharine M., eldest daughter of Judge S. **BAILEY**. Memphis Eagle & Enquirer, 5/31/1854. Died—On the morning of the 28th of April, 1859, Elizabeth Hart, infant daughter of William H. and Kate M. Lake. The friends and acquaintances of the family are invited to attend the funeral from the residence of Henry Lake, Esq., this morning....Services by Rev. T. J. **DRANE**. Memphis Daily Avalanche, 4/29/1859.

Married, In Fayetteville, Tenn., on the 26th February, 1854, by Rev. C. D. **ELLIOTT**, James B. **LAMB**, Esq., of Memphis, Tenn., and Miss Elizabeth F., daughter of Dr. Wm. **BONNER**. Memphis Daily Appeal, 3/6/1857. (Author's note: 1854 is probably a misprint error of the paper.)

The subscribers have taken the large store on Front Row...for the purpose of carrying on a direct importation of all kinds of Birmingham and Sheffield Goods connected with the Hardware business...R. T. **LAMB** & Co. Daily Enquirer, 4/25/1847. We regret to learn that R. T. Lamb, Esq., a citizen of this place, highly esteemed in the different walks of life, died of cholera, in the city of New York, on the 6th instant. Memphis Eagle, 8/16/1849.

S. H. **LAMB**, Madison street, Memphis, respectfully informs country merchants and others, that he has constantly for sale a general assortment of the most approved School, Classical, Theological, Medical, Law and Miscellaneous Books...Daily Enquirer, 11/4/1847.

Died. At his residence, near Memphis, on the 8th inst., of congestive fever, Dr. Sylvanus **LAMB**, in the 30th year of his age. Formerly of Parkersburg, Va. The Parkersburgh and Fairmont Va. Papers will copy. Memphis Daily Eagle, 10/9/1848.

Died, At his residence in Mississippi county, Arkansas, on the 1st inst., Wilie B. **LAMB**, aged 39 years, only brother of J. B. **LAMB**, Esq., of this city. Memphis Daily Appeal, 11/6/1857.

We publish this morning the professional card of Mons. M. Etienne **LAMBERT**, who designs permanently locating in our city as a professor of the French and Italian languages. Prof. Lambert is a graduate of Paris University and has been engaged as a teacher of the languages in this country for the past four years. Laterly he came from Florence, Ala. ....Memphis Daily Appeal, 3/2/1856.

We regret to announce the death of E. S. **LAMPHIER**, a well-known druggist for a number of years in this city. The sad event occurred at 10 o'clock Tuesday night. Memphis Daily Appeal, Thurs., 8/18/1859.

Died, In Memphis, Tennessee, July 5th, Lorenzo Dimon, only son of L. D. and Jane Biers(?) **LAMPMAN**, aged 5 months. Memphis Daily Appeal, 7/7/1857.

Died, In Jackson, Tenn., on the 21st of October, Mrs. Anna Terrell Lancaster, wife of Samuel **LANCASTER**, Esq., in the 59th year of her age. She was the eldest daughter of the venerable Capt. John **LYNCH**, formerly of Lynchburg, Va., who died in Madison county in the year 1842, and was descended from a long line of honorable and patriotic ancestors. Memphis Daily Appeal, 11/3/1858.

Married, At the residence of Dr. W. G. **LANCASTER** on the 22d July, 1852, by G. M. **BARTLETT**, Esq., Dr. John B. **LANCASTER**, of Texas, to Miss Lucy V., daughter of the late Richard **LAKE**, of this county. Memphis Daily Appeal, 7/26/1852.

Married, on Thursday evening, 23d inst., by Rev. J. H. **GRAY**, Mr. Wm. T. **LAND** to Miss Margaret Ann **BAIN**, all of Memphis. Daily Memphis Enquirer, 12/25/1847.

Died, On Tuesday, 8th inst., Mrs. Amanda S. Lane, consort of D. J. **LANE**, of Fayette county, Tenn. Weekly Appeal, 12/25/1846.

Mary Priscilla Lane, wife of the Rev. G. W. **LANE**, and daughter of much esteemed and excellent Samuel **HERRON** (deceased) died at her home, Central Academy, Panola county, Miss., on the 6th of April, 1859; aged twenty-three years and nine months. She received a liberal education at Oakland, Yallobusha county, and at Union Female College, Oxford, Miss. Memphis Daily Avalanche, 4/16/1859.

Married, On the 9th instant by Josiah **HORNE**, Esq., Mr. J. B. **LANE** to Mrs. M. A. **ZELLES**, all of this city. Memphis Daily Appeal, 10/11/1859.

Married, In Jackson, Tenn., on Wednesday, the 2d inst., by Rev. Dr. Rivers, of Florence, Ala., J. Jay **LANE**, Esq., of New Orleans, to Miss Alice **HUBBARD**, all of the former place. Memphis Daily Appeal, 3/3/1859.

Died, On the evening of the 19th inst., from the effects of a burn received on the morning of the same day, Euena(?) Hill, only daughter of J. M. and J. E. **LANE**. Aged 18 months. Memphis Daily Appeal, 1/24/1858. Died, On the 23d inst., of diptheria, after a week of painful suffering, Henry Flavel, son of J. M. and J. E. Lane, aged nearly 6 years, at Hickory With, Tenn. Memphis Daily Appeal, 9/29/1859.

Died, On Saturday morning, 11th inst., in this city, at the residence of his son, F. **LANE**, Esq., Mr. Sampson **LANE**, in the 82d year of his age. Memphis Daily Appeal, 12/13/1852. Died, On Monday evening last, near Horn Lake, Mrs. Polly Lane, wife of the late Sampson Lane, and mother of Flecther and D. J. **LANE**. She was one of the old early mothers of Memphis, and was 84 years of age....Memphis Daily Appeal, Wed., 5/27/1857.

Died, At Hickorywithe, Tenn., September 23d, Mrs. Jane Lane, wife of J. M. **LANE**, Esq., aged 32 years. Memphis Appeal, 10/7/1851.

Taken up by Joseph B. **LANE**, living in the 10th district, one white horse........Weekly Appeal, 9/25/1846.

Married, On the 20th inst., by the Rev. Mr. McAleer, Michael **LANGAN**, Esq., to Mrs. Eliza **MILLAR**, both of this city. Weekly Appeal, 10/24/1845.

Married, On the evening of the 5th instant in Panola county, Miss., by Rev. James **BATES**, Mr. J. E. **LANGFORD** and Miss Harriet J., daughter of Mr. Pannel **TAYLOR**, all of Panola county. Columbus (Miss.) papers please copy. Memphis Daily Appeal, 2/11/1857.

Married, On the 10th inst. by Dr. Goodlet, Mr. D. P. **LANIER** to Miss Nancy R. **FRAZIER**, both of Davidson county, Tenn. Memphis Eagle & Enquirer, 3/17/1853.

Married, In this city on the 15th inst., by the Rev. W. H. **HYER**, Mr. John C. **LANIER** to Miss Mary Louise, daughter of Dr. Nat. **HOWCOTT**. Memphis Daily Appeal, 12/17/1852. The friends and acquaintances of John C. and Mary L. Lanier are invited to attend the funeral of their child, Robert Eldridge, from Calvary Church, at 9 o'clock this (Wednesday) morning, 18th inst. Services by the Rev. D. C. **PAGE**. Died, On the 17th instant, Robert Eldridge, son of John C. and Mary L. Lanier, aged nineteen months and eleven days. Memphis Daily Appeal, 7/18/1855.

Married, On Tuesday evening, 15th inst., by Rev. J. H. **GRAY**, Mr. J. S. **LANPHIER**, Merchant of this city, to Miss Virginia, daughter of Mr. E. **WOODARD**, of this county. American Eagle, 7/18/1845. Died, In this city, early on the morning of the 26th inst., in the 23d year of her age, Virginia, wife of J. S. Lanphier, and daughter of Elbert **WOODARD**. Memphis Daily Appeal, 5/28/1848.

Died, at the house of William **MONTGOMERY**, Esq., Norment Mills, near Bolivar, Tenn., on the 3d of May, 1856, John **LAPINE**, only son of John and Elizabeth **LAPINE**, in the 21st year of his age. The deceased was a stranger in a strange place, far from the land of his birth and intimate acquaintants, yet in his last trials he found himself surrounded by a doting mother, an affectionate father, and trusty friends....Memphis Daily Appeal, 5/14/1856.

We learn from Mr. Booker, clerk of the steamer Return, that a young man named John **LARKIN**, of this city, a cook on the steamer Return, fell overboard on Monday last, a short distance above Des Arc, and was drowned. The deceased had relatives in this city. The body was not recovered. Memphis Daily Avalanche, Sat., 3/19/1859.

Married, At the residence of the bride's father in this city on the 26th instant, Mr. Edward **LASSEMAN**, of Yallobusha county, Miss., to Miss Lydia A. **McILVAIN**. Also, at the same place, Mr. Geo. P. **LOWE**, of Miss., to Mrs. Phoebe **DAVIS**, all of this city. Memphis Daily Appeal, 8/28/1858.

Married—At Covington, on Tuesday evening the 14th ult. Mr. Francis S. **LATHAM**, editor of this paper, to Miss Jane Catharine, daughter of James N. **SMITH**, Esq. of the above place. Memphis Enquirer, 12/2/1837. House and Lot for Sale—I offer a bargain in the House and Lots where I now reside. They were purchased cheap and will be sold at cost, on six, twelve and eighteen months credit. There are five rooms in the house, a good garden and outhouses, situated in the most pleasant and desirable part of Memphis, and is one of the most convenient and handsome places in the town. F. S. Latham, Nov. 8, 1839. Memphis Enquirer. The undersigned, having entered upon his duties as Post-Master of Memphis, withdraws all editorial connection with this paper. Its editorial department will be conducted by Mr. Edward J. **CARRELL**...F. S. Latham. Memphis Eagle, 5/24/1849. Died, at 2 o'clock this morning Sept. 5th, Harriet, infant daughter of F. S. and Jane C. Latham. The friends of the family are invited to attend the funeral this evening at 4 o'clock, at their residence on Main corner of Beal street. Memphis Daily Eagle, 9/5/1850. The friends and acquaintances of F. S. and Jane C. Latham are respectfully invited to attend the funeral of their infant son, Robert....this morning....Memphis Daily Appeal, 6/30/1859.

Married, On the 19th instant by Rev. W. Carey **CRANE**, Mr. Henry J. **LATHAM** and Miss Mary E. **JONES**, all of Hernando, Miss. Memphis Daily Appeal, 2/20/1856.

Married. On the 8th instant, by S. W. **LEDBETTER**, Esq., John M. **LATTA** to Miss Margaret M. **COCHRAN**, all of this county. Daily Eagle, 2/22/1848.

The friends and acquaintances of John **LAUDERDALE** are requested to attend his funeral this (Friday) Morning at 9 o'clock, at the residence of his father, Vance Street, South Memphis. The Volunteers are requested to meet at 8 o'clock this morning at Dr. Curtis' office….for the purpose of attending the funeral of John Lauderdale, their brother in arms in Mexico. Daily Enquirer, 8/20/1847.

Married, On Wednesday, January 19th, by J. **WALDRAN**, Esq., Jerome **LAUDOLPHOS** to Ellen **CARNES**; all of this city. Memphis Daily Appeal, 1/21/1853.

Married, At the Episcopal Church in this city, on the evening of Tuesday last, by the Rev. Dr. Page, Mr. Albert T. **LAVALLETTE**, to Miss Louisa Jane **McMANUS**, both of this city. Nashville papers will please copy. Memphis Appeal, Friday, 1/3/1851. Married, On Tuesday evening, October 9th, at the residence of J. H. **DAY**, Esq., by Rev. Dr. Harrison, Mr. Albert T. Lavallette, of Memphis, to Miss Sallie C. Day, of Jackson, Tenn. Memphis Daily Appeal, 10/13/1855.

Married, On the 22d instant, at the residence of the bride's parents, in Arkansas county, Ark., by Rev. H. C. **HORTON**, Mr. W. D. **LAVENDER**, of New York, formerly of Nashville, Tenn., and Miss Nannie W. **ROSS**. Nashville papers and New York Herald please copy. Memphis Daily Appeal, 4/28/1857.

A young man, Mr. Henry **LAW**, connected with the house of Messrs. A. T. **WELLS** & Bro., died last evening of typhoid fever. Mr. Law was a native of New York, and was much esteemed by his circle of friends and acquaintances. His funeral will be attended from the First Presbyterian Church this evening. Memphis Daily Appeal, 1/22/1856.

Mrs. Margaret **LAW** accidentally fell into Wolf river near the saw mills last Sunday and was rescued from a watery grave by a young German by the name of Andrew **ADAMS**, who came very near being drowned himself by the frightened and drowning lady. Memphis Daily Appeal, 7/4/1855.

A young lady by the name of Alice **LAWLESS**, living with her sister on Court street, east of Second, died suddenly yesterday morning from the effects of an over-dose of laudanum taken Wednesday night. Medical service was procured, but too late to do good. Coroner Waldran held an inquest and a verdict returned in accordance with the above facts. Memphis Daily Appeal, 9/5/1856.

A man named Pat **LAWLESS**, who was confined in the city prison for a misdemeanor, died very suddenly yesterday morning under such circumstances as to warrant an inquiry into the case by the coroner. After investigation the jury returned a verdict of death from disease. Memphis Daily Appeal, 12/21/1859. The report that the late John **LAWLESS**, who died suddenly Tuesday, had died in jail, was erroneous. He breathed his last in his room, at the Merchant's Hotel….Memphis Daily Appeal, 12/22/1859.

We learn that Thomas **LAWLESS**, a blacksmith by trade, and at the time employed by Mr. Danbury, of this city, was drowned day before yesterday in the Wolf river. Memphis Daily Appeal, 6/24/1856.

Died: On the 12th inst., after a brief attack of cholera, whilst upon the Mississippi river, Capt. B. L. **LAWRENCE**, of this city. His funeral will take place at 9 o'clock this morning from the residence of Mrs. James **LAWRENCE** on 3d street. Weekly Memphis Eagle, 7/19/1849. [From the Memphis Appeal.] It is with feelings of the most painful regret that we are called upon to announce the death of Capt. B. L. Lawrence, who departed this life on the evening of Thursday last, between 2 and 3 o'clock, in the 43d year of his age. He died on board the steamboat Pitser Miller, of which boat he was acting at the time, as pilot, on her return from Cincinnati and just as she reached this city. He had been afflicted with diarrhea for several days previously, which he had temporarily checked until the morning of the day of his decease, when he was seized with cholera, and was in a few hours a corpse. It may be said that he literally died at the wheel, and in the discharge of duty of which no one had a higher appreciation. He was the last of five worthy brothers, all of whom have died in our midst, and who were among the earlier citizens of Memphis.—His remains were consigned to the tomb by the Masonic fraternity, of which he was a most worthy member, after a beautiful and eloquent eulogium pronounced by Maj. Jas. **PENN**…. Memphis Enquirer, Sun., 7/15/1849.

Died—At his residence in this place, on the morning of Saturday last, the 13th inst., of pulmonary disease, James H. **LAWRENCE**, in the 44th year of his age...Tribute of Respect – The following resolutions were adopted by the Board of Mayor and Alderman of the City of Memphis, upon learning the decease of James H. Lawrence, late city Collector ...Weekly Appeal, 12/26/1845. During the period of nearly 25 years in which Mr. L. was a citizen of this place, few men have sustained a like character with him, as a man of integrity and uprightness.....The deceased was a consistent member of and a ruling elder in the 1st Presbyterian church of this city.....Although he left behind him an interesting and afflicted family, he confidently committed them into the hands of a covenant-keeping God.....American Eagle Weekly, 12/19/1845.

Died, on the 1st inst. Wm. Lawrence, infant son of Mr. John B. **LAWRENCE** of this town. Memphis Advocate, 3/8/1828. Died, in this city on the 5th inst., Mr. John B. Lawrence, in the 49th year of his age. American Eagle, 7/14/1843. Died—On the 5th inst., at his residence in this city, Mr. John Lawrence; one of the earliest citizens of the place. The Appeal, 7/7/1843.

Married, On the 17th ultimo at the residence of D. S. **WRIGHT**, Esq., by Rev. J. W. **KNOTT**, Mr. R.(?) L. **LAWRENCE** to Miss Liddia A. **STAILEY**, all of this city. Memphis Daily Appeal, 4/1/1859.

Robt. **LAWRENCE**, (Late of Memphis, Tenn.,) Has settled in New Orleans, and tenders his services as a General Agent, and Commission. Memphis Enquirer, 9/16/1837.

Married, on Thursday evening last, 4th inst., by Rev. George W. **COONS**, Mr. William **LAWRENCE**, of this city, to Miss Frances C. Armour, daughter of David **ARMOUR**, Esq., of Shelby county. Daily Enquirer, 11/6/1847.

Married. On the 8th of April by Rev. W. S. **BURNEY**, Maj. W. H. **LAWSHE** to Miss M. C. **MARKETT**, all of Lafayette county, Miss. Memphis Appeal, 4/24/1855. At a regular Communication of Water Valley Lodge, No. 132, the following preamble and resolutions were unanimously adopted: Whereas, Our beloved Brother, W. H. Lawshe, has been suddenly called from this Lodge below, to the Celestial Lodge above....Resolved, That we sincerely and deeply sympathize with the bereaved widow, father, brothers and family of our deceased brother.... Water Valley, Miss., Sept. 9, 1859. Memphis Daily Appeal, 9/20/1859.

Married, On the evening of the 16th inst., by Rev. B. **MILLER**, Wm. A. **LEA**, Esq., to Miss Martha E., daughter of Dr. R. A. **BROWN**, all of Macon, Tenn. Memphis Eagle & Enquirer, 6/22/1852.

H. L. **LEAF**, Dealer in Western Produce. Corner of Centre Landing and Water street. Daily Enquirer, 2/26/1847.

Died of Typhoid Pneumonia, near Brownsville, Tenn., on Monday, the 6th day of December, 1852, Dr. E. H. **LEAKE**, aged 24 years, 7 months and 8 days. The deceased was born April 28th, 1828, in the county of Goochland, Va. A few years since he emigrated to the city of Memphis, became a student of the Botanico Medical College, and in the usual course of time, graduated at that Institution. For a little more than one year preceding his death, he was associated with Dr. N. **HOWCOTT**, of this city, in the practice of Dental Surgery. A few weeks ago he left, apparently in good health, on a visit to one of his aunts and while gone, met with his death as above mentioned. Thus has the seemingly unkind hand of the great destroyer torn from the bosoms of loving brothers and sisters....Christian Advocate, other city papers and papers of Richmond, Va., please copy. Memphis Eagle & Enquirer, 1/4/1853.

Married, On the 26th ult., by the Rev. Mr. Alston, Dr. E. M. **LEAKE**, of this county, to Miss Catherine T. Watkins, daughter of Col. Joseph **WATKINS**, of Fayette county, Tenn. The Appeal, 4/5/1844. Died—Friday, the 13th inst., at the residence of Col. T. **LEAKE**, after a lingering illness, Benjamin Scott Leake, youngest son of Dr. E. M. and C. T. Leake, of Camden, Ark.—aged eight months. Daily Enquirer, 8/19/1847.

161

Married, At the residence of T. C. **CRENSHAW**, on Tuesday evening last, by the Rev. Geo. W. **COONS**, Dr. Virginius **LEAKE**, to Miss Martha A. **FIELD**; all of Shelby county. Memphis Eagle, Thurs., 10/11/1849.

Married. On Thursday evening, 4th instant, by the Rev. Mr. Ware, Mr. R. W. **LEAKS** to Miss Lucy Ann, daughter of M. J. **ANDERSON**, Esq., of Haywood county. Memphis Daily Appeal, 1/10/1855.

Died: At his residence in the vicinity of Memphis, on the 23d of August, Charles A. **LEATH**, in the 29th year of his age. The disease which terminated his life was scrofula, with which he had been afflicted for several years.....And what was harder still to part with was his kind and faithful mother, and his fondly attached brother and sister and their family....Weekly Memphis Eagle, 8/30/1849.

Married. On the 13th inst. at the Methodist Church in this city, by Rev. J. W. **KNOTT**, Mr. P. M. **LEATH** and Miss Vallie M. **LEATH**, of this city. Memphis Whig, 7/14/1855.

Married, At Pulaski, on the 10th inst., D. M. **LEATHERMAN**, Esq., of Memphis, to Miss Eliza Jane, daughter of Hon. L. M. **BRAMLETT**, of Pulaski. American Eagle Weekly, 7/18/1845. D. M. Leatherman, Esq., of this city, was elected by the Legislature on Saturday last, Prosecuting Attorney for the 11th Judicial Circuit, for 6 years from the expiration of the term of the present incumbent. Daily Enquirer, 10/30/1847. Died, On Wednesday last, 26th inst., in the 30th year of her age, at the residence of her husband, D. M. Leatherman, Esq., Eliza Jane, second daughter of Judge Bramlett of Pulaski, Tenn. The funeral obsequies were performed on yesterday by Rev. G. W. **COONS**, in whose congregation the deceased was a communicant, and the remains deposited in Winchester Cemetery...Mrs. Leatherman died of a disease of the lungs...Memphis Eagle & Enquirer, 5/28/1852.

Joseph S. **LEAVETT** Is now opening another lot of those prime long leg calf Boots...Daily Enquirer, 3/4/1847.

Married, On the 15th inst., in the vicinity of Memphis by the Rev. Jno. H. **GRAY**, Mr. C. A. **LeCOQ** to Miss Susan A. **RUDISILL**, all of this city. Memphis Daily Appeal, 9/20/1852.

Francis H. **LE COQ**, Painter, Has removed his shop to Shelby Street, near the Gayoso and would respectfully inform the public, that he is ready, at all times, to execute all sorts of work in Painting and Glazing. Daily Enquirer, 1/25/1847.

Died, In this village on Monday, February 7th, B. H. **LEDBETTER**....*Panola* (Miss.) *Picayune*. Memphis Eagle & Enquirer, 2/23/1853.

John W. **LEDBETTER** & Co. Cotton Factors and Commission Merchants, No. 4 Front Row, Memphis, Tenn....Memphis Daily Appeal, 10/27/1858.

Married. Near Germantown, on the 12th inst., by A. L. **YANCEY** Esq. S. W. **LEDBETTER** Esq., to Mrs. S. H. **WESSON**. Memphis Eagle, 5/18/1848.

It was rumored in this city yesterday that Capt. James **LEE**, late of the *Kate Frisbee*, had died recently at the Hot Springs, in Arkansas. Capt. Lee has been at the Springs during the past month for the benefit of his health. He was one of the oldest and most popular steamboatmen on the western waters....Memphis Daily Appeal, 12/20/1859.

Died. At Durhamsville, in this State, on the 11th ultimo, after a painful and protracted illness, Mrs. Mary Lee, widow of the late Phillip **LEE**, Esq., of Westmoreland county, Va., in the 86th year of her age....She was the daughter of the Rev. Thomas **SMITH**, born during the period of the Colonial dissentions with the mother country....Memphis Daily Appeal, 1/2/1855.

Paris House Confectionary. V. **LEFORT**, Respectfully informs the citizens of Memphis, that he has opened his establishment in Andrews' new Buildings...Daily Enquirer, 1/19/1847.

Married: By the Rev. J. H. **GRAY**, on the 26th June, Dr. N. E. **LEGGET**, of Hudsonville, to Mrs. E. P. **COWAN**, of Marshall co., Miss. Memphis Daily Eagle, 7/4/1848.

Married, On the 18th inst., at the residence of the bride's father, by the Rev. Mr. Sternheim, Mr. J. H. **LEHMAN** and Miss Caroline **STRAUSS**. Memphis Daily Appeal, 9/19/1856.

Junius E. **LEIGH**, Attorney at Law, Memphis, Tenn…Office on Main street, East side, between Court Square and Madison streets. Memphis Daily Eagle, 6/13/1848.

Married, On the 21st inst., at the residence of the bride's father, J. J. **RAWLINGS**, Esq., by Rev. A. M. **BRYAN**, Mr. N. F. **LeMASTER** and Miss Olivia A. Rawlings, all of Shelby county. Memphis Daily Appeal, 10/24/1857.

Brother Charles P. **LEMONS** was born September the 18th, 1806, in Rockingham county, North Carolina, and removed with his neighbors to Williamson county, Tenn., in 1811; from thence to Fayette county about the year 1830. He professed religion at Wesley camp ground and joined the Methodist E. Church at the same meeting, and was for many years a steward in said church. He married Susan **BUFORD**, in 1840, who died in the fall of 1842. Brother Lemons died in the 42d year of his age, after an illness of 24 days, October 15th, 1847…Memphis Appeal, 11/20/1847.

Married. In Fisherville, Tenn., on the 21st day of February, 1855, by Dr. W. G. **LANCASTER**, Mr. Thomas **LEMY** to Mrs. Martha F. **LITTLE**, daughter of Wm. **HAMRIED**, Esq. Memphis Daily Appeal, 2/28/1855.

Died, on Monday morning, Mr. Thomas F. **LENNOX**, co-proprietor of the Memphis Theatre. Memphis Eagle, Thurs., 10/18/1849.

Departed this life at the residence of her son-in-law, Col. Charles **POLK**, Mrs. Lucy B. **LENOIR**. Mrs. Lenoir was born in Charlotte City, Va., June 1, 1780(?). Died in Jackson Parish, La., September 1, 1858….For fourteen years she was a consistent and pious member of the Protestant Episcopal Church….Memphis Daily Appeal, 9/16/1858.

Died on the 4th inst. at Hickory Wythe, Fayette Co., Tenn., after a short and painful illness of 36 hours, Mrs. Elizabeth Lenow, aged 29 years, wife of James **LENOW**, of the firm of J. & J. Lenow. Mrs. L. was born in Isle of Wight co., Va., and emigrated from Southampton with her husband in the spring of '39. She has left a bereaved husband and three infant children to lament their irreparable loss. Memphis Enquirer, 3/13/1840.

Died—On the 28th inst., at Richard **LEAKE's** Esq., Mary Sophia, aged one year and eight months, daughter of James and Indiana H. **LENOW** of this city. Memphis Daily Appeal, 7/31/1847.

Married, On Thursday the 9th inst., by the Rev. B. **ASKEW**, Capt. Joseph **LENOW**, merchant of the firm of J. & J. Lenow, of Hickory Wythe, Tenn., to Miss Frances Catherine, daughter of the late Francis E. **BROWN**, dec'd., all of Fayette county, Tenn. The Appeal, 1/10/1845. Died on the 4th inst., Joseph Francis, son of Joseph and Frances Lenow, at the tender age of 2 years, 3 months and 19 days. He was the only son of his affectionate parents…. Memphis Daily Appeal, 8/16/1848.

Died—In this place on the 18th inst. Benjamin **LEONARD**, formerly of Pittsburg, Pa., but more recently of Marietta, Ohio, in the 50th year of his age. Memphis Enquirer, 1/25/1839.

Married, On Saturday, 11th inst., by Rev. Dr. Finley, Mr. Charles E. **LEONARD**, to Miss Mary J. **LEWIS**, all of this city. Memphis Daily Appeal, 1/13/1851.

The friends and acquaintances of Peter **LEONARD**, of Crittenden county, Arkansas, are invited to attend the funeral of his son, Michael, This (Sunday) Morning at half-past 11 o'clock, at the Mound City Ferry Landing, in Memphis. Memphis Daily Appeal, 6/14/1857.

Married. On Thursday evening, 13th inst., in South Memphis, Mr. T. **LEONARD**, to Miss Martha A. Brown, daughter of Mr. John **BROWN**, all of this city. Memphis Eagle, 4/17/1848. Died, In this city, on Monday evening, the 28th inst., William Carroll Leonard, infant son of Thomas and Martha Ann Leonard, aged 1 year, 8 months and 26 days. Memphis Daily Eagle, 10/30/1850.

The subscriber having determined to engage in the Mercantile Business, would sell at a fair price, the following property, to wit: A small Farm, 8 acres...with good frame houses...about one mile south of South Memphis...Hernando road. Also, a Farm in Crittenden county, Arkansas, opposite Memphis, with houses and a fine orchard on the premises. Also, a House and Lot on Beal street, South Memphis—house suitable for a small store..Thomas **LEONARD**. Memphis Daily Eagle, 7/20/1848.

Married—On Wednesday, the 18th inst. at the residence of Maj. John H. **BILLS**, in Bolivar, by Rev. Wiley B. **PECK**, Mr. William W. **LEONARD**, to Miss Lucy N. Polk, daughter of the late John **POLK**, deceased. Memphis Advocate, 4/28/1827.

Died, twelve miles Southeast of Oxford, on the 8th ultimo, Mrs. Lizzie Lester, daughter of William **COOKE**. She was born in Philadelphia, Penn., November 29th, 1829, and lived in the city of her birth until January 11th, 1853, when she married Dr. J. D. **LESTER**, and moved with him to Mississippi, where she became the mother of two children, the death of one being prior to her own—the other is still living....Memphis Daily Appeal, 3/26/1856.

Married. On Wednesday evening the 7th inst. by J. M. **KIRK**, Esq., Mr. Jas. R. **LESTER** to Miss Lucy A. **SHELTON**, all of the vicinity of Bone Yard, Tishomingo county, Miss. Memphis Daily Appeal, 3/13/1855.

Departed this life on Saturday, the 22d inst., Wm. H. **LESTER**. His remains will be taken from the Carolina House, Shelby street, at 4 o'clock, P.M.....Daily Memphis Enquirer, 9/23/1849.

Hall of Morning Sun Lodge, May 14, A.D., 1859. Whereas, The Supreme Architect of the Universe has removed from time to eternity our brother, W. W. **LETTLE**, who has long been a worthy member of our order....Memphis Daily Appeal, 5/29/1859.

Married, In this city on the evening of the 12th inst., by Rev. Mr. Garrett, Mr. Wm. **LEVERETT**, to Mrs. Mary A. **LITTLEFIELD**. Memphis Daily Appeal, 6/16/1851.

Married, On Saturday evening, 3d inst., by the Rev. Mr. Alemany, Mr. Cajetan **LEVESQUE**, to Miss Ann **TOOKE**, all of Memphis, Tenn. Quebec and Montreal papers copy. Daily Enquirer, 7/7/1847. Died, On Friday evening last, the 18th inst., Mr. Cajeton Levesque. Mr. L. was a native of Canada and was born in the year 1809. For the last nine years he has been a resident of this city. He leaves a wife and two children to bemoan his loss. Memphis Eagle & Enquirer, 6/20/1852.

Died—In this city on Sunday the 28th inst., Hellen P., youngest child of Joseph S. and Eliza L. **LEVETT**, aged 17 months and 5 days. Daily Enquirer, 3/31/1847. Died, on Friday noon, March 2d, Byrd Powell, infant son of Jos. S. and E. L. Levett, aged seventeen months and seven days......Daily Memphis Enquirer, 3/6/1849.

Married, In New York, on Wednesday, August 19th, by Rev. Mr. Isaacs, of Wooster Street Synagogue, J. **LEVEY**, Esq., of New Brunswick, N.J., to Miss Sarah R.(?) **BARNETT**, of Memphis. Memphis Daily Appeal, 8/28/1857.

Married, On the 18th instant at the residence of the bride's mother, at Trenton, Tenn., by Rev. Mr. Seay, R. A. **LEVY**, of the steamer Daniel Boone, to Miss C. S. **CRAWFORD**, of the former place. Memphis Daily Appeal, 7/28/1858.

Died, At Germantown, on the morning of the 25th inst., Mrs. Elizabeth Lewellen, consort of Peter A. **LEWELLEN**, in the 34th year of her age. Memphis Daily Appeal, 11/29/1852.

Died, In this city, on the 20th inst., Mrs. Nancy **LEWELLING**, aged 60 years, a native of Virginia, but for many years a resident of Mississippi...Memphis Eagle, 1/25/1849. The friends of J. W. **LEWELLING** are respectfully invited to attend the funeral of his Mother, Mrs. Nancy Lewelling, this evening at 3 o'clock, from his residence adjoining the Episcopal Church. Memphis Eagle, 1/22/1849.

The friends of the late S. W. **LEWELLING**, are invited to attend his funeral from the South Memphis Methodist Church, at 4 o'clock, this afternoon. Memphis Appeal, 2/13/1851. Died, in this city, on the 12th inst., of Pneumonia, Stephen W. Lewelling, formerly of North Carolina, and for the last three years a resident of this city...Memphis Appeal, 2/14/1851.

Married, By Rev. B. **MEDLIN**, February 2, 1858, Mr. Benjamin T. **LEWIS** to Miss Sarah C. **RICHARDSON**, at her grand-father's, Daniel **GOBER**, all of Fayette county, Tenn. Memphis Daily Appeal, 2/12/1858.

Married, On the 3d inst., by Rev. E. E. **PORTER**, Mr. David **LEWIS** to Miss Isabella **WALKER**. Memphis Daily Appeal, 12/21/1859.

Died, On Saturday the 10th inst., of pneumonia, in this county, Mrs. Mary Lewis, consort of E. B. **LEWIS**, aged 38 years. Memphis Daily Appeal, 9/13/1859.

Granville **LEWIS**, Attorney at Law. The Appeal, 10/4/1844.

Died—At the Redford House on Wednesday, May 4th, of chronic Diarrhea, Major Henry **LEWIS**, a citizen of Madisonville, St. Francis county, Ark., in the 49th year of his age. Memphis Daily Avalanche, 5/6/1859.

To Nancy **LEWIS**, James **LEWIS**, Elizabeth **LEWIS**, Mary **LEWIS**, Sarah **LEWIS**, William **LEWIS**, & Crawford **LEWIS**, minor children of Crowell **LEWIS**, deceased, & heirs at law of William **LEWIS**, deceased. Take Notice. That we shall petition the county court of Shelby county, at their April Sessions, 1827, for commissioners to be appointed to divide between us, the children of Henry **LEWIS**, deceased, & the children of Crowell Lewis, deceased, all legal heirs of the said William Lewis, deceased, 573 acres of land, lying in said county of Shelby...being part of an 823 acre tract granted by the state of Tenn. to the heirs of the said William Lewis, deceased...Reding **LEWIS** & son & heir of the said William Lewis. Jackson Gazette, 10/7/1826

Died, at the residence of his brother, Patrick F. **LEWIS**, Clinton, Miss., on the 30th September, Chas. W. **LEWIS**, formerly of this city. Memphis Enquirer, 10/8/1846.

Robert W. **LEWIS**, Hardin **LEWIS**, and Benj. **WILSON**, having entered into co-partnership and established a Brick Yard on the Pigeon Roost road at the Bayou, and immediately upon the bounds of the Corporation of Memphis.....Robt. W. Lewis & Co. Memphis Enquirer, 9/2/1837.

Married, On Tuesday evening the 5th inst. by Rev. J. H. **GRAY**, Mr. S. S. **LEWIS** to Miss Laura Amaryllis, daughter of Jno. **HOUSTON**, Esq. Weekly Appeal, 5/15/1846.

Died, Last night, Victor, aged 18 months, son of O. H. and L. O. **LIDE**. The friends and acquaintances of the family are invited to attend the funeral from their residence on Second street, between Washington and Poplar streets, this morning at 11 o'clock. Services by Rev. Mr. Drane. Memphis Daily Appeal, 6/5/1858.

Report of the Board of Health, For the last 48 hours to 12 o'clock, M., July 16th.....Michael **LIDEN** (Irishman) 25 y'rs. Reported Cholera.....Daily Memphis Enquirer, 7/17/1849.

Two weeks since, the consort of Mr. Jas. **LIGON**, a young man living on Big Creek, in this county, presented him with two boys and a girl, at one birth! The two parents, together, we understand, weigh 200 pounds. Is there any county, or any couple of the same size, in the Union, that can 'hold a priming' to this? Memphis Eagle & Enquirer, 5/14/1853.

Died—In this city on Tuesday, the 28th instant, William **LIGHTON**, about 60 years of age. The deceased was born at Raspberry Hill, county Derry, Ireland. He resided in Kentucky for some years previous to his death, where he joined the volunteers in the present was with Mexico; came with them as far as this place, where he was taken sick. He was an honest man, and a true and genuine patriot to his adopted country. Louisville papers please copy. Weekly Appeal, 7/31/1846.

The friends of Owen **LILLY** and family are respectfully invited to attend the funeral of his son Denis, from their residence on Main street, South Memphis, this morning at 9 o"lock. Memphis Daily Appeal, 10/23/1857. Died, In this city on Friday evening, of typhoid fever, Philip, son of Owen and Catherine Lilly, aged 23 years. The friends of deceased are invited to attend his funeral from his late residence on Main street....Memphis Daily Appeal, Sun., 11/8/1857.

All persons indebted to the estate of the late Mrs. Mary **LINCH**, deceased, are requested to come forward....Thomas **BURK**, Administrator. Memphis Daily Appeal, 9/10/1853.

Died—On the 24th December, John C. **LINCOLN**, formerly of Sparta, Tenn., but for the last three years a resident of this city. Daily Enquirer, 1/4/1847.

Died, In this city on the 2d inst., at the residence of her brothers, William and David C. **WILLIAMS**, Mrs. Lucy **LINDOWER**, aged twenty-one years. Memphis Daily Appeal, 11/4/1858.

We have announced heretofore that Mr. E. A. **LINDSEY**, late of Mount Sterling, Ky., had become a permanent citizen of Memphis. It now gives us pleasure to qualify that announcement with the assurance that he has become associated in business with Mr. C. S. **FICKLEN**, late of Maysville, Ky....Messrs. L. and F. deal largely in the most desirable description of western produce....Memphis Daily Avalanche, 3/31/1859.

On Sunday night last at half past twelve o'clock the steamer Grey Eagle, one of our Cincinnati packets, descending met the Sultana ascending in shute 35, thirty-five miles above Memphis. As the boats approached each other the Grey Eagle attempted to pass the Sultana on the Island side, thus giving the Sultana the Tennessee side to pass up. It appears that the Sultana also wished to pass on the Island side. A collision became imminent. The Grey Eagle immediately began backing water, rung her bell, hailed the Sultana, and told her to back water also. The Sultana, however, did not back, and struck, with her bow, the Grey Eagle just aft the boilers on the larboard side...the water and steam rushed out, scalding very badly six persons, whose lives are despaired of. One of the engineers, James **LINDSEY**, is lost, supposed to have been scalded and that he jumped overboard, as he remained at his post. One fireman, name not known, is supposed to have been lost in the same way.....Memphis Enquirer, Tues., 6/13/1848.

We were pained yesterday morning to hear of the sudden death of Col. M. W. **LINDSEY**, who died of Cholera the day previous at his residence on the rail road, near Colliersville.—Col. Lindsey had just returned from New York, and as we learn, contracted the disease on the river. He had for some years been a citizen of Memphis....He had practiced his profession here with great success, and was justly regarded as one of the ornaments of the bar....Memphis Appeal, 9/14/1854. At a meeting of the members of the Memphis Bar, convened at the office of the Clerk and Master of the Chancery Court, in the City of Memphis, on Saturday morning the 16th inst., to discharge the melancholy duty of paying the last tribute of respect to the memory of their deceased brother, Mathew W. Lindsey....Memphis Daily Appeal, 9/17/1854.

Married. At Holly Springs, Miss. on the 21st inst. by Rev. G. W. **SILL**, Dr. J. D. M. **LITCHFIED** and Miss Brooks Lucas, daughter of Col. P. W. **LUCAS**, all of that place. Memphis Whig, 6/25/1855.

The friends and acquaintances of Mr. C. A. **LITTLEFIELD**, are invited to attend the Funeral of his late wife, Mrs. Elizabeth Littlefield, at 3 o'clock this (Monday) evening, from the residence of Mr. Jas. **JUNKINS**, Union street. Divine service by Dr. Hall. Memphis Daily Appeal, Mon., 5/12/1851.

Died, In Gonzales county, Texas, on the 8th January, Mr. Fleming **LITTLEFIELD**, after a long illness of some 28 days of Typhoid Fever. Mr. L. was a long resident of Panola county, Miss., and moved to this county some two years since. He left a wife and three children to mourn his loss; and since he has been here, he has won for himself many warm friends....Memphis Eagle & Enquirer, 2/2/1853.

Married, On Tuesday, 4th inst., by Rev. Sam'l **DENNIS**, Mr. J. A. **LITTLEFIELD**, of this city, to Miss M. A. **BAIRD**, of Shelby county. Weekly Appeal, 8/14/1846.

California Emigrants. The list of names is not complete as a full report of the various companies has not been presented; and several of the names on the list of the company have determined to go on another boat...Memphis Mess. Thos. **MORAN**, J. D. S. **SULLIVAN**, John **McKEON**, M. **GAFFNEY**, C. **SLEEPER**, Henry **WILLIAMS**, Jos. **WHITE**, Perry **WHITE**, Dr. J. H. **HOLMES**, M. **RUDULPH**, Jas. H. **ANTHONY**, E. **HOUSTON**, Jas. **LITTLEFIELD**. Memphis Daily Eagle, 3/21/1849.

Tribute of Respect. Hall of Gravel Hill Lodge No. 232, May 2d, 1856.} Resolved, That we deeply lament the loss of our beloved brother, C. S. **LITTLEJOHN**, who departed this life on the 26th of April, 1856....Memphis Daily Appeal, 5/14/1856.

For Sale. An Unsurpassed Plantation on the Mississippi River. The subscriber, intending to remove his negroes further south for the purpose of engaging in the cultivation of sugar, offers for sale his highly improved plantation, lying at the foot of the 2d Chickasaw Bluffs, five miles below Randolph. The tract contains 1100 or 1200 acres....The improvements consist of an excellent frame dwelling house, four large new cribs, nineteen new cabins....J. B. **LITTLEJOHN**. Memphis Eagle & Enquirer, 1/1/1853.

Married, In Louisville, Ky., on the 1st inst., by Rev. J. H. **LINN**, Mr. Steven W. **LLEWELLYN**, of Memphis, Tenn., to Mrs. R. Ann **POWELL** of Louisville. Memphis Eagle, 5/10/1850.

Married—On yesterday, Col. Gardner B. **LOCKE** of this place, to Miss Mary Jane, only daughter of Dr. J. B. **PRESCOTT**, of this place, and late of Louisiana.... Memphis Enquirer, 7/20/1836. Died, On Saturday evening, 30th ult., Louisa Beckford, daughter of Gardner B. and Mary Jane Locke, aged 1 year, 8 months and 8 days. American Eagle, 10/13/1843. Died, On Wednesday morning, April 22d, Ella, infant daughter of G. B. and M. J. Locke. Memphis Daily Appeal, 4/23/1857. Our whole community have been pained to learn that Col. G. B. Locke died at his residence in this city, of pulmonary consumption, on Wednesday night, 28th inst. Col. Locke is one of our oldest citizens and business men....We extract the following biographical sketch of him from the Memphis City Directory for 1856-7: "The subject of this brief notice....was born in Rutherford county, Tenn., on the 27th day of August, 1810. In the spring of 1827 he settled in Raleigh, the county seat of Shelby county, and taught school for six months ....In the fall of the same year he entered the store of Bayles & Davis, as a clerk, and has resided in Memphis ever since....In the prosecution of his business as an auctioneer and real estate broker, in which he is virtually the pioneer....Before he attained his majority he was elected colonel-commandant of the militia of Shelby county....In 1836, when the call was made upon Tennessee for volunteers....he raised a company for service in Florida....The remoteness of Memphis....and the large numbers....which flocked to the standard....prevented the company being received. He has filled the offices of recorder, tax collector, marshal, alderman and mayor of the city...." Memphis Daily Appeal, 12/30/1859.

Married, On the 27th of August, 1856, by Rev. P. J. **ECKLES**, Mr. J. **LOCKHART**, of LaGrange, Tenn., and Miss Virginia **THOMPSON**, of Byhalia, Marshall county, Miss. Memphis Daily Appeal, 9/17/1856.

Died, At LaGrange, Tenn., on the 23d inst., of inflammation of the brain, Robert Chambers Lockhart, of Coahoma county, Miss., son of Octavia F. and the late John J. **LOCKHART**, aged fourteen years nine months and fourteen days....Memphis Daily Appeal, 4/28/1859.

Married. On the 19th inst., by the Rev. Mr. ALSTON, Eggleston LODWICK, Esq., of Portsmouth, Ohio, to Miss Rhoda GATES, of this City. Weekly Appeal, 1/22/1847.

Died, In this city at 5 o'clock on yesterday, Mr. Charles LOFLAND, one of our oldest and most respected citizens. Memphis Appeal, 1/4/1851. Masonic Funeral Notice. The members of "South Memphis Lodge No. 118" and "Angerona Lodge, No. 168," will meet at their respective Lodge Rooms, to-day (Saturday) at 10 o'clock, A.M., to attend the funeral of our late Brother, Charles Lofland, from the 2d Presbyterian Church...Memphis Appeal, 1/4/1851. Masonic.... Resolved, That our warmest sympathies and condolence, are hereby given to his children, who are deprived at so early an age of paternal affection ...Memphis Daily Appeal, 1/14/1851.

Married—On Thursday evening last, by Rev. Mr. Coons, in this city, Mr. William O. LOFLAND to Miss Emily J., daughter of William CLARK, formerly of East Tenn. Memphis Enquirer, Sat., 10/31/1846. Died, on yesterday, Clark, infant son of Wm. O. and Emily Lofland of this city, aged 7 months. Memphis Enquirer, 7/13/1848. The splendid flouring establishment of our enterprising fellow-citizen, Mr. Wm. O. Lofland, the erection of which we have heretofore noticed, is now in successful operation, and the Mill is now turning out a quality of flour unsurpassed by that of any establishment in the northwest...Memphis Appeal, 1/10/1851.

Died, On Thursday morning the 3d inst., at her residence, Island No. 40, a few miles above this city, Mrs. Catherine M. LOFTIN, formerly of Jackson, Tenn. Memphis Eagle & Enquirer, 6/5/1852.

Died, On the 31 day of July of consumption, in DeSoto county, Miss., Mr. J. S. LOGAN, of this city, aged 39 years. Memphis Daily Appeal, 8/28/1858.

Married: On the 1st inst. by Rev. J. H. GRAY, Mr. Thos. H. LOGWOOD, of Fayette county, to Miss Mary N. DRIVER, of this city. Memphis Whig, 11/3/1855. It will be seen by his card that our talented young friend, T. H. Logwood, Esq., late of Sommerville, has removed to this city and will hereafter prosecute his profession here. We doubt not that he will win his way to an eminent position at the Memphis bar. Memphis Daily Appeal, 1/16/1856. Died, On the 26th instant, of convulsions, Henry Driver, infant son of Gen. T. H. and Mary S. Logwood, aged two months. Memphis Daily Appeal, 7/28/1859. Died, On the 1st instant, of consumption, Mrs. Mary S., consort of Gen. T. H. Logwood, aged 23 years. The friends and acquaintances of the family are requested to attend her funeral from the family residence on corner of Beal and Lauderdale streets....Memphis Daily Appeal, 10/2/1859.

Died, In New Orleans on the 10th ult. of a pulmonary affection, from which he had been suffering a long time, Col. Gabriel W. LONG, formerly and for many years, a well known citizen of this county. Memphis Eagle & Enquirer, 3/2/1853.

Married, On the 22d instant at Oxford, Miss., by Rev. J. N. WADDEL, Mr. G. A. LONGSTREET to Miss Hattie W. WENDEL. Memphis Daily Appeal, 3/25/1859.

J. G. LONSDALE & Co., having sold out their stock of Groceries in this city, with the view of closing up their business, request all those who are in their debt...Memphis Eagle, 8/13/1847. The friends and acquaintances of J. G. & Eliza Ann Lonsdale are invited to attend the funeral of their infant daughter, Sophia Page, from their residence in South Memphis, this evening at 5 o'clock. Memphis Eagle & Enquirer, 5/27/1852. Departed this life on Wednesday, the 26th inst., Sophia Page Lonsdale, infant daughter of John G. and Eliza Ann Lonsdale, of this city...Memphis Eagle & Enquirer, 5/29/1852.

The Pillar, of Corinth, Miss., of October 31, says that Absolom LOONEY committed suicide about a mile from that place on Friday last, by cutting his throat with a razor. It is supposed that he was laboring under a aberration of mind, caused by pecuniary embarrassment. He was about fifty years of age. He leaves a wife and several children to mourn his loss. Memphis Daily Appeal, Tues., 11/3/1857.

Married, On Tuesday evening last, at Fort Pickering, Col. D. LOONEY, to Miss Mary, only daughter of Hugh ROLAND, Esq. Weekly Appeal, Friday, 7/4/1845. Died, In Columbia, Tenn., on the 21st inst.,

David Looney, son of Col. David and Mary Looney, of this city, aged 16 months. American Eagle, 9/2/1847.

We regret to chronicle the death of Jos. W. **LOONEY**, which took place at Manhatten, Clay county, Kansas, on the 21st ult. Mr. Looney, it will be remembered, left here about six weeks ago in company with others for Pike's Peak. At that time he was in the enjoyment of very good health, but the fatigue of traveling and camp life were too severe for his constitution, and he sunk under them. A wide circle of friends will mourn the loss of a good man and an estimable citizen—*Enquirer*. Mr. Looney was a brother of the Messrs. Looney of this place, and was at the time of his death about thirty-seven years of age....Memphis Daily Avalanche, 5/4/1859.

Married—In this county, on the 2d inst., by the Rev'd. P. P. **NEELY**, Mr. Robert F. **LOONEY**, of Memphis, to Miss Louisa M. **CROFFORD**, of this county.—Columbia Observer. Daily Enquirer, 11/16/1847.

Married, On the 12th of August, 1857, at the residence of _____ Lorance, by J. **WALDRAN**, Esq., Mr. Daniel __. **LORANCE** to Miss Virginia T. **RODGERS**, all of Shelby county. Memphis Daily Appeal, 8/14/1857.

Died, At the house of David **GILLELAND**, near Durhamville, Tenn., on the 27th March, 1853, Mrs. Mary E. Lott, consort of Cornelius **LOTT**. Memphis Eagle & Enquirer, 4/5/1853.

Mr. Henry E. **LOTT**, in a very graceful and well written salutatory, took charge of the City Column of the Eagle and Enquirer yesterday morning. Mr. L. is modest and unassuming.... Memphis Daily Appeal, 10/6/1852. Died, in this city on the 26th of June, Henry E. Lott, in the 28th year of his age. The deceased was born at Fairmont, in the State of Virginia, and resided there up to about ten years ago, when he came to this city and entered into business....Memphis Daily Appeal, 7/11/1855.

Died. On the 29th ult., at his Iron Works, in Perry County, Tenn., Col. C. I. **LOVE**, of Nashville. Memphis Enquirer, 8/19/1837.

Married, On the 21st inst., at the residence of J. L. **BEASLEY**, Esq., in this city, by Rev. C. C. **CONNER**, Mr. H. W. **LOVING** and Miss Sallie **BLOCK**, all of this city. Memphis Daily Appeal, 10/23/1857.

Died, At Holly Springs, Miss., on last Sunday, the 24th inst., Mr. Thomas N. **LOVING**, in the 76th year of his age. Nashville papers please copy. Memphis Daily Appeal, 10/30/1858.

James **LOW**, the subject of this memoir, was born on the 7th day of October, A.D. 179, and departed this life on the 29th day of December, A.D. 1854 at his residence in Marshall county, Mississippi, where he had resided ever since 1838(?)—the time he left South Alabama and became a citizen of this State. In 18__, when quite young he emigrated from Pendleton county, Georgia to South Alabama, where he married Jane **HUMEL**(?), the lady of his choice with whom he ever lived in the most fond regard up to the 2d of June, 1854, the time of her decease; a few months only before his departure to another and better world, leaving a large family of children, with many relatives and friends to mourn their loss....As a member of the Baptist Church....Memphis Appeal, 1/24/1855.

In the past week only 5 deaths have occurred, viz: Preston **LOW**, aged 23; Wm. **CRAWFORD**, pauper, aged 30; R. C. **SLAUGHTER**, aged 44; S. C. **DREDMAN**, aged 25(?); negro girl, aged 7—all of cholera. Daily Memphis Enquirer, 4/20/1849.

Married, On Tuesday the 25th instant, by the Rev. Samuel **GILLILAND**, Mr. Thos. B. **LOW** of Hardeman co., to Miss Viola L. **DELOACH**, of Shelby co., near Germantown. Memphis Appeal, 4/2/1848.

Died. On Thursday morning, 25th inst., Henry Flavio, son of J. Henry A. and Ida **LOWNES**, aged 3 years and 6 months. Weekly Memphis Eagle & Enquirer, 5/31/1854. Died, On Sunday morning, the 21st inst.,

Powhattan Lownes, infant son of J. H. and Ina **LOWNES**, aged 8 months and 22 days. Memphis Weekly Appeal, 5/26/1858.

Departed this life in Crittenden county, Ark., on the 15th of January, 1859, Mrs. Nancy Ann, consort of James **LOYD**, in the 25th year of her age....A few moments before she closed her eyes forever, she called her husband, mother and brother to her bedside....soon she would be with her babe and many relatives that had gone before her....Memphis Daily Appeal, 2/26/1859.

Oliver **LUCAS**, Esq., late of Louisville, Ky., and spoken of as a talented gentleman, has become associated in the editorial management of the "Avalanche." We extend to him a welcome to our city and hope that he may find it a pleasant home, socially and pecuniarily. Memphis Evening Ledger, 1/29/1858.

Married, On the evening of the 15th instant at Calvary church, by Rev. Dr. White, Mr. Walker R. **LUCAS** to Miss Mollie R. **THOMPSON**, all of this place. Memphis Daily Appeal, 12/17/1859.

Married, By J. **WALDRAN**, Esq., 15th inst., Mr. Anderson **LUMKINS**, to Mrs. Isabella **KENNEDY**, all of this county. Memphis Daily Eagle, 9/18/1850.

Died. At Seguin(?), Texas, on the 29th ult., Col. Jon_ W. **LUMPKIN**. Col. Lumpkin was a native of Georgia and removed to Panola county, Miss. about the year 1839, and represented that county in the Senatorial branch of the Legislature. From Mississippi he removed to Memphis and regarded this city as the place of his residence at the time of his death....Memphis Daily Appeal, 1/21/1855.

Died—At North Mount Pleasant, on the 30th March, 1842, Elijah **LUMSDEN**, aged 80 years. He was at the siege of Ninety-six, under General Green. American Eagle, 4/14/1842.

On Friday evening, Col. **LUNDY**, a well known citizen of this county, was stepping out of the door of his residence, situated four miles from Memphis, on Cane Creek, on the Hernando road, when a gun, which he held in his hand cocked, ready to shoot an ox, was accidently discharged, and the ball passed up through his chin, killing him instantly. Memphis Eagle, 11/18/1850. Land and Negroes for Sale. By virtue of a decree made at the present term of the Chancery Court, sitting in Memphis, I will sell at auction, on the 18th day of January next, at the residence of the late Joshua C. Lundy, deceased, on the Hernando road, about three miles from Memphis, three Negro Slaves and one hundred Acres of Land, belonging to the dec'd., the land being the same on which he was residing at his death, and which he bought from one Wesley **BLACKMAN**.... William L. **LUNDY**, Adm'r of the estate. Memphis Daily Appeal, 1/3/1851.

The friends and acquaintances of the late Isham G. **LUNDY** are respectfully invited to attend his funeral from his late residence at 10 o'clock this morning. Memphis Daily Appeal, 8/19/1857.

It is reported that Dr. Wm. L. **LUNDY**, formerly of this city, fought a duel in Nicaragua with a Capt. West, in which the latter was seriously wounded. Memphis Daily Appeal, 8/20/1856.

....These sad reflections are suggested by the death of my friend, my collegemate, N. P. **LUSHER**, of Memphis, Tenn. Graduating in June, 1858, in a class that numbered larger than any ever before, at the University of North Carolina....Feb. 13, 1859. Memphis Avalanche, 2/14/1859. On Saturday, 5th inst....departed this life, in New Orleans, Nathaniel Pearson Lusher, a native of Mississippi, in the twentieth year of his age; son of Henry M. **LUSHER**, of this city, and grandson of the late Nathaniel **PEARSON**, formerly of North Carolina....The remains of the deceased have been brought to this city from New Orleans, and in a few days will be removed to Pontotoc, Miss., for interment by the side of his mother....Memphis Daily Appeal, 2/13/1859.

Died, at his residence in Yallabusha county, Miss., on the morning of the 1st instant, Maj. Robert **LUSK**, aged 64 years, 4 months and 4 days....The deceased was a native of Union District, South Carolina, and removed to this county some eight years since. For more than thirty years he has been an active and zealous member of the Old School Presbyterian Church....In him his widow has lost her joy, his aged mother her earthly hopes....Memphis Daily Appeal, 7/10/1855.

Married—In Huntingdon, Carroll County, on Tuesday the 20th ult, Mr. Joseph **LUTER** to Miss Lucy **GREEN**. Memphis Enquirer, 4/5/1836.

Married by Rev. J. E. **DOUGLASS**, May 4th, in Marshall county, Miss., Doctor Archibald M. **LYLES** and Miss Margaret D. **CRADDOCK**. Memphis Daily Appeal, 6/4/1859.

Married, On the 5th inst., at Corydon, Indiana, by Rev. Dr. Ryan, Frank W. **LYNN** to Miss Mary Ida **LICESTER**. Memphis Daily Appeal, 9/13/1859.

Died. In this city, on the 26th of January last, of Pneumonia, Mary Adela, daughter of John T. and Minerva **LYNN**, of St. Louis, Mo., aged one year and eight months. St. Louis and Pittsburg papers please copy. Memphis Daily Appeal, 2/15/1855.

Luxahoma Lodge No. 145, A.F.A.M., was convened May 5th, A.T. 5856, for the purpose of attending the burial of Brother S. H. **LYON**, who, before his death, requested to be buried with Masonic honors....Died, at his residence in DeSoto county, Miss., on the 3d day of May, 1856, Brother S. H. Lyon, in the 64th year of his age. He died of consumption....Brother Lyon was ....one of the first settlers in North Mississippi....an affectionate husband and father....Memphis Daily Appeal, 6/3/1856.

Married, Thursday evening, February 21st, at the residence of Col. James D. **RUFFIN**, of DeSoto county, Miss., by Rev. Wm. Carey **CRANE**, President of Mississippi Female College, Mr. James S. **LYTLE**, of St. Louis, Mo., to Miss Ellen Ruffin, youngest daughter of the late James **RUFFIN**, of Panola county. St. Louis and Louisville papers copy. Memphis Daily Appeal, 2/27/1856.

Doctor J. C. **MABRY**, Having located himself in Memphis, offers his services to the citizens and public generally, in all the branches of his profession. He can at all times be found at his office, on the South side of Winchester St., recently occupied by Dr. **McCOULL**...Memphis Enquirer, 1/23/1838. Died in this city on 31st ult., of Bilious Pneumonia, Dr. Jno. C. Mabry, in the 33rd year of his age...Dr. Mabry was a native of Edgefield District, South Carolina, a State for which he ever expressed the warm affection of a devoted son...After all, to have a son so loved and honored by strangers, and to be surprised with the news of his death before they heard of his sickness, must be a severe blow to the distant parents....he made a profession of religion about a week before his death, when he had the happiness of being received into the Catholic Church...Memphis, April 13th, 1845. Weekly Appeal, 4/18/1845.

Married, At Mount Paran church, Marshall county, November 2, by Rev. S. S. **GILL**, Mr. Ovid **MABRY**, of DeSoto county, Miss., to Miss Lucy R. **JEFFRIES**, of Lafayette county, Miss. Memphis Daily Appeal, 11/9/1859.

Married, On Wednesday morning, the 13th inst., at the residence of Moses **NEELY**, Esq., by Rev. R. R. **EVANS**, Mr. Benjamin **MACKLIN**, of Pulaski, Tenn., to Miss Roxanah S. **NEELY**, of this county. Memphis Eagle & Enquirer, 4/27/1853.

Married, On the 5th instant in this city by Esq. Horne, Mr. S. B.(?) **MACLEMORE** to Mrs. Ann **McCALL**. Memphis Weekly Appeal, 4/14/1858.

Donald **MacLEOD**, formerly of Washington City and late of Memphis, has been lecturing recently at Louisville, with distinguished success. Memphis Eagle & Enquirer, 1/15/1853. Donald MacLeod, Esq., formerly assistant editor of the Memphis Eagle, has returned to his native country—Scotland....Memphis Eagle & Enquirer, 2/12/1853.

Died, On the 23d of May, 1859, at the residence of her daughter (Mrs. Susan E. **MARKHAM**) in Tipton county, Tenn., Mrs. Eleanor Howe **MACON**, in the 66th year of her age....Richmond (Va.) Enquirer and Montgomery (Ala.) papers please copy. Memphis Daily Appeal, 5/31/1859.

Died, Near Whiteville, Hardeman county, of billious cholic, on Sunday night, 20th inst., Col. John T. **MACON**. The deceased was one of the oldest and best citizens of the county in which he lived...Memphis Appeal, 7/24/1851.

Died, August 11, Duff Macpherson, son of M. E. and C. G. **MACPHERSON**, aged seventeen months and eighteen days. Memphis Daily Appeal, 8/13/1857.

Died, On the fifteenth instant, of yellow fever, Mr. Ambrose **MADDEN**, aged twenty-nine years....His funeral will take place this morning at ten o'clock, at his brother's residence on Court street. Memphis Daily Appeal, 9/16/1855.

Died—At his residence in South Memphis, yesterday, Mr. F. **MADDING**, constable of the Southern corporation. His disease was cholera...He was attacked with cholera on Wednesday night, about 9 o'clock, and such was the rapid progress of the disease....that he died yesterday at 12 ½ o'clock.....Daily Memphis Enquirer, 6/22/1849.

Married, In St. Louis on December 24th, by the Rev. J. **GOODLER** (?), Dr. J. W. **MADDOX**, of Memphis, to Miss Harriet V. **SHERWOOD**, of the former city. Memphis Daily Appeal, 1/4/1851.

Married: On the 17th by Rev. J. H. **GRAY**, D.D., Mr. R. D. **MADDOX** to Miss Susan **FOSTER**, all of LaGrange, Tenn. Memphis Evening Ledger, 12/31/1857. Married, On the 23rd ult. by Rev. J. H. **GRAY**, D.D., Mr. R. D. **MADDOX** to Miss Sue **FOSTER**, all of LaGrange, Tenn. Memphis Daily Appeal, 1/1/1858.

Married, On the 1st inst. in this city, by Rev. W. M. **EWING**, Dr. S. C. **MADDOX** to Miss Sallie E. **BOLTON**. By the same, Mr. P. G. **TRICE** to Miss Mollie L. **BOLTON**—all of Shelby county. Memphis Daily Appeal, 11/2/1859.

It is our painful duty to announce the occurrence of two fatalities in connection with the festivities which have just closed. The death of Fritz **MAENHOUSER**, a member of the Washington Rifles, has already been announced. He died of sun-stroke, Saturday evening, on the way to the scene of the encampment, having been stricken down in the ranks while on the route to the Fair Grounds. The deceased was a native of Germany, a tailor by trade, and left a wife and two children to mourn his sad fate. His remains now rest in Winchester Cemetery....Memphis Daily Appeal, Wed., 7/6/1859.

At Fort Pickering on Saturday evening last, a little boy, a son of F. **MAESTRI**, while gathering blackberries, fell into a dry well, which, being full of gas, caused the death of the little unfortunate in a few moments. Memphis Appeal, Mon., 7/12/1852.

Died, In this city about _ o'clock yesterday morning, of inflammation of the stomach, Mrs. Mary Magevney, wife of Michael **MAGEVNEY**, aged about forty years. Memphis Daily Appeal, 6/6/1855.

Married—On Sunday 31st May, at his residence, by the Rev. W. L. **CLACEY**, Mr. Eugene **MAGIVNEY**, to Miss Mary **SMITH**, both of this place. Memphis Enquirer, 6/5/1840.

Common Law & Chancery Court of Memphis. Thomas **MAGUIRE** vs. Melvina **MAGUIRE**. Petition For Divorce filed in the Common Law side of said court, December 30, 1852. It appears to the Clerk, from affidavits of the complainants, filed herein, that the defendant in this cause is a non-resident of the State of Tenn. It is therefore ordered that publication be made for three successive weeks in the Memphis Eagle and Enquirer, a newspaper published in the city of Memphis, requiring said defendant to appear before the Judge of said Court, at the next term thereof, to be held at the Court House in the city of Memphis, on the first Monday in March next, and plead or demur to complainant's petition, otherwise the same will be taken for confessed and set for hearing ex parte....Memphis Eagle & Enquirer, 1/2/1853.

Died, On the 19th inst., James L. **MAHAFFY**, aged 44 years. On the 22d inst., Alice Gray, second daughter of the late James L. Mahaffy, aged 4 years and 4 months. Memphis Whig, 6/24/1856.

Married, on the 3d instant, by Rev. J. H. **GRAY**, Mr. James T. **MAHAFFY** to Mrs. Mary L. **CAMPBELL**, all of this city. Memphis Enquirer, 7/5/1849. Died, suddenly, yesterday evening, at 4 o'clock, Robert, eldest son of Mr. James T. Mahaffy. The friends of the family are invited to attend the funeral, this morning at 10 o'clock, at the family residence near Exchange Square, Front Row. Services by Rev. G. W. **COONS**. Memphis Enquirer, 3/17/1849. Died—In this city, on Friday evening, Mrs. Mary Ann Mahaffy, consort of Mr. J. T. Mahaffy. Mr. Mahaffy has been sorely afflicted. On the morning of the same day he lost an infant son, and it is only about a week since an elder son was suddenly taken away by death. Daily Memphis Enquirer, 3/25/1849. Died, On the 19th inst. James L. Mahaffy, aged 44 years. On the 22d inst., Alice Gray, second daughter of the late James T. Mahaffy, aged 4 years and 4 months. Memphis Whig, 6/24/1856.

Died, In this county, 7th instant, Michael **MAHAR**, aged about 60 years, a native of the county Tipperary, (Ireland.) He was remarkable for candor, honesty, correct and fair dealing, and of an Independent, liberal, and generous heart. A Friend. Weekly Appeal, 4/23/1847.

Arrived in this city yesterday, an old citizen of Memphis who two years ago emigrated to California—Billy **MAHONEY**—a cistern builder....Memphis Daily Appeal, 2/24/1857.

More Cases of Sun Stroke....The fatal case was that of a laborer named John **MAHONY**, employed in the foundry of Messrs. Street, Hungerford & Co. He was attacked about ten o''lock, while exposed to the rays of the sun, in the Navy Yard, and died in a few minutes afterward....Memphis Daily Appeal, 7/22/1859.

Married, In this city on the 10th instant, by Esq. Waldran, Mr. Frank **MAIER** to Mrs. Julia C. **GEORGE**, all of this city. Memphis Weekly Appeal, 5/19/1858.

Wine, Liquor, and Cigar Store. Wm. **MAJOR** & Co., (Court Street). Have just received and will keep constantly on hand, a fine assortment of Brandies, Gin, Rum, Monongahels and Irish Whiskey...Weekly Appeal, 12/11/1846. Died, In this city on the 18th inst., Hester P. B. Major, daughter of William and Mary Ann Major, in the 9th year of her age. Memphis Daily Appeal, 2/27/1848.

Died, On Tuesday the 22d, at his residence in North Memphis, Wm. **MAJORS**, aged 50 years ....Memphis Whig, 4/23/1856.

Married, On Thursday night, the 3d of December, by Rev. Mr. Bateman, Mr. E. W. **MALLORY** to Miss Maria West **PENN**, both of this city. Memphis Weekly Appeal, 12/8/1858.

Died, In this city, on Saturday morning last, 8th inst., of Consumption, Mrs. Martha Elizabeth Mallory, wife of Eugene W. **MALLORY**, in the 23d year of her age. The deceased was an exemplary member of the Christian Church of this city...Memphis Appeal, 5/11/1852.

Married, On the 23d of February at the residence of Dr. I. D. Na____, St. Francis county, Ark., by Rev. W. H. ____, Dr. J. B. **MALLORY**, of Lamar, Marshall county, Miss., to Miss Sue G. **HART**, of LaGrange, Tenn. Memphis Weekly Appeal, 3/24/1858.

Died, In Hernando about three weeks since, Mr. James **MALLORY**. American Eagle, 2/14/1842.

Married, In Marshall county, Miss., on the 9th inst., Mr. John W. **MALLORY**, of this city, to Miss Martha A., daughter of R. S. **PARHAM**, Esq. Memphis Eagle, 1/25/1849.

Died, at Jefferson, Texas, on the 7th of last month, after a short illness, Jane Adaline, daughter of Col. George **ELLIOTT**, of Sumner county, Tennessee and wife of Dr. H. H. **MALONE**, formerly of the same place....As a daughter she was kind and affectionate; the joy of the old homestead, around whose happy hearth an aged father and mother and loving brothers and sisters gathered....But a few months since she left with him who loved her best, and who, in death, felt her last pulse, and saw her heart's last throb, to go to the place where she died, amid strangers and in a distant clime. None were there to receive her dying blessing but her husband and two interesting boys, of tender years, whom cruel death has decreed motherless and left orphans for ever....Memphis, August, 1855. Memphis Daily Appeal, 8/12/1855.

Married, On the 16th instant, in Athens, Ala., at the residence of Major J. Nichlas **MALONE**, the bride's uncle, by Rev. J. E. **DOUGLASS**, President of Marshall Female Institute of Mississippi, Mr. S. Edward **MALONE**, of Marshall county, Miss., to Miss Roxanna Q. Malone, daughter of Mr. N. C. **MALONE**, of Tishomingo county, Miss. Memphis Daily Appeal, 3/20/1859.

Died—On the 13th inst., in Shelbyville, Tenn., John Steele, youngest son of Dr. R. C. **MALONE**, of this place, aged 2 years. American Eagle Weekly, 9/26/1845.

Married, On the 2d inst. by the Rev. H. S. **PORTER**, Mr. Z. H. **MANEES**, (of the firm of Sharpley & Manees,) to Mrs. Minnie L. **BROWN**, both of this city. Nashville papers please copy. Memphis Eagle & Enquirer, 6/4/1853.

Married: In this city, on the 8th inst., Maj. Wm. H. **MANEES**, to Miss Fannie, daughter of Col. S. R. **BROWN**, of Memphis. Weekly Memphis Eagle, 7/26/1849.

Died, on Monday the 6th inst. Mr. Reuben **MANEFEE**, a citizen of this place. Memphis Advocate, 8/11/1827.

A difficulty occurred yesterday....in the northern part of the city, between Elijah **ENGLAND** and Patrick **MANEY**, during which England struck Maney on the head with a heavy piece of timber, fracturing his skull, and causing his death a few hours afterward....Memphis Daily Appeal, 11/6/1859.

Married, On Wednesday evening, the 26th ult., at the residence of Dr. P. **WILSON**, in Haywood county, Tenn., by Rev. Geo. W. **YOUNG**, Mr. W. B. **MANN** and Miss Victoria V. Wilson, daughter of Dr. P. Wilson. Memphis Daily Appeal, 12/2/1856.

We are pleased to notice in our advertising column that Capt. Wm. C. **MANN** and Mr. Wm. **WORSHAM**, late of the good steamboat Memphis, have secured the elegant and comfortable passenger packet, Mattie Wayne, to ply between this port and Cincinnati....Memphis Appeal, 2/23/1853.

Died. In this city on the 27th inst., Edwin **MANNING**, of consumption. The friends of the family are invited to attend his funeral from Wesley Chapel....Memphis Daily Appeal, 11/28/1854.

The friends and acquaintances of R. S. **MANNING** are invited to attend his funeral from his late residence on the Memphis and Tennessee Railroad, at 11 o'clock. Services by the Masonic order. Memphis Daily Appeal, 2/25/1859. At a called meeting of Jeremiah Lodge No. 158, held.... Friday, February 25th, A.D., 1859....the following resolutions were unanimously adopted: Whereas, It has pleased an All-wise God....to remove from our midst Brother Reubin S. Manning, who departed this life on yesterday morning....Memphis Daily Appeal, 3/1/1859.

Married. On Wednesday the 15th, near Rienzi, Miss. by Rev. Mr. **GILLENWATERS**, Mr. Samuel **MANSFIELD**, of Memphis, Tenn., to Miss Mary B. Robertson, daughter of Major William **ROBERTSON**. Memphis Daily Appeal, 8/18/1855.

I Have 1140 acres of Land, sixteen miles from Memphis, DeSoto, Miss., well improved, for which I will take 10 dollars per acre, cash. Josiah **MAPLES**. Memphis Daily Appeal, 9/14/1855.

Died, In Memphis on Thursday, 27th inst., at 8 o'clock A.M., of scarlet fever, Sargeant S. Prentiss, infant son of Dr. John T. and Ophelia S. **MARABLE**, aged 1 year, 6 months and 21 days....Louisville and Clarksville papers and the Nashville Christian Advocate please copy. Memphis Daily Appeal, 3/29/1857.

Through the politeness of Dr. E. **MARCY**, of this city, we have been favored with the perusal of an interesting letter from his brother, the gallant Capt. R. B. **MARCY**, whom Col. Johnston, the commander of the Utah expedition, had dispatched to New Mexico, for the purpose of purchasing horses and mules to replace those that perished in the march of the expedition from Fort Laramie to Fort Bridger….Memphis Weekly Appeal, 3/17/1858.

Married, On the 8th of January, by the Rev. Mr. Evans, Mr. Sidney **MARKHAM**, of Nonconnah, Tenn., formerly of New Hartford, Conn., to Miss Columbia A. **BELL**, of Shelby county, Tenn. Memphis Appeal, 3/5/1851.

We regret to observe announced in our New Orleans exchanges, the death of James B. **MARKS**, formerly a resident of this city, and a native of Louisiana. He died on the 16th(?) inst. after a long and painful illness…..Daily Enquirer, 2/23/1847.

Died, On Friday, the 13th inst., of pneumonia, Mr. James **MARKUM**, aged 73 years….He was with General Jackson in the Indian wars and at the battle of New Orleans. At the time of his death, he was a member of the firm of D. M. Moore & Co. He leaves a wife and three children ….Memphis Daily Appeal, 2/18/1857.

Married. In Oxford, Miss. on the 30th ult. at the residence of Prof. Lewis **HARPER** of the University of Mississippi, by Judge A. B. **LONGSTREET**, E. R. **MARLETT**, M.D., of Syracuse, N.Y., to Miss Fannie, second daughter of the late Dr. Kial(?) **WRIGHT**, of the same place. Memphis Daily Appeal, 4/5/1855.

John L. **MARLING**, Esq., one of the editors of this paper, has been nominated by the President and confirmed by the Senate, as Charge d'Affaires to Guatemala….Memphis Daily Appeal, 8/10/1854.

Died—In this city, on Wednesday 24th inst., C. D. **MARMON**, aged 24 years. Weekly Appeal, 8/7/1846.

Married, On Monday evening, 15th inst., by Esq. Waldran, Mr. N. **MARONEY** to Miss Elizabeth C. **HARDEN**, all of this city. Memphis Daily Appeal, 11/16/1852.

An Irishman named Patrick **MARONEY**, says the *Evening News* of yesterday, was killed this morning, at the junction of Jackson street and the Mississippi and Tennessee Railroad. He was on a platform car and as the passenger train was approaching he jumped off for the purpose of driving some cattle from the track, when his foot slipped and he fell across the tract, and before he could recover himself the train passed over him, cutting himself almost in too. Memphis Daily Appeal, 4/16/1856.

Died, On the 5th instant, Major George W. L. **MARR**, aged about seventy-five years. The deceased served and was wounded in the Creek war under Gen. Jackson, and in 1815 was elected to Congress from the Clarksville District. In 1821 he removed to Obion county, where he has ever since lived, and several times represented that county in the Tenn. Legislature. Memphis Daily Appeal, 4/18/1856.

Married, On the 6th inst., at the Episcopal Church, by the Rev. Dr. Page, Acting Master Robert A. **MARR**, U.S.N. to Miss Mary F., youngest daughter of Capt. E. A. F. **LAVALLETTE**, U.S.N. Memphis Eagle, 4/8/1850.

Married, By Rev. J. J. **SLEDGE**, at the residence of the bride's father, J. W. **MARROW**, Esq., to Miss Henrietta **NUNER**, all of Lafayette county, Miss. Memphis Daily Appeal, 2/18/1858.

W. F. Tucker Lodge I.O.O.F. No. 48, Harrisburg, Miss., June 28, 1857. Whereas, by a decree of an All Wise Providence, our esteemed Brother, J. Y. **MARRS**, has been taken from our midst….Resolved, That the neighborhood and community have lost an estimable citizen and the Methodist Church a worthy and zealous communicant….Resolved, That we extend our sincere sympathies to his surviving parent and relations….Memphis Daily Appeal, 7/7/1857.

Married, On the 21st inst. by Rev. B. F. **GRIFFIN**, Samuel J. **MARSH** to Miss Parmelia **LONG**, all of Tipton county, Tenn. Memphis Daily Appeal, 6/25/1859.

Died, In this city, on Saturday 27th inst., at 4 o'clock, P.M., Wm. **MARSH**, formerly of Giles county. Aged 44 years. Memphis Appeal, 9/30/1851.

Officer Morgan was yesterday brought before Justices Rose and Hill on a charge of murdering Elijah **MARSHALL**, on Tuesday morning....Memphis Daily Appeal, Sat., 9/10/1853.

Marshall Female Institute. The Second Session will open on Monday, the 31st of July, and continue twenty-one weeks...It is situated in the country, one mile north of the Stage Road from Holly Springs, to Memphis, twenty miles from the former place, thirty from the latter, and four miles from North Mt. Pleasant...James **MARSHALL**, President. Memphis Daily Appeal, 7/18/1848.

Married, On Thursday evening the 25th inst., at the 1st Presbyterian Church in this city, by the Rev. Mr. Henderson, Mr. James **MARSHALL**, of this city, to Miss Margaret **FUTHEY**, of Tipton county, Tenn. Memphis Eagle & Enquirer, 3/31/1852.

Married, On the 3d inst. at Collierville, Ten. by the Rev. Samuel **WATSON**, Dr. Jefferson H. **MARSHALL** to Miss Elizabeth D. **WARE**. The Appeal, 9/20/1844.

A meeting of Scotchmen was held at the Worsham House, Saturday evening, Nov. 3d for the purpose of taking into consideration the organization of a branch of St. Andrews' Society in this city. Mr. Robert **MARSHALL** having been called to the Chair, and Mr. R. R. **McDONALD** appointed Secretary....Dr. J. Stewart **McKENZIE** opposed the formation of any Society.... *Resolved,* That Wm. **POOLEY** be appointed Treasurer....Memphis Daily Appeal, 11/6/1855.

Died, in Dandridge, Ten., on the 4th ult., Andrew Russell **MARTIN**, in the 25th year of his age. Daily Enquirer, 10/8/1847.

Married, On the morning of the 11th inst. at the residence of Dr. Jameson, by Rev. Joseph R. **HAMILTON**, Mr. G. F. **MARTIN**, Esq., to Miss Virginia L. **JAMESON**, both of Marshall county, Mississippi. Memphis Daily Appeal, 11/17/1857.

It will be seen elsewhere in this morning's issue that G. Alex. **MARTIN** has, owing to continued ill health of himself and family, changed his location from Brownsville, Tenn., to this city. Memphis Daily Appeal, 8/16/1856.

Died, On the evening of the 27th inst., at Flora Lake, Mrs. Martha Ann Martin, wife of Dr. George Alexander **MARTIN**, aged 44 years and 17 days. Thus has passed away a tender and faithful wife, an affectionate mother, a true woman. The deceased was a native of Kentucky and at different periods a resident of Arkansas and Tennessee....Memphis Daily Appeal, 10/29/1856.

J. D. **MARTIN**, M.D., Offers his professional services to the citizens of Memphis and vicinity. Office on Court Square, South side....Memphis Daily Appeal, 9/23/1852.

Married, On the 23d inst. at the residence of the bride's father, near Laconia, Ark., by the Rt. Rev. Bishop Otey, Mr. Jackson **MARTIN**, of Tallahatchie county, Miss., to Miss Mary B. **WARFIELD**. Memphis Weekly Appeal, 3/31/1858.

Married, At the Second Presbyterian Church on the 21st instant by Rev. Dr. J. H. **GRAY**, Dr. John A. **MARTIN**, of White county, Ark., to Miss Alice, daughter of James **ARMOUR**, of this city. Memphis Daily Appeal, 11/23/1855.

Married, At the residence of Col. C. C. **WHITE**, near Byhalia, Marshall county, Miss., on the 25th inst., by Rev. S. __. **STARK**, Dr. Jno. D. **MARTIN**, of Memphis, Tenn., to Miss Rosalie A. **WHITE**. Memphis Daily Appeal, 11/26/1857.

Notice. The insolvency of the estate of Samuel P. **MARTIN**, having been suggested by the Administrator, all persons having claims...Memphis Daily Appeal, 1/7/1851.

Married, On the evening of the 31st ult., by the Rev. Thomas **TAYLOR**, Dr. James M. **MASK** and Miss Elizabeth J. McKinnie, daughter of David **McKINNIE** – all of Hardeman county. Memphis Eagle & Enquirer, 1/20/1852.

The James Laughlin left here last evening on her usual trip to Napoleon. Captain Dick **MASON** has charge of her now....Memphis Appeal, 8/8/1854.

Died at the Central Hotel in Memphis, on Tuesday the 14th of January, after an illness of but one day of Cramp Cholic, in the 23d year of his age, Mr. John H. **MASON**, formerly of Holly Springs, Mississippi. He has left an aged mother, and kind and affectionate brothers...The Appeal & American Eagle Weekly, 1/17/1845.

Married, In this city, on Sunday evening, by Rev. Geo. W. **COONS**, Mr. Joseph T. **MASON**, to Miss Ann Maria, daughter of the late John **McCOULL**, Esq. of Spotsylvania county, Va. Weekly Appeal, Fri., 11/28/1845.

Married, On the 23d inst., by the Rev. John **GAILER**, Dr. James A. **MASSEY**, of Shelby County, Tenn., to Miss Mary H. daughter of W. D. **CROOK**, Esq. of Marshall county, Miss. Weekly Appeal, 1/2/1846. Died, At his residence in Shelby county, on the 11th inst., after an illness of twenty days, Dr. Jas. A. Massey, aged 27 years, 11 months. Memphis Appeal, 10/22/1852. At a regular communication of Wood Lawn Lodge No. 211 of Free and accepted Masons, on the 4th of December, 1852, the following resolutions were unanimously adopted: Whereas, It has pleased the Great Worshipful Master above to remove from the Lodge Militant to the triumphant Lodge above our much esteemed friend and Brother, Dr. James A. Massey...That we deeply sumpathize with his bereaved widow and fatherless children; also with his aged and afflicted parents.... Memphis Appeal, 12/15/1852.

Died—In LaGrange, Tenn., September 10, 1858, of an apoplectic illness, Pamela L. Massey, relict of Joshua W. **MASSEY**, who lived and died in Queen Ann's county, Maryland. The deceased was born of ancient and honorable family in Kent county, (Massey's x Roads) Maryland, on the 22d day of March, 1785(?). Early widowed, her thoughts and energies became absorbed in the education of her children....Her only daughter, whose husband had by the same pestilence a few days preceded her, having been cut off by the epidemic of 1853, at New Orleans, leaving a large family of orphaned children of tender infancy, she betook herself promptly to their support and education....Baltimore, Centreville and Chestertown, Maryland, papers please notice. Memphis Daily Appeal, 9/14/1858.

Married, On Thursday evening, the 18th inst., at the residence of the bride's father, by Rev. Mathew **WEBBER**, Mr. James R. **MATEER** and Miss Laura E. **JONES**, all of this city. Memphis Daily Appeal, 9/19/1856.

Died, in this city, on Sunday morning last, Mr. James **MATH**. The friends and acquaintants of P. G. **MATH** are invited to attend the funeral of the deceased, from his late residence, corner of Main and Huling streets, at three o'clock This Afternoon. Memphis Daily Appeal, 12/24/1856.

One of the most melancholy affairs that has occurred in our city for many years, took place about half past one o'clock yesterday, which resulted in the instant death of W. C. **MATHEWS** and the shooting of Mr. Joseph **WILLIAMS**, who is reported as dying at the time of writing this article ....It seems that some twelve months ago, while on his way to California, Mr. Williams left a parrot with the family of Mrs. Young....Yesterday, being on his return home to England from California, he called and got the parrot and took it to the boarding house of Mrs. Dalman...while at dinner he was called out by Mr. Benjamin **CONNER**, a daguerreotypist, and was asked what he would take for the bird. Williams informed him that he did not wish to dispose of it, when Conner declared he would have it any how and started to walk off with it, designing to return it to Mrs. Young, whose family had formed a great attachment for it. Williams made an effort to recover it, when Conner drew a repeater and deliberately shot him, the ball taking effect in the left breast, just below and in front of the arm pit. He then started off leisurely to Mrs. Young's, his boarding house, when he was pursued by officer O'Neal with some citizens, whom he threatened to shoot....In his effort to escape he passed the house of Mathews, on Second street, who, hearing the calls of O'Neal, to take him, that he was guilty of murder, started in pursuit in company with his brother, and chased him as far as Adams street bridge, where Mathews fired one or two shots at him. Conner then turned and fired three times at Matthews, the third shot taking effect in the heart, killing him instantly. Conner was then arrested and lodged in jail....He has been a citizen of Memphis some twelve months, and is said by those who know him, to be a rather quiet, inoffensive young man, and was never known to be in a difficulty before....Mr. Mathews was a clever, industrious young man and has left an aged and widowed mother....Mr. Williams is also a young man, but a comparative stranger in our city and was just on the eve of leaving for Baltimore. There is said to be no hope of his recovery....Memphis Daily Appeal, 5/1/1856. Williams, the man who was shot by Conner, on Wednesday last, died of the wound about noon on yesterday....Memphis Daily Appeal, Tues., 5/6/1856.

Married, On Tuesday evening, 18th inst., by Rev. R. C. **GRUNDY**, at the Owen House, in this city, Mr. Geo. **MATONE** to Miss Louisa **CHEEK**, all of Ark. Memphis Daily Appeal, 10/20/1859.

Married, On Thursday evening, the 3d instant, by Rev. B. F. **THOMAS**, Mr. C. G. **MATTHEWS**, of Shelby county, Tenn., and Miss Ann J. Buchanan, at the residence of her father, the Rev. B. B. **BUCHANAN**, of DeSoto county, Miss. Memphis Daily Appeal, 2/6/1857. Married, On December 10th, by Rev. Wm. Carey **CRANE**, Mr. M. F. **MATTHEWS**, of Shelby county, Tenn., and Miss Sarah L. Buchanan, eldest daughter of Rev. Dr. B. B. **BUCHANAN**, of DeSoto county, Miss. Memphis Daily Appeal, 12/13/1856.

Married, On the 24th inst. by Elder W. J. **BARBEE**, at the residence of Col. J. E. **MATTHEWS**, of DeSoto county, Mr. Samuel W. **MATTHEWS** to Miss Matilda Jane **McDONALD**. Memphis Daily Appeal, 12/31/1857.

Married. On the 24th of December, 1850, by Rev. John **WILSON**, Mr. John G. **MATTHEWS**, of Graves co., Texas, to Miss Sarah Jane **STRONG**, of Tipton co., Tenn. Austin Gazette, (Texas) will please copy. Memphis Daily Appeal, 1/7/1851.

Died, On the morning of the 21st instant, "Little Lulie," infant daughter of Sam. W. and Mattie J. **MATTHEWS**, aged 3 months and 11 days. Memphis Daily Appeal, 2/24/1859.

Died, On the 24th ult. of typhoid pneumonia, at the residence of his father near Saulsbury, Hardeman county, Tenn., L. B. **MAULDIN**, aged 32(?) years and 11 days. Memphis Weekly Appeal, 12/8/1858.

Married, On the morning of August 30th, at the residence of the bride's father, by Rev. J. W. **ROGERS**, Rector of St. Thomas Church, Somerville, Tenn., Mr. Abram **MAURY**, of Memphis, to Miss Mary J. **HANCOCK**, of Hardeman county, Tenn. Memphis Daily Appeal, 8/31/1859.

Died, In this city, on Sunday morning, 25th inst., of consumption, Mary Rebecca, consort of J. S. **MAUS**, aged 22 years. Memphis Eagle & Enquirer, 1/28/1852. J. S. Maus, the keeper of a Family Grocery and Produce Store, suddenly dropped dead yesterday morning. His disease is supposed to have been apoplexy. Memphis Daily Appeal, 7/10/1852.

Died: In this city, at the residence of his brother, on Sunday evening, August 19th, Mr. Joseph S. **MAUS**, in the ___ year of his age. Mr. M. was a very worthy and industrious young man; for several years past he had been employed in the different printing offices of the city, and had acted as Secretary of the Memphis Typographical Society. He was correct and unobtrusive in his deportment. Weekly Memphis Eagle, 8/23/1849.

Death of Jesse E. **MAXWELL**.—We neglected yesterday to chronicle this painful intelligence ....He died at Hardin Springs but his body was brought to this city for burial, and now sleeps in Elmwood Cemetery.....Memphis Daily Appeal, 7/9/1856.

Married, In DeSoto county, Miss., on Sunday last, Mr. Thomas A. **MAXWELL**, of this county, to Miss Mary C. **FARRIS**, of the former place. The Daily Eagle, Wed., 2/16/1848.

Married, On the 28th instant at the residence of F. E. **WHITFIELD**, Esq., by Rev. C. R. **HENDRICKSON**, Mr. Benjamin **MAY** and Miss Demetria A., daughter of S. R. **SIMMONS**, Esq., of Fayette county. West Tennessee Whig please copy. Memphis Daily Appeal, 4/30/1857.

Departed this life on Monday evening, September 17, 1855, Mrs. Mary G., consort of Charles **MAY**, in the 33d year of her age after an illness of nine days. Her disease was a violent attack of the autumnal congestive fever....Mrs. M. was a member of the Methodist Episcopal Church in this city. As a lady, a wife, a sister, a friend, and above all, as a christian....The deceased leaves a deeply afflicted husband and an only son to mourn....Memphis Daily Appeal, 9/19/1855.

Died, On Sunday morning, the 17th instant, in the twenty-second year of her age, at her residence on Main street, Fannie N., wife of Charles **MAY**. Memphis Daily Appeal, 5/26/1857.

Married, On Wednesday evening at 4 o'clock, at Bell Grove, in this vicinity by Rev. Mr. Bryan, Charles **MAY** to Miss Fanny V., daughter of Peter **HEISTON**, Esq. Memphis Whig, Fri., 5/23/1856.

We announce this morning the nuptials of Charles **MAY**, Esq., and one of the fairest daughters of Memphis. The union was celebrated at Wesley Chapel, yesterday, and the happy pair, accompanied by a gay party, embarked on the steamer J. H. Lucas for St. Louis last evening.... Memphis Daily Appeal, 6/17/1859.

Died, In this city Sunday evening, 30th ult., after a short illness, Wm. **MAY**, in the 30th year of his age. The funeral will take place from the residence of Mr. Chas. **MAY**, on Union street....This Morning....Memphis Daily Appeal, 11/1/1859.

Married, On Thursday, December 23d, at the residence of C. M. **GUYER**(?), by Rev. A. M. **BRYAN**, Mr. James **MAYDWELL** to Miss Sophia **HA_ISON**, both of this city. The happy parties left for Louisville on a bridal tour on the steamer Moses McLellan. Lexington, Ky., Louisville and St. Louis papers please copy. Memphis Weekly Appeal, 12/29/1858.

Married, On the __th instant at Asberry Chapel, by Rev. J. _. Meriweather, Mr. Thomas **MAYDWELL** to Miss Lucy **FLEASHART**, both of this city. Louisville and Lexington (Ky.) papers please copy. Memphis Daily Appeal, 7/27/1859.

We are pained to learn that Mr. Virgil **MAYFIELD**, late of the firm of F. Lane & Co., of this city, was yesterday thrown from his horse and instantly killed. The accident happened somewhere on the Horn Lake Road. His remains will be taken on_____ this morning, to the residence of his _____-in-law, Mr. Garrett **LANE**, in Fayette county for interment. Memphis Daily Appeal, 10/14/1855.

On yesterday morning between eleven and twelve o'clock, a painful accident occurred on the Memphis and Ohio Railroad. When within about five miles of the city, the engineer of the train discovered some distance ahead, a man sitting on the track, and gave the alarm; the man arose and the engineer, thinking that he would get off the track, did not lessen the speed of the locomotive. When, too late, it was discovered that the man was still on the track. The cars ran over him, cutting off both legs and mutilating one of his hands....Memphis Daily Appeal, 2/1/1857. ....The name of the victim was Samuel **MAYNARD**. We learn from Maj. Houston that he died before 7 o'clock, the same evening on which the accident occurred. Memphis Daily Appeal, 2/5/1857.

Married, On the 5th inst. in Fayette County, Tenn., by Elder F. M. **FREEMAN**, Mr. James A. **MAYO** and Miss Mary A. **BLAIR**, all of that county. Memphis Whig, 1/10/1856.

Died, In Fayette county, Tenn., on the 30th of March, 1850, Mrs. Sally E. **MAYO**, aged 54 years. Memphis Daily Eagle, 5/10/1850.

Married, Recently, in Madison county, Mr. W. H. **M'ADOO** and Miss Susannah **HAYNES**, and also, Mr. Sion W. **BOON** and Miss M. L. **PYLES**. Memphis Daily Appeal, 4/15/1856.

R. C. **M'ALPIN**, Attorney At Law—Has settled in Memphis and will attend the Circuit Courts, of the counties of Tipton, Haywood, Hardeman, Fayette and Shelby. Memphis, March 8, 1827. Memphis Advocate, 4/28/1827.

Died, On the 3d of December, of pneumonia, in the 62d year of his age, Mr. Wm. **M'ATEER**. He leaves many friends to mourn his loss. Memphis Daily Appeal, 12/16/1859.

Died, on the 11th inst. Newton M'Cleary, jun., son of Mr. James A. **M'CLEARY** of this place – aged about six years. Memphis Enquirer, 10/13/1838.

Married, on the 23d of November by Rev. Mr. Griffin, Mr. R. G. **M'CLEVAIN**, late of Lancasterville, S. C., to Miss L. L. **PULLIN**, all of Tipton county, Tenn. Memphis Weekly Appeal, 12/8/1858. (Author's Note: spelled **McELVAINE** in another paper.)

Married, On the 29th of August, 1855, by Rev. Absalom **JEHU**, at the residence of Judge **McASH**, Mr. John C. **M'COULEY** to Miss Ella **McASH**, all of White county, Ark. Memphis Daily Appeal, 9/20/1855.

Married, On the 28th ult., by Rev. Reuben **BURROW**, Mr. John R. **M'CREIGHT**, merchant of Mt. Zion, Tipton county, Tenn., and Miss K. W. **HILLIARD**, of Fayette county, Tenn. Memphis Daily Appeal, 11/5/1857.

Died, In Wittsburg(?), St. Francis county, Ark., on the 11th instant, Richard **M'REE**, aged about 48 years, formerly of Jackson, Tenn. West Tennessee Whig will please copy. Memphis Daily Appeal, 1/17/1851.

Married, By Rev. E. J. **WILLIAMS**, near Hernando, on the 4th day of February, 1857, Mr. Samuel R. **McALEXANDER**, of Marshall county, Miss., and Miss Eliza J. **CLIFTON**, of DeSoto county, Miss. Memphis Daily Appeal, 2/7/1857.

Married, At Franklin, Tenn. on the 19th inst. by Rev. A. M. **CUNNINGHAM**, Miss Narcissa H., daughter of R. C. **FOSTER**, Esq., of that place, and Mr. John W. **McALISTER**, of Florence, Alabama. Memphis Eagle & Enquirer, 1/25/1853.

Married, Near the Artesian Springs, Madison county, Miss., on the 20th inst., by Rev. J. A. **DICKSON**, Mr. H. Connor **McCAIN**, of Tipton county, Tenn., to Miss M. Clemmie, second daughter of Col. Thomas **SIMPSON**. Memphis Daily Appeal, 12/28/1859.

Died, On the 14th instant near Portersville, Tipton county, Tenn., Mr. James M. **McCAIN**, aged about 49 years, formerly of Mecklenburg county, South Carolina; disease consumption. Memphis Daily Appeal, 3/24/1859.

Married, On the evening of the 13th of February by Rev. J. **WILSON**, Mr. W. R. **McCAIN** and Mrs. Letitia **SIMONTON**, daughter of John and Martha **STRONG**, all of Tipton county, Tenn. Memphis Daily Appeal, 3/12/1856.

Died, August the 16th, Mary Malcolm, infant daughter of Malcolm and Mary **McCALLUM**, aged 6 months. Memphis Appeal, 8/24/1852.

Departed this life at the residence of her husband, Dr. Wm. H. **McCARGE**, in DeSoto county, Miss., Sunday morning, October 19th, Mrs. Lucy A. McCarge....She was born in Madison county, Ala., November 23d, 1823, and was the second child of Robert and Eliza F. **PAYNE**, and was nearly grown when her parents removed to the State of Mississippi. She was married August 10th, 1843. She embraced religion and was baptized into the fellowship of the Baptist Church in the year 1846....She has gone to the bright land of spirits, leaving her husband and five children of tender age....Memphis Daily Appeal, 10/23/1856. Married, Near Olive Branch, Miss., on the 7th instant, by Rev. Wm. Carey **CRANE**, Dr. Wm. H. **McCARGO** to Mrs. Frances K. **PAYNE**, all of DeSoto county. Memphis Daily Appeal, 9/14/1858.

Two shooting affrays came off in our city on Saturday night last. One in North Memphis, a Mr. Tanzy, said by the evening paper to be from Louisville and connected with the late riot there, shot a man by the name of D. **McCARNON**. The weapon used was a horse pistol loaded with buck shot. The charge entered McCarnon's head, killing him instantly. Liquor was the cause.... Memphis Daily Appeal, 11/20/1855.

On Monday evening Michael **McCARTY**, an Irishman who has lived in this city for the past two years, and who was boarding in the alley north of Winchester street, complained to his friends that a fellow boarder had insulted and threatened him, and that he was in fear of his life, and also that he dare neither sup nor sleep in the boarding house while the man was there. He was invited to sup with a relative in the neighborhood and did so. After dark he left, saying he should sleep at the house of a friend. Yesterday morning his lifeless body was found lying in the street in front of the boarding house. His scalp was cut at the back of his head....Memphis Daily Appeal, 11/11/1857.

Executor;s Sale of Desirable Lane, Will be sold, on the premises, on the 12th of Nov next, if not previously sold, 640 acres of Land....lying in Fayette county, Tenn., 3 ½ miles east of Moscow and 1 mile north of the Memphis and Charleston Railroad....L. C. **McCAUGHAN**, Ex'tor of K. A. **McCAUGHAN**, dec'd. Memphis Daily Appeal, 10/13/1855.

Married, Near Whiteville, Hardeman county, Tenn., on Tuesday evening, 4th inst., by Rev. Phillip **WALKER**, Mr. Hampden **McCLANAHAN**, of Jackson, Tenn., to Miss Lucy K., daughter of Maj. John C. **GREEN**, of the former place. Memphis Daily Appeal, 2/14/1851. Died, Of consumption, in Jackson, Tenn., at 4 o'clock yesterday morning, Mrs. Lucy McClanahan, wife of Hampton McClanahan, Esq. Memphis Daily Appeal, 3/24/1859.

Died, Of consumption, at the residence of Dr. D. H. **WILLIAMS**, in Henderson county, Tenn., on Friday last, John D. **McCLANAHAN**, in the 22d year of his age....He had been a regular employee in the Appeal office for some years, in which establishment he served a regular apprenticeship in the art of printing, and at the time of his death was an an excursion among his relatives in search of health. The fell destroyer consumption, however, was relentless....Memphis Daily Appeal, Thurs., 3/10/1859.

Died. Of Consumption, in Lauderdale county, Ala., on the 29th November last, Robert **McCLANAHAN**, Sheriff of the county, aged 35 years....Memphis Daily Appeal, 12/8/1855.

Died.—At the residence of Samuel **McCLANAHAN**, in Jackson, Tenn., on Tuesday morning, 6th instant, of congestion of the lungs, Nelson **McCLANAHAN**, in the 27th year of his age. The deceased was a native of Laurens District, S.C., but had been for the last 20 years, a citizen of the place in which he died...At the summons of his country, he entered the war with Mexico, in which he served with honor and distinction as a lieutenant in the 14th Infantry, under Col. Trousdale...Memphis Appeal, 5/12/1851. Died, Suddenly, in Jackson, Tenn., on Friday evening last, Mrs. Louisa McClanahan, wife of Samuel McClanahan, Esq., in the – year of her age. The deceased was a native of Abbeville District, South Carolina, and had been from early womanhood an exemplary member of the Presbyterian Church....In all the relations of life, mother, friend and neighbor, she fully exemplified all those traits of character which adorn the true christian. In the maturity of life she has gone home after having raised a large family....Memphis Daily Appeal, Sun., 11/1/1857.

Married, On the 23d inst. at the residence of Col. Crawford, in DeSoto county, Miss., by Rev. Robt. **FRAZIER**, Mr. Wm. J. **McCLANE**, of Memphis, to Miss Mary A. **CRAWFORD**. Memphis Daily Appeal, 2/26/1853.

Died, On Tuesday morning last, 17th inst., of consumption, on the Tennessee River, James D. **McCLELLAN**, Esq., of Jackson, Tenn. The deceased had been for many years a prominent member of the Jackson bar...useful and exemplary, as a husband, fond and devoted...Memphis Daily Appeal, 2/23/1852. Died, On Friday last, Mrs. Isabella C. McClellan, widow of the late James D. McClellan, Esq., of Jackson, and the only surviving sister of our friend, Col. C. D. **McLEAN**, of this vicinity....Memphis Daily Appeal, Fri., 10/30/1857.

Married, In the vicinity of Sommerville, at the residence of Mrs. Sarah B. **TROTTER**, by the Rev. Phillip **TUGGLE**, on the 29th August, T. D. G. **McCLELLAN**, M.D., to Miss F. E. **PORTER**. Daily Memphis Enquirer, 9/5/1848.

Married—In Somerville, on the 24th inst., by the Rev. R. H. **JONES**, William B. **McCLELLAN**, Esq. Editor of the Granada Bulletin, Mississippi, to Miss Caroline **RAWLINGS**, of this county. Memphis Enquirer, 9/1/1836.

Married, On the 26th(?) ultimo, by S. W. **LEDBETTER**, Esq. at the residence of Mr. W. **PURRYER**, Mr. Jackson **McCLUER** and Mrs. **HARRIS**, both of this county. Memphis Eagle & Enquirer, 1/4/1853.

Rev. Ed. **McCLURE**, the newly elected Rector of Grace Church, has arrived in the city.... Memphis Daily Appeal, 10/30/1859.

A dissipated man, named James **McCODE**, was found by a policeman lying in Main street.... yesterday afternoon, in a very low condition, from the effects of dissipation and exposure to the sun. He was at once conveyed to the jail-yard, and died in a very short time....Memphis Daily Appeal, 7/19/1859.

Married—On the 9th inst., by the Rev. Henry W. **SALE**, Mr. Malcolm **McCOLLEM** to Miss Mary A. Thomas, daughter of John W. **THOMAS**, Esq. of Shelby. Somerville Reporter, 12/14/1839.

Married, On Tuesday, 2d inst., at Middle Haddam Conn., by Rev. Sylvester **NASH** Mr. Jas. M. **McCOMBS**, of this city, to Miss Elizabeth W. **NASH**, of the former place. American Eagle Weekly, 9/26/1845. Jas. M. McCombs & Co., Dealers in Hard-ware and Iron. Sign of the Broad Axe, Front Row, just below the Railroad, Memphis, Tenn. Memphis Enquirer, 6/18/1846. Died, On Thursday, the 3rd instant, of croup, Harry Sylvester, eldest son of J. M. and Elizabeth W. McCombs, aged 4 years and 12 days...Memphis Daily Eagle, 10/4/1850.

P. **McCONNEL**, the unfortunate individual who was run over by a wood train on the railroad this side of Lagrange, died Thursday of this week. Memphis Daily Appeal, Fri., 2/22/1856.

Married, In Haywood county, Tenn., on the 7th inst., by Rev. J. L. **CHAPMAN**, James **McCONNELL**, Esq., of this city, to Mrs. Catharine M. **FIELD**, of Haywood county. Memphis Appeal, 12/15/1852.

Died, In this city, (of yellow fever,) on the 8th instant, Mr. James **McCOOL**, aged about thirty years. The deceased was a bricklayer by trade and supposed to have relatives in New York. New York and Brooklyn papers please copy. Memphis Daily Appeal, 10/13/1855.

Married, On Wednesday morning, 10th instant, at the residence of the bride's father, by Rev. H. **WALSH**, Mr. Joseph M. **McCORKLE** to Miss Jennie, daughter of A. R. **HUTCHENSON**, all of DeSoto county, Miss. Memphis Weekly Appeal, 3/24/1858.

Died in this place, on the 20th inst. after a short illness of bilious spasmodic cholic, Frederic A. **McCOULL**, in the 18th year of his age. He was a native of Virginia, and had resided but a few months in our town. He was universally esteemed, and died much lamented. Memphis Enquirer, 7/29/1837.

Dr. J. M. **McCOULL**, Tenders his professional services to the citizens of Memphis and its vicinity. Memphis Enquirer, 1/7/1837.

Died: On the evening of the 14th instant, Mrs. Mary Ann, late consort of Mr. J. W. **McCRACKEN**. The friends and acquaintances of Mr. J. W. McCracken are respectfully invited to attend the funeral of his wife, Mrs. Mary Ann McCracken from his residence in Moseley's Avenue. Memphis Whig, 8/15/1855.

Married, On the 24th of November, near Flewellen's __ Roads, DeSoto county, Miss., by Rev. Wm. Carey **CRANE**, Mr. David J. **McCRAKEN** to Miss Martha L. Wolf, eldest daughter of Mr. James **WOLF**, all of DeSoto county. Memphis Daily Appeal, 12/1/1857.

Died. On the 16th February, at the Covington Hotel, of Pneumonia, William **McCRAW**, in the 27th year of his age. He was a native of East Tennessee, having been a resident of Covington for several years past, leaves many relatives and friends to lament their deplorable loss…as a friend he was kind and true, as a brother warm and affectionate, as a son devoted and obedient, as a Free-Mason he was of high order and good standing, as a Son of Temperance he was ever true to the pledge. Memphis Daily Appeal, 3/11/1851.

Chickasaw Lodge, No. 8, I.O.O.F. Memphis, May 10, 1852. Whereas, It has pleased an all wise Providence to remove from time to eternity, in the prime of life, our beloved brother, Alexander **McCREADY**, who died at Steubenville, Ohio, on the 18th of April, 1852, with Consumption …Memphis Eagle & Enquirer, 5/21/1852.

Married, On Tuesday evening, the 4th inst., at the residence of Mrs. Howard, by Rev. Mr. Philip **TUGGLE**, Mr. M. **McCULL_H**, formerly of Columbus, Ohio, to Mrs. Mary Jane **HOWARD**, of this city. Memphis Daily Appeal, 8/5/1857.

A recontre took place on Sunday last at the livery stable of Mr. John **EDGAR**, in which Mr. Thomas **McCULLY** met his death at the hands of Edgar. Deceased received three wounds from a knife, and expired almost immediately. As the matter is undergoing judicial investigation we forbear comment. Mr. McCully was a member of the Sons of Temperance, by which fraternity his remains were buried on Sunday afternoon. Memphis Enquirer, Tues., 6/27/1848. (Author's note: In another article the name was given as **McCULLA**.)

On yesterday afternoon the steamer *J. M. Convers* touched at our landing and left a man in a dying state, in charge of a negro drayman, who received orders to convey him to the Hospital. On the way, the dying man called for water, which was furnished him by the driver, and the dray proceeded on its way to the Hospital. Arrived at the gate of that building, the negro was horror-struck to find that on his dray was a corpse….Coroner Waldran held an inquest upon the body and a verdict was returned that deceased, whose name, from a paper on his person, is believed to be Cornelius **McCURE**, came to his death from a disease supposed to be diarrhea….It was presumed that Mr. McCure had been employed on the boat at one time as a deck hand…. Deceased was about thirty-five years of age. Memphis Daily Appeal, 10/11/1856.

Married, On the 11th instant by Thomas T. **RIVES**, Esq., at the residence of the bride's father, Mr. _. A. **McDANIEL**, of Corinth, to Miss Ellen V. **HARDIN**, of Saulsbury, Tenn. Memphis Weekly Appeal, 5/26/1858.

Married, On Wednesday the 28th ult., by the Rev. D. K. **CRENSHAW**, Dr. A. C. **McDONALD** to Miss Mary Ann **SHELTON**, all of this County. Memphis Eagle & Enquirer, 5/2/1852.

We learn that Mr. Edward **McDONALD**, living in the upper end of town, was shot and seriously wounded, by Ransom **ELLIOTT**, on Wednesday night. The wound is not considered mortal. Elliott was examined before Esq. Rose, and committed for trial. Memphis Enquirer, 8/25/1848.

The friends and acquaintances of Mr. and Mrs. J. R. **McDONALD** are invited to attend the funeral of their little son, Willie, from their residence on Alabama street this afternoon at 4 o'clock. Memphis Daily Appeal, 3/25/1857.

A very sudden death occurred at the rooms of the City Dispensary....Yesterday. A laborer, whose name was James **McDONALD**, applied to the attending physician for treatment, but, before he received attention, the patient fell upon the floor and died. Esquire Horne held an inquest upon the body yesterday morning and the verdict of the jury was that the deceased had died from natural causes. Memphis Daily Appeal, 7/2/1859.

Died, At the residence of Dr. J. J. **TODD**, eight miles east of Memphis, on the morning of the 15th of August, Andrew **McDOWELL**, aged 42 years. New York Herald and Day Book please copy. Memphis Daily Appeal, 8/19/1857.

Married, At Fort Pickering, on the 11th inst., by Jesse **WALDRAN**, Esq., Matthew **McDOWELL** to Miss Sarah E. **LOW**, all of Fort Pickering. Memphis Eagle & Enquirer, 3/16/1852.

Married, On the 18th instant by Rev. Wm. Carey **CRANE**, Mr. Thomas J. **McDOWELL**(?), of Dallas county, Texas, to Miss Mary P. **HUGHES**, of Marshall county, Miss. Memphis Weekly Appeal, 3/24/1858.

The Subscribers Academy will open the 4th of September at the school house, Washington Street. By request, evening classes, in all the branches of an English, Classic 1, and Mercantile education, including book keeping by double entry, will be formed at the same time...J. A. **McEVOY**. Memphis Daily Appeal, 8/15/1848.

The friends and acquaintances of the late Mr. Alex. **McELHERAN** are respectfully invited to attend his funeral this evening....Services....at the Second Presbyterian Church. Memphis Daily Appeal, 7/10/1859.

Married, On the evening of July 25th at the residence of the bride's father, by Rev. J. W. **KNOTT**, Mr. T. B. **McEWEN** to Miss Annie M. **OWEN**, all of this city. Memphis Daily Appeal, 7/29/1857.

The Rev. J. W. **McFARLAND**, Pastor of the Second Methodist Church of this city, departed this life on Monday last. His disease was typhoid fever....Mr. McFarland formerly resided in Gibson county, in this State, where his remains are to be taken. Memphis Appeal, 7/19/1854.

Married, At the residence of the bride's mother in Florence, Ala., by George W. **SNEED**, Esq., Mr. John H. **McFERRIN**, of North Mount Pleasant, Miss., to Miss Elizabeth S. **ARMS**, of Florence, Ala. Mobile Register copy. Memphis Daily Appeal, 11/15/1859.

Married, In Columbus, on Tuesday evening, the 5th instant, by Rev. James A. **LYON**, Edward J. **McGAVOCK**, Esq., of Nashville, Tenn., and Miss Ella W., daughter of Col. A. F. **YOUNG**, of Columbus, Miss. Memphis Daily Appeal, 5/12/1857.

Petition for Divorce. Mary Ann McGee, vs. James **McGEE**. In the Circuit Court of Shelby County, Tennessee, at Raleigh. It appearing to the satisfaction of the Clerk, from the Petition of the complainant in this behalf filed, duly sworn to, that the defendant, James McGee, is a non-resident of the State of Tennessee; it is ordered that publication be made in the Memphis Weekly Appeal for thirty days, requiring said defendant, James McGee, to appear at the next term of the Circuit Court of Shelby county, Tennessee, to be held at the Court House in the town of Raleigh, on the third Monday in September next....Memphis Daily Appeal, 7/21/1858.

Philip **McGEE** who boarded at Mrs. Ross' in the Navy Yard, went home Sunday evening in a drunken condition and was very troublesome and annoying to the inmates of the house. This conduct was tolerated, however, until yesterday morning, when he was ejected by one James **DOGHER**, Mrs. Ross' brother. After he was thrust out, McGee proceeded a few yards and fell dead. Esquire Horne held an inquest upon the body yesterday and the jury rendered a verdict that the deceased had died of violence at the hands of some one unknown to them. Memphis Daily Appeal, Tues., 8/9/1859.

Married. At the residence of Augustus **FESMIRE**, Lafayette county, Miss., on the 30th day of November last by Rev. J. W. **PENDER**, R. G. **McGEE**, Esq., to Mrs. Martha **BLOODWORTH**, both of Lafayette county. Raleigh, N.C. Standard please copy. Memphis Daily Appeal, 12/13/1854.

Report of the Board of Health, For the last 48 hours to 12 o'clock, M., July 23. Child of Mr. Thos. **McGEE**, aged 11 months. Bowel Affection. Child of Mr. John **NEWBOLE**, aged 16 months. Bowel Affection ...Memphis Enquirer, 7/24/1849.

The friends and acquaintances of E. **McGEHEE** are respectfully invited to attend the funeral of his infant son, Edward, at 4 ½ o'clock P.M. this day, from his residence. Divine services by Rev. T. A. **WARE**. Memphis Daily Appeal, 7/20/1856.

Died, At his residence in Panola county, Miss., on the 25th ult., Hugh **McGEHEE**, Esq., an old and highly esteemed citizen of that county. Mr. McGehee was, we believe, a native of Georgia, and was a brother of the late Abner **McGEHEE**, the well-known philanthropist of South Alabama. Memphis Daily Appeal, 8/1/1855.

Married, On Thursday evening, the 14th inst., at the residence of John **TRIGG**, Esq., in this vicinity, by the Rev. Geo. W. **COONS**, Mr. J. O. **McGEHEE** to Miss Racheal C. **TRIGG**, all of Jackson, Tenn. Memphis Eagle, 2/16/1850.

Died. In this city on the 12th inst., Henderson **McGOWN**, of Batesville, Ark., formerly of Middle Tennessee, aged about thirty years. Memphis Daily Appeal, 7/16/1854.

The friends and acquaintances of Mr. John **McGRATH** are respectfully invited to attend the funeral of his infant daughter, This Evening at 4 o'clock from his residence on the corner of Winchester and Third streets. Memphis Daily Appeal, 6/3/1858.

Died, On the 8th of July last, at Fall River, Massachusetts, John **McGRAW**, in the 30th year of his age. The deceased resided for a number of years in Memphis....Memphis Daily Appeal, 9/12/1856.

Married, On the 1st instant by Rev. E. Darwin **ISBELL**, Mr. Thomas **McGUIRE** to Miss Phebe **STODDARD**, all of this city. Memphis Eagle & Enquirer, 5/4/1853.

On a flat boat at the river about 10 o'clock yesterday morning, two men named Michael C. **GAUNTLY** and Henry **McGUYER** got into a quarrel which led to a fight; during the struggle Gauntly seized a saw and struck McGuyer with it, so that he fell into the water. He contrived however to catch hold of the side of the boat, but Gauntly continued to assail him until he sunk into the river to rise no more. Gauntly was taken into custody. Memphis Daily Appeal, 11/3/1857.

Died, In this city, on the 7th inst., Mr. James **McINTERFER**, aged 30 years. Illinois and Michigan papers please copy. Memphis Eagle, 1/11/1850.

James Torry on yesterday killed J. **McKANNA**, in the office of Esq. Rose, by shooting him through the body. We learn that a case was under examination before Esq. Rose, and Torry was a witness. McKanna was introduced to discredit Torry. After each had been examined, a few words passed between them, when McK. struck T. two or three blows with a stick, upon which Torry drew a pistol and shot McKanna through the body, which caused his death in 15 minutes. At the time of writing this paragraph Torry is under examination before the proper Court, and we will say nothing to prejudice the case. Memphis Enquirer, 5/31/1849. James **TORREY** has been held to bail by the examining Court, to appear and attend his trial at the next Circuit Court, for the shooting of James McKanna.....The remains of Mr. McKanna were interred yesterday evening, and were attended to their last resting place by a large procession, consisting of the Fire

Company, of which he was a member, and a large concourse of citizens. It is altogether a sad affair. Memphis Enquirer, 6/1/1849. (Author's note: Name given as **McKINNEY** in another newspaper.)

Died—In this vicinity on the 23d ult., Alexander, son of Mr. A. A. **McKAY**, in the third year of his age. The Appeal, 1/5/1844. Died, at the residence of his parents, near Memphis, on the 18th inst., William Thomas, infant son of Mr. A. McKay, aged 10 months and 5 days. American Eagle, 7/3/1846.

Married, On the 25th instant at the residence of the bride's father, Col. Allen A. **PITTMAN**, in Prairie county, by Rev. J. W. **MOORE**, Mr. John _. **McKAY** to Miss Mollie B. **PITTMAN**. Memphis Weekly Appeal, 4/14/1858.

Death of James R. **McKEE**—We are advised by letter of the death of J. R. McKee, in Belmont county, Ohio. The deceased had been engaged as a compositor on the *Bulletin* of this city for several years....it was feared by his many friends that he would not survive to reach his home, but consumption, that "plague of the printer," allowed him the respite of a few weeks, and he died under his father's roof, surrounded by his first and firmest friends. Memphis Daily Appeal, 7/22/1859.

Died—On Sunday evening the 18th instant, at the residence of his brother, William, of pulmonary consumption, Nicholas **McKEON**, Jr., aged 24 years – youngest son of Nicholas **McKEON**, of Street county, Westmeath, Ireland. His remains were taken to the Catholic Church......American Eagle, 6/23/1843.

Died, In this city, on the 22d inst., P. **McKEON**, in the 31st year of his age. The deceased was a native of Street Parish of Street County Westmeath, Ireland; and for the last eight years a resident of Memphis. Memphis, 2/24th. Memphis Enquirer, 2/26/1846.

Married—On Thursday, 24th inst., by Rev. Mr. Allimane, Mr. Thos. **McKEON**, to Miss Mary **HUGHES**, all of this city. Memphis Enquirer, 9/26/1846. On yesterday afternoon about four o'clock, Joseph McKeon, son of Thomas McKeon, was thrown from a horse on Third street near Exchange. He is about six years of age.... Memphis Daily Appeal, 11/14/1856. The young son of Mr. McKeon....died between four and five o'clock last evening. The friends and acquaintances of Thomas and Mary McKeon are requested to attend the funeral of their son, Joseph P. McKeon, from their residence on Poplar street, between Second and Third....Memphis Daily Appeal, 11/15/1856.

Died, At the residence of Mr. Wm. **McKEON**, his son, Michael B. McKeon, age 8 years, 3 months. Memphis Daily Appeal, 11/2/1856. Died, On Saturday, 1st instant, Michael B., son of William and Margaret McKeon, aged eight years and three months. Little "Miky," as he was familiarly called, was afflicted from infancy with a torturing disease and at times suffered most excruciating pain. During one of these spells of intense suffering he breathed his last, after an illness of only a few hours....Memphis Daily Appeal, 11/6/1856.

Married—On Monday evening last in this city, by the Rev. P. W. **ALSTON** Mr. Joseph **McKIBBIN** of Memphis, to Miss Anna Maria, daughter of George M. **CROCKETT** of Gallatin, Tenn. The Appeal, Fri., 6/14/1844.

B. F. **McKIERNAN**, Attorney at Law, Will practice in the Circuit and County Courts of Shelby and the adjoining counties; and also in the Supreme and Chancery courts at Jackson. Office on Exchange street. The Appeal, 9/15/1843. Criminal Court. The fall term of this court, the Hon. B. F. McKiernan presiding....Memphis Daily Appeal, 10/8/1857.

Married. By the Rev. H. M. **KERR**, in Purdy, Tenn., on the 6th inst., Jas. F. **McKINNEY**, attorney at law, to Miss Julia A. Adams, daughter of B. B. **ADAMS**. Memphis Daily Eagle, 1/18/1848.

Died, Near Saulsbury, Tenn., December 3d, of Pneumonia, Mrs. Mary Eliza, wife of Mr. John R. **McKINNIE**(?). Memphis Weekly Appeal, 12/15/1858.

Married, On the 16th inst. by Rev. Jno. **WILSON**, Mr. William **McKINSTRY**, Jr., of Fayette county, Tenn., to Miss Eliza **DAVIS**, of Tipton county, Tenn. Memphis Weekly Appeal, 12/29/1858.

Died. In the vicinity of Dyersburg on the 23d of June, of Congestive Chill, Mr. James **McKNIGHT**, aged 60 years. The deceased was a native of Laurens district, S. C., whence he emigrated to West Tenn. 27 years ago, where he has ever since resided....Memphis Appeal, 7/8/1853.

The telegraph has announced the death of Logan **McKNIGHT**, at New Orleans, who died suddenly on Monday of disease of the heart. He was the eldest son of Virgil **McKNIGHT**, Esq., of Louisville, and was the agent of the Bank of Kentucky in New Orleans....The deceased was the brother of M. **McKNIGHT**, Esq., of the firm of Gates, Wood & McKnight, of this city. Memphis Daily Appeal, Fri., 4/8/1859. The remains of the late Logan McKnight, Esq....were on board the steamer *Eclipse* yesterday. They are to be taken to Louisville for interment. Memphis Daily Appeal, 4/10/1859.

Died, yesterday morning of scarlet fever, after three weeks of intense suffering, Margaret McKnight, aged about nine years, youngest daughter of Mrs. Mary **McKNIGHT**, of this city. Memphis Daily Appeal, 6/22/1856.

Died—On the 4th inst., at the residence of A. B. **SHAW**, Mrs. Elleanor **McLAIN**, with consumption, aged 43 years. Memphis Appeal, 10/7/1848.

Died. At the residence of her father at 10 o'clock last evening, Elizabeth, daughter of G. **McLEAN**, aged 6 years, 2 months. Friends and acquaintances are invited to attend her funeral at her father's house on the Raleigh road this evening. St. Louis papers please copy. Memphis Appeal, 7/22/1854.

The following are all the deaths for the week ending May 30th: George **McLEAN**, aged 45, Cholera.....Memphis Daily Eagle, 5/31/1849.

Died—In this town, on the morning of the 2d inst., at the residence of Mr. F. S. **LATHAM**, after two days sickness of the Congestive Fever, Calvin Rush, son of James A. **McLEARY**, of Randolph, in the 15th year of his age. Memphis Enquirer, 12/6/1839.

Our friend, Andrew J. **McLEMORE**, of San Francisco, California, is now on a visit to his old friends and relatives in this city....Memphis Daily Appeal, 4/1/1857.

Married, At the residence of S. B. **MALONE**, Columbus, Miss., by the Rev. E. P. **NEALY**, Mr. John C. **McLEMORE**, Jr., of Memphis, Tenn., to Miss Mary Louise, daughter of the late Dr. **NELSON**. Memphis Appeal, 7/28/1851. Died. On Saturday evening last at the residence of her husband, Mrs. Mary L., wife of John C. McLemore, Jr., near Colliersville in this county. Memphis Daily Appeal, 1/23/1854.

By Virtue of Decree of the Circuit Court of Shelby coun., Tennessee, at January Term, 1856, upon the ex-parte petition of U. T. **McLEMORE**, et. al., heirs of Joel **McLEMORE**, deceased, I will proceed to sell at auction, in front of the Court-House door in Raleigh, on the 7th Day of April Next, 1150 acres of valuable land, lying at the junction of Big Creek and Loosa Hatchie river, known as the McLemore plantation....Rob't. L. **SMITH**, Clerk. Memphis Daily Appeal, 2/28/1856.

Died—In this city, on the 3d inst., of Consumption, Mr. Norman **McLEOD**, of Arkansas. The Appeal, 12/13/1844.

The friends and acquaintances of Col. J. H. and Caroline R. **McMAHAN** are respectfully notified that the funeral of their son, Francisco De Moreton(?) will take place from their residence on Vance street, near Shelby, This Friday Morning at 9 o'clock. Service by Rev. T. L. **GRACE**, at the Catholic Church. Memphis Daily Appeal, Fri., 7/1/1853.

187

A laborer named Michael **McMAHAN** was accidentally killed yesterday, while working under the bluff below Shaw's wharf boat, by a portion of the bank falling on him…Memphis Eagle & Enquirer, 3/28/1852.

J. H. **McMAHON** is a candidate for Clerk of the Circuit and Commercial Courts of Shelby County, at the next March election. Daily Enquirer, 11/5/1847.

On Friday last, a man named John **McMAHON** died very suddenly, in the upper part of the city, and was buried within two hours after his death. Suspicion having arisen as to the cause of his death, and reports having gone abroad that he had been foully dealt with, his remains were exhumed on Saturday last and an investigation had. Although several marks were found upon his face and head, it is supposed they were occasioned by falls. There was no doubt, we understand, that he froze to death….Memphis Daily Appeal, 1/13/1857.

Return of John C. **McMAHON** from Nicaragua.—This gentleman, a son of the Rev. W. H. **McMAHON** of DeSoto county, Miss., passed through this city on Friday last on his return home from his expedition to Nicaragua….Memphis Daily Appeal, 8/3/1856.

An affray occurred Tuesday night at the residence of James **ROARKES**, eight miles from the city, between Mr. Roarke and Philip **McMANUS**. Mr. Roarke was insulted by McManus, whereupon Roarke assaulted McManus with his fist. McManus resented the assault and drew a knife, which Mr. Roarke wrenched from his hand, turning upon him and inflicting two or three fatal wounds, from which he died immediately….Memphis Daily Appeal, Thurs., 10/13/1859.

Died. At the residence of his son, near Kossuth, Miss., on the 5th inst., Col. A. **McMILLAN**, formerly a highly respectable citizen of Lawrence county, Ala. Memphis and Nashville papers please copy. Memphis Daily Appeal, 6/8/1856.

Married, On the 16th inst., by J. **WALDRAN**, Esq., Alexander **McMILLAN** and Ann **HIGGINS**—all of this city. Memphis Eagle & Enquirer, 1/18/1852.

James **McMILLAN** was yesterday morning severely wounded by Isaac **BOLTEN**, at the slave depot of Bolton & Co., with pistol shots. Bolton shot four times at McMillan, wounding him twice….The difficulty arose out of the sale of a free negro, whom Bolton alleges McMillan sold to him for a slave….P.S.—Since writing the above article we learn that Mr. McMillan has died from the effects of his wounds. Memphis Daily Appeal, 5/24/1857.

Died. On Sunday morning the 6th of August at the residence of her daughter, Mrs. Sarah **TRIGG**, in this vicinity—Mrs. Jane **McMILLAN**, in the 69th year of her age. Memphis Appeal, 8/9/1854.

The Mayor was authorized to pay the balances due J. B. **McMURRY**, late a policeman, to those who buried him. Memphis Daily Appeal, 10/17/1855.

Married, In this city on the 22d inst., by Rev. T. L. **GRACE**, Mr. John **McNALLY**, of Pine Bluff, Ark., to Miss Mary **FLAHERTY**, of Memphis. Memphis Weekly Appeal, 4/28/1858.

The friends and acquaintances of John **McNAMARA** are respectfully invited to attend the funeral of his wife This Evening at 4 o'clock, from his residence on Market street. Memphis Daily Appeal, 8/26/1858.

Died, On Sunday night last, John **McNAMARA**, aged thirty-two years. Mr. McNamara was the cashier of the house of Apperson & Co….He has left three children orphans. Memphis Daily Appeal, Thurs., 3/31/1859. Notice, As the guardian of the children of John McNamara, dec'd., I will lease for a term of years the vacant lot on Market street, fronting the lot on which Frazer **TITUS** lives. I will also rent by the year, the house in which said McNamara lived at the time of his death, adjoining the above….Daniel **McNAMARA**, Guardian. Memphis Daily Appeal, 8/21/1859.

Married, On Thursday evening, at St. Peter's Church, by Rev. Mr. **GAWGLAUGH**, Mr. Michael **McNAMARA** to Miss Maggie I. **McNAMARA**, all of this city. Memphis Daily Appeal, 5/14/1859.

Died—At his residence in Coffeeville, Mississippi, on Tuesday, the 3d inst., Albert T. **McNEAL**, Esqr., attorney at law. In the death of this amiable and excellent man…the community in which he lived have to mourn the loss of one of their most valuable citizens—an affectionate wife and child, a beloved husband and father. The deceased was a native of Maury county, Tenn., but resided from early youth to manhood in Bolivar; he graduated in the year 1832, at Cumberland College, Nashville, with the first honours of his class, and commenced the practice of law at Coffeeville, in the year 1834 where he resided until his death…His body was, at his request, conveyed to Bolivar and there intered, according to the rites of the Protestant Episcopal Church …The Appeal, 9/20/1844.

Died—In Bolivar, at the residence of her father on Sunday evening the 16th inst., Priscilla, only child of Maj. E. P. and Anna **McNEAL**, after a protracted illness of nine weeks. The deceased was a member of the Episcopal Church….Memphis Daily Appeal, 7/22/1854.

Died, at her residence in Bolivar, Ten., on the 8th inst., Mrs. Clarissa McNeal, aged 64 years. Mrs. McNeal was the relict of the late Capt. Thomas **McNEAL**, who was one of the first settlers of Hardeman county…Whether as a wife, mother or neighbor, she was all the fondest affection could have wished her to be…Weekly Appeal, 12/11/1846.

Married. At Fisherville, Tenn., on the 11th(?) instant by Dr. H.(?) B. **RAMSEY**, J. B. **McNEELY** to Mrs. Margaret **McNEELY**, all of Shelby county, Tenn. Memphis Daily Appeal, 1/16/1855.

Married. On the 17th inst. in this city by Rev. Dr. Porter, Mr. J. H. **McNEIL** to Miss A. P. **SLEDGE**. Raleigh, N.C. and Huntsville, Ala. papers please copy. Memphis Daily Appeal, 4/20/1855.

Gainesville Lodge No. 75 was convened on Monday night, April 7th, A.L. 5856, for the purpose of attending to the burial of Brother John **McNEIL**, who requested before his death, to be buried with Masonic Honors….At Oak Bluff, Green county, Arkansas, on the 7th day of April, A.D. 1856, Brother John McNeil died, in the 34th year of his age, a worthy member of our Lodge. Brother McNeil was the son of George and Nancy **McNEIL**, of Claiborne county, Tenn….He died of Consumption….Memphis Daily Appeal, 4/25/1856.

Died—On the 4th instant, on board the steamer P. H. White, Mr. A. G. **McNEILL**, aged about 25 years, son of Mr. George B. **McNEILL**, of Arkansas. He is supposed to have died of Cholera, or something resembling that disease. He was buried about 150 miles above Little Rock…..He has left many relations and friends to lament his early death. Daily Memphis Enquirer, 4/22/1849.

Died, at his residence near LaGrange, Fayette county, July 4th, Alexander **McNEILL**, in the 63rd year of his age. Mr. McNeill was a native of Moore county, North Carolina, which he represented in the House of Representatives of the Legislature for several years. He emigrated to Fayette county in 1834 and has constantly devoted himself to the pursuit of agriculture since his removal to Tennessee….As a neighbor and friend, husband and father, he has proved himself equal to all the ____ which devolved upon him….Fayetteville *North Carolinian* and *Observer* please copy. Memphis Daily Appeal, 7/8/1857.

We regret to record the death of Mr. Danl. **McNEILL**, an old resident of Marshall county, Miss. The sad event occurred recently at the plantation of the deceased in Louisiana….Memphis Daily Appeal, 10/11/1859.

Married, On the 21st instant at the residence of H.(?) **VAN PELT**, Memphis, by Rev. J. H. **GRAY**, D.D., Mr. J. H. **McNEILL**, of Louisiana, to Miss Minerva **ARMSTRONG**, of this place. Memphis Daily Appeal, 7/22/1859.

I offer for sale the plantation whereon I now live, containing 320 acres…. comfortable Dwelling House, with brick chimnies, 2 shops, Negro houses, Gin, Cotton Press and Mill…situated 14 miles South-East of

Memphis, Shelby county, Tenn. and ¼ (?) of a mile from the Mississippi State Line. Phillip **McNEILL**. Memphis Weekly Eagle, 1/25/1849.

Died. At the residence of her husband, near Memphis, on the 20th inst. Mrs. Frances McNutt, consort of the Rev. A. G. **McNUTT**, in the 32d year of her age.....American Eagle, 7/3/1846. Died. In Elbridge, Illinois, on the 9th inst., Rev. A. G. McNutt, recently of this vicinity. Weekly American Eagle, 6/3/1847.

Departed this life, on Sunday evening last, of pulmonary consumption, David M. **McPHERSON**, aged 33 years. The deceased was a native of Pennsylvania, but for several years a resident of the Western District of Tennessee.....His remains were conducted to the Episcopal Church.... American Eagle, Fri., 7/14/1843.

We learn that on Monday evening last, Mr. Thomas **McPHERSON**, of DeSoto county, Miss., was shot and killed by Mr. Morrison **FUTRELL**, of the same county. Both parties lived near Tatesville, and were of respectable family. Futrell, we learn, fled immediately and had not been apprehended at last accounts. Memphis Daily Appeal, Thurs., 10/18/1855.

Married, In LaGrange on the 24th ult. by Rev. D. C. **WELLS**, Mr. John **McQUIRK**, of Holly Springs, to Miss S. A. **MAHAFFY**. Memphis Eagle & Enquirer, 6/3/1853.

Married, On the 26th of October by Rev. Mr. Metcalf, Mr. A. J. **McQUISTON**, A.M., of Drew county, Ark., (late of Tipton county, Tenn.,) to Miss Mary, daughter of J. W. **McKINSTRY**, of Lafayette county, Tenn. Memphis Weekly Appeal, 12/8/1858.

It is with sincere regret that we notice in the Matamoros Flag of the 22d ult. the death of Maj. C. C. **McRAE**, the father of a worthy and estimable citizen of Memphis. The Flag says: "We attended last evening the funeral of Major Charles C. McRae, aged about 70, a native of the parish of East Feliciana, La., but for the last 25 years a resident of Mexico. The deceased came to this city in June last, from Chihuahua, where he has resided for many years. In his illness he was watched by kind and sympathizing friends, and although cut off by death in a city where he was an apparent stranger, a large procession of our citizens followed him to the grave. He has several children residing in his native parish in Louisiana, and one son residing in Memphis, Tenn., to whom the intelligence of his death will be sorrowful tidings. We ask the New Orleans and Memphis papers to be the herald of the mournful news." Daily Enquirer, 10/7/1847.

Married Last evening, at the residence of Dr. K. P. **WATSON**, by the Rev. Dr. Gray, Mr. W. B. **McREE** of Covington, Tenn., and Miss Sophronia A. **WEAVER**, of this place. Memphis Daily Eagle, 10/11/1850.

We call attention to the advertisement of Mr. John A. **McROBERTS**, who proposes to teach youth in this city. He has long experience in his profession and bears a high reputation.... Memphis Eagle, 12/20/1850.

Married. On Saturday, March 10th by J. **WALDRAN**, Esq., Jas. A. **MEADER** Esq., to Miss Almira L. **KINGSBURY**, all of this city. Memphis Appeal, 3/14/1855.

Maj. H. H. **MEANS**, formerly an old resident of this city, has just returned from California, looking in good health. Memphis Eagle & Enquirer, 6/25/1852.

We regret to learn that Mr. J. P. **MEANS**, a venerable and well-known citizen of Shelby county, who lived about three miles East of Raleigh, lost his life yesterday morning by injuries sustained by the fall of a tree near his residence. The deceased survived his injuries but about two hours. He was about seventy-five years of age, and was an old citizen of the county. Memphis Daily Avalanche, 3/22/1859.

Died. In Prairie Co., Ark., Mr. Jas. H. **MEANS**, of consumption, aged 29 years. Mr. Means was formerly an estimable citizen of our city and was one of the firm of J. H. Means & co. He married the daughter of our old and much beloved citizen, Dr. W. G. **GRANT** and has left an affectionate wife and child to mourn his loss. His remains were brought to our city for interment. Memphis Daily Appeal, 4/5/1855.

Married—In this city, on Thursday evening the 15th inst., by the Rev. Geo. W. **COONS**, Dr. John H. **MEANS** to Miss Sarah Ann, daughter of Prof. Geo. R. **GRANT**. Daily Enquirer, 4/17/1847.

Married, In Somerville, Ten. on the 11th inst., Mr. Thos. M. **MEANS**, of Memphis, to Miss Ann E. **BOLEY**, of Somerville. Memphis Daily Appeal, 10/21/1853.

Departed this life on the 3d inst. Mary Moore, daughter of Thos. Moore **MEANS**, aged two years, one month, and twenty two days….Memphis Enquirer, 9/5/1846.

Died. On the 9th inst. in this city, Mrs. Rachel Means, wife of Maj. W. B. **MEANS**. The subject of this notice had been for many years a pious and consistent member of the Presbyterian church, and when she died was a communicant in the 1st Presbyterian church in this city. She together with her husband emigrated some years since from South Carolina to this state. At the time of her death she had been a resident of this city about one year…all the duties which devolved upon her as a church member, a friend, a wife and a mother…Weekly American Eagle, 10/15/1846.

Married.—On last evening, by the Rev. Mr. Coons, Wm. **MEANS**, Esq., to Mrs. **PHOEBUS**, all of this city. Memphis Appeal, 10/29/1847.

Died, In Macon, Tenn., on Wednesday, the 28th ultimo, Nannie, daughter of John H. **MEBANE**, of Fayette county, Tenn., aged 13 years. Memphis Weekly Appeal, 5/26/1858.

Law Side of the Common Law and Chancery Court of the City of Memphis. A. W. **MEEK**, vs. Elizabeth T. **MEEK**. Petition for Divorce. In this cause it appearing by complainant's bill, duly sworn to, that Elizabeth T. Meek is a non-resident of the State of Tennessee. It is therefore ordered that publication for four successive weeks be made in the Memphis Daily Appeal….requiring said defendant to appear at the July term of this Court, commencing the 1st Monday of July, 1858, and answer, plead or demur to plaintiff's petition, or the same will be taken for confessed, and set for hearing *ex-parte*. Memphis Daily Appeal, 6/2/1858. Married, On Monday, August 2d, at the office of J. **WALDRAN**, Esq., by that gentleman, Mr. A. W. Meek and Miss Elizabeth **HERDSTER**, all of this city. Memphis Daily Appeal, 8/3/1858.

A difficulty occurred yesterday between Mr. J. P. **MERCER**, Engineer of the Memphis and Ohio Railroad, and Joe **ABLE**, which resulted in the use of pistols and seriously wounding the former. They were in the Empire House at the time of the occurrence and had been discussing a matter connected with railroad matters, when words were multiplied until they both simultaneously arose and drew pistols. Mercer had a small revolver and fired and missed; Able returned the fire with a large repeater; took a position behind the door and fired twice and missed. Mercer at the same time was advancing upon him, and before the third fire of Able's, he had neared him sufficiently to strike the back of Able's head with his pistol while in a bending position. Able then fired his third ball, which entered Mercer's left side just below the lower rib, glancing round his intestines and was taken out near the spine….Memphis Daily Appeal, 9/1/1855. J. P. Mercer, whom we noticed yesterday morning as being shot by Joe Able, was reported in a very critical condition last evening….His wife, who is a beautiful and intelligent woman, came in the cars yesterday evening to attend him. We learn, since writing the above, that Mr. M. died about half past 11 o'clock last night. Memphis Daily Appeal, 9/2/1855. We were in error yesterday in stating that Mr. Mercer….was an engineer on the Memphis and Ohio railroad. We should have said *contractor* and not engineer. Memphis Daily Appeal, 9/3/1855.

Cigars, 20,000 No. 1 Regalia Cigars, just received per steamer Missouri, and for sale cheap by H. B. & C. B. **MEREDITH**. Memphis Daily Appeal, 2/23/1848.

On Monday, the 28th of September at Macon, Tenn., Mrs. Millie __. Meredith, consort of J. D. **MEREDITH**, was taken from earth to Heaven, after an illness of forty-eight hours. Aged, 20 years. Farmville and Richmond papers please copy. Memphis Daily Appeal, 10/8/1857. Married, On Tuesday morning, 3d inst., by Rev. R. C. **GRUNDY**, D.D., at the residence of the bride's father, near Somerville, Tenn., J. D. Meredith, Principal of the Macon Collegiate Institute, to Miss Mary, eldest daughter of Levy

KETCHUM, Esq. Memphis Daily Appeal, 8/5/1858. Died, April 27th, Mittie Marion, only child of Prof. J. _. **MEREDITH**, of Macon, Tenn., and the late Mittie R. **LEWIS**(?), of King and Queen, Va. Memphis Weekly Appeal, 5/5/1858.

Married, On the 3d inst. by Rev. N. **SULLIVAN**, Mr. F. A. **MERIWETHER**, of Madison county, Tenn., to Miss E. A. **HARDY**, of Fayette county, Tenn. Memphis Eagle & Enquirer, 3/18/1853.

Married. On Wednesday, August the 22d by Rev. Dr. Gray, Mr. Chas. G. **MERRIMAN** and Miss Martha L. **WHITE**....Memphis Daily Appeal, 8/23/1855.

Married—In New Haven, Conn., Oct. 4th, J. E. **MERRIMAN**, of the firm of Merriman & Clark, Memphis, to Miss Emeline S. **WILCOX**, of the former place. American Eagle, 10/20/1843. Died, On Saturday 3rd inst., Edward, son of James E. and Emeline S. Merriman, aged 10 months. American Eagle Weekly, 5/9/1845. James E. Merriman, Watch-Maker, (From Wall Street, New York) North Side of Exchange Square, Memphis, Tenn. American Eagle, 2/7/1842.

Married, On the 10th inst., by Rev. German **BAKER**, Mr. C. S. **MERRIWETHER** to Mrs. Louisa A. **BANKS**, at the residence of the latter, in DeSoto county, Mississippi, near Hernando. Memphis Daily Appeal, 11/12/1857.

Trial of Wm. **PETERSON** for Murder. Few persons in this section of the country will fail to recall, on reading the above name, the vague details given at the time of one of the most cold-blooded and frightful murders ever perpetrated. The indictment charges William Peterson with the willful murder of Thomas **MERRIWETHER**, on the 25th of May, 1851...The prisoner was brought into court, and pled not guilty to the following indictment, which was read...He is quite a youth—not apparently exceeding twenty years of age...At times, especially when the beautiful and evidently lady-like widow of the deceased came into court to testify to the clothes found on the body...Memphis Daily Appeal, 5/24/1852.

Married, in this city, last evening, by the Rev. Dr. Page, Capt. R. Sidney **GOUGH**, of New York, to Miss Maria **MERRYWEATHER**, of Memphis. Daily Enquirer, 9/3/1847.

We are authorized to announce Jefferson **MESSICK** Esq., a candidate for the office of Register of Shelby County. American Eagle, 10/6/1843.

Our old friend, Jo. **METCALF**, late of Louisville, has settled himself permanently amongst us, as will be seen by reference to his card and will be pleased to serve his friends and the public at large with his most excellent beverages. Memphis Daily Appeal, 4/23/1856.

Married, On yesterday the 11th inst by James **ROSE**, Justice of the Peace, in this city Mr. Charles **MEYER** to Miss Eliza **NELSON**. Memphis Eagle & Enquirer, 2/13/1853.

Carriage Making – W. H. **MIDDLETON** has removed one mile from Memphis, on the State Line road, where he intends to carry on the above business in co-partnership with J. **HOLCOMB**. Memphis Enquirer, 10/27/1838.

Married, near Hudsonville, Miss., on the 25th May, Mr. Isaac E. **MILAM** to Miss Maria L. **HOWELL**. Memphis Daily Appeal, 6/7/1848 Married, At the residence of Col. C. W. **SANDERS**, Chicot county, Ark., on Tuesday, November 24th, by Rev. Mr. Williams, Mr. James B. **MILES**, of that county, to Miss E. E. **HILL**, of LaGrange, Tenn. Memphis Daily Appeal, 12/6/1857.

Married, On the morning of the 22d October, by Rev. Joseph R. **HAMILTON**, President of the Cold Water Baptist Female Seminary, at the residence of B. A. **FORD**, Esq., near Waterford, Marshall county, Mississippi, Rev. ____nah D. **MILLER**, pastor of the Baptist Church in Elizabethtown, Kent county, Miss., and Miss Margaret __. **FORD**. Memphis Daily Appeal, 10/27/1857.

Married—In this place, on Wednesday evening last, by the Rev. Jeptha **HARRISON**, Mr. Albert L. **MILLER**, (of the firm of Miller & Cannon) to Miss Esther Amanda **WALLACE**, of Cabarrus county, North Carolina. Memphis Enquirer, Fri., 4/17/1840.

Died, At Benicia, California, December 7 Major Albert S. **MILLER**, of the 2d U.S. Infantry. [Maj. Miller was, we believe, a son of Judge Pleasant **MILLER**, late of Jackson, Tennessee.] Memphis Eagle & Enquirer, 1/26/1853.

Pursuant to a Decree of the Chancery Court at Memphis, rendered in the case of B. F. **MILLER** and B. A. **MASSEY**, adm'rs. Of Ward W. **MILLER**, dec'd., vs. the creditors of said Ward Miller, I will, on Thursday the 10th of April, 1856, on the premises, proceed to sell....Lot of Land, containing about eight and one-third acres, lying on the new Raleigh road....Memphis Daily Appeal, 3/30/1856.

Married, by the Rev. S. T. **TONERAY**, on Sunday 28th ult., Mr. Benjamin F. **MILLER** to Miss Eliza **SMILEY**. The Appeal, 8/2/1844.

Died. At the residence of Col. James **WORD**, in Tishamingo County, Mississippi, on the 29th ult., Florence Miller, the only child of Professor and Mrs. H. V. M. **MILLER**, of this city, aged 9 years and 4 months. American Eagle, 8/5/1847.

Married. At the 1st Methodist Church in this city, on Monday evening, 17th instant, at 8 o'clock by Rev. J. W. **KNOTT**, Mr. J. B. **MILLER**, of Memphis, to Mrs. M. A. **BRADFORD**, of Coahoma county, Miss. Helena papers please copy. Memphis Daily Appeal, 10/17/1854.

Married. On the 26th of July by the Rev. J. K. **BOYCE**, Mr. J. M. **MILLER**, of Fayette county, to Miss M. J. **WRIGHT**, of Tipton county, Tenn. Memphis Appeal, 8/8/1855.

The friends and acquaintances of J. W. **MILLER** are invited to attend his funeral This Morning at 10 o'clock, from his residence, corner of Vance and Causey street, South Memphis. Memphis Daily Appeal, 3/24/1857.

We announced some days since, says the Nashville Union of the 2d, that Capt. Joseph **MILLER** had been severely wounded by a pistol shot in the thigh, by a man named Jones.—We regret that it is now our painful duty to announce his death from the wound. He died on Thursday, after having suffered much. Capt. Miller was one of the oldest steamboat Captains on the Western waters, and leaves behind a numerous circle of friends to deplore his loss. He was a bold, fearless, frank and energetic man--few men had warmer friends—his loss to his family is irreparable. Weekly American Eagle, Thurs., 1/7/1847.

Married, In this city, at the Catholic church, on Saturday last, by the Rev. Joseph S. **ALEMANY**, Mr. Marshall J. **MILLER**, of Louisville, Ky., to Miss Eudora R., daughter of Judge **BARRY** of this city. Weekly Appeal, Fri., 8/21/1846.

Married, Yesterday evening, 31st ultimo, on Court street, by Rev. James H. **OTEY**, Oliver R. **MILLER**, Esq., of Ripley, Miss., and Miss Julia M. **YOUNG**, of Memphis. Memphis Daily Appeal, 1/1/1857.

Died, Near Germantown, on the 10th inst., Mr. R. A. **MILLER**, in the 45th year of his age. Mr. M. was a native of Prince George County, Va., and at an early period of his life moved to Cumberland county, Ky., thence to this county in 1832. Kentucky & Virginia papers please copy. Memphis Eagle & Enquirer, 2/23/1853.

We are pained to learn that Richard E., a son of R. H. **MILLER**, Esq., about four years of age, lost his life yesterday morning under the following circumstances: The little fellow had been afflicted with chills, and Mr. Miller applied to an apothecary for quinine, and received morphine instead. The morphine was thus administered by mistake, and proved fatal yesterday morning. Memphis Daily Appeal, 7/8/1859.

Died, On Tuesday, August 10th, of intermitting fever, Robert B., son of Robert B. and Nancy M. **MILLER**, aged five months and seventeen days....Memphis Daily Appeal, 8/11/1858.

Died. Near Portersville, Tenn. on the 25th instant, Amanda H., daughter of S. B. and E. A. **MILLER**. Memphis Daily Appeal, 8/1/1854.

About the year 1838, I transferred by deed to John W. **QUARLES**, (then of Virginia, now of Memphis, Tenn.,) the one sixth part of the Estate of my deceased brother, (Thomas R. **MILLER**, of Texas,) upon the following conditions, viz: The said Quarles was to pay the sum of eight hundred dollars, go to Texas with certain papers and deliver them into the hands of the then Administrator, and to attend in person to the settlement of the said Estate, all of which, he, the said Quarles has failed to do. Finding that Quarles would not attend to the business according to agreement before the act of limitation would take effect, I was compelled to engage the services of a certain Mr. John P. **HAWKINS** to attend to the same. I therefore consider the contract "null and void," and that he has no interest in the same, and forewarn all persons from trading with said Quarles for any interest that he may profess to have. Edward H. **MILLER**, Prince Edward County, Va. Memphis Daily Eagle, 4/21/1848.

A serious difficulty occurred in this city yesterday, which resulted in the death of a citizen named Miller. From the evidence before the Coroners jury, it appeared that W. W. **MILLER** and J. L. **PHILLIPS** were partners in business, but a difficulty occurring between them sometime since, their business affairs were in the hands of a receiver. A fresh misunderstanding taking place yesterday, Miller attacked Phillips with a stick which he had in his hand. After a few blows Phillips drew a pistol and snapped it, but it missed fire, when Miller seized a weight and made at the former. Phillips now drew a bowie-knife and inflicted some three or four wounds upon Miller, about the chest and region of the heart, from which he died in a very few moments...The jury returned a verdict that he came to his death by the hands of Phillips. Phillips gave himself up, and was bound over in the sum of $1000 for his appearance at the next term of the Court...Memphis Eagle & Enquirer, 4/9/1852.

Died. In Haywood county, Tenn. on the morning of July 31st, after a long and painful illness, Mrs. Mary A. E. Miller, consort of Wm. **MILLER**, in the 51st year of her age. Memphis Daily Appeal, 8/6/1854.

Died, In Gibson county, Tenn. on the 30th of October, Wm. Blount **MILLER**, son of the Hon. Pleasant M. **MILLER**, aged about 28 years. Memphis Daily Appeal, 11/4/1855.

Married, On the 14th inst. by Rev. J. W. **KNOTT**, Mr. Wm. H. **MILLER** and Miss Mollie J., youngest daughter of Geo. **GRAINGER**, Esq. Cincinnati and Pittsburg papers please copy. Memphis Whig, 2/15/1856. Died, On the 21st instant at half past 5 o'clock, William George, only child of William H. and Mary J. Miller. The friends and acquaintances of his parents and those of Mr. George Grainger, are respectfully invited to attend the funeral This Afternoon at 2 o'clock, from the residence of George **GRANGER**, on the Raleigh road. Memphis Daily Appeal, 10/22/1858.

Col. Wm. P. **MILLER**—We were gratified in again shaking hands a few days since, with Col. Miller, late from Texas. He has arrived at his home in Randolph, after many hardships and imprisonment in the cause of Texian liberty, and, as is not uncustomary, a victim of persecution and ingratitude of some who have been most benefitted by his services. Our citizens will remember the Colonel having visited our town a few months since, with a gallant band of martial heroes, volunteers in the Texian wars, who marshalled through our streets, under the waving folds of their silver star. Col. Miller has taken about 500 soldiers into Texas; and has been a most efficient and valuable officer in the early history and struggles of the infant republic. On his return thro' New Orleans, he was presented with a beautiful Texian banner, by the patriotic ladies of that city, as a testimony of regard for his services; whilst President Houston, in gratitude for the same services, took from him his sword. Col. Miller is popular with both the people and army of Texas, and a Committee of Congress, appointed for the purpose, shielded Col. M. from the persecution of the President, as unjust and arbitrary. President Houston is by no means popular with either the citizens or army. Memphis Enquirer, 9/9/1837.

Married, On the 20th inst. by the Rev. Philip **ALSTON**, Willie B. **MILLER**, of this city, to Miss Louisa E. Pope, daughter of John **POPE**, Esq., of Shelby county. Weekly Appeal, 5/23/1845. Died, On Monday, 21st Oct., 1850, LeRoy Pope, infant son of Willie B. and Louisa P. Miller, aged thirteen months. The friends and acquaintances of the family are invited to attend the funeral this morning, at 10 o'clock, from the residence on Madison street. Memphis Daily Eagle, 10/22/1850.

Married, on Wednesday evening, 24th inst., at the residence of Mr. Thos. **JAMES**, in South Memphis, by Rev. R. C. **GRUNDY**, D.D., Mr. Geo. **MILLERTH** to Miss Elizabeth D. **JAMES**. Memphis Weekly Appeal, 12/1/1858.

Married, In this city on the 29th inst. by Rev. R. C. **GRUNDY**, D.D., Mr. Green **MILLS** to Miss Mary __. **HICKS**. Memphis Daily Appeal, 12/30/1857.

Married, in Helena, Ark., on Thursday, 19th inst. by Rev. Mr. Hyer, Mr. Isaac C. **MILLS**, of this city, to Miss Mary F. (or E.), daughter of Allen W. **HICKS**, Esq. Memphis Enquirer, 11/24/1846.

Married, In Germantown, Tenn., at the residence of the bride's father, September 23, by Rev. R. R. **EVANS**, Rev. J. D. **MILLS** to Miss Emily T. **LUCKEN**. Also, on the same day, and at the residence of the bride's father, and by the same, Mr. S. C. **GARNER**, of Memphis, and Miss Matilda A. **MOLITER**, of Germantown. Memphis Daily Appeal, 9/26/1858.

Col. John F. **MILLS**—This gentleman has, within the last few days, become a citizen of our city, having sold his place in Phillips county, Ark....Memphis Daily Avalanche, 4/5/1859.

Married, At Holly Springs by Rev. Mr. Watson, Mr. Patrick **MILLS** to Miss H. **TOMSON**, all of that place. Memphis Daily Appeal, 7/24/1857.

A young man named E. F. **MIMS**, fell from the steamer Arctic, on Saturday night last 5 miles below Randolph, and was instantly killed by the wheel. His trunks were marked "Utica, Miss." Memphis Appeal, 12/21/1852.

Married—On the 25th inst., by the Rev. Mr. **CROPPER**, Mr. Wilson **MISENHEIMER** to Miss Hetty **SLOUGH**, all of this county. Memphis Enquirer, 12/29/1838.

Married. On the 28th ult. in this vicinity by Rev. H. S. **PORTER**, Mr. Jonathan **MITCHEL** to Miss Susan A. **BELOAT**. Memphis Daily Appeal, 1/4/1855.

Joseph W. **LITTLE**, who murdered, in the most demoniac manner, David L. **MITCHELL**, Sheriff of White County, Tenn., on the 11th of March, while executing a writ upon him, was seen at Randolph on Wednesday evening, but made his escape...He will undoubtedly take a boat at Memphis, or above, on his way to Texas. Five Hundred Dollars reward is offered for his apprehension by Jabez B. **MITCHELL**, of Sparta, Tenn...He is described as being about six feet and one inch high, with blue eyes and black hair, and complexion rather swarthy—tolerably slender built; two of the fingers of his right hand are crooked—the little finger and the one next to it; he is about 23 years old. Memphis Enquirer, 4/8/1837.

Another Revolutionary Hero Gone. Jesse **MITCHELL**, departed this life, on the 3d of September, 1847, at the residence of Daniel **HOKE**, in De Soto County, Miss., in the 88th year of his age. Memphis Appeal, 9/29/1847.

Married, On Tuesday evening, 4th(?) inst., at the residence of the bride's father, by Rev. R. C. **GRUNDY**, D.D., Mr. Wm. Bayles **MITCHELL** to Miss Annie E., daughter of Col. Geo. **PATTISON**, of this city. Memphis Daily Appeal, 1/7/1859.

Married, On Thursday evening the 4th inst., at Calvary Church by Rev. C. T. **QUINTARD**, Mr. Wm. Bedford **MITCHELL** and Miss Sallie, eldest daughter of Dr. A. P. **MERRILL**, all of this city. Memphis Daily Appeal, 6/6/1857.

Fellow Citizens – I offer myself as a Candidate for the Office of Justice of the Peace, of Civil District No. 13 in Shelby county, Ten., at the ensuing March election. My local residence (being at Fort Pickering)...John **MIXON**. American Eagle, 2/21/1842.

Married, In Tipton county on the evening of the 19th July, by the Rev. David **CUMMINS**, Mr. John W. **MOARHEAD** to Miss Harriet A. **RICE**, late of Prince Edward Co., Va. American Eagle, 8/4/1843.

Married, On the 17th of April by Rev. J. K. **BOYCE**, Rev. W. S. **MOFFATT**, of Obion county, Tenn., and Miss M. Jane, daughter of the Rev. John **WILSON**, of Tipton county, Tenn. Memphis Daily Appeal, 5/3/1856.

Married, At the residence of the bride's father near Fisherville, on the 18th of January by Dr. W. G. **LANCASTER**, Mr. W. H. **MONCRIEF** to Miss Mary Adeline **SANDERLIN**, all of Shelby county, Tenn. Memphis Daily Appeal, 1/22/1858.

Died, On Thursday last, in this city, of pneumonia, Mattie May, daughter of H. A. and M. J. **MONTGOMERY**. Little Mattie was in the eleventh month of her age....Memphis Daily Appeal, 4/6/1856.

Married—In this city, on the 2nd inst. by the Rev. Samuel **WATSON**, Mr. Stewart R. **MONTGOMERY** to Miss Thulina **KNOX**. Memphis Enquirer, 1/3/1840.

Died, On Saturday, 20th March, Mrs. Louisa Montgomery, consort of Wm. H. **MONTGOMERY**, in her 39th year. Mrs. M. was one of the oldest residents of Memphis—having been born here...She leaves a husband and five children...She had been for some time a member of the Baptist Church. Memphis Eagle & Enquirer, 3/31/1852.

Whilst the steamer James Robb was on her way up from New Orleans, a panic was spread among the passengers on board, by the alarm of fire. Mr. **MOON** who was one of the passengers, and destined for this place, was so severly effected by the panic, that he sank down in a chair and died almost instantly. He had with him a considerable amount of money and valuable baggage, all of which were safely delivered to his relatives in Memphis....Memphis Eagle & Enquirer, 1/29/1853.

We are pained to learn that a letter has been received, announcing the death, at Vera Cruz, of Lt. Asbert G. **MOON**, late of this city. Lt. M. received his commission in the army under the provision of the Ten Regiment Bill, and left here some 2 or 3 months since for the seat of war. He was, we believe, placed on duty at Vera Cruz, where he died of the vomito. He has left many friends to mourn his early doom. Daily Enquirer, 9/2/1847.

Married. In this City on the 14th inst. by Dr. T. **SANDERS**, Mr. D. M. **MOON** to Miss A. J. **GARRETT**. By the same on the same night, Mr. J. P. **HAYMAN** to Miss E. A. **SNODEN**. Memphis Daily Appeal, 12/24/1854.

Married: At Willow Cottage, the residence of her father, in this county, on the evening of the 19th instant, by the Rev. Mr. Hyer, Mr. I. N. **MOON**, of New Orleans, to Miss S. G. A. Goldsby, only daughter of Mr. T. T. **GOLDSBY**. Memphis Daily Eagle, 10/24/1848.

Married—On Wednesday, the 2_th ult., by the Rev. Wm. **HYER**, Mr. J. N. **MOON**, of the firm of Miller & Moon of this city, to Miss Harriet, only daughter of Andrew **REMBERT**, Esq. of Shelby county. The Appeal, Fri., 3/1/1844.

We learn that Jacob N. **MOON**, Esq., has been elected President of the Memphis Branch of the Planters Bank...Mr. M. is an old and highly respected citizen, long and extensively engaged in business in this city...Weekly Memphis Eagle, 10/4/1849.

Died, At the residence of Mr. James **BOWERS**, in Panola, Miss., on Thursday, the 24th inst., of Pneumonia, Mrs. Christiana **MOORE**, aged seventy-two years, four months and four days. Memphis Daily Appeal, 12/31/1857.

Married. On the 11th by Rev. Dr. Porter, Mr. D. A. **MOORE** and Miss Ann Eliza **BROOKSHAW**, all of this city. Memphis Daily Appeal, 4/14/1855.

Married, On the 9th instant at the Baptist Church in Hernando, Miss., by Rev. James **DENNIS**, David T. **MOORE**, of Johnson county, North Carolina, to Miss Annie D. Hancock, daughter of James **HANCOCK**, of Newborn county, North Carolina. Memphis Weekly Appeal, 11/17/1858.

I wish to sell the valuable farm on which I now reside, lying on the Pigeon Roost Plank Road, 18 miles from Memphis, in De Soto county, Miss., containing 720 acres of land....Ellis **MOORE**. Memphis Appeal, 8/1/1854.

We left Memphis on Saturday morning amid the din of music and the shouts of the thousands assembled at the depot....The "Georgia" train was freighted with the lady delegates, a portion of the Fire Department, the Mayor and seven of the City Council, with such others of the delegation as could get seats....On the route from Memphis to Huntsville we were repeatedly cheered by assemblages convened at different stations....Prior to leaving Huntsville....Nothing of remarkable interest transpired....until we arrived at Whitesides, a station fifteen miles West of Chattanooga....about three-fourths of a mile from Whitesides, at a place known as the Aetna Mining Company, when all of a sudden we found ourself on the bottom of the car and a man lying on top of us....This sad mishap was occasioned by the breaking of the fore break of the first passenger car, which caught the wheel immediately behind it, throwing that car off the track, and dragging with it the baggage car....Mr. Moore, who was killed, was standing on the platform at the time of the accident....Mr. George **MOORE**, a member of the Relief Fire Company, was so badly injured that he died at Chattanooga....Memphis Daily Appeal, 6/2/1857. The remains of Mr. Geo. Moore....were yesterday attended to their last resting place in Winchester Cemetery....Memphis Daily Appeal, 5/28/1857. Tribute Of Respect.—Whereas, It has pleased an inscrutable Providence to remove from our midst our late brother, George W. Moore, be it therefore Resolved, That we, his brother members of Memphis, Lodge No. 6,I.O.O.F....Memphis Daily Appeal, 6/3/1857.

Married, On the 21st inst., by the Rev. J. H. **GRAY**, Mr. James **MOORE**, of N. Orleans, to Miss Elizabeth **McIVER**, of Shelby co., Tenn. Memphis Daily Eagle, 12/25/1848.

Married—On Wednesday evening, 6th inst., at the residence of John **MAGEE**, De Soto County, Miss. by the Rev. Samuel **WATSON**, Mr. Jesse **MOORE**, of Memphis, to Miss Margaret Ann **JONES**, of the former place. Memphis Daily Appeal, 10/10/1847. Died, In this city yesterday, July 25th, Mrs. M. A. Moore, consort of Jesse Moore, aged 29 years. Memphis Daily Appeal, 7/26/1857.

Married, At the residence of Mr. Jacob **KUYKENDALL**, on the 7th instant, in Panola county, Miss., by Rev. J. W. **BATES**, Mr. Jesse **MOORE**, of this city, to Mrs. Martha E. **KUYKENDALL**, of the former place. Memphis Daily Appeal, 10/9/1858.

Died, At his residence on Linden street, Friday evening, July 30, John **MOORE**, aged one hundred and one years, and eighteen days. He was a native of Ireland, but came to this country at a very early age, and resided for many years in Kentucky. He was a soldier under Gen. Wayne in the Revolution, and also under Gen. Scott in the late war...He had been long a worthy member of the Masonic fraternity, and of the Methodist Episcopal Church...He has left a wife of advanced age, and a numerous family to deplore his departure, though taken in the fullness of time. Memphis Appeal, 8/2/1852.

Died, On the 28th ult., Mrs. Mary E., wife of John **MOORE**, and daughter of Emeline N. and Tilman **GREGORY**, aged 17 years and 4(?) months. She was married last January and left a lovely infant, two months old....Like the morning star, hath passed away an affectionate daughter, a kind sister, devoted wife and tender mother, from her afflicted relatives. Memphis Daily Appeal, 12/9/1856.

Married, On the 1st of December by Rev. John **WILSON**, Mr. John A. **MOORE** to Miss M. J. **McCLUSKIN**, both of Tipton county, Tenn. Memphis Daily Appeal, 12/24/1857.

Married, In Jackson county, Ark., on the 16th instant by A. L. **YANCEY**, Esq., Mr. John C. **MOORE** to Miss Mary E. Gregory, daughter of Tilman **GREGORY**, all of that county. Memphis Daily Appeal, 2/3/1856.

Married. In Marshall County, Mississippi, on the 27th inst. by Rev. Joseph **DOUGLASS**, Dr. Thomas E. **MOORE**, of Bolivar, Tenn., to Miss Susan, daughter of Maj. J. **MORGAN**. Memphis Daily Appeal, 4/1/1855.

Married, On Thursday 29th inst., by the Rev. C. T. **HALLY**, Mr. Thomas W. **MOORE** to Mrs. Sarah **HARTWELL**, all of this county. Memphis Daily Eagle, 9/3/1850.

Died, At her residence in DeSoto county, Miss., on the 1st of March, Mrs. Judith C. Moore, wife of Major Wm. **MOORE**, in the 51st year of her age, leaving a devoted husband and three children....Memphis Weekly Appeal, 3/24/1858.

Died, Of typhoid fever, at 10 minutes past 8 o'clock on the evening of the 9th May, 1853, at the residence of her father, in Yalobusha county, Miss., Miss Harriet Ann Gillespie Moore, eldest daughter of Wm. D. and Charlotte **MOORE**....The North Carolina Argus and Southern Christian Advocate will please copy. Memphis Eagle & Enquirer, 5/20/1853.

Died, At his residence in Marshall county, Miss., on the 1st May, 1857, Maj. James **MOORING**, in the sixty-third year of his age. Major Mooring was a native of Georgia, but removed to Mississippi about twenty years since....He was buried by his Masonic brotherhood....Memphis Daily Appeal, 5/10/1857.

We are grieved to announce the demise of our friend, Mr. Joseph **MOREHEAD**, for several years past employed in this office as clerk and traveling collector...He left us in ____ health about three weeks since, to visit our parents in Mississippi, and was attacked with pneumonia, at the residence of Rev. James **WATSON**, in DeSoto county, where he died, on Saturday evening, after a week's illness. Memphis Appeal, Wed., 3/12/1851.

Died, in Danville, Ky., on the 22d of May, Rev. T. H. **MOREHEAD**, son of Mrs. Jane S. Morehead, near Memphis, in the 31st year of his age....In the autumn of 1845, he graduated at Centre College, Danville, and entered Union Theological Seminary in the summer of 1846; at which he completed his studies preparatory to entering the Gospel Ministry, and was licensed to preach by the Presbytery of the Western District, at its meeting in April last....he bade them farewell, and set out on his return to Virginia, which he had selected as the field of his operations.....On the evening of the 21st of May, he reached Danville, in the stage, having felt somewhat unwell during the day....But that scourge of the earth, Cholera, had seized him.... Memphis Eagle, 6/7/1849. Having taken out Letters of Administration on the Estate of my brother, T. H. Morehead, this is to notify all persons having claims against him to present them......J. S. **MOREHEAD**, Adm'r. Weekly Memphis Eagle, 10/18/1849.

Married, On the 24th inst. at the residence of the bride's mother, by Rev. Edward E. **PORTER**, Mr. William T. **MOREHEAD**, of Arkansas, to Miss H_ttie L. **LUDISILL**, of Memphis. Arkansas *Traveler* please copy. Memphis Daily Appeal, 12/27/1857.

Married, In Jackson, Tenn., on the 28th ult., by Rev. C. **McKINNEY**, Mr. Emmet T. **MORGAN**, Esq., of Covington, Tenn., and Miss Sarah A., first daughter of R. W. **WILSON**, Esq., of Jackson. Memphis Daily Appeal, 8/1/1858.

We are informed that our friend Col. George W. **MORGAN**, well known to our readers as a talented poetical correspondent of the Appeal...is announced as a candidate for the office of General of Brigade, in this division of the Tennessee militia...Memphis Daily Appeal, 5/15/1852.

Married, On the 24th inst., at the residence of the bride's father, in Memphis, by Rev. A. M. **BRYAN**, Mr. J. B. **MORGAN**, of Hernando, Miss., to Miss Lizzie A. **DOUGHERTY**. Also, at the same time and place, Mr. J. M. **SIMMS**, of DeSoto county, Miss., to Miss Mollie O. **DOUGHERTY**. There is a touching beauty in the thought of the two sister brides launching out into the sea matrimonial at the same instant.... Memphis Daily Appeal, 11/25/1857.

We learn from the Hernando North Mississippian, that the Hon. John A. **MORGAN**, formerly Probate Judge of DeSoto county, died at his residence on the Plank Road, on the 7th inst. Memphis Eagle & Enquirer, 3/12/1853.

Died. In this town on Sunday last, John H., infant son of John H. and Martha Ann **MORGAN**, aged 10 months. Memphis Enquirer, Sat., 9/16/1837.

Married. At Calvary Church in this city, on the 4th inst. by Rev. Dr. Page, Mr. St. Clair M. **MORGAN**, of Nashville, to Miss Maria Percy, youngest daughter of Col. John **POPE**. Memphis Appeal, 5/5/1854.

Died, suddenly on the 11th inst., of scarlet fever, William Wellbourn, aged 17 months and 3 days, only child of Dr. W. N. **MORGAN**, of Germantown, Tenn. Weekly Appeal, 3/27/1846. Died, At Germantown on the 26th of May last, at the residence of his son, Dr. Wm. N. Morgan, Mr. John **MORGAN**, aged 83 years....The aged and remarkable gentleman, whose death we have recorded, has been a resident of this place for the last ten or twelve years.... Huntsville, Ala., and Richmond, Va., papers copy. Memphis Daily Appeal, 6/5/1858.

We regret to learn from a dispatch received by Col. Wm. **MORIN** yesterday, that his son, Marshal **MORIN**, Esq., who was keeping the Union House at Holly Springs, Miss., was shot yesterday morning and was killed by the shot....Memphis Daily Appeal, 6/5/1858.

Patrick **MORONOY** and his wife, Bridget, having separated, by mutual consent, Patrick Moronoy will be no longer responsible for any debts of her contracting. Daily Memphis Enquirer, 7/10/1849.

Our friend Mr. John C. **MORRILL**, of South Memphis, and foreman of the Appeal Job Office, is with his amiable family, in great distress on account of the loss of his little son, a child about six years of age, who strayed from home yesterday, and has not yet been found. He is supposed to have been accompanied by a son of Wm. **CRANE**, Esq., still younger than himself. Any information in regard to them will be thankfully received...Memphis Appeal, 3/4/1852. Mr. John C. Morrill of this place, well known as a practical and energetic printer has established himself at Des Arc, Prairie County, Ark., where he intends to commence the publication of a Democratic paper, to be called the "Arkansas Citizen."....Memphis Appeal, 8/12/1854.

Married. In Jackson, Tenn. on the evening of the 23d instant, Jno. M. **MORRILL**, Esq., to Miss Georgiana M. **LEA**. Memphis Daily Appeal, 5/2/1855. Died. In Jackson, Tenn. on the 20th of October, Mrs. Georgie, consort of Mr. John M. Morrill and daughter of Rev. Lorenzo **LEA**, in the 21st year of her age. Memphis Daily Appeal, 11/4/1855.

On Thursday afternoon the good steamer *Kate Frisbee*, having on board about one hundred and fifty souls, left the port of Memphis, bound on a pleasure excursion up the river to Fogleman's Island, to see Charley **MORRIS**, whom everybody hereabout knows, become united to the daughter of the largest proprietor on the island. It was quarter before six o'clock when the *"Kate"* slipped her moorings and backed out from the landing....The *Frisbee* speeded on her way, with light-hearted beings on board and soon the music from Bradford's celebrated band called a portion of the human freight on board to join in the mazes of cotillions. The dance was kept up until the boat arrived at Fogleman's Island, when all, save the crew of the boat, proceeded to the house of the bride's father, where, at ten o'clock, "Charles Fox Morris, Esq., and Miss Mississippi **FOGLEMAN** were united in the bonds of matrimony by Rev. Dr. Gray."....After the "knot" was tied, the party adjourned to the boat, where in the course of an hour or two a splendid supper was set....After the table was cleared away, the band struck up a lively tune, and soon dancing was again commenced and kept up until after four o'clock. The boat arrived at Memphis about five o'clock and those who had not gone to bed on board the boat started home....Memphis Daily Appeal, Sat., 3/14/1857.

Married, in Iowa City, IL.(?), on the 2d April, General Eastin **MORRIS**, late of this city, to Mrs. Eliza **REAGAN**. Memphis Enquirer, 5/5/1846.

Over two weeks ago, Mr. I. G. **MORRIS**, Civil Engineer, who had been a sub-contractor on the Little Rock Railroad over the river, left the place where the men were at work saying that he was going to look at the flood. He did not return, but eventually his horse came back without the rider. Fears for the safety of Morris induced a search and the remains of the unfortunate man were found last week at Black Fish creek. How he had come by his death was a mystery....The deceased was well known in this city where some of his relations are residing. Memphis Daily Appeal, 5/20/1858.

Died, At Cockrum, Miss. on the 9th inst., in the 23d year of her age, Mrs. Harriet Elizabeth, consort of Dr. Joseph W. **MORRIS**, after a protracted illness of two months....—*North Mississippian*. Memphis Eagle & Enquirer, 3/26/1853.

Miss Tennessee Morris, daughter of Mr. M. **MORRIS** was drowned on Tuesday last, by falling in a small branch, within about two miles of Memphis, on the Raleigh road, where she was found dead. She is supposed to have taken a fit and fallen in the creek. Weekly Appeal, Fri., 4/24/1846.

Died, In this place at the residence of his brother, M. H. **MORRIS**, Esq., after a protracted illness, Mr. Thos. **MORRIS**, late of Memphis, in the 28th year of his age. [Pontotoc, (Miss.) Paper. Memphis Daily Appeal, 9/23/1852.

Married, Near Fisherville, on the 6th inst., at the residence of the bride's mother, by Dr. W. G. **LANCASTER**, Mr. Robert **MORRIS**, of Independence county, Ark., and Miss Nancy M. **GREEN**, of Shelby county, Tenn. Memphis Daily Appeal, 10/13/1857.

Died, In Stewart county, in this State, August 19th, Mrs. Polly Morris, consort of W. G. **MORRIS**.... Memphis Daily Appeal, 9/1/1858.

We are authorized to announce Maj. Walter B. **MORRIS** as a candidate for the office of Mayor of South Memphis; the election takes place 1st Saturday in January next. The Daily Eagle, 12/15/1846. Another of the pioneer citizens of Memphis is gone. Major Walter B. Morris is dead. He died at his residence in Fort Pickering on Saturday morning at 2 o"lock, after a protracted illness, in the 57th year of his age and was buried yesterday afternoon. The Masonic order of which he was a brother, were present and followed his remains to the grave. Memphis Daily Appeal, 1/9/1854.

Married, On Thursday, June 5th, by Rev. W. Carey **CRANE**, of Hernando, at the residence of her mother, in DeSoto county, Miss., Mr. A. D. **MORRISON**, of Memphis, and Miss E. R. K.(?) **STEVENSON**. Memphis Daily Appeal, 6/6/1856.

Married. On Sunday evening at the residence of Mrs. M. **REED** by Jas. **ROSE**, Esq., Mr. Charles **MORRISON**, of the Theatre, to Miss Amelia M. **JACKSON**, of this city. Memphis Daily Appeal, 2/13/1855.

The friends and acquaintances of the late Col. D. **MORRISON** are respectfully invited to attend his funeral from the U.S. Hotel, at 11 o'clock this morning. Divine services by Rev. J. H. **GRAY**. Masonic Notice. The members of South Memphis and Angorona Lodge are requested to meet at the lodge room Odd Fellows Hall, at 10 ½ o'clock this morning to attend the funeral of the deceased brother, the late Col. D. Morrison. Memphis Daily Appeal, 9/17/1852.

On the 7th inst. Mr. James **MORRISON**, a citizen of Chesterville, Pontotoc county, Mississippi, committed suicide, while under the influence of liquor, by cutting his throat with a razor, near severing his head from his body. He leaves a wife and children to mourn his awful death....Memphis Daily Appeal, 5/16/1857.

Married, In Dyersburg, on the 20th(?) inst., at the residence of Mr. Watkins, John **MORRISON**, Esq., of Fort Pickering, to Mrs. Martha **MORRIS**, of Sumner county, Tenn. Nashville and Gallatin papers copy. Memphis Daily Appeal, 12/30/1859.

Married, At the residence of Fanny **FARLEY**, on the 28th ult., by Elder C. B **YOUNG**, Mr. John C. **MORRISON** to Miss Susan F. **FARLEY**, all of Panola county, Miss. Memphis Daily Appeal, 3/8/1859.

Married. Near Edwardsville, Illinois, April 3, 1855, by Rev. Mr. West, Mr. Thos. W. **MORRISON**, of Edwardsville, and Miss Jenny Morrison, daughter of the late David **MORRISON**, of Memphis, Tenn. Memphis Whig, 4/23/1855.

We regret to learn that Col. Wm. M. **MORRISON**, Agent for the Northern Railroads in this city, died on the wharf-boat of A. B. Shaw & Co., yesterday morning. Col. M. was highly respected and beloved by the many of our citizens who formed his acquaintance during his sojourn amongst us...Memphis Daily Appeal, 8/18/1852.

Circular of the Botanico Medical College, Memphis, July 28th, 1847...The gentlemen constituting the Professional Board for the ensuing session are as follows: James **WEAVER**, M.D., Professor of Anatomy and Professor of Surgery. Amariah **BIGGS**, M.D., Professor of Physiology and Pathology. O. L. **SHIVERS**, M.D., Professor of Materia Medica and Medical Botany. M. **GABBERT**, M.D., Professor of the Theory and Practice of Medicine. Hugh **QUINN**, M.D., Professor of Midwifery and the Diseases of Women and Children. Rev. Wm. **HYER**, A.M., Professor of Chemistry and Pharmacy. G. W. **MORROW**, M.D., Demonstrator of Anatomy...P. S. **GAYLE**, Prest. Wm. D. **WILKERSON**, Sec'y. Daily Enquirer, 9/1/1847. Married, By the Rev. Charles A. **WALKER** at the house of T. B. **NORMAN**, Esq., Prof. G. W. **MORROW** and Miss Dathula V. **PRICE**, all of Hardeman county, Tenn. Memphis Daily Appeal, 4/2/1856.

Married. On the 19th instant by Rev. P. H. **WALKER**, Prof. W. B. **MORROW**, M.D., of New Castle, Tenn., to Mrs. Martha Jane **SMITH**, of Middleburgh, Tenn. Memphis Daily Appeal, 7/22/1855.

The friends and acquaintances of the late Q. L. **MORTON** are respectfully invited to attend his funeral, from the First Presbyterian Church, This (Saturday) Evening at 3 o'clock. I.O.O.F. The members of Chickasaw Lodge No. 8 are requested to meet at their Hall at 2 ½ o'clock, punctually....respectfully invited to attend the funeral of our late brother, Q. L. Morton. Memphis Daily Appeal, 3/14/1857.

Died: In New Orleans, on the 21st inst., of injuries sustained by the explosion of the steamer Concordia, on which boat the deceased was clerk, Mr. John F. **MOSBY**, formerly of this city, in the 34th year of his age. Memphis Daily Eagle, 9/30/1848.

Died—In this town, on Monday last, Mrs. Martha **MOSBY**. Memphis Enquirer, Sat., 5/27/1837.

Died—On the morning of the 26th ult., after a very short illness, Mrs. Susan H., consort of Mr. Sam'l **MOSBY**, Merchant of this city, in the 20th year of her age...The Appeal, 7/5/1844.

Married—On Tuesday morning last, by Rev. P. W. **ALSTON**, Mr. Samuel **MOSBY**, merchant of this place, to Miss Sarah Samuel, daughter of Col. Samuel **LEAKE**, of Shelby county. Memphis Enquirer, Thurs., 7/23/1846.

Accident—We regret to learn that the Sheriff of this county, J. B. **MOSELEY**, Esq., received quite a severe injury on Thursday last, by falling with his horse and buggy over the bridge on the Raleigh road just this side of the residence of Col. John **POPE**.....Injury to one of his ancles, and pretty sore contusions in the region of the back and hip, were the only results...Memphis Enquirer, 9/26/1846.

Died, In this city yesterday, at 12 o'clock, Judith Scott, aged five years and twenty-one days, daughter of John B. and Martha E. **MOSELEY**. Their friends and acquaintances are requested to attend her funeral this evening at 3 o'clock from the residence of Col. S. R. **BROWN**, on Second street. March 22nd, 1853. Memphis Eagle & Enquirer.

Samuel F. **MOSELEY**, is elected to the Texas Legislature. He lives in Cass county. He was elected by a respectable majority so says the Jefferson Democrat. He formerly lived here and the above intelligence may be gratifying to his friends. Memphis Daily Appeal, 12/23/1847.

Died—In Memphis, on the 21st of January, Henry W. **MOSELY**, Esq. Southern Statesman, 2/4/1832

Married, On Thursday evening last, by the Rev. Geo. W. **COONS**, Maj. John B. **MOSELY** of this city, to Miss Martha E., daughter of Col. S. **LEAKE**, of this county. American Eagle, Thurs., 11/12/1846.

Died, At Fort Pickering, on Friday last, after a few hours illness, Mrs. Sarah **MOSELY**, daughter of Hugh **ROLAND**, Esq. American Eagle, Fri., 9/22/1843.

Died, In this vicinity, of Scarlet Fever, George **MOSSBERG**. Memphis Daily Appeal, 10/23/1856.

Married. At Snowdoun, in Marshall County, Miss., on the evening of the 22d inst. by Rt. Rev. James H. **OTEY**, Col. Christopher H. **MOTT**, of Holly Springs, to Miss Sallie A. **GOVAN**, of Snowdoun. Memphis Daily Appeal, 12/24/1854.

Married, In this city on Thursday evening, the 24th inst., by the Rev. Mr. Davidson, Mr. Samuel C. **MOUNT** to Miss Margaret **WYANT**, all of this city. Memphis Eagle & Enquirer, 6/26/1852.

We learn that Mr. John **MOUTON**, formerly Superintendent of the Memphis Gas Company, was recently killed by a railroad casualty in Connecticut. His many friends in this city, we know, will deeply sympathize with his aged parents in his untimely loss. Memphis Whig, 11/6/1855.

Caroline **MUHLENBURG**, a young German girl, who had been in this country only three weeks, fell dead in the streets in front of the Presbyterian Church, corner of Main and Beale streets, yesterday evening about 3 o'clock. The Coroner's jury returned a verdict of death from visitation of God, "or in other words, *coup de soleil*. She was arriving at the time in the capacity of servant somewhere in South Memphis. Memphis Appeal, 7/4/1854.

Married, On the evening of the 12th inst. by Rev. Wm. Carey **CRANE**, Hon. Robt. **MULDROW**, of Octibbeha(?) county, to Miss Ann Eliza Oliver, daughter of Major Simeon **OLIVER**, of DeSoto county. Memphis Daily Appeal, 1/19/1858.

A personal recounter occurred yesterday afternoon on board the *Kate Frisbee* between Maj. Thomas **MULL**, of Marshall county, Mississippi, and W. R. **HUNT**, Esq., of this city, in which the first mentioned gentleman received a wound by a pistol shot from which he soon died. Pistols were used on both sides....Memphis Daily Appeal, 11/10/1857.

A man whose name was ascertained to be Cornelius **MULLIN**, was found Sunday morning, in the vicinity of the bayou and Jefferson street, quite dead. He had evidently died from exposure....Memphis Daily Appeal, 11/15/1859.

Married, On the 24th instant by Rev. Dr. _____, Mr. David **MUNCRIEF**, of Fisherville, to Mrs. Mary **RUDISILL**, of Raleigh. Memphis Weekly Appeal, 3/31/1858.

Married. In this city, at the Henrie House, on the 22d inst., by the Rev. Mr. Dennis, Mr. Theophilus **MUNFORD**, of Munfordville, Ky., to Miss M. E. A. **BAYLISS**, of this city. Weekly American Eagle, 12/24/1846.

Married: In Des Arc, Ark. on Thursday evening the __th inst. by R. **McIVER**, Esq., Mr. David W. **MUNROE**, of Memphis, Tenn., to Miss Fanny K. **BAXTER**, of that place. Memphis Whig, 10/23/1855.

Married, On the 17th ult. by Rev. John **CARROLL**, at the residence of the bride's father, Rev. Wm. **THOMPSON**, of Prairie county, Ark., Mr. L. W. **MUNROE** to Miss America **THOMPSON**, all of Prairie county, Ark. Memphis Weekly Appeal, 3/3/1858.

Died. On the 8th inst., in this vicinity, Mrs. Eliza M. Munson, wife of Mr. A. **MUNSON** of this place....American Eagle, 3/18/1847.

Married, On Thursday, the 15th inst. by the Rev. Benedict J. **SPALDING**, Dr. Geo. W. **MURPHY**, of this city, to Miss Mary Ann McManus, of Bardstown, Ky., daughter of the late Charles **McMANUS**. Memphis Enquirer, 1/24/1846. Died In this city on Thursday last, of Consumption, Dr. George W. Murphy. Memphis Appeal, Sat., 5/17/1851.

A serious affray occurred on Friday evening last at Phillips' Bayou, on St. Francis river, between Thomas B. **WILKERSON** and Hugh **MURPHY**, in which the former shot the latter, killing him in a short time. There were several standing about at the time of the melee, and a man named John **TURNER** was also shot, killing him instantly. Wilkerson fled and has not yet been arrested. Memphis Daily Appeal, 8/6/1856.

Died, on the 31st ultimo, at the residence of Mr. Charles **LEATH** near this city, Captain Thomas B. **MURPHY**, late of Decatur, Ala., in the 49th year of his age...As a husband, father, friend and brother, he sacrificed every selfish consideration in the punctilious discharge of the duties which devolved upon him...Although a stranger, a large number of the masonic fraternity accompanied his remains to the grave, where the usual ceremonies were performed. His zeal and devotion for the order justly entitled him to such support.....Memphis Enquirer, 5/5/1846.

Married, On the 26th inst. at the residence of the bride's parents, by Rev. Mr. Lynch, Mr. W. T. **MURPHY** to Miss Lizzie P. **HALEY**, both of this city. Memphis Daily Appeal, 7/28/1859.

About 12 o'clock last night...we were disturbed by the cries of—"watch," "man killed." The alarm was caused by the murder of Mr. G. W. **MURRAY**, keeper of a billiard saloon on Madison street. It appeared that Mr. Murray and a Mr. Hudson were engaged in playing cards in the bedroom back of the saloon, when a difficulty occurred; words passed and Hudson, with a knife in his possession, some eight inches in length, plunged it to Murray's heart. He died almost instantly...Hudson was arrested soon afterwards...and lodged in jail...Memphis Weekly Appeal, 1/9/1856.

Died, at his residence in this city on yesterday (5th inst.) Jas. B. **MURRAY**, formerly of Harrisburg, Pa., but for several years a resident of this city. He funeral takes place this evening from his residence on Market Square, to which the friends of the deceased are respectfully invited. Daily Enquirer, 10/6/1847.

Died, On the 23d inst. at his residence in Hardeman county, after a lingering illness of many months, Col. John **MURRAY**, aged about 80 years. Col. Murray was one of the first who entered this county, and will be recollected by all who were concerned in the land business, as a Surveyor and locator. Perhaps none of those early adventurers shared so largely the hardships incident to their vocation as the deceased; he literally lived in the wild forest for several years and although social in his disposition, he seemed to prefer at all times a border life...Weekly Appeal, 10/31/1845.

In pursuance of a deed of Trust executed to me on the 22nd day of February 1847, by Robert J. **MURRAY**, to secure certain debts therein specified, I will expose to public sale...on the 28th day of March 1848...Lots No. 90 and 91...Said deed of Trust is of record in the Register's Office of Shelby County, in Book W, pages 238 and 239. R. M. **ROBERTS**, Trustee. Memphis Daily Eagle, 4/6/1848.

The friends and acquaintances of William **MURRAY** are respectfully invited to attend his funeral This Evening at 3 o'clock from his residence, foot of Exchange street. Memphis Daily Appeal, 10/31/1856.

Died. In Jackson, Tenn. on Wednesday morning, the 19th instant, Mrs. Alethea Murrell, wife of Mr. John **MURRELL** and only surviving daughter of the late Dr. A. A. **CAMPBELL**, of that place. The deceased has left an aged mother, a disconsolate husband and a little daughter....From early life Mrs. Murrell had been a devout member of the Presbyterian Church....Memphis Daily Appeal, 7/25/1854.

Married. In Germantown on the 21st inst. by Thomas C. **BLAKELY**, Esq., Mr. John **MYERS** to Mrs. Annie Francis **GIBSON**, all of Germantown. Memphis Daily Appeal, 3/24/1854.

Married, On Thursday the 21st ult. by Rev. S. W. **HALL**, Mr. W. B. **MYERS**, of Collierville, Tenn., to Miss Sarah Eliza **NEWTON**, of McNairy county. Memphis Eagle & Enquirer, 5/5/1853.

Married, on Thursday, 10th inst. by Rev. Mr. Coons, Mr. Thos. B. **MYNATT**, to Miss Martha Hill **VAN PELT**, all of this city. Weekly Appeal, 12/11/1846. The friends and acquaintances of Thomas B. Mynatt are invited to attend the funeral of his brother, William **MYNATT**, from his residence on Union street, This Morning at 10 o'clock. Died, In this city at 1 o'clock A.M. yesterday, Mr. William Mynatt, for nine years an *attache* of the Appeal Office....Mr. Mynatt was born in Knoxville on the 29th of September, 1824, and was consequently in the thirty-third year of his age. He was the son of the late Mr. C. and of Mrs. Harriette **MYNATT**, of this city, and leaves behind him an affectionate mother and brother and a large circle of warmly attached friends to mourn his premature loss....Memphis Daily Appeal, 4/7/1857.

Died, Near Grand Junction, in Hardeman county, Tenn., on the 17th inst., Lewis Matthews, infant son of John W. and Isabella J. **NABORS**, aged one month and one day. Memphis Weekly Appeal, 12/1/1858.

Married, By Rev. J. T. **MERRIWETHER**, Mr. Robert C. **NALL**, of Obion county, Tenn., to Mrs. Mary A. **TIPPETT**, of Memphis. Memphis Daily Appeal, 8/26/1859.

Four Horses will be sold at public auction...at the stable in the Navy Yard...Thomas B. **NALLE**, Act'g Navy Agent. Memphis Appeal, 6/24/1848.

Died, Of inflammation of the lungs, on the 13th inst., on board steamer "Martha Washington," bound up, Madeline Gertrude, daughter of E. W. and S. A. **NANCE**, aged 3 years, 4 months, and 15 days. Her remains were deposited in the Butler Cemetery of this place. Memphis Eagle, 4/17/1849.

Died, At his residence in Dyer county, Tenn., on the 11th day of February, 1856, of palsy, Col. William **NASH**, aged sixty-five years. The deceased served in Captain James' Company of Volunteers from Madison county, Kentucky, in the war of 1812, was wounded at the battle of the river Raisin, in Canada, resided in Dyer county since 1842, lived in retirement, denied by frowning fortune all the luxuries and many of the comforts of life...He lived respected and esteemed by all who knew him and died regretted by a large circle of friends. Memphis Daily Appeal, 3/20/1856.

Married, On the 7th inst. by J. **WALDRAN**, Esq., John **NEAGLE** to Miss Margaret A. **DOUGHERTY**, all of this city. Memphis Eagle & Enquirer, 3/10/1853.

Married, On the 14th September by Rev. B. H. **RUSSELL**, Rev. James H. **NEAL** of Grass Valley, California, to Miss Sarah Ann **BOARDMAN**, of Shelby county, Tenn. Memphis Daily Appeal, 11/26/1857.

Married, At the residence of the bride's father on the 20th day of September, 1857, by J. M. **THOMPSON**, Esq., James L. **NEALY**, of _radley county, Arkansas, and Miss Elizabeth **LYNN**, of Shelby county, Tenn. Chester *Standard* (S.C.) please copy. Memphis Daily Appeal, 10/3/1857.

We are authorized to announce James **NEEL** a candidate for Register of Shelby county at the ensuing March election. Daily Enquirer, 11/5/1847.

Died, In Madison county, Tennessee, near Jackson, on the 26th of June, Mrs. Rosana M. Neely, consort of Samuel **NEELY**, Esq. Mrs. Neely was in the 67th year of her age. The deceased had been a resident of the county 22 years. Her native State was South Carolina, York district. She joined the Presbyterian Church at the age of 20 years....Memphis Daily Appeal, 7/7/1857.

Married. In this city on the 3rd instant by Rev. H. S. **PORTER**, Mr. Jas. F. **NEIL**, of the firm of Ferguson & Neil, to Miss Catharine **WILLIAMSON**. Memphis Daily Appeal, 1/4/1855.

Pleasant Hill, Shelby Co., Ten. Departed this life, on the 23d ult., at half past 8 o'clock, A.M., Mrs. Eliza P. Nelson, consort of Charles I. **NELSON**, Esq., after a painful illness of ten or fifteen days...By this dispensation of Divine Providence her companion has lost a kind and affectionate wife; five lovely and interesting children, all of whom are daughters, are bereaved of a pious and affectionate mother, and the infant Christian Church, of which she was a devoted member....The Appeal, 8/16/1844.

The undersigned, Administratrix of the estate of John J. **NELSON**, dec'd., requests all indebted to said estate to settle the same.....Rachel **NELSON**, Adm'rix. Weekly Appeal, 10/9/1846.

Died at his residence in Lauderdale county, on the 19th ult., Dr. John J. **NELSON**, aged 33 years. The deceased was born in Louisa county, Virginia and emigrated to this State in 1839, where he soon became a successful practitioner...In his death the country has lost a valuable citizen...and his bereaved wife a devoted and affectionate husband...Memphis Appeal, 10/26/1852.

Died; in Shelby county, Tenn., on the 25th day of July, 1847, Mrs. Mary E. Nelson, consort of John W. **NELSON**, in the 42d year of her age. The deceased has left an affectionate husband, and numerous friends and relatives to mourn her loss....She had expected very soon to have connected herself with the Presbyterian Church....As wife, friend, and mistress, she was all that could be desired....Richmond (Va.) Whig, Enquirer and Watchman of the South, please copy. Daily Enquirer, 8/11/1847.

Information Wanted. Littlebury **NELSON**, son of Abraham **NELSON**, of Langville, Ark., was to start from Martin co., N.C., about the first of November last, for St. Francis county, Ark., and has not since been heard from. He is 18 years old, has light hair, and is about 5 feet, 2 or 3 inches high. Any information respecting him will be thankfully received by his father, who resides at or near Langville, Ark.....Memphis Eagle & Enquirer, 6/17/1853.

Died, In Columbia, Ten., on 24th October last, at the residence of Mr. P. **NELSON**, Maj. J. W. **NELSON**, of Shelby county, in the 66th year of his age. Maj. Nelson was one of our best citizens, and his death will create a void in the large circle of his friends and acquaintances, who are left to mourn his loss. Memphis Daily Appeal, 11/4/1852.

Lieut. E. M. **ANDERSON** of this city writes the following letter to Mr. S. O. **NELSON** of N. Orleans, informing him of the particulars of the death of his gallant and noble brother, Lieut. F. B. **NELSON**, of this city. P_an Del Rio, three miles from Cerro Gordo, April 19th, 1847. My Dear Sir.—The melancholy duty has devolved upon me of disclosing to you the death of your brother and our beloved Nelson. At the head of his command and foremost in the charge he fell!! His last words were "Come on my brave boys." He fell near the fort from a musket ball in his heart....I would particularly recommend to you his two friends and mess-mates, Benj. **OLIVER** and Cornelius **DONAHUE**. He was devoted to them, as were they to him....Gen. Pillow requests that you have a coffin made and sent to him at Vera Cruz; as he intends returning home to visit his family, in the course of a month, he will, if furnished with a coffin, bring his body....Respectfully your friend, truly, E. M. Anderson. American Eagle, 5/13/1847. Died: At the residence of her father, Samuel **TANNER**, Esq. in Athens, on the 27th ult., after a protracted and painful illness, Mrs. Martha A., wife of S. O. Nelson, of New Orleans, aged 39 years. Memphis Whig, 9/12/1855.

Died, On the morning of the 30th ult., of Measles, Martha, infant daughter of Wm. B. and Maria **NELSON**. The friends of the family are requested to attend the funeral, this morning, at 10 o'clock, from their residence on Jackson street. Services by Rev. Dr. H. S. **PORTER**. Memphis Eagle & Enquirer, 5/1/1852.

Married, On the 9th instant at the residence of Mr. Asa R. **CHILTON**, Byhalia, Marshall county, Miss., by Rev. P. J. **EXCHOLS**, President of Byhalia Female Institute, Mr. Nathan **NESBITT**, of DeSoto county, to Miss Rebecca **LOVE**, of Marshall county. Memphis Weekly Appeal, 11/24/1858.

Married. On the 3rd of January, 1855, by Rev. E. E. **HAMILTON**, R. N. **NESBITT**, Esq., to Miss Martha R. **THOMAS**, all of Somerville. Memphis Appeal, 1/9/1855.

Married, near Germantown, Tenn., on the 18th inst., by A. L. **YANCY**, Esq., Mr. Wm. D. **NESBIT** of DeSoto county, Miss., to Miss Margaret L. **MORGAN** of Shelby county, Ten. Memphis Enquirer, 5/20/1848.

Died, In this city at the residence of Rev. B. H. **CAPERS**, on Monday evening, the 14th inst., Frank Wade, son of Albert G. and Amanda Capers **NEVILLE**, aged one year and eight months....Memphis Daily Avalanche, 3/16/1859.

Married. On the 21st inst. at the residence of Mrs. **BOYCE**, in Panola county, Miss. by Rev. Mr. Young, John **NEVINS**, Esq., of Shelbyville, Tenn., to Miss Sarah **PEARSON**, of Pleasant Mount. Memphis Daily Appeal, 7/25/1854.

We are pained to learn the death of Rev. Thos. J. **NEWBERRY**, for many years a citizen of this city, and for several years pastor of the Presbyterian Church at Raleigh. He died last Sabbath, on board the steamer E. W. Stephens, whilst descending the Ohio River, near Evansville, Indiana, of cholera. He was a useful and excellent gentleman, and was, we learn, to have been united in marriage with a lady in the vicinity of Raleigh, last night. Weekly Memphis Eagle, Thurs., 7/5/1849.

We are requested to state that Mrs. Ellen **NEWBURN**, for some years a resident in the Lunatic Asylum at Nashville, is now entirely well in mind and body, and can now be restored to her friends who reside in this place, but whose address the Superintendent is not acquainted with. Memphis Daily Appeal, 2/2/1852.

Died, At his residence on Main street, on Thursday, March 10th, at twenty minutes past 11 o'clock P.M., Mr. O. P. **NEWBY**....Services at his residence by Rev. Mr. Steadman. Memphis Daily Appeal, 3/11/1859.

Mr. Geo. **NEWELL**, clerk of the H.R.W. Hill, died of yellow fever on board that boat yesterday. He contracted the disease while in New Orleans. Memphis Daily Appeal, 8/29/1855.

Married—in Memphis, on the 13th inst., by Rev. P. W. **ALSTON**, Dr. J. C. **NEWNAN** to Miss Martha **LITTLEFIELD**, both of Mississippi. Memphis Enquirer, 8/15/1846.

Died, On yesterday, 30th inst., Thomas Carroll, son of John and Margaret **NEWSOM**—aged three years one month and ten days. Memphis Daily Appeal, 8/31/1858.

Died, On the 18th instant, of pneumonia, at his residence on President's Island, Mr. Thomas **NEWSOM**—only brother of Mr. John **NEWSOM**, tax collector for this city—in the 36th year of his age, leaving a wife and three children to lament his death. Mr. N. was born in Sussex county, Virginia, and has resided in this county for the last 24 years....Memphis Eagle & Enquirer, 1/23/1853.

Married, At Flewellen's X Roads, DeSoto county, Miss., June 7th by Rev. Wm. Carey **CRANE**, Dr. Charles E. **NEWTON**, late of Harrison county, Va., and Miss Martha V. Farmer, daughter of Maj. Jos. W. **FARMER**, of DeSoto county. Memphis Daily Appeal, 6/11/1857.

Married, On the 26th of May by the Rev. E. H. **WHITMORE**, Mr. George W. **NICHOLS** to Miss Ann **WELLONS**, all of this city. Memphis Eagle & Enquirer, 5/28/1853.

Died, in this city, on Monday, May 31st, Mr. Walter **NICHOLS**, Merchant, aged 38 years. May peace attend his exit from a world of trouble and sorrow. May Divine consolation sustain his bereaved family in a distant land. Daily Enquirer, 6/3/1847.

Hon. A. O. P. **NICHOLSON**. This gentleman left his home, near this place, on Wednesday last, for Washington City, where he goes to assume the editorial control of the Union....during the short time he occupied a seat in the United States Senate he won for himself a reputation which ranks him among the best statesmen of the Republic....Memphis Appeal, Sat., 9/10/1853.

Died: On the 24th July, in South Memphis, Elizabeth P., consort of O. NICHOLSON, in the forty-second year of her age. Trenton Star Spangled Banner please copy. Memphis Eagle, 8/3/1849. Died, on the 1st Sept. in South Memphis, Francis E. infant daughter of O. Nicholson; aged 3 years and 6 months. (Trenton Star Spangled Banner please copy.) Daily Memphis Enquirer, 9/5/1849.

Commander Wm. C. NICHOLSON, Naval Commandant at this port, arrived here on Wednesday last. He was preceded by a high reputation as an officer and a gentleman. Memphis Appeal, Sat., 10/18/1851.

Married, On the 23d inst., by Rev. H. S. PORTER, D.D., Mr. Tabot NICOLSON, of Madison county, to Miss Elizabeth HATHAWAY, of this city. Memphis Daily Appeal, 8/26/1852.

Married, In Haywood county, on Tuesday the 4th inst. by the Rev. J. E. BRIGHT, Mr. Wm. C. NIXON, of Memphis, to Miss Margaret L., daughter of David HAY, Esq. American Eagle Weekly, 3/14/1845.

Married, On Wednesday evening, 5th instant, at Mr. Harrison's on the Raleigh plankroad, by Rev. R. C. GRUNDY, D.D., Mr. Wm. S. NOBLIN to Miss Charlotte A. GARNER, all of Shelby county. Memphis Weekly Appeal, 5/12/1858.

The Nashville Gazette states that Mr. Theo. NOEL, of Memphis, Tenn., has just secured a patent for an improvement in winding watches...Memphis Daily Appeal, 1/8/1852.

Died, Suddenly, at Germantown, in this county, on Monday night last, Thomas J. NOLAND, aged 57 years....His remains were deposited in Elmwood Cemetery, near this city. Memphis Daily Appeal, Fri., 9/4/1857.

We take pleasure in calling attention to the law card of Judge John A. NOOE, late of Alabama, who has become permanently located at this place....Memphis Whig, 11/21/1855.

Died, Of Pneumonia, on the 7th inst., in the 36th year of her age, Mrs. Elenor B., consort of Col. John R. NORFLEET, of Marshall county, Miss. The deceased was a daughter of the late William COOPWOOD of DeSoto county. She was married in the year 1840 and leaves her husband and four children to mourn her loss. Memphis Daily Appeal, 12/22/1857.

Died, on the 12th inst., John Wesley, infant son of Mrs. Fanny NORMAN, aged three months and three days. Memphis Daily Appeal, 1/22/1859.

Married, On the 18th instant by Rev. J. GAINES, Col. L. NORMAN to Miss S. J. B. JONES, all of Boone Yard, Miss. Memphis Weekly Appeal, 6/2/1858.

The friends and acquaintances of T. B. and Maria NORMENT are invited to attend the funeral of their son, Charlie, from their residence on Vance, between Hernando and DeSoto, at 3 o'clock P.M. to-day. Services by Rev. A. M. BRYAN. Memphis Daily Appeal, 2/19/1858.

Died—On the 21st inst., Margaret Elizabeth, youngest daughter of Richard and Sarah NORRIS, aged 4 years and 4 months and 17 days. Baltimore Republican and Argus please copy. The Appeal, 6/28/1844.

Mr. E. O. NORTON, well and favorably known as a railroad man, has located permanently in this city and will be connected with the freight business on many of our northern and eastern roads. Memphis Daily Appeal, 10/20/1859.

We are authorized to announce Messrs. J. I. ANDREWS and S. A. NORTON, as candidates for re-election as Aldermen of the 4th Ward. Memphis Daily Appeal, 2/23/1848.

Married, On Wednesday evening last, at the residence of Elija **PULLIAM**, Esq., by the Rev. Wm. **HYER**, Mr. Stephen A. **NORTON** of Memphis, and Miss Elmira **PULLIAM**, of Shelby county. American Eagle, Thurs., 12/16/1847.

We take pleasure in calling public attention to the law card of Judge John A. **NOVE**, late of Tuscumbia, Alabama.—Judge Nove has settled permanently in Memphis....Memphis Daily Appeal, 11/22/1855.

Serious Railroad Accident. Yesterday evening, as the cars were coming in from Germantown, Mr. V. S. **NUNNEMAKER** fell from the tender and had his left arm so severely lascerated as to render amputation necessary and it was accordingly taken off near the shoulder....Mr. Nunnemaker was removed to the hospital and was doing very well late yesterday evening....Memphis Appeal, 1/25/1853. Died, At the hospital in this city on Monday, 31st January, of cerebral inflamation, Mr. V. S. Nunnemaker....Memphis Appeal, 2/2/1853. ....It will be gratifying to his friends abroad to learn that every attention was paid him....Memphis Eagle & Enquirer, 2/1/1853. (Author's note: spelled **NUNEMAKER** in this article)

The friends and acquaintances of Michael **NUSS** are invited to attend the funeral of his son Jacob, from his residence on Washington street, This (Sunday) Evening at 2 o'clock. Memphis Daily Appeal, 6/7/1857.

Married, At Jackson, Tenn., on the 11th instant, by Rev. A. W. **JONES**, Mr. W. J. **OAKES**, of Jackson, Tenn., to Mrs. Margaret E. **LYON**, of Des Arc, Ark. Memphis Daily Appeal, 4/17/1859.

Married. At the residence of Mrs. Rutherford on the evening of the 22d instant, by Rev. J. W. **KNOTT**, Mr. Oliver H. **OATES**, of White county, Ark., to Miss Virginia O. **WILBORNE**, of this city. Memphis Daily Appeal, 3/27/1855.

The friends and acquaintances of the late Maj. S. K. **OATES** are invited to attend the funeral of his late daughter Mary J. Oates, from his late residence on Union street at 8 o'clock this Sunday morning, July 23d, 1854. Memphis Daily Appeal.

Died, On the 4th inst., at the Hickory Wythe Springs, Fayette County, Tenn., Mr. Thomas J. **OATES**, aged 37 years. The city papers of Raleigh, N.C. will please copy. American Eagle, 6/17/1847.

Nothing affords us more pleasure than to announce that our esteemed fellow townsman, Mr. Michael **O'CONNOR**, who was supposed to have been drowned from the steamer St. Francis, is yet in the land of the living. He arrived in the city yesterday evening, alive and vigorous, having been left at a wood yard, and expresses the opinion that he is worth half a dozen dead men yet. We extend him our most cordial congratulations on his restoration to his home and friends. Memphis Daily Appeal, 8/3/1853.

A bricklayer by the name of Peter **O'HANLAN**, who recently came to this city from St. Louis, fell from a building on which he was at work last Friday, and died in about six hours afterwards. He had no family, but is understood to have relatives in Augusta, Ga....Memphis Daily Appeal, Sun., 9/11/1859.

...Mr. Robert T. **O'HANLON** has assumed the management of the Race Course in the neighborhood of this city...Memphis Eagle, 9/6/1849.

Died, In this city on the 20th instant, Benjamin F., infant son of Benjamin and Sarah **O'HAVER**, aged eleven months and fourteen days. Memphis Daily Appeal, 5/24/1852.

Died, In this city, June 9, 1859, Mrs. Mary O'Herren, consort of Mr. Wm. **O'HERREN**, aged twenty-six years. Memphis Daily Appeal, 6/11/1859.

Died, on yesterday morning, at ½ past 7 o'clock, at the residence of his son-in-law, J. W. **FOWLER**, Esq., of Congestive Chill, Col. W. J. **OLDHAM**, aged 57(?) years, who emigrated from North Carolina to Mississippi some 15 years since...Services by the Rev. M. **COONS**. Memphis Daily Eagle, 5/18/1850.

Mr. William **OLDHAM**, a native of Dublin, Ireland, fell senseless to the ground on the corner of Main and Union streets and expired while he was being conveyed to the hospital. His death is supposed to have been superinduced by the extreme heat of the weather in connection with rather intemperate habits—habits no doubt contracted while in the army, from which he was but recently discharged. We learn that he had been in the city only since Monday evening. His remains were decently interred in Winchester Cemetery....Upon his person were found....a number of letters....2 or 3 from an affectionate sister, dated at Presentation Convent Dublin. From these papers we glean the following facts: He was enlisted as a private in Company D, Capt. Macrae, 3d infantry on the 2d day of February, 1849, for five years and was discharged at the expiration of his term of enlistment....and at the date of his discharge 32 years of age. He served in the expedition against the Navajoe Indians under Col. Washington, in 1849(?) and under Col. Sumner in 1852. He was honourably discharged at Albuquerque, New Mexico, on the 2d day of February, 1854....Memphis Appeal, Thurs., 7/27/1854.

Married, On the 12th inst. in Abbeville District, South Carolina, by Rev. Mr. Sloan, Mr. David T. **OLIVER**, of DeSoto county, Miss., to Miss Sallie C., youngest daughter of Capt. Jas. W. **FRAZIER**. Memphis Daily Appeal, 11/28/1857.

Married, In South Memphis, by the Rev. N. M. **GAYLORD** of the Universalist church, on Tuesday evening 28th inst., Mr. Elijah **OLIVER** to Miss Eliza Ann **JONES**. Weekly Appeal, 8/7/1846.

Geo. S. **OLIVER**, the engineer who was injured by attempting to leap from the cars of the Grenada road, died a short time after being brought to his home in this city on Friday evening last. Memphis Evening Ledger, Mon., 1/18/1858.

Married, On the 20th(?) instant at the residence of the bride's mother, by Rev. G. **WINFIELD**, Col. S. H. **OLIVER**, of Memphis, to Miss Hennie V. **ROAN**, of Pine Bluff, Ark. Memphis Daily Appeal, 10/26/1859.

Died, on Sunday morning last, Thomas J. **OLIVER**, of the firm of Oliver & Hancock, in the 44th year of his age. Memphis Appeal, Wed., 2/23/1848.

Died, At his residence in Fort Pickering, Wednesday, August 18th, Jesse **OLMSTED**, Esq., aged 63 years...Memphis Appeal, 8/19/1852.

Married, On the 12th inst., at the residence of the bride, Mr. E. **O'NEAL**, of Mississippi, and Miss Z. A. **McGOWAN**. Memphis Daily Appeal, 2/13/1857.

The Killing of John **O'NEAL**—We hear several conflicting accounts of the killing of an Irishman named O'Neal by a negro belonging to Mr. Rawlings, which occurred on Tuesday last. One account we copied in yesterday's paper from the *Evening News*. All the information about comes from Mr. Rawlings' negroes who were present at the time of the homicide or soon after. They state, we learn, that a controversy arose between the white man and the negro; that the former struck the negro in the face, whereupon O'Neal was stricken down with a clab-board, from which blow he died the day after....Memphis Daily Appeal, Fri., 9/25/1857.

Married, On the 13th inst. at the Verandah Hotel, by Jesse **WALDRAN**, Esq., Mr. Joseph **O'NEILL**, of Gaines' Landing, Ark., and Mrs. Virginia **GARLAND**, neice of Mr. J. M. **FADLEY**, of Memphis, Tenn. Memphis Daily Appeal, 4/15/1856.

We are pained to announce the death of Mr. Frederick **ORGILL**, of New York, who was formerly a clerk in the house of Holyoake, Lowns & Co., of this city, and the brother of Mr. Edmund **ORGILL**, of the House of Orgill Brothers & Co., hardware merchants, the successors of Lowns, Orgill & Co....He died in New York city yesterday morning....of hemorrhage of the stomach. Memphis Daily Appeal, 9/14/1859.

Married, At Pittsfield, Mass. in St. Stephen's Church, on Thursday, September 6th, by Rev. R. T. Parvin, Miss Annie Merrill, youngest daughter of Mr. Justus **MERRILL**, of Pittsfield, to Henry A. **ORNE**, of Memphis, Tenn. Memphis Daily Appeal, 9/19/1855.

Married, On Thursday evening, November 26th, at the residence of Capt. B. G. **GARRETT**, by Rev. Mr. Collins, Mr. George W. **ORR** and Miss M. A. **SPARKS**—all of this city. Memphis Evening Ledger, 11/27/1857.

We yesterday received the following note from Rev. E. H. **OSBORNE**, Pastor of the Second Baptist Church. It will be a matter of sincere regret to his numerous friends in this city, that he has determined to resign the Pastoral charge which he now holds....Memphis Daily Appeal, 2/1/1855.

Taken up by Jesse **OSBURN**, living 18 miles east of Raleigh, near the Covington road, one dark bay horse....Memphis Enquirer, 1/14/1837.

Died, In Columbia, Tenn., at the residence of her father, after five days illness of bilious pleurisy, Sarah McGavock, daughter of the Rev. James Harvey **OTEY**, aged sixteen years and eleven months...American Eagle, 6/24/1847.

Married, on Wednesday evening, 5th inst., by the Rev. Joseph E. **DOUGLASS**, Mr. John **OUSLER**, of Fayette County, Tennessee to Miss Mary N. **CONNILLY**, of Marshall County, Mississippi. Daily Memphis Enquirer, 4/26/1848.

Doctor Joseph B. **OUTLAW** – Having removed to Memphis, offers his services to the inhabitants thereof and of the surrounding country. His residence and office are on Poplar street, directly fronting the Presbyterian Church. Dr. O. deems fit to say, that he liberally enjoyed the advantages of our best Eastern Colleges and Hospitals, and has been extensively engaged in practice for more than twenty years, the last three of which having been in this country. American Eagle, 3/3/1843.

We regret sincerely to announce the death of Mr. W. **OVENS**, of the firm of Skeggs & Ovens, of our city. He died of the prevailing disease on Wednesday night. Mrs. Ovens, who was also attacked at about the same time that her husband was, died early yesterday morning....Memphis Daily Appeal, Fri., 10/19/1855. Our readers will remember that a morning or two since we chronicled the death, by yellow fever, of Mr. and Mrs. Ovens, two very highly respectable citizens of South Memphis. In their death, they left behind them seven orphan children,--the oldest not more than thirteen or fourteen years old,--with an aged grandmother in their charge. After the burial of their parents, Mr. Skeggs, the partner of Mr. Ovens, rented a house on Winchester street, in North Memphis, with the view of removing the children from the infected District....The neighbors became alarmed at the contigulty(?) of children who had been where yellow fever was and we learn that the landlord was remon____ with by Mr. Kehoe and Mr. and Mrs. _____ until the children were removed....with their aged grandmother and forced back to the home of their desolation....Memphis Daily Appeal, 10/20/1855. Capt. Pepper, of the *Hickman*, took charge of the late Mr. and Mrs. Ovens' children yesterday, for the purpose of carrying them to Cincinnati....Memphis Daily Appeal, 11/18/1855.

The friends and acquaintances of Rev. F. A. and Elizabeth H. **OWEN** are respectfully invited to attend the funeral of their son, Wilber Fisk, at the First Methodist Church this morning at 11 o'clock. Memphis Eagle & Enquirer, 6/3/1853.

The Franklin Review of the 6th instant mentions the occurrence of a difficulty in Williamson county, on Wednesday last between two brothers – Jabez and Richard **OWEN** – in which the latter was killed, by being repeatedly stabbed with a knife...Memphis Daily Appeal, 8/10/1852.

Died. On Saturday, 14th inst., Hellen, youngest daughter of Miles and Martha A. **OWEN**, aged 4 months and 27 days. American Eagle, 8/19/1847. Died—On Friday, 23d inst., William, second son of Mr. Miles and Martha A. Owen. Memphis Enquirer, 10/31/1846. Our citizens were aroused about 11 o'clock last night, by the alarm of fire, which was discovered to proceed from the roof of the large and beautiful brick dwelling of Mr. Miles Owen on the corner of Madison and Third Streets.—The building was entirely consumed, the engines being inefficient by the scarcity of water in the vicinity. The furniture was mostly saved, in a damaged state. It is supposed to have been the work of some of the family servants Memphis Appeal, 1/10/1851. Died, On the morning of the 11th inst., Ida, daughter of Miles and Martha A. Owen. Her funeral will take place at 4 o'clock this evening, from her father's residence, corner of Madison and Third streets. Memphis Daily Appeal, 8/12/1858.

Married, In Hinds county, Mississippi, at the residence of John A. WATSON, Esq. by the Rev. C. K. MARSHALL, Miss Margaret L. MURPHY to P. A. OWEN, Esq., of New Orleans, formerly of Memphis. Memphis Eagle & Enquirer, 1/6/1853.

Died, at the residence of his mother, Mrs. Melissa OWEN, Edge Hill, Lauderdale county, Tenn., on Friday evening, 12th instant, Mr. Samuel P. OWEN, aged 29 years, after a painful illness of more than three weeks....Memphis Daily Appeal, 10/25/1855.

Married, On the 30th April, 1856, by W. W. BAKER, Esq., Mr. Thomas B. OWEN, of Lafayette, Miss., and Miss Mary A. LIPSCOMB, of Coffeeville, Miss., formerly of Decatur, Alabama. Memphis Daily Appeal, 6/10/1856.

Died in this vicinity, on Friday last, 2d inst., at 20 minutes past 12 o'clock, Mrs. Margaret, consort of Col. William E. OWEN, in the 35th year of her age. A native of Belfast, Ireland—the deceased removed in early life to the United States, and after passing some years in the Eastern States, removed in 1836 to Nashville, Tenn., where she resided until united in wedlock to Colonel Owen, in the fall of 1843....For many years an exemplary member of the Protestant Episcopal Church...Eagle. The Appeal, 8/9/1844.

Died, In Des Arc, on the 26th ult., Virginia L., daughter of William L. and Narcissa E. OWEN, aged one year and ten months. Memphis Daily Appeal, 5/11/1859.

Died—In this city, on Thursday last, about 3 o'clock P.M., Mr. George J.(?) OWENS, aged 33 years. Mr. Owen was a native of Kent, but has been a citizen of Memphis for ten or twelve years....Daily Memphis Enquirer, Sat., 7/28/1849.

Married, On the 27th inst. by Rev. J. W. KNOTT, Mr. Henry OWENS and Miss Martha A. TATE, all of this city. Memphis Daily Appeal, 3/28/1856.

Married, by Rev. Reuben BURROW, on the 10th May, 1847, Mr. V. OZMONT, of this city, to Miss E. V. HENDERSON, daughter of Mrs. MAYES, of Fayette Co., Tenn. Daily Enquirer, 5/13/1847.

Married – On Thursday evening, 17th inst., by N. G. CURTIS, Esq., Mr. Calvin PADGETT to Miss Phoebe J. WELSH, all of this county. Daily Memphis Enquirer, 5/20/1849.

Married, On the 16th instant by Esquire Waldran, Mr. Wesley PADGETT and Miss Clarissa McQUEEN, all of Fort Pickering. Memphis Daily Appeal, 9/18/1856.

Died, On Sunday morning, the 14th, Eliza Ormsby Page, wife of the Rev. D. C. PAGE, Rector of Calvary Church. Thus, "having the testimony of a good conscience; in the communion of the Catholic Church....Memphis Daily Appeal, 10/16/1855. The funeral services for Mrs. Page, wife of the beloved Pastor of the Episcopal Church in this city, will take place this morning at 9 o'clock, at the church. Services by Rev. Dr. Quintard. Memphis Whig, 10/15/1855. The Rev. David C. Page, having accepted a call to the Rectorship of St. Paul's Church in Erie, Penn., desires that all letters and papers for him may be directed accordingly. Memphis Daily Appeal, 11/12/1856. Died, At the residence of Dabney MINOR, Esq., in Marshall county, Miss., on the morning of the 1st instant, of pulmonary consumption, Robert Ormsby PAGE, son of the Rev. David C. and E. O. Page, aged 22 years. Louisville and New Orleans papers please copy. Memphis Daily Appeal, 4/5/1859.

Married, At Bolivar, on Friday evening, 11th inst., by Rev. Mr. Taylor, Mr. James A. PAINE, Merchant of Jacksonport, Ark., and Miss Mary P. POSTON, of Hardeman county. Memphis Daily Appeal, 7/15/1856.

Married, On the morning of the 1st inst., at the residence of ----- Finley, in Holly Springs, by Rev. Dr. Payne, Mr. Joseph N. PAINE, of Memphis, to Miss Laura B. FENNER, of Holly Springs, Miss. Memphis Daily Appeal, 12/4/1857.

Married, In Philadelphia on the 13th inst., by Rev. John Jenkins, D.D., Mr. W. D. PAINTER, of Memphis, to Miss Bettie T. THOMPSON, of the former place. Memphis Daily Appeal, 9/16/1859.

Married, In this city last evening by Rev. J. W. SCOTT, Mr. Stephen PALMER to Mrs. Rachel NEWSOM. Memphis Daily Appeal, 8/20/1857.

Died, Yesterday morning, Frances, youngest daughter of William and Margaret PALMER, aged 19 months and 19 days......Memphis Daily Appeal, 5/5/1848.

Married, On the 24th June, by the Rev. Mr. Winfield, Doctr. John Stephen PALMORE to Miss Sarah E. Isbell, daughter of Capt. Thomas H. ISBELL, all of Fayette County, Tenn. The Richmond (Va.) papers will please copy. Weekly Memphis Eagle, 7/19/1849.

Died, at the residence of her husband, Spring Hill, Fayette county, Tenn., on the 17th day of October, 1852, Mrs. Susan E. PALMORE, in the 45th year of her age, after a lingering and painful illness of more than 12 months. The deceased was born in Buckingham county, Virginia and emigrated to this State in 1845...In her death society has lost an ornament and her bereaved husband and children a devoted wife, and mother...Richmond, Va. Papers please copy. Memphis Daily Appeal, 11/4/1852.

Died, On the 12th instant, Mr. Thos. J. PARDUE, aged 40 years and 5 months....Services by Rev. Wm. L. ROSSER. Memphis Daily Appeal, 10/13/1859.

Married, By Rev. Mr. Flagg at the residence of the bride's father, near LaGrange, on Wednesday evening, 28th inst., Mr. Jos. J. PARHAM, of this city, to Miss Cornelia Michie, daughter of Maj. Chas. MICHIE. Memphis Weekly Appeal, 5/5/1858.

Report of the Board of Health. For the last 48 hours, ending 12 o'clock M, July 2d....Mrs. Irabela PARIETE, cholera....Memphis Enquirer, 7/3/1849.

Married, On the 31st ult. by Rev. J. W. BATES, Mr. F. H. PARISH, of Glasgow, Ky., to Miss S. A. ANDERSON, of DeSoto county, Miss. Memphis Daily Appeal, 9/2/1859.

The death of Mr. A. G. PARK, of this city, was announced in St. Louis on the 3d inst....The deceased was not simply a mechanical daguerreotypist—he was an artist and possessed the soul and inspiration of the true artist. He has made some of the best pictures of that style ever taken, and the work that attracted so much attention at the world's exhibition in Paris and New York, winning the prizes, was the result of his genius and skill....Memphis Daily Avalanche, 2/9/1859.

Died, in this city, on the 22d inst., of inflammation of the peritone_m, Andrew PARK, aged 32 years. Memphis Enquirer, 6/25/1846.

Married, On Thursday evening last in the immediate vicinity of this city, by the Rev. G. W. COONS, W. __. TAYLOR, Esq., of Marshall county, Miss., to Miss Ann E. Park, daughter of David PARK, Esq. Memphis Appeal, Sat., 4/2/1853.

Died—On the morning of the 11th instant, James B., eldest son of David and Jane PARK, in the 22d year of his age. After 17 years of suffering, such as seldom falls to the lot of mortals, he has gone to his rest.....Confined for six months prior to his death, to his bed and racked with incessant pain.....Nashville papers will please copy.—Eagle. Weekly Appeal, 4/17/1846.

We were much pained yesterday to hear of the death of our esteemed fellow-citizen, David **PARK**. He died suddenly, as we learn, of appoplexy. He was among the oldest and most highly respected citizen of Memphis and was a man of fine social qualities and of great business capacity. Peace to his ashes. Memphis Daily Appeal, 3/7/1856.

Taken up by John **PARK**, living 10 miles east of Memphis, near the State Line Road, one sorrel mare...The Appeal, 10/27/1843.

Married, On Wednesday evening, the 7th inst., by Rev. T. L. **GRACE**, Mr. Jno. **PARK** to Miss C. Martina **GALLAGHER**, all of this city. Memphis Daily Appeal, 7/9/1852.

Married—On Thursday the 18th inst. by the Rev. Jeptha **HARRISON**, at the residence of Doct. Wyatt **CHRISTIAN**, Mr. Wm. **PARK**, to Miss Rebecca **COCKE**, both of this city. Memphis Enquirer, 10/20/1838.

Miss Rebecca Park, daughter of our fellow-townsman, Wm. **PARK**, took the premiums for the best composition read at the commencement and examination exercises ___ the Florence Synodical Female College....Memphis Daily Avalanche, 7/14/1858.

Died, at his residence in Dyer county, Tenn., on Saturday morning, December 6, 1856, after an illness of four days, of pneumonia, Daniel E. **PARKER**, Sr., Esq., aged 67 years and 5 months. Esq. Parker had been a resident of Dyer county for nearly thirty years—widely known as a most worthy and useful citizen....His family are deprived of an excellent, affectionate and provident husband and father....Danville, Va., papers please notice. Memphis Daily Appeal, 12/20/1856. Died, of pneumonia, after an illness of eight days, at her residence in Dyer county, Tenn., on the 14th inst. at 8 ½ o'clock, A.M., Mrs. Martha Parker, (widow of Daniel E. Parker, Sr., Esq., lately deceased,) aged 62 years, 10 months and 10 days....Mrs. Parker was one of the best of wives, kindest of mothers....She was for many years....a member of the Cumberland Presbyterian Church....Danville (Va.) papers please notice. Memphis Daily Appeal, 12/27/1856.

Dentistry—Geo. H. **PARKER**, M.D., offers his professional services to the citizens of this place and vicinity. The claims which he offers for their patronage are a very extensive experience in every branch of his profession, and a diploma from the University of Pennsylvania at Philadelphia. Ladies attended at their residence...Memphis Enquirer, 4/5/1839.

Married, On the 11th instant at the residence of Dr. Eldridge, Col. George L. **PARKER**, of Memphis, and Miss C. L. **LUNDIE**, of Shelby county. Memphis Daily Appeal, 12/13/1855.

Died, On Monday morning, November 29th, of dyspepsia, Thomas Parker, eldest son of R. A. **PARKER**, Esq., in the 21st year of his age. Memphis Appeal, 12/1/1852. Died, In this city, on Tuesday evening last, Miss Mary Ann, daughter of Mr. and Mrs. R. A. Parker, in the 16th year of her age. Memphis Appeal, Thursday, 2/3/1853. Died, In this city on the morning of the 2d inst., at 6 o'clock, A.M., after a brief illness, at the residence of her father, in the 17th year of her age, Miss Martha Ann Parker, second daughter of R. A. Parker, Esq.....Thus has a second stunning blow fallen upon our worthy and excellent fellow-citizen, R. A. Parker, Esq. Within the short space of one month, a son, of much promise, and now a daughter....Memphis Eagle & Enquirer, 2/3/1853.

Married, On the 25th instant in Tipton county, Tenn., at the residence of the bride's father, by Rev. Jas. **HOLMES**, Mr. R. A. **PARKER**, Jr., of this city, and Miss Sallie J. **FLOWERS**. Memphis Weekly Appeal, 6/2/1858.

Samuel W. **PARKER** vs. Elizabeth Parker, Bill for Divorce...The bill charges that complainant had heretofore married the defendant; that over two years ago defendant had willfully absented herself from his bed and board without any just cause, and therefore prays a Divorce. Memphis Enquirer, 3/4/1837.

Married, On Sunday, September 16th, at Baker's Chapel by Rev. Mr. Baker, Dr. E. M. **PARKS**, of DeSoto county, Miss., to Miss C. M. **GIBBS**, of Marshall county, Miss. Memphis Daily Appeal, 9/18/1855.

Died, On Thursday morning, January 29th, little Jimie Bailey, only son of William and Lou. **PARR**, aged two years, eight months and seventeen days....Lincoln Journal and Fayetteville Observer please copy. Memphis Daily Appeal, 2/8/1857.

Married, In Bolivar, November 2d, at the residence of Major John H. **BILLS**, by the Rev. H. **CHAMBERLAIN**, Thomas A. **PARRAN** to Miss Maria E. **WOOD**. Memphis Daily Appeal, 11/10/1848.

Married—On Thursday evening, the 28th ult....Mr. Thomas O. **PARRAN** to Miss Nancy Carr, daughter of Thomas D. **CARR**, Esq., all of Shelby county. Memphis Advocate, 3/1/1828.

David M. **PARRISH**, one of the heirs of William S. **PARRISH**, dec'd will take notice that the undersigned will file a petition in the next Circuit Court, to be holden at the Court House in Covington, to have laid off and set apart to them the dower interest which Lucinda **JAMES**, formerly Lucinda **PARRISH**, wife of the late William S. Parrish, has in and to three tracts of land lying in Tipton County, one of 120 acres, one other for 120 acres and one for 82(?) acres, owned by said William S. Parrish; at the time of his death one of the tracts of 120 acres was occupied by said Parrish. You as one of the heirs at law of said Parrish can attend and make objections, of any you have. Purly **JAMES**, Lucinda James. Weekly American Eagle, 8/27/1846.

Married, On the 24th inst., at the Carolina House, by the Rev. Samuel **DENNIS**, Dr. David M. **PARTEE** to Mrs. Susan B. **NEWBY**—all of this city. Memphis Daily Eagle, 1/25/1850.

Died, on the 16th September instant at the residence of her father, Col. Hiram **PARTEE**, near Ripley, Lauderdale county, Tennessee, Louanna Partee, in the twelfth year of her age....So that whether sustaining the relation of school girl, or playmate, or sister, or daughter, little "Tennie" always won the warmest affections....Nashville *Union* please copy. Memphis Daily Appeal, 9/24/1856.

Married, On the 20th of September by Rev. Mr. Crosby, Mr. A. S. **PASCHALL** to Miss C. M. **FLETCHER**, all of Pontotoc county, Miss. Memphis Daily Appeal, 10/13/1855.

Died—In Water Valley, Miss., August 4, 1858, Kate, only child of J. M. and Paulina **PASCHALL**, aged one year eight months and fourteen days....Memphis Daily Appeal, 9/28/1858.

Married, At the late residence of Mr. Brooks, in DeSoto county, Miss., on the morning of the 10th ult., by Elder C. B. **YOUNG**, Mr. R. H. **PASLEY**, son of Austen **PASLEY**, of Panola county, to Miss Elizabeth **BROOKS**. Memphis Daily Appeal, 3/8/1859.

Masonic. At a regular communication of South Memphis Lodge No. 118, held at the Lodge Hall, on the evening of April 9th, A.D. 1847, the following preamble and resolutions were unanimously adopted:-- Whereas, it has pleased the Supreme Architect of the Universe to remove from our midst our esteemed and worthy brother, Robert H. **PATILLO**, Esq...Weekly Appeal, 4/16/1847. At a meeting of the members of the Memphis Bar..submitted the following resolutions....Resolved, that we have learned, with deep and unaffected regret, the death of our professional brother R. H. Patillo.....Weekly American Eagle, 4/15/1847.

Married, On the 31st of July by Rev. R. R. **EVANS**, Mr. Geo. C. **PATRICK** to Miss Susan C. **TEMPLETON**, all of Shelby county. Memphis Daily Appeal, 8/2/1856.

Died. On yesterday, Leonidas Knox, youngest son of J. M. and M. K. **PATRICK**. Also, died, at the same time and place, Robert Greenville, son of E. M. & L. **PATRICK**. American Eagle, 6/3/1847. Our city fire-bells sounded their startling alarm about half-past eight o'clock last night, some vile incendiary having set on fire the cotton warehouse of Mr. J. M. Patrick, containing some 1500 bales of cotton. The fire was extinguished, though not until several bales had become more or less burnt...The Daily Eagle, 2/29/1848.

Our friend Isaac M. **PATRIDGE**, late of the Memphis *Whig*, leaves on the cars this morning for Holly Springs, to assume the editorial control of the *Times*, published at that place. During his short residence in this city, he had collected around him a circle of warm personal friends...Memphis Daily Appeal, 8/1/1856.

Married, On the 21st ult., by the Rev. D. **COFFEY**, Mr. B. M. **PATTERSON**, Jr., to Miss Tempie P., daughter of Wm. **BATTLE**, Esq.; all of this county. Memphis Eagle, 11/8/1849. Died, Of consumption, at the Dunlap Springs, near Bolivar, on the 31st of July ult., Mrs. Tempe Patterson, consort of Bernard M. Patterson, jr. and daughter of William and Chloe Battle, of Shelby county, Tenn. Memphis Daily Eagle, 8/10/1850.

Married, On the 6th inst. by Rev. A. M. **BRYAN**, our young friend, Billy **PATTERSON**, of the firm of P. M. Patterson & Bro., to Miss Maggie B. **CHESTER**, all of this city....The happy couple left on the *Ingomar*, on a bridal tour for the Crescent City, last Wednesday evening.... Memphis Daily Appeal, Friday, 1/8/1858. Mr. William M. **PATTERSON**, one of our enterprising omnibus men, returned to the city yesterday, on the *Ingomar*, from a bridal trip to New Orleans....Memphis Daily Appeal, 1/19/1858.

Married, At the residence of the bride's father in DeSoto county, Miss., on Thursday, 3d December, by Rev. W. C. **ROBB**, Pugh T. **PATTERSON**, of Memphis, Tenn., to Miss Mary __. Rozell, daughter of Col. Y. P. **ROZELL**. Nashville *Union* and North Carolina *Standard* please copy. Memphis Daily Appeal, 12/5/1857.

Report of the Board of Health....In the last 24 hours the following deaths have occurred....Wm. **PATTERSON**, taken from a flatboat yesterday evening, and died last night of Cholera. Memphis Eagle, 1/9/1849.

...For Sale. My house and lot, on Madison street, between Main and Second streets...Alex. **PATTISON**, jr. Memphis Appeal, 8/10/1852.

The friends and acquaintances of Col. George **PATTISON** are invited to attend the funeral of his wife This Afternoon....at the family residence on Vance street. Services by Dr. Grundy. Memphis Daily Appeal, 9/2/1859. ....But few Christians have exemplified this more strongly than did Mrs. Sallie G. Pattison, who died at her residence in this city, on the morning of the 1st inst. Her maiden name was **TRABUE**. She was a native of Adair county, Ky., and became the wife of Col. George Pattison in 1831. In 1837 she made a public profession of religion and joined the Presbyterian Church in Clarksville, in this State. She moved with her husband to Memphis in 1844, and soon after became a member of the Second Presbyterian Church....She was one of the original founders of the Memphis Orphan Asylum....She has left several sons and one daughter to mourn with their father....when they came she had the entire seven to encircle her bed upon their knees....Memphis Daily Appeal, 9/18/1859.

We are requested by the family of the late Geo. **PATTISON**, Jr., to state that the remains of the deceased will be interred this afternoon; the exercises will take place at the house of Mr. Pattison on Vance street....The remains of the late Geo. Pattison arrived at this city last evening over the Memphis and Charleston railroad....Memphis Daily Appeal, 11/22/1859. Died, On Sunday, November 13th, in the city of Brooklyn, at the house of Mr. Wm. M. **JUNKS**, George Pattison, of this city, in the 22nd year of his age....When Col. Pattison, his father, removed to Memphis, George was but a child....Though he died far away from home, it is unspeakably comforting to his family to know that he was not among strangers, but at the house of a friend....Memphis Daily Appeal, 12/4/1859.

Wm. H. **PATTISON**, Commission Merchant. This gentleman, for a long time connected with the well known and substantial house of Lowe, Pattison & Co., New Orleans, has located in our city....Memphis Daily Appeal, 8/22/1855.

Died, In this city on the 2d inst., Mrs. Lucy H. Paul, wife of W. P. **PAUL**, Esq., of Memphis, and daughter of John **McINTOSH**, Esq., of Nashville. Disease—Inflammation of the Bowels. Nashville papers please copy. Memphis Daily Appeal, 5/6/1857.

Died. On the evening of the 10th instant at his residence in De Soto county, Miss. oF typhoid pneumonia, Mr. C. B. **PAYNE**, in the 49th(?) year of his age. Fayetteville papers please copy. Memphis Daily Appeal, 1/14/1855.

Married, in Memphis, on Tuesday 18th instant, by the Rev. B. S. **FANT**, Wm. Edwin A. **PAYNE** to Miss Martha J. **BLACKER**(?), both of DeSoto County, Mississippi. Daily Memphis Enquirer, 1/20/1848.

Married, On the 2nd inst., at the residence of Col. Wm. **POLK**, near Centre Hill, Miss., by Rev. J. M. **RODGERS**, Mr. Robt. **PAYNE** to Miss Mollie l. **McGOWAN**, all of Marshall county, Miss. Memphis Daily Appeal, 12/3/1857.

Died, At Centrehill, Mississippi, on the 29th day of April last, Mrs. Maria S. Payne, consort of Robert **PAYNE**, in the 29th year of her age. She was a native of Charlotte county, Virginia.... Memphis Daily Appeal, 5/19/1857.

The friends and acquaintances of the late Dr. James S. **PEACOCKE** are invited to attend his funeral from his residence on Adams street, between Fourth and Fifth....Services by Rev. J. O. **STEADMAN**. St. Louis and Fredericksburg (Va.) papers please copy. Memphis Daily Appeal, 2/20/1859.

Died—At Hickory Grove, in Shelby county, on the 1st day of December, Julia Ann, daughter of Samuel H. and Condice **PEAKE**, aged 11 years, 1 month and 13 days. Memphis Enquirer, 12/8/1838.

A. **PEARCE**, Esq., died at his residence in this city on the 5th instant. The deceased was a native of Virginia, but removed to Mississippi in the year 1836 and settled at Holly Springs, where he studied Law with Mr. Nelms, and was admitted to practice and formed a partnership with his Patron and Preceptor. In the year 1848 he was appointed to the honorable and responsible office of Judge of the County Court. Having been apprised of the sickness of his venerated mother and feeling it to be an act of filial peity to visit her and administer to her wants in her last hours, he resigned his Judgeship and returned to Virginia. On his return to Mississippi he resumed the practice of Law in partnership with Mr. McCampbell. He removed to this city in 1841, and formed a partnership with the late R. H. **PATELLO**, Esq. In the year 1846 he was elected a member of the Legislature of Tenn. In the Fall of 1849....he ruptured a blood vessel in the Lungs, which resulted in his death by consumption on the 5th instant....Memphis Appeal, 4/13/1853. (Author's note: There is obviously an error in dates, but this was copied as printed.)

Died—In this city, on Wednesday morning, the 19th inst. Walter Benjamin, son of Benjamin and Susan P. **PEARCE**, aged nine months and one day. The Appeal, 6/21/1844.

Married, In this city at the residence of Mr. B. W. **BURCH**, on the 3d inst., by Rev. Mr. Bateman, Dr. J. A. **PEARCE** and Miss Sallie A. **FEAGAN**, all of Mississippi. Natchez papers please copy. Memphis Weekly Appeal, 3/17/1858.

Married: On Thursday night the 25th inst. at the residence of Col. Sam'l. R. **BROWN**, by the Rev. McPherson, Dr. J. S. **PEARSON** to Mrs. Fannie **MANESS**, all of this city. Memphis Whig, 10/27/1855.

Married. At the Bluff City Mills, by Rev. J. R. **HENDRICKSON**, Mr. Moses **PEARSON**, of this city, to Miss Mary M. **DOBKINS**, of McMinnville, Tenn. Memphis Daily Appeal, 2/3/1855.

Married, On Thursday, the 29th of January, by the Rev. Mr. Cowin, Mr. Burlin **PEEBLES**, formerly of Greensville county, Virginia, to Miss Mary E., daughter of Joshua C. **LUNDAY**, Esq., of Shelby County, Tenn. Memphis Enquirer, 2/3/1846.

Died, In Fayette county, near Somerville, Tenn., on the 1st inst., Mrs. Georgiana M., consort of Etheldred D. **PEEBLES**, aged 33 years. North Carolina and Virginia papers please copy. Memphis Daily Appeal, 12/4/1855.

Died, At her residence near Chulahoma, Marshall county, Miss., on Wednesday the 26ᵗʰ inst. at 11 o'clock, A.M., Mrs. Charlotte **PEEL**. Memphis Eagle & Enquirer, 1/29/1853.

Married, On the evening of the 22d ult., at the residence of Major James **ALEXANDER**, by Rev. J. R. **HAMILTON**, Mr. Thos. J. **PEEL** to Miss Olivia T. **ALEXANDER**, of Marshall county, Miss. Memphis Daily Appeal, 10/9/1858.

Married, In this city on the 28ᵗʰ inst., by J. **WALDRON**, Esq., Mr. H. D. **PELL**(?) to Miss Susan **BONDURANCE**, all of this city. Memphis Weekly Appeal, 10/13/1858.

Maj. Geo. M. **PENN**, an old and highly respected citizen, died at his residence, in this place, on Friday last, after a lingering illness of several weeks. Memphis Appeal, Mon., 8/30/1852.

J. L. **PENN**, Attorney at Law, Memphis, Tenn. Memphis Enquirer, 1/31/1846. Married, on Tuesday evening, the 25th inst., at the residence of Seth **WHEATLEY**, Esq., by the Rev. Dr. Page, James Lyttelton **PENN**, Esq., to Miss Nannie B. Balch, daughter of the late John K. **BALCH**, all of this city. Memphis Enquirer, 4/28/1848. It is our painful duty to announce the death of James L. Penn, Esq., a prominent young lawyer of this city. He died in Fayette county on Sunday, after a long and painful illness.—He has thus been cut down in the prime and vigor of manhood, leaving a large circle of friends and relatives to mourn his premature loss....Memphis Appeal, Tuesday, 7/19/1853. On Tuesday last the mortal remains of James Lyttleton Penn, late a member of this Bar—of bright and hopeful promise—were consigned to their last resting place....Mr. Penn was a native of Lynchburg, in the State of Virginia, from whence his father removed in 1825, to the State of Alabama. He completed his education at Union College, Schenectady, New York....He read law in the office of James W. **McCLUNG**, Esq., in the city of Huntsville, Ala., in his 20ᵗʰ year....From thence, in the latter part of 1845, he removed to this city....Memphis Appeal, 7/25/1853.

Wagon Road from Memphis to California. Correspondence of the Memphis Appeal.] Fort Belknap, Texas, December 1, 1857. Messrs. Editors: The only apology I have to offer you for my remissness in the performance of the promise made to you in Memphis, and renewed at Des Arc, that of keeping you posted regularly in regard to the progress of the El Paso and Fort Yuma Wagon Road Expedition, is this....from the time it passed Fort Chadborne, (about the 20ᵗʰ September,)....Superintendant Leach, accompanied by his immediate command, had reached Franklin, on the Rio Grande, on the 21ˢᵗ of October last, having had altogether a pleasant trip across the Texas plains....We reached this place one month ago to-day. Here Captain D. C. **WOODS**, commander of the ox train, has concluded to go into winter quarters....No deaths, so far as I am informed, have occurred, in this or in the mule train, from disease; and only one from accident. This was the case of Frederick **DELF**(?), a Prussian by birth. He was a teamster in the mule train, and got run over by his wagon near Hot Springs, Ark., at which place the poor fellow soon afterward died of his injuries. He hailed from the State of Illinois, where he enlisted in this service, and is said to have funds and property there. Another serious but not fatal accident of this kind happened in the ox train in the case of John B. **PENNINGTON**, a man who enlisted in your city, (of which place he had been for some time a citizen, I believe.) He had his thigh and two of his ribs broken, and his chest considerably injured. His recovery was despaired of, and he was left at Little Rock, Ark., where the accident happened, in charge of a physician. When recovered sufficiently to travel, as creditable to his *pluck*, it may be mentioned that he pursued and overtook the train, on the confines of this State, and is again in its service. It will, perhaps, be interesting to you, to be informed that the Memphis "b'_oys," connected with this train, have generally acquitted themselves handsomely—so much so, that certain of them have been appointed to positions which entitle them to a little *extra* consideration. Mr. W. P. **WILLARD** has received the place of Secretary to Capt. Woods; Mr. James H. **CRAFT** that of one of the Wagon-Masters; and Mr. G. Y. **BROWN** that of Commissary....McK. Memphis Daily Appeal, 1/19/1858.

The Memphis, Capt. Jim **PEPPER**, is due to-morrow from Cincinnati...Memphis Daily Appeal, 3/15/1856. Capt. James H. Pepper—This gentleman has disposed of his interest in the Memphis and Cincinnati Packet Company and, we are pleased to learn, has determined to engage in business in this city....Memphis Daily Appeal, 6/30/1859.

Married, At Rising Sun, Indiana, on Thursday evening, 30th ult., by the Rev. H. G. **DURBIN**, Mr. Robert D. **PERCIVAL**, of this city, to Miss Fanny **BANKS**. Memphis Appeal, 4/7/1848.

Married, In Brownsville, Haywood co., Tenn., on Thursday, the 5th inst., by the Rev. J. E. **BRIGHT**, Dr. Benjamin F. **PERKINS**, of Claiborne Parish, La., and son of Nicholas **PERKINS**, Esq., of this county, to Miss Jane W. Proudfit, daughter of William **PROUDFIT**, Esq., of this place. The Franklin Review and Raleigh, N.C. papers will please copy. Memphis Eagle & Enquirer, 2/14/1852.

Died—On Tuesday, the 15th ult., at the residence of her brother, George W. **PERKINS**, Esq., in DeSoto county, Miss., Miss Elizabeth S., daughter of the late Nicholas **PERKINS** of Williamson co., Tenn., in the 19th year of her age. The Franklin Review will please copy. Weekly Appeal, 10/9/1846. Died, In DeSoto county, Mississippi, at the residence of her father, on the 5th inst., Angelina Maria Perkins, second daughter of George W. Perkins, Esq., aged 14 years and 1 day, of Typhoid Fever....Columbia and Franklin, Tenn., and Hernando, Miss., papers please copy. Memphis Eagle & Enquirer, 2/6/1853.

Died, In this vicinity on Sunday evening, 5th instant, Walter Wrenn, infant son of J. and Mrs. E. A. **PERKINS**, aged about 18 months. Memphis Daily Appeal, 9/9/1858.

Married: At the residence of Mr. A. J. **HENRY**, in South Memphis, on Wednesday evening, by Rev. P. S. **GAYLE**, Mr. John A. **PERKINS**, of Hernando, Miss. to Miss Jane T. **HOTCHKIS**, of this city. Memphis Daily Eagle, Fri., 7/14/1848.

Died, February 21st....infant son of John R. and Penelope R. **PERKINS**, aged four months.... Early Grove, Miss., Feb. 27th, 1859. Memphis Daily Appeal, 3/3/1859.

Died, In this vicinity on the 17th inst., in the sixty-first year of her age, Mrs. Eliza H. Perkins, wife of Col. Jno. P. **PERKINS**, formerly of Haywood county and daughter of Col. Richard **NIXON**, late of North Carolina. Memphis Daily Appeal, 10/19/1855.

Died, at his late residence, Poplar Grove, Williamson county, Tenn., on Sunday 6th of August, 1843, Col. Nicholas Tate **PERKINS**. The Appeal, 8/25/1843.

Two Houses and Lots for rent, suitable for family residence; but so connected as to be suitable for a boarding house...Apply on the premises, on Main between Adams and Jefferson streets, Memphis...Wm. M. **PERKINS**. Daily Enquirer, 5/22/1847.

Married, On Thursday evening 21st ult. in Madison county, Tenn., Mr. Merlin **PERRY** to Miss Ann **BOON**. The Appeal, 10/6/1843.

Married, On the 19th instant at the residence of the bride's father in Hardeman county, by Rev. Thomas **TAYLOR**, Mr. W. F.(?) **PERRY**, of Fayette county, to Miss Charity Chapman, daughter of Col. **CHAPMAN**. Memphis Weekly Appeal, 6/2/1858.

By order of "Morning Sun Lodge No. 186,' of free and accepted Masons: By an all-wise, yet inscrutable providence, our fraternity has been called to mourn the loss of our beloved brother, A. S. **PERSON**, who departed this life May 31st, 1852...Resolved, Therefore, That in the death of Bro. P. we have lost a Mason good and true, an estimable citizen, an affectionate husband, and a tender father...Memphis Eagle & Enquirer, 6/4/1852.

Married. On Wednesday evening, the 15th inst., by the Rev. Allen **WYNNE**, Mr. Amos **PERSON**, to Miss Matilda C. Redditt, daughter of Mr. Sharke **REDDITT**, all of this country. American Eagle, 1/1/1848

Died—In Shelby county on the 15th ult., in the 44th year of his age, Col. Thomas **PERSON**, one amongst the earliest settlers of this District. Southern Statesman, 7/2/1831

Married, On the evening of the 22d instant, near Collierville, by Rev. P. C. **HALLEY**, at the residence of Wm. **BIGG's**, Mr. J. R. **PERSONS** to Miss Bettie **BIGGS**, all of Shelby county, Tenn. Memphis Weekly Appeal, 3/3/1858.

On Wednesday last Mr. Robert F. **PERSONS**, of this county, living in the vicinity of Shelby depot, on the Memphis and Ohio Railroad, was killed in his saw mill by the kam rod, which flew off while the mill was in motion and struck him on the head, fracturing his skull. He lived only a few hours after he was struck. It is a little remarkable that his wife had a presentiment that he was going to be killed, and implored him on Wednesday morning not to go to the mill, following even as far as the yard-gate….Memphis Daily Appeal, Sat., 5/21/1859.

Married, On the 1st instant at the house of Mr. Wm. **PARAM**, Maury county, by Rev. J. T. **PICKETT**, Dr. George B. **PETERS**, of Bolivar, Tenn., to Miss Jessie H. **McKISSACK**, of Maury county. Memphis Weekly Appeal, 6/16/1858.

I have for sale the Residence and 183 ½ acres of land belonging to Thomas **PETERS**, Esq., lying on the State Line Road and the Memphis and Charleston Railroad, 21 miles east of Memphis, at Bray's Station. The improvements consists of a dwelling, built in Gothic Style, 9 large rooms and 2 small ones….Apply to Thos. Peters, on the premises….Memphis Daily Appeal, 12/25/1856.

The County Court of Shelby county yesterday elected J. W. A. **PETTIT** Chairman of the Quorum Court, Josiah **HORNE** Coroner….Memphis Evening Ledger, 1/5/1858.

Married, In Memphis, on the morning of the 27th inst. by Rev. Mr. Rains, James **PETTIT**, Esq., of Somerville, and Miss Georgia Cooper, daughter of George P. **COOPER**, of this vicinity. Memphis Daily Appeal, 10/28/1857.

Married, In Tuscumbia, Ala., on Wednesday evening, Aug. 13th, by the Rev. N. A. **PENLAND**, Mr. Jas. T. **PETTIT**, of Memphis, Tenn., to Miss Jane Foster, daughter of Wm. **COOPER**, Esq., of Tuscumbia. Memphis Daily Eagle, 8/20/1850.

Died—On Monday the 21st September, Eliza Jane, wife of Col. J. W. A. **PETTIT**, of this City, in the 30th year of her age, after an illness of 4 months…..The deceased was a native of Hancock county, Georgia, and previous to her removal to Memphis, had resided several years at Eufaula, Alabama….In the death of this excellent lady, an affectionate husband and five dear children are left to mourn….Weekly Appeal, 9/25/1846. Notice is Hereby Given, That in conformity with the city charter, the Board of Mayor and Aldermen of Memphis have established a system of Public Schools within the limits of the city, which will go into operation by the 1st of September next…John W. A. Pettit, Superintendent Public Schools. Daily Memphis Enquirer, 8/3/1848.

Wm. Henry **PETTY** of Mobile, died in Havanna on the 7th ult. He was a native of Fayetteville, Tenn. He was a lawyer, and member of the last Legislature of Alabama from Franklin county. Memphis Eagle & Enquirer, 4/22/1853.

We learn by letter from Washington, that Dr. C. **PEYTON**, of our city, has been appointed Surgeon in the army, and has been ordered to Fort Smith, Ark., to accompany a body of troops from the place to California. A Corps of Topographical Engineers has been ordered to make reconnaissance and survey a nearer and more Southward route to San Francisco, and Dr. P. accompanies them to report on the medical topography of the country. Daily Memphis Enquirer, 3/29/1849.

Col. Ran. **PEYTON**, a brother of the Hon. Bailie **PEYTON**, committed suicide a few days since in Sumner county, by shooting himself. He had been laboring under an alienation of the mental faculties for three or four years. Memphis Enquirer, 8/4/1846.

Married, Yesterday afternoon, by J. **HORNE**, Esq., at his office, Monsieur Gotlieb **PFISTERER** to Mlle. Theresia **BEHRENS**, all of this city. Memphis Daily Avalanche, 4/15/1859.

Married. On the morning of the 22d inst. at the residence of the bride's father, (Mr. Benjamin **NORRIS**, near this city) by Rev. J. W. **KNOTT**, Mr. Benjamin F. **PHELON**, of this city, and Miss Mary S. Norris. Memphis Whig, 5/23/1855.

The subscriber respectfully informs the public, that he has removed his shop to the corner of Poplar and Second Streets, where he continues to carry on the Blacksmithing Business...Isaac **PHELON**. Memphis Enquirer, 6/13/1849. Died, In this city on Sunday morning, the 18th inst., at the residence of her husband, Mrs. Julia, consort of Isaac Phelon, in the 37th year of her age. The deceased leaves a husband and family of four children...Memphis Daily Appeal, 1/21/1852. We learn that our old friend, Isaac **PHELAN**, who has for a number of years been extensively engaged in the foundry and manufacturing business in this city, designs making New Orleans his future home....Memphis Daily Appeal, 10/30/1858. It is with feelings of sincere regret that we announce the death of Col. Isaac Phelon, late of this city. The sad event occurred at the residence of Murray **PHILLIPS**, Esq., near Louisville, Ky., on the 3d inst. The deceased was well known in this community, and enjoyed the confidence and esteem of all with whom he had business or social relations. Memphis Daily Appeal, 10/9/1859.

The friends and acquaintances of the late John F.(?) **PHILLIPS**, are requested to attend his funeral this morning at 10 o'clock, from the residence of Tilman **BETTIS**, Esq. Memphis Appeal, 2/25/1851.

Married. On Tuesday evening, December 26th, 1854, in St. Peter's Church, Columbia, by Rev. D. **PISE**(?), Mr. Lemuel H. **PHILLIPS** to Miss Annie Maria, daughter of James **WALKER**, Esq. Also by the same, at the same time and place, Mr. Ed. F. **LEE** to Miss Jane Virginia, daughter of Dr. I. B. **HAYS**, all of this place. [Columbia Herald] Memphis Daily Appeal, 1/16/1855.

Married: Near Somerville on the 21st inst. by Rev. Y. **MORAN**, Mr. R. S. **PHILLIPS** and Miss C. M. **POWELL**, all of Fayette county. Memphis Whig, 11/22/1855. Married, On the evening of the 20th inst., at the residence of her father by Rev. Mr. Moran, Mr. R. S. Phillips to Miss C. M., daughter of W. **POWELL**, Esq., all of Fayette county. Memphis Daily Appeal, 11/22/1855.

On Wednesday last, the 8th inst., H. W. **BASS** and Samuel W. **PHILLIPS** of DeSoto county, Mississippi, got into an affray in which Bass stabbed Phillips in the abdomen with a pocketknife, causing his death in 36 hours afterward....Memphis Daily Appeal, 10/12/1856.

Married—At the residence of William **LAWRENCE**, Esq., near Memphis, on Wednesday evening, the 9th inst., Mr. Thomas **PHOEBUS**, Editor of the Memphis Advocate, to Miss Sophia **BROWN**. Jackson Gazette, 4/19/1828

Died, on the 30th of November, at his residence in Fayette county, Tennessee, John G. **PICKENS**, in the 38th year of his age. The deceased was for many years a member of the Cumberland Presbyterian Church, and died in the full triumph of a living faith. At a meeting of North Mount Pleasant Lodge No. __, of Free and Accepted Masons, the following preamble and resolutions were adopted: Whereas, It hath pleased Almighty God, the Supreme Architect of the Universe, in His infinite wisdom to remove by death our Brother, John L. Pickens....Memphis Daily Appeal, 1/3/1857.

Died, At 3 o'clock, on the morning of the 24th instant, Miss Maria T. Pickett, second daughter of Mrs. Ann F. **PICKETT**, of this city,,,The cause which produced this disastrous result occurred during the late Fair given by the Odd Fellows of this city, when the dress of this interesting young lady accidentally came in contact with a candle, by which it took fire, when she and her sister and another young lady, became enveloped in flames,,,The Huntsville (Ala.) Advocate and Banner of Peace, Lebanon, Tenn. please copy. Memphis Daily Eagle, 12/27/1850.

Edward **PICKETT**, Attorney At Law, Memphis, Tenn. Office South side of Court Square.... Memphis Daily Appeal, 9/23/1852.

Col. Edward **PICKETT**, Jr. This gentleman, who was formerly connected in an editorial capacity with this paper, since Editor of the Natchez *Free Trader* and late Editor and Proprietor of the Vicksburg *Sentinel*, has retired from the latter journal and announces his intention....to remove to this city for the purpose of practicing the profession of the law....Memphis Daily Appeal, 2/28/1857.

Married, In this city, on the 9th inst., by Rev. Dr. Gray, A. **PIERCE**, Esq., to Miss P. C. **PATILLO**, all of Memphis. Memphis Appeal, 1/13/1851.

Various reports having been circulated by the officers of the steamer Saxon and others to the effect that I had given up charge of the steamer Coro No. 2, I deem it proper to state that they are wholly groundless, and that the Coro No. 2 will continue in the trade until my new boat is ready to take her place, which will be in a few weeks. John **PIERCE**, Capt. Memphis Appeal, 10/16/1851.

Intelligence received in this city yesterday from California, assures us of the death of Captain John **PIERCE**, late of this city. The sad event occurred in Los Angelos county. The deceased leaves a wife and interesting family in this city. Memphis Daily Appeal, 7/6/1859.

Married, Near Fort Pickering on Wednesday, the 7th inst., by Esquire Richards, Dupay **PIERRE** to Miss Nancy **SNOWDEN**, all of this vicinity. Memphis Daily Appeal, 9/8/1859.

Married, In Rutherford county, recently, Benj. F. **PINKERTON** and Macinda **GUM**. John M. **SINCLAIR** and Sarah B. **FLOWERS**. Robt. R. **CALDWELL** and Tennessee S. **BUCHANAN**. Henry R. **ANDERSON** and Nancy E. **BAXTER**. Joseh M. **THREET** and Caroline **EVINS**. Memphis Daily Appeal, 4/15/1856.

Obituary. It is my melancholy duty to record the death of one of the most amiable and noble ladies of this, my near vicinity, Mrs. Clarissa **PIPKIN**....She was born August 15th, 1814, and died December 1st, 1855, four miles East of Raleigh, Shelby county, Tenn. She made an early profession of christianity and at the age of sixteen years joined the Baptist Church at Holly's Spring, Wake county, North Carolina....She leaves a bereaved husband, three sons and two daughters to deplore their untimely loss. Peace to her ashes! A Friend. Rosstown, Shelby county, Tenn., Dec. 12, 1855. Wake county, N.C., papers please copy. Memphis Daily Appeal, 12/15/1855.

Died, At his residence four miles east of Raleigh, in this county, on the 8th instant, Jesse **PIPKIN**, in the __ year of his age. The deceased was one among our most worthy planters and had been, for some years previous to his removal to Shelby, a citizen of Madison county, in this State...North and South Carolina papers will please copy. Memphis Daily Appeal, 4/15/1856.

The funeral of Thos. **PITMAN** Jr., will take place from the First Presbyterian Church on to-morrow, (Sunday) at 3 o'clock....Memphis Eagle, 3/24/1849.

We are authorized to announce Allen A. **PITTMAN** as a candidate for Sheriff at the approaching March election. Memphis Eagle, 12/13/1849.

Died—In this city on Sunday, the 18th inst., of consumption, Gilly **PITTMAN**, formerly of Buckingham county, Va., in the thirty-third year of his age....His remains were yesterday interred in Elmwood, being attended to his last resting place by his friends and relatives. Richmond Enquirer please copy. Memphis Daily Appeal, 9/20/1859.

Died, on Saturday evening, October 16, C. Bias Pittman, aged 13 years, 1 month and 23 days, son of Thomas **PITTMAN**, Sr., deceased, and Jane D. Pittman, from injuries received by being run over by the cars of the Memphis and Ohio Railroad....Memphis Daily Appeal, 10/19/1858.

Married, On the 11th instant, at Des Ark, Arkansas, by Rev. Daniel L. **GRAY**, Mr. Thomas F. **PITTMAN**, of Memphis, to Miss Mary, daughter of Major William **HOUSTON**, of the former place. Memphis Weekly Appeal, 5/26/1858.

Commander Charles T. **PLATT**, of New York, has been ordered to the command of the Memphis Depot & Dock Yard, in place of Capt. Nicholson, who has been granted leave of absence for three months....Memphis Eagle & Enquirer, 1/16/1853

Married, In LaGrange by Elder W. C. **ROGERS**, Rev. George **PLATTINBURG**, of Aberdeen, Miss., and Miss Josephine **HOWARD**, of LaGrange, Tenn. Memphis Daily Appeal, 9/18/1855.

Died: In Morning Sun, Shelby co., Tenn.; at the residence of Wm. **WASH**, Esq., on the night of the 17th inst., Dr. Charles J. **PLEASANTS**, in the 36th year of his age. Dr. Pleasants was the brother of the lamented John Hampton **PLEASANTS**, the able and talented editor of the Richmond [Va.] Whig, and emigrated from Richmond to Shelby county in the year 1841, and has practiced successfully his profession ever since....His numerous friends here sincerely sympathize with his distant relatives, particularly the aged surviving parent....Weekly Memphis Eagle, 8/23/1849. (Author's note: Name of deceased given as James J. Pleasants in another article.)

Married, On Monday evening the 11th inst. by Rev. G. W. **COONS**, Mr. Jas. E. **PLUMMER**, jr., to Miss Mary K., daughter of Littleton and Mary K. **HENDERSON**, all of Memphis, Tenn. Memphis Daily Appeal, 4/13/1853.

Died, On the 30th September at Ladies Valley, El Dorado county, California, Mr. Nathan F. **PLUMMER**, formerly of Shelby county, Tenn., after a brief illness. He was a member of the Macon Presbyterian Church....Aged, forty five years. Charlotte and Sauls____, North Carolina papers will please copy. Memphis Daily Appeal, 11/19/1857.

Died in this city on Tuesday, July 5th, 1853, after a long and painful illness, Hugh **PLUNKET**, aged 23 years. The deceased was a native of the county of Fermaugh, Ireland, and emigrated to this city about two years ago, where he had earned for himself an enviable reputation by that industry, perserverance and strict integrity which characterised him through life. The news of his death will be received with feelings of unfeighned sorrow by the companions of his youth, with whom he was an universal favorite. May he rest in peace. Memphis Daily Appeal, 7/7/1853.

Died, On the 12th instant at the residence of her father, James **MOORING**, in Marshall county, Mississippi, Mrs. Eliza C., consort of S. R. **POINTER**, of Arkansas county, Arkansas, in the 24th year of her age. Memphis Daily Appeal, 7/19/1856.

Married, On the 6th instant, by the Rev. Wm. H. **BARKSDALE**, of Lawrence county, Ala., Mr. Charles E. **POLK**, of Kossuth, Tishomingo county, Miss., and Miss Cornelia E. **FAIRCLOTH**, of Brickville, Ala. Memphis Daily Appeal, 8/13/1856.

Died—In Bolivar, on the 14th instant, of scarlet fever, Mary Eliza, infant daughter and only child of Horace M. and Ophelia J. **POLK**; aged seven Months, wanting two days. Weekly Appeal, 4/25/1845.

Died, At his father's residence near Bolivar, on the 19th inst., Edward McNeal, only child of Marshall T. and Eveline **POLK**, aged twenty months and one day. Memphis Daily Appeal, 9/28/1858.

Our community on last week was called to mourn over the death of one of the best and most amiable of our younger citizens. Thomas Gilchrist, son of General Thomas G. and Mary **POLK**, aged thirteen years and ten months, was accidentally killed by the discharge of his gun on the 9th inst....Holly Springs, Miss., April 11th, 1853. Memphis Eagle & Enquirer, 4/16/1853.

Died, Yesterday at 2 o'clock, P.M., Henry Otto, son of John H. and Catharine W. **POLLOCK**, aged 11 years and 6 months. The friends of the family are requested to attend the funeral this afternoon at 5 o'clock, from their residence on Beal street, between Main and Shelby. Memphis Eagle & Enquirer, 6/3/1852.

Died, at his residence in St. Francis county, Ark., on the 13th of June, James H. **POOL**....To his bereaved wife: Your brightest consolation will be found in training the hearts of his lovely children to obey you and love their Redeemer....Memphis Daily Appeal, 7/8/1859.

Married, At the residence of Col. Wm. **WILLIAMS**, in Shelby county, on Wednesday, the 25th of Sept., 1850, by the Rev. Mr. J. E. **DOUGLASS** of the Marshall Institute, Mr. Drew H. **POPE**, of Desoto county, Miss., to Miss Nannie M. **BUSTER** (?). Memphis Eagle, 10/2/1850.

Married—At Snowdown, the residence of Hon. A. R. **GOVAN**, in Marshall Co., Miss., on Tuesday evening last, by Rev. S. M. **WILLIAMSON**, John **POPE**, Esq., of Shelby County, Tenn., to Miss Elizabeth Hemphill, daughter of the late Morgan **JONES**, Esq., of Wilmington, N.C. Memphis Enquirer, Friday, 11/8/1839. The friends and acquaintances of Col. John Pope, are invited to attend the funeral of his wife, Elizabeth, at 9 o'clock this (Thursday) morning from his residence, on the Raleigh road. Memphis Eagle & Enquirer, 6/24/1852. Died, on the 23d inst., at the residence of her husband in Shelby county, Elizabeth Hemphill, wife of Col. John Pope. She was a native of Wilmington, Delaware, and on a visit to her sister at the South was married, and has for twelve years resided in this county...In the retirement of her country home she assiduously cultivated the minds of her children, whose teacher she was...The deep and anxious grief with which the eldest son, about ten years of age, hung around his mother in her dying moments, was a beautiful testimony how truly that heart, which is now chilled by the icy hand of death, must have vibrated with all the sensibilities of a mother's love! Memphis Eagle & Enquirer, 6/27/1852.

Married, At noon on the 8th of January, at Calvary Church by Right Rev. Bishop Otey, Hon. John **POPE** and Madame Adela Clara **CHAMBLISS**, all of this vicinity. Memphis Daily Appeal, 1/9/1857.

The Oaks for sale. Having recently purchased elsewhere, I offer for sale, the handsomely improved Plantation, on which I at present reside, consisting of nine hundred acres of Land, situated 4 miles east of Memphis, on the Memphis and Summerville Plank Road...Jno. **POPE**. Memphis Eagle & Enquirer, 2/25/1852.

Died, On the morning of the 11th instant, Percy Pope, son of LeRoy and Mary **POPE**, in the 13th year of his age. Services from Calvary Church at 4 o'clock P.M. Memphis Daily Appeal, 5/12/1857.

Married, In this city, on the 6th instant, at the residence of Dr. G. W. **ACRES**, by Rev. J. W. **KNOTT**, Mr. M. **POPE**, of Walnut Camp, Ark., to Miss Julia F. **McCLAREN**, of Macon, Tenn. Richmond Whig and Enquirer please copy. Memphis Weekly Appeal, 4/14/1858.

Married, At Elmwood, in this county, on Thursday evening last, by Rev. Mr. Knott, Mr. Oswold **POPE**, Merchant of this city, to Miss Sallie P., daughter of Dr. A.B.C. **DUBOSE**. Memphis Daily Appeal, Sat., 5/3/1856.

Death of William **POPE**, Esq. The remains of this gentleman arrived at the wharf on Saturday, on board the Autocrat. He had been on a visit to his plantation in Mississippi, and while riding out, on the 21st inst., his horse was affrighted and starting suddenly, threw him from his saddle, instantly killing him. His family were here daily expecting his arrival, when his corpse was landed. Mr. Pope was a resident of Huntsville, Ala.....Memphis Daily Appeal, 3/28/1848.

Died, in this city on yesterday morning of Pneumonia, Mrs. Eliza A. C. Porter, consort of Dr. D. M. **PORTER**, aged 42 years. The friends and acquaintances of the deceased are requested to attend her funeral from the Cumberland Presbyterian Church at half past 10 o'clock, A.M. Daily Memphis Enquirer, 9/30/1849.

Died—On the 7th ult., in Lockhart, Texas, Dr. David Montgomery **PORTER**, formerly a citizen of Memphis, and partner of Dr. James **YOUNG**. Dr. Porter was extensively known throughout Texas and Mississippi, and the last six years a resident of Lockhart….an active member and Ruling Elder of the Cumberland Presbyterian Church for the last twenty-three years….we sincerely sympathize with his bereaved wife and children….Memphis Daily Avalanche, 5/10/1859.

Married, At Hampden Sidney, Virginia, on the 28th of May by Rev. S. B. **WILSON**, D.D., Mr. Ed. E. **PORTER**, of Memphis, Tenn., to Miss Mattie C. Rice, youngest daughter of the Rev. Benjamin H. **RICE**, D.D., of the former place. Memphis Daily Appeal, 6/6/1855. Died, On the evening of the 12th, Anna M., infant and only daughter of Rev. Edward E. and Mattie C. Porter—aged two years and six months. Memphis Daily Appeal, 5/15/1859.

Died, on the 4th inst., at his plantation in Bolivar county, Miss., Rev. Elias R. **PORTER**. His funeral will take place this evening at 3 o'clock, from the residence of Miles **OWEN**, corner of Third and Madison streets. Burial service by Rev. J. T. C. **COLLINS** at the grave. Memphis Daily Appeal, 12/8/1857.

The Rev. Herschel S. **PORTER**, D.D. This distinguished divine, who has been presiding Pastor of his church in Philadelphia for the last eight years and has won a high and wide-spread reputation, arrived in our city on yesterday, and will take charge of the Cumberland Presbyterian Church in this city…Memphis Appeal, 9/6/1851. Married, On the 14th inst. by Rev. B. **MILLER**, Rev. Dr. H. S. Porter to Miss Martha Persons, daughter of the late Turner **PERSONS**. Memphis Eagle & Enquirer, 6/16/1853. Died, On the 10th instant at the residence of Mr. John **PERSONS**, in Shelby county, Eugenia, daughter of Rev. H. S. and Mrs. M. A. Porter, aged one year and two months and ten days. Memphis Whig, 8/11/1855. Rev. Dr. H. S. Porter.—It becomes our melancholy duty to announce the death of the learned and faithful Pastor of the First Cumberland Presbyterian Church of this city. After an illness of four days, he departed this life at his residence at 5 o'clock, A.M., on yesterday. His disease was bilious fever, which was probably contracted from over-exertion in the ministerial labors which he has been zealously performing for the last three weeks during a revival occasion….His remains were attended to Morris Cemetery yesterday by a large procession of his congregation and friends. Memphis Daily Appeal, 10/6/1855. ….At a meeting of the faculty of the Memphis Medical College….Dr. Herschel S. Porter, Professor of Natural History, etc., has been suddenly removed from us by death…Memphis Daily Appeal, 10/7/1855.

Died, October 6th, Jeremiah J., only son of J. C. and A. E. **PORTER**, aged 18 months. Richmond, Va. papers please copy. Memphis Daily Appeal, 10/9/1856.

Married: In this city, on Tuesday, the 25th inst., Mr. James **PORTER** to Miss Amelia Harris, daughter of A. O. **HARRIS**, Esq., all of this city. Memphis Daily Eagle, 7/27/1848. The friends and acquaintances of Mr. James H. Porter are invited to attend the funeral of his late wife, Mrs. Amelia Porter, this evening at 3 o'clock, from the Episcopal Church. Memphis Daily Appeal, 3/5/1851.

Died, In this city on Friday night last, Mrs. Mary Ann **PORTER**, of Jackson, Tenn., widow of the late Capt. Porter, of this city, and eldest daughter of the late Judge **HASKELL**, of Jackson. While on a visit to her relatives in this city, Mrs. Porter was attacked with the prevailing fever ….She had for a number of years been a consistent member of the Episcopal Church….She has left behind her….an orphan son and daughter, of tender years….Memphis Daily Appeal, Sun., 10/28/1855.

I respectfully invite you to examine my "Iron Rack Press," built on the bluff in front of the Richmond House in this city. The principle of its power is the screw, which bears equally on both ends of the follower, while the levers to which the power is applied remains at the point most favorable to its action…P. W. **PORTER**. Daily Enquirer, 4/2/1847. We are pleased to see that our fellow-townsman, Col. P. W. Porter, the inventor of the self-loading Rifle, is now on a visit to his family here….Col. P. has been absent in Massachusetts during the last year or more, perfecting his arrangements for the manufacture of the war-arresting fire-arm. Memphis Eagle & Enquirer, 2/9/1853. Died, In this city, at half past nine o'clock on the 7th inst., Col. P. W. Porter, of this city. The deceased has been a citizen of this place for several years past....Memphis Daily Appeal, 11/9/1856.

Married, On the 23d inst., by Rev. Mr. Horton, Mr. R. H. **PORTER**, of Fayette county, Tenn., and Miss Mollie **FOWLER**, of Panola county, Miss. Memphis Daily Appeal, 12/27/1856.

Died, In this city on the 14th inst., Miss Sarah Jane **PORTER**. Memphis Daily Appeal, 9/15/1855.

Died. In Paris, Henry county, Ten. on the 15th ult. Col. William **PORTER**, aged 49 years. The Appeal, 10/6/1843.

It is with no ordinary feelings of pain that we announce the demise of our friend Capt. Wm. N. **PORTER**, lately commander of the "Eagle Guards", from this city, now on service in Mexico. We learn from the *Picayune* of Sunday that he arrived in New Orleans on the steamer McKim on Friday, on his way to Memphis, and died at the St. Charles Hotel on the evening following. His remains were brought here yesterday morning by the same boat which conveyed the melancholy intelligence to his bereaved family, and were deposited in the cenotaph of "Butler Cemetery," from whence they will be conveyed to the tomb to-day at 10 o'clock. Capt. Porter's disease was chronic diarrhea, from which he had been a sufferer for several months. He was trying to reach his family here, but the satisfaction of dying among his kindred has been denied him by an inscrutable Providence...Tri-Weekly Memphis Enquirer, Saturday, 12/5/1846. Obituary – The remains of Capt. Porter were removed from the cenotaph on Sunday afternoon, and interred with the rites of the Episcopal Church, and the usual honors of the Masonic Fraternity, of which he was a zealous and warm-hearted member....Tri-Weekly Memphis Enquirer, Tuesday, 12/8/1846. William **PORTER**, son of the late Col. Wm. N. Porter, (who commanded a company from Memphis in the Mexican War) committed suicide on last Tuesday, in his room at the Lucky House, in this city, by administering to himself a dose of *strychnine*. Porter came to Jackson some four or five days ago, since which time he has been passing about the streets in a melancholy mood....A while after breakfast on the ill-fated morning of his death, he went to Mr. J. C. **COCK**, a gentleman connected with the Lucky House, and asked for a few sheets of paper, saying he wanted to write some letters....after a short time returned to Mr. Cock with a letter written, which he got Mr. C. to fold up and direct to "Mrs. Nancy Porter, Salem, Miss.," whom he told Mr. Cock was his half sister; though, as we know he has no such relative, we suppose to be his wife....He was only about 18 years old....where he was making his home when he came here a few days ago, we have not learned. He leaves a wife and one child, we think in Mississippi—*Jackson (Tenn.) Whig.* Memphis Daily Appeal, Wed., 11/3/1858.

Married—In Nashville, on Wednesday evening last, by the Rev. R. B. C. **HOWELL**, Mr. Robert **PORTERFIELD** to Miss Mary Figuers, daughter of Dr. M. **FIGUERS** of this place. American Eagle, 4/7/1842.

Died.—On Tuesday morning, 2nd inst. Mrs. Margaret Jane Ports, consort of Doct. Samuel H. **PORTS**, in the 24th year of her age...By her death she has left an afflicted husband, with a large circle of relatives and friends, to mourn her irreparable loss. Daily Enquirer, 2/24/1847.

John **POSTLETHWAITE**, Forwarding and Commission Merchant, Randolph, Tenn. Memphis Enquirer, 9/2/1837. We regret to notice among the deaths announced in the New Orleans papers of the 4th, that of Mr. John Postlethwaite, of the house of Crockett, Garland & Co., and for many years a merchant in Randolph, this State; he fell a victim to the prevailing fever. He was a most estimable man, and a native of Lexington, Ky. American Eagle, 9/16/1847.

Married, On the 15th inst., by the Rev. Mr. Gale, Dr. Geo. N. **POSTON**, of Cadiz, Ky., to Miss Eliza E.(?) daughter of Jno. T. **MURRELL**, Esq., of this city. The Daily Eagle, 2/17/1848.

Died: In this city on Friday evening, the 23d instant, Mollie H., eldest daughter of H. H. **POTTER**, aged 18 years, of consumption. Memphis Whig, 11/24/1855.

Died, Of Pneumonia, in Panola county, Miss., on the 30th of April, Col. John W. **POTTS**, in the forty-sixth year of his age. He was a native of Mecklinburg, N.C., and emigrated to Panola county in the year 1849....Memphis Daily Appeal, 5/12/1857.

Died, Of Typhoid fever, at the residence of W. H. **STREET**, in this vicinity, February 19th, 1850, Benjamin F. **POWEL**, in the 23d year of his age...He made profession of religion when quite young, and soon afterwards became a member of the Cumberland Presbyterian Church, at Winchester, Tenn.... Memphis Daily Eagle, 3/2/1850.

Notice is hereby given that the undersigned has taken out letters of administration upon the estate of Ellen **POWEL**, dec'd....Geo. R. **POWEL**, Adm'r. Memphis Daily Appeal, 6/25/1854.

On Saturday night between twelve and one o'clock a difficulty occurred at the Metropolitan Restaurant, between Capt. Wm. **POWELL** and Mr. G. W. **REDDICK**, a barkeeper in the establishment, which resulted in the death of the former gentleman at the Worsham House, at seven o'clock on Sunday evening, and the slightly wounding of Reddick....Powell suffered greatly during the day, but early in the morning, having become conscious that he could not survive, requested a friend to take his papers and money ($740) to his wife at Burlington, New Jersey....where he desired also his remains to be conveyed....Captain Powell had only been in our city about two months....He was, we understand, a native of Philadelphia, where he resided a number of years. Apparently, he was about thirty years of age at the time of his death. He has left a wife and child besides numerous relations....Memphis Daily Appeal, Tues., 1/13/1857.

Married, On the 28th July by Esq. Waldran, Benj. F. **POWERS** and Miss Sarah J. **ELAM**, all of Memphis. Memphis Daily Appeal, 8/7/1856.

Married, On the 28th instant in this city, by Rev. Mr. Barbee, Mr. C. L. **POWERS** and Miss Lucy L. **SMALL**. Memphis Daily Appeal, 1/31/1857.

Married. In this city on Wednesday evening last, 6th instant, by Rev. Mr. Saunders, Mr. Edward **POWERS** to Miss Sarah A. E., eldest daughter of John G. **BINGHAM**. Memphis Daily Appeal, 9/8/1854.

G. W. **PRATT**, Piano Forte Dealer, Front Row, Memphis, Tenn. Memphis Daily Appeal, 10/14/1847.

Died, On yesterday morning, Mrs. Anna Prescott, consort of Jedediah **PRESCOTT**, in the 42d year of her age. The friends and acquaintances of the family are requested to attend her funeral this (Wednesday) evening at 3 o'clock, from J. **PRESCOTT's** residence on Market street, East of the Bayou. Memphis Daily Appeal, 2/11/1852. Died, In this city on the evening of the 31st October, 1858, Josiah Prescott, third son of Jedediah Prescott, in the 34th year of his age. The friends and acquaintances of Josiah Prescott are requested to attend his funeral from the residence of Levi **PRESCOTT**, in North Memphis, at 10 o'clock This Morning. Memphis Daily Appeal, 11/2/1858. Died, On Sunday morning last, November 13, 1859, Jedediah Prescott, in the 63rd year of his age. The friends and acquaintances of Jedediah Prescott are requested to attend his funeral from his late residence in North Memphis, This Afternoon. Memphis Daily Appeal, 11/15/1859.

Died, In this city, May 6th, 1858, Mrs. Mary Jeffries Prescott, consort of Jesse P. **PRESCOTT**, in the 25th year of her age. Memphis Weekly Appeal, 5/12/1858.

Died, on the 10th inst., of consumption, Hannah W., wife of Levi **PRESCOTT**, in the 54th year of her age....Memphis Daily Appeal, 1/12/1848. Married, at Cincinnati, Ohio, on the 14th inst., by the Rev. H. **JEWELL**, Mr. Levi Prescott, of this city, to Mrs. Mary E. **KING**. Daily Memphis Enquirer, 8/26/1848.

All persons who do not list their taxable Property and Polls by the 10th February, may expect to pay double taxes besides costs, (list to be handed to my Deputy, Oscar F. **PRESCOTT**.) James **ROSE**, Revenue Commissioner for the 5th Civil District. Daily Enquirer, 2/6/1847. Died, On yesterday evening, April 2d 1851, of consumption, after a protracted illness of three months, Mrs. Ann R. W. Prescott, wife of Oscar F. Prescott—aged 26 years. The friends and acquaintances are invited to attend her funeral from his residence, north Memphis, this Thursday evening.... Memphis Daily Appeal, 4/3/1851. Married. On Sunday evening, 18th, by S. R. **RICHARDS**, Esq., Mr. Oscar F. **PRESCOTT**, of this city, to Mrs. Mary **DAVIS**, of Boston, Mass. Memphis Daily Appeal, 2/21/1855.

Died: On the night of Friday, the 11th instant, Mrs. Mary, consort of Mr. Thomas **PRESTON**, and daughter of the late David **CRAIGHEAD**, at the residence of her husband, in Arkansas, opposite Randolph. Weekly Memphis Eagle, 5/17/1849.

Married, In Jackson, Tenn., on the 10th instant, by Rev. C. **McKINNEY**, Col. Walter E. **PRESTON**, of Arkansas, to Miss Fannie Middleton, second daughter of General S. J. **HAYS**. Memphis Weekly Appeal, 3/24/1858.

Married, On the 17th instant at the residence of the bride's father, Z. **BAILEY**, Mr. A. O. **PREWITT** to Miss Louvenia Bailey, all of Hardeman county, Tenn. Memphis Daily Appeal, 2/22/1859.

Married, Near Grand Junction, at 9 o'clock A.M., on Tuesday, the 21st inst., at the residence of T. J. **VALENTINE**, by Rev. Levin **SAVAGE**, Mr. Joseph H. **PREWITT** to Miss Mollie, daughter of E. **HILL**, Esq. At the same time and same place, and by the same, Mr. John **ARNETT** to Miss Sallie, daughter of Thomas **SMART**, deceased. Memphis Weekly Appeal, 12/29/1858.

Died, On the 17th instant, in Grand Junction, Thomas Valentine, infant son of Dr. N. H. and Mary S. **PREWITT**, aged 6 weeks. Memphis Daily Appeal, 10/21/1858.

Died, In Hardeman county, Tenn., Patrick H. **PREWITT**. He was born 14th June, 1800, departed this life 7th October, 1858, aged 58 years. Memphis Daily Appeal, 10/21/1858.

Married: On Thursday 7th inst., at the residence of Mr. Jno. **NEWSOM** in this city, by Rev. Wm. **HYER**, Mr. Cartwright **PRICE**, to Miss Emily, daughter of Capt. Wm. D. **AKIN**, of this city. Memphis Eagle, 9/9/1848.

Married—By the Rev. Mr. Gilliland of LaGrange, Mr. Edwin H. **PRICE**, of this place, to Miss Mahia A. **RUFFIN**, of Hardeman County, Tennessee. Memphis Enquirer, 5/11/1836. Departed this life on the 24th ultimo, at the residence of his father-in-law, Major James **RUFFIN**, of Panola, Miss., Edwin H. Price. The deceased was a native of Richmond, Va., and removed from that place to Memphis in the year 1834, where he has resided since, prosecuting his business as a druggist, with a fidelity which won for him the confidence of all who had the pleasure of his acquaintance. Mr. Price fell a victim thus early in life, at the age of 31, to that insideous disease, consumption....He has left behind him to mourn, his untimely loss a wife and three children.... Weekly Appeal, 5/9/1845. Married, On the 19th June, 1856, by Rev. S. G. **STARK**, at the residence of Major D. S. **WHITE**, step-father of the bride, Panola county, Mississippi, Mr. Thomas J. **DURRETT**(?), of Hart county, Georgia, and Miss Elizabeth H., daughter of the late Edwin H. Price, of Memphis, Tennessee. The Augusta *Constitutionalist* and Richmond *Enquirer* will please copy. Memphis Daily Appeal, 7/13/1856.

Married, On the 17th inst. by the Rev. G. W. **DAY**, Mr. Elijah **PRICE**, of Memphis, to Miss Mary **SWINK**, of Medon, Madison county, Tenn. Memphis Eagle & Enquirer, 4/24/1853.

In Circuit Court of Shelby County, Tenn. Mary A. Price vs. Elisha **PRICE**. Petition for Divorce. Upon application, and it appearing to the Clerk of said Court from the petition in this behalf, that the defendant is a non-resident of the State of Tennessee, ordered that publication be made in the Memphis Weekly Appeal....for four successive weeks, requiring said defendant to appear within the three first days of the next term of said Court, to be held at the Court House in the town of Raleigh, on the third Monday in January next....or the same will be taken for confessed and set for hearing ex-parte. Memphis Daily Appeal, 12/18/1855.

Married—On Thursday evening, June 2d, by Rev. R. C. **GRUNDY**, D.D., Mr. Henry J. **PRICE** and Mrs. Augusta B. **TRICE**, all of this city. Memphis Avalanche, 6/4/1859. Died, On yesterday after a short illness, Mrs. Augusta B. Price, aged about 22 years, the wife of H. J. Price and only child of Hume F. and Elizabeth C. **HILL**. Her funeral will take place this afternoon....from the residence of Judge Hill at the corner of Shelby and Trezevant streets. Memphis Daily Appeal, 9/7/1859.

Died, Near Moscow, Ten. on Thursday, the 24th of August after a short but painful illness...Mrs. Elizabeth Price, wife of the Rev. John **PRICE**, deceased, late of Fayette Co., Tenn., in the 54th year of her age...Lincoln Journal please copy. Memphis Daily Appeal, 8/30/1848.

Died—Of consumption, at the residence of his brother, in the vicinity of this city, on yesterday morning at 4 o'clock, William R. **PRICE**, formerly of Richmond, Va., and for many years a resident of this city, as one of the firm of Anderson, Walker & Co.—in the 27th year of his age. The remains of the deceased were interred yesterday morning at 10 o'clock with military honors, by the "Memphis Blues", of which company he was a member. The Appeal, 1/5/1844.

Died, On the 25th inst., in DeSoto county, Miss., of typhoid fever, Joseph _. Prichard, son of Benj. **PRICHARD**, late of Williamson county, Tenn. Nashville papers please copy. Memphis Weekly Appeal, 3/31/1858.

Died, On the 15th December, after a short illness, James Henry, only son of Doctor A. W. **PRIDE**, aged 3 years, 7 months and 12 days. Nashville *Union and American* and other Nashville papers will please copy. Memphis Daily Appeal, 12/17/1857.

I offer for sale my Plantation, one of the best in the county, consisting of 500 acres of Land.... The farm lies ten miles south of Eastport, on Big Bear Creek, at the mouth of Clear creek....The above land lies in Tishomingo county, Miss. I will sell very cheap, as I wish to go to Texas.... address me at Cripple Deer, Miss. E. M. **PRIDE**. Memphis Appeal, 10/27/1854.

Died, at his residence in Shelby county, Tenn., on the 1st inst., Rev. William **PRIDDY**, in the 75th year of his age. Richmond (Va.) *Enquirer* and *Whig* and Somerville *Star* please copy. Memphis Daily Appeal, 8/6/1856.

Died, In Nashville, on the 18th instant, Mrs. Naomi, wife of Rev. J. C. **PROVINE** and daughter of Enoch **ENSLEY**, Esq. Memphis Daily Appeal, 10/21/1855.

Married—On Thursday evening, 15th inst., by Rev. Mr. Dennis, Mr. J. M. **PROVINE**, Merchant, to Miss Sarah Ann **WREN**, all of this city. Memphis Enquirer, 10/17/1846. J. M. Provine, Real Estate and Collecting Agent, Memphis, Tenn. Office in the Overton Block. Memphis Daily Appeal, 9/9/1853. The friends of J. M. and S. A. Provine are requested to attend the funeral of their daughter, Mollie, at their residence on Hernando road This (Sunday) Afternoon at 3 o'clock P.M. Services by Rev. A. M. **BRYAN**, D.D. Memphis Daily Appeal, 9/13/1857. Died, On Saturday, the 12th inst., in this vicinity, of congestion of the brain, Mollie, daughter of Mr. J. M. and Mrs. Sarah A. Provine, aged ten years and one day. Nashville and Texas papers please copy. Memphis Daily Appeal, 9/16/1857.

Clerk's Sale. Of Highly Valuable Well Improved Plantation and Other Lands in Shelby County! R. A. **PRUDEN** vs. The minor heirs of James **PRUDEN**, deceased. Petition to sell real estate for division. By virtue of an interlocutory order of the County Court of Shelby county, at Aug term, 1855, of said Court, in the above cause, I will offer to the highest bidder on the premises, on Saturday, November 17th, 1855, the following tracts of land, belonging to the heirs of James Pruden, deceased, to wit: One tract containing 291 acres, lying in Shelby county....Memphis Daily Appeal, 10/11/1855.

Married, On the evening of the 21st ult., at the residence of Wm. H. **YOUNG**, Esq., by Rev. J. R. **HAMILTON**, Mr. Adam R. **PRYOR** to Miss Elizabeth A. **YOUNG**, all of Marshall county, Miss. Memphis Daily Appeal, 10/9/1858.

Died, At the residence of Mrs. L. I. **ARMSTRONG**, Lawrence county, Ala., on the 14th instant, Mrs. Emily A. **PRYOR**, daughter of A. **McKISSACK**, of Hernando, Miss., aged 31 years. Memphis Weekly Appeal, 5/26/1858.

Married. In San Antonio, Texas, on the 10th of October last, Mr. F. J. **PRYOR** to Miss S. F. **DAVIS**, formerly of Memphis. At the same time and place, Mr. A. A. **MUNCEY** to Miss Mary E. **SAPPINGTON**, late of this city. Memphis Daily Appeal, 11/7/1854.

Died, at his residence, Marshall county, Mississippi, on Tuesday the 12th inst. at 9 A.M., Green **PRYOR**, Esq., after a long and painful illness, aged 57 years, 1 month, and 3 days. The deceased (who was the father of one of the editors of this journal) was born in Pittsylvania county, Virginia, on the 9th of March, 1796. His father died within a few months after his birth; and his mother, marrying again in the course of four or five years, soon afterwards removed with her husband and family to Williamson county, Middle Tennessee, where he resided until he grew to man's estate. Before attaining his majority, he had enlisted as a volunteer in the armies of the United States, and fought with our troops under Gen. Jackson at Talladega, the Horse Shoe, and at the battle of New Orleans.—Soon after his return from the wars, he married and settled in Maury county, Tenn.....He afterwards resided a few years near Florence, Lauderdale county, Ala., and then removed to Hardeman county, West Tenn., where he remained 17 years; that is, from 1825 to 1842. Since 1842, he has resided at Cool Springs, Marshall county, Miss.... Memphis Eagle & Enquirer, 4/17/1853. (Author's note: J. P. **PRYOR** was an editor of this newspaper at this time.)

Coroner Waldran, on Wednesday night, held an inquest on the body of C. W. **PUCKETT**, who was shot on the Fair Grounds on the second day of the late Fair. A *post mortem* examination was made, from which the surgeons drew the conclusion that the ball had lodged near the spine, after passing completely through the lungs. The verdict of the jury was, that the deceased was shot with a pistol in the hands of F. G. **BUTLER**....After lying about four days he was attacked with intermittent fever, after which he became jaundiced and then had several attacks of epistaxis, the last being very profuse and exhausting, and that he died on the 4th of November....Memphis Daily Appeal, 11/6/1857.

Whereas Letters of Administration having been granted to the undersigned by the County Court of Shelby county, on the estate of John A. **PUCKETT**...Douglas **PUCKETT**. Memphis Daily Eagle, 4/9/1850.

Died, On yesterday morning, 3d inst., Henry Pugh, son of H. R. **PUGH**, in the 6th year of his age....Memphis Daily Appeal, 6/4/1857.

James **PUGH**, private in Capt. Freeman's company, East Tennessee Battalion, died on Sunday night last, a few miles above Cairo, on board the steamer C. Conner.—His remains were brought to our city, and interred on Tuesday evening. Memphis Appeal, Thurs., 10/21/1847.

Married, At the residence of Dr. F. C. **GARDNER** in Fayette county, Tenn., Mr. Lafayette **PULLIAM** and Miss Susan **GARDNER**. Memphis Daily Appeal, 1/27/1857.

Married: On the evening of the 22d inst., by Rev. S. W. **SPEER**, D.D., Mr. M. P. **PULLIUM** to Miss Kate Adams, daughter of Geo. W. **ADAMS**, Esq., all of LaGrange, Tenn. Memphis Daily Appeal, 1/1/1858.

Taken up by Rebecca **PURCE**, living about 3 miles south of Raleigh, on the Pigeon Roost road, one sorrel mare...Memphis Enquirer, 1/14/1837.

Died, On Saturday, the 3d inst., of dysentery, Eugene, son of Dr. R. F. and Ann Eliza **PURNELL**, aged four years, one month and twenty-three days. Memphis Eagle, 11/8/1849. Died, On the 17th inst., William Henry, son of A. E. and late Dr. Purnell, aged 2 years and 6 days. Memphis Daily Eagle, 9/20/1850.

Married—On the 15th inst. at the residence of J. S. **WELBOURN** by the Rev. Mr. Goodwyn, Mr. E. M. **PURSLEY** to Miss Frances M. **BATES**. Daily Enquirer, 3/19/1847.

J. M. **PURSLEY**, Attorney at Law, Memphis, Tenn. Memphis Daily Appeal, 4/22/1848.

Married, At Brown's Ferry, Limestone county, Alabama, on the 25th of September, by Rev. E. M. SWOOPE, Mr. John W. PURYER, of Courtland, Lawrence county, Ala., to Miss V. B. Hawkins, of Marshal county, Miss., daughter of Adam HAWKINS, deceased. Memphis Daily Appeal, 10/6/1855.

Died—At Hernando, Miss. 23d ult. James W. PUTNAM, Mayor of that place, and a most worthy and valuable citizen. The Appeal, 10/6/1843.

James QUAILEY, an old man, and an Irishman by birth, was killed in the chain gang department of the calaboose, on Thursday night, by a fellow countryman named Cargen. Cargen was committed by the examining Magistrate, to await his trial for the deed, at the next term of the criminal court. Memphis Evening Ledger, Mon., 12/28/1857.

Died, at the Desoto House, South Memphis, on Friday, the 21st inst., Samuel W. QUARLES of Cornerville, Giles county, Tenn., one of the volunteers belonging to Capt. Milton HAYNES' company of calvary. N.B. Pulaski, Whig and Courier will please copy. American Eagle, 8/27/1846.

Died In this city, on the 31st day of August, 1851, of chronic inflammation of the stomach and bowels, Mrs. Elizabeth QUARMBY, of England, in the 44th year of her age. Memphis Daily Appeal, 9/2/1851.

The subscriber has prepared himself with stables and lots to Board Horses, by the week or month, and intends paying particular attention to that business. He will keep on hand a plentiful supply of corn and fodder. His residence is two and a half miles from Memphis on the Raleigh road. D. C. QUEEN. Memphis Enquirer, 2/15/1839.

Departed this life on Wednesday, the 18th inst., of bilious pleurisy, Mr. Vivant QUENICHET, of this county, in the 52d year of his age, leaving a widow and 4 children to bemoan an irreparable loss. The deceased immigrated to this county in January, 1830, from Denwiddie county, Va. At a very early age he became a professor of religion, and attached himself to the Methodist Episcopal Church....Memphis Enquirer, 9/22/1838.

The friends and acquaintances of Thos. QUIN are requested to attend the funeral of his wife Lydia R. Quin, on Sunday Evening the 24th inst. at the Episcopal Church. Services by the Rev. Dr. Page. Daily Memphis Enquirer, 6/23/1849.

Married, On the 30th inst., at the residence of Mr. Ruck, in South Memphis, by the Rev. Tobias DICKEY, Mr. Josiah QUINCY to Miss Virginia BLOOMINGTON, all of this city. Memphis Eagle & Enquirer, 2/3/1852.

Married, By the Rev. G. H. WHITEMORE, at the Whitemore House, Mr. James W. QUINN to Miss Mary CROSS, all of this city. Memphis Daily Appeal, 11/4/1858.

Died: On the 13th inst. at 4 o'clock A.M., Mr. Eugene R. RACINE, of yellow fever. Mr. Racine was a native of Louisiana, but was early in life sent to France, where he was educated. After completing his education he returned to this country and some six or seven years ago, settled in Memphis, where he continued to reside until his death....Memphis Whig, 10/15/1855.

Married, in this city at the First Presbyterian Church, on the 23d inst., by Rev. James O. STEADMAN, Mr. Wm. L. RADFORD to Mrs. F. C. LAWRENCE, all of Memphis. Memphis Daily Appeal, 10/24/1855.

Shelby Male High School, Near Germantown, Tenn. The Second Annual Session of this Institution will commence on the First Monday of September....A. M. RAFTER, Principal and Professor of Natural Science and Professor of Ancient Languages; Rev. R. R. EVANS, Professor of Mental and Moral Philosophy; T. B. JOHNSON, Professor of Mathematics and Principal of Commercial Department; Signor Carlo DeHARO, Professor of Modern Languages....Memphis Daily Appeal, 7/17/1855.

A little boy, about 7 or 8 years of age, was left on the wharf-boat a few days since. He says his name is John **RAGAN**, and that he was left by a woman off of a steamboat. The little fellow says he has a sister in the Asylum at St. Louis, and that his father and mother are dead. Mr. Thomas **FORD**, living on Gayoso street, has kindly taken charge of him, subject to any demand that may be made by those entitled to his charge. Memphis Daily Appeal, 7/21/1852.

Died, On Tuesday, October 16, at his residence near this city, Mr. Marcus B. **RAGAN**, in the 68th year of his age....Memphis Daily Appeal, 10/27/1858.

The funeral of the late Marcus B. **RAGAN** will be preached by Elder T. J. **DRANE**, at the First Baptist Church, to-day....Memphis Daily Appeal, 1/9/1859.

I am very anxious to sell my residence, about half a mile from the Gayoso House, fronting the Hernando road; there is a large brick building with 8 rooms and 2 passages and portico in front,--also, a large brick kitchen, smokehouse and store room, with 13 acres of land, and as good a well of water and as fine a cistern as any in the State...Geo. O. **RAGLAND**. Weekly Appeal, 1/16/1846.

Our community was startled yesterday evening by the announcement that Dr. Nathaniel **RAGLAND** was dead....Our information is that he died of a carbuncle near the spine, between the shoulders. He was one of the oldest and most highly respectable citizens of Shelby county.... Died, In this city at 2 o'clock yesterday afternoon, Dr. Nathaniel Ragland....Memphis Daily Appeal, 8/13/1859.

Nathaniel A. F. **RAGLAND**, Attorney At Law, Memphis, Tenn. The Appeal, 10/4/1844. Died. Suddenly on Monday evening last at the residence of his brother, in this vicinity, Nathaniel A. F. Ragland, Esq. [North Alabamian, Nov. 3rd] Memphis Daily Appeal, 11/7/1854.

H. William **RAGONOT**, Engraver on Wood. Memphis Daily Appeal, 10/6/1852.

Died, On the 20th inst., Mr. Jonas **RAMSOUR**, in the 64th year of his age. For many years he had been a consistent member of the Presbyterian Church. The greater part of his life was spent in Lincoln county, North Carolina....In the year 1843 (or 1848?) he emigrated to the neighborhood of Lamar, Marshall county, Mississippi, where he continued til his death....He has left behind him a family who knew how to appreciate his virtue....Lincolnton (N.C.) papers please copy. Memphis Daily Appeal, 9/1/1857.

Mr. Alfred **RANDALL** of Stanley county, N.C., took passage on the steamer *Julia Dean*, at Wattinsaw for this city. The boat stopped to wood at Hawkin's woodyard at ten o'clock on Thursday morning, when Mr. R., in stepping from the steamer to the wood-boat, fell and broke his neck. He died in ten minutes after the accident. His corpse was brought to the city last evening and placed in charge of Mr. Holst, city sexton, who will deposit it in a vault, where his friends, who it is understood will send for it, can obtain it. Mr. Randall paid a visit to Arkansas for the purpose of selecting a farm and, as we understand, having selected a location, it was his intention to bring his family which is a large one, to our sister State, and there make a permanent residence...Mr. R., we learn, was between fifty-five and sixty years of age and that he was a man of considerable property in North Carolina...Memphis Daily Appeal, Sat., 4/19/1856.

Died, At the residence of A. B. **McGINNIS** in this city, on the 27th instant, John W., son of David **RANDALL**, near Nashville, Tenn. Nashville papers please copy. Memphis Daily Appeal, 9/28/1855.

Died, At his residence near Collierville, Shelby county, Tenn., on the 23d October, 1859, Mr. John **RANDOLPH**, aged 40 years. Mr. Randolph was born in Madison county, Ala., on 23d day of October, 1819, and was therefore just 40 years of age, having died upon the anniversary of his birthday. He emigrated while a young man to Monroe county, Miss., where he married Mrs. S_atera **WILLIS**, and lived for several years. He then removed to Shelby county, Tenn., where he lived beloved by all who knew him until his death....The new-made grave in the churchyard bedewed as it is with sincere tears of sorrow....The deceased leaves a devoted wife and an affectionate niece, the only members of his family....Mr. R. died of that most terrible of all diseases, consumption....Huntsville, Ala., and Aberdeen and Columbus, Miss., papers please copy. Memphis Daily Appeal, 11/13/1859.

Married. By the Rev. H. M. **KERR**, on the 30th December last, Mr. David C. **RANKIN**, to Mrs. Nancy C. **RANKIN**, all of McNairy co., Tenn. Memphis Daily Eagle, 1/18/1848.

Married, On Wednesday the 30th ult. by the Rev. W. D. F. **SAWRIE**, Mr. Thos. A. **RASH** of Germantown, to Miss Mariella J., daughter of Col. Richard **LEAKE**, of this county. Memphis Enquirer, 9/16/1837.

Died—In Memphis, on the night of the 10th inst., Mr. Isaac **RAWLINGS**, merchant, and one of the oldest and most respected citizens of Memphis. Somerville Reporter, 9/28/1839. Notice – All persons indebted to the estate of Isaac Rawlings deceased, are required to come forward and make immediate payment. W. J. **RAWLINGS**, Administrator of the estate of Isaac Rawlings, dec'd. Oct. 18, 1839. Memphis Enquirer.

The funeral of the late J. H. **RAWLINGS** will take place from the family residence, on the Randolph road....this afternoon. Memphis Daily Appeal, 7/6/1859. It becomes our painful duty this morning to announce the death of one of our oldest and most highly respected citizens, Mr. J. H. Rawlings. He breathed his last....Tuesday night last, and his remains were deposited in their last resting place yesterday evening....Memphis Daily Appeal, Thurs., 7/7/1859. Letters of Administration having been obtained by the undersigned, upon the estate of John H. Rawlings, at the August term, 1859, of the County Court of Shelby county, all persons indebted to said estate are hereby requested to come forward....Sarah J. **RAWLINGS**, Administratrix. Memphis Daily Appeal, 8/24/1859.

Married. In this city on Thursday evening, 2d inst., by Rev. Dr. Porter, Mr. J. J. **RAWLINGS**, of the firm of Webb & Rawlings, to Mrs. Sophia **LOWRY**. Memphis Daily Appeal, 11/5/1854.

Married on the 9th inst., by Rev. J. H. **GRAY**, Mr. Jackson C. **RAWLINGS** to Miss Jane C. **McCAY**, all of this city. Memphis Enquirer, 5/16/1849.

Died—At her residence in Shelby County on the morning of the 20th inst., Mrs. Sarah Ann Rawlings, consort of Mr. Joseph **RAWLINGS**. Mrs. Rawlings has been cut off in the bloom of life, leaving behind her a deeply afflicted husband, an infant too young to be sensible of its irreparable loss, and warmly attached friends to lament her early leave of them. She was amiable in her disposition, kind and benevolent of heart, fascinating in her manners, with a well directed education.....Memphis Enquirer, 6/24/1837.

Married—On Tuesday, 10th inst., by the Rev. Mr. Dennis, Mr. Jos. J. **RAWLINGS**, to Miss Lucinda **BROWN**, all of this county. Memphis Enquirer, 3/13/1840.

Died, On Saturday last, about 10 o'clock, A.M., Mrs. Mary A. Rawlings, consort of Joseph J. **RAWLINGS**, Esq., of this city. Memphis Daily Appeal, Mon., 10/4/1852.

Married, On the 27th inst. by Rev. J. T. C. **COLLINS**, John E. R. **RAY**, Esq., of this city, to Miss Mary Smith **HUDSON**, of Marshall county, Mississippi. Memphis Daily Appeal, 11/29/1855.

Died. In this city, on the 5th of Cholera, Mr. James O. **RAYMON**, a native of Tuscaloosa, Alabama, aged 33 years, leaving a wife and four children to lament his loss. Weekly Memphis Eagle, 6/14/1849.

We have been furnished by the clerk, Mr. Saml. P. **READ**, with a detailed manifest of the steamer Amanda, from Hatchie River....Memphis Daily Appeal, 2/21/1853.

Died, In this city, on Tuesday morning, the 14th inst., George Edward, youngest son of Geo. R. and Grace A. **REDFORD**. Memphis Enquirer, 7/16/1846. Died, on Sunday the 6th inst., of measles, Susan Price, infant daughter of Geo. R. and Grace A. Redford, aged two years. Richmond, Va. Papers will please copy. Memphis Eagle & Enquirer, 6/8/1852. Died, On Tuesday morning, 5th instant, of Pneumonia, Elwood, youngest son of Geo. R. and Grace A. Redford, aged 8 months and 3 days. Richmond, Va. papers please copy. Memphis Daily Appeal, 4/6/1853.

The Funeral of Mrs. Margaret Elizabeth **REDMAN** will take place at the Episcopal Church, this afternoon at 3 ½ o'clock. The friends of her husband and of her father are requested to attend. Daily Memphis Enquirer, 3/24/1849.

Married, at the residence of Thomas **BOND**, Esq., in Haywood County, on the 23d inst., by the Rev. A. J. **SPIVY**, Capt. Reub. T. **REDMAN**, of Arkansas, to Miss Margaret E. **BLOOM**, of Memphis. Memphis Enquirer, 4/28/1848.

Married, On the 25th October at the residence of Madame Shurtleff, by Rev. H. **HORTON**, Mr. J. M. **REDUS**, of Louisiana, to Miss Mary Jane **POLK**, of Memphis. Memphis Daily Appeal, 10/27/1859.

Col. David **REED**, late a citizen of this place, has moved to Memphis where he will engage in the practice of Law. Col. R. only lived here about six months, but during that time he made many warm and strong friends....—*Jackson, Tenn., Whig.* Memphis Daily Appeal, 1/27/1857.

Married, On the 5th instant by Rev. J. E. **DOUGLAS**, at the residence of her father, Mr. G. W. **REED**, of Somerville, Tenn., and Miss Myra D. **GOBER**, of Fayette county. Memphis Daily Appeal, 8/12/1856.

Married, On Thursday 11th inst., by the Rev. J. H. **GRAY**, Mr. Thomas **REED**, of Denmark, to Mrs. Catherine B. **GREEN**, of Memphis. American Eagle, 11/18/1847.

Married, On Tuesday, November 20th, at the residence of E. J. **ELAM**, Esq., by Rev. T. J. **DRANE**, Thos. B. **REED** to Miss Laura A., daughter of Henry **COOPER**, Esq., all of Memphis. Memphis Weekly Appeal, 12/8/1858.

Married, On Sunday evening, 3d instant by Hume F. **HILL**, Esq., Mr. James R. **REESE** and Mrs. Latiessa(?) **FULLERTON**, all of this city. Memphis Daily Appeal, 2/5/1856.

Married, In Fayette county, on Thursday night, the 14th inst. by the Rev. Mr. Williamson, Mr. Thos. C. J. **REEVES** to Miss Nancy W. **HOLMES**. Memphis Eagle & Enquirer, 4/19/1853.

We are authorized to announce Wm. P. **REEVES** a candidate for re-election to the office of Register of Shelby County. American Eagle, 10/6/1843.

The friends and acquaintances of Mr. Benjamin **REID**, of the firm of Reid & Shelton, are requested to attend his funeral This Morning....from the First Methodist Church. Memphis Daily Appeal, 3/19/1859.

Married, On the 8th inst. in Macon, Tenn., by Rev. A. D. **METCALFE**, Mr. John B. **REID** to Miss L. Wallace Neal, daughter of T. G. **NEAL**, Esq. Memphis Daily Appeal, 2/17/1859.

Married, At the residence of her father, on Thursday morning, 2d inst., Mr. John B. **REID** and Miss Nannie R.(?), daughter of Col. Henry **DAY**, all of DeSoto county, Miss. Memphis Daily Appeal, 6/14/1859.

Married, On the 16th instant by Rev. B. **MEDLIN**, Dr. R. A. **REID** to Miss Lydia H. **BROWN**, all of Macon, Fayette county, Tenn. Memphis Weekly Appeal, 3/3/1858.

Died—At his residence in this town last evening, Mr. Thomas **REID**. Memphis Enquirer, 4/12/1836.

Married. In Elba, Fayette county, Tenn., on the 26th ult. by Elder M. W. **WEBBER**, Mr. Wm. C. **REID** to Miss Eliza Ann, daughter of Mr. David **BENTLEY**. Memphis Daily Appeal, 7/17/1855.

Died—In this city, on Thursday, 4th inst., Dr. Charles E. **REINHARDT**, formerly of Raleigh, and a native of North Carolina; he was an upright, benevolent, and excellent citizen, and at his death an Elder in the First Presbyterian Church. Memphis Appeal, 11/7/1847. Married. On Tuesday, at the residence of W. S. **WELLS**, by the Rev. T. J. **NEWBERRY**, Daniel L. **MILLER**, M.D., of Whiteville, Miss. to Miss Margaret S., daughter of the late Dr. C. E. Reinhardt. Memphis Eagle, 4/5/1848.

Died, In this county, on the 29th April, Andrew **REMBERT**, Esq., one of the early settlers of this county and a native of Georgia. Mr. Rembert was a truly benevolent and exemplary man and a worthy member of the Methodist Church; his loss will be severely felt, not by his relatives alone, but by all within the influence of his acquaintance, and especially the poor within the vicinity of his late residence. American Eagle, 5/23/1845.

Died, On Monday morning, 8th instant, at 10 o'clock, at the residence of his mother, in the vicinity of Memphis, James A. **REMBERT**, in the 22d year of his age. Memphis Daily Appeal, 6/10/1856.

Married—At Lebanon, Tenn., July 23, Mr. L. C. **REMBERT**, of this county, to Miss Mary Jane, youngest daughter of Thomas **JACKSON**, Esq. American Eagle Weekly, 8/1/1845. I will sell the plantation on which I reside, situated nine miles from Memphis and two miles east of the Hernando plank road, containing five hundred and twenty-eight acres....L. C. Rembert. Memphis Daily Appeal, 10/7/1853.

Married, On Wednesday evening, 6th(?) instant, by Rev. Dr. Page, Mr. Lewellyn C. **REMBERT** to Miss Mary E. Ragland, daughter of Dr. N. **RAGLAND**, all of Shelby county. At the same time and place, Mr. C. Devereux **DUNLAP**, of Louisiana, to Miss Sarah Virginia Ragland. Memphis Daily Appeal, 7/8/1853.

Married—On the 9th instant, by the Rev. Jno. C. **JOHNSON**, Mr. S. S. **REMBERT**, to Miss Ann, daughter of Benj. **DUNKIN**, Esq., all of this county. Memphis Enquirer, 2/21/1840. I have determined positively to sell out my plantation, etc., consisting of 400 acres of hilly land; 400 acres of cleared land...900 acres in the woods...Twelve miles North-east of Memphis, Shelby county, Tenn. S. S. Rembert. Memphis Enquirer, 1/27/1848.

Departed this life on the 26th ult., Mrs. Louisa Rembert, consort of Samuel **REMBERT**, Esq., of this county, in the 58th year of her age.....Memphis Enquirer, 5/5/1838.

Married, At the residence of the bride's father on the morning of the 11th inst., by J. N. **LYNN**, Esq., Mr. B. P. **RENFRO** to Miss Margaret E. **CATHY**. Also at the same time and place, Mr. J. M. **ADKINS** to Miss Mary **BOYD**—all of DeSoto county, Miss. Memphis Daily Appeal, 12/14/1859.

Doctor G. A. **RENNER**, A Graduate of Gotten University in Germany, Having practiced medicine in the U.S. for 12 years, located himslef at Moscow, Fayette Co., Tenn., about the first of July last, and having since purchased the Moscow Hotel, is now prepared for the accomodation of invalids from a distance, who might otherwise be deprived of his medical aid...Memphis Daily Eagle, 1/16/1846.

Married, On the 26th instant, at Nashville, by the Rev. R. A. **LAPSLEY**, D.D., Dr. J. Houston **REYNOLDS**, of Memphis, to Miss Jane W. Trabue, daughter of Charles C. **TRABUE**, of that city. Memphis Eagle, 10/2/1850.

Married, At the Christian Church, Memphis, on Tuesday evening, May 26th, by Elder J. E. **MERRIMAN**, Mr. Thomas B. **REYNOLDS** and Miss Fannie E. **TOOF**. Memphis Daily Appeal, 5/27/1857.

New Clothing Establishment. The subscribers take great pleasure in informing their friends and the public generally, that they are now receiving at their house on Front Row, between Washington and Adams streets...a choice selection of Ready Made Clothing...Daniel **RHODES** & Co. Daily Enquirer, 11/4/1847.

On Sunday night a rencountre took place between William D. **BELL** and Benj. **RICE**, about three miles Northeast from the city, near Strong's Mills, on the new Raleigh road, in which the latter was killed by the discharge of a shot gun in the hands of the former. It seems that Rice had been driven from his house by the high water and was camping out until the water should subside. Having lost his wife a short time before, he had engaged with Bell and his wife to come and live with him and take care of his infant child....Memphis Daily Avalanche, Tues., 4/19/1859.

At a stated communication of Memphis Lodge No. 91 of Free and Accepted Masons, held at the Masonic Hall, on the evening of the 24th instant, the following gentlemen were duly elected for the ensuing six months, and subsequently installed into the offices annexed to their respective names, as follows: James **RICE**, Jr., W.M.—Tobias **WOLF**, S.W.—M. **VANDERBILT**, J.W.—Geo. A. **WOOD**, Secretary—Wm. **CHASE**, Treasurer—C. **VAN CAMPEN**, S.D.—H. W. **SEALE**, J.D.—Jno. S. **WILLIAMS**, S. & T. Appointments: Edward **DASHIELL** and Wm. J. **WOODS**, Stewards. M. **GABBERT**, Physician. Memphis Enquirer, 1/1/1848. James Rice, Jr., Attorney at Law. Office on Main street...Daily Memphis Enquirer, 6/1/1848.

Married—By J. **WALDRAN**, Esq., on the 12th inst., James J. **RICE**, Esq., and Miss Victoria Elizabeth **FAUST**, all of this city. Memphis Daily Avalanche, 6/14/1859.

Tax Sales. State of Tennessee—Shelby county—February Term, 1823—Whereas, Samuel R. **BROWN**, Sheriff and collector of the public taxes for the county of Shelby, reported to court the following tracts of land, as having been omitted to be returned for the public taxes for the year 1822....John **RICE**, 5000 acres grant 294 Big Hatchie; Same 5000 grant 293 Big Hatchie; Heirs of Benj **WHITE**, 640 entry 119 Big creek; Samuel & James **TORGY** 5000 on Mississippi; Minos **CAMRON** 55 acres entry 770; Abner **PILLOW** 600 No. 621 Wolf river; Anthony **BLEDSOE**, 4000 acres No. of claim 406 on Big Creek; Same 506 acres No 179....The foregoing tracts of land will be offered for sale....Memphis Advocate, 11/3/1827.

Died—At his residence in this vicinity, on Saturday, 26th inst., Captain Jos. M. **RICE**, Sen., aged 56 years. Memphis Eagle, 6/7/1849.

Married, On the 22d inst., at the residence of the bride's uncle, Dr. James **NEWBORN**, Haywood county, Tenn., by Rev. C. C. **CONNER**, Mr. Levi **RICE**, of Memphis, to Miss Sarah P. **HOLLAND**. Memphis Daily Appeal, 7/24/1858.

The trial of W. D. and Josiah M. **RICE**, which has been occupying the attention of the Criminal Court for several days past, closed yesterday. The jury brought in a verdict of "guilty of voluntary manslaughter" as to Josiah M. Rice, and he was sentenced to five years labor in the Penitentiary; Wm. D. **RICE** was acquitted...Memphis Daily Appeal, 3/22/1856.

Died: On the 13th instant of Disease of the Heart, F.(?) **RICHARDS**, aged 73 years. Pittsburg and Cincinnati papers please copy. Memphis Whig, 8/15/1855.

At a general meeting of the Stock Holders of the City Exchange Company, held on the 13th instant, Lewis R. **RICHARDS**, was appointed cashier, and Isaac G. **WILLIAMS** Secretary. Daily Enquirer, 4/7/1847.

Died at the Herron House on Friday morning the 12th inst., after a lingering illness, Van Buren, only son of Dr. W. and Elizabeth **RICHARDS**, aged seven years, seven months and twelve days. Kentucky papers please copy. Daily Enquirer, 8/20/1847.

The friends and acquaintances of W. and L. C. **RICHARDS** are respectfully invited to attend the funeral of their daughter Mary Elizabeth, from their residence on Jackson street, Fort Pickering, on Sunday morning, 18th inst....Services by Rev. Mr. Thomas. Memphis Daily Appeal, 7/16/1859. Died, On the 15th of July, 1859, Mary Elizabeth, daughter of Walter and Lucinda Richards, aged four years, four months and twenty-five days....Memphis Daily Appeal, 7/27/1859.

At Marion's Grove, Madison county, Tenn. on Saturday, 31st ultimo, a man by the name of Willis **RICHARDS** was shot and killed by Mr. Cullin **JACKSON**. It seems that the parties were in a quarrel when Jackson drew a pistol and shot Richards in the breast, who expired in a few minutes. Jackson ran away and at last accounts had not been heard from. Memphis Daily Appeal, 1/9/1854.

Married, On the 24th inst. at St. Mary's Church, by Rev. G. P. **SCHETSKY**, B.D., Mr. C. A. S. **RICHARDSON** to Miss Mary F. Woods, daughter of the late James **WOODS**, all of this city. Memphis Daily Appeal, 12/25/1857.

Married, On the 7th inst. at Dyersburg, Tenn., by Rev. Mr. Hamilton, Mr. D. M. **RICHARDSON** and Miss Mollie F. **PHILLIPS**, all of Dyer county, Tenn. Memphis Daily Appeal, 10/18/1857. Married, In Dyer county, on the 7th inst., Dr. David M. **RICHARDSON** and Miss Mary F. **PHILLIPS**. Also Mr. Andrew **HART** and Miss----- **WEBSTER**. Memphis Daily Appeal, 10/21/1857.

The funeral sermon of Phillip Richardson, the son of Gen. R. V. and M. E. **RICHARDSON**, will be preached this morning at 10 o'clock in Asbury Chapel, by Rev. J. T. C. **COLLINS**. Memphis Daily Appeal, 12/27/1857. Died, In this city on Friday evening last, 7th instant, Mrs. Elizabeth A. **RICHARDSON**, mother of General R. V. Richardson, of this place. Memphis Daily Appeal, 1/11/1859.

Married, On the 10th instant at Jackson, Miss., by Rev. C. K. **MARSHALL**, Prof. Wilson G. **RICHARDSON**, of the Mississippi University, and Miss Louisa V. **KENNON**, of Tuscaloosa, Ala. Memphis Daily Appeal, 4/17/1856.

Married – On the 27th inst., at the residence of Mr. Samuel **STUCKY**, by Rev. Dr. N. **HOWCOTT**, Mr. David L. **RIDGWAY** to Miss Mary R. **STUCKY**,--All of this city. Daily Memphis Enquirer, 3/29/1849.

Married. In Somerville, Tenn. on the 15th inst. by the Rev. Mr. Collins, Mr. Henry A. **RIDLEY** to Miss Mary E. **SMITH**. Memphis Daily Appeal, 9/19/1853.

Colliersville, July 27, 1855. Messrs. Editors: Sometime since I attached myself to the "new-fangled order," commonly designated Know-Nothings; and wishing to withdraw from the Order, I wrote to an officer of the council which I joined, (or was at the time I joined,) about ten days ago, and not receiving an answer, I have thought it best to disconnect myself from the Order through the columns of the Appeal, as I wish to be free to vote for whom I please. Yours, respectfully, Jas. W. **RIDOUT**. Memphis Daily Appeal, 7/29/1855.

Tribute of Respect. Exchange Buildings, June 15, 1857. At a meeting of the German Washington Rifle Company, held this evening, a Committee was appointed to draw up suitable resolutions in regard to the death of our Captain, J. F. **RINGWALD**. Whereas, It has pleased our Almighty God to call hence, by the visitation of death, in the prime of life, our much esteemed and beloved friend and fellow-soldier, Captain J. F. Ringwald; by his untimely death our Company has lost a very useful and popular Commander....the widow a kind and generous husband, and the children an indulgent and affectionate father....Memphis Daily Appeal, 6/16/1857. Angerona Lodge No. 188, Memphis, Tenn. At a special meeting of this Lodge, held in their Hall on Friday, the 12th June, the following report was made....In the Providence of God we are called upon to lament the death of our esteemed brother J. F. Ringwald....the true and upright Mason....Memphis Daily Appeal, 6/14/1857. Our city was yesterday painfully startled by the announcement of the sudden death of Mr. F. Ringwald....one of our most respected citizens....Captain Ringwald was a native of Germany, but had been a citizen of Memphis for a number of years....His remains will be deposited in Elmwood Cemetery....Memphis Daily Appeal, 6/12/1857.

E. F. **RISK**, thankful to his friends and the public generally, for their liberal patronage, would inform them that he continues to keep constantly on hand a large assortment of plain and japanned Tin Ware, Cooking Coal Stoves and Castings...Daily Enquirer, 4/2/1847. Died, In this city on Tuesday, the 10th inst., at 11 o'clock P.M., Charles, infant son of E. F. and Jane H. Risk—aged 11 months. Cincinnati papers please copy. Memphis Daily Appeal, 8/12/1852. Died, On Saturday, the 15th instant, George M., infant son of E. F. and Jane H. Risk, aged eleven months and four days. Memphis Daily Appeal, 12/18/1855.

Married, On the 25th inst. at the residence of Mr. Higgs, by Rev. J. T. C. **COLLINS**, Mr. W. W. **RITCHIE**, of the firm of Stout & Ritchie, to Miss Kate J. **BUTLER**, both of this city. Memphis Daily Appeal, 8/29/1858.

We are authorized and requested to announce Thomas **RIVERS**, of Sommerville, a candidate for the office of Brigadier General of the 23d Brigade of Tennessee Militia, vice Gen. Jos. R. **WILLIAMS**, resigned. Memphis Enquirer, 11/14/1846.

Married, In Lynchburg, Virginia, on the 19th of March by Bishop Early, Hon. Thomas **RIVERS**, member of Congress from the Tenth District of Tennessee, and Miss Lucretia, daughter of Col. Thomas **DILLARD**. Memphis Daily Appeal, 4/1/1856.

Died, On Friday morning at Col. Sam'l **LEAKE's**, in this county, Mrs. Elizabeth Rivers, wife of General Thomas **RIVERS** of Sommerville, and daughter of William and Elizabeth **DICKSON**, of North Alabama; aged about 23 years. Mrs. Rivers had been in bad health for more than a year, and was returning home hoping she had recovered, when she was attacked with the Pneumonia, and after an illness of a few days, died. Memphis Daily Appeal, 12/8/1852.

We regret to announce the sudden death, either by accident or violence, of Mr. George **RIVES**, son of the late Col. Peter G. **RIVES**. The sad event occurred Thursday evening, at the residence of his Brother, Mr. John **RIVES**, thirteen miles below this city, in Arkansas. With a gun in his possession, the deceased, accompanied by a black boy, was engaged at some duty in the corn field, Thursday afternoon, during which time Mr. R. wandered a short distance from his companion. While Mr. R. was absent from the negro the gun was discharged, and the black boy soon afterward came upon the deceased, and found him shot through the right side, and quite dead....The remains were interred at the residence of his brother, in Arkansas, last evening. The deceased was well known in this city. Memphis Daily Appeal, Sat., 8/13/1859.

Died, In Marshall county, Miss., on the 20th of March, Mrs. Martha L. Rives, wife of Thomas **RIVES**, of Fayette county, Tenn....She, with her family of little daughters, was on a visit to her father's....She had been for years a member of Protestant Episcopal Church....Mrs. Rives has left a husband and three interesting little daughters....Memphis Whig, 4/3/1855.

Died—On this 29th inst., after a short illness, George D., son of Dr. Wm. **RIVES**, of this place, in the 12th year of his age.....Weekly Appeal, 6/6/1845.

Married. On Tuesday, 28th instant, by Rev. J. H. **GRAY**, Mr. Marcus **RO_OU** to Miss Minna **BAWER**, all of this city. Memphis Daily Appeal, 8/29/1855.

Died, On Monday, the 3d instant, Mrs. M. B.(?), wife of Dr. H. _. **ROBARDS**. Memphis Weekly Appeal, 5/5/1858.

We are pleased to see that Rev. Wm. C. **ROBB**, Pastor of the First Methodist Church of this city, has returned to his charge, from a visit to the North, and that he is recruited and invigorated in health and spirits. He will, we are requested to state, recommence his stated duties in his church, Sabbath morning next at the usual hour. Memphis Daily Appeal, 8/19/1853. Married, On the evening of the 25th instant at the residence of her father, in DeSoto county, Miss., by Rev. Philip **TUGGLE**, Miss Margaret J. **MILLER** to the Rev. Wm. C. Robb, Presiding Elder of the Memphis District. Memphis Daily Appeal, 10/27/1855. Memphis Conference.—This religious and intelligent body, after a session of seven days, closed its deliberation night before last and adjourned to meet at Jackson, Tenn., next year. The appointments for the Memphis district are Rev. W. C. Robb, Presiding Elder; Rev. Thomas A. **WARE**, Pastor of Wesley chapel; Asbury chapel, Rev.'s J. T. **COLLINS** and Samuel **WALTON**. Rev. F. A. **OWEN**, book agent and member of Wesley Quarterly Conference. Memphis Whig, 11/23/1855. Our whole community received a sudden shock on Friday morning last by the announcement of the death of Rev. W. C. Robb, which occurred on the previous day, at the residence of his father-in-law, in DeSoto county, Miss....Rev. W. C. Robb was born in Sumner county, Tenn., of pious and highly respectable parents, where he received his early education, and afterwards prosecuted the study of the law until he was admitted to the bar. Soon after this event he removed to Grenada, Miss., the residence of an only sister....At a general revival of religion in Grenada he embraced a Christian's faith....resolved to enter immediately upon studies preparatory to the ministry, connected with the Methodist Episcopal Church....For the last three years he has been acting in the capacity of Presiding Elder in the Memphis district....His remains were deposited in their final resting place in Elmwood Cemetery....Memphis Weekly Appeal, 3/17/1858.

A boy about sixteen years old by the name of Joseph **ROBBINS**, near Germantown, came to his death on Saturday evening in the following melancholy way: He was riding or leading a mule and had fastened the halter by which he was led round his wrist. The mule took fright and throwed the boy in some way and run dragging him some two miles; when the mule stopped the boy was found dead. Memphis Daily Appeal, 9/18/1855.

Married, on the 16th May, Mr. H. M. **ROBERTS** to Mrs. C. A. **AMMONS**—all of Hardeman county. Weekly Appeal, 6/12/1846.

Died, At 4 o'clock P.M. on the 3d inst., at Lawrenceburg, Tenn., Miss Julia C. **ROBERTS**, sister of Prof. H. R. **ROBERTS**, of the city. Memphis Weekly Appeal, 12/8/1858.

Married, On Sunday evening, 8th inst., by the Rev. J. P. **DAVIDSON**, Mr. M. P. **ROBERTS** to Miss Sarah E. **GILBERT**, both of this vicinity. Daily Enquirer, 8/11/1847.

The death of Capt. Chas. D. **ROBERTSON** is announced. The sad event occurred recently at the residence of a relative a short distance above New Orleans. Capt. **ROBINSON** was one of the oldest steamboatmen on the western waters, and commanded the first regular packet between this port and New Orleans. He was an experienced boatman and a genial companion. Memphis Daily Appeal, 8/13/1859. (Author's note: The 2 different spellings were copied as written.)

Married, On Wednesday evening, 9th inst., at the residence of the bride's mother, near Fisherville, by Dr. W. G. **LANCASTER**, Mr. Elijah **ROBERTSON**, of Marshal county, Miss., to Mrs. M. B. **MORELAND**, of Shelby county, Tenn. Memphis Daily Appeal, 6/17/1858.

Died, on the 2d inst., at the residence of her brother in Edmondson county, Ky., Mrs. Kitty B.(?) Robertson, consort of G. A. **ROBERTSON**, of this vicinity, in the thirty-fifth year of her age....as wife, mother and friend, she ever exhibited the true Christian character. Having joined the Methodist Episcopal church at the age of twelve years....She leaves a husband and two or three children, besides relatives and friends, to mourn her untimely death....But consumption ....marked her for its victim....Memphis Weekly Appeal, 5/19/1858.

Died. Of scarlet fever, near Tatesville, Miss., June 17, Richard, only son of Mrs. Lenora **ROBERTSON**, aged ten years, ten months and thirteen days...Memphis Whig, 6/27/1856.

Married, on Wednesday evening last, by the Rev. Mr. Gray, Wyndham **ROBERTSON**, Esq., to Miss Judith M. **POPE**, all of this city. Enquirer, Friday, 9/24/1847. Wyndham Robertson, Jr., Attorney at Law—Memphis, Tenn., will practice regularly in the counties of Shelby, Tipton and Hardeman, and in the Court of Appeal, at Jackson. Memphis Daily Appeal, 12/13/1847.

By virtue of a decretal order of the Circuit Court of Shelby county, Tenn., at January term, 1852, on the petition of W. J. **ROBINS** and others, I will...on the first Monday in February nest, proceed to sell 246 acres of Land, lying in the 7th civil district of Shelby county, Tenn., on the waters of Fletcher Creek, and the Lagrange road from Raleigh, and being the dower of Julia Robins, widow of Benj. **ROBINS**, deceased, as the property of Benjamin Robins, deceased ...Memphis Eagle & Enquirer, 1/20/1852.

We learn that yesterday afternoon....at Collierville in this county, an affray occurred during which Mr. F. B. **ROBINSON** was shot and killed by Mr. B. G. **PERSON**. The occurrence, our authority informs us, grew out of an old grudge. We have received no particulars of the unfortunate affair. Memphis Daily Appeal, 8/5/1859.

Married. On the morning of the 8th instant by Rev. J. W. **KNOTT**, Mr. G. N. **ROBINSON**, of the firm of Robinson, Morgan & Co., and Miss Mary L. **SCALES**, of Marshall county, Miss. Memphis Daily Appeal, 8/9/1855.

We learn that a fatal affray occurred on Sunday last, a few miles beyond Marion, Crittendon county, Ark., between David **STANLEY** and James **ROBINSON**, resulting in the death of the latter....Memphis Whig, Tues., 9/25/1855.

The friends and acquaintances of James **ROBINSON**, Esq., are requested to attend the funeral of his wife, from his residence in the country, to-day at 10 ½ o'clock. Services by Rev. Mr. Steadman. Memphis Daily Appeal, 1/3/1857.

Died, At the residence of James **ROBINSON**, on Trigg avenue, on Friday, the 7th inst., Molly Mason, daughter of D. E. and Eliza M. **ROBINSON**, of Texas, aged two years and six months. Memphis Daily Appeal, 8/8/1857.

Married, By Esq. Waldran, on the 2d inst., Mr. Luke **ROBINSON** and Mrs. Rebecca **BICKEL**, all of this city. Memphis Weekly Appeal, 3/17/1858.

Died, In Randolph, on Saturday last, of congestive fever, Thomas **ROBINSON**, Esq., aged 50 years. One of the oldest residents of Randolph, his humane and generous virtues _____ him the esteem of his fellow men, who deeply lament the loss of his influence and usefulness. Memphis Enquirer, Sat., 8/19/1837.

Died, At Jackson, Tenn., on March 5th, Florence Ione, infant daughter of Tracy and L. Bettie **ROBINSON**, aged 4 months and 26 days. Memphis Weekly Appeal, 3/17/1858.

Married—On Tuesday evening, by the Rev. P. W. **ALSTON**, at the Residence of Mr. A. **KERNAHAN**, Mr. Wm. **ROBINSON** to Miss Isabella **PATTERSON**. The Appeal, Friday, 6/14/1844. The undersigned having administered on the estate of the late Wm. Robinson, Esq., propose to sell at private sale…Isabella Robinson, Admr's. Memphis Daily Eagle, 9/5/1850.

Among the deaths from yellow fever, occurring on Sunday evening last, we have to announce that of Mrs. Amanda Roche, wife of F. G. **ROCHE**, Banker, of the firm of C. W. Cherry & Co. It is only a week or two since Mr. Roche was bereaved of a little daughter, but in the death of the partner of his bosom, the strokes of Providence have fallen doubly heavy upon him. Memphis Daily Appeal, 10/16/1855.

Married, On the 7th instant at the residence of the bride's father, in Fayette county, Tenn., Mr. B. **RODGERS**, of Marshall county, Miss., to Miss M. E. **CARPENTER**. Memphis Weekly Appeal, 12/15/1858.

Died—At Holly Springs, on the 5th inst. Mr. James **RODGERS**, of this county, aged 77 years—the father of Maj. John B. **RODGERS** of this vicinity. Weekly Appeal, 9/19/1845. Died, At the residence of Dr. J. Y. **CUMMINS** in Holly Springs, Miss., on the 5th instant, Mr. James **ROGERS**, of Shelby county, Tenn., aged 77 years. American Eagle Weekly, 9/26/1845.

James and William **RODGERS** vs. Elizabeth **RODGERS**, et. al., heirs and distributees of Cullen **RODGERS**, dec'd. By virtue of a Decree of the County Court of Shelby County, made in the above cause, at the January Term, 1857, of said Court, I will offer at public sale on Tuesday, February 10th, 1857, on the premises, The Tract of Land belonging to the estate of Cullen Rodgers, dec'd., about 8 miles east of Raleigh, on the LaGrange road, containing 200 acres….Memphis Daily Appeal, 1/11/1857.

Died. At the residence of Mr. Lemuel **FARRAR**, in this county, on Wednesday last, Maj. John B. **RODGERS**, in the 56th year of his age. Maj. R. was a native of South Carolina, but for many years a most estimable citizen of this county, from whence he removed two years since to Walnut Bend, Arkansas, where he was extensively and successively engaged in planting…and has left a numerous family to lament his death. Memphis Appeal, Tuesday, 10/7/1851. Died—On the 27th(?) ult., Mrs. Malinda Rodgers, in the 53d year of her age, wife of Maj. John B. Rodgers, of this vicinity, leaving a large family and an afflicted husband. Memphis Daily Appeal, 1/2/1848.

Mrs. Mary L. Rodgers, of this city, mother of Thos. A. **RODGERS**, recently connected with the Ledger office, died on the morning of the 26th inst., at 5 o'clock. Memphis Evening Ledger, 10/29/1857.

Married, On Monday, the 17th inst., at the Navy Yard, by the Rev. Geo. W. **COONS**, F. A. **ROE**, passed Midshipman, U.S.N., to Miss Bettie **SNYDER**, of this city. Weekly Memphis Eagle, 9/20/1849.

The eastward bound mail train, which left on the Memphis and Charleston Railroad on Monday evening, met with a sad accident about twenty-two miles from this city....the engineer saw two large oxen come upon the track ahead of him....the accident could not be averted, the locomotive striking the cattle with great force, and flying off the track, taking with it the baggage car and a second-class passenger car. Mr. A. T. **ROGERS**, the conductor of the mail train, was in the mail car at the time of the collision, but stepped on the platform to see what was the matter, (as is supposed,) and was caught between the cars and his legs so mutilated that amputation became necessary....but he was so exhausted in the time that elapsed before he could be extricated from the wreck, that he only survived the shock a few moments. Mr. Rogers was well and favorably known in Fayette county, Tenn., where he was raised, and where his father, Mr. Robert R. **ROGERS**, resides....His remains were brought to this city yesterday evening, and will be taken hence to his father's residence for interment....Memphis Daily Avalanche, Wed., 5/18/1859.

Married. On the morning of the 26th inst. at Oxford, Miss., by Prof. J. N. **WADDEL**, D.D., Hon. D. F. **ROGERS** to Miss M. C. Robinson, daughter of Thos. H. **ROBINSON**, Esq., of the University Hotel. Memphis Daily Appeal, 10/29/1854.

Died, At Memphis, September 6th, Edwin Francis, youngest son of Dr. E. D. and Elizabeth **ROGERS**, aged 19 months and 25 days. Memphis Daily Appeal, 9/9/1857.

Married, At Calvary Church by the Rev. J. W. **ROGERS**, Mr. H. H. **ROGERS**, of Brownsville, Tenn., to Miss Eliza **ROSE**, of this city. Memphis Weekly Appeal, 12/15/1858.

Married, In this county on Thursday last by the Rev. J. W. **ROGERS**, Dr. W. E. **ROGERS**, of Brownsville, Tenn., to Miss Elizabeth, daughter of Wm. **BATTLE**, Esq. Memphis Eagle & Enquirer, 6/4/1853. We take pleasure in asking the attention of the citizens of Memphis and vicinity to the professional card of Dr. W. E. Rogers. We have known Dr. Rogers long and well, and know him to be a safe and skillful physician. His field of labors for many years has been in Brownsville and Haywood county, where he enjoys a high reputation. He has now selected Memphis as his future home....Memphis Daily Appeal, 1/13/1858.

A young man by the name of James H. **ROGERS**, died yesterday of bilious fever. He was a member of Mechanics' Fire Co. No. 4, and his funeral was attended yesterday by the company in full uniform. Memphis Daily Appeal, 9/15/1855.

Married, On the 29th ult. at the residence of Mr. Joshua **ECKLIN**, near Fisherville, by Dr. Wm. G. **LANCASTER**, Mr. James H. **ROGERS** to Miss Harriet A. **PATRICK**, all of Shelby county. Memphis Daily Appeal, 12/4/1855.

Married, On the 30th ult. by Hume F. **HILL**, Esq., Mr. John **ROGERS** and Miss Hatty **BOTTO**, all of this city. Also, by the same, on the 30th ult., Mr. Thomas **REEVES** and Miss Rosa **BOTTO**, all of this city. Memphis Daily Appeal, 5/1/1859.

Wholesale and Retail Clothing Store, on Front Row...George **ROHR**, Clothier. Daily Enquirer, 11/17/1847.

We are authorized to announce Hugh **ROLAND** as a candidate for re-election for Justice of the Peace for the 14th Civil District, at the ensuing March election. Memphis Appeal, 2/6/1848. Hugh Roland versus Robertson **TOPP**. This suit was brought to recover wages due plaintiff, for work and labor done on the Gayoso House as an architect, in the years 1841 '42 etc....The jury gave plaintiff $600. Memphis Daily Eagle, 3/31/1848. Died, At his residence in Fort Pickering, on Tuesday, 25th inst., Hugh Roland, Esq., Architect, aged 55(?) years. Mr. Roland was, we believe, a native of Pennsylvania and emigrated to

Nashville, in this State, a great many years ago. He attained and held an eminent rank in his profession, a large number of the public edifices of Tennessee and Kentucky having been built under his direction…Memphis Eagle & Enquirer, 5/28/1852.

The body of Joseph **ROLAND**, who was drowned at the wood-yard of J. A. **HARRIS**, Esq., 12 miles below town, from a skiff while attempting to board the steamer Atlantic, on the 12th of January last, has been found and buried. The sum of fifty-four dollars was found in his pocket, which is in the hands of Dr. Wm. **RIVES**, to whom his friends, living in St. Louis, it is said, will apply. Memphis Eagle & Enquirer, 2/20/1853.

Married, At Forest Grove, Fayette county, Tenn., on Wednesday, January 18, by Rev. L. C. **ROBERTS**, Mr. John W. **ROOK** to Miss Martha K. **MEARS**, of Marshall county, Miss. Memphis Daily Appeal, 1/19/1859.

Married, In this county, on Tuesday, 26th ult., by the Rev. M. **THREAT**, Mr. E. H. **ROOT** to Miss Caroline **POOL**. The Appeal, 1/5/1844.

Married, On the 11th inst. by Rev. James W. **BATES**, Mr. Geo. F. **ROOTES**, of St. Louis, Mo., to Mrs. Cypressa C. **VANCE**, of Panola county, Miss. Memphis Daily Appeal, 8/13/1859.

Died. On the 5th inst. at the residence of Captain Nat **ROBERTS**, Green **ROPER**, at the advanced age of 82 years. Mr. Roper was born in South Carolina and removed to Hardeman county in 1817….—Bolivar Dem. 25th. Memphis Daily Appeal, 4/29/1855.

Married, On Thursday, the 28th of April, by J. **WALDRAN**, Esq., Mr. Andrew **RORBURG** to Miss Louisa **MILLER**, all of this city. Memphis Daily Appeal, 5/1/1859.

Died, at the residence of his brother, (Capt. Alfred H. **ROSE**, of this county,) on the 3d inst., David E. **ROSE**, M.D., late of Pulaski, Giles Co., Tenn., in the 27th year of his age. He had just commenced the practice of medicine with every prospect of becoming eminent and useful in his profession…..The Appeal, 9/27/1844.

Married, On Thursday evening last, by Rev. P. W. **ALSTON**, Mr. Frederic **BAXTER**, of New Orleans, to Miss Mary E., daughter of James **ROSE**, Esq., of this city. Weekly Appeal, Friday, 8/8/1845. We are authorized to announce James Rose, Esq., as a candidate for re-election to the office of Justice of the Peace, for the 5th Civil District. The Daily Eagle, 2/16/1848. Our citizens were yesterday morning painfully shocked by the announcement of the sudden death of James Rose, Esq. It seems that he had left the city soon after breakfast in a buggy with H. F. **HILL**, Esqr. to attend the sitting of the County Court at Raleigh, when about three miles from town, he suddenly swooned away, without any premonitory symptons of disease, and in less than five minutes was a corpse.—He is supposed to have died with a disease of the heart….For years before our residence in Memphis, Mr. Rose had been an executive officer of the law in our city….His funeral will take place from Calvary Church at 3 o'clock this evening. Divine Services by Rev. D. C. **PAGE**. Memphis Daily Appeal, 4/3/1855.

Married, On Wednesday, October 29th, at the residence of Jos. A. **GREEN**, Esq., Mr. James **ROSE**, of this city, and Miss Mary F. **NEWMAN**, of Tipton county, Tenn. Memphis Daily Appeal, 10/30/1856.

For Sale Or Rent—For one year, my plantation on Big Creek, containing from five to six hundred acres….Apply to Major D. **DUNN**. I have also appointed Major Dunn my Attorney in fact. Robert H. **ROSE**. Memphis Advocate, 3/22/1828.

Married—On Wednesday last, by the Rev. P. W. **ALSTON**, Maj. Samuel **ROSE**, of Randolph, to Miss Prudence W., eldest daughter of Maj. Jno. W. **JONES**, of this county. Memphis Enquirer, Fri., 9/7/1839.

Death of W. A. **ROSE**.—We were pained to learn of the death of this gentleman on yesterday, which occurred at Natchez, Mississippi, on his way to New Orleans for his health, which had been declining for several months. Memphis Daily Appeal, 10/27/1857. The remains of Wm. A. Rose, who died at Natchez on Monday, are expected to arrive this morning by the steamer *H. D. Newcomb*. Memphis Daily Appeal, Wed., 10/28/1857.

Wm. **ROSELLE**, Esq. This gentleman arrived in the city yesterday to assume the duties of news and commercial editor of the Memphis Appeal. We clip the following flattering notice of him from the Cincinnati *Enquirer*, with the press of which city he has long been connected as a reporter and editor....Memphis Daily Appeal, 10/3/1857.

Married, On the 14th inst., by Rev. D. J. **PARKER**, Dr. Grant T. **ROSS** to Miss Lenora **DOUGHTUY**, all of San Felipe, Texas. Memphis Daily Appeal, 9/29/1859.

Married, on the 28th ult., at the residence of E. S. **GILES** Esq. by the Rev. D. P. **COFFEY**, Mr. Thomas J. **ROSS**, to Miss Ann Frances **MICKILBERRY**. The Appeal, 4/5/1844.

Died, In DeSoto, Miss., on the 2d inst., in the fifty-first year of her age, Mrs. Adline Rossel, consort of Stephen **ROSSEL**. The subject of this notice was a pious and consistent Christian, a member of the M. _. Church, a devoted wife and affectionate mother, and a kind mistress. Memphis Daily Appeal, 9/30/1858.

Medical Card. The undersigned having formed a partnership respectfully announce to the citizens of the surrounding country, that they are prepared to attend punctually to the practice of the various branches of their profession...Office on the Covington road, half a mile east of Pleasant Ridge Meeting House, Shelby county, Tenn. Dr. F. L. **ROULHAC**, Dr. J. M. **CHASE**. Memphis Enquirer, 8/8/1846.

Died—On Wednesday morning last, Abner Turner, only daughter of William and Margaret **ROUNDTREE**, aged four months and twenty-five days. Memphis Daily Avalanche, 5/6/1859.

Married, On yesterday by Rev. J. O. **STEADMAN**, D.D., Mr. R. **ROWELL**, of DeSoto county, Miss., and Miss Ellen C. Neely, daughter of Mr. William **NEELY**, of this vicinity. Memphis Daily Appeal, 3/13/1857.

Jo. C. **ROWLAND**, Late of Philadelphia, Having located permanently in Memphis, respectfully offers his professional services to the citizens of Memphis and vicinity...Memphis Daily Appeal, 6/8/1852.

Married, On the 3d inst. by Rev. John **BRICE**, Mr. _. W. **ROWLETT**, of Blackmore, Ark., to Miss Amelia H. **LIGON**, of Henderson county, Ky. Memphis Weekly Appeal, 11/17/1858.

Died, Of consumption, on the 18th inst., at the residence of E. W. **ROWLETT**, in Mississippi county, Ark., Robert B. **ROWLETT**, in the 27th year of his age. Memphis Daily Appeal, 12/24/1856.

Died—On the 12th inst., at the residence of Mr. Joseph D. **ALLEN** of this place, Mr. Wm. H. E. **ROWNES**, aged about 26 years. Mr. R. formerly resided in Lawrenceburg, Ia., but has been a citizen of this place for the last three or four years.....He had no relatives here, but he received every attention that his situation required during his illness. Daily Enquirer, 1/19/1847.

Sale of Negroes & Personal Estate: Will be sold to the highest bidder, at the late residence of Joseph T. **ROYALL**, dec'd., 10 miles South-east from the town of Memphis, on the Hernando plank road, on the 29th of December next, the crops of corn, fodder, etc...Isham G. **LUNDY**, Adm'r of Joseph T. Royall, deceased. Memphis Daily Appeal, 11/30/1852.

Married, At the residence of Mr. Wm. **JOINER** in this county, at 4 o'clock yesterday morning, by Rev. Mr. Bateman, Mr. D. R. **ROYSTER** and Miss Eva **JOINER**, all of Shelby county. Memphis Weekly Appeal, 11/24/1858. Departed this life on the morning of the 13th inst., at the residence of her husband, Mrs. Evelina, consort of D. R. **ROYSTER**, in the twenty-first year of her age. Raleigh Register and Richmond Enquirer please copy. Memphis Daily Appeal, 9/17/1859.

Notice. Will be sold at the late residence of David **ROYSTER**, deceased, near Col. Leake's on the Stage Road, on the 15th day of this Month, all the stock, consisting of horses, mules, cattle, hogs and sheep; two good wagons, corn oats, fodder, hay, etc. Plantation utensils and many other things.....At the same time and place, will be rented the Plantation, containing 300 acres cleared land, having on it a good gin and horse mill, and a full supply of the finest water. J. W. **ROYSTER**, R. W. **ROYSTER**. The Appeal, 1/5/1844.

Married – On Wednesday evening last, by the Rev. J. H. **GRAY**, Frank W. **ROYSTER**, of Memphis to Helen M., only daughter of Henry **LAKE**. Richmond papers please copy. Weekly Memphis Eagle, Thursday, 5/31/1849. Died, At the residence of Henry **LAKE**, Esq., near Memphis, on Thursday night the 29th instant, about nine o'clock, Henry Lake, son of Frank W. and Ellen Royster, aged thirteen months and six days. Memphis Daily Appeal, 6/2/1851. Died, On the evening of the 7th inst., Richard W., infant son of F. W. and Helen F. Royster, aged sixteen months....Memphis Daily Avalanche, 2/9/1859.

Married. On Tuesday the 27th of February by Rev. Thos. P. **WARE**, Dr. B. L. **ROZELL**, of Desoto county, Miss., to Miss Lizzie **LYON**, of Jackson, Tenn. Memphis Daily Appeal, 3/2/1855.

I am offering for sale a very valuable tract of land, 3 ½ miles east of Memphis, containing 590 acres, 200 in cultivation; the balance well timbered...For information apply to Solomon **ROZELL** adjoining said place. R. A. **ROZELL**. Weekly Appeal, 1/16/1846.

Died, At his residence near this city, on Tuesday last, Solomon **ROZELLE**, one of our oldest and most highly respected citizens. Mr. Rozelle was one of the pioneers of West Tennessee, having first settled in Henderson county, where he resided until 1829 or '30, when he removed to this vicinity. He died at a very advanced age and has left behind him a large and highly respectable family of children, besides the partner of his bosom, who has shared with him through a long period of years....Memphis Daily Appeal, Thursday, 8/28/1856. Died, In Marshall county, Miss., on the 28th of August last, of typhoid fever, after an illness of five weeks, Rev. C. W. **ROZELLE**, youngest son of the late Solomon Rozelle, of this vicinity, in the 36th year of his age....In early manhood he connected himself with the Methodist Episcopal Church....Memphis Daily Appeal, 9/6/1856.

Died—On Friday morning, 20th inst., Mr. Jno. **RUDISH**; so extensively known as Auctioneer. He was an Odd Fellow and was buried with the ceremonies of that order; a large number of members attending. Weekly Appeal, 11/27/1846.

Died, At his residence on the 10th inst., Mr. A. Wallace **RUDISILL**. His funeral will take place from the Third Presbyterian Church, This Morning....Memphis Daily Appeal, 1/11/1859.

Died: At her residence on Exchange street on the 10th instant, Mrs. Ann M. **RUDISILL**, aged 58 years. Charlotte, N.C. papers please copy. Memphis Whig, 10/11/1855.

Married—On Thursday last, by the Rev. Mr. McNutt, Mr. J. C. **RUDISILL**, to Miss Chloe Ann **EDWARDS**, all of this county. Memphis Enquirer, Sat., 11/24/1838.

Died, At the residence of his mother, one and a half miles Northeast of Memphis, on the 5th instant, of Congestive Fever, James L. **RUDISILL**, aged twenty-six years. Memphis Daily Appeal, 10/7/1856.

Died, At Arkadelphia, Ark., on the 19th ult., Mrs. Aelissa Rudisill, of this county, and relict of the late John **RUDISILL**, of this city. Memphis Daily Appeal, 2/1/1859.

T. S. **RUDOLPH** and Z. **RUDOLPH**, Jr. Having this day associated together for the purpose of conducting a Wholesale and Retail Cash Dry Goods Store...Front Row, between Washington and Adams street. Daily Enquirer, 10/15/1847.

Mr. Zebulon **RUDOLPH**, formerly of this city, and for many years an attache of the Enquirer staff, died of consumption on the 25th ult., in Izzard county, Ark., aged 62 years. Memphis Whig, 2/23/1856.

C. **RUDZINSKY**, Esq., a Lieutenant of the United States Army, who was staying at the Gayoso, was found yesterday morning sitting upright in his bed ____. He was suffering from consumption. He had no friends in the city and no clue is possessed as to where they may be addressed. Memphis Daily Appeal, 8/19/1858.

Died, On the 21st ult., at Beechwood, Prince George county, Edmund Quintus **RUFFIN**, aged nearly 14 years, eldest son of Edmund **RUFFIN**, Jr.—*Rich. (Va.) Enq.* Memphis Eagle & Enquirer, 4/7/1853.

Died, In Hardeman county, on the morning of the 24th ult., Col. James F. **RUFFIN**, about 35 years of age. American Eagle Weekly, 12/5/1845.

Married, on Sunday, 27th ult., at the Methodist Episcopal Church, in Memphis, by Rev. Wesley **WARRETT**, Dr. Jno. M. **RUFFIN**, of Panola County, Miss., to Miss Mary V. **COLEMAN** of DeSoto County, Miss. Tri-Weekly Memphis Enquirer, 10/3/1846.

Died in this city on the 18th inst., of a congestive chill, Mrs. Mary Ruffin, the wife of Major William **RUFFIN** and a daughter of the late Walter **SHELTON**, Esq. Mrs. Ruffin was a native of Henrico county, Virginia, and spent much of her youth in the city of Richmond and adjoining counties....She removed with her father to the Western District of Tennessee, about 20 years since and married her beloved and attached husband in Somerville, in the vicinity of which they resided for many years....For the last 3 years their home has been in Memphis....She left no child to share the poignant grief of that bereaved husband. Memphis Daily Eagle & Enquirer, 5/31/1853. The friends and acquaintances of Major William Ruffin, President of the Gas Company, are invited to attend his funeral at 10 o'clock A.M. to-morrow (Monday) the 20th inst., from the residence of _. _. Turnage, Esq., on Jefferson street. Memphis Daily Appeal, 7/19/1857. Died, In this city on the evening of Saturday, the 18th inst., of Bilious Dysentery, Maj. William Ruffin—a much esteemed and justly valued citizen. Maj. Ruffin was born in King William county, Virginia, in 1978, whence he emigrated to West Tennessee, and settled near Somerville in 1831, and thence removed to Memphis in 1851. He was the son of James **RUFFIN** and Mary **ROAN**, the sister of John **ROAN**, a distinguished statesman and representative of Virginia in the United States Congress from early manhood to venerable old age, through the period of that State's most brilliant history, beginning almost with the establishment of the National Independence, and continuing, with short interval, to 1835....The Richmond, Virginia, papers will please copy. Memphis Daily Appeal, 7/22/1857. (Author's note: The birth date of 1978 is obviously a misprint by the paper.)

Married, At the residence of the bride's father, in Panola county, Miss., on the 12th inst., by Rev. Stephen G. **STARKS**, Mr. William **RUFFIN**, of Memphis, to Miss Sallie _. **WHITE**. Memphis Daily Appeal, 1/27/1858.

Married, At Calvary Church at half-past eight o'clock last evening, by Rev. G. **SCHETKY**, G. P. **RUMBAUGH**, Esq., and Miss Anna F. Trezevant, daughter of Col. J. T. **TREZEVANT**, Esq., all of this city. Memphis Daily Avalanche, 5/19/1859. Married....G. P. C. Rumbaugh, Engineer of the Memphis and Little Rock Railroad....Memphis Daily Appeal, 5/22/1859.

Married—On Monday Evening last, by the Rev. Mr. Stone, Mr. Jas. M. **RUMMELL**, of Lee, Massachusetts, to Mrs. Elizabeth **VAUGHN**, of Memphis. Memphis Daily Appeal, Wed., 8/23/1848.

Married, By Rev. H. C. **HORTON**, Mr. Charles **RUNHOLY** to Miss Mollie **GILES**—all of this city. Memphis Daily Appeal, 11/2/1859.

Died—At the residence of his brother-in-law, Mr. John **DAVENPORT**, on Friday the 15th inst., Washington D. **RUNKLE**, aged about 26 years. American Eagle, 4/21/1842.

We have been kindly furnished with a copy of an interesting letter from Mr. A. C. **RUSSELL**, formerly of this city, now in California. From it we shall make copious extracts in our next. Mr. Russell writes cheeringly of his health and pecuniary prospects. Memphis Appeal, 1/18/1851. We had the pleasure of a visit yesterday from our old friend A. C. Russell, Esq., of San Francisco, who is stopping at the Gayoso

House. Mr. Russell is a native of Tennessee, and was formerly connected with the press of this city, first as compositor in the office of the "Eagle," and afterwards as editor and proprietor of the "Commercial Journal"....the hardships which the early emigrants to California had to encounter having made little or no impression on his East Tennessee constitution....His present visit to "the States" has reference to the establishment of a new paper at San Francisco....Memphis Eagle & Enquirer, 3/15/1853. Married, Last evening, the 16th inst., at the residence of Mr. **HOLDEN**, on Second street, by the Rev. Dr. H. S. **PORTER**, Andrew C. Russell, Esq., of San Francisco, Cal., to Miss Katherine Erskine **PICKETT**, of this city. Memphis Eagle & Enquirer, 3/17/1853.

Married, On the 17th inst., by Justice Waldran, Mr. John **RUSSELL** to Miss Fanny **BARTON**, all of this city. Memphis Eagle & Enquirer, 6/19/1852.

Married—On Thursday evening last, by the Rev. Mr. McAleer, Capt. E. F. **RUTH** to Mrs. Mary A. **ELLIOTT**, both of this city. The Appeal, Friday, 5/17/1844. We had the pleasure yesterday of shaking by the hand our old friend and former townsman, Capt. E. F. Ruth, who has returned to our city after an absence of some two and a half years. The Capt. is in "fine plight," having fattened some fifty pounds, and is seemingly as gay and hale as in days of yore ere the hand of time had left its impress on his brow. Memphis Daily Appeal, 5/20/1851.

Married, In this vicinity on Thursday evening, the 7th inst., by Esquire Horne, Mr. Edward **RUTHER** to Miss Mary **CAMPBELL**, all of Shelby county, Tenn. Memphis Daily Appeal, 7/9/1859.

Married. On Thursday evening, the 15th inst. Mr. Harrison **RUTLAND**, to Miss Penina **HATHAWAY**, both of this county. American Eagle, 1/1/1848.

Ranaway, About the 18th May, from the subscriber, five miles south of Germantown, Shelby County, Tenn., my negro boy, Charles...Stephen W. **RUTLAND**. Daily Enquirer, 6/11/1847.

Married, In Shelby county, Tenn. on the 12th inst., by the Rev. M. J. **BLACKWELL**, Mr. Wilie N. **RUTLAND** to Miss Martha Jane **RAMEY**. Memphis Eagle & Enquirer, 5/16/1852.

Married, At Early Grove, on the 10th inst. by Rev. J. W. **ROGERS**, Rector of St. John's Church, Mr. Fredrick **RYAN** to Miss Margaret **FREEMAN**, all of Marshall county. Memphis Daily Appeal, 10/16/1855.

The man named Patrick **RYAN** so severely injured last week during the row on the Hernando Road, died on Sunday last, in South Memphis. An inquest was held by Justice Waldran...Michael **RYAN** was discharged yesterday from the charge of murdering Patrick Ryan, no proof appearing against him. Memphis Daily Appeal, Tues., 12/9/1851.

A fatal affray occurred yesterday morning between one and two o'clock, between Mr. T. **RYAN**, of this city, and Mr. Lyon, of Jackson, Tenn., in which the former was shot dead. Memphis Appeal, 10/29/1854.

At a meeting of the Board of Health at 12 o'clock M., Friday, Jan. 5, the following deaths were reported, as having occurred in the last 24 hours: Joseph **RYNE**, at the Hospital, taken from a flatboat, Cholera. Nicholas **ELLIOTT**, taken out of the streets in the night by the police, and soon died—cause unknown. John **HETHER**, on a flatboat, of Chronic Diarrhea, as reported by his physician. Memphis Daily Eagle, 1/6/1849.

Esq. Horne, the Coroner, yesterday held an inquest over the body of a child of four years old, named Wm. **SADDLER**, who was found, in the morning, drowned in the Bayou. It appeared that on Wednesday morning the child was seen playing in the swelled waters of the Bayou; soon afterward it was missed, and its fate was uncertain until the body was found yesterday morning, floating on the surface. The mother of the little boy had left for St. Louis the day before, placing her son in charge of a female residing on Smoky Row, near Auction street, close by the Bayou....Memphis Daily Appeal, Sat., 6/12/1858.

We are authorized to announce John **SAFFARANS**, Esq., as a candidate for Mayor, at the approaching Municipal Election in March next. Daily Enquirer, 1/7/1847.

We had the pleasure yesterday of interchanging salutations with our esteemed friend, the President of the late Whig Club of this city, Col. John L. **SAFFARANS**, whose pleasant countenance we do not remember to have seen since the ever memorable disaster which befell the universal whig party in November last. On inquiring as to his whereabouts during the interval, he informed us that he had just returned from an exploring expedition up the rolling fork of Salt River....Memphis Appeal, 1/21/1853.

Another of our oldest, most respected and most enterprising citizens has gone. Colonel Daniel **SAFFARRANS** died at Dunlap Springs, near Bolivar, on the 11th inst. He has been suffering for many months from an ineradicable disease which strikes down so many of the bravest, and best, as well as the gentlest of the world—pulmonary consumption. In quest of alleviation he visited Cuba last winter, and on his return, in the spring, went to Dunlap Springs where he passed the summer. Col. Saffarrans was born on the 22d of February, 1799, in the State of Virginia. Early in life he removed to Gallatin, in this State, where by energy, industry and attention to business, he acquired wealth and position....his death will be sincerely lamented by a large circle of friends and by an attached family. The friends of the late Daniel Saffarrans are requested to attend his burial at Elmwood Cemetery....Memphis Daily Appeal, 9/16/1858.

Married, On the 23d ult., at the residence of Andrew **TAYLOR**, by Elder George **PLATTENBURG**, Mr. John **SAFFARRANS** and Mrs. M. G. **HUMPHREYS**. At the same time and place, Mr. John W. **BROWN** and Miss F. M. **JONES**, all of Shelby county. Memphis Daily Appeal, 7/1/1856.

An Italian by the name of James **SALARI**, was found dead in his bed yesterday morning at his sleeping room....He died of apoplexy. Memphis Whig, 9/25/1855.

Died, in Fayette county, on the 20th ult., very suddenly, Rev. Henry W. **SALE**, in the 61st year of his age. American Eagle Weekly, 12/5/1845.

By virtue of a deed of trust executed to me by the late William H. **SALE**, on the 12th day of August, 1848, which was duly recorded in the Register's Office of Shelby county, Tenn., on the 11th Sept., 1848.... Memphis Daily Eagle, 12/28/1850.

Died, On the 16th May, at the residence of her son, near Memphis, Mrs. Elizabeth **SAMPLE**, aged 79 years and ten days. Charlotte, N.C. papers please copy. Memphis Daily Appeal, 5/18/1856.

Died, In Memphis, May 5th, 1856, William Marlin **SAMPLE**, aged two years and seven months. Memphis Daily Appeal, 5/9/1856.

Died, on the morning of the 8th June, at the residence of Mrs. A. C. **THURMAN**, in this vicinity, William R. **SAMPSON**, in the 37th year of his age, after an illness of several months. The deceased was a native of Goochland County, Va., but for the last 18 years a resident of this state. Richmond, Va., Whig and Enquirer copy. Daily Enquirer, 6/15/1847.

Married, On the 13th inst. at the residence of Captain R. M. **MASON**, by Rev. J. L. **CROSS**, Mr. John P. **SAMUELS** to Mrs. Frances A. **JONES**, all of Shelby county, Tenn. Memphis Daily Appeal, 11/16/1859.

Died, at the residence of Stephen **ENGLISH**, Esq., on the 6th of August, 1854, Benjamin **SANDEFORD**. He was born in Halifax county, North Carolina, March 12th, 1770....He was and had been an accepted member of the Old Baptist Church for many years....He was married to Martha **GARDINER** on the 22d of May, 1794, and afterwards emigrated to Warren county, Georgia in 1797, lived there 20 years and represented that county in the Legislature for the year 1817, being a warm advocate of the Jacksonion school of politics. He removed from there to the northeast part of Shelby county, Tenn., in the year 1827, where his eventful life of usefulness as a citizen terminated, aged 84 years, 4 months and 24 days, leaving a widow....and an interesting number of descendants from him, numbering one hundred and thirty souls. Warrenton (Ga.) papers please copy. Memphis Daily Appeal, 8/31/1854.

Died, in Nashville, on the 29th ultimo, Mrs. W. L., widow and relict of the late J. B. **SANDERS**, M.D., in the 43d year of her age, and for many years a resident of this place.....She has left five children to mourn their irreparable loss. Memphis Enquirer, 4/9/1846.

Married, On the 20th instant at the residence of Geo. **HULM**, Madison county, Miss., Mr. Joseph B. **SANDERS**, of DeSoto, and Miss Eva **DENSON**, of the former county. Memphis Daily Appeal, 11/27/1856.

Pursuant to a decree renewed at the March Term, 1852, of the Common Law and Chancery Court, of the City of Memphis, in the case of L. **HENDERSON**, adm'r. of M. L. **SANDERS**, deceased, vs. the heirs of M. L. Sanders...Memphis Eagle & Enquirer, 5/6/1852.

At a meeting of a portion of the officers and employees of the Memphis and Ohio Railroad, on Saturday, September 26th, 1857, called on account of the death of Samuel M. **SANDERS**, one of their associates and friends. Mr. J. T. **TREZEVANT** was called to the chair....Resolved, That we deeply and sincerely sympathize with his kind and affectionate mother and also with his aged grand-parents, who are called upon to follow their only son to his long, long home.... Died, Near Brownsville, at the residence of Dr. Watkins, on the night of the 25th inst., Sam'l Sanders, an attache of the Memphis and Ohio Railroad. Memphis Daily Appeal, 9/27/1857.

Died—On the 30th ult., Frances Susan, aged 13 months & 11 days, infant daughter of Thomas A. & Elizabeth Ann **SANDERS**, of Shelby County, Tennessee. Memphis Enquirer, 4/7/1838.

Married, In Belton, Texas, December 17th, X. B. **SANDERS**, Esq., late of this city, to Miss Annie E. **SURGHNON**. Nashville and Columbia, Tenn., papers please copy. Memphis Daily Appeal, 1/27/1858.

Married. On Thursday evening, the 13th inst. by the Rev. Bishop Otey, James **SANDS** to Jessie Maria, daughter of the late J. **OLMSTEAD**, Esq. Memphis Eagle & Enquirer, 1/15/1853. Among the recent deaths at New Orleans by the prevailing epidemic, we notice those of Mr. James Sands and his wife, formerly of this city. Mrs. Sands' maiden name was Jessie M. Olmsted and as such will be recognized by a large circle of friends and acquaintance. Mr. Sands died on Thursday, the 18th, and his wife on Saturday, the 20th. [Whig. We knew Mr. Sands well and esteemed him highly. He as well as his lady were from Pittsburgh. They had been recently married. Memphis Daily Appeal, 9/1/1853.

We are pained to have to record the death of Mr. J. W. **SANGSTER**, grocer and commission merchant, of the late firm of Copeland & Sangster. He died yesterday morning as we learn, of congestive chill. Memphis Daily Appeal, 9/11/1855. We committed an error in announcing the death of Mr. J. W. Sangster in our yesterday's issue. It should have been R. D. **SANGSTER**, his brother, who is residing at his house....Memphis Daily Appeal, 9/12/1855. Married, On the 29th of October, in Haywood county, Tenn., by Rev. Wm. **SMITH**, Mr. J. W. Sangster, of Memphis, to Miss Mollie A., daughter of James A. **WADDELL**, Esq. Memphis Daily Appeal, 11/1/1856.

Married, On the 27th inst., by J. **WALDRAN**, Esq. Mr. W. H. **SANGSTER** to Miss E. C. **KILSEY**, all of this city. Memphis Eagle, 5/29/1850.

Died, Thursday, June 2, 1859, at his residence in this county, three miles from the city, F. **SANNONER**, in the 69th year of her age....Memphis Daily Appeal, 6/3/1859.

Married.—On Wednesday evening last, 2d inst. by Rev. Mr. Whelock, Mr. John A. **SANNONER** to Miss Mariah B., eldest daughter of Samuel P. **WALKER**, Esq., all of this city. Memphis Appeal, 11/4/1853.

Died—On the 15th instant, in this city, Florence, infant daughter of Dr. M. B. and Eliza A. **SAPPINGTON**—aged two years and ten months. The funeral service will be performed at the Episcopal Church at 10 o'clock, this morning by the Rev. Mr. Alston. Weekly Appeal, 9/19/1845. Died, On the evening of the 14th inst., Edwin Hickman, only son of Dr. M. B. and Mrs. E. A. Sappington, aged 16 months and 17 days. Memphis Appeal, 4/16/1848. Dr. Mark Brown Sappington, through a Card in the Appeal, addressed to Quarter Master Anderson, tenders his medical services, gratis, to the sick or wounded volunteers, during their sojourn in the city...Daily Enquirer, 6/2/1847. The friends and acquaintances of the late Dr. M. B. Sappington are invited to attend his funeral this afternoon at 4 o'clock from his residence on Madison street. Memphis Appeal, 11/20/1852. Died, In this city on the morning of the 19th inst., of Congestion of the Brain, Dr. M. B. Sappington, in the 51st year of his age. Dr. S. was one of the earliest settlers in Memphis and long a prominent physician and citizen...He has left behind him a large and interesting family to mourn his decease. Memphis Daily Appeal, 11/22/1852.

Married, On Wednesday the 10th inst. by Rev. Wm. G. **GRAY**, Dr. Hugh K. **SAUNDERS**, of Tippah county, to Miss Agnes V. **FOSTER**, of Pontotoc county, Mississippi. Memphis Daily Appeal, 10/23/1855.

Died, At the residence of E. M. **MATTHEWS**, in Lafayette county, Miss., on Sunday evening last after a brief illness, Mrs. Mary E., consort of Ro__ S. **SAUNDERS**, of this city, in the 24th year of her age. She was interred Sunday, at College Hill in a burying ground where repose several members of her family....Memphis Daily Appeal, Tuesday, 7/21/1857. Died, On the 15th inst., at the residence of E. M. **MATTHEWS**, in Lafayette county, Mississippi, William M., infant son of Rolfe S. **SAUNDERS**, of this city. Memphis Daily Appeal, 9/17/1857.

At becomes our painful duty to announce the death of our friend, Napoleon B. **SAUNDERS**, who breathed his last at the residence of Mr. Benjamin **WRIGHT**, in this city, last Sunday, 28th February....He was a native of Maury county, in this State, but came when quite a youth to Memphis, where he grew up....His remains were escorted to their last resting place in Winchester Cemetery yesterday....Memphis Weekly Appeal, 3/3/1858.

Died, At his residence, in South Memphis, on the 16th inst., of an affection of the lungs, Dr. Thomas F. **SAUNDERS**, in the 45th year of his age. Memphis Daily Appeal, 9/22/1851.

Died, On the 18th inst. at Memphis, Mrs. Eugenia L., wife of Rev. Ben N. **SAWTELLE**, in the twenty-sixth year of her age....Memphis Daily Appeal, 4/24/1859.

Died, At Richland, Mississippi, of Typhoid Fever, on the 10th of October, William P. **SAYLE**, formerly of this place, and brother-in-law of Governor James C. **JONES**. Memphis Daily Eagle, 11/13/1850.

...The undersigned will sell on liberal terms a valuable tract of land containing one thousand acres, situated in the north east part of Shelby county, Tenn., on the west fork of Beaver Dam creek, in the 11th district and ranges four and five, twenty-five miles from Memphis and fifteen from Randolph. There is about 40 acres cleared on the tract, comfortable cabin, etc. The land is known as the Williams tract, and upon application to Mr. Wm. **BATTLE** in the neighborhood, will be shown to any person who may wish to purchase. For particulars apply to Maj. James **CONNER**, Tuscumbia, Ala., or the undersigned at Decatur. John F. **RHEA**, Executor of Jos. **SCALES**, dec'd. Memphis Enquirer, 1/7/1837.

Died, in this city on Thursday, 21st instant, Mr. Timothy **SCANNELL**. His friends and acquaintances are invited to attend his funeral from the Catholic Church, this morning at 10 o'clock. Memphis Daily Appeal, 8/22/1856.

Mr. Geo. W. **SCHABEL** died on Sunday morning, from the effect of the pistol shot received from the hands of Mr. Ward. He was a young man much respected in this community, and has left a wife and child to mourn his untimely loss.—His remains were followed by a large concourse of citizens, among whom were a large number of the order of Odd Fellows, to the cenotaph on Sunday, where they will remain until the return of his family, who were absent in Mississippi. Memphis Eagle & Enquirer, Tues., 3/23/1852.

In pursuance of a decree entered at the March Term 1848 of the Commercial and Criminal Court of Memphis, in the case of the heirs of John F. **SCHABEL**, dec'd, ex-parte Petition to sell Real Estate, I will proceed to sell, on Saturday, the 17th day of June next....in front of the Banking House of the late Farmers and Merchants Bank on Jefferson street…..the lot on which said banking house is situated….—Said Sale being made to enforce the lien heretofore reserved and for the payment of a note due by the said Farmers and Merchants Bank, for sixteen hundred and ninety-five dollars, the balance due by said Bank for said property. Wm. T. **AVERY**, Clerk. Memphis Daily Eagle, 4/18/1848.

Married. On Thursday the 29th ult. at the residence of Col. S. R. **BROWN** by the Rev. H. S. **PORTER**, D.D., Mr. James F. **SCHABELL** to Miss Mary E. Saffarans, daughter of Mr. John **SAFFARANS**, of this city. St. Louis, Nashville & Louisville papers please copy. Memphis Eagle & Enquirer, 1/1/1853.

The Members of South Memphis Lodge, No. 118, are required to meet at their Hall, at half past three o'clock this evening, to attend the funeral of Bro. H. **SCHAFFNER**…The friends and acquaintances of Henry Schaffner are invited to attend his funeral, from his residence on Desoto street, between Union and Beale, this afternoon…Memphis Eagle & Enquirer, 5/12/1852.

Married, On the morning of the 30th July, by Elder C. B. **YOUNG**, Benjamin F. **SCHALIONS** and Miss Ann **BISHOP**, all of Panola county, Miss. Also, on the 31st, Allen F. **BETTS**, of DeSoto, and Miss Adeline **BRACKINRIDGE**, of Panola county. Memphis Daily Appeal, 8/9/1856.

Died, On the 26th inst., Miss Mary Eliza Schenck, aged 19 years, daughter of J. P. **SCHENCK**, of Franklin, Ohio. Memphis Daily Appeal, 12/28/1859.

….The Rev. G. P. **SCHETKY**….has resigned the pastorship of Grace Church, Memphis, in consequence of being appointed to the Parish of St. Andrews, New Jersey….Memphis Daily Appeal, 10/23/1859.

Married, By J. **WALDRAN**, Esq., on the 16th inst., A. C. **SCHIEK** to Miss Pauline **TUNFTMEISTER**, all of this city. Memphis Daily Avalanche, 6/18/1859. (Author's note: names given as **SCHIEN** and **TURFFRINSTER** in Memphis Daily Appeal, 6/18/1859.)

The Rev. J. **SCHWALM** will preach his farewell sermon, in the German language, at the First Presbyterian Church, on tomorrow (Sunday) at 2 o'clock P.M., as there is no hopes to form a congregation at this time. Daily Memphis Enquirer, 9/15/1849.

Died, At Mississippi City, on the morning of the 27th inst., of congestion, Mrs. Elizabeth Scott, wife of Hon. Charles **SCOTT**, of this city. But a few weeks since, Mrs. Scott, in buoyant health, left home to visit a beloved and only sister then temporarily residing on the sea coast, near Mississippi City, and to afford a son, then in feeble health, the benefit of sea-bathing….Mrs. Scott was born and educated near Nashville in this State, and in 1840, soon after her marriage, removed with her husband to Jackson, Miss., where she continued to reside until her removal to this city, about eighteen months since….Memphis Daily Appeal, 7/28/1859.

Died. At Paducah, Ky. on the 12th of July, after a painful illness of twelve days, John A. **SCOTT**, of Yorkville, Gibson county, Tenn. Memphis Daily Appeal, 8/16/1854.

Married. At Nashville on the 27th ult. by the Rev. Dr. Edgar, Mr. G. H. **SCRUGGS**, late of Huntsville, Ala., (and of the firm of Bellows & Scruggs,) to Miss E. C. **SIMPSON**, of Nashville. Memphis Eagle & Enquirer, 2/5/1853.

Plantation For Sale. The undersigned offers for sale the well known and most desirable tract of land situated within one mile of Germantown and fourteen of Memphis, belonging to the estate of Robert **SCRUGGS** dec'd; containing about 400 acres, rising 200 under cultivation—having good water, fine orchards, good buildings, new gin house, etc…R. S. **SCRUGGS**, Executor, Maria **SCRUGGS**, Executrix. Weekly American Eagle, 6/12/1846.

The friends and acquaintances of Mrs. Frances **SEALE** are invited to attend the funeral of her son Robert, This Morning….from Calvary Church. Memphis Daily Appeal, 1/5/1859. We stated yesterday that a boy was accidentally shot on Monday by the discharge of a pistol at a gunstore ….by an employee in the store named Bowman. The boy, whose name was Robert **SEALE**, and who was fourteen years of age, lingered through the night and yesterday morning he expired…. The boy was the son of a widow….Memphis Daily Appeal, 1/5/1859.

The whigs of Shelby in Convention at Raleigh on Monday, made, we will say, the very best nomination they could have made, and a very excellent one under any circumstances. For no man in the county, and but very few, if any, in the State, are better qualified to discharge the duties of Representative, than Col. Granville D. **SEARCY**…Weekly Memphis Eagle, 5/10/1849.

N. W. **SEAT**, M.D. – Memphis, Tenn. Office on Court Square,--the one formerly occupied by Archibald WALKER. The Appeal, 7/7/1843.

By virtue of the powers in me vested by Deed of Trust, executed by Nathaniel W. **SEAT**, dated July 20th, 1847, registered in the Register's office for Shelby county, in Book X, page 260 and 261, I shall expose for sale, on the 26th day of May, 1849…the following described lots in South Memphis…Sam'l **VANCE**, Trustee. Weekly Memphis Eagle, 5/17/1849.

Married—In Fayette county, on the 24th ult. Mr. John H. **SEAWELL** to Miss Louisa A. **HENDON**. Memphis Advocate, 5/3/1828.

Died—In Randolph, on the 25th ult. Newman **SEAWELL**, son of Mrs. Seawell (widow)—aged about seven years. Memphis Enquirer, 10/13/1838.

From the card of Sterling T. **SEAWELL**, Esq., it will be seen that he has commenced the practice of the law in Indianola, Texas….Memphis Daily Appeal, 2/23/1853.

Died—In Louisville, Kentucky, on 2__ th July, ult., Joseph Franklin Seawell, son of Lieut. W. B.(?) **SEAWELL**, U.S.A., aged 2 years and ___ months. Memphis Daily Appeal, 8/10/1847.

The undersigned, (acting under assurances from Washington that the company will be received,) propose raising a company to go to Mexico, as part of the ten regiments recently authorized by Congress…Those who may wish to go, will report themselves to either of the undersigned, or at the auction store of Seawell & Co. W. H. **SEAWELL**, S. T. **SEAWELL**, W. P. **VADEN**. Daily Enquirer, 2/25/1847.

Died, In Brownsville, Haywood county, July 21st, Georgeannia, eldest daughter of Mr. and Mrs. M. M. **SEAY**, aged three years ten months and six days. Memphis Weekly Appeal, 7/28/1858.

Married. At Andrews' Chapel, in this city, on Sunday the 2nd inst. by the Rev. Thos. **LANGFORD**, Bro. Wm. T. **SEAY**, of Jackson, Tenn., to Miss Mag, second daughter of the Rev. W. W. **ROBB**, of Nashville.—Brother Seay and Sister Robb are both members of Finn Social Degree, No. 1—the bride having passed the chairs in that degree.—*Nashville Organ*. Memphis Eagle & Enquirer, 1/16/1853.

Married, At the Second Presbyterian Church on the 10th inst., by Rev. J. H. **GRAY**, Dr. N. M. **SEED** and Miss Virginia E. **LAW**, all of this city. Memphis Whig, 6/12/1856.

Married, On the morning of the 11th inst….by Hume F. **HILL**, J.P., at his office, Mr. R. B. **SEERIGHT** to Miss Louisa A. **DAVIS**—the residence of the parties unknown. Memphis Daily Appeal, 5/13/1859.

We are authorized to announce Russel **SEGER** a candidate for Town Constable, at the approaching March election. Daily Enquirer, 1/5/1847.

Married, On Tuesday, the 8th of March, by Rev. Robt. J. **ALCORN**, of Memphis, Tenn., Dr. J. E. **SEGMAN**, of Pine Bluff, Ark., to Miss Kate **ALCORN**, of Coahoma county, Miss. Memphis Daily Appeal, 3/15/1859.

The funeral of Mr. **SEHAD**, a soldier who did gallant service and lost a leg under Gen. Taylor, in the Mexican war, will take place to-day, t 10 o'clock A.M., from the residence of Mr. Windroth, opposite the navy yard. Memphis Eagle, 9/3/1850.

Married, In Memphis on the 20th April by the Rev. Mr. Hendrickson, Mr. Charles **SEIG**, of Cincinnati, to Miss Elizabeth Marshall, daughter of Robert and Jane **MARSHALL**, formerly of Cincinnati. Cincinnati papers please copy. Memphis Eagle & Enquirer, 4/22/1853.

Married, On Thursday evening, 25th inst., by Rev. R. C. **GRUNDY**, in South Memphis, Mr. Joseph **SELIGMAN** to Miss Mary E.(?) **DAVENPORT**. Memphis Weekly Appeal, 12/1/1858.

Died, On the 13th instant, Fannie Gertrude, daughter of Benjamin and Sarah P. **SETTLE**, formerly of Rockingham county, North Carolina, three years and five months of age. Raleigh Standard and Greensboro Patriot please copy. Memphis Daily Appeal, 3/21/1857.

Died, In Marshall county, on Monday morning, 15th inst., of congestive chills, William Josiah Settle, son of David and Jane N. **SETTLE**, aged eleven years, one month and twenty-seven days. Memphis Weekly Appeal, 3/24/1858.

Died—June 21st, Wilder, infant son of John and Melinda **SEVIER**, aged one year, nine months and one day. Memphis Daily Avalanche, 6/22/1859.

Died, On the 23d inst., near Raleigh, Tenn., Mrs. Lucy L. Sewall, wife of E. G. **SEWALL**. Memphis Daily Appeal, 6/25/1859.

Married, On the 30th of November, 1859, at the bride's uncle's, Major B. S. **TAYLOR**, by Rev. J. L. **CROSS**, Mr. Edward G. **SEWALL** to Miss Mattie J. **TAYLOR**, all of Shelby county, Tenn. The New Orleans Picayune will please copy. Memphis Daily Appeal, 12/7/1859.

_____ J. **SHACKELFORD** departed this life at the residence of his father, S. W. **SHACKELFORD**, in _____ of Pontotoc, Miss., on the 29th of March in the 36th year of his age. The subject of the above notice was born in _____, Va., on the 21st of October, 1819.--....a printer by trade and was for many _____ a resident of Memphis where he worked in the office of the "Appeal"....In the year 1844 he was engaged in _____ and editing the "Western Spy," a _____ published in the town of Somerville, Tenn.-- _____ much from his disease (consumption)....left a father and mother, and two brothers to mourn his loss. Memphis Daily Appeal, 5/13/1855.

The funeral of Clifford, son of George and Martha **SHALL**, will take place from the Worsham House this evening at half-past three o'clock....Memphis Daily Appeal, 4/9/1857.

About 12 o'clock yesterday noon Michael **SHALLER**, an old citizen of this place, fell suddenly dead near Court Square. It seems that he was taken suddenly with a very severe hemorrhage of the lungs or stomach, and, after walking some thirty paces, fell upon the pavement in a lifeless condition. He was instantly taken care of and treated by Dr. Creighton, but the stream of life had flown, and he expired in a few minutes. Mr. Shaller for some years past has resided in Cincinnati, but had recently returned to Memphis, with the view of making this his future home, and, as we are informed, was in daily expectation of the arrival of his family. He was for many years connected with Mr. Keller, of this city, in the clothing business....The friends and acquaintances of M. Shaller, deceased, are respectfully invited to attend his funeral....from Morris Cemetery, in South Memphis to the Catholic graveyard. Memphis Daily Appeal, 10/12/1858.

The friends and acquaintances of D. W. **SHANKS** are invited to attend the funeral of his late wife, from his residence on Union street This Afternoon....Services by the Rev. Doctors Grundy and Bryan. Memphis Daily Appeal, 2/8/1859. Died, On Wednesday, February 9th....Mattie Niles, only daughter of D. W. Shanks....Memphis Daily Appeal, 2/10/1859.

Funeral Invitation. On Thursday, July 31ˢᵗ, Thomas A., infant son of David W. and Caroline **SHANKS**. Their friends and acquaintances are invited to attend his funeral from their residence on the corner of Beal and Second street this evening at 4 o'clock. Services by Rev. Bishop Otey. Memphis Daily Appeal, 8/1/1856.

The particulars published in the city papers of the death of Dr. F. T. **SHANKS**, we are authoritatively informed, were not entirely correct. He was at his uncle John **THOMPSON's**, whose plantation adjoins his own, on Swan Lake, near the Arkansas river, twenty-five miles below Pine Bluffs. He had spent the day with Mrs. Thompson and her sister. After tea, and while in the room with the ladies, he was examining a pocket pistol that he had borrowed to take with him on an excursion that he contemplated taking, with several other gentlemen, to the bottom, for the purpose of examining some land. The pistol was accidentally discharged, the ball entering the side of his head, rendering him immediately insensible and speechless, and producing death in a short time. The melancholy accident occurred on the 16ᵗʰ instant. Memphis Daily Appeal, 5/24/1857. Died, In Arkansas county, on the 16ᵗʰ instant, Dr. F. T. Shanks, aged 27 years, son of Dr. L. **SHANKS**, of Memphis, Tennessee. The remains having been brought to Memphis…. Memphis Daily Appeal, 5/24/1857. (Author's note: Name given as Frank in another article.)

Died, August 2d, Rebecca Jane, aged three years and ten months, youngest daughter of Dr. Lewis **SHANKS**. Tri-Weekly Memphis Enquirer, 8/6/1846. Died—On the 8th inst. Rebecca Thompson, aged 18 months, daughter of Doctor Lewis Shanks, of this town. Memphis Enquirer, 7/14/1838.

Married, In Grenada, Miss., on the 8ᵗʰ inst., by Rev. J. W. T. **AULD**, Col. D. W. **SHANNON**, of Ark., and Miss Arabella E. **ABEL**, of Grenada. Memphis Daily Appeal, 4/15/1856.

Dr. J. D. **SHANNON**, Having located himself in Memphis, tenders his services, in all the various branches of his profession…Office on the west side of Main street, one door north of Jefferson…Daily Enquirer, 7/1/1847.

Married, On Tuesday evening, the 23d inst., by the Rev. Geo. W. **COONS**, Mr. W. B. **SHAPPARD**, of Nashville, to Miss Cordelia C., youngest daughter of Mr. G. **FRIERSON**, of this city. Memphis Eagle, 11/1/1849.

Letters of administration having been granted to the undersigned at the March term of the County Court, of Shelby County, Tenn., on the estate of Ann T. **SHARP** dec'd, notice is hereby given to all who are indebted to said estate, to call and pay the same. Miles **OWEN**, Administrator. Memphis Daily Eagle, 3/24/1848.

Married. At the residence of Col. George F. **CROCKETT**, in San Augustine county, Texas, on Thursday evening the 4ᵗʰ ult. by Rev. A. J. **LOUGHBOROUGH**, Dr. B. F. **SHARP**, of San Augustine county, to Miss Mary **CROCKETT**, late of this city….Memphis Daily Appeal, 8/3/1854.

In pursuance of the provisions of a deed of Trust made by John M. **SHARP**, bearing date the 28th day of April 1843, I will expose to public sale…on Fridday 5th day of February next…the following described tract of land, situated in the County of Shelby…containing 96 acres, and granted by the State of Tennessee to John M. Sharp, by Grant No. 5089…on an Island in the Mississippi River being the second Island above the mouth of Wolf River, and commonly known as the "Old Hen"…Sylvester **BAILEY**, Trustee…Weekly Appeal, 1/8/1847.

Capt. John M. **SHARPE**.—This gentleman, who so much distinguished himself as Captain of the Mississippi Rifles in the bloody and memorable battle of Buena Vista, is at present on a visit to his only child, the wife of our esteemed townsman, Col. C. H. **WILLIAMS**, who, we regret to learn, is seriously sick….Memphis Daily Appeal, 5/7/1859.

Died, At the residence of R. H. **JACKSON**, of Fayette county, Tenn., on Wednesday, the 2d inst., in the 30ᵗʰ year of her age, Mrs. Mary, consort of Mr. Samuel **SHAVER**, formerly of East Tennessee, and more lately of Batesville, Ark., and daughter of the late Hon. Samuel **POWELL**, of Hawkins county, East Tennessee. Memphis Daily Appeal, 1/12/1856.

A little son of A. B. **SHAW**, aged about six years, fell down the staircase from the second story of his residence on Union street, just beyond the bayou, yesterday afternoon, and was killed by the accident. The little fellow's neck was broken, causing his death instantly. Memphis Daily Appeal, 7/15/1859.

Doctor John D. **SHAW** Has settled himself in the Town of Raleigh, Shelby County; where he offers his professional services in the practice of Medicine, Surgery, and Obstetricks....Memphis Advocate, 2/23/1828.

On the Death of Samuel Jackson Shaw. Died, Saturday, January 21st, aged 3 years, 4 months and 2 days....(The above is, we understand, a tribute from a very little Miss to the memory of a young friend, an interesting little son lately lost by our friend, Capt. Shaw.—Ed. Eagle) Memphis Weekly Eagle, 1/25/1849. Died, Saturday, at the residence of his father, on Union street, Samuel Jackson Shaw, son of A. B. and E. J. **SHAW**, aged 3 years 4 months and 2 days. Memphis Daily Eagle, 1/22/1849. Died, On the 10th inst., Able Byron, infant son of Capt. A. B. and Elenor J. Shaw, aged ten months and twenty-two days. Memphis Whig, 6/12/1856. The friends of the family are invited to attend the funeral from their residence on Union street...Memphis Daily Appeal, 6/11/1856.

Married, On the 5th inst. at Idlewild, residence of W. S. **WELLS**, Shelby county, Tenn., by Rev. Henry **WALSH**, Capt. Alexander **SHAW**, of DeSoto county, Miss., to Mrs. Mary E. **REINHARDT**, of Shelby county, Tenn. Memphis Whig, 2/8/1856.

A difficulty occurred at Bolivar on Thursday night, about 9 o'clock, between two young men named Langstreet **CRISP** and Thomas **SHAW**, in which the former was shot. After some words had passed between them, Crisp drew a pistol and taking hold of the barrel, commenced beating Shaw on the head with it. At the third of fourth blow the pistol went off, shooting Crisp through the heart, killing him instantly. The jury returned a verdict that he came to his death by his own hands...Memphis Eagle & Enquirer, Sat., 4/3/1852.

Died, In Hardeman county, on the 15th inst. Mr. Willie C. **SHAW**, formerly of Fayette, aged about 26 years. American Eagle Weekly, 9/26/1845.

At a meeting of the Phi-Sigma Society of the University of Mississippi, held on the 24th of October, the following resolutions were passed: Whereas, It has pleased our kind Benefactor to remove from earth our highly esteemed brother, Edward **SHEEGOG**, who departed this life on the 31st day of August, in the 17th year of his age....Resolved, That we tender our deep and heartfelt sympathies to his much-agrieved parents and kindred....Memphis Daily Appeal, 10/27/1857.

A young man by the name of John **SHEEHAN**, was killed last evening about 9 P.M., near Maddox's Livery stable, by an Irish girl by the name of Mary **MORIARTY**. It appears that Mary had been led somewhat astray from the path of virtue by the pretensions and declaration of her seducer, when, finding that he was not disposed to make reparation for the wrong, she made two fatal stabs with a dirk upon his person. The first stab was in the abdomen, the second struck his heart, and he died instantly. The woman was immediately arrested and lodged in the Calaboose to await trial. [At a very late hour last evening we heard a very different version of the above affair; we forbear giving them.] Memphis Daily Appeal, 9/2/1855.

Died on Monday afternoon, the 5th inst., at 4 o'clock, at the Commercial Hotel, after a lingering and painful illness, which she bore with christian resignation, Mrs. Margaret Shelby, consort of John **SHELBY**, Esq., a Merchant of this place....She is gone where spirits of her own pure nature dwell, leaving a disconsolate husband and an afflicted circle of friends.....Louisville, Ky., and Natchez, Miss. papers please copy. Weekly Memphis Eagle, 3/8/1849.

Died, At half past 7 o'clock, on the 28th inst., Susan Armstrong, only daughter of A. P. and M. E. **SHELDON**, and grand daughter of Col. Daniel **SAFFARANS**, aged 3 years and 6 months…Services at the Episcopal Church. Memphis Eagle & Enquirer, 2/29/1852.

Married, On the 8th instant in Tuscumbia, Ala., at the residence of the bride's mother, by Rev. A. M. **KLINE**, Mr. Asa **SHELTON**, of Memphis, to Miss Martha E. **ROSS**, of the former place. Memphis Daily Appeal, 3/9/1859.

Married, At the Cumberland Presbyterian Church on the evening of the 23d inst., by Rev. Dr. A. M. **BRYAN**, Mr. B.(?) W. **SHELTON** to Miss Maggie A. **HARDING**, all of Memphis. Memphis Daily Appeal, 2/24/1858.

Married, At Elysian Grove, Fayette county, Tenn., on the 21st August, by Rev. Wm. M. **McFERRIN**, Rev. J. W. **SHELTON** and Miss M. A. **CROSS**, both formerly from North Carolina. Weekly Memphis Eagle, 9/6/1849.

Married, On the 30th ult. by Rev. H. M. **WILKINSON**, at the residence of Lovet **SPIVEY**, Esq., of Drew county, Ark., formerly of Mississippi, Mr. John __. **SHELTON**, of Florence, Desha county, Ark., late of Fayette county, Tenn., and Miss Virginia Ann **SPIVEY**. Memphis Daily Appeal, 1/9/1857.

Died, On the 4th day of August, 1856, Mrs. Martha P. Shelton, consort of John F. **SHELTON**, Esq., and daughter of the late Drury and Sarah **MILAM**, of Lincoln county, Tennessee. Observer, Fayetteville, Tenn. please copy. Memphis Daily Appeal, 8/16/1856.

Married, On the 21st inst. in Limestone county, Ala., by Rev. Robert **VANHOOSE**, Mr. Lee B. **SHELTON**, of West Tennessee, to Miss Laura O. **RAMSEY**, of Limestone county. Memphis Daily Avalanche, 4/26/1859.

Married, In Lauderdale county, on the 30th July, by the Rev. Joseph H. **BORUM**, Mr. R. A. **SHELTON**, to Miss Nancy, daughter of Thomas **DURHAM**, Esq. Weekly American Eagle, 8/14/1846.

Married, In Tipton county, on the morning of the 5th inst., at the residence of the bride's father, by Rev. A. M. **BRYAN**, Mr. Samuel R. **SHELTON** to Miss Sallie B. **RUTHERFORD**. Memphis Daily Appeal, 5/7/1857.

Stone Cutting. The subscriber has located himself in Memphis, and is prepared to furnish to order all kinds of work in his line……Thomas **SHELTON**. The Appeal, 1/26/1844.

We learn from the Carrollton *Democrat* that Charles Palmer **SHEPPARD**, Esq., of that town, died of pulmonary consumption on the 14th inst. Mr. Sheppard was one of the most distinguished and successful lawyers in the portion of Mississippi in which he resided….In a practice of about fifteen years he had acquired a considerable fortune….Mr. Sheppard was a native of Virginia, but received his classical education at the University of Nashville….Mr. Sheppard was the brother-in-law of our fellow-citizen, A. H. **CALDWELL**, Esq. Memphis Daily Appeal, 3/23/1855.

For Sale.—The subscriber being about to remove to New Orleans, offers for sale low and on time, 93 acres of choice Land, of the "Porterfield Tract," in the bottom near to, and southeasterly of the town limits of Randolph. Also, 5 town lots, including his residence. I. De Blois **SHERMAN**. Randolph, 2/25/1842. American Eagle Weekly, 2/28/1842.

Married—On Tuesday evening, the 18th inst., by Rev. E. M. **SWOOPE**, Benj. **SHERROD**, Jr., to Ella, daughter of Col. Richard **JONES**, all of Courtland, Lawrence county, Ala….Memphis Daily Avalanche, 5/27/1859.

Mr. Daniel **SHERRY** died of yellow fever in this city on Friday night. We did not hear that Mr. S. had been down the river, but his business detained him we believe constantly on our own steamboat landing.

and in intercourse with steamers having yellow fever patients on board. Memphis Daily Appeal, Mon., 9/26/1853.

Strayed or stolen from the subscriber on the night of the 17th inst., an iron gray horse...J. **SHETTER**, Germantown. Memphis Daily Appeal, 5/21/1848.

Married. In Murfreesboro, Tenn. on December 25th, Elijah M. **SHETTLESWORTH**, Esq., of Jackson county, Ark., to Miss Martha J. Jamison, daughter of H. D. **JAMISON**, Esq., of Rutherford county. Memphis Daily Appeal, 1/11/1855.

We yesterday had the pleasure of sitting down to the amply spread board of the fine steamer James Laughlin, in honor of the birth-day of her commander, Capt. John **SHIRLEY**...Memphis Whig, 4/18/1856.

At a regular meeting of Augusta Lodge No. 45, of Free and Accepted Masons, the following preamble and resolutions were unanimously adopted: Whereas, It hath pleased an Allwise God to remove from our midst, our highly esteemed and much lamented brother, John **SHIVERS**, who departed this life on the 24th of June, A.D., 1855, at his residence in Augusta county, Arkansas; Resolved, That in the death of our worthy Brother, his wife has lost an affectionate husband, his children a kind father....Memphis Daily Appeal, 8/21/1855.

Married. On Thursday 11th of August by the Rev. H. T. **JONES**, Dr. R. B. **SHORE** to Mrs. Olive G. **LYNCH**, all of this county. Memphis Daily Appeal, 9/3/1853.

Married, on the 26th of October, by the Rev. Mr. Taylor, of Fayette, at the residence of J. **GRAY**, Dr. Robert **SHORE** to Miss Sarah E. **MOORNING**, both of Shelby County. Daily Memphis Enquirer, 11/3/1848.

Married. On the 18th(?) inst. at the residence of Moses **NEELY**, by the Rev. Mr. Foster, Mr. W. **SHORTER** to Miss Felicia **NEELY**, all of this county. Weekly Memphis Eagle & Enquirer, 5/31/1854.

Died, In this city on Thursday morning last, at the residence of his father, of typhoid fever, Thomas J., son of Geo. S. **SHROYER**, aged 26 years. Memphis Daily Appeal, Sat., 10/16/1852.

Masonic Funeral Notice. The members of South Memphis Lodge No. 118 and Angernon Lodge No. 168, are requested to meet at their Hall, on this day, Wednesday, 5th inst...to attend the funeral of our late Bro. Joseph D. **SHUBERT**...Memphis Daily Appeal, 11/5/1851.

Married, In Oxford, Miss., on the 12th(?) inst., at the Presbyterian Church, Mr. A. L. **SHUTWELL** of Louisiana to Miss Julia M. Brown, daughter of Col. James **BROWN**. Memphis Daily Appeal, 7/19/1859.

Married, on the 9th inst., in this city, by the Rev. J. H. **GRAY**, Mr. Joseph **SIDLE**, of New Orleans, to Miss Mary Jane Houston, daughter of John **HOUSTON**, Esq. Daily Memphis Enquirer, 5/12/1848.

Married—On the 26th of April, 1859, by Rev. Mr. Erwin, Mr. J. P. **SIGMAN**, of Mississippi, to Miss Josephine **THOMAS**, of North Carolina. Memphis Daily Avalanche, 5/3/1859.

The friends and acquaintances of the late A. J. **SIGNAIGO** are respectfully invited to attend his funeral at nine o'clock this morning from his residence on Adams street, opposite the Catholic Church. Memphis Daily Appeal, 10/13/1855.

Married, On Sunday, August 8th, by Rev. T. L. **GRACE**, Mr. J. Augustin **SIGNAIGO** to Miss Theresa **AIROLO**. Natchez and St. Louis papers please copy. Memphis Daily Appeal, 8/10/1858. Died, In this city on Sunday morning last, Mrs. Theresa Signaigo, wife of G. A. **SIGNAIGO**, in the sixteenth year of her age. Memphis Daily Appeal, Tues., 5/17/1859.

Married, On the 4th instant by Rev. J. W. **KIRK**, at the residence of the bride, Mr. Lion R. **SIMMONS** to Mrs. N. H.(?) **COUSAR**, both of Bolivar county, Miss. Memphis Daily Appeal, 12/11/1859.

Ho! For Texas. I offer for sale the tract of Land on which I reside, containing about 1200 acres…This farm is 29 miles east of Memphis, in the southwest corner of Fayette county, between Macon and Colliersville…S. R. **SIMMONS**. Memphis Daily Eagle & Enquirer, 6/3/1852. Died, On the 21st August, Mrs. Mary M., consort of S. R. Simmons, of Fayette county, Tenn. Memphis Daily Appeal, 9/30/1856.

Married, On the 23d inst., by Rev. T. J. **DRANE**, Mr. Thos. A. **SIMMONS** to Miss Martha M. **GIBBS**, all of Memphis, Tenn. Memphis Weekly Appeal, 12/29/1858.

Married. In Fayette county on Thursday evening, March 2d, Mr. W. J. **SIMMONS** to Miss Mary W. **MILLER**. Memphis Appeal, 3/7/1854.

Died, On the 11th instant, Collin Tarpley, son of J. T. and Annie V. **SIMMS**, aged twenty months. Memphis Daily Appeal, 7/13/1856.

Married, At the residence of the bride's father, by Rev. Z. H. **WHITEMORE**, on the 21st inst., Mr. P. S. **SIMONS** and Miss S. A. **ROBERTSON**, daughter of Col. Robertson, all of this city. Memphis Daily Avalanche, 3/23/1859.

Died, Of scarlet fever on the 18th instant, James L., son of Dr. James L. **SIMPKINS**, of DeSoto county, Miss., aged __ years. Tallahassee (Fla.) papers please copy. Memphis Daily Appeal, 1/26/1856.

Early yesterday morning a man named John **SIMPSON**, while laboring under a fit of *mania a potu*, jumped from the window of a house on the Raleigh road and killed himself. He leaves a wife and children to mourn his loss. Memphis Daily Appeal, 5/1/1857.

Married, On Wednesday evening, 4th inst., by the Rev. I. L. **CHAPMAN**, Mr. Granville S. **SIMS** to Miss V. A. **HAYNES**, all of this city. Memphis Daily Appeal, 8/6/1852.

Died, in Shelby county, Tennessee, July 7th, 1849, Mrs. Emily, consort of Mr. James **SIMS**, in the eighteenth year of her age…She had but recently settled in our neighborhood…. Providence be sanctified to the good of her bereaved and disconsolate husband, and the family of the deceased. The Holly Springs papers will please copy. Memphis Eagle, 7/12/1849.

Death of Leroy **SIMS**, Esq. A friend just returned from Holly Springs, brings the melancholy tidings of the death of this most worthy and excellent man. He died on Monday last at his residence in Holly Springs, Mississippi, after a protracted and painful illness extending through several weeks. Mr. Sims was one of the most noted mail-contractors in the Union…Memphis Daily Appeal, 2/6/1856.

Died, At the residence of his father, E. D. **SINCLAIR**, in Lafayette county, Mississippi, on Wednesday, the 16th day of September, 1857, William Henry **SINCLAIR**, aged eighteen years, eleven months and twenty-five days. Memphis Daily Appeal, 9/25/1857.

Died, On the 4th ultimo, in Denmark, Tenn., after a brief illness of one week, Margaret A. Sinclair. Died, On the 10th ultimo, in Denmark, Tenn., after a long and painful illness of twenty-one days, with typhoid fever, at the residence of her father, Peter **SINCLAIR**, Mollie W. Sinclair. It is by the rude hand of Death that another one of life's priceless gems has been snatched away from the fond embraces of a kind father and mother and loving brothers and sisters….Memphis Daily Appeal, 12/10/1857.

A Tribute of Respect….It now becomes our sad duty to pay this last and melancholy tribute to the remains of William H. **SINCLAIR**, who was a member of the Sophomore Class of the University of Mississippi ….Memphis Daily Appeal, 12/13/1857.

Married, At the bride's plantation on the Yazoo river, by Rev. J. S. **MONTGOMERY**, on Wednesday, the 9th inst., the Hon. Otho R. **SINGLETON**, M.C., from this District, to Mrs. Eliza **LOUGHBORO**, of this county. The happy couple left immediately on the steamer Hope *en route* for Washington....*Yazoo (Miss.) Banner.* Memphis Daily Appeal, 11/15/1859.

Died, "In the Communion of the Catholic Church," on Christmas Eve, at his residence in Hinds county, Mississippi, George G. **SKIPWITH**, Esq., aged 49. Memphis Daily Eagle & Enquirer, 1/6/1853.

Married, At Calvary Church on the evening of the 24th inst., by Rev. G. **SCHETSKY**, Peyton **SKIPWITH**, Esq., to Miss Mary Isbella **COLLIER**. Memphis Daily Appeal, 3/27/1859.

University of Memphis. The Literary Department of this Institution has been reorganized by the appointment of S. L. **SLACK**, A.M. and W. L. **SLACK**, A.M. to the chairs of Mathematics, Natural Science, etc...By order of the Trustees, B. F. **FARNSWORTH**, President. Memphis Enquirer, 11/5/1846.

Married, At the Commercial Hotel in this city, by Judge Hume F. **HILL**, Mr. William **SLADE** to Miss E. _. **LANE**, both of Hernando, Miss. Memphis Daily Appeal, 6/28/1856.

Married. On yesterday evening on Madison street by Hume F. **HILL**, Esq., Jno. **SLAPPEL** to Catherine **WITTEG**, both of this city. Memphis Daily Eagle & Enquirer, 2/1/1853.

Married, On December 4th by Rev. B. F. **GRIFFING**, W. R. **SLATE** to Miss Caroline **HEARNY**, all of Tipton county, Tenn. Memphis Weekly Appeal, 12/8/1858.

An Irish woman named **SLAUGHTER**, wife of a member of the Tennessee Calvary, threw herself from the ferry boat, into the Mississippi, on Sunday evening last, and was drowned. She was going over to the camp to bid her husband farewell, and it is supposed that distraction at the thought of parting with him drove her to the desperate deed. She is represented as having sustained an exemplary character. Her body was rescued from the waves after life was extinct. Memphis Enquirer, Tues., 7/28/1846.

Memphis Volunteers Killed and Wounded—We are indebted to Mr. M. L. **SLAUGHTER** for the following corrected list of the killed and wounded, received in a letter from his brother, who was present and in the battle—Enquirer. Killed—Lieut. Chas. **GILL**, Lieut. Fred B. **NELSON**, Thos G. **STAINBACK**, Chas. A. **SAMPSON**, Sergt. A. L. **BYNUM**, R. L. **BOHANNON**, _____ Robertson,--7. Wounded.—Ben. **OLIVER**, Thos. **GOODWIN**, Josiah(?) **PRESCOTT**, Chas. C. **ROSS**, B. **PLUNKETT**, A. **GREGORY**, John **GREGORY**, all severely; John P. **ISLER**, slightly—8. Weekly American Eagle, 5/13/1847.

Married. By the Rev. Thomas P. **DAVIDSON**, Mr. Martin L. **SLAUGHTER**, to Miss Mary E. **FLESHEART**, all of South Memphis. American Eagle, 12/2/1847.

Departed this life on Thursday, the 22d inst., of consumption, Mrs. Ann D., wife of Joel M. **SLEDGE**, of Chulahoma, Miss. Daily Memphis Enquirer, 7/2/1848.

William A. **SHELBY**, Administrator of James K. **SLOAN**, dec'd. versus John **SLOAN**, and the Creditors of James K. Sloan deceased. The bill in this cause having been filed by the administrator, for the purpose of suggesting the insolvency of the estate of James K. Sloan dec'd...American Eagle, 7/1/1847.

Died. In this city on Tuesday morning, at the residence of E. **McDAVITT**, Mr. Joseph Lapsley **SLOSS**, in the 26th year of his age. Mr. Sloss was a native of Kentucky.....he was a devoted member of the Methodist Episcopal Church...American Eagle, Thurs., 10/14/1847.

Died, In this city, on the evening of the 22d, Thomas Haywood, infant son of James O.(?) and Martha Ann **SLOVER**, aged three months and nine days. Memphis Daily Appeal, 7/24/1856.

Died, On Tuesday morning, 8th instant, Clara Rebecca, infant daughter of Wm. H. and Sallie Jane
SLOVER (STOVER?), aged 1 year, 3 months and 13 days. Ripley, Miss. and East Tennessee papers
please copy. Memphis Daily Appeal, 1/16/1856.

Married—On Thursday, the 1st inst., at the Episcopal Church, by the Rev. P. W. **ALSTON**, Henry D.
SMALL, Esq. to Miss Mary Jane **CARY**, all of this city. Memphis Enquirer, 1/6/1846. We regret to
announce that the family of our friend Henry D. Small, Esq., met with a sad affliction last evening, which
will in all probability result in the death of a little boy about twelve years of age....The little fellow was
caught on the track of the Mississippi and Tennessee railroad, near the family residence, in the southern
suburbs of the city, last evening, and was knocked down by the locomotive, the wheels passing over him in
such a manner as to entirely sever one foot from his body, while the other was so horribly crushed as to
render amputation necessary....Memphis Daily Appeal, 11/12/1859. Died, On Saturday morning, the 12th
instant, at the residence of his parents in South Memphis, Frank, son of H. D. and Mary J. Small. Memphis
Daily Appeal, 11/13/1859.

Died, On July 25th, at her residence in Raleigh, Tenn., of Typhoid Fever, in the 74th year of her age, Mrs.
Ann **SMITH**. Memphis Daily Appeal, 7/28/1858.

....Miss Mary Elizabeth Smith, daughter of the late Calvin M. **SMITH**, Esq., was, for more than 16 years,
confined to a sick couch....by the constant watchful care of her affectionate mother, Mrs. Col. **McLEAN**,
of this vicinity....For some years she had been a member of the Methodist Episcopal Church....On Monday
night, the 7th of March, her Pastor again visited her and remained with her until she finally sunk to rest, at 2
o'clock, on Tuesday morning....Memphis Daily Appeal, 3/15/1853.

On Wednesday evening Edward **SMITH**, a native of Ireland, resident in this city, was admitted into the
Hospital suffering from an attack of jaundice. Nothing peculiar was observed in his manner and he ate his
supper with apparent heartiness. After undressing, he inquired among the patients for a knife to cut a piece
of tobacco from his plug. None of them having one, he took from the mantle-piece a razor, with which one
of the patients had shaved himself that afternoon. Suddenly he drew up his shirt and, plunging the sharp
blade into his left side, drew it with one horrid gash across his abdomen, completely disemboweling
himself! The other patients, who were all Irishmen, set up a shriek of horror, but were too much alarmed to
approach the wretched man, who continued, with violent strokes, to cut yet deeper into his mutilated body,
while at the same time, he declared that he would cut down any one who should attempt to prevent him
executing his desperate design of self-murder. Alarmed by the outcries, the Hospital Steward, Mr. Hu_ton,
entered the room. The man, who was still cutting with the razor, staggered a few steps towards Mr. Huston,
muttered some words, which in the excitement were not understood, then fell to the floor a
corpse!....Memphis Daily Appeal, Fri., 12/11/1857.

Married, On Thursday the 5th inst., at the residence of Dr. Porter, by Rev. H. S. **PORTER**, Mr. Edward L.
SMITH, of the firm of Crystal & Smith, of Memphis, to Miss Sarah V. **HATHAWAY**, of Nashville.
Memphis Daily Appeal, 2/7/1852.

Departed this life on Friday evening, the 15th instant, of Consumption, Frances **SMITH**, aged two years.
Her funeral will take place at 7 o'clock this morning from Butler street. Memphis Daily Appeal,
8/17/1856.

Married, In this city, on Wednesday evening, at the residence of Thos. H. **ALLEN**, Esq., Frederick W.
SMITH, Esq., Teller in the Union Bank, to Miss Cynthia C. **ALLEN**. Memphis Eagle, Sat., 4/14/1849.

Married, By Rev. Dr. Page, on the 19th inst., Catherine D. **WORMELEY** to Dr. Geo. A. **SMITH**, all of
this city. Memphis Eagle, 4/26/1849.

Died, In the vicinity of Brownsville, on the 12th of October, 1855, Sallie M., infant daughter of George C.
and Adelia **SMITH**, of Memphis, Tenn., aged 14 months and thirty days. Memphis Daily Appeal,
10/26/1855.

Died. In this city on Wednesday, 23d instant, Mary Washington, daughter of Mr. and Mrs. Geo. W. **SMITH**. Memphis Appeal, 8/25/1854.

Married—On Thursday evening last, by Rev. Mr. Cropper, George W. **SMITH**, Attorney at Law, of this place, to Miss Mary **DUNN**, of this vicinity. Memphis Enquirer, Friday, 4/19/1839. It is our sad and painful duty to have to record the death of the eldest son of Geo. W. Smith, Esq., of this vicinity, a lad of some ten or twelve years old. Evening before last, while riding through a lane near his father's residence, he saw a number of little girls ahead of him, and with the view, we suppose, of frightening them, ran his pony after them. Coming in too close contact with the hindmost of the children, we suppose, he checked his pony too suddenly, when he was thrown against the fence and lay for awhile apparently senseless and speechless. After a few minutes, however, he remounted and rode home, but died about 10 o'clock at night....The friends and acquaintances of Geo. W. Smith are requested to attend the burial of his son This Day at 10 o'clock A.M., from his residence, two miles east of Memphis, on the Poplar street road. Memphis Daily Appeal, 10/26/1856.

Married, In this city, on 10th inst., by Rev. Mr. Dennis, Mr. George Y. **SMITH**, to Miss Emily **PEYTON**. The Daily Eagle, 12/16/1846.

Died, In this city, on the 15th inst., H. G. **SMITH**, 3d Clerk of the Marshall Ney, in the 30th year of his age, of Cholera contracted in New Orleans. Memphis Weekly Eagle, 1/18/1849.

Married, On the 12th instant at the residence of J. C. **RICHMOND**, Esq., near College Hill, Miss., Mr. H. P. **SMITH** and Miss Matilda **RICHMOND**. Memphis Daily Appeal, 5/14/1857.

Died, On the 26th of September, of pneumonia, a short illness, at Napoleon, Ark., Mr. Henry **SMITH**. He resided for a number of years in Hinds county, Miss....Memphis Daily Appeal, 10/6/1859.

Henry G. **SMITH**, Attorney at Law. The Appeal, 12/13/1844.

Married. At Salem Church on the 3rd inst by Rev. John **WILSON**, J. G. **SMITH**, Esq. to M__ _arah E. **ALLEN**, all of Tipton county. Memphis Daily Appeal, 1/18/1854.

We are pained to announce the death of Mrs. Smith, wife of our esteemed associate of the Eagle and Enquirer. She breathed her last about 7 P.M.... The friends and acquaintances of J. Watt **SMITH** are invited to attend the funeral of his wife, from his residence on Linden street, at 9 o'clock this morning. Memphis Whig, 10/15/1855. It is our melancholy duty to record the death of one of the most noble men of our city, J. Watt Smith, associate editor of the *Eagle and Enquirer*....Mr. Smith's death was caused more by his over-taxed and sensitive mind than by disease; untiringly he watched by the bed of a dear wife until she had "passed away," when, disheartened and overwhelmed with grief at the thoughts of his loneliness and dear little children, he took to his bed, and never rose again....Mr. Smith was born in this State and was about thirty-five years of age at his death. He has been connected with some paper, either in this State, Alabama or Louisiana, from early manhood....He came to this city in 1852....But none will suffer so deeply and bitterly as his dear, affectionate little daughter, two larger sons and a sickly babe....Memphis Daily Appeal, 10/20/1855.

Died, Near Brownsville, Ten., on the 3d instant, Mrs. Sarah Smith, consort of Jacob C. **SMITH**, in the 56th year of her age...She had been for many years a pious and consistent member of the Baptist Church...Weekly Appeal, 3/26/1847.

Married, At the First Baptist Church in this city, on Wednesday, the 2d inst., by Rev. C. R. **HENDRICKSON**, Mr. Jas. H. **SMITH**, of Shelbyville, Ky., to Miss Mollie J. Drane, daughter of Rev. T. J. **DRANE**, of this city. Louisville Journal and Courier please copy. Memphis Daily Appeal, 12/4/1857.

We regret to learn that Mr. James Hudson **SMITH**, of Memphis, and formerly of the firm of Smith, Carroll & Co., of this city, was attacked by cholera at Baton Rouge yesterday morning at 8 o'clock, and died at 8 P.M.—N.O. Eve. Pic. 3d inst. Memphis Daily Eagle, 3/15/1850.

Married. On the 6th instant by the Rev. J. W. **KNOTT**, Mr. James M. **SMITH**, of LaGrange, and Miss Harriett C., daughter of the Rev. R. H. **JONES**, of Memphis. Memphis Daily Appeal, 3/8/1855.

Married, On Thursday, the 5th instant, at the residence of Mr. Henry **TOWNSEND**, in Tipton county, Tenn., by the Rev. Lewis **ADAMS**, Mr. James S. **SMITH** to Miss J. W. **TOWNSEND**, all of that county. Memphis Daily Appeal, 8/13/1858.

Married, In this vicinity on Sunday evening, the 28th of September, by B. H. **ESTES**, Esq., Joel Rob't. __. **SMITH** and Miss Caroline, youngest daughter of A. **WRIGHT**, Esq., late of North Alabama. Memphis Daily Appeal, 10/7/1856.

Died, On Tuesday morning, 6th inst., at the residence of J. L. **WEBB**, in this city, Mr. John G. **SMITH**, of Tipton county, Ten., formerly of Granville county, N.C. Nashville and N.C. papers please copy. Memphis Daily Appeal, 5/7/1851.

The friends and acquaintances, as also the Brethren of the Independent Order of Odd Fellows, are respectfully invited to attend the funeral of John H. **SMITH**, (a member of Madison Lodge, Huntsville, Ala.,) from Mrs. Murry's boardinghouse, Front Row, at 9 o'clock This Morning. Memphis Daily Appeal, 8/21/1858.

We learn from a private letter....that Mr. John J. **SMITH**, long a resident of this city, died at the residence of his uncle, in Alabama, on the 6th instant. Mr. Smith has been engaged as a compositor in the office of the *Morning Bulletin* from the commencement of that journal until within a few weeks past....Memphis Daily Avalanche, 5/10/1859.

Married, Near Germantown, on Thursday the 11th inst., Dr. John P. **SMITH**, to Mrs. M. C. **REID**. Weekly Appeal, 9/19/1845.

Married, On Tuesday, the 27th inst., by the Rev. Thos. J. **NEWBERRY**, Mr. Joseph L. **SMITH** to Miss Drue J. **DOTY**; both of Raleigh. Memphis Daily Appeal, 7/1/1848.

We learn that our gifted townswoman, Miss L. Virginia **SMITH**, has returned from New Orleans, after concluding an arrangement for the publication in a collected form of her many fugitive poems to the daily and periodical press. Memphis Appeal, 5/14/1852. Married, At the residence of Col. J. T. **TREZEVANT** on Wednesday evening, 12th last, by Right Rev. Bishop Otey, Mr. John **FRENCH**, of McMinnville, Ten., to Miss L. Virginia Smith, of this city....May the bright planets shine gently and genially upon the union of our young Memphis poetess with the happy stranger who hath borne her off upon the good steamer Bulletin to the capital city of the Sunny South. Memphis Daily Appeal, Thurs., 1/13/1853.

Died, On the 6th instant, Marie Josephine, daughter of Lemuel and Lavenia **SMITH**, in the eighth year of her age. Memphis Eagle, 10/10/1850.

Married, In Marshall County, Miss., on Tuesday 23d ult. by Rev. N. R. **JARRATT**, Mr. Lemuel **SMITH**, jr. of Memphis to Miss Lively **CHEAIRS**, of Marshall County, Miss. Memphis Daily Eagle, 1/3/1846.

Married, at Raleigh, Tenn., on Wednesday, 11th instant, by Rev. Sam'l **DENNIS**, Mr. R. L. **SMITH** to Miss Mary Jane **DEWOODY**. Daily Memphis Enquirer, 7/15/1849.

Married, On Wednesday evening, 23d inst., at the Cumberland Presbyterian Church, by Rev. A. M. **BRYAN**, Mr. Rufus **SMITH**, of the firm of R. F. Carson & Co., to Miss Adelaide, daughter of the late Dr. John A. **WILSON**, of Holly Springs. Memphis Daily Appeal, 9/25/1857.

The Hon. S. A. **SMITH** was married on Wednesday, 16th inst., at the residence of F. W. **LEA**, Esq., Bradley county, to Mrs. Lavenia **HENDERSON**, daughter of the late Hon. Luke **LEA**. Memphis Daily Appeal, 5/24/1855.

Died, In Cincinnati, on the 19th inst., Mrs. Ruth Smith, wife of Samuel W. **SMITH**, aged fifty-one years. Memphis Daily Appeal, 11/24/1857.

We regret to learn that the Grocery establishment of Mr. T. Lee **SMITH**, of Raleigh, was entirely destroyed by fire on Saturday night last—loss estimated at 4 or $5000.—Supposed to have been the work of an incendiary. Memphis Daily Appeal, Tues., 4/8/1851.

Married, In Henderson county, Wednesday, October the 1st, by Rev. Joseph **JOHNSON**, Dr. Theodore A. **SMITH** and Miss Ellen E. **RAGAN**. Memphis Daily Appeal, 9/30/1856.

Married. At Bolivar, Tenn., on the 28th ult. by Rev. Louis **JANSON**, Thomas R. **SMITH**, Esq., to Miss Kate Miller, daughter of Pitser **MILLER**, Esq. Memphis Eagle & Enquirer, 5/4/1853.

Mr. W. Hy. **SMITH**, of the Nashville *Banner*, and a brother to our late and lamented friend, J. Watt **SMITH**, of the *Enquirer*, is now in our city. His business, though a melancholy one, we hope will be made somewhat pleasant by the desire of many to extend to him all the proper testimonials of friendly feeling for his own as well as his departed brother's sake. Memphis Daily Appeal, 11/3/1855.

Died, On the 9th instant, William J., only son of W. J. and M. A. R. **SMITH**. Memphis Daily Appeal, 9/14/1856.

Mr. W. Sidney **SMITH** left our city on the fine steamer Belle Key last night, en route for Washington City, via Louisville and the northern cities. During his brief stay here, he formed many friends, who admire him for his many virtues and noble bearing. Memphis Eagle & Enquirer, 5/29/1852.

Married, by the Rev. Colin **McKINNEY** of Jackson, on the 18th inst., Mr. Wm. **SMITH**, of Memphis, to Miss Cintha(?) Jane, eldest daughter of the late Philip **WARLICK**(?) Esq. of this County—Jackson Republican. Memphis Daily Appeal, 1/29/1848.

Married. At Willow Glenn, Fayette Co., on Thursday, the 10th ult., by Rev. W. **BERTON**, Mr. Wm. C. **SMITH**, of Memphis, to Miss Sallie A. **COTTON**, of Fayette Co. American Eagle, 6/17/1847.

Married—On the 12th inst., by Wm. **CHASE**, Esq., Mr. Wm. C. **SMITH** to Miss Permelia **ELLISON**, all of Memphis. Daily Enquirer, 8/14/1847.

Married—On the 18th of February, 1846, by the Rev'd. Mr. **HARVELL**, Dr. Wm. F. **SMITH**, to Miss Francis J. **MAN**, of Marshall County, Miss. Lynchburg Virginia will please copy. Memphis Enquirer, 3/17/1846.

Married, On the 28th instant at the residence of J. M. **WILLIAMSON**, Esq., near this city, by Rev. Dr. White, Mr. Wm. F. **SMITH**, of Milton, N. C., to Miss M. Ellen **HUNTINGDON**, of Parish St. Mary, La. Memphis Daily Appeal, 7/30/1859.

We are authorized to announce Wm. J. **SMITH,** Mechanic, for the office of Major of the 154th Regiment of Tennessee Militia, at the election about to be ordered by the Brigadier General. Memphis Appeal, 8/9/1852.

Wm. R. **SMITH** is solicited by many voters, to suffer his name to be run for Mayor of the City of Memphis, and will please let us hear from him as soon as possible. Memphis Daily Appeal, 2/23/1848.

Our city, for two or three weeks prior to Thursday last, was entirely exempt from cholera disease. But the cool, damp change in the weather, or other cause, has produced several cases, nearly all of which have terminated fatally...On Friday, Mr. Albert G. Smith, son of Wm. R. **SMITH**, sexton...Yesterday, Mr. Thomas W. **ERSKINE**, of Nashville, travelling agent of the Union Bank...Memphis Eagle, Thurs., 5/24/1849.

Died, At the residence of his father, near Brownsville, Haywood county, on the morning of the 4th instant, of consumption, Mr. William C. SMITH, in the twenty-eighth year of his age...Memphis Daily Appeal, 5/9/1856.

Married, On the 6th inst., by the Rev. Dr. Page, Mr. James L. SMITHER, of Texas, to Miss Caroline MARKHAM, of this city. Memphis Daily Appeal, 1/8/1852.

Alfred A. SMITHWICK, J. B. Carr's Brick Building Front-Row, is now opening and prepared to exhibit a new, full and complete assortment of Fall and Winter Goods. The Appeal, 10/4/1844. Married, on the morning of the 14th inst., in Columbia, Tenn., by the Rev. Mr. Mack (?), Alfred A. Smithwick, merchant of Memphis, to Miss Mary Louisa LAW, of the former place. Tri-Weekly Memphis Enquirer, 10/20/1846. Died, On the 24th instant, Mary Louise, consort of A. A. Smithwick, of Memphis. Funeral services by Rev. Dr. Grundy, from the Second Presbyterian Church this evening at 4 P.M. Memphis Daily Appeal, 7/25/1858.

Married, On Thursday evening, the Rev. Mr. Gray, Mr. James F. SMITHWICK, of Tallaloosa, to Miss Lucy V. STRANGE, of this city. American Eagle, Thurs., 12/2/1847.

Departed this life on 21st ult., of permanent disease of the bowels, Isaac N. SNEAD, aged 31 years two months and two days....Daily Enquirer, 3/17/1847.

Died. On the 24th ult., William Henry, infant son of W. H. and E. SNEAD, aged 10 months and 22 days. American Eagle, 10/1/1846. Died, On Thursday the 27th ult., Mary Emmer, infant daughter of Eliza and Wm. H. Snead, aged 1 year, 9 months and 27 days. Memphis Eagle & Enquirer, 6/2/1852.

John L. T. SNEED, Attorney at Law, Will attend regularly the Courts of Shelby, Fayette and Hardeman Counties, Tenn. and Marshall and Tippah Counties, Miss. Office in LaGrange, Tenn. Memphis Enquirer, 3/9/1848. Married, In Hardeman county, on Sunday, the 27th, by the Rev. _____ Harris, John L. T. Sneed Esq., of La Grange, to Miss Mary Ashe Shepperd, daughter of the late William SHEPPERD, Esq. Memphis Eagle, 8/30/1848. We are pleased to learn that our efficient and accomplished District Attorney, J. L. T. Sneed, Esq., has removed to Memphis and will hereafter take up his residence in our midst....Memphis Appeal, 11/7/1853.

Married, On the 10th inst., at the Second Presbyterian Church, by Rev. J. H. GRAY, Dr. N. M. SNEED and Miss Virginia E. LAW, both of this city. Memphis Daily Appeal, 6/12/1856.

Volunteers Arrived. Capt. W. T. SNEED, we understand, reached home night before last...Daily Enquirer, 6/19/1847.

Died, In Fayette county, on the 10th inst., William M. SNEED, Esq., formerly of Oxford, N.C., in the 70th year of his age. Memphis Enquirer, 3/25/1849.

The undersigned having qualified at the October Term, 1847, of the Shelby County Court, as executor of the last will and testament of Nathan SNOWDEN, deceased, hereby notifies all those indebted to said estate....J. S. EDWARDS, Executor. Memphis Daily Appeal, 11/1/1848.

Married, On Tuesday evening, the 30th ult., by the Rev. Mr. COTTINGHAM, Mr. P. M. SNYDER, of Memphis, Tenn., to Miss Mary Elizabeth HARTWELL, of Poinsett county, Ark. Weekly Appeal, 7/17/1846. Died, On Wednesday morning, the 4th inst., in the town of Wittsburg, St. Francis county, Ark., Mrs. Mary E. Snyder, consort of Peter M. Snyder, formerly of Memphis, Tenn., aged 21 years. Memphis Eagle & Enquirer, 2/14/1852.

I offer for sale my House and Lot on Second street, opposite Mr. Blythe's new building. The house is a fine two story brick, with high basement, has nine well finished rooms, a handsome portico, galleries back, and a neat yard in front, shut in by iron railing....S. C. SNYDER, M.D. Memphis Daily Appeal, 8/30/1855.

The subscriber will re-open his School, at his residence, Richland, near Beaver Dam Forks Post Office, Tipton County, Tenn., on the 1st Monday in April next...Wm. M. SOMERVELL. Memphis Eagle, 2/15/1849.

Some of our readers will remember that about a week ago David SORLEY was nearly drowned in the Bayou, owing to his horse falling with him there. He has been in a somewhat debilitated condition since that time, and on Monday on walking out in the fierce heat of the sun, he was unable to withstand its effect, and was seized with the peculiar congestive symptoms known as sun-stroke; the consequences were fatal....Memphis Daily Appeal, 7/20/1859.

Married. On the 5th day of September by Rev. J. O. STEADMAN, Mr. George D. SOUTHALL, of this city, to Miss Belle CHAMBLIN, of Mt. Sterling, Ky. Memphis Daily Appeal, 9/7/1855.

Mr. William H. SOUTHALL and three negro men were drowned by the capsising of a skiff on Tuesday last, while crossing a bayou near Southall's residence on the Mississippi River, sixteen miles above Memphis....Memphis Eagle & Enquirer, Fri., 1/28/1853.

Married. On the 21st instant by H. S. PORTER, D.D., Mr. Joseph SOWENS to Miss Sarah P. C. MORGAN, all of this city. Memphis Daily Appeal, 9/23/1854.

Married. On the 2nd inst. by Rev. J. S. PORTER, Mr. Henry SPAULDING to Miss Pane H. POSEY, all of this city. Memphis Appeal, 5/3/1854.

Married, On the evening of the 18th inst., by the Rev. Wm. HYER, Jno. H. SPEED to Miss Mary E. DEADRICK, all of this city. Weekly Memphis Eagle, 4/26/1849.

Died, On the 9th of August, 1859, at the residence of Mrs. Susan STEVENSON, in Memphis, Mrs. Eliza Jane SPEER, in the 56th year of her age. Memphis Daily Appeal, 8/12/1859.

Died—In this city, of cholera, on the 8th instant, Henry Clay Spence, aged about 5 years—also, John C. Spence, aged about 8 years. These were the children of Mr. John C. and Mrs. Elizabeth SPENCE.....Daily Memphis Enquirer, 6/16/1849.

Married, On the 25th inst., by Rev. G. W. DILL, Mr. John E. SPICER, of Memphis, to Miss Mary Jane Matthews, daughter of Dr. B. D. MATTHEWS, of North Mt. Pleasant, Miss. Memphis Appeal, 11/30/1852.

Died, of Consumption, on the 19th of July, 1855, in the 27th year of his age, Horace SPICKERNAGLE. The deceased was a native of Kentucky and migrated to this city with his father when but two years of age, where he has ever since resided....Left an orphan when but sixteen years of age, by the death of his father, (his mother having died several years previous,) with two younger brothers and a sister depending in a great measure on his exertions for support ....His occupation was that of Printer....He leaves a young wife and an infant daughter.... Memphis Daily Appeal, 7/28/1855.

Died. At the residence of Mrs. Sappington, on yesterday, September 16th, John SPICKERNAGLE, of Billious Fever, aged 14 years....Memphis Daily Appeal, 9/17/1853.

Died—In this city, on the 13th inst. after a protracted illness, Edward H., infant son of John and Mary SPICKERNAGLE. The Appeal, 10/20/1843. Pursuant to a Decree made at the November Term, 1852, of the Common Law and Chancery Court of the city of Memphis, in the case of Wm. E. BUTLER and W. B. MORRIS vs. Mary J. SPICKERNAGLE, et. al. heirs of Jno. M. Spickernagle, I will on Tuesday the 3d May, 1853....proceed to sell....Memphis Daily Appeal, 3/23/1853.

Died—At his residence in South Memphis, on Saturday evening last, the 12th inst., Mr. William SPICKERNAGLE, an old and respectable citizen of this town. He was highly esteemed by all who knew him, for his honesty, kindness and liberality. Weekly Appeal, 7/18/1845.

Died, In this city on Sunday night, Mr. William T. SPICKERNAGLE, aged nineteen years. This young and estimable man, it appears, fell a victim to his own goodness. He attended a friend who was sick of the yellow fever on the "Bluff City," until his death, and there contracted the disease. He has left a widowed mother and good sister to mourn their irreparable loss. Memphis Daily Appeal, 9/4/1855.

The first Bird store in Memphis. Signor A. SPINETTO Has the pleasure to inform the Ladies and Gentlemen of Memphis and the vicinity, that he has opened a splendid Bird Store in Memphis, on Main street, north of Adams...Memphis Eagle & Enquirer, 1/20/1852.

Died. In this city, on Friday night last, at half-past 10 o'clock, Mr. Alfred S. SPIVEY, of the house of W. B. Miller & Co., aged about 26 years. The deceased was a native of Gates county, North Carolina, but for some years a resident of this city. He was intimately known to but few, who, with his two brothers, residents of this place, deeply mourn and lament his sudden and untimely end. Raleigh (N.C.) papers will please copy. Weekly Memphis Eagle, Thurs., 10/18/1849.

Died, On the 2nd inst., Henry C., youngest son of J. and Callie SPIVEY....Memphis Daily Appeal, 9/3/1857. Died, on Wednesday, September 2d, after a brief illness, Henry Clarke, son of Jacob and Caledonia Spivey, aged two years and ten months....MemphisDaily Appeal, 9/15/1857.

We learn from the Army and Navy ____ that Surgeon W. A. SPOTTSWOOD has been ordered to the Memphis Navy Yard, to supply the place of Surgeon J. W. PLUMMER recently detached on "waiting orders." Surgeon Spottswood arrived at his post a few days since....He was, we believe, detached from the Navy Yard at Pensacola, Florida. Memphis Daily Appeal, 7/18/1854.

Married, At the residence of Mrs. Celina J. JACKSON, in Amite county, Miss., on the 14th inst., by Rev. M. S. SHIRK(?), Dr. T. J. SPURLOCK, formerly of Jackson, Tenn., to Miss A. J. ROBINSON, of Amite county. Memphis Daily Appeal, 4/27/1859.

Married. In Lafayette county, Miss., on the 19th inst., by Rev. Dr. Stanford G. BURNEY, Rev. Geo. T. STAINBACK to Miss Clara B. GRADY, all of that county. Memphis Daily Appeal, 10/29/1854.

Six companies of the 4th Regiment, namely two from East, two from Middle and two from West Tennessee, arrived on Thursday, on the steamer Iowa....They brought the remains of Lieutenant Charles GILL, Richard L. BOHANNAN and Thomas STAINBACK, all of this city.....Memphis Daily Appeal, 7/15/1848.

Married, On Monday, 31st of October, by Rev. R. H. RIVERS, Mr. W. E. STAINBACK, of Somerville, Tenn., to Miss Laura C. BUTTS, of Florence, Ala. Memphis Daily Appeal, 11/8/1859.

Married, June 21st by Rev. J. E. DOUGLAS, Mr. George W. STAMPS to Miss Matty M. Joyner, daughter of Rev. Thos. JOYNER, near the Marshall Female Institute, Marshall county, Miss. Memphis Daily Appeal, 6/22/1858.

Departed this life April 15, 1859, near Collierville, Tenn., Mrs. Nicholas Ann Stamps. She was born May 1829 in Lawrenceburg, Tenn. She was the daughter of Nicholas PERKINS, Esq., of Williams county, Tenn., known as "Dan River Nicholas," and was one of fifteen children, three of whom only survive. She was early left an orphan, and spent the years of her girlhood at the house of her brother, Col. G. W. PERKINS, then living in Hardeman county....She was married to Geo. A. BRINKLEY in March, 1844. Three children, the issue of this union, survive to mourn, at a tender age, the loss of a most devoted mother. After Mr. Brinkley's death she resided with her brother, Col. G. W. Perkins, of DeSoto county, Miss., until her marriage with Capt. Jerome B. STAMPS, December 13, 1855. One little boy, the issue of this union, is left behind to miss a mother's tender care....She professed religion at the Big Spring Baptist Camp Ground,

Madison county, Tenn., and subsequently united with the Presbyterian Church....Her funeral discourse was preached by Rev. Wm. Carey **CRANE** at Salem Presbyterian Church, Shelby county, Tenn....and her remains are deposited near that church....Franklin Review and Mississippi Baptist please copy. Memphis Daily Avalanche, 4/27/1859.

Married, On the 16th inst. by Rev. Mr. Hoge, Mr. Robert _. **STANARD**, of Richmond, Va., to Miss Martha Virginia **COWAN**, of Memphis. Memphis Daily Appeal, 12/30/1857.

Died—In this city on the 15th Inst., of apoplexy, Benjamin **STANTON**, of Memphis, Tenn., formerly a merchant of Mobile, Ala.—N.O. Bulletin of Wednesday. Tri-Weekly Memphis Enquirer, Tues., 9/22/1846.

Died on Thursday, 10th inst., Hallowell, only son of Hon. F. P. **STANTON**, aged two years. Weekly Appeal, 12/11/1846. Died—In this place, on Sunday night 30th ult., Jeptha Fowlkes, aged about one year and eight months, only child of Frederic P. Stanton, Esq. Memphis Enquirer, 8/19/1837. Died—At the residence of F. P. Stanton, Esq., Walter Scott, aged five months, his only child. Memphis Enquirer, 5/31/1839.

Died, on Friday, 13th inst., Mr. Richard **STANTON**, formerly of Alexandria, Va., in the 57th year of his age. Weekly Appeal, 11/20/1846. We recently copied from one of our city papers a bare annunciation of the death of Mr. Richard Stanton, of this city, and formerly of Alexandria, District of Columbia. Mr. Stanton was the father of Hon. F. P. **STANTON**, member of Congress from this district and at the time of his death filled the office of principal clerk in the U.S. Navy establishment in this city ...American Eagle, 11/26/1846.

We had the pleasure of a visit yesterday from Hon. Richard H. **STANTON**, late Representative in Congress from Kentucky, and a brother of the Hon. F. P. **STANTON**. Memphis Daily Appeal, 8/9/1857.

Married, On Tuesday morning last, by the Rev. Mr. Moore, William N. **STANTON**, Esq., of Memphis, Tenn., to Miss Sophia, daughter of Mr. Arthur **JOHNSON** of this place. Hagerstown Torchlight. Weekly Appeal, Friday, 8/21/1846. ...we have the painful duty of announcing the demise of one of our confreres. Wm. N. Stanton, Esq., editor of the "Memphis Daily Appeal," is no more. He died at the residence of Mr. Gookin, in South Memphis, at 3 o'clock on the morning of Thursday last, 21st, after a painful illness of 2 days. His disease was paralysis, of so violent a character that from the moment of the attack to its final and afflicting consummation, he was able neither to speak or move....Mr. Stanton was in the beginning of his 28th year. Educated for the Bar, he had recently entered upon editorial life as a profession. By his demise a youthful wife and infant daughter are left widowed and fatherless, and the hopes of relatives and friends for his future distinction and usefulness suddenly nipped in the bud....Daily Enquirer, 10/23/1847.

Died, In this city on the 21st inst., at the Richmond House, Mr. Chas. C. **STANWOOD**. Mr. S. had been but a short time in the city, and was recently from Hernando, Miss. Although a stranger, every attention was shown him by the physician who waited upon him, and other friends, during his illness. Weekly Memphis Eagle, 11/29/1849.

Died. In Springfield, Tenn., on the 9th inst., of scarlet fever, Jo. C. Stark, Jr., son of Jo. C. and Lamiza A. **STARK**, aged 2 years, 2 months and 22 days. Also, on the 15th inst., of the same disease, Thomas Ridly Stark, son of the same, aged 4 years, 4 months and 4 days. Memphis Eagle & Enquirer, 4/26/1853.

The friends and acquaintances of J. B. and S. **STARKE** are invited to attend the funeral of their infant daughter Angie this Saturday morning at 10 o'clock, from their residence on Pontotoc, between Shelby and Main. Memphis Daily Appeal, Sat., 5/9/1857.

Died. On board steamer Missouri, on Sunday the 9th inst., after a painful illness of two days, Peter Burrell, age three years, nine months and six days, son of Col. P. B. and Adaline **STARKE**, of Miss. Memphis Eagle, 1/11/1848.

Notice. It becomes my painful duty to announce to the public, that whereas my wife Eliza hath this day (27th Dec. 1847,) left my bed and board, without any reasonable cause, that I will not be accountable for any of her contracts, or liable for any that she may make; nor that any one may credit her thinking that I will pay it, for I am resolved to pay none. L. R. **STARKES**. Memphis Daily Appeal, 1/19/1848.

We regret to announce the death of Rev. S. G. **STARKES**, Principal of the State Female College, near this city. At a meeting of the Board of Trustees of the State Female College, held on Saturday, October 8th, 1859....the following resolutions were adopted: We have heard with unfeigned regret of the decease of the Rev. S. G. Starkes, ...who departed this life at Iuka, Miss., on the morning of the 7th inst....Memphis Daily Appeal, 10/9/1859.

Died. On Friday last, near Morning Sun, in this county, of congestive fever, Emma, only daughter of C. A. and Mildred **STARR**, aged 11 years and six months. Weekly Memphis Eagle, 9/20/1849.

....We are pained to record the death of Mrs. Starr, consort of Mr. Richard A. **STARR**, at Guyandotte, Va...Memphis Daily Eagle, 7/27/1850.

Died. On Sunday evening last at the residence of R. S. **MANNING**, in DeSoto county, Miss., Mrs. Mary A. **STATEN**, in the 52d year of her age. Memphis Eagle & Enquirer, Sat., 6/3/1853.

Departed this life, on the 10th ult., in Denmark, after a painful illness of twenty-one days, with typhoid fever, Mollie W. St. Clair, daughter of Peter **ST. CLAIR**, Esq....the affectionate hand of a loving mother was there to wipe the death damp from her brow....Memphis Daily Appeal, 1/6/1858. Died, In Oakland Grove, Prairie county, Ark., after an illness of 13 days, with pneumonia, Jas. W. St. Clair, eldest son of Peter St. Clair, late of Madison county, Tenn., aged 19 years, 11 months and 3 days. Memphis Daily Appeal, 1/8/1859.

Married. In Wilmington, Del. On the 3rd instant by Rev. Mr. Wynkoof(?), Rev. J. O. **STEADMAN**, pastor of the First Presbyterian Church in this city, to Miss Mary A. **HAYDEN**, of Wilmington. Memphis Daily Appeal, 1/17/1855.

Married, On the 3d inst., by the Rev. J. H. **GRAY**, Mr. Sam'l. W. **STEEL**, of DeSoto county, Miss., to Miss Mary Ann Neely, daughter of Mr. Wm. **NEELY**, of this vicinity. Memphis Daily Appeal, 8/6/1852.

The remains of Thomas J. **STEEL** were interred yesterday in Winchester Cemetery....The deep affliction of his immediate relatives as well as the friendly feeling those present had to the deceased before his death, cast a gloom on every countenance such as is not always seen on such occasions. Memphis Daily Appeal, 6/3/1855.

We regret to have to announce the death of Charles **STEELE**, Esq., an old, well known, and highly respected citizen, who was long engaged as a steamboat agent in this city. He died at nine o'clock yesterday at Dunlap's Springs. Memphis Daily Appeal, 8/14/1858. We mentioned yesterday the death of the lamented Chas. Steele. He was about forty years of age. The friends and acquaintances of the deceased are requested to meet at Mr. Potter's, No. 38 Front Row, at 4 o'clock this afternoon to attend the funeral. The religious services will be conducted by the Rev. Mr. Schetky. Memphis Daily Appeal, 8/15/1858.

Married. In this city on the evening of the 15th instant by Rev. Dr. Porter, Mr. F. E. **STEINBACK**, of Memphis, and Miss Elizabeth J. **PICOT**, of New York. Memphis Daily Appeal, 2/17/1854.

Married. On the evening of the 28th ultimo by Rev. C. R. **HENDRICKSON**, Mr. Lewis **STELLE** and Mrs. Sarah J. **DOUGLASS**. Memphis Daily Appeal, 3/2/1855.

Died. In this city on Friday evening, 4th instant, at 8 o'clock, P.M., Ambrose **STEPHENS**, in the 51st year of his age. The deceased was a native of New Haven, Ct., and had been a resident of Memphis since 1846....The father of the deceased was killed on the Canada frontier, during an engagement in the war of

1812. The deceased left 3 orphan children to mourn his irreparable loss....He was interred yesterday with Masonic honors by the Masonic fraternity of this city.... Memphis Daily Appeal, 3/7/1853.

Married. Also on the 17th inst., by (S. W. **LEDBETTER**), Daniel **STEPHENS** to Miss Ann B. **McDONALD** of this county. The Daily Eagle, 2/22/1848.

BBLS Plantation Molasses....for sale by John H. **STEPHENSON**. American Eagle Weekly, 12/26/1845.

Married—On Tuesday, 4th inst., by Rev. Mr. Dennis, Mr. John **STERLING** to Miss Araminta A. **SMITH**, all of this city. Memphis Enquirer, 8/6/1846. Notice is hereby given, that the undersigned has been qualified as Administratrix of John Sterling deceased, late of Shelby county, Tenn.—All persons indebted to said....Col. Charles D. **McLEAN** is my legally authorized agent. A. A. **STERLING**, Adm'x. Jan. 4, 1848. Memphis Daily Appeal, 1/5/1848.

Married, In Jackson on Thursday, June 5th, (at the residence of her father, John W. **CAMPBELL**, Esq.,) by Rev. C. **McKINNEY**, Mr. Robert **STERLING** and Miss Penelope P. Campbell. Memphis Daily Appeal, 6/14/1856.

Married, Near Cockrum, Miss., on the 18th inst., by Rev. Mr. Johnson, Mr. O. H. P. **STEVENS** to Miss Kitty C. **PRYOR**. Memphis Daily Appeal, 5/26/1859.

Died, On the evening of Thursday, November 3d....Wm. **STEVENSON**, of hemorrhage of the lungs. Memphis Daily Appeal, 11/4/1859. Masonic Tribute. At a stated meeting of South Memphis Lodge, No. 118, at Memphis, Tenn., on 11th instant, the following was presented, to-wit: Whereas, It has been the will of the Supreme Architect of the universe to call from labor our late brother, Wm. **STEPHENSON**....That in his death, his companion, his wife, has lost an affectionate husband....Memphis Daily Appeal, 11/17/1859.

Petition for Divorce. William **STEVENSON**, vs. Nanc_ M. **STEVENSON**. Common Law and Chancery Court of Memphis, (Law Side). In this cause it appearing to the Clerk and Master in vacation by the petition of plaintiff, that the defendant is a non-resident of the State of Tennessee....requiring the said defendant to appear at the November Term, commencing on the first Monday in November next, and plead, answer or demur to plaintiff's petition or the same will be taken for confessed and set for hearing *exparte*. Memphis Daily Appeal, 10/7/1858.

Married, On the evening of the 16th, at the residence of Dr. Welch(?), of Raleigh, Tennessee, by Rev. A. M. **BRYAN**, D.D., Andrew **STEWART**, of Des Arc, Arkansas, to Miss Josephine T. **PHARR**, of the former place. Memphis Daily Appeal, 9/18/1857.

At a meeting of the Board of Managers of the Elmwood Cemetery, held this day, the following resolutions were unanimously adopted: *Resolved*, That we have heard this morning, with astonishment and unfeigned regret, the announcement of the death of E. Pinckney **STEWART**, Esq., late President of the Elmwood Cemetery....Memphis, Feb. 8, 1859. Memphis Daily Avalanche, 2/9/1859.

Married on Monday evening, the 14th inst. by the Rev. Mr. Stewart, Mr. John **STEWART**, to Miss Elizabeth **BOND**, both of this county. American Eagle, 1/1/1848.

Married. At Raleigh, Ten., on Wednesday evening, 18th inst., by Rev. D. L. **GRAY**, M. D. L. **STEWART**, Esq., to Miss Sallie, daughter of Dr. Daniel and Amelia **COLEMAN**, all of Raleigh. Memphis Appeal, 10/20/1854. We deeply regret to learn that Saml. V. **STEWART**, a brother of our worthy townsman, M.D.L. Stewart, Esq., was killed on the 17th instant, at Yazoo City by A. Pinkney **HEAD**. The affray grew out of some domestic difficulty. Mr. Stewart was Coronor and Deputy Sheriff at the time of the affray. The parties met in the street by appointment armed with double barreled guns. Both parties fired and Stewart received a charge of buck shot in his heart. He died instantly. Head fled and has not been heard from. Mr. Stewart leaves a large family to mourn his sudden and melancholy loss. Memphis Daily Appeal, 5/28/1856.

Married, On the 23d inst. at Asbury Chapel, South Memphis, by Rev. L. D. **MULLINS**, Mr. W. L. **STEWART**, of the firm of Stewart & King, to Mrs. Susan R. **LOGAN**, of this city. Memphis Daily Appeal, 12/27/1857.

....About half-past eight o'clock last evening, William James **STEWART** was shot and killed near the corner of Main and Gayoso streets, by a young man named Cyrus **OBERLY**. The circumstances of the affair are as follows: It seems that the parties formerly lived in Allegheny City, Pa., and that Stewart, the deceased, had married Miss Oberly, a sister of Cyrus Oberly, in opposition to the wishes of her friends. A separation was brought about after the marriage, and the wife of Stewart came with her family to reside in this city. The deceased, who is a flatboat pilot, arrived in this city recently, and in company with a gentleman named Cook essayed to see his wife last evening, at the residence of the family, in Beale street, but was unsuccessful. When he left his wife's residence he pursued his way, in company with his friend, up Main street. When the two arrived at the intersection of Main and Gayoso streets, they were accosted by young Oberly, who had followed them, it seems. The deceased and his companion turned about and were confronted by the young man, who, without ceremony, drew a pistol and fired at Stewart, the ball taking effect in the left side, just above the hip and causing death almost immediately ....Oberly is a printer by trade, and is about twenty years of age. The deceased was apparently twenty-eight years of age....Memphis Daily Avalanche, 1/20/1859.

Died, At the residence of G. Sharland **PHILLIPS**, near Somerville, Tenn., on the 30th ult., Mrs. Ariana **STITH**, in the 75th year of her age. Nashville (Tenn.) and Petersburgh (Va.) papers please copy. Memphis Daily Appeal, 12/9/1856.

Died, In this city, March 16th, at 7 o'clock A.M., Miss Susan **STOCKLAGER**, aged twenty-three years, of Consumption. The funeral of the deceased will take place from Asbury Chapel, at 10 o'clock A.M. To-day. Services by Rev. P. **TUGGLE**. Memphis Daily Appeal, 3/17/1857.

Married, On Wednesday evening, by the Rev. Mr. Gray, Miss Lucy Jane, daughter of John **TRIGG**, Esq., to Mr. Charles A. **STOCKLEY**, all of this city. Weekly Appeal, Fri., 5/22/1846.

Died. In Sonora, on the 7th of March last, of small-pox, Alexander **STOCKTON**, a native of Tennessee, aged about 20 years. Memphis Eagle & Enquirer, 5/10/1853.

P. G. **GAINES**, Adm'r. of the estate of William **STOCKTON**, dec'd...The Complainant in this cause having filed his bill, suggesting the insolvency of said Estate...Memphis Daily Appeal, 9/1/1848.

Married, by Rev. R. C. **GRUNDY**, D.D., at his residence in Memphis, on Wednesday, February 9th(?), at High Noon, Mr. Henry **STODDARD**, of Dayton, Ohio, to Miss Sarah L. C. **KEMPER**. Memphis Daily Appeal, 2/10/1859.

On Tuesday, December 21st, about two o'clock, two men by the name of **RAINEY** (Wm. and John), went to Augusta, Ark., and having a misunderstanding with a youth by the name of Daniel **NIBLET**, they (the Raineys) went into Mr. Richmond **STOKER**'s house, which some twelve months since, they had been forbidden to enter under any pretext whatever. John Rainey seized young Niblet by the collar and jerked him out of Stoker's house. Mr. Stoker fearing that they (the two Raineys) would kill young Niblet, ran to pull them (the Raineys) off, when they turned upon him (Stoker) with a spear-cane and bowie-knife, cutting and stabbing him in a most horrid manner, from the effects of which he died in a few minutes—not, however, until he had so severely beaten Wm. Rainey that he was unable to escape—he now being in custody. John Rainey, however, made his escape, and is now at large....Jno. Rainey is nearly 6 feet high, dark complexion, about twenty or twenty-one years old, heavy head of coarse black hair, bobbed off behind....Rainey went from the neighborhood of Collierville to Augusta, and Mr. R. Stoker went from Jackson, Tenn., to Augusta. Memphis Weekly Appeal, 12/29/1858.

Married, On the 29th of December by Rev. W. Carey **CRANE**, at his residence, A. W. **STOKES**, Esq., of Hernando, Miss., and Miss Maggie **McKENSIE**, of Brooklyn, New York. Memphis Daily Appeal, 1/4/1857.

Died—After an illness of two days of congestive fever, Emma, only daughter of C. A. and Mildred **STONE**, aged eleven years and six months. The Richmond Whig and Enquirer will please copy. Daily Memphis Enquirer, 9/18/1849.

Died, Of Apoplexy, at his plantation, near Pine Bluff, Ark., on Wednesday the 29th ult., Dr. James B. **STONE**, formerly of Franklin, Tenn., in the 30th year of his age. Memphis Daily Appeal, 1/5/1859.

Married. In this county on Thursday, 1st inst., by Rev. E. D. **ISBELL**, Mr. Lemuel S. **STONE**, of this city, to Miss Narcissa M. **NEWSOM**, of Madison county. Memphis Daily Appeal, 6/3/1854.

Married, On the 7th instant in this city, by Rev. J. T. C. **COLLINS**, Dr. W. E.(?) **STONE** to Miss Alice **BYRNE**, both of Memphis, Tenn. Memphis Daily Appeal, 10/13/1858.

Married, On Tuesday evening last by Rev. Mr. Evans, Mr. William **STONE** to Miss Mary Jane, daughter of Wm. T. **BETTIS**, Esq., near Germantown, Shelby county. Memphis Daily Appeal, Sun., 2/7/1858.

On Monday last at Fisherville, in this county, at the store of Messrs. Ammons & Baker, O. P. **STONER**, a sprightly youth aged 16 years, was suddenly killed, by the accidental discharge of a pistol. The pistol belonged to young Stoner, and while in the possession of Mr. A. W. **SMITH**, was accidentally discharged, the ball taking effect in the left temple of young Stoner, causing his death in a few hours. Memphis Eagle & Enquirer, Sun., 3/13/1853.

Married, On the 3d instant at the residence of the bride's father, in this city, by Rev. C. A. **DAVIS**, Capt. Adrian **STORM** to Miss Carrie, second daughter of Joseph **WILLIS**, Esq. Memphis Daily Appeal, 11/5/1859.

Married, On the morning of the 17th February last, at the residence of Col. Ro. **WEIR**, near San Antonio, Texas, Mr. C. L. **STORY**, of Lockhart, and Miss Mary E. **SANDERS**, formerly of Memphis. Nashville papers please copy. Memphis Daily Appeal, 3/18/1857.

Died, At Washington City, on Saturday, September 26th, 1857, John Kirby, infant son of the Rev. W. C. and Mary E. **STOUT**, of North Mount Pleasant, Marshall county, Mississippi. Aged 6 months and 23(?) days. Memphis Daily Appeal, 10/9/1857.

Died, On Tuesday evening, 29th inst., of Consumption, Mr. William S. **STOUT**, in his 23d year. The funeral will take place This Afternoon at 3 o'clock from the residence of Mrs. Simms on Madison street. Memphis Daily Appeal, 12/30/1857.

Married, At Calvary Church, in Memphis, Tenn., on the evening of the 7th of April, by Rev. Dr. White, George **STOVALL** to Miss Laura J. Williams, daughter of the late Hon. C. H. **WILLIAMS**, of Lexington, Tenn. Memphis Daily Appeal, 4/9/1859.

Married, On the 13th inst. by Rev. Mr. Luckadoo, Mr. Wm. J. **STOVALL** to Miss Sue E. **LEFTWICH**, all of Shelby county. Memphis Daily Appeal, 2/16/1859.

The friends of the late Mrs. Caroline T. **STOW** are invited to attend her funeral at the Second Presbyterian Church at 10 o'clock A.M. Eufaula, Ala., papers pleast notice. Memphis Daily Appeal, 11/15/1859.

On Thursday afternoon a difficulty occurred on Beal street, near Causey, between two brothers named Joseph and Jacob **STRAHL**, which resulted in the latter striking the former with a cleaver, inflicting a ghastly wound upon his forehead. It was feared yesterday morning that the injured man could not survive, but we are pleased to state that at a late hour last night his physicians pronounced his would not dangerous. Memphis Daily Appeal, 10/11/1856.

Married, In DeSoto county, Miss., on Wednesday evening, 15th inst., by Rev. M. H. **NEAL**, Col. James **STRAIN**, of Memphis, to Miss Eliza C., daughter of Abner **WIMBERLY**, Esq. Knoxville, Ten. papers copy. Memphis Appeal, 10/17/1851. Died. On Sunday morning, 23d inst., Eliza C. Strain, wife of James Strain, aged 39 years. Memphis Eagle & Enquirer, 1/27/1853.

Died, At the residence of his Brother, near Horn Lake Landing, Miss., on the 17th instant, Joseph A. **STRAIN**, in the 26th(?) year of his age. Knoxville *Whig* please copy. Memphis Daily Appeal, 6/19/1856.

Died, on the 25th of August, at the Military Institute Norfolk, Va., of Yellow Fever, after a short illness, Gideon A. **STRANGE**, aged 17 years and 6 months....Having been a student of the Military Institute at Norfolk, he was during the vacation (prior to the appearance of the Yellow Fever in that city) on a pleasure trip out at sea, and returned during the height of the epidemic, to find that the friends he left behind him had fled. All intercourse with the city from abroad being suspended, he was compelled to remain and battle with the "King of Terrors," ....Memphis Daily Appeal, 9/7/1855.

Died. In St. Louis, on the 25th ult., Mrs. Mary H., consort of Jesse A. **STRANGE**, formerly of this city. Memphis Eagle, 6/14/1849.

Married, On the 2d inst., at the Tabb Street Presbyterian Church, Petersburg, Va., by the Rev. A. B. **VAN ZANDT**, John P. **STRANGE**, Esq., of this city, to Miss Mary J. **LAMB**, of the former city. Memphis Daily Eagle, 7/16/1850. Died. In Petersburg, Va., on the 18th ult., Calvin, infant son of J. P. and M. J. Strange, aged 12 months and thirty days. Memphis Daily Appeal, 7/27/1854. Died, On the 14th instant, at night, of Erysipelas, Jeannie Campbell, infant daughter of John P. and M. J. Strange. Memphis Daily Appeal, 3/17/1857. Died, In this city, on the 17th inst., Mrs. Mary J., wife of John P. Strange. Memphis Daily Appeal, 3/18/1857.

The two grand moral pictures, the Temptation of Adam and Eve, and the Expulsion from Paradise, being an improvement upon the celebrated pictures by Duburfe, are offered for sale. During the last 12 months they were exhibited in the principal towns in Tennessee, and some of the adjoining States, and have been universally admired as the finest specimens of art. The sale of these Paintings has been rendered necessary by the recent death of Josiah **STRANGE**, the artist by whom they were executed. Persons who may be disposed to purchase can apply to me at Huntingdon, or to C. **MICHIE**, Esq. at La Grange, at which latter place the paintings may be examined. Henry **STRANGE**, Adm'r. Daily Enquirer, 3/24/1847.

Married, On the evening of the 9th instant at Calvary Church, by Rev. C. T. **QUINTARD**, Mr. Wm. R. **STRANGE** and Miss Maria E., daughter of Dr. A. P. **MERRILL**, all of Memphis. Memphis Daily Appeal, 2/10/1857.

Married: At Mr. B. R. **TREZEVANT's**, near Germantown, on Tuesday evening last, by the Rev. Mr. Gray, Dr. Asa S. **STRATTON** to Miss Mary F. **CHAMBERLIN**. Also, at the same place, C. C. **CADWELL** to Miss Emily E. **ROSS**. Weekly Memphis Eagle, Thurs., 7/19/1849.

Died. In this city, on last Monday, September 10th, in the sixtieth year of his age, Henry **STRATTON**. Mr. S. was a native of Bedford county, Va. Twenty-eight years of his life were spent in Simpson co., Ky. Thence he removed to Holly Springs, Miss., and finally to this city, in which place for the last three years he has been engaged in mercantile affairs....Weekly Memphis Eagle, 9/20/1849.

Married, On Thursday evening, the 18th inst., by the Rev. J. H. **GRAY**, John T. **STRATTON**, Esq., to Miss Emma P., daughter of the late J. B. **FERGUSON**, all of this city. Memphis Daily Appeal, 9/19/1851.

The funeral of Mrs. Margaret M. **STRATTON** will take place to-day, Thursday, 21st inst., at 10 A.M. from the family residence on Second street....Services by Rev. A. M. **BRYAN**. Memphis Daily Appeal, 1/21/1858.

Married, At the residence of the bride's father, near Memphis, on Thursday evening, the 5th inst., by Rev. C. G. McPHERSON, Mr. W. H. STRATTON to Miss Sallie A., daughter of W. B. WALDRAN, Esq. Memphis Daily Appeal, 5/7/1859.

The friends and acquaintances of Mr. Anthony and Mrs. Frances H. STREET, are requested to attend the funeral of their son, William Gallespie, from the Cumberland Presbyterian Church…this Tuesday evening. Memphis Daily Appeal, Tues., 5/6/1851.

Died—At Fort Pickering, on the 25th ult., Mr. Edwin STREET, aged 31 years, In his death society has lost a worthy and estimable citizen. American Eagle Weekly, 7/4/1845. The creditors of the late Edwin Street, are hereby notified to bring forward their claims, properly proven, and present them to the undersigned as Administrator…Wm. H. STREET, Adm'r. Weekly Appeal, 7/11/1845. Died—At Fort Pickering on the 2d inst., Mrs. Eliza Street, widow of the late Edwin Street, aged about 25 years. American Eagle Weekly, 7/4/1845.

Married, On the 11th inst., at Cedar Hill, Haywood county, Tenn., by Rev. T. A. WARE, James A. STREET, of Memphis, and Miss Leana M. MEAUX, of said county. Memphis Whig, 6/13/1856.

Clerk's Sale. Joseph STREHL, Adm'r. of Jno. STREHL, dec'd, vs. Nicholas STREHL. Pursuant to a Decree, made in this cause at the July Term, 1852, of the Law Side of the Common Law and Chancery Court of the city of Memphis, I will, on the 1st Monday—being the 6th day--of September next, proceed to sell…the Real Estate mentioned in the petition…Memphis Daily Appeal, 8/11/1852.

Married, At the residence of the bride's mother, Mrs. E. P.(?) MINOR, of Somerville, on Tuesday, 29th December, Mr. S. M. STRICKLAND, of Mississippi, to Miss Sallie V. Minor. Memphis Daily Appeal, 1/3/1858.

Died, In this county on Monday, June 30th, G. B. STRICKLING, in the 26th year of his age. He was an exemplary member of the Baptist Church…Memphis Daily Appeal, 7/3/1856.

Married, On the 22d of January by Rev. E. H. GREEN, Mr. Charles STRONG, son of the late W. J. STRONG, Esq., and Miss M. Ann, daughter of the late M. M. DICKSON, all of Tipton county, Tenn. Memphis Daily Appeal, 2/1/1857.

Walter STROUD, of Coffee county, Tenn., was beaten to death on the 4th inst., near Murfreesborough, by two men named Lavender and Woodall. Memphis Eagle & Enquirer, 6/15/1852.

Early yesterday morning a man named Anthony STROUP, a carpenter of German descent, who came to this city from New York State, and who was boarding at the Exchange Hall….was found lying in a dying condition, opposite his boarding house. His head was hurt and bleeding, and shreds of hair, to some of which the skin adhered, were lying about the spot dabbled in blood. Dr. Hartz was sent for, who discovered on probing the wound….that the man's skull was competely broken in over the right ear….The Doctor states that recovery is impossible. Memphis Daily Appeal, 9/1/1858.

Married. At Ellenwood, near this city, the residence of Col. Wm. O. CHILTON, on Tuesday the 8th inst. by the R't Rev'd Bishop Freeman, Colonel Charles Calvert STUART, of Chicot county, to Miss Harriet E., daughter of Col. Wm. O. CHILTON, of this county.—*VanBuren (Ark.) Intelligencer*. Memphis Eagle & Enquirer, 3/27/1853.

Died, In DeSoto county, Miss., at the residence of his brother, Charles S. STUART, on the 13th of July, 1859, of gastro enteritis, Dr. Wm. C. STUART, son of Atabalina and Ann STUART. He was born in Decatur, Ala., June 8, 1832. Was a graduate of the University of Mississippi, and graduated last March at the University of Pennsylvania….Memphis Daily Appeal, 7/27/1859.

State of Tennessee, McNairy County, May Rules held in the Clerk's office of the Circuit Court before the Clerk and Master, etc. Petition to Divide or Sell Shares. Benjamin **SANDERS**, Jr., Administrator of Robert **STUBBLEFIELD**, Dec'd, versus Mary **STUBBLEFIELD**, Jefferson **STUBBLEFIELD**, John H. **STUBBLEFIELD**, Andrew J. **COFFMAN**, Casper **McBRIDE**, Felix G. **MONK**, David **ROBERTS**, James **GEORGE**, Carrall **RUNNELS**, husband of Amanda **RUNNELS**, formerly Amanda **MOORE**, Wm. C. **SAUNDERS**, husband of Martha **SAUNDERS**, formerly Martha **MOORE**, and Washington F. **MOORE** by his guardian, Benjamin **SAUNDERS**. It appearing to the satisfaction of the clerk and master, from the petition and affidavits of petitioners, that Jefferson Stubblefield, Casper McBride, David Roberts and Carrall Runnels, are non-Residents of the State of Tennessee: it is therefore ordered that publication be made in the American Eagle...commanding the said non-residents to appear at the next term of the Circuit Court...in the town of Purdy, on the fourth Monday in August next...Weekly American Eagle, 5/27/1847.

Common Law Court. Thos. **MORRISEY**, administrator of the estate of Wm. **STUBBLETON**, vs. Gayle & Dent, for selling wrong medicine, thereby causing death, the plaintiff recovered $1,500. Memphis Evening Ledger, 12/1/1857.

Died, In this city on Thursday....of pleurisy, in the 38th year of his age, S. C. **SUIT**. Memphis Daily Appeal, Fri., 11/4/1859.

A laborer named John **SULLIVAN**, was killed yesterday evening, while engaged in digging sand under the bluff, below the wharf-boat, by the bank falling upon him...Memphis Eagle & Enquirer, 4/23/1852. (Author's note: Name given as James in another newspaper.)

An Irishman, named Thos. **SULLIVAN**, from this city, was killed on Tuesday last, by the falling of an embankment on the Memphis and Charleston Railroad, near Cold Water Springs. He, with a number of others, were engaged in excavating, when the accident occurred. Memphis Daily Appeal, Thurs., 7/17/1856.

Married, In Memphis, at the Christian Church on Monday, August 23d, 1858, by Elder W. J. **BARBEE**, Mr. A. J. **SUMPTER** to Miss Martha Ann Want, daughter of Walter **WANT**, Esq., all of this city. Louisville, Ky., and New Albany, Ind., papers please copy. Memphis Daily Appeal, 8/29/1858.

We learn from the Memphis Enquirer that a murder was committed in that place on Saturday the 25th ult. The person killed was John **SUPPLE**, an Irish laborer, and the murderer's name is John **WILLIAMS**, also a laborer. Williams has been committed to jail, being unable to procure bondmen to the amount of $1,000 for his appearance to trial. Somerville Reporter, 2/1/1840.

Married, Near Memphis, Tenn., at the residence of the bride's parents, on the 22d December, by Rev. Phillip **TUGGLE**, Rev. _. B. **SURATT**, of the Louisiana Conference, to Miss Alice **TATE**, of this county. By the same, on the 3d inst., Mr. John **SLAUGH** to Mrs. Elizabeth **HOLMES**, all of this county. Memphis Daily Appeal, 12/25/1857.

Married. At Helena, Ark. on Thursday morning the 2d inst. by Rev. Reuben **JONES**, R. F. **SUTTON**, Esq. to Miss Anna **HICKS**, both of that place. Memphis Daily Appeal, 2/13/1854.

The copartnership heretofore existing, under the name of Wm. Swaim & Son, was dissolved on the 21st of July last, by the decease of the said Wm. **SWAIM**, and the business is now, and will be in future, conducted exclusively by the subscriber, who has had the sole charge of the manufacturing of the Panacea and Vermifuge for the last fourteen years.....James **SWAIM**. Daily Enquirer, 3/21/1847.

On yesterday about twelve o'clock, as the freight train on the Memphis and Charleston Railroad was approaching the Grand Junction, a brakeman, named **SWAN** (son of Policeman **SWAN** of this city,) fell from the hindmost car, his head coming in contact with the rail, causing almost instant death. His remains were taken to Holly Springs, where his mother resides. Memphis Daily Appeal, 6/14/1857.

Died, At the residence of his brother, Hon. G. **SWAN**, in Knoxville, Tennessee, on the 9th inst., Mr. John J. **SWAN**, of this city, in the 29th year of his age. The deceased was raised in this place….In 1846 he volunteered for the Mexican war and was in the battle at Cerro Gordo….—*West Tennessee Whig*. Memphis Daily Appeal, 8/23/1857.

Married. In Nashville on the 15th instant by the Rev. Dr. Edgar, Mr. S. H. **SWAN**, of this place, to Miss Martha C. **SWAN**, of Nashville. Memphis Daily Appeal, 11/28/1853.

J. T. **SWAYNE**'s Law Office…Howard's Row, Memphis, Tenn…Memphis Enquirer, 1/18/1848. Married, In this city on Tuesday evening, by the Rev. G. W. **COONS**, Col. J. T. Swayne, to Miss Mary C., daughter of Ethel H. **PORTER**, Esq. Memphis Daily Appeal, 5/1/1851.

The N.O. Tropic of Friday last contains the following: Jumped Overboard – J. S. **SWEENEY,** of Memphis, on the *Memphis*, down yesterday, jumped overboard on the night of the 19th. He left a note in his berth with these words—"I am on my way to Heaven." Mr. Sweeney we understand was a generous and well educated native of Ireland and taught school in this vicinity……American Eagle Weekly, Fri., 12/5/1845.

We are authorized to announce John L. **SWEENEY**, as a candidate for Alderman of 5th Ward. Memphis Daily Appeal, 2/23/1848.

Married—On Tuesday 20th Inst., by the Rev. Samuel **WATSON**, Mr. Samuel M. **SWEETLAND** of the firm of James Woods & Co., to Miss Martha A., daughter of the late D. H. **ABERNATHY**, all of this city. Daily Enquirer, 4/22/1847. The friends and acquaintances of Saml. Sweetland, are respectfully invited to attend the funeral of his late wife, Martha A., at half-past ten o'clock, this morning, from the Second Presbyterian Church. Memphis Eagle & Enquirer, 1/1/1852.

Died, on the 22d inst. at his residence in Fayette county, Tenn., in the 68th year of his age, Wm. **SWIFT**, Esq. The deceased was born in Hanover county, Virginia, October 26, 1791, and served as a young soldier in the American Army in 1812, in the war with Great Britain. In the year 1835 he emigrated to Fayette county, where he passed the remainder of his days as a useful and respectable planter….In his last hours he was consoled by his bereaved and affectionate family….The Richmond (Va.) Enquirer will please copy. Memphis Weekly Appeal, 12/1/1858.

Married, At the residence of T. P. **AYDLETT**, in this city, on Tuesday evening, the 13th inst., by Bishop Otey, Mr. C. C. **SWOOPE**, Esq., of Ala., to Miss Fannie **HUTCHINS**, of Memphis. Memphis Daily Appeal, 7/17/1858.

It is with most profound grief that we announce the death of George A. **SYKES**, Esq., which melancholy event occurred at his residence in Tunica county, Miss., on the 14th instant.—His death was caused by congestive chills. His remains, accompanied by his family, arrived here last evening on the steamer Daniel Boone, on their way to Columbia, Tenn., the place of residence of his wife's family, where they will be interred….Memphis Daily Avalanche, 6/17/1859. ….At the time of his death he was but a young man— scarcely beyond thirty years of age—and yet he had been twice honored by the people of his county with a seat in the Legislature of his State….He leaves a widow and one child to mourn….Memphis Daily Avalanche, 6/18/1859.

Married—May 4th by Rev. J. E. **DOUGLAS**, in Marshall county, Miss., Doctor Archibald M. **SYLES** and Miss Margaret D. **CRADDOCK**. Memphis Daily Avalanche, 6/4/1859.

Geo. **SYPERT**, a ____ man in the employ of Mr. E. F. R__k, while engaged yesterday in guttering the new house being erected on Union street for Gen. Williams, fell from the top and was killed….He is a nephew of Stephen **SYPERT**, of Jackson and has other relatives living in Middle Tennessee. Memphis Daily Appeal, 8/15/1857.

On Wednesday last a jury of inquest was held on the body of a Mrs. **TABNER**, on Poplar St., who was found drowned in a well about daylight of that morning. She was first discovered by her husband, who called in the neighbors to his assistance; but when the body was extricated it was found that life was extinct. Verdict of the jury—"Drowned by accident." Daily Enquirer, Fri., 3/5/1847.

Died, in this city, on the 25th inst., Mr. Geo. **TABOR**, formerly of Mount Morris, Livingston County, New York. Mr. T. was a consistent member of the Baptist Church, and during his short residence in Memphis, his future home, he had won for himself the esteem and friendship of all who knew him. The Daily Eagle, 11/28/1846.

Married, In New Albany, Indiana, on the 14th instant, by the Rev. B. F. **ROLLINS**, Mr. __. V. **TADLOCK**, of Covington, Tenn., and Mrs. Margaret O. **KENDLE**, of New Albany. Memphis Daily Appeal, 8/30/1856.

Married, In this city on the evening of the 2d inst., at the residence of the bride's mother, by Rev. Dr. Bryan, D.D., Mr. J. **TAGG**, of the firm of Jones & Tagg, to Miss Hattie **WYANT**, all of Memphis, Tenn. Memphis Daily Appeal, 11/4/1858.

The Funeral of Matilda W. Tagg, wife of Joseph **TAGG**, will take place on next Sabbath afternoon at 3 o'clock, November 23d, at the Cumberland Presbyterian Church. Services by Rev. A. M. **BRYAN**. Memphis Daily Appeal, 11/22/1856.

Died, On Monday, 3d instant, at the residence of Mrs. Young, Mrs. Wm. **TAIT**. Memphis Daily Appeal, 9/4/1855.

Married, In Collierville, Tenn., by Rev. Thos. **JOINER**, Mr. F. D. **TALLEY** to Miss Ella **CREWDSON**, all of Collierville. Memphis Daily Appeal, 7/14/1858.

Died, On the 15th of August, 1857, in Brownsville, Tennessee, Robert S. **TALLIAFERRO**, aged 38(?) years. Memphis Daily Appeal, 8/16/1857.

Married, On the 18th instant in the vicinity of Luxahomo, DeSoto county, Miss., by Rev. Mr. Watson, Mr. E. **TALLY** to Miss N. M. **WHITE**. Memphis Daily Appeal, 7/21/1855.

Married, In this city at the residence of Mr. M. _. **COCHRAN** on Second street, Mr. Fletcher H. **TALLY** to Miss M. C. **LEAKE**. Memphis Weekly Appeal, 3/3/1858.

W. F. **TANNEHILL**, Jefferson street, announces to his friends and the public, that he has commenced receiving a full and choice assortment of Books and Stationary.....Weekly Appeal, 12/18/1846. Died: In this city, last evening Eliza Dewees, daughter of W. F. and E. A. Tannehill. The friends and acquaintances of the family are requested to attend the funeral this afternoon at 4 o'clock, from their residence on Court street. Memphis Eagle, 9/13/1849. W. F. Tannehill, Esq., died in this city yesterday. Mr. T. was well-known in this city, Nashville and Louisville, and his wide circle of friends will deeply sympathise with his afflicted family in their melancholy bereavement. Memphis Daily Eagle, 11/16/1850. Chancery Sale of a Town Lot. Pursuant to a Decree, made at the November Term, A.D. 1852, of the Common Law & Chancery Court, of the city of Memphis, in the case of Alexander **ALLISON** vs. Eliza Tannehill and others, legal heirs of William F. Tannehill, deceased; I will, on Monday, the 2d day of May, 1853.... proceed to sell to the highest bidder....as part of lot No. 338, situated on Adams street....Memphis Daily Appeal, 4/23/1853.

On last evening between six and seven o'clock, a murder was perpetrated on the Memphis and Charleston Railroad, between Beal and Union streets. The name of the murdered man is W. A. **TANNER**, late a salesman in the mercantile house of Candee, ____ & Co., Main street. The body was discovered a short time before the arrival of the cars....When found, life was not quite extinct, but the victim could not speak....The dead body was taken to the house of his mother, who lives on the outskirts of the city, and with whom he resided. Mr. Tanner was an exemplary member of the Cumberland Presbyterian

Church....He was about twenty-five years of age.... Memphis Daily Appeal, 2/10/1857. The funeral of the victim, Wm. G. **TANNER**, took place in the afternoon....Memphis Daily Appeal, 2/11/1857.

Married. In Rutherford county, Tenn., on the 26th day of June last, by the Rev. William **EGLETON**, James C. **TAPPAN**, Esq., of Helena, Ark., to Miss Mary E., daughter of Hon. Samuel **ANDERSON**, of the former place. Memphis Daily Appeal, 9/1/1854.

Married, On Thursday evening last, by J. **WALDRAN**, Esq., Joseph C. **TARKINTON** to Miss Martha L. **DAVIS**; also Mr. A. T. **FLEMING**, to Miss Matilda **ELLISON**, all of this city. Memphis Eagle & Enquirer, Sat., 2/14/1852.

Married, On the 17th inst., at the residence of the bride's mother, in Tipton county, Tenn., by Rev. Jos. Jno. **SOMERVELL**, Mr. Wm. N. **TARWATER**, of Memphis, Tenn., to Miss Georgie M. **SOMERVELL**, of Tipton. Memphis Daily Appeal, 11/22/1859.

Coroner Horne held an inquest on Sunday on the body of a German named Edward **TASS**, who committed suicide in L. **SOLHEIN's** carpenter shop, on Washington street, at eleven o'clock in the morning, by shooting himself in the temple with a pistol. It appeared that the unfortunate man had once been in good circumstances in Chicago. A large amount of money he had invested was lost during the troubles of the panic. He removed to Paducah, Ky., where his wife, an accomplished lady, taught music. He came down here a short time ago in quest of employment, but not succeeding, he fell into despair, and took a vain refuge in suicide. What sad tidings for his poor, heart-broken wife. Memphis Daily Appeal, Tues., 9/28/1858.

Died, In this city, on the 9th inst., John Henry, son of Jesse M. **TATE**, aged 14 years, 4 months and 23 days. Memphis Eagle & Enquirer, 6/16/1852.

Died, yesterday morning at 9 o'clock, of whooping cough, James Carnes, infant son of Samuel and Mary A. **TATE**, of this city, aged 5 months. Daily Memphis Enquirer, 6/6/1849. Died, On the night of the 20th inst., Michael Gabbert Tate, infant son of Samuel and Mary A. Tate, aged sixteen months and eighteen days. Memphis Eagle & Enquirer, 6/22/1852. I wish to sell my Plantation, twenty miles east of Memphis and three quarters of a mile of the Memphis and Charleston Railroad, adjoining the plantation of Col. E. W. **KENNY** on the south. There are 850 acres in the tract....Sam. Tate. Memphis Daily Appeal, 11/4/1854.

Married, At Hernando, Miss., on the 5th inst., by the L.D. **MULLENS**, T. S. **TATE**, of Memphis, to Mrs. Lucy A. **FOOTE**, of DeSoto county. Memphis Daily Appeal, 10/6/1859.

Died, At his residence near Somerville, Fayette county, Tenn., on the 2d of April, 1858, B. S. **TATUM**, Sr., in the 57th year of his age. The deceased was an old resident of Fayette county, having resided there upwards of twenty years. Memphis Weekly Appeal, 4/14/1858.

Married, In Somerville on the 6th instant by Rev. Moses **GREEN**, Mr. Bartlett **TATUM** and Miss Catharine **APPLEBERRY**, all of that place. Memphis Daily Appeal, 8/9/1856.

Died, In Macon, Tenn., on the 6th inst., Mrs. Rebecca H. Tatum, wife of E. W. **TATUM**, and a member of the Presbyterian Church. Only a week previous, her first and only child, an infant daughter but a few weeks old, had been committed to the tomb...Memphis Daily Eagle, 9/24/1850.

Died—of congestive fever, on Friday the 30th of August, in the 37th year of her age, Mrs. Clarrisa Taylor, consort of A. **TAYLOR**, Esq. of Shelby county, Ten., and daughter of Mr. William **POLK**, of Arkansas. Mrs. Taylor...left behind five children.....The Appeal, 9/13/1844.

Election in South Memphis. Our twin sister city, the younger portion of the "two in one" which makes Memphis, held an election for Mayor last Saturday...The candidates were Dr. Murphy (unsuccessful) and A. B. **TAYLOR**, Esq., (successful, beating his opponent by 18 votes). His (newly elected) Honor, A. B. Taylor, is, therefore, chief magistrate of so much of this "clearing" as lies beyond the middle of Union street, southwards, for 1849 A.D. Memphis Eagle, 1/11/1849. The unadjusted balances due the city of Memphis have been placed in the hands of George **DIXON**, Attorney, for collections....A. B. Taylor, Mayor. Memphis Daily Appeal, 10/15/1853.

Died, March 10th at the residence of Andrew **TAYLOR**, near Collierville, Willie, son of Isaac and Eliza **TAYLOR**, aged three years and eleven months. Memphis Daily Appeal, 3/18/1857.

Married, On Wednesday evening, June 30, at Calvary Church, by Rev. Dr. White, Archibald H. **TAYLOR**, Esq., and Miss Lucy Ruffin, daughter of E.(?) K. **TURNAGE**, Esq., all of this city. Memphis Daily Appeal, 7/2/1858.

Married, On Sunday morning the 13th inst. at the residence of F. **BAXTER**, Esq., by Rev. Mr. Wardwell, Dr. Arthur K. **TAYLOR** and Miss Susan P. Rose, daughter of the late James **ROSE**, Esq., all of this city. Memphis Whig, 1/14/1856.

Married—Last evening by the Rev. J. H. **GRAY**, Dr. B. F. **TAYLOR** of Whiteville, Tenn., to Miss Ann _____ Stanton, daughter of the late Richard **STANTON**, Esq. of Memphis. Memphis Appeal, 11/5/1847.

Married. In Shelby county on the 21st inst. by Rev. A. T. **WYNNE**, Mr. B. T. **TAYLOR**, to Mrs. Martha H. **WARD**. Memphis Appeal, 9/23/1854.

Died. On the 4th of August, Charles **TAYLOR**, of Desoto co., Miss., in his 80th year, formerly of Madison co., Ala. Huntsville Democrat please copy. Memphis Daily Appeal, 8/9/1854.

Married, On Thursday, the 18th instant, by Rev. J. T. C. **COLLINS**, Mr. George **TAYLOR** and Miss Rachel **MURPHEY**, all of this city. Memphis Daily Appeal, 9/21/1856.

Sale of Family Furniture. On Thursday the 28th inst...at the residence of J. R. **TAYLOR**, on Beal street, a few yards from Second street, South Memphis, I will offer for sale, by virtue of a deed-in-trust, to me executed, by said Taylor, a large lot of household furniture...H. **ROLAND**, Trustee, J. E. **PHILLIPS**, Auc'r. Daily Enquirer, 1/22/1847.

It is with no ordinary feelings of mortification that we announce the death of Dr. James **TAYLOR**, late of this county, formerly of Haywood county, Tennessee. He died on Saturday morning, 20th inst., after a short, but painfull illness; leaving an amiable wife and several interesting children to mourn his loss.— Eldorado (Ark.) Union. Weekly Appeal, 3/26/1847.

The undersigned offers for sale his Plantation in the county of Tipton, containing four hundred and sixty three acres...This land is situated on the head branches of Beaver Dam creek, six miles south of Covington, and within one mile of the Mountain Academy, under the charge of the Rev. James **HOLMES**...James A. **TAYLOR**. Memphis Daily Eagle, 8/2/1848.

Married, On Wednesday, the 20th inst., at the residence of her father in this county, by the Rev. Mr. Bryant, Mr. James H. **TAYLOR**, to Miss Mary E., daughter of Elijah **ARRIONETT**. Memphis Eagle, 12/25/1848.

Married, On the 3d of November, at the residence of the bride, in Panola county, Miss., by Rev. W. **DUPUY**, Mr. Jas. R.(?) **TAYLOR**, of this city, and Miss Elgenia A. **MORGAN**. Columbus (Miss.) papers please copy. Memphis Daily Appeal, 11/8/1857.

Married. At the residence of Mr. C. C. **CLEAVES** on the evening of the 21st instant, by Rev. J. W. **KNOTT**, Mr. John H. **TAYLOR**, of the late firm of Strange, Goodwin & Co., and Miss Sallie W. **STRANGE**, all of this city. Memphis Daily Appeal, 3/23/1855. Died, In this vicinity on Thursday, the 10th inst., Lucy Myrtle, daughter of John H. and S. W. Taylor, aged 1 year, 7 months and 24 days. Memphis Daily Appeal, 6/13/1858.

Married, At the residence of her father, Dr. R. C. **HANCOCK**, in DeSoto county, Miss., on Wednesday evening, August 13th, by Rev. Mr. Matthews, Mr. John H. **TAYLOR**, of Memphis, and Miss Violet __. Hancock. Memphis Daily Appeal, 8/16/1856.

Married, on Wednesday evening, 29th ult., in this city, by Rev. Thomas **TAYLOR**, Mr. John P. **TAYLOR**, to Miss Jane E. **MANNING**, both of this city. Daily Enquirer, 10/2/1847. Died, On the 3d instant, Mrs. Jane E. Taylor, consort of John P. Taylor, of this city....Memphis Daily Appeal, 12/4/1856.

Married, On the evening of the 2d inst., at the residence of the bride's father, in Tipton county, Tenn., by Rev. J. J. **SOMERVILLE**, Mr. John P. **TAYLOR**, of this city, to Miss Mary L. **SMITH**. Memphis Daily Appeal, 6/5/1858.

Married—At Memphis, on Wednesday evening last, by the Rev. A. T. **SCRUGGS**, Mr. John W. **TAYLOR** to Mrs. Lucy M. **NASH**, all of that city. American Eagle, 4/7/1842. The friends and acquaintances of John W. and Lucy M. Taylor are invited to attend the funeral of their infant son John W., from their residence, corner of Third and Jackson Streets, to-day at 10 o'clock. Memphis Daily Appeal, 6/9/1851.

Died. On Monday, the 12th inst., at the residence of Gen. Jos. R. **WILLIAMS**, South Memphis, of Typhoid Pneumonia, Mrs. Elizabeth M. O. Taylor, widow of the late Lewis C. **TAYLOR**, Esq. [Clarksville, Tenn. papers and the South Western Christian Advocate, Nashville, will please copy.] Weekly Memphis Eagle, 3/22/1849.

Died, On the 8th inst., of Pulmonary Consumption, Mark M. **TAYLOR**, in the 63[rd](?) year of his age. Nashville and Panola (Miss.) papers please copy. Memphis Daily Appeal, 12/12/1857.

Married, On Thursday evening, October 6, at the residence of the bride's uncle, Jesse M. **TATE**, Esq., by Rev. Mr. Davis, Dr. Richard H. **TAYLOR** to Miss Vollie **GIFT**, all of this city. Memphis Daily Appeal, 10/9/1859.

Married—In Denmark, Madison county, on the 3d inst., Thomas H. **TAYLOR**, Esq., merchant of Memphis, to Miss Jane, first daughter of Dr. John **INGRAM**. Weekly Memphis Eagle, 5/17/1849.

Married, by Elder T. J. **DRANE**, on 13th inst., near this city, at the residence of Capt. Joseph **LENOW**, Mr. W. P. **TAYLOR** to Miss Maria **LENOW**. Memphis Daily Appeal, 1/15/1858. ....on 13th inst., near this city, at the residence of Capt. Joseph Lenow, Mr. W. P. Taylor to Miss Fannie **LENOW**. Memphis Daily Appeal, 1/16/1858.

Died. On the 26th of December, 1854, at his residence in Tipton county, Ten., Major William **TAYLOR**, formerly of Mecklenburg, Va., in the 65[th](?) year of his age....Richmond (Va.) Enquirer please copy. Memphis Daily Appeal, 1/7/1855.

Dr. Wm. V. **TAYLOR** Has located himself in Memphis, and offers his professional services to his friends and the public. Office on Main street, a few doors above Madison—Residence corner of Court and Third streets. Memphis Daily Appeal, 8/25/1848. The friends and acquaintances of Dr. Wm. V. Taylor and family are invited to attend the funeral of their son, Leonard H. Taylor, from their residence on Poplar street, this (Thursday) evening at __ o'clock. Services by Rev. D. C. **PAGE**. Memphis Daily Appeal, 11/30/1854.

Died, At his residence in Jefferson county, Ark., July 27th, Isaac **TEAGUE**, in the 62d year of his age. Memphis Advocate, Eagle and Enquirer and Jackson Whig please copy. Memphis Daily Appeal, 9/21/1858.

Married, At the residence of Mrs. Emma **BROWNING**, in DeSoto county, Miss., on the 7th instant, by Rev. J. **ROBINSON**, Mr. Wm. A. **TEAGUE** to Mrs. Emma Browning. New Orleans Picayune please copy. Memphis Daily Appeal, 4/23/1859.

Married. On the 16th inst., by the Rev. Mr. Hodge, John H. **TEMPLE** to Miss Catherine E. **MALTBIE**, both of this city. American Eagle, 9/23/1847.

On the 4th Mr. O. G. **TENNY**, living on Causey street, fell dead from the same cause.—*Evening News of yesterday.* Memphis Daily Appeal, 7/9/1856. (Author's note: cause – sun stroke.)

Married—On the 29th June, by Rev. Joseph **FRANE**, Mr. Henry **TEST**, of Memphis, to Miss Elmira, daughter of Thos. **SMITH**, of York, Pa. Memphis Enquirer, 7/16/1846.

The friends and acquaintances of Mr. Henry **TEST** are requested to attend his funeral from his residence on Miami street, above Poplar, on Saturday morning....Services by Rev. A. H. **THOMAS** at the First Methodist Church. Memphis Avalanche, Fri., 2/11/1859. Died, On Thursday evening, February 10th, Mr. Henry Test, aged about forty-three years. Memphis Daily Appeal, 2/12/1859.

Died. On the 28th instant, Bias Price, infant son of Westly and Mary Ann **TEST**, aged 1 year, 9 months and 20 days. American Eagle, 8/5/1847.

Married, On Wednesday, 4th inst., by the Rev. Dr. **HAWKS**, Mr. Wm. **THATCHER**, Merchant of Shreveport, La., to Miss Elizabeth P. Hill, daughter of Col. Allen **HILL** of this city. American Eagle, 8/12/1847.

Died, On Sunday morning, March 27th, 1859, in Raleigh, Shelby county, Tenn., at the residence of Sam'l **ALLEN**, Esq., Asa S. **THOMAS**, formerly of Blairsville, Pa., but for many years past a citizen of Raleigh and well known as the efficient and popular Deputy Clerk of the County Court at the county seat, which office he held at the time of his death....Memphis Daily Appeal, 3/30/1859.

Married, On Thursday, December 4th, 1856, by Rev. Wm. Carey **CRANE**, Rev. B. F. **THOMAS** and Miss Lydia M. Bledsoe, daughter of Mr. Benj. **BLEDSOE**, all of DeSoto county, Miss. Memphis Daily Appeal, 12/7/1856.

Married, On Wednesday, May 13th, at the residence of Turner W. **HARRIS**, near Big Creek, Shelby county, Tenn., by Rev. Dr. R. C. **GRUNDY**, Mr. C. C. **THOMAS**, of Memphis, and Miss Maggie E. **BATEMAN**. Memphis Daily Appeal, 5/14/1857.

Died. At the residence of her father in Marshall county, Miss., on Monday, 3d of January, 1853, in the 12th year of her age, Margaret Louis, daughter of Col. Charles L. **THOMAS**. Memphis Eagle & Enquirer, 1/9/1853.

Married, on the 22d inst., by N. G. **CURTIS**, Esq., Mr. Daniel **THOMAS** to Miss Mary **LAWS**, all of this county. Memphis Enquirer, 4/24/1849.

Soon after eight o'clock last night as John **THOMAS**, a cook on the *Kate Frisbee*, was walking along Court street on the north side a little above Front Row, a pistol was fired, by whom is not known. Thomas and some persons with him ran towards the spot, on the way towards the corner of Front Row, Thomas received a fatal stab from the hands of an individual not at this writing certainly known. He exclaimed to a companion: "Williams I am killed," fell upon the pavement, and was in a few minutes a corpse....Thomas was a young man of irregular life, he was formerly a member of the No. 5's Fire Company and his body was laid out in their engine house, he having no family in town....Memphis Daily Appeal, 9/11/1858. The funeral of the late John Thomas, who was killed in this city on Friday evening last, was attended by large delegations from the different fire companies, on Saturday afternoon. He was a member of Fire Company No. 5. Memphis Daily Avalanche, Mon., 9/13/1858.

Died. On the 16th inst., in this city, Mrs. Frances A. Thomas, wife of Mr. William **THOMAS**, of the firm of Kirk and Thomas, of this place....American Eagle, 12/24/1846.

The friends and acquaintances of William and Virginia **THOMAS** are invited to attend the funeral of their daughter, Virginia Carr Thomas, from their residence on Market street, east of the Bayou, to-day (Wednesday) at 3 o'clock. Memphis Daily Appeal, 4/8/1857.

Married, On the 12th instant, by E. **BRAY**, Esq., at the residence of John **SAMPLES**, Mr. Wm. **THOMASON** and Miss Lucinda **SAMPLES**, all of Shelby county. Memphis Daily Appeal, 3/17/1857.

Married, At the residence of the bride's father, near Macon, Tenn., September 11th, by Rev. R. L. **WALLER**, James A. **THOMPSON**, Esq., and Miss Mary K. **BLAYDES**. Memphis Daily Appeal, 9/13/1856.

Pursuant to a decretal order of the Circuit Court of Shelby County, at the January term, 1848, I will on the 22d day of April next, at the Court House door in the town of Raleigh, expose to public sale...one hundred (100) acres of Land, as the property of James P. **THOMPSON** dec'd., the widow waving her dower. Said Land is situated on the waters of Big Creek, being the same tract conveyed to him by Carr **CRENSHAW** and E. L. **CRENSHAW**. Memphis Daily Eagle, 3/11/1848.

Died, At the residence of his father, near Hickory With, Tenn., Mr. James W. **THOMPSON**, aged near 20 years, of Inflammation of the Stomach and Bowels, after a painful suffering of 18 days. Memphis Eagle & Enquirer, 6/24/1852.

From papers found on the person of the man found dead on the plank road, it is supposed that his name was James W. **THOMPSON**, of Lynchburg, Virginia. Circumstances also induce the belief that Thompson was insane at the time, and had wandered off to die on the highway. A post mortem examination proved that his brain was diseased at the time. Memphis Daily Appeal, 8/19/1853.

Married, At the residence of Mrs. E. T. **HUNT**, in Panola county, Miss., on Wednesday morning, 13th inst., by Rev. J. H. **GRAY**, D.D., Dr. John **THOMPSON**, of Oxford, Miss., to Miss Laura E. **HUNT**. Memphis Daily Appeal, 1/14/1858.

Died, At his mother's residence in Hardeman county, on the 2d September, John L. **THOMPSON**, of congestive fever, aged 22 years, 10 months and 23 days. In the death of this young man, a fond mother lost the most affectionate of sons. He has left many brothers and sisters...The Appeal, 9/20/1844.

Married, In Shelby county on Wednesday evening, May 28th, by Rev. Jeremiah **BURNS**, Mr. Lycuragus **THOMPSON**, of this city, and Miss Mary C., daughter of Randolph **WEBB**, dec'd., late of this county. Raleigh (N.C.) papers please copy. Memphis Daily Appeal, 5/30/1856.

Died, On the 10th instant, near Germantown, Tenn., Ida, infant daughter of N. N. and Mary L. **THOMPSON**. Memphis Daily Appeal, 11/11/1855.

Bath House—Phil. **THOMPSON**, next door to the Commercial Hotel, is now prepared to give warm, Cold and Shower Baths, at all hours, from sunrise till 10 o'clock at night. Daily Enquirer, 4/3/1847.

Died, In this city on Tuesday the 10th inst., Juliet, wife of Phillip H. **THOMPSON**, Esq., in the 23d year of her age. Nashville papers and Louisville Journal please copy. Memphis Whig, 6/13/1856.

Died. On Saturday, the 8th inst., at his residence on the State Line Road, one mile east of Memphis, R. H. **THOMPSON**, in the 41st year of his age. Memphis Daily Eagle, 4/13/1848.

Died, At his residence, in Hardeman county, Thos. **THOMPSON**, aged 63 years, of congestive fever, on the 21st day of August. Mr. Thompson...has left an amiable wife and numerous family of children...The Appeal, 9/20/1844.

Married, In Wilmington, N.C., by the Rev. Dr. Drane, on the 18th ult., Gen. Waddy **THOMPSON**, of Greenville, S.C., to Miss Cornelia, eldest daughter of Col. John D. **JONES**. Memphis Daily Eagle, 12/4/1850.

Married, On Tuesday, 20th inst., in Shelby county by Rev. A. H. **NELSON**, D.D., Mr. William G. **THOMPSON**, Esq., of Memphis, and Miss Mary H. **NELSON**, of Shelby county. Memphis Daily Appeal, 10/22/1857.

Jas. B. **THORNTON**. Attorney at Law, Memphis, Ten. Daily Enquirer, 2/6/1847.

Died—At the residence of the Rev. M. W. **WEBBER**, on Wednesday the 17th inst., Dr. Fendel **THURMAN**, in the 42 year of his age, after a protracted and lingering disease of more than six months...The Appeal, 7/26/1844.

Married, On the evening of the 16th instant by Rev. R. **BURROW**, Mr. Jno. P. **THURMAN** and Miss Sallie E., eldest daughter of Robert **ECKRIN**, Esq., all of this county. Richmond, Va. papers copy. Memphis Daily Appeal, 9/27/1856.

Thomas J. **THURMAN** died of Pneumonia at his late residence in Hardeman county, Tenn., forty-two years of age, a native of Wilkes county, N.C., and a resident of this immediate vicinity twenty years, leaving behind him a disconsolate widow, six children, and a concourse of relations and friends to mourn his exit from this life....Memphis Appeal, 2/7/1853.

I will slaughter and have for sale at the Upper Market House, on Saturday morning next, one of the fattest and finest Bullocks...P. W. **THURSTON**. Memphis Daily Eagle, 4/21/1848.

Married, On the 7th inst. by Rev. E. H. **GREEN**, Mr. Rob't. **TICER** and Mrs. ----- **FLEN_KEN**, both of Tipton county, Tenn. Memphis Daily Appeal, 10/23/1857.

Married. On Tuesday 7th inst., by the Rev. M. J. **HANNER**, Mr. John W. **TIMBERLAKE**, of Va., to Miss Elizabeth Ann, eldest daughter of Chas. T. **HOWARD** Esq., of Middleburg, Hardeman county, Tenn. Memphis Enquirer, 1/10/1840.

Died, On Saturday morning at the residence, corner of Second and Jefferson streets, James, son of Mrs. **TIPPETT**, aged fourteen years. [This is the third child the same lady has lost within a month.] Memphis Daily Appeal, 12/27/1857.

Died, On the morning of the 4th inst., Bennie, second son of Rev. H. H. and Mary Ann **TIPPETT**, aged 12 years and 1 month. Also, on the evening of the 5th, Willie, third son of the same family, aged 7 years and 4 months. Memphis Daily Appeal, 12/6/1857.

Masonic Funeral Notice. The Members of Angerona Lodge, No. 168, will meet this evening...for the purpose of attending the burial of our late brother, E. **TITUS**. Died—At his residence in Arkansas, on yesterday morning, August 7, at 8 o'clock, Mr. E. Titus. The friends of the deceased are requested to attend his funeral this evening, at 4 o'clock, from the residence of F. **TITUS**. Memphis Daily Appeal, 8/8/1851.

Died—At his residence in Red River county, Texas, on the __1st November last, Col. James **TITUS**, father of F. **TITUS**, of this city. The deceased was one of the oldest and most respectable residents of this county previous to his removal to Texas, and was well known both in this State and Alabama, where he had a large circle of warmly attached friends, to whom this intelligence will be a source of sincere sorrow. The Appeal, 1/12/1844.

Died, At Hernando, Miss., on Sunday afternoon, Mr. Robert **TITUS**, silver-smith, recently of Memphis and formerly of Boston, Mass. American Eagle, Fri., 9/22/1843.

Married, In this vicinity on Wednesday evening by Rev. Mr. **BETHELL**, Mr. Robert E. **TITUS** of this place, to Miss Indiana, daughter of Geraldus **BUNTYN**, Esq. of this vicinity. American Eagle, Friday, 5/25/1843. Departed this life at Bersheba Springs, Warren County, on Saturday, the 3d instant, Mr. Robert E. Titus, of the firm of F. & R.E. Titus of this city, in the 28th year of his age. He visited the Springs for the benefit of his sadly bereaved consort, whose health was delicate, and was himself violently attacked with billious fever, which terminated his earthly career in something less than two weeks.....The Appeal, 8/16/1844.

A man by the name of James **TOBIN** was most brutally murdered on Thursday night about 11 o'clock on board A. B. Shaw & Co.'s Wharf-boat...The deed was committed on the forecastle of the boat, with a large knife, which was plunged into his breast, producing death instantly...but had no papers by which his residence could be indicated. Memphis Eagle & Enquirer, Sat., 5/1/1852.

Married, On Tuesday, the 14th inst., by the Rev. Samuel **WATSON**, Edward S. **TOD**, of this city, to Miss Emma R., daughter of Joel **HALL** of Shelby county. Tri-Weekly Memphis Enquirer, 4/23/1846.

Died. At his residence in this city on Monday evening, April 9, 1855, Mr. Edward S. **TODD**, in the 37th year of his age. Mr. Todd was a native of Philadelphia, of a highly respectable family and was educated by Prof. Bache(?). He came to this place in 1836 and engaged on the Memphis and Lagrange Railroad as a Civil Engineer, in which branch of science he was thoroughly educated. After the suspension of that work he settled in Memphis, where he remained until his death. He was for many years City Engineer....He leaves a wife to mourn the loss....Philadelphia papers please copy. Memphis Daily Appeal, 4/17/1855.

Died, on the 6th inst., in Macon, Tenn., John **TODD**, in the 45th year of his age....Memphis Daily Appeal, 10/12/1856.

Married, At the residence of the bride's father in Felicity, Ohio, on Thursday, October the 18th, by Rev. W. **RUTLEDGE**, Miss S. Amanda **FALLIN** and John W. **TODD**, Esq., of Memphis, Tenn. Memphis Daily Appeal, 10/25/1856.

Died, On Tuesday evening the 2d inst., of scarlet fever, Frank, the only son of Dr. T. H. **TODD** of this county, aged two years and nine months. Weekly American Eagle, 6/12/1846. Died, In Shelby county, Tenn., 10 miles east of Memphis, on the 10th inst., after a protracted illness of some four months, Mrs. Burchett R., consort of Dr. T. H. Todd of this county, in the 32d year of her age...as a mother, she stood an example...devoted husband and two sweet children, a son and daughter...The Huntsville Democrat and Lincoln Journal will please copy. Memphis Eagle & Enquirer, 3/17/1852.

Married, On Wednesday, at the residence of T. S. **AYRES**, Esq., by Rt. Rev. J. H. **OTEY**, D.D., Dr. Thos. **TODD** to Mrs. Mary **AYRES**, all of this city. Memphis Daily Appeal, 2/16/1856.

Died—Near Bolivar, on Sunday the 3d inst., Mrs. Emily Todd, consort of Maj. Wm. **TODD**, and daughter of J. J. **WILLIAMS**, Esq. Memphis Enquirer, 5/8/1840.

Died, On the morning of the 2d instant, James Otey, third son of Henrietta and Charles **TOMES**, deceased. Nashville and New York papers please copy. Memphis Daily Appeal, 7/3/1858.

Died, In this city on Monday, the 31st October, of consumption, John Franklin **TOMPKINS**, aged 33 years. He was a native of New York city, and a short time resident of this city. His remains were cared for and attended in funeral by the Sons of Malta, of which he was a member....He leaves behind a young and much afflicted wife to mourn his loss. New York, New Orleans and Louisville papers copy. Memphis Daily Appeal, 11/1/1859.

Died, On Friday the 12th instant, at the residence of his father in South Memphis, Robert Emmet **TOMPKINS**, aged 16 years. Memphis Daily Appeal, 11/13/1852.

We regret to learn that the Rev. S. T. **TONCRAY**, one of our oldest citizens, departed this life yesterday at his residence in the upper part of town. Mr. T., though living in humble circumstances, and occupying a comparatively small space in the public eye, was one of the most estimable and useful members of the community. By occupation a silversmith, he possessed a genius for invention, and an ingenuity and skill in all things within the range of handicraft, that we have never known equalled. In this respect he has left no successor, and his loss will be severely felt. He was, too, a good man in the Christian sense of the term.— Of his own means, the fruit of the labor of his hands, he had build a handsome little Church, of which he was the pastor.—Enquirer of the 12th. American Eagle, 2/18/1847.

We learned by the telegraph from Louisville yesterday that Mr. John S. **TOOF**, the well known local editor of the *Bulletin*, was united in the bonds of matrimony Thursday evening, to a young lady of that city. Memphis Daily Appeal, Sat., 12/24/1859. Married, At the residence of the bride's brother in Louisville, on the 26th inst., by Rt. Rev. Bishop Spaulding, Mr. John S. Toof, of Memphis, to Miss Agnes **McCANN**, of Louisville. Memphis Daily Appeal, 12/28/1859.

Married, In Fort Madison, Iowa, on the 31st July, by Elder Jas. H. **BACON**, Miss Mary J., daughter of Rev. Daniel **BATES**, and Mr. S. C. **TOOF**, of this city. Memphis Daily Appeal, 8/5/1856.

Married, On Wednesday evening, 11th inst. by the Rev. Mr. Coons, Mr. J. A. **TOON**, to Miss Caroline H. **DICKSON**, both of this city. The Appeal, Fri., 12/13/1844.

Whereas, we, members of the Chickasaw Lodge No. 8, of the I.O.O.F. have received the mournful intelligence of the death of our beloved brother Jesse A. **TOON**, who departed this life on the 26th day of June, 1847, in the county of Henderson in this State...American Eagle, 7/22/1847. I will expose at public sale on Saturday, 11th day of March, at the house of Franklin **MADDING** on the Hernando road, near Judge **KING's** residence, sundry articles of household and kitchen furniture, rifle gun, etc.—belonging to the estate of Jesse A. **TOONE**. John **HOUSTON**, Adm'r. Memphis Daily Appeal, 2/25/1848.

Married—At Nashville, on the evening of the 29th (?) April last, by the Rev. J. T. **EDGAR**, Robertson **TOPP**, Esq. of this place, to Miss Elizabeth **VANCE**, of that city. Memphis Enquirer, 5/13/1837. Whig Electoral Ticket – Robertson Topp, of Shelby. Memphis Enquirer, 3/13/1840.

Last evening at half past seven o'clock, a number of Irish people got into a difficulty on Winchester street, between Main and Front Row, when Charles **WINTER** and Patrick **TORPEY** engaged in a violent quarrel; the latter, it is asserted, struck the former with a brick, who in return shot at him twice with a revolver, the second shot reaching the heart. The wounded man attempted to retreat, but fell into a bystander's arms and died in less than half an hour....Torpey was the man who has had charge of Court Square since it was thrown open to the public. Memphis Daily Appeal, 7/4/1858.

Died. On the 28th of March, in California, after a painful illness of many months, Miss L. E. Torrey, consort of James A. **TORREY**, formerly of this city. The deceased was born December 16, 1816 in the State of Kentucky, but had resided several years in Memphis, from whence she went to California some two years ago, suffering with that slow yet fatal disease, Consumption ....She leaves her aged mother and only brother (John W. **HAWTHORN**) in this city to mourn her loss. Memphis Whig, 5/4/1855.

Married, On Tuesday evening, the 2d inst., by Hume F. **HILL**, Esq., Capt. James A. **TORRY**, of the Nicaraguan army, and Miss Nancy M. **PATTERSON**, of this city. Memphis Daily Appeal, 2/6/1858.

Married, On Tuesday evening, July 1st, by Hume F. **HILL**, Esq., Mr. Wm. **TOURTELLO**(?) to Mrs. Anna **KIRBY**, all of this city. Memphis Whig, 7/2/1856.

Married, On the 25th of January by Rev. N. H. **McFADDEN**, Dr. Isaac **TOWELL** to Miss Artimessa **GLASS**, all of Tipton county. The Yazoo Democrat will please copy. Memphis Daily Appeal, 2/1/1856.

Married, In Marshall county, Miss., on the 11th instant by Rev. Mr. Fagg, at the residence of Mr. Charles L. **THOMAS**, Mr. Edward A. **TOWNES**, of Yallobusha county, to Miss Mary W. **THOMAS**. Memphis Daily Appeal, 1/20/1856.

Died—On the 23d of July last, at the residence of Maj. John **BELL**, Henderson County, Ten., of the Bilious fever, Col. Joel (?) R. **TOWNES**, formerly of this county, but recently of White County, Arkansas. He has left many friends and relatives to mourn his untimely death.... Memphis Enquirer, 8/12/1837.

Having located myself in Memphis, at No. 83 Front Row, between Adams and Washington streets, for the purpose of doing a wholesale and retail Grocery business...John E. **TOWNES**. Memphis Eagle, 10/4/1848.

Married, On Thursday the 5th inst. by Rev. P. W. **ALSTON**, Mr. David **TOWNSEND**, merchant, to Miss Elizabeth, daughter of Sam'l **McMANUS**, Esq., all of this city. The Appeal, 12/13/1844. Died. On Friday last, 3d instant, Mary Hackney, infant daughter of David H. and Elizabeth Townsend, aged about two years. American Eagle, 9/9/1847. Died, at the Galt House, Louisville, Ky., at 4 o'clock P.M., on the 5th inst., John Moore, infant son of David H. and Elizabeth A. Townsend, of this city, aged 1 year and 9 months....The innocent babe now sleeps along side of a little sister (nearly the same age) who preceded him about two years since.... Daily Memphis Enquirer, 6/14/1849.

Married. On the 14th instant by the Rev. Louis **ADAMS**, Gen. Wm. **TOWNSEND** to Miss A. **FOSTER**, all of Tipton county, Ten. Memphis Daily Appeal, 3/17/1855.

For sometime a pretty Irish girl of seventeen, residing in the neighborhood of the gas works has been engaged to be married to a fellow countryman named Stokes, to whom she was deeply attached. The banns were published three times in the Catholic Church. On Sunday week the day of marriage came, Margaret **TRACEY**, that was her name, prepared for the occasion, but her lover came not. Her grief and shame may be imagined, but in the course of the week the false youth contrived by excuses and carresses to obtain her consent to making last Sunday the happy day. The poor girl was satisfied, but who can describe her overwhelming feelings when her heartless lover again was absent and on being interrogated declared that it was not his intention to marry her. This was more than the afflicted girl could bear, she rushed to the Bayou, swollen by the floods, and in the liquid depths sought a refuge from cruelty and disappointment. Yesterday morning her body was recovered and an inquest was held over it by Esq. Horne. The verdict returned was "voluntary drowning." Memphis Daily Appeal, Tues., 6/22/1858.

Yesterday Esq. Horne held an inquest over the body of Jno. **TRACEY**, who was found dead in his bed at the house of J. D. **LYNCH**, on Front Row opposite the Navy Yard. Verdict—died from appoplexy. Memphis Daily Appeal, 6/29/1858.

Married, At the New Magnolia House, New Orleans, on the 6th instant, by Rev. Linas **PARKER**, Thomas G. **TRACY**, Esq., and Miss Lizzie **HALL**, of Louisville, Kentucky. Memphis Daily Appeal, 2/14/1856.

Married, On Wednesday, 3d inst., at the residence of A. T. **PEGUE**, Esq., Jackson, Tenn., by Rev. Amos **JONES**, Mr. D. C. **TRADER**, of the firm of Goggin, Trader, Holt of this city, to Miss Kate **MAY**, of Jackson. Memphis Daily Appeal, 8/5/1859.

Mrs. Caroline A. Trader, consort of William **TRADER**, born in Hertford county, North Carolina, removed to Tennessee in 1835, and departed this life at Memphis, Tenn., on the 23d January, 1846, at 3 o'clock, A.M...An exemplary member of the Presbyterian church....Memphis Enquirer, 2/3/1846.

Married, on the night of Sunday, 12th inst., by the Rev. N. M. **GAYLORD**, Mr. Wm. **TRADER**, of Memphis, Tenn., to Miss Mary Frances, eldest daughter of Mr. William S. **PAMPLIN**, of Henderson, Ky. Tri-Weekly Memphis Enquirer, 7/14/1846.

Died, On the 3d inst., in this city, of pneumonia, Mr. John **TRAINER**, aged 46 years. The deceased was a resident of Memphis for the last eight years, during which time he had gained for himself the reputation of an honest man, a doting husband and kind parent. Memphis Weekly Appeal, 3/17/1858.

A fatal affray occurred in Germantown on the 23d inst., between Wm. **TRAMMELL** and Wm. A. **JOICE**, by which the former was killed, having been repeatedly stabbed by the latter…Joice has not been arrested, but it is understood that he has not fled the country; and will probably surrender himself for trial. Memphis Daily Appeal, 1/28/1852.

Married, In Madison county, Miss., at the residence of Mrs. Mary G. **HERNDON**, by Rev. H. _____, Mr. A. _. **TREADWELL**, of Memphis, to Miss Maggie Q. **HENDERSON**. Memphis Weekly Appeal, 12/1/1858.

Died, In this city of cholera infantum, on the 14th inst., Wade, infant son of Allison C. and Rebecca E. **TREADWELL**. Franklin, Tennessee papers please copy. Memphis Daily Appeal, 9/18/1857.

Married, On the 22d inst., near Fisherville, in Shelby county, W. L. **TREADWELL**, Esq., of Memphis, to Miss Louisa A. **FARABEE**. Memphis Weekly Appeal, 12/29/1858.

Died—Near La Grange, Tenn., on the fourth inst., Mrs. Margaret Trent, wife of Dr. William H. **TRENT**, in the 38th year of her age…Exemplary in all her estates, as wife, mother, friend and mistress…Weekly Appeal, 9/12/1845.

English & Classical School Near Germantown. The undersigned having purchased a small farm near Germantown, will, on the 12th October, open a school, near his residence, on the State line road one mile and a half above the village…..Tuition for session of 5 months, will be $8, $12 ½ and $20, according to the branches studied. B. R. **TREZEVANT**. Weekly American Eagle, 10/1/1846. Died: At Pembroke Cottage, on the 27th July, Charles Leopold, youngest son of B. R. and Rachael G. Trezevant, aged one year and ten months. Weekly Memphis Eagle, 8/9/1849. Died—On the evening of the 19th Mary E., daughter of B. R. and Rachael Trezevant, aged 8 years. Weekly Appeal, 9/26/1845.

Attention Militia, The 154th Regiment, composed of the 5th, 12th and 13th civil districts, will parade on Tuesday the 10th inst. at 10 A.M., on the premises between the Gayouso House and Fort Pickering. As I have within my possession the names of every man in this regiment, subject to the military duty, I will enforce the law most rigidly, against all delinquents. Every man who stays home, instead of turning out on parade, shall pay his fine. J. T. **TREZEVANT**, C.C. 154th Reg. T.M. The Appeal, 10/6/1843.

Died—On the 25th ult. at his father's residence, four miles east of Memphis, in the 14th year of his age, James E. son of Col. James **TREZEVANT**, formerly of Southampton county, Va. The Richmond Va. Papers are respectfully requested to give the above an insertion. Memphis Enquirer, 9/2/1837.

Died, At 8 o'clock on Monday evening, May 19th, 1856, Louisa R., wife of John Pollard **TREZEVANT**, in the 32d year of her age. The friends of the family are invited to attend the Funeral Services, at Calvary Church, Memphis, this Evening at 4 o'clock. Memphis Daily Appeal, 5/21/1856.

Departed this life on the evening of the 4th inst. Francis O. Trezevant, son of Lewis C. **TREZEVANT** of this place; aged six years and nine months. Memphis Enquirer, 7/8/1837. Died On the evening of the 17th inst., at Dr. W. W. **TUCKER's**, Peter (?) P. son of Lewis C. Trezevant of this place, in his tenth year. Memphis Enquirer, 8/19/1837. Died. In this town the 10th inst., Richard Augustus, infant son of Lewis C. and Rebecca D. Trezevant. This is the third affliction of the kind that has befallen the bereaved parents within a few weeks…Memphis Enquirer, 9/16/1837. Married, On Thursday morning, 24th instant, at Calvary Church by Rev. Mr. Wardwell, Miss Elizabeth Cocke Trezevant, daughter of Dr. Lewis C. Trezevant, dec'd., and George DeBenniville **KEIM**(?), of Pottsville, Pennsylvania. Memphis Daily Appeal, 4/25/1856.

Died, On Tuesday May 4th, 1852, at the residence of her son N. M. **TREZEVANT**, Mrs. Mary B., relict of the late James **TREZEVANT**, of this county, formerly of Southampton county, Va. Her friends are invited to attend her funeral at the First Methodist Church, this (Wednesday) afternoon...Memphis Eagle & Enquirer, 5/5/1852. Died, On the 29th inst., Zoe Trezevant, infant daughter of N. M. and A. Trezevant, aged 1_ months. Memphis Daily Appeal, 11/1/1857.

Married, On Thursday evening, the 30th November, by Rev. G. W. **COONS**, Mr. Nathaniel M. **TREZEVANT** to Miss Amanda A. **AVERY**. Memphis Daily Eagle, 12/5/1848.

Married. In this city on Thursday afternoon the 12th instant by the Rev. John H. **GRAY**, Mr. John R. **TRICE** to Miss Augusta B., only daughter of Hume F. **HILL**, Esq. Memphis Daily Appeal, 1/13/1854.

We understand, says the *Southern* (Ky.) *Patriot*, that our friend, Tandy H. **TRICE**, Esq., recently a citizen of this place, has associated himself with Mr. J. M. **McCOMBS**, of Memphis, Tenn., in the wholesale and retail Hardware business....Memphis Daily Appeal, 2/23/1856.

Married. On Monday evening, 21st inst., at the residence of Col. Jas. H. **MURRAY** in this county, by Rev. Dr. D. L. **GRAY**, Judge Wm. C. **TRICE**, of Ark., to Mrs. Sarah **BUTLER**, State of Kentucky. Memphis Daily Appeal, 8/26/1854.

An affray occurred at a negro ball, on the Raleigh road, just beyond the city limits, Saturday evening between a white cooper named Frederick **TRIETE**, a citizen of north Memphis, and a party of negroes. Triete, it is said, interfered with the festivities, and was set upon by a number of negroes, one of whom struck him on the head with a club, fracturing his skull and causing his death yesterday....Memphis Daily Appeal, Wed., 9/7/1859.

Died—In Madison County, on Friday the 28th July last, Henry (?) **TRIGG**, formerly of this county, aged 21 years. He was highly esteemed by all who knew him, and died universally lamented. Memphis Enquirer, 8/12/1837.

The friends and acquaintances of James **TRIGG** are invited to attend the funeral of his wife at 9 o'clock, A.M., Thursday, 12th instant, from the residence of John **TRIGG**. Memphis Daily Appeal, 7/12/1855.

Died—On Sunday, the 10th instant, after a severe and protracted illness, Mary Letitia W., infant daughter of Mr. & Mrs. John **TRIGG**, of this city. The Appeal, 9/15/1843. At a meeting of the Directors of the City Exchange Company of Memphis, John Trigg, Esq. was elected President, and H. R. **PHUGH** Esq. appointed Secretary. Memphis Enquirer, 5/9/1846. ....Thus has "passed away" the gentle life and spirit of Julia, in her sixteenth spring, the daughter of Mr. John **TRIGG**, of this city. The pestilence passed over her invalid form whilst visiting New Orleans with her fond and sorrowing parents....Weekly Memphis Eagle, 4/19/1849.

The friends and acquaintances of Mr. John **TRIGG** are invited to attend the funeral of his late wife at 4 o'clock this evening, from his residence two miles from the city. Memphis Daily Appeal, 7/14/1854. Died. In the vicinity of the city on the 13th inst., Mrs. Elizabeth P. Trigg, consort of John Trigg, Esq...Memphis Daily Appeal, 7/15/1854.

Married, On Monday last by Rev. Mr. Cobb, John **TRIGG**, Esq., to Mrs. Julia **CHESTER**, all of this city. Memphis Daily Appeal, Thurs., 12/13/1855.

Married, In this city on Thursday last, 14th inst., Mr. John **TRIGG** and Miss Martha **HASKELL**. Memphis Daily Appeal, 1/16/1858.

We were yesterday shown a letter from Mr. A. T. **FARISH** to Mr. Lansom **TRIGG**, announcing the death of the latter gentleman's son, Mr. James Trigg, of diarrhea, in the hospital, in Marysville, Upper California, on the 19th June...Memphis Daily Eagle, 8/13/1850.

Married, In Rutherford county, on Thursday evening, 24th ult., by the Rev. Dr. Lapsley, Mr. Thomas B. **TRIGG**, of Memphis, to Miss Susan N., 2nd daughter of Col. R. L. **WEAKLEY**, of Rutherford county. American Eagle, 7/8/1847.

Died, On the 24th of July at Moscow, Tenn., of chronic diarrhea, J. M. **TRIPP**, of this city. Memphis Daily Appeal, 8/5/1856.

Married, In Jackson, Tennessee, on the 29th instant, Mr. G. W. **TROTTER**, of this city, and Miss S. E. **MERIWEATHER**, of the former place. Memphis Daily Appeal, 5/1/1857.

It is our sorrowful duty to announce the death of Col. Cincinnatus **TROUSDALE**, one of the Swamp Land Commissioners for the State of Arkansas, and brother to one of the editors of this paper. He expired at Helena, Ark., on last Thursday, 3d instant, after a long and painful illness of nearly four weeks....He was just thirty-two years old. The deceased had resided in Arkansas for about 11 years, where he practiced the profession of the law until the declaration of war with Mexico, when he joined Col. Yell's Regiment of volunteers....After the war he resumed the practice of the law at Dover, Pope county. In 1851, he was appointed by Gov. Roane a member of the board of Swamp Land Commissioners....He was interred at Helena on the 4th instant by his brethren and friends of Telula Lodge, No. 2, I.O.O.F.....Memphis Appeal, 2/9/1853. (Author's note: Leon. **TROUSDALE**, Editor.)

Married, At the residence of the bride's father, John W. **RECORD**, Esq., near Holly Springs, Miss., by Rev. Mr. Paine, Captain J. M. **TROUSDALE**, of Franklin, La., and Miss Anna Almira Record. Memphis Daily Appeal, 8/23/1856.

Married, On Thursday evening, 28th ult., at the residence of the bride's father, by Rev. Richard **HINES**, Mr. N. W. **TROUT** to Miss Catharine W., eldest daughter of I. N. **HENKEL**, Esq., all of this city. Memphis Daily Appeal, 5/1/1859.

Married, In Germantown, on the 5th inst., by S. W. **LEDBETTER**, Esq., Mr. George W. **TRUEHEART**, to Mrs. Maria **SCRUGG**, both formerly of Virginia. Memphis Daily Eagle, 12/16/1850.

Died—In this place on Sunday morning last, after an illness of only a few days, Capt. James W. **TRUELOVE**, Superintendent of the Memphis Foundry, aged 50 years.....He was a kind father ......His remains were attended to their last resting place by a respectable concourse of our citizens, together with the resident brethren of the masonic fraternity – of which he was a zealous and worthy member. Memphis Enquirer, Fri., 2/1/1839.

Dr. W. J. **TUCK** has removed his Office to Front Row, over the Book Store of C. C. **CLEAVES**. Memphis Daily Eagle, 1/6/1846. It is with regret the most sincere and profound that we announce this morning the death of Dr. W. J. Tuck, of this city, which occurred on yesterday morning. Dr. Tuck was a physician of considerable eminence....Dr. Tuck was for the past two years the Secretary of the Board of Health....His death was caused by a severe attack of cramp colic. Memphis Daily Avalanche, 6/15/1859. ....Drs. Walker, Shanks and Robards were appointed a committee to prepare an obituary, to be published in the Nashville Medical Journal, and the New Orleans Medical and Surgical Journal. Memphis Daily Avalanche, 6/17/1859. ....He was a native of Virginia, and died at the age of forty-three....The remains of the deceased were interred in the Elmwood Cemetery yesterday afternoon. Memphis Daily Appeal, 6/15/1859.

Married, On Monday evening, 31st ult., at the residence of Jas. **FLAHERTY**, on Union street, by Rev. Mr. Davis, Benjamin **TUCKER** to Mrs. Susan **VINING**—all of this city. Memphis Daily Appeal, 11/2/1859.

Died: On the 14th inst., Edwin Richard, son of H. J. and Mrs. A. E. **TUCKER**, aged one year and eight months. Memphis Whig, 10/15/1855.

Married, On the 2__th instant, by J. **WALDRAN**, Esq., J. R. **TUCKER** and Mrs. N. C. **STELL**, all of this city. Memphis Daily Appeal, 9/27/1856.

Married, On the 8th of December by Rev. John **WILSON**, of the Methodist Church, Mr. Jas. **TUCKER**, of Fayette county, Tenn., to Miss Laura, daughter of Thomas S. **CAROTHERS**, Esq., of Tipton county, Tenn. Memphis Daily Appeal, 12/24/1857.

Died, At her residence near this city, on Monday the 17th instant, in the 43d year of her age, Mrs. C. C. Tucker, daughter of the late Col. James **TREZEVANT**, and widow of Dr. W. W. **TUCKER**, for many years a citizen of this county. Memphis Weekly Appeal, 5/26/1858.

At a meeting of the Board of Health, Sunday, 12 M., January 7, the following deaths were reported in the last 24 hours....William **TUCKER**, aged 45 years, disease not reported. Jessee **KIRK**, aged 32 years, disease consumption. Memphis Eaily Eagle, 1/8/1849.

Capt. A. W. **TUFTS**, formerly proprietor of the United States Hotel, (now Worsham House) in this city, died at Jackson, La., on the 27th ult. Memphis Whig, 11/8/1855.

Married. In this city on the 26th inst. by Rev. H. S. **PORTER**, Mr. P. K. (or R.) **TUFTS** and Miss Love E. Mulford, oldest daughter of J. H. **MULFORD**, Esq., all of this city. Memphis Whig, 6/27/1855.

Died, In this city on the 9th inst., at the residence of Elbridge T____, Mary C. Tuley, youngest daughter of J. W. and P. H. **TULEY**, of New Albany, Indiana, and grand-daughter of Rev. Seth **WOODRUFF**, aged 18 years. New Albany and Louisville papers please copy. Memphis Daily Appeal, 2/10/1857.

Married: In Georgetown, Ohio, on the 20th ult., by the Rev. J. R. **GIBSON**, Mr. J. D. **TULFORD**, of Memphis, Tennessee, to Miss Mary Ann **KING**, of the former place. Memphis Daily Eagle, 8/5/1848.

Married, In this city on the 4th(?) inst., by Rev. Mr. Lowry, Mr. R. J. **TURESTINE** and Miss Julia E.(?) **POWELL**. Dyersburg Recorder copy. Memphis Daily Appeal, 11/5/1857.

Married, in this county, on Wednesday evening, T_____ J. **TURLEY**, to Miss Flora C. **BATTLE**. American Eagle, Fri., 5/5/1843.

Thos. J. **TURLEY**, Attorney at Law—Memphis, Tenn. Memphis Appeal, 12/13/1847. We are pained to record the death of one of our most estimable citizens and eminent lawyers, Thomas J. Turley, Esq., of the law firm of Wright & Turley, expired yesterday afternoon at 3 o'clock, after an illness of about ten days....Memphis Daily Appeal, 8/2/1854.

Died—In this city, on Sunday evening, 12th inst., William Payne, only son of the Hon. Wm. B. **TURLEY**...He was an only son! In him were centred his parents' devoted affections and his sisters' pure and holy love.....Memphis Enquirer, 7/23/1846. The community on yesterday was thrilled with surprise and sympathy by the sudden announcement of the death of the Hon. Wm. B. Turley, Judge of the Memphis Court of Common Law and Chancery. On Friday morning, stepping from the door of the hotel at Raleigh, he fell, and his cane, being broken, pierced his lift side near the region of the heart, inflicting a terrible wound of which he died on Tuesday night—Judge Turley was a native of Tennessee and throughout his career was an ornament of the bar and of the bench...Memphis Daily Appeal, Thurs., 5/29/1851. The remains of the Hon. Wm. B. Turley, were yesterday borne to the Winchester Cemetery, escorted by the Masonic Fraternity and a large procession of citizens. Funeral services were held at the residence of his brother, Thomas J. **TURLEY**, Esq...Memphis Daily Appeal, 5/30/1851. Married, In Jackson, Tenn., on Tuesday morning, 21st inst., by Rev. Mr. McCulloch, Mr. Alexander **HENDERSON**, to Miss Mariah, daughter of the late Hon. Wm. B. Turley. Memphis Appeal, 10/25/1851.

Married—At Holly Springs, Miss., on the evening of the 29th(?) ult., by the Rev. Daniel **BAKER**, Rufus K. **TURNAGE**, Esq., of Memphis, to Miss Emily Sneed Taylor, daughter of Dr. W. V. **TAYLOR**. Memphis Daily Appeal, 10/5/1847.

Married, On the 9th inst. by Rev. Peter **CULP**, Mr. W. G. **TURNAGE**, Esq., of Tipton county, to Miss Sallie, daughter of Henry **MELTON**, of Fayette county. Memphis Daily Appeal, 12/27/1857.

Married, On the 24th inst. at the residence of Jno. W. **HAWTHORNE**, by Rev. Dr. Gray, Mr. Chas. J. **TURNBULL**, of Nicaragua, to Miss Frank G., eldest daughter of J. A. **TORREY**, of California. Memphis Whig, 2/26/1856.

We learn with sorrow that on Saturday last Mrs. **TURNER**, wife of our esteemed fellow citizen of the Citizens' Bank, was suddenly stricken down by appoplexy at Huntsville, Ala., and expired in a few minutes. The numerous friends of herself and family in this city and elsewhere, will learn this sad intelligence with unfeigned sorrow. Memphis Daily Appeal, Tues., 6/22/1858.

Married, In Little Rock at the residence of Mr. Alexander **GEORGE**, on Tuesday evening the 20th inst., by Jas. D. **FITZGERALD**, Esq., Mr. Charles **TURNER** to Miss Madaline **KOUNTZ**, both of that city. Memphis Whig, 5/29/1856.

Married, on Wednesday, 19th of April, near Germantown, by the Rev. P. S. **GAYLE**, H. P. **TURNER**, M.D. to Miss Frances A. Morgan, daughter of John **MORGAN**, Esq. Daily Memphis Enquirer, 5/4/1848.

I offer for sale 500 acres of Land on the waters of Nonconnah Creek, immediately on the Hernando road, adjoining the lands of Wm. **PERSONS**, Wesley **BLACKMORE**, Geraldus **BUNTYN**, and the heirs of Richard J. **PERSONS**, about 4 miles from the town of Memphis ...The subscriber will remain in the county till about the 20th inst...James **TURNER**. American Eagle, 12/16/1847.

Died—On the 29th of July, at the residence of her grandfather, Col. Jesse **ALLIN**, Martha W. **TURNER**, aged eight years and four months. The Tri-Weekly Memphis Enquirer, 8/13/1846.

Died—On the 2d inst., in this city, after a protracted illness of one month, Mrs. Maria Turner, wife of Mr. W. D. **TURNER**, in the 34th year of her age. She has left a disconsolate husband, three affectionate children and a numerous circle of friends to mourn her death....Memphis Enquirer, and Jackson, Ten. paper will please notice. Weekly Appeal, 3/12/1847.

Died, In this city, on Saturday last, of congestive fever, Mr. William **TURNER**—aged about 50 years. Memphis Daily Appeal, Wed., 9/24/1851.

Married, In Austin, Miss., on the 13th instant, Mr. Wm. **TURNER** to Miss Dianitia A. **NEBLET**(?). Memphis Daily Appeal, 5/20/1858.

Administrator's Sale. I will sell on Monday, the 31st inst., at the late residence of James **TWEEDLE**, deceased, (on President Island,) about 60 head of cattle,....30 or 40 stock hogs, one wagon, one ox cart, all the farming utensils, household and kitchen furniture, etc....Felix M. **FLETCHER**, Admin'r. Memphis Daily Appeal, 1/24/1853.

Dr. John W. **TWEEDY**, Late of Courtland, Alabama, having removed to Memphis, offers his professional services to the public. Office No. 23 Front Row....Memphis Daily Appeal, 3/3/1857.

Died, in this city, on Tuesday, 24th inst., Charles W. **TWITCHELL**, of Pensacola, Fla., aged 23 years. Daily Enquirer, 8/26/1847.

On Wednesday evening last, one of Dr. Dockery's wagons return from Memphis with a white man dead in the wagon, who was identified by the name of John **TYLER**. He had formerly lived at Mr. Robinson's, 9 ½ miles Southeast of Memphis. It appears that John Tyler, on the morning of Wednesday last, at or near a shoe shop, close to the bayou, Southeast of Memphis, got into the wagon sick. He told the driver that he wanted to be hauled to Mr. Tipton's, on the Hernando Road. Some 10 miles from Memphis....he died, consequently he was brought to this place....He was decently interred. "Monterey," Hernando, Miss. Memphis Appeal, 9/19/1848.

Died, At the residence of Mr. A. A. **McKAY**, in this vicinity, on Saturday evening last, Mr. Wm. **TYSON**, of Madison county, Tenn. The Daily Eagle, Tues., 2/22/1848.

Died—In this county, on Tuesday morning last of bilious pleurisy, Jno. W. **TYUS**, in the 36th year of his age. The deceased was a native of Virginia – a kind father and husband, and one of the best of citizens.... Memphis Enquirer, Fri., 3/29/1839.

Married, On Tuesday, the 18th instant, at the residence of the bride's father, near Fisherville, by Dr. W. G. **LANCASTER**, Mr. Benjamin **UMPHRIES** to Miss Sarah E. **DUVAL**, all of Shelby county, Tenn. Memphis Daily Appeal, 7/27/1858.

Married. On the 12th inst. in Fisherville, Mr. Sylvester **UMPHRIES** to Miss Mary Ann, daughter of Joseph **DARBY**. Memphis Daily Appeal, 7/30/1854.

We regret to hear that G. W. **UNDERHILL**, Esq., of the firm of Martin, Underhill & Co., died at Louisville on Friday last, after a protracted illness. Mr. Underhill had long resided in Arkansas and was at the time of his death the member elect from Crittenden county to the State Legislature....Memphis Daily Appeal, 9/10/1854.

The friends and acquaintances of the late Geo. W. **UNDERHILL** are requested to attend his funeral from Winchester Cemetery at half-past 10 o'clock, this (Saturday) morning, December 16th. Services by Rev. D. C. **PAGE**. Memphis Daily Appeal, Sat., 12/16/1854.

The undersigned having taken out letters of Administration on the estates of Albert G. **UNDERWOOD** and A. B. **McGINNIS**, deceased, requests all persons having claims against said estates to present them.... A. **WRIGHT**, Joseph **LENOW**, Administrators. Memphis Daily Appeal, 11/8/1855.

We learn in a private note to the editor from the Postmaster at Helena, Ark....that an affray occurred in that place on Saturday last, between Jas. M. **CLEVELAND**, Esq., editor of the "Star," and Q. K. **UNDERWOOD**, Esq., editor of the "Shield." They fought with pistols and knives. Mr. Underwood was mortally, and Mr. Cleveland dangerously wounded....Memphis Whig, Tues., 9/25/1855.

Died, In Hopefield, Ark., on Thursday last, at 6(?) o'clock A.M., of pneumonia, Mrs. Clementine Underwood, wife of Mr. W. C. **UNDERWOOD**, aged nineteen years. The remains of the deceased were brought to this city and deposited in Winchester Cemetery yesterday. Memphis Daily Appeal, Sat., 2/20/1858.

We learn from the Helena (Ark.) Bulletin, that Mr. Washington L. **UNDERWOOD** formerly of Anderson county, in this State, committed suicide at Helena on the 20th inst., by shooting himself through the heart. He, with his wife, says the Bulletin, had taken dinner at his brother's Judge **UNDERWOOD**'s house, of which the deceased partook heartily. A few minutes afterwards, he stepped into another room, drew his pistol and shot himself through the heart...He was in the 34th year of his age. Pecuniary embarrassment and ill health are assigned as the causes of the fatal deed. Memphis Daily Appeal, 8/28/1851.

Died—On Wednesday, 30th ult. Hiram, son of William and Emeline **UNDERWOOD**—aged 16 months. Daily Enquirer, 7/2/1847. The Henrie House. The subscriber has this day leased the above building and is fitting up for the reception of boarders...Wm. Underwood. Daily Memphis Enquirer, 3/10/1848. New Livery Stable: Corner of Adams and Second Streets...Wm. Underwood. Memphis Daily Appeal, 10/1/1852.

Married, On the 25th ultimo by the Rev. Mr. Thompson, Major J. H. **UNTHANK**, of Hernando, Miss., to Miss Mary Bell, eldest daughter of Gen. R. P. **NEELY**, of Hardeman county, Tenn. Memphis Daily Appeal, 8/3/1855. J. H. Unthank, Esq.—The card of this gentleman, Attorney and Counsellor at Law, will be seen in to-day's paper. He was for some time a practitioner in Mississippi, and comes recommended as a clever man and a good lawyer. Memphis Daily Appeal, 12/13/1855.

Married: On the 19th inst., at Raleigh, by the Rev. T. J. **NEWBERRY**, Mr. J. H. **UPDEGRAFF**, to Miss Sarah T. **AKIN**, both of this city. Memphis Daily Eagle, 9/22/1848. (Author's note: spelled **AIKEN** in another newspaper.)

Married, On Tuesday 6th, at the residence of James **EPPES**, by Rev. Mr. Watson, Mr. James R. **UPSHAW** and Miss Bettie W. **EPPES**. Memphis Whig, 5/7/1856.

We are requested to announce Capt. M. T. B. **UPSHAW**, of Shelby County, as a candidate for Brigadier General, in place of Gen. T. C. **McMACKIN** Resigned. The Appeal, 10/27/1843.

Died, At his residence in Hardeman Co., Tenn., on the 14th Inst., William **USHER** Esq., in the 43 year of his age. Mr. Usher emigrated to this State from Richmond County, North Carolina in 1832, left behind him a large circle of relatives and friends and sought a home in the far West, among strangers...He has left a bereaved wife, four daughters and a wide circle of friends.... Memphis Daily Appeal, 3/30/1848.

The friends and acquaintances of Antonio and Mary **VACCARO** are respectfully invited to attend the funeral of their child Mary, This (Sunday) Afternoon, at 3 o'clock from their residence on Adams street. Memphis Daily Appeal, 9/20/1857.

All persons having claims against the estate of Wm. **VADEN**, deceased, will present them for payment....Wm. P. **VADEN**, Adm'r. of Wm. Vaden deceased. Memphis Daily Eagle, 4/12/1848.

We understand that Mr. Wm. P. **VADEN** is getting up a volunteer company at Germantown, and that some 30 men promptly enrolled their names.—They are marching to Green Bottom to-day, and thence to Col. Leake's, to give our gallant young men in those districts an opportunity to join them.....The Weekly American Eagle, 5/29/1846.

Married, on the 28th inst., by Elder B. W. **STONE**, Mr. Cornelius **VAN CAMPEN** to Miss Elizabeth **MEALY**, both of this city. Memphis Enquirer, 6/30/1848. Died, On Sunday, 20th instant, Luther M., infant son of Cornelius and Ellen Van Campen. Memphis Daily Eagle, 10/22/1850.

Died, In this city on the 12th inst., of consumption, at the Bybee House, Mr. Elisha **VANCE**, aged about 26 years. Memphis Daily Appeal, 1/13/1857.

Married—In Hernando, on Monday, the 16th inst., at the residence of S. A. **WELLS**, by Rev. J. W. **BATES**, Mr. John D. **VANCE**, of Panola, Miss., to Miss Ann L. **THORP**, of Memphis, Tenn. Memphis Daily Avalanche, 5/18/1859.

Died, On Saturday, the 17th inst., William Davis, infant son of M. D. and Margaret **VANCE**—aged one year seven months and fifteen days. Memphis Daily Appeal, 7/20/1858. Died, On Monday, July 18, Rutha Adaline, daughter of M. D. and Margaret A. Vance, aged four years, six months and eighteen days. Memphis Daily Appeal, 7/21/1859.

Married: At the residence of Abijah(?) Allen, on the 7th inst., by John M. **GRIGGS**, Esq., Mr. Robert L. **VAN METER** to Miss Eliza **ADAMS**, all of St. Francis county, Arkansas. Memphis Daily Eagle, 9/12/1848.

Death of Henry **VAN PELT**, Senior Editor of the Appeal. We are suddenly called upon to discharge the mournful duty of announcing the death of our associate and friend, Henry Van Pelt...He breathed his last on yesterday morning in the 54th year of his age...Henry Van Pelt was a native of Kentucky and he possessed in an eminent degree the warm, impulsive and generous nature which popular _____ has attached to the people of that State.—He began his editorial career there about thirty years ago, from

Kentucky he came to Tennessee and pursued his professional avocation for a number of years in Franklin and Nashville. On the 21st of April, 1841, he established the Appeal...Memphis Daily Appeal, 4/24/1851.

Married: On the 29th inst. at the Second Presbyterian Church by Rev. J. H. **GRAY**, Mr. J. W. **VAN WAGENER** and Miss Annie P. Wolf, eldest daughter of Tobias **WOLF**, Esq., all of this city. Memphis Whig, 10/30/1855. By a dispatch received last evening we learn that Mr. J. W. Van Wagenen, of our city, died at New Orleans yesterday of consumption. Mr. V.W. had but lately married and was on a tour with his young bride for the purpose of improving his health. His death must be a severe bereavement to his beautiful wife and kind relatives. His remains will be brought up on the *Niagara*. Memphis Daily Appeal, 1/26/1856. Died—In New Orleans, on the 25th day of January, Mr. J. W. Van Wagenen, son of Mrs. Eliza W. **WARD**, of this city, in the 28th year of his age...Memphis Daily Appeal, 2/13/1856.

George C. **VAN ZANDT**. Late Engineer and Architect of the Memphis Navy Yard, tenders his professional services to the citizens of Memphis and vicinity....Memphis Daily Appeal, 10/27/1854.

Married, At the residence of R. H. **BONNER**, in Marshall county, Miss., on Thursday, 6th inst., by Rev. S. **PARHAM**, Mr. A. J. **VAUGHAN**, jr., of Missouri, and Miss Martha J. **HARDAWAY**, of Marshall county. South Side (Va.) Democrat will please copy. Memphis Daily Appeal, 11/8/1856.

Died, at the residence of Mr. S. **FLEETWOOD**, in Shelby county, on Saturday the 1st inst. Mr. Richard C. **VAUGHAN** (only son of Mr. William **VAUGHAN**,) in the 29th year of his age, a native of Mecklenburg Co. Va. He left a wife and three children to lament his loss. Memphis Advocate, 12/8/1827.

The friends and acquaintances of Mr. W. K. **VAUGHAN** are invited to attend his funeral This Day, at half-past 3 o'clock P.M. from the residence of Mr. Davenport....Memphis Daily Appeal, 11/22/1857.

Died. In Germantown, Tenn. on the 3rd instant, Wm. **VAUGHAN**, aged about 90(?) years, having been a resident of the county for thirty years. Memphis Daily Appeal, 1/10/1855.

Married—On Monday the 12th inst., at the residence of Robert A. **MOTLEY**, Esq., in this county, Mr. James A. **VAUGHN**, late of Virginia, to Miss Elizabeth A. **MOTLEY**. Memphis Enquirer, 11/18/1848.

Married, At the residence of E. P. **STEWART**, Esq., on the 14th inst., by Rev. J. H. **GRAY**, D.D., Mr. L. **VEST** to Miss Sarah A. **WASSON**, all of this city. Memphis Whig, 2/16/1856.

Married, On Thursday evening, 13th inst., at the residence of Rev. C. G. **McPHERSON**, by Rev. C. A. **DAVIS**, Algenon S. **VIGUS**, of this city, and Miss Mary J. **PICKETT**, of Port Byron, New York. Memphis Daily Appeal, 10/15/1859.

Died—On the morning of the 5th inst. of billious fever, in Crittenden county, Arkansas, Miss Ann, daughter of Amos and Mary **VINCENT**, in the 13th year of her age. The Appeal, 7/7/1843.

Departed this life, in Covington, on the 19th day of October, of pulmonary consumption, Mrs. Lucy W. Vincent, consort of Wm. B. **VINCENT**, in the 25th year of her age. By this seeming affliction of Providence, four sweet little daughters are left motherless, and their father to mourn the loss of an affectionate wife and mother. Memphis Enquirer, 11/22/1839.

We learn that Mr. O. K. **VINING**, an Englishman, for some years a dry goods clerk in this city, but more recently a clerk at the Memphis and Charleston Railroad depot, disappeared unceremoniously to parts unknown, on Monday last, leaving behind him a wife uncared for. The desertion, as we understand, was wholly without cause, and has taken the friends and acquaintances of the parties completely by surprise, as Mr. Vining has generally borne a good character while in this city. Memphis Daily Appeal, Thurs., 11/22/1855.

Died, On the 4th December, 1852, in the 27th year of her age, after a short and severe illness, Jane Maria, the beloved and affectionate wife of Owen Keen **VINING**, of this city...Died, In this city, on the 10th

December, 1852, James William, infant son of Owen K. and the late Jane Maria Vining, aged 10 days. Memphis Daily Appeal, 12/16/1852.

The friends and acquaintances of R. **VIRGESON** and lady are respectfully invited to attend the funeral of their infant daughter, This Day, at 3 o'clock, P.M., at his residence on Madison street, near Third. Services by Rev. Dr. Bryan. Memphis Daily Appeal, 10/21/1857.

We regret to record the death of Robert **VIRGESON**, an old and well known citizen of this city, which occurred at his residence on Saturday morning last. His death was sudden and unexpected....Mr. Virgeson removed to this city from Pennsylvania, his native State, in 1847, and has been ever since that time extensively engaged in business as a house carpenter and builder. He died at the age of thirty-three years, leaving an interesting family....His funeral, which took place yesterday afternoon, was attended by the members of the Independent Order Odd Fellows, of which he was an accepted member. Memphis Daily Avalanche, Mon., 5/30/1859.

Married, On yesterday evening, at the residence of R. **PERRY**, Esq., by the Rev. Mr. Henderson, Hiram **VOLLENTINE**, Esq., Atty at Law, to Miss Eliza **JONES**, all of this city. Memphis Appeal, 4/17/1851.

Daniel **VOLMER**, son of Gen. Volmer, of this city, has disappeared in a most mysterious manner and his friends are considerably alarmed thereat. He has not been seen since Monday week. Fears are entertained that he has met with foul play. Memphis Daily Appeal, Thurs., 3/26/1857.

On the evening of the 2d inst., a difficulty occurred over a card table at Bender's coffee house on Main street, west of Washington, between two men named Wache and Bunger, and although high words passed between the two, nothing serious at the time resulted from it. A day or two afterwards, Mr. Wache visited the same establishment and (as we were informed yesterday) Bunger followed him in and stabbed him in the side...Mr. Wache, who is better known as Count **WACHE**, was taken to the hospital where, after lingering in great agony, he expired on Sunday evening. Count Wache was a native of Hungary but lived a long time in Prussia, from which country he fled on account of political opinions that conflicted with the monarchical form of government of that kingdom....the Grand Jury have found a _____ bill against Ferdinand **BUNGER** for murder. The police are in search of him. Memphis Daily Appeal, Tues., 11/18/1856.

Married, In Madison county, on the 9th instant, by Rev. Mr. Merriwether, B. B. **WADDELL**, Esq., of this city, and Miss Fannie L. **TARVER**, of Madison county. Memphis Daily Appeal, 6/12/1857.

Died, In this city on the 29th inst., Cornelius B. **WADE**, in the 18th year of his age. He was a native of Bridgeport, Conn. During the past year he was a resident of this city....His funeral will take place from the Second Presbyterian Church....Memphis Daily Appeal, 1/30/1859.

Married, on the 13th May, by the Rev. _____, Mr. J. **WADE** to Miss Frances C. **McKAUGHAN**. Weekly Appeal, 6/12/1846.

Married, On the 20th ult. at Salem, Miss., by Rev. H. G. **SPENCER**, Mr. B. W. J. **WAFFORD**, of Kickapoo, Anderson County, Texas, to Miss Fanny E. **AYRES**, of Tippah county, Miss. "Presbyterian Herald," Huntsville, Texas, please copy. Memphis Daily Appeal, 7/20/1855.

Married, In this city on Wednesday evening last, by the Rev. D. E. **BURNS**, Mr. J. H. **WAGGENER** to Miss Sallie A. **CHEEK**, all of Memphis. Memphis Daily Appeal, Fri., 10/24/1851.

Died, Near Raleigh, Tenn., on the 16th instant, Willie Karr, only son of Col. W. W. and Margaret S. **WAIR**, aged eight months and fifteen days. Memphis Daily Appeal, 5/21/1856.

Married. On the 1st by Rev. C. R. **HENRICKSON**, Mr. James S.(?) **WALDRAN** to Miss Malinda A., daughter of Mr. John **NEAL**, all of this city. Memphis Daily Appeal, 9/3/1853.

The friends and acquaintances of W. B. and S. A. **WALDRAN** are requested to attend the Funeral of their infant son, this morning...from the Cumberland Presbyterian Church...Memphis Daily Appeal, 9/30/1851. The friends and acquaintances of Wm. B. and S. A. Waldran are invited to attend the funeral of their daughter Julia from their residence This Evening....Memphis Daily Appeal, 11/2/1859.

Married, on the 22d inst. the Rev. Wesley **WALK**, to Mrs. Sarah **HARGES**, both of Fayette County, Ten. Memphis Enquirer, 4/1/1837.

Married, On Thursday evening, the 14th inst., by Rev. A. M. **BRYAN**, Mr. Alex C. **WALKER** to Miss Allie J. Cayce, daughter of M. C. **CAYCE**, Esq., all of Memphis. Memphis Daily Appeal, 10/16/1858.

Married, At Monticello, Carrol Parish, La., on Tuesday, the 8th inst., by Rev. J. W. **MOSELEY**, Mr. Andrew G. **WALKER**, of Columbia, Tenn., and Miss Susan W., eldest daughter of Hon. Thos. W. **WATTS**. Memphis Daily Appeal, 4/15/1856.

Married, In the town of Macon, Tenn., by Rev. C. **CONNER**, Dr. Edmond J. **WALKER** to Miss Sallie K. **REID**, all of that town. Memphis Weekly Appeal, 12/8/1858.

Married, On Monday evening, the 22nd inst., by the Rev. G. W. **COONS**, H. C. **WALKER**, Esq., of this city, to Miss Lizzie A. Trigg, daughter of John **TRIGG**, Esq., if this vicinity. Memphis Eagle & Enquirer, 3/24/1852.

Married, Last Friday, by Rev. M. **GRAY**, Henry C. **WALKER**, Esq., Cashier of the Union Bank of Tenn., to Miss Margaret B., daughter of John **TRIGG**, Esq., all of this city. American Eagle, 6/19/1846. Died— at the residence of her father, John Trigg, Esq., in this vicinity, on the 13th inst., Margaret B. Walker, wife of Henry C. Walker, Esq...As a child, a wife, a sister, and a friend, she had won the affections of all who surrounded her....The subject of this notice was born January 7th, 1828, and was united in marriage to Henry C. Walker, Esq., June 10th, 1846, so that for nearly 3 years, she rendered bright and happy the existence of her devoted husband ..Weekly Memphis Eagle, 5/17/1849.

Yesterday afternoon Knox, the second son of our friend J. Knox **WALKER**, Esq., was thrown from his horse, and his foot catching in the stirrup, he was dragged for some distance, his head on the ground, until he was so much bruised and mangled, as to cause his immediate death. He was about ten or twelve years of age....Memphis Daily Appeal, 8/2/1857. Died, Gideon Pillow Walker, aged two years and six months, youngest child of Mr. and Mrs. J. Knox Walker. Funeral services from the residence of J. Knox Walker, on Central avenue, To-Day. Memphis Daily Appeal, 10/27/1859.

Died: On Saturday evening, Melville, son of Dr. J. M. **WALKER**. The friends of the family are invited to attend the funeral, at 10 ½ o'clock this morning, from the residence of the family in South Memphis. Services by Rev. J. H. **GRAY**. Memphis Daily Eagle, Monday, 11/13/1848. Died, on the 2d inst., at the residence of Dr. J. M. Walker, South Memphis, after an illness of eighteen days duration, Mary M., youngest daughter of Dr. J. M. and Mary A. Walker, aged 4 years and 2 months. Memphis Appeal, 9/7/1852.

Married, On the morning of the 6th instant by Rev. Thos. P. **STONE**, at the residence of J. M. **PREWIT**, Esq., Mr. Jno. A. **WALKER**, of DeSoto county, Miss., and Miss Callie Prewit, of Drew county, Ark. Memphis Daily Appeal, 8/12/1856.

Married, At Charlottsville, Va., on the 27th ult., by Rev. D. Davis, Mr. Marsh **WALKER**, of the city of Memphis, and Miss Celia **GARTH**, of the former place. Our young friend has arrived at home with his beautiful and accomplished Virginia bride....Memphis Daily Appeal, 12/9/1856.

Departed this life on Saturday night last, the 13th inst., Mrs. Mary **WALKER**, Sen'r., in the 59th year of her age. The deceased was a native of Buckingham county, Virginia, but for many years a resident of this city. The demise of this amiable lady and affectionate mother seems to demand something more than a mere announcement....The subject of this brief memoir embraced a "saving faith" in early life and united with the Protestant E. Church.....Daily Enquirer, 2/17/1847.

Married—At Brook Hall, by Rev. Mr. Glenn, on the evening of the 28th May, Mr. Robert L. **WALKER**, merchant, of the firm of Walker & Greer of this city, to Miss Sarah Ann, daughter of Col. Wm. **BYARS**, of Washington Co., Va. The Appeal, 6/14/1844.

Married. In the vicinity of Cuba, in this county, on Saturday evening, the 18th inst., by Henry P. **THOMPSON**, Esq., Mr. Thomas **WALKER**, aged nineteen years, to Mrs. Katherine **PLUMMER**, aged about thirty-seven years, consort of Marcus **PLUMMER**, dec'd., all of this county. Memphis Eagle & Enquirer, 6/24/1853.

Thomas **WALKER**, of Hernando, Miss., was found dead on Thursday evening, 1st inst., in that place in the stable of Mr. J. **NEWBERRY**. Cause—intemperance. Memphis Eagle & Enquirer, Wed., 3/9/1853.

Died, On the 22nd ult., at his residence near Holly Springs, Miss., Maj. Robt. H. **WALL**, in the 57th year of his age. Memphis Daily Appeal, 5/8/1859.

Married, by the Rev. Mr. Chase, on Wednesday evening 7th inst., A. **WALLACE**, Esq., to Miss Mary **DENNIS**, all of this city. Daily Enquirer, 7/9/1847.

The friends and acquaintances of Mr. and Mrs. A. **WALLACE** are respectfully invited to attend the funeral of their infant son this day....from their residence on Union street. Memphis Daily Appeal, 5/5/1859.

Married, On Tuesday, May 3d, near Horn Lake, at the residence of the bride's brother, by Rev. Mr. **MANNING**, Mr. J. G. **WALLACE** to Miss Sallie W. **MANNING**, all of Mississippi. Memphis Daily Appeal, 5/6/1859.

Died. At the residence of her husband, Panola county, Mississippi on the 3rd of March, Mrs. Eliza Wallace, consort of Dr. John P. **WALLACE**—aged about 29 years. The deceased was the daughter of the late Major James **RUFFIN**, recently of Hardeman county in this State and originally of Virginia....she was adorned with all those graces which make up the character of a dutiful daughter, a loving mother, and an affectionate wife and sister....Memphis Eagle & Enquirer, 3/6/1853.

Married, On the 1st inst., by the Rev. Geo. W. **COONS**, Mr. Rhea **WALLACE** to Miss Sarah **HICKS**, all of this city. Memphis Appeal, 3/4/1848.

Coroner Waldran held an inquest yesterday over the body of William **WALLACE**, found dead in a wagon near the ice house in the southern part of the city. The jury returned a verdict that he came to his death by the hands of Providence. He was about 35 years of age and had been in bad health for some time. Memphis Eagle & Enquirer, 5/13/1852.

Died. On the morning of the 25th ult. at the residence of his father in Panola county, Miss., William C. **WALLACE**, aged 21 years and 7 months....Memphis Daily Appeal, 6/9/1854.

The members of the Hibernian Relief Society and the friends and acquaintances of John **WALSH** are invited to attend his funeral, from his residence, corner of Main and Market streets, on Sunday morning...Services at the Catholic Church. Memphis Daily Appeal, Sat., 5/29/1852.

Coroner Horne yesterday held an inquest over the body of John J. **WALSH**, who died in jail....The crime for which he has been compelled to pine in a dungeon and herd among outcasts was *insanity*!....He was relieved by death from his sufferings yesterday....Memphis Daily Appeal, 7/14/1858.

Married, By Rev. A. H. **THOMAS**, at the residence of Col. Thomas(?), Mr. James R. **WALT**, of the firm of Walt & Johnson, Memphis, to Miss Mary L. **BATEMAN**, of Tipton county, Tenn., Memphis Daily Appeal, 12/13/1859.

The friends and acquaintances of Rufus P. and Jane **WALT** are requested to attend the funeral of their infant daughter, Anna, This (Saturday) Morning, May 30th, at 10 o'clock, from the residence of H. B. **JOINER**, on Poplar street. Services by Rev. J. N. **TEMPLE**. Memphis Daily Appeal, 5/30/1857.

Married. At the residence of Col. L. J. **DUPREE**, on Thursday, the 16th inst., by Rev. D. C. **PAGE**, Mr. Edward C. **WALTHAL**, of Coffeeville, Miss., to Miss Sophie A. **BRIDGERS** of Holly Springs. Memphis Daily Appeal, 8/17/1855. Died, on Monday evening, November 26th at Coffeeville, Mississippi, Sophie A., wife of Edward C. Walthall, Esq....Memphis Daily Appeal, 12/2/1855.

Married, On Thursday evening, September 23d, at the residence of her father, by the Rev. Joseph E. **DOUGLASS**, Mr. James C. **WALTON**, of Fayette county, Ten., to Miss Martha A. E., daughter of Mr. John C. **McGEHE**, of DeSoto county, Miss. Memphis Appeal, 10/16/1851.

Died—Of congestive fever, on Saturday the 23d inst., at 8 o'clock P.M., Mrs. Ann Ward, consort of Col. Edward **WARD** of Shelby county. She was a native of Amelia County, Va., and at the time of her death was in the 61st year of her age; during the last 45 of which, she was the wife of the bereaved and afflicted husband.....For twenty years she was an exemplary member of the Presbyterian Church....Memphis Enquirer, 9/30/1837. Plantation For Sale – New Life, the residence of the late Col. Edward Ward, of Shelby county, Tennessee, lying on the waters of Big Creek, thirteen miles south of Randolph, and 23 north-east of Memphis, containing about 1000 acres of land, 400 of which are cleared and under good fence. The premises contain a good dwelling-house and necessary out-buildings for a large family, a gin-house, and mill ...Memphis Enquirer, 7/21/1838.

Died, In this city yesterday morning....Horace R. **WARD**, Jr., after an illness of two weeks, aged 22 years 8 months and 3 days. The friends and acquaintances of the family are respectfully invited to attend the funeral from the family residence, corner of Shelby and Vance streets....this morning. Memphis Daily Appeal, 8/25/1859.

Married, In this city on Tuesday evening, 12th inst., by Rev. M. **WARE**, Mr. Jacob C. **WARD** and Miss Pauline M., daughter of Littleton **HENDERSON**, all of this city. Memphis Daily Appeal, 2/15/1856.

....Died, at the residence of his father one mile south of Ripley, Tenn., on the 29[th](?) December, 1854, John M. Wardlow, son of Joseph and Mary **WARDLOW**, in the 20th year of his age.... Christian Advocate please copy. Memphis Daily Appeal, 1/12/1855.

Died, In Wesley, Mrs. Martha Ware, consort of Wm. W. **WARE**, aged 23 (?) years. American Eagle, 12/9/1847.

Notice is hereby given that the undersigned has taken out letters of administration upon the estate of Isaac H. **WAREHAM**, deceased ....Geo. **DIXON**, Adm'r. Memphis Daily Appeal, 6/8/1854.

Married, In this city on the evening of the 10th inst., at __ o'clock, by Rt. Rev. James H. **OTEY**, Bishop of Tennessee, Mr. Noah D. **BELK**(?), of Keokuk, Iowa, to Miss Harriet G., eldest daughter of Mr. and Mrs. W. P. **WARFIELD**, of this city. Memphis Daily Appeal, 11/11/1857.

Married, Near Germantown, on Thursday the 11th inst. by Rev. J. H. **GRAY**, Mr. John G. **WARNER** to Miss A. M. **McIVER**. Weekly Appeal, 9/19/1845.

Married, On the 21st of September, at the residence of her mother, by the Rev. J. M. **ROGERS**, of Shelby county, Ten., Mr. Wm. M. **WARNER**, Jr., of this county, to Miss Ilia A. **BLOCKER**, of DeSoto county, Miss. New Orleans Picayune please copy. Memphis Appeal, 10/12/1852.

Married, On the 9th instant by Rev. J. T. C. **COLLINS**, Miss Matilda, daughter of Wm. **WALKER**, Esq., of this city, to Mr. Archibald **WARREN**, of Wheeling, Va. Memphis Daily Appeal, 6/11/1858.

Married, On the 4th inst. by the Rev. Doctor **BASKERVILL**, Mr. Asberry **WARREN**, of Fayette co. to Miss Eliza A., daughter of J. J. **WILLIAMS**, Esq., of Hardeman county, Tenn. Memphis Appeal, 8/10/1847.

Married. At the residence of Maj. E. P. **McNEAL**, in Bolivar, Tenn., on the 7th of April by the Rev. Mr. **JANSEN**, Dr. Daniel E. **WARREN**, of Fayette county, Tenn., to Miss Sallie A., only daughter of the late Willis **WILLIAMS**, of Clarksville, Tenn. Memphis Eagle & Enquirer, 4/12/1853.

To Undertakers—Sealed proposals will be received by the undersigned until 1st April next, for furnishing materials and building a Methodist Church on Jas. **WARREN**'s land, 5 miles east of Raleigh...For a more particular description of said house, persons wishing to bid, will call on James Warren. Joseph **LOCKE**, J. N. **MASSEY**, Thos. **HILL**, James Warren, Commissioners. Memphis Enquirer, 3/21/1836.

Married—On the 19th inst., by the Rev. A. **DAVIDSON**, Mr. Samuel H. **WARREN**, of Fayette county, to Miss Emily Ann **KIMBROUGH**, of Shelby. Memphis Enquirer, 11/29/1839.

Married, On the 19th inst., by John T. **MACON**, Esq., Mr. Wm. T. **WARREN**, to Miss Emeline G. Crowder, daughter of Wm. B. **CROWDER**, Esq., all of Hardeman co., Tenn. Memphis Eagle, 11/27/1850.

Married, At the Central House in this city, on Tuesday evening, the 1st inst., by Rev. J. H. **GRAY**, Dr. **WARRINGTON**, of Pontotoc, Miss., to Miss Emma **GLASS**, of this place. Memphis Daily Appeal, 1/3/1856.

Hall of Morning Sun Lodge, No. 144, A.D. May 23, 1859. At a called communication of the Morning Sun Lodge, the following resolutions were adopted respecting the death of Wm. **WASH**, Esq.: Whereas The All-wise and Supreme Architect of the Universe has seen it fit to remove from time to eternity our much esteemed brother, Wm. Wash, who was an old citizen of the comm'y, and one of the founders of our Lodge, on the 22d inst....in the 43d year of his age....We were pained yesterday to hear of the death of our old friend, Esq. Wm. Wash, of Morning Sun, and a member of the firm of Wash & Baker, in this city.... Memphis Daily Appeal, 5/24/1859.

Died—In Wesley, on the 9th inst., Henry C. **WATKINS**, aged 23 years. He died in the arms of Jesus. Memphis Enquirer, 8/19/1837.

The Mutual Assurance and Trust Company of Memphis. Joseph S. **WATKINS**, President, J. J. **FINLEY**, Secretary. Memphis Enquirer, 12/1/1846.

Attention Volunteers!! Under the late requisition of the Governor of Tennessee, calling for two Regiments of Volunteers from the State, to serve for five years or during the war...the undersigned proposes to raise a company in the city of Memphis and its vicinity...Lucien M. **WATKINS**. Memphis, September 19, 1847. Memphis Daily Appeal.

Died at Somerville, on the 15th, of Apoplexy, Mr. Thomas **WATKINS**, senior. Memphis Enquirer, 1/31/1840.

Yesterday Mr. Wm. **WATKINS**, a bricklayer of this city, fell from the walls of the Odd Fellows' Hall, now in progress of construction, to the ground, a distance of about 70 feet. At dark yesterday evening he was still living, and hopes were entertained that he would survive. Weekly Memphis Eagle, 11/1/1849.

Married, In this city on Tuesday last, by Rev. Mr. Drane, A. J. **WATSON**, of Brownsville, Tenn., to Miss Harriet S. **BAUGH**, of this city. Memphis Daily Appeal, Thurs., 10/6/1859.

Mr. Thos. H. **WILLIAMS** and Mr. David **WATSON** were instantly killed near Hickory Wythe, Fayette co., on Wednesday. They were engaged repairing the road, and when the cloud came over they retired to a small hickory bush as a temporary shelter from the rain.—A large tree some distance off was struck by the electric fluid, and literally torn to pieces. A portion of the electricity appears to have descended upon the hickory, which was very little damaged, although its violence was so great as to kill two men instantly and badly injure seven or eight others. American Eagle, Thurs., 6/24/1847.

Died, of bilious cholic, at her residence in Williamson county, Tenn., on the 31st ultimo, Mrs. Jane Watson, widow of the late Capt. John **WATSON**, of that county and mother of Mrs. David M. **CURRIN**, of this city. She was in the 67th year of her age. Richmond Enquirer please copy. Memphis Daily Appeal, 8/2/1855.

Botanic Physician. Dr. K. P. **WATSON** having located permanently in Memphis, tenders his professional services to the public...Daily Enquirer, 2/6/1847. Married—On the 13th inst., by the Rev. Mr. Jones, Dr. K. P. Watson, of this city, to Miss Nannie A. **WEAVER**, of Sommerville, Tenn...Daily Memphis Enquirer, 9/15/1849. We had the pleasure yesterday of welcoming home our former townsman, Dr. K. P. Watson. The Dr. has been spending some two or three years in the practice of his profession in California, but, as will be seen from his card, has returned to take up his abode again in Memphis....Memphis Daily Appeal, 10/13/1855.

Attention is called to the Law Card of S. Y. **WATSON**, Esq., who has recently removed to this city, having graduated at the Law School at Lebanon....Memphis Daily Appeal, 10/27/1854.

Married—In this county, on Thursday, 26th ult., by the Rev. Sam'l **WATSON**, Mr. George M. **WATSON**, of Union co., Arkansas, to Miss Frances C. **DUKE**. Weekly Memphis Eagle, 5/10/1849.

Died, In this vicinity on yesterday morning, Samuel, youngest son of Rev. S. and Mary A. **WATSON**, aged two years and one month. Memphis Weekly Appeal, 5/26/1858.

Married, On Wednesday morning, 24th inst., by Rev. Saml. **WATSON**, at the residence of Dr. K. P. **WATSON**, in this city, Dr. J. A. **WATSON**, of Arkansas, to Miss L. A. E. **BROOKS**. Memphis Eagle & Enquirer, 3/27/1852.

Married, On Wednesday 29th ult. by Rev. S. G. **STARKS**, Mr. Wm. H. **WATSON**, (of the firm of Watson & Williams) to Miss Virginia I. **ABERNATHY**, both of this city. Weekly Appeal, 11/7/1845. Died. At Elysian Fields, Harrison co., Texas, Virginia, wife of Wm. H. Watson, formerly of this city. Memphis Daily Appeal, 4/21/1855.

Died, In this city, on Tuesday morning the 17th inst., Mr. Wm. **WAUHOP**, late of Halifax county, Va. The deceased was extensively known in his native State as a gentleman of important business relations and of high social position...Memphis Daily Eagle, 9/20/1850.

Dr. C. S. **SWAN**, formerly of this city, and his partner, Dr. C. C. **WEBB**, who was the son of G. W. **WEBB**, and was born and raised in Bledsoe county, Tenn., were on Sunday the 22nd inst., at West Point, White county, Arkansas, in their professional capacity as dentists. They were staying at the house of Col. Rodgers, where they were called upon by Isaac **FELSENTHRALL**, a German residing at Searcy, who, we are informed, had levied upon their horses for a debt he claimed was due him. A dispute arose between him and Dr. Webb; the lie was given, and a fight took place. Dr. Webb had a walking cane, his opponent a pistol, with which he shot him in the abdomen. Dr. Birney fetched a loaded gun and offered it to Webb. The latter said he was a dead man and could not shoot, but he implored Dr. Birney to shoot for him. The Doctor did so, hit Felsenthrall in the head, and he fell dead. Dr. Webb soon afterward expired....Memphis Daily Appeal, 11/28/1857.

Married, On the 2nd inst., in the town of Macon, Tennessee, by S. B. **DOUGAN**, Esq., Mr. Howell **WEBB** to Mrs. Temperance **KIZER**. Memphis Daily Appeal, 7/7/1857.

Died—On Saturday morning, 27th instant, about 2 o'clock, A.M. after an illness of 48 hours, with hemorrhage of the lungs, Mr. Oran **WEBB**, partner in the house of Henry & Webb, of this place, and recently from Louisville. Mr. Webb had been a resident of Memphis about 4 months .....He leaves an interesting and sorrowing wife, with a tender child. His distant relatives may be consoled to know that every attention which skill or friendship could suggest was bestowed upon him in his last illness.....His wife left here on Sunday for Louisville, Ky., with the corpse, to bury among her relatives in that city her husband and her grief. The Appeal, 2/2/1844.

Married, On the 1st inst., at Lagrange, Ten., by the Rev. Rob't V. **TAYLOR**, Mr. Rob't C. **WEBB** to Miss Lizzie E. **DORCH**. Memphis Appeal, 5/6/1851.

Married, On the 27th inst., Mr. Thos. **WEBB**, merchant of Middleburg, Tenn., to Miss Emma, daughter of Rev. Milton N. **HAMER**. Memphis Weekly Appeal, 6/2/1858.

Died—Of dropsy of the brain on Tuesday 29th Oct., Adelia Augusta, daughter of William and Harriet **WEBB**, recently of Cincinnati, Ohio, aged 4 years and 9 months. Memphis Enquirer, 11/1/1839.

Married, At Dublin, Shelby county, Tenn., October 14th by Dr. Wm. G. **LANCASTER**, E. B. **WEBBER** to Miss Sarah Ann **EDMONDSON**, all of Shelby county. Memphis Daily Appeal, 10/23/1855.

Married. On the 19th inst. by Rev. H. S. **PORTER**, Mr. John L. **WEED** and Miss Maria A. **IAMS**—all of Memphis. Memphis Appeal, 4/21/1854.

At a regular meeting of Sommerville Lodge No. 24, I.O.O.F., the following resolutions were passed: *Resolved*, That in the death of our worthy brother George T. **WEIGNWRIGHT**, who died at his residence in Fayette county, Tenn., on the 5th of February, '51, we think society has sustained a loss of one of its most excellent and useful citizens...Memphis Daily Appeal, 3/1/1851.

Married, In Baltimore, on the 21st of January last, Andrew **WEIR**, of the U.S.Navy, to Miss Mary R. **ALLEN**, of Norfolk, Virginia. The Daily Eagle, 2/17/1848.

Died. Saturday, July 5th, 1856, Mrs. Susan M. Weir, aged 25 years, wife of Geo. F. **WEIR**, Esq., formerly of Galveston, Texas...The ties that bound her to this earth—to a devoted husband and to her little children, have been rudely sundered...Memphis Whig, 7/9/1856. The friends and acquaintances of Mr. George F. Weir are invited to attend the funeral of his late wife, Mrs. Susan M. Weir, from his residence on the corner of Union and Desoto streets, this Sunday evening at 4 o'clock. Funeral services by Father _____. Memphis Daily Appeal, 7/6/1856. Died, On Saturday the 5th instant, Mrs. Susan M., wife of George F. Weir...The tender ties that bound her to a devoted husband and an aged mother....Memphis Daily Appeal, 7/11/1856.

Married—On Tuesday, March 19th by the Rev. Mr. Toncray, Mr. Caswell **WELCH** to Mrs. Elizabeth **FINDLEY** all of this vicinity. The Appeal, 3/29/1844.

Married, At 7 o'clock, Tuesday morning, October 5th, in this city, at the residence of the bride's mother, by Rev. W. H. **LEIGH**, our highly esteemed and talented young friend, M. D. **WELCH**, Esq., Clerk of the Supreme Court at Jackson, in this State, to Miss Sallie E. Harris, eldest daughter of the lamented William R. **HARRIS**, late of the Supreme Bench of Tennessee.... Jackson papers please copy. Memphis Daily Appeal, 10/7/1858.

Married, by the Rev. ____ Clarkson, on the 20th inst. Mr. Thos. **WELCH** to Mrs. Martha **McCLOSKY**, all of this city. Daily Memphis Enquirer, 1/23/1848.

Died, On Tuesday the 13th instant, at residence in Chicot county, Ark., Mrs. H. C. Wellborn, wife of A. C. **WELLBORN**, formerly a resident of Shelby county, Tenn. Mrs. Wellborn was in her 25th year. She leaves a husband and four small children to the bitterest grief. The Memphis and Huntsville (Ala.) papers will please copy. Memphis Daily Appeal, 7/25/1858.

Departed this life on the 10th instant, at Covington, Tenn. Mr. Cyrus **WELLER**, late editor of the Arkansas Times & Advocate, aged twenty-five years and ten months. He was a worthy member of the Presbyterian Church. He has left an affectionate wife and one son....The Appeal, 12/27/1844.

Died, at the Gayoso House, in this city, on Tuesday, the 14th inst., Mr. Francis A. **WELLS**, aged 40 years, a native of Colchester, Conn., but for many years a steamboat pilot on the Mississippi River....Though far from his family and kindred, he received in his last days all the kindness and attention that could be bestowed by sumpathising friends. Connecticut papers please notice. Daily Enquirer, 9/16/1847.

Died, At Well's Station, Shelby county, on Monday, the 17th instant, William Swan, son of Samuel A. and Mary T. **WELLS**, aged 12 days. Memphis Daily Appeal, 5/20/1858.

Married, In Rahway, New Jersey, on the 11th inst. by Rev. _._. Sheddam(?), Mr. W. E. **WELLS**, of this city, to Miss Annie P., eldest daughter of Jacob L. **WOODRUFF**, of the former place. Memphis Daily Appeal, 8/26/1857.

Wells & Wray, Dealers British, French, India and American Dry Goods...2d door north of Washington st. Front Row. Wm. S. **WELLS**, J. Rich. **WRAY**. Daily Enquirer, 11/4/1847.

Died. On Wednesday afternoon last of congestive chills, Mrs. Martha Welsh, aged 40 years, consort of Mr. Thomas **WELSH**, of this vicinity. The deceased had been a resident of Memphis for the last 16 or 17 years....Memphis Eagle & Enquirer, Fri., 5/20/1853.

Married, In Brownsville, on the 16th inst. by Rev. Mr. Collins, Mr. J. P. **WENDEL**, Professor of Music in the Brownsville Female Seminary, to Miss Julia B. Bradford, daughter of the late Carroll **BRADFORD**. Memphis Daily Appeal, 7/17/1857.

Died—At Fort Pickering, on the 1st instant, Mr. William **WENDELL**, aged 53 years. He was greatly afflicted with Cancer, and after trying the most approved remedies, from the medical faculty, about Nashville, where he has resided for many years, he sought the aid and skill of Doctor Gilbert, but so far had the disease advanced, that his case was considered hopeless by that gentleman from the date of his arrival here, about four months ago...The Appeal, 9/15/1843.

A melancholy and unusual occurrence came to light yesterday, which, as near as can at present be ascertained, confirms the self-destruction of a German gentleman who had lately came to our city. The gentleman, Dr. Randolph **WENDEROTH**, arrived here on the 17th of December last from Cincinnati, for the purpose of establishing a German paper. He had been engaged as an editor of a German periodical at Indianapolis, Indiana...On last Tuesday, a week ago yesterday, he was noticed to appear very melancholy and recklessly inclined, and left his boarding place, the "Germania House," and was seen but once afterwards in the vicinity of Fort Pickering. On yesterday, finding that Dr. Wenderoth did not return and being somewhat fearful as to his fate, his trunk was broken open, where a letter was found addressed to Mr. H. **KATTMANN**. It stated that before that letter was read he should have committed his own destruction, but that he could not, for many reasons, make known the cause for so rash an act. He only expressed the wish that his brother in Indiana might be informed of his death. His fate has not yet been learned, but it is of course to be presumed that he has either deceived others very much or himself, as no tidings of him can be gathered. Memphis Daily Appeal, Wed., 2/6/1856.

Married, on the 28th of March, by the Rev. J. **VINCENT**, Mr. A. **WESSON** to Mrs. Susan H. **THOMSON**, all of the County of Shelby and State of Tenn. Daily Enquirer, 4/11/1847.

Coroner Waldran held an inquest on the body of Mrs. Mary **WEST** yesterday, and the jury rendered a verdict that she came to her death by destitution and disease. It had been rumored about that she died from the effects of blows received from her husband, but from the testimony of Dr. Porter and others, it was evident that this rumor was incorrect. Memphis Eagle & Enquirer, 6/9/1852.

Married. On Thursday, the 24th inst., at Madrid Bend, Obion county, Tenn., by Rev. M. **ROBERTS**, Dr. E. **WESTBROOK** and Miss Jinnie R. **MERRIWETHER**. Memphis Whig, 5/30/1855.

I offer for sale the tract of land on which I now reside, for fifteen dollars per acre, three hundred cleared, one hundred and forty-seven timbered, lying eight miles above Gallagher and two miles of Shelby

Depot....Also 620 acres adjoining the said tract....S. T. **WESTBROOK**. Memphis Daily Appeal, 11/23/1856.

Taken up by Benjamin **WESTE**, living 13 miles east of Raleigh, on the Lagrange road, one bay mare...Memphis Enquirer, 1/14/1837.

The announcement was made by telegraph yesterday morning that a gentleman named W. H. **WESTON** had been killed by Capt. Jackson in Hopkinsville, Ky. The deceased was a young lawyer of fine promise, and had taken up his residence in this city but a few months ago. He had but recently been united in marriage with a daughter of Hon. W. L. **UNDERWOOD**, of Kentucky. Memphis Daily Appeal, 9/4/1859. Correction—we gave, on Saturday last, the particulars of the shooting affray between Capt. Jas. Jackson, of Christian county, Ky., and Mr. W. H. Weston, of this city. We have since learned that the gentleman who received the fatal shot was not Mr. W. H. Weston, Jr., but the father of that gentleman, whose name is identical with that of his son. The younger Weston was also on a visit to Kentucky at the time, but was not present at the scene of the affray. Memphis Daily Appeal, 9/6/1859.

At a meeting of the citizens of Memphis, held at Johnson's Hotel for the purpose of paying a tribute of respect to the memory of their lamented fellow citizen, Hugh **WHEATLEY**,--....Whereas, it has been the will of Divine Providence to call from among us our highly esteemed friend and fellow townsman, Dr. Hugh Wheatley, who, less than four days ago was enjoying all the blessings of health....Memphis Enquirer, 2/18/1837. The subscriber having qualified as administrator of the estate of the late Dr. Hugh Wheatley, hereby notifies all persons having claims against said estate ...Seth **WHEATLEY**. Memphis Enquirer, 3/11/1837.

Married, On Wednesday, February 27th at the residence of Mrs. R. **CROOK**, of Marshall county, Miss., by William **MOFFAT**, Esq., Captain F. **WHEATLEY**, of Fayette county, Tenn., and Miss Rachel **KOONCE**, of Marshall county. Memphis Daily Appeal, 3/2/1856.

Married—On the 16th inst., by the Rev. Dr. Edgar, Seth **WHEATLEY**, Esq. Attorney at Law, of Memphis, to Miss Mary, daughter of the Hon. William A. **COOK** of this city—Nashville Whig. Memphis Enquirer, 4/26/1839. Died, In this city, on the 23d December, Mrs. Mary C. Wheatley, consort of Seth Wheatley, Esq. Her mother had been consigned to her grave scarce a week, when the daughter's spirit was called to accompany her...and a young and beloved niece preceded her but a few days...Memphis Daily Eagle, 1/3/1850. At a meeting of the members of the Memphis Bar, convened at the office of the Clerk and Master of the Chancery Court of the city of Memphis, on Monday morning the 7th inst., to pay the last tribute of respect to the memory of their deceased brother Seth Wheatley....Memphis Daily Appeal, 6/8/1858.

Married, On Thursday evening, the 25th instant, by Rev. George W. **COONS**, at the residence of Col. F. M. **FLETCHER**, in this vicinity, W. W. **WHEATLEY**, Esq., of this city, to Miss Marian **CARTER**, from Kentucky. Memphis Daily Eagle, 4/27/1850.

Died, In this city, on Saturday evening last, of Typhoid Fever, Jas. L. **WHEATLY**, Esq., a young and promising member of the Memphis Bar. Memphis Eagle & Enquirer, 4/20/1852. On Tuesday morning the 20th inst., the members of the Memphis Bar, convened...to pay the proper tribute of respect to the memory of their deceased professional brother, James L. Wheatley...He was a native of Virginia. A few years since he removed to this city...He died on the 17th inst., in the 27th year of his age...Memphis Eagle & Enquirer, 4/22/1852.

Married—On Thursday the 3d of October, at the residence of Seth **WHEATLY**, Esq., by Rev. P. W. **ALSTON**, Col. Miles **CAREY**, of De Soto county, Miss., to Miss Susan C. **WHEATLY**, of Memphis. Memphis Enquirer, 10/11/1839.

Died, In this city on the 21st inst. of typhoid fever, Chas. **WHEATON**, aged 38 years. The friends of A. G. **WHEATON** are invited to attend the funeral of his brother, Chas. Wheaton, from No. 75 Front Row. Memphis Daily Appeal, 9/22/1855.

Died—On Tuesday night about 10 o'clock, Sure (or Sere) Beckwith, son of Doctor S. M. and Sarah C. **WHEATON**, in the 17th year of his age….The Raleigh (N.C.) Register will please copy the above. Weekly Appeal, Fri., 5/23/1845.

Married, On the 19th inst. by Rev. C. R. **HENDRICKSON**, Mr. Benjamin H. **WHEELER**, of Cincinnati, and Miss Margaret E. **RODGERS**, of this city. Memphis Daily Appeal, 11/21/1853.

Died.—At Fort Smith, Ark., on Sunday 13th inst., Mr. Jeremiah **WHEELER**. Mr. W. arrived at this place, a few days previous to his death on board the steamer C_____, on his way to Fannin county, Texas, where he said he had a son living. He was taken sick soon after he arrived and died as above _____, leaving four orphan boys. He wife died in Memphis last May.—Fort Smith Herald. Memphis Appeal, 2/29/1848.

Married, At the residence of _____ Ayres, Esq. in this county on the evening of the 5th inst. by W. C. **ROBB**, Mr. Joseph C. **WHEELER**, Merchant, of Carrolton, Miss., to Miss Matilda E. **AYRES**, daughter of _____ Ayres, Esq. Memphis Daily Appeal, 4/7/1853. (Author's Note: Blanks copied from newspaper.)

Died, At the residence of Joseph A. **GREEN**, Tipton county, on the 1st of March, Mary, eldest daughter of Rev. J. A. and Ellen R. **WHEELOCK**. The friends and acquaintances are respectfully invited to attend the funeral services from the Memphis and Ohio Railroad Depot, this Morning….Services by Rev. Mr. Hines at Winchester Cemetery. Memphis Morning Bulletin, 3/3/1859.

The public are respectfully informed that there will take place in the First Methodist Church, on Friday evening, the 4th inst.,….an examination of the Pupils of the Tennessee Institution for the instruction of the Blind, for the purpose of exhibiting their progress in the studies pursued by them…The Scholars will be exercised in reading by means of embossed letters, Writing, Geography, Arithmetic, Etc…E. W. **WHELAN**, Principal of the Institution. Daily Enquirer, 6/4/1847.

Married, In Shelby county, Tenn., on the 13th instant, by Rev. A. D. **METCALF**, Mr. A. W. **WHITAKER**, of Mississippi, and Miss C. Minerva **DONELSON**. Memphis Daily Appeal, 2/19/1856.

Died. In this city on Saturday morning 19th inst., of Typhoid Pneumonia, Mr. Richison **WHITBY**, in the 59th year of his age. The deceased was a native of South Carolina, having been born in Waterburg District, June 5, 1794. He emigrated to Shelby county, Ten. in 1826, where he has since lived….He has left behind him a disconsolate wife and five children to mourn a loss to them irreparable. Memphis Appeal, 2/22/1853. All persons indebted to the estate of the late Richeson Whitby, deceased, are requested to come forward….Perminta **WHITBY**. Adm'trix. Memphis Daily Appeal, 4/21/1853.

Married, At Henry **HARRIS'** on the 20th by Rev. J. C. **CROSS**, Mr. Abram **WHITE**, of McLemoresville, to Mrs. Elizabeth **BROOM**, of Memphis. Memphis Daily Appeal, 12/22/1855.

Married, July 2d, 1859, by J. **WALDRAN**, Esq., Mr. Charles **WHITE** to Miss Julia **BORDEN**, all of Fort Pickering. Memphis Daily Appeal, 7/6/1859.

Married, In Memphis, on 12th instant, by J. **HORNE**, Esq., Mr. David **WHITE**, Second Engineer on the Daniel Boone, to Mrs. Jane **HARDING**. Memphis Daily Appeal, 7/13/1858.

Died, On the 15th inst. at his residence in Panola county, Miss., Major David S. **WHITE**, aged forty-nine years….Memphis Daily Appeal, 3/18/1859.

For Sale.—Five hundred acres of Land, lying __ miles east of Memphis on the State Line road. Apply on the premises to Eppy **WHITE**. Memphis Daily Eagle, 4/15/1848. Married, On Thursday, the 25th inst., by the Rev. Geo. W. **COONS**, William P. **BLACKSTONE**, Esq., of Kentucky, to Miss Louisiana C. **WHITE**, daughter of Col. Eppy White, of this county. Memphis Daily Eagle, 1/27/1849. Col. Eppy White, one of the oldest citizens of Shelby county, died very suddenly on Sunday last, at his residence eight miles from this city. Memphis Daily Appeal, Wednesday, 5/13/1857. Died, At his residence, on the 10th instant, of apoplexy, Col. Eppy White, in his sixty-sixth year. Col. W. was a native of Georgia. He moved to this county in 1830....He leaves a large family and many relatives to mourn his loss. Eutaw (Ala.) papers please copy. Memphis Daily Appeal, 5/16/1857.

Married, On Wednesday last, March 30, Col. F. M. **WHITE**, of Memphis, to Miss Catharine **GARDNER**, of Augusta, Ga. Memphis Daily Appeal, 4/5/1859.

Married, On Tuesday evening the 11th inst., at the residence of Mrs. Turner, in this city, by Rev. Dr. B. F. **HALL**, Mr. J. **WHITE** to Miss M. J. **TURNER**, all of this city. Memphis Daily Appeal, 11/15/1851.

The funeral of the late Col. J. D. **WHITE**, will be preached at the Cumberland Presbyterian Church in this city, on Sabbath morning next, 1st proximo. Services by Rev. S. G. **BURNEY**. Memphis Eagle, 8/31/1850.

Married. Near Tuscumbia, Alabama, on the 5th instant by Rev. Wiley **REID**, Mr. James M. **WHITE**, of the firm of Alexander & White, of this city, to Miss Mary, daughter of Col. F. T. **ABERNATHY**. Memphis Daily Appeal, 12/9/1854.

New Firm. John D. **WHITE**, Wm. B. **WALDRAN** & Jesse M. **TATE**, have this day associated themselves together under the firm and style of White, Waldran & Tate, for the purpose of conducting a Grocery and Commission Business...The Appeal, 2/2/1844. The undersigned having been qualified as Executors of the last will and testament of the late John D. White, request all persons owing his estate to come forward....W. B. **WALDRAN**, G. L. **HOLMES**, Ex'rs. Weekly Memphis Eagle, 12/13/1849. At a called meeting of Germantown Lodge No. 95, held at their Hall, in Germantown, on the 7th day of September, 1849, for the purpose of paying the respect due to the memory of our deceased brother, the late John D. White, it was, on motion, Resolved, That we sincerely lament the departure of our esteemed brother, who was highly estimated as a good Mason, a good citizen, an honorable man, and exemplary in the discharge of all his duties as a citizen and head of a family....Daily Memphis Enquirer, 9/13/1849. Married, On Wednesday evening, 1st inst., by the Rev. Geo. W. **COONS**, the Rev. Wyly M. **REED**, of Leighton, Alabama, to Miss Mary Carolina, daughter of the late Col. John D. White, of this county. Memphis Daily Appeal, 1/4/1851.

The friends and acquaintances of the late John D. **WHITE**, Jr., are invited to attend his Funeral, at his mothers—six miles East of Memphis --this, Friday evening...Memphis Daily Appeal, Fri., 6/20/1851.

Died, at the residence of her parents, corner Tennessee and Butler streets, infant daughter of Joseph and Matilda **WHITE**....Memphis Daily Appeal, 7/2/1859.

Died. In Clarke county, Ark., on the 1st inst., Mary, consort of Oscar L. **WHITE**, Esq., formerly of Memphis, Tenn. American Eagle, 12/16/1847.

Married. At Bolivar, Tenn., 22d inst., by the Rev. Phillip **WALKER**, Mr. R. S. **WHITE**, of Shelby county, and Miss Mary C. **BRIGHT**, of the former place. Memphis Whig, 3/29/1855.

On the 5th of February next I will sell at auction....Seven Lots, belonging to the estate of Richard M. **WHITESIDES**, deceased....Henry G. **SMITH**, Agent for Thomas **WHITESIDES**. Memphis Eagle & Enquirer, 1/26/1853.

Married, On Monday, 12th instant, at Holly Springs, by Rev. Mr. Rogers, Mr. Luke J. **WHITFIELD**, of Columbus, and Miss Elenora J. **HARRIS**, of the former place. Memphis Daily Appeal, 5/15/1856.

Died: On Saturday, the 11th inst., Sarah Janet, infant daughter of Thomas and Emma **WHITFIELD** of this city....Weekly Memphis Eagle, 8/16/1849.

The friends and acquaintances of the late Thomas **WHITFIELD** are respectfully invited to attend his funeral, which will take place this (Thursday) morning, at 10 o'clock from his residence on Moseby street. Services by Rev. Dr. Page. Memphis Daily Appeal, Thurs., 11/1/1855.

Died, At his residence in Tipton county, Tenn., on the evening of the 16th instant, Capt. Daniel R. **WHITLEY**, aged 55 years. Capt. Whitley was a native of Johnson county, North Carolina; removed to the Western District of Tennessee at an early day, where, by his untiring energies and superior business qualities, he had arisen to the very first rank among the planters of his county. He was an affectionate husband, a tender father....Memphis Daily Appeal, 10/19/1856.

Married: At the residence of Mr. A. J. **HENRY**, in South Memphis, on Wednesday evening, by Rev. P. S. **GAYLE**, Mr. L. Miltman **WHITMAN** to Miss Sarah E. **HENRY**, all of this city. Memphis Daily Eagle, Fri., 7/14/1848.

Married, In Holly Springs on the 12th inst., by Rev. J. T. C. **COLLINS**, Mr. J. L. **WHITMORE**, of Memphis, to Miss Ella E.(?) **SMITH**, of Marshall county, Miss. Memphis Daily Appeal, 1/15/1858.

Died, On the 5th inst., Virginia, infant daughter of Mr. and Mrs. R. **WHITNEY**, aged 14 months and 18 days. The friends and acquaintances of the family are invited to attend her funeral at 10 o'clock this morning, from their residence on Second street, nearly opposite the post office. Services by Rev. Mr. Knott. Memphis Daily Appeal, 8/6/1856.

Died—In this place, on the 30th ult., Mr. John H. **WHITSETT**, in the 27th year of his age. Memphis Enquirer, 9/2/1837.

Died, On Tuesday last, the 5th instant, at 5 o'clock, John Sanburn, infant son of W. W. and E. J. **WHITSETT**, aged 14 months and 15 days. American Eagle, 9/8/1843. Died—In this place on Thursday the 18th inst., George Cheatham, son of W. W. Whitsett, aged five years. Memphis Enquirer, 7/19/1839. Died, At his residence, on Market Square, in this city, on Friday evening, 28th instant, at 7 o'clock, of Apoplexy, Mr. W. W. Whitsitt, in the 52nd year of his age....Memphis Appeal, 10/29/1853.

Died on Monday 26th instant at 12 o'clock M., of inflamation of the brain, William Wiley, son of Samuel H. and Elizabeth J. **WHITSITT**, aged 11 months and 22 days. The friends and acquaintances are respectfully invited to attend the funeral from the residence of Mrs. W. M. **WHITSITT**, Market square, this morning at 10 o'clock. Memphis Daily Appeal, 3/28/1855.

Died—Of congestive fever, on Sunday, 2__th inst., Sarah, daughter of Mrs. Sarah **WHITSITT**, of this place, aged 12 years. Memphis Enquirer, Sat., 8/26/1837.

We are authorized and requested to announce Mr. William **WHITSITT**, Sen. (Whig) as a candidate to represent the people of Shelby county in the next session of our State Legislature. Memphis Enquirer, 3/22/1839.

It becomes our painful duty to announce the death of our father, Rev. William **WHITSITT**, at his farm in Phillips county, Ark., on Friday last. The deceased was born in North Carolina, and was a resident of this city for twenty five years. He removed from here in 1852, and settled at the place where he died. Memphis Evening Ledger, Sat., 11/14/1857.

A German, by the name of Shelby **WHITTATER**, in the employement of Messrs. Saffarans & Co., was on a spree Tuesday last, and after drinking pretty freely of the ardent, he went to his room and lay down.—Yesterday morning his bed companion woke up as usual and before leaving endeavored to wake him up, when it was discovered that he was dead. He had died sometime during the night without a struggle and without awakening his companion...Memphis Eagle & Enquirer, 4/15/1852. (Author's note: Name given as **WHITINGTON** in the list of internments.)

Married, On Thursday evening, February 21st, by Rev. W. W. **KEEP**, Dr. **WHITTON**, of Pontotoc county, Miss., to Miss Susan A. **BOONE**, of this city. Memphis Daily Appeal, 2/26/1856.

We are pained to learn that Willie, eldest son of W. J. **WICKS**, President of the River Bank, _____ a horrible death yesterday afternoon about one o'clock. It seems that he was grazing a pony in his father's _____, two and a half miles from the city, having the halter strap wrapped around his waist. The pony became vicious and the poor boy was dragged the lot, being unable to releave himself. When assistance came it was too late to be of any avail and the mangled body of the lad was carried to his home, where he soon breathed his last....The boy was eleven or twelve years of age. Memphis Daily Appeal, 4/1/1857.

Married, On Thursday, October 30th, at the residence of the bride's father, near Oakland, Tenn., Mr. Jas. **WIGGINS** and Miss Julia **WRAY**, all of Fayette county. Memphis Daily Appeal, 11/10/1857.

Married, On the 14th inst., in Tipton county, Miss., by the Rev. A. **SLOVER**, Dr. Martin L. **WIGGS** to Miss Sallie E. Finger, only daughter of John M. **FINGER**. Memphis Daily Appeal, 8/1/1858.

Mr. N. **WILCOX**, of the house of J. E. Merriman & Co., was buried yesterday. He was a young man of most excellent qualities and was admired for goodness and nobleness by those who knew him best. Memphis Daily Appeal, 10/25/1855.

Married—On last Thursday evening, by the Rev. J. H. **GRAY**, Mr. John **WILDBERGER** to Miss Caroline, daughter of Mr. E. **CHEEK**. Weekly Memphis Eagle, 5/24/1849.

Married, On the 4th inst., in Petersburg, Va., by the Rev. Dr. D. S. **DOGGETT**, Mr. D. W. C. **WILDER**, of Memphis, Tenn., to Miss Margaret A. **BOISSEAU**, of Petersburg, Va. Memphis Eagle, 9/18/1850. Died, On Friday the 28th of May, Sarah Cornelia, infant daughter of D. C. and M. A. Wilder, aged 9 months and 4 days. Memphis Eagle & Enquirer, 6/2/1852. New Drug Store. D. C. Wilder & Co., Druggists & Apothecaries, Main street...Memphis Daily Appeal, 9/1/1851. We learn just before going to press that the wife of our esteemed citizen, D. C. Wilder, died very suddenly last night. Memphis Whig, 5/12/1856.

Died—On Sunday morning, Mrs. _____ Wilder, consort of Daniel S. (?) **WILDER**, Merchant of this city, after a long and painful illness. Tri-Weekly Memphis Enquirer, Tues., 3/10/1846.

Married, On the 1_th inst. at the residence of Mr. Oliver, by Rev. John **BATEMAN**, Mr. M. D. L. **WILDS** to Miss L. C. **BELOTE**, all of this city. Memphis Weekly Appeal, 11/24/1858.

Married. On Thursday evening the 16th in this city by L. R. **RICHARDS**, Esq., Mr. S. J. **WILEY** to Miss Amelia **POWERS**. Memphis Daily Appeal, 6/24/1853.

Married, On Tuesday, 20th January, near Fisherville, Tenn., Mr. Thos. **WILEY** to Miss R. J. **STEPHENSON**, all of Shelby county. Memphis Daily Appeal, 1/27/1857.

Died, in this county, on the 27th ult., Francis **WILKERSON**, Esq., aged about 71 years. Mr. Wilkerson was born in Pitt county, North Carolina in 1776—imigrated to Davidson county, Tenn., in 1811—removed to Williamson county in 1814, thence to Hardeman county in 1829.—He was, in the fullest acceptance of the term, "a gentleman of the old school."...an affectionate husband, a kind father, an indulgent master, an honest man...Middleburg, Tenn., 4/8/1847. Weekly Appeal, 4/23/1847.

Died, In Granada, Nicaragua, of fever, on the 8th of November last, Capt. Douglas J. **WILKINS**, late of the Nicaraguan army, in the twenty-third year of his age. And thus has passed away one just reared to maturity by loving parents, whose constant care and attention seemed alone to prolong the life of one so delicate. Memphis Daily Appeal, 12/21/1856.

Married, On the 29th ult. by Rev. E. _. **GREEN**, Mr. Geo. **WILKINS** and Miss Nancy **SHAW**, both of Tipton county, Tenn. Memphis Daily Appeal, 11/5/1857.

Married, At Brooklyn, L.I., March 21st, 1850, by Rev'd. F. K. **FARLEY**, James S. **WILKINS**, of Memphis, to Miss Mary P. **CLARKE**, of Brooklyn. Memphis Daily Eagle, 4/17/1850.

Married, On the 15th inst., General Wm. **WILKINS** to Mrs. **SMITH**; both of Tipton county, Tenn. Memphis Daily Appeal, 7/30/1852.

Dr. Wm. **WILKINS**—This gentleman, late of Louisville, has located permanently in this city....Memphis Daily Appeal, 1/12/1859.

Died, In this city, on yesterday...Caledonia, infant daughter of J. and M. A. **WILKINSON**. Memphis Daily Appeal, 8/8/1851.

Married. On the evening of the 5th inst. at the residence of Maj. William **MOORE**, in DeSoto county, Miss., by the Rev. Stephen G. **STARKS**, Mr. Robert **WILKINSON**, (of the firm of Wilkinson, Pryor & Co., of Memphis) to Miss Lucy A. Banks, daughter of the late Henry **BANKS**, Esq., deceased. Memphis Daily Appeal, 10/6/1853.

Died last evening at 6 o'clock, Mrs. Susan H. **WILKINSON**. Aged 57 years. The funeral will take place this (Saturday) evening at 3 o'clock, at the house of her son, Jno. **WILKERSON**, on Third Street....Memphis Daily Appeal, 11/18/1854. (Author's note: Spelling copied as printed.)

Married. On the 2d instant by the Rev. E. H. **GREEN**, Mr. J. W. **WILLEY** to Miss Nancy **MILLER**, both of Tipton county, Tenn. Memphis Daily Appeal, 8/8/1855.

Died, At his residence in Somerville, Tenn., on the 18th inst., after a protracted and painful illness, Mr. John **WILLFONG**, in the 56th year of his age. Memphis Daily Appeal, 12/23/1855.

Married. On the 7th instant at the residence of Isaac **LUKEY**, Esq., of Drew county, Ark., by Rev. Thomas **STONE**, Mr. Arthur **WILLIAMS** to Miss Martha H. **DONALDSON**. At the same time and place, by Nathan **BRANSON**, Esq., Mr. Jno. L. **DONALDSON** to Miss Melissa **WOODWORTH**. Memphis Daily Appeal, 3/18/1855.

Married, In Hardeman County, on Thursday, the 30th ult., by the Rev. Mr. Walker, Mr. C. H. **WILLIAMS** to Miss Mary A., eldest daughter of Leven **BROWNING**, Esq. Memphis Daily Appeal, 11/4/1851.

The friends and acquaintances of C. H. **WILLIAMS** are requested to attend the funeral of his wife, at his residence this evening....Memphis Daily Appeal, 5/24/1859.

Died, On Saturday evening, February 2d, Erneast Jones, aged 16 months, son of D. C. and Mary C. **WILLIAMS**. Memphis Daily Appeal, 2/5/1856.

Married: On the 12th inst., by James F. **BATTS** (or **BATTE**), Esq., Mr. David **WILLIAMS**, to Miss Mary A. **BEARDON**, all of Shelby county. Weekly Memphis Eagle, 8/23/1849.

Married. On the 28th(?) December, 1854, at the residence of Hall **JARMON**, Esq., near Florence, Ala., Mr. Duke **WILLIAMS**, Jr., of Somerville, to Miss S. S. **KENNEDY**. Memphis Daily Appeal, 1/9/1855.

Married, On the 26th inst., near Collierville, at the residence of the bride's mother, Mrs. E. C. **GILLILAND**, by Rev. Wm. M. **McFERRIN**, Rev. E. **WILLIAMS** to Miss A. P. **SMITH**. Memphis Weekly Appeal, 12/1/1858.

E. P. **WILLIAMS**, Blacksmith and Finisher, North side of Court Square, between Main and Second Streets, Memphis, Tenn., Still carries on the above business in all its various branches, at the same stand occupied by him for the last 10 years...Daily Enquirer, 11/4/1847.

Married, By J. **WALDRAN**, Esq., on the 30th of May, 1852, Mr. Elijah **WILLIAMS** to Miss Louisa H. **HARRIS**, all of this city. Memphis Eagle & Enquirer, 6/1/1852.

Died, At the residence of H. S. **KING**, near Horn Lake, Shelby county, Tenn., on the 4th inst., Mrs. Fanny R. **WILLIAMS**, late of Danville, Boyd county, Ky., in the 78th year of her age. Memphis Daily Appeal, 9/8/1857.

Married. On the 31st July in the vicinity of Memphis by the Rev. M. **STEDMAN**, Frank **WILLIAMS**, Esq., of the house of Williams, Phillips & Co., of New Orleans, to Miss Catharine J., youngest daughter of John **TRIGG**, Esq. Memphis Daily Appeal, 8/4/1854. Died. At the residence of her father, Col. John Trigg, near this city, on Monday evening, Mrs. Kate Williams, consort of Frank Williams, Esq., New Orleans, in the 19th year of her age. Memphis Whig, Tues., 3/6/1855.

Died, In this city on the morning of October 2, 1858, at the residence of G. J. **WILLIAMS**, Ruth, infant daughter of Joseph and Caroline **WILLIAMS**, of West Baton Rouge, La., aged 11 months and 10 days. Memphis Daily Appeal, 10/3/1858.

I Have for sale in separate tracts 2,610 acres of valuable Land, situated on and near the dividing line of Shelby and Fayette and Memphis and Ohio Railroad....Purchasers are specially invited to see me at my residence in the neighborhood of Hickory Wythe....H. B. S. **WILLIAMS**. Memphis Daily Appeal, 12/25/1856.

Married. On Thursday evening, 30th ult., at the residence of Mr. John S. **McGEHEE**, Panola county, Miss., by the Rev. M. H. **NEAL**, J. D. **WILLIAMS**, of Memphis, to Miss Kate **McGEHEE**, of Pontotoc county, Miss. Memphis Daily Eagle, 4/8/1848.

Married, On the 4th inst. by the Rev. Doctor Baskervill, Mr. Asberry **WARREN**, of Fayette co. to Miss Eliza A., daughter of J. J. **WILLIAMS**, Esq., of Hardeman county, Tenn. Memphis Appeal, 8/10/1847.

Information Wanted of James **WILLIAMS**, Jr., who volunteered at Memphis last year in Capt. Porter's company of cavalry. He was in the battle of Vera Cruz and a friend who was with him on his return to New Orleans, in the ship Edith, states that he left the latter place in company with 2 or 3 Tennesseans. He was in a precarious state of health, and it is thought he may not have come farther than Memphis, on his way home. When last seen he had about $200 in gold—since which time he has not been heard of. Volunteers, particularly those of the cavalry company, would confer a lasting favor and place under the deepest obligation of gratitude an affectionate father and mother, by giving any information possible of their lost son. Address: James **WILLIAMS**, Lawrenceburg. October 7, 1847. Daily Enquirer, 10/12/1847.

Married, On the 2d instant, Mr. John **WILLIAMS**, of Haywood county, to Mrs. M. E.(?) **HUMPHREYS**. Memphis Weekly Appeal, 12/15/1858.

Married, On the evening of Tuesday last, by the Rev. Mr. Coons, Mr. John S. **WILLIAMS**, to Miss Frances S. **LAWRENCE**—all of this city. Weekly Appeal, Fri., 4/17/1846.

Notice is hereby given to the members of the Masonic Fraternity, that the regular meetings of Memphis Lodge No. 91, are held from and after this time, on the second and fourth Thursdays ...Jno S. **WILLIAMS**, Sec...Daily Enquirer, 3/28/1847.

Married, In Mississippi county, Ark., on Tuesday evening, March 23d, by Rev. Mr. Morris, John W. **WILLIAMS**, Esq., to Miss Anna Hickman, eldest daughter of Col. Elliot H. **FLETCHER**. Memphis Weekly Appeal, 4/7/1858.

Died at the residence of Gen. Joseph R. **WILLIAMS**, in this city, on the evening of the 26th ult., Mrs. Elizabeth, consort of the late Capt. John **WILLIAMS**, of Nashville. It was the good fortune of the writer, but a few years since, to partake for a brief period of the generous hospitality of the esteemed and accomplished lady, whose decease is noted above, and rarely, if ever, had a sense of more perfect domestic happiness been presented to his eye, than the one it was then his pleasure to behold. Happy in the presence of husband, daughter and sons, whose healthful and gay contenances....Since that time, how desolate has Death made that home. The daughter in her youth and beauty, the husband in the prime of life, and one son in the vigor of early manhood, have in rapid succession, passed away from the communion of loved ones on earth....And when the widowed wife, and sorrow-smitten mother, would have fled from the hearth, around which were gathered so many memorials of her bereavement, and sought in the society of her only surviving son some respite from the sad memories of other and happier days, the fell despoiler of all her fondest hopes attended her in her flight, and ere her destination was reached, fastened upon her frail and stricken frame....and while her mortal remains await the return of an only son, to be deposited by the side of those of her family who have preceded her, 'tis gratifying to numerous friends to believe that their spirits have been re-united above. Daily Enquirer, 4/2/1847.

Married, On the 12th May, by the Rev. M. B. **LOWREY**, at the residence of Mrs. E. M. O. **TAYLOR**, in Arkansas county, Ark., Gen. Jos. R. **WILLIAMS**, of Memphis, to Miss E. H. Taylor, daughter of Lewis C. **TAYLOR**, Esq., dec'd. Weekly Appeal, 6/6/1845. The friends and acquaintances of Gen. Joseph R. Williams are respectfully invited to attend the funeral of Mrs. Henrie E. Williams to-day at 10 ½ o'clock, from his residence on the corner of Main and Beal streets, South Memphis. Daily Memphis Enquirer, 11/26/1847. Notice. The Independent Order of Odd Fellows are respectfully requested to meet at their Hall this morning at 9 o'clock, to attend the funeral of the wife of our Wo. Patr. Jos. R. Williams. Daily Memphis Enquirer, 11/26/1847. Married—On the 2d inst., in Hinds co., Miss., Gen. Joseph R. Williams, of Memphis, to Miss Jane T. Wilkins, daughter of Dr. Benj. **WILKINS**. Weekly Memphis Eagle, 5/17/1849. Died—In Memphis, on the 23d inst. of croup, Eugene L., infant son of Gen. Joseph R. Williams...Weekly Memphis Eagle, 5/31/1849.

All persons indebted to the estate of Nancy G. **WILLIAMS**, dec'd. will please make immediate payment....Wm. S. **WILLIAMS**, Executor. Memphis Daily Appeal, 7/29/1854.

Married, On the 30th ultimo at Jackson, Tenn., Nat. W. **WILLIAMS**, Esq., of Holly Springs, Miss., to Miss Paradise Huntsman, of the former place, and daughter of the late Hon. Adam **HUNTSMAN**. Memphis Daily Appeal, 6/6/1855.

Married, On the 1st instant, at the residence of the bride's father, by Dr. W. G. **LANCASTER**, Mr. P. M. **WILLIAMS** to Miss M. C. **BRET**, all of Shelby county, Tenn. Memphis Daily Appeal, 9/8/1858.

Married, In Nashville, Tenn., on the 4th inst., at 11 o'clock A.M., by Rev. Dr. Edgar, Dr. R. N. **WILLIAMS**, of Arkansas, to Miss Mary Morgan, daughter of Samuel D. **MORGAN**, Esq. Memphis Weekly Appeal, 5/12/1858.

Captain Russel **WILLIAMS** of the steamer Excell, died of cholera on board his boat at Davenport. Memphis Daily Appeal, 8/4/1854.

Married, In Ashley county, Ark., on the 1st inst., Mr. Samuel J. **WILLIAMS**, of West Baton Rouge, La., to Miss Lavinia **MEEK**. Memphis Weekly Appeal, 12/15/1858.

The friends and acquaintances of W. and _. C. **WILLIAMS** are respectfully invited to attend the Funeral of their deceased sister, Mrs. Nancy Dudly, the wife of G. W. **DUDLY**, deceased, from their residence on Vance street, second house from DeSoto, east. Memphis Daily Appeal, 6/1/1858.

At a meeting held by the members of South Memphis Division, No. 70, Sons of Temperance, the following preamble and resolutions were unanimously adopted, expressive of our regret at the untimely loss of our friend and brother W. W. **WILLIAMS**, who departed this life on the 27th inst...Resolved: That the various papers of the city be requested to publish the foregoing, and that a copy of the same be sent to his bereaved relations...Memphis Daily Appeal, 8/2/1848.

Found, On the 11th inst., a small sum of money, which the owner can get by describing and paying for this advertisement. Apply at William S. **WILLIAMS'** Land Office...Memphis Daily Appeal, 1/13/1848.

Married, In this county, on Thursday evening, 22d inst., by the Rev. S. M. **COWAN**, Maj. William S. **WILLIAMS**, of Hernando, Miss., to Mrs. Nancy G. **BUSTER**, of this county. Weekly Appeal, 1/30/1846.

The friends and acquaintances of A. G. **WILLIAMSON** and Wm. Kenan **HILL** are invited to attend the funeral of Mrs. A. G. Williamson, from the Second Presbyterian Church this morning at 11 o'clock. Memphis Daily Appeal, 5/16/1856. Died, On Thursday, May 15th, at the residence of her mother, Mrs. Juliet Hill, wife of Rev. A. G. Williamson, aged 27 years and six months.... Memphis Daily Appeal, 5/17/1856. Married, On Tuesday, 21st inst., at Oxford, Miss., by Rev. S. J. **REID**, Mr. A. G. Williamson, of this city, to Miss Kate M. **ROBINSON**, of the former place. Memphis Daily Appeal, 9/22/1858. Died, On Wednesday morning, December 14, Kate M., the beloved wife of Mr. A. G. Williamson, leaving behind her a babe twelve days old. Mrs. Williamson was formerly Kate M. Robinson, of Oxford, Miss....Memphis Daily Appeal, 12/16/1859.

Married, At the residence of the bride's father, near Hernando, yesterday, by Rev. A. G. **WILLIAMSON**, Mr. F. H. **WILLIAMSON**, of the firm of Fransiola & Williamson, of this city, to Miss Mary E. **McGOWEN**. Memphis Daily Appeal, 7/14/1858.

The friends and acquaintances of Mr. James D. **NEILL** are invited to attend the funeral of his in-law, Miss Agnes M. **WILLIAMSON**, from his residence on St. Patrick street this morning at 11 o'clock. Memphis Whig, 11/6/1855. We regret to announce the death of Miss Agnes J. Williamson, a beautiful and very intelligent young lady of our city. She died of the late prevailing disease. She had for some time past been engaged as a teacher of one of our highest grade city schools....Memphis Daily Appeal, 11/6/1855. ....Miss Williamson was a native of Pennsylvania....Memphis Daily Appeal, 11/7/1855.

Died. On Tuesday evening, the 6th instant, at the residence of her son-in-law, Mr. James Q. **NEILL**, Mrs. Eunice **WILLIAMSON**, aged 58 years, of yellow fever. Memphis Daily Appeal, 11/7/1855.

Died.—At Gonzales, Texas, on the 13th ult., Geo. N. **WILLIAMSON**, Esq. Mr. W. had been a resident of Lavacca County and is supposed to have relations in Tennessee or North Carolina. Memphis Daily Appeal, 9/12/1854.

Married, At Christ Church, Holly Springs, on Thursday, the 4th instant by Rev. J. W. **RODGERS**, Rector of St. Thomas' Hall, Gen. H. E. **WILLIAMSON** and Miss Darthula O. Bradford, daughter of Gen. A. B. **BRADFORD**. Memphis Daily Appeal, 10/16/1855.

Married, On the 12th of August, 1857, at the residence of the bride's father, near High Hill, Tenn., by Rev. J. L. **CROSS**, Mr. J. **WILLIAMSON**, of Nashville, to Miss Mollie T. **BROOKS**. Memphis Daily Appeal, 8/28/1857.

Universalist Church, Concert Hall, Exchange Alley, Rev. J. D. **WILLIAMSON**. Daily Enquirer, 2/28/1847.

Married, In this city on the evening of the 23d inst., at the residence of Mr. J. J. **ROBINSON**, by Rev. J. T. C. **COLLINS**, Mr. J. L. **WILLIAMSON** to Miss Emma J. **CORNWELL**, all of this city. Memphis Weekly Appeal, 6/30/1858.

All persons having claims against Jesse **WILLIAMSON**, deceased, will present them....H. T. **LEMMON**, Executor. Memphis Daily Appeal, 8/26/1855.

Married, on the 18th inst., by the Rev. Alex **LITTLEJOHN**, Calvin W. **CHERRY**, of the firm of Cherry, Henderson & Co., New Orleans, to Miss Anna Maria, daughter of Lewis P. **WILLIAMSON**, Esq., of Fayette county, Tenn. Memphis Enquirer, 7/27/1849.

Died, On Friday, September 14th, Jas. Edward Williamson, aged 2 years, 8 months, son of Julie and R. A. **WILLIAMSON**. Memphis Daily Appeal, 9/16/1855.

We have the sad duty to record the melancholy and horrible death of this estimable man—Maj. R. A. **WILLIAMSON**, Superintendent of the Memphis and Ohio Railroad. This fearful accident occurred yesterday morning about 9 ½ o'clock, some sixteen miles from town, on the "Hatchie Bridge," over the waters known as Griffin's creek, some three hundred yards from the Shelby depot. Mr. W. was on the train as it passed the bridge and in the hindmost car, and it is supposed that he placed his head far out of the train's passage, and was looking backward when his head came in contact with a post of the bridge, killing him instantly...Maj. W. was a native of Baltimore and has long been known as connected with important railroad enterprises in our country. For many years he had been engaged on the Memphis and Charleston road...when he resigned his position and was placed in the same official capacity over an important railroad in Georgia. From that State he was called to superintend the Memphis and Ohio road...Maj. Williamson was forty-five years of age and fortunately has left no wife and children to mourn his loss....Memphis Daily Appeal, 1/18/1856.

Married, On Thursday evening last, by Rev. Saml. **DENNIS**, Mr. Samuel B. **WILLIAMSON**, merchant of this city, to Miss Mary E., daughter of Mr. Wm. **EANES**, of this county. American Eagle Weekly, Friday, 5/9/1845. The friends and acquaintances of S. B. & Mary E. Williamson are invited to attend the funeral of their infant daughter, Mary Eliza, from their residence on Madison street, this (Monday) evening.... Services by the Rev. H. S. **PORTER**. Memphis Appeal, Mon., 1/26/1852.

The friends and acquaintances of Thomas T. **WILLIAMSON**, are invited to attend his funeral this afternoon at 3 o'clock, from the residence of his brother S. B. **WILLIAMSON**, on Jefferson street. Memphis Daily Eagle, 11/3/1847. S. B. Williamson, Admr. of T. T. Williamson, decd. Vs The Creditors of said Estate....Those indebted to said estate are requested to make payment to Samuel B. **WILLIAMSON**, Admr....Memphis Daily Eagle. 10/16/1848.

Married, At Goodwood, in this county, on the 12th of August, by G. M. **BARTLETT**, Esq., Mr. James C. **MALONEY**, of Tipton county, to Miss Clarvan F. **WILLIS**, of Shelby county. Memphis Appeal, 8/16/1852.

Died, In Sacramento City, Calif., on the 26th of January last, John **WILLIS**, formerly of La Grange, Tenn. North Carolina papers please copy. Memphis Daily Eagle, 4/16/1850.

Died, On Thursday, May 8th, at Wyalusing, at the residence of Col. H. L. **HOLCOMBE**, Marshall, Texas, Maj. N. M. **WILLIS**, of Lagrange, Fayette co., Tenn., aged 38 years. Memphis Appeal, 6/3/1851.

Died, At the residence of his father on the 22d of November, 1856, Dr. Wm. H. **WILLIS**, aged twenty-four years, one month and twenty days. Dr. Willis....recently commenced the practice of medicine in Marshall county, Miss....he was attacked with typhoid fever, and returned to his father's house to die....Also, at the same place, of typhoid fever, on the 12th December, 1856, Ruffin **WILLIS**, brother of Dr. Wm. H. Willis, and youngest son of Henry **WILLIS**, aged nineteen years, eight months and twenty-seven days. Ruffin N. Willis was a young man....Fayette County, Tenn. Memphis Daily Appeal, 1/18/1857.

Taken up by John **WILLISON**, living 13 miles east of Memphis, one grey filly.....Memphis Enquirer, 1/14/1837.

Died, At Chulahoma, Miss., on the 27th of February last, Mr. Joshua H. **WILLOUGHBY**, after a painful illness of three months. The deceased was a member of the Methodist Church....Memphis Daily Appeal, 3/5/1857.

Died. At their residence in Prairie county on the third of December, Mrs. Mary, wife of E.(?) F. **WILLS**, late of Memphis, aged 44 years. Memphis Whig, 12/19/1855.

Died. In Tipton county, on the 25th ult., Mrs. Ann E. Wills, consort of Mr. E. L. **WILLS**, in the 18th year of her age. Weekly Memphis Eagle, 2/8/1849.

Married, at the residence of Jas. _. **EPPS**, Esq., on the 12th instant by Rev. _. R. **EVANS**, Mr. Sam'l. M. **WILLSON** to Miss Mary E. **VAUGHAN**, all of Shelby county. Memphis Daily Appeal, 6/12/1855.

Died, In this city, on Wednesday, December 30th, Mr. John C. **WILROY**, formerly of Virginia, in the 46th year of his age. Virginia papers please copy....The members of Memphis Lodge No. 6, I.O.O.F., will meet at their hall at 2 o'clock P.M. to-day....to attend the funeral of our late brother, John C. Wilroy....Memphis Daily Appeal, 1/3/1858.

Married—In this city, by Rev. Mr. Starks, on the 24th ult., Mr. Alfred **WILSON** to Miss C. L., daughter of Col. T. J. **DOBYNS**. Memphis Enquirer, 1/6/1846.

Married—In this County, on Thursday evening 31st ult., by William H. **EAMES**, Esq., Maj. David **WILSON**, of Fayette County, Tenn., to Miss Sarah, daughter of Wilson **LURRY** Esq., of Shelby County. Daily Memphis Enquirer, 9/3/1848.

The friends and acquaintances of Captain David **WILSON** are invited to attend his funeral This Morning....at his late residence, two miles southeast from the city on McLemore street; interment at Elmwood Cemetery. Died, at his residence near this city, on yesterday morning, Captain David Wilson, in the 60th year of his age. Memphis Daily Appeal, 2/26/1859.

Married. On the 2d day of August by Rev. John G. **PARKER**, Col. David L. **WILSON**, of Shelby county, Tenn., to Miss Mary E. **BATTE**, of Rankin county, Miss. Memphis Daily Appeal, 8/9/1855.

I wish to sell my House and Lot on Main street, north of Adams. It has a front on Main street of 50 feet and runs back to Front Alley 148 ½ feet. Wishing to settle on a farm, I am determined to sell...Edward J. **WILSON**. Memphis Daily Appeal, 8/11/1852.

Married, On the 15th inst., at Forest Hill, Hardeman county, Tenn., by the Rev. Henry **WARREN**, Mr. Geo. **WILSON** of Milton, N.C., to Miss Mary Elizabeth, daughter of Samuel H. **SMITH**, Esq. Weekly Appeal, 2/20/1846.

Married—On the 10th inst., by the Rev. Jeptha **HARRISON**, in the Presbyterian Church Memphis, Tenn., Mr. Luther **PERRY**, of Boston, to Mrs. Harriet B. **WILSON**, widow of the late Dr. O. J. S. **WILSON**, of New Orleans. Memphis Enquirer, 11/15/1839.

At a stated meeting of Clinton Lodge, No. 54, of Free and Accepted Masons, held in Bolivar, Tenn., on Monday evening, May 5th, 1851, the following Preamble and Resolutions were unanimously adopted: Whereas: It hath pleased Almighty God to remove from our midst, our worthy brother, J. C. **WILSON**, a Master Mason, and long a useful and worthy member of our Lodge...Resolved, That we truly and deeply sympathise with his disconsolate widow and distressed relations in their sad bereavement. Resolved, That we will, on Sunday, the 25th inst., as a Lodge, move in procession to the Episcopal Church, in this place, where a funeral discourse will be delivered...Memphis Daily Appeal, 5/20/1851.

We were pained yesterday to learn of the death of Maj. J. M. **WILSON**, an old and highly respectable citizen, and for some years Marshal of our city. His funeral will take place from his residence in the Navy Yard at 11 o'clock this morning. Memphis Daily Appeal, 11/22/1856.

James **WILSON**, Esq., of Williamson, was killed last Friday by the accidental discharge of his gun. Memphis Whig, Thurs., 6/12/1856.

Married, On the 23d inst. at the residence of Dr. A. J. **BARBEE** in Haywood county, Tenn., Mr. Joel E. **WILSON** to Miss Isabella F. **BARBEE**. Memphis Daily Appeal, 7/30/1856.

Married, At the residence of the bride's father, on the 15th of December, by Rev. John **WILSON**, Mr. A. Jamison **WILSON** to Miss Eliza H., second daughter of W. R. **McCAIN**, all of Tipton county, Tenn. Memphis Daily Appeal, 12/24/1857.

Died, In Holly Springs on Sunday last, Dr. Jno. A. **WILSON**. Dr. Wilson was for many years a citizen of Memphis....His remains will be buried in Morris Cemetery to-day....Memphis Daily Appeal, 4/21/1857. Masonic Tribute. Departed this life on the morning of the 19th inst., at Holly Springs, Miss., Brother John A. Wilson, after a painful illness of several weeks....In his death the Fraternity are deprived of a faithful Brother; the community of a useful citizen and his children of a kind and indulgent parent....Memphis Daily Appeal, 4/24/1857.

Married, On the 1st inst. by Rev. Mr. Thomas, Mr. John B. **WILSON** to Miss Mary **HOUSTON**, all of Shelby county, Tenn. Memphis Daily Appeal, 12/8/1857.

Married – In this city, on the 9th inst., by Rev. J. H. **GRAY**, Mr. W. J. **KEEN** to Miss M. E. R. **WILSON**. Memphis Enquirer, 11/11/1848.

Death Of A Courtesan—The lifeless body of a poor, unfortunate woman, named Malinda **WILSON**, was found in an out building, in South Memphis, yesterday. She had evidently died of exposure and dissipation. Memphis Daily Appeal, 12/10/1859.

A young man named Robert **WILSON** was overcome by the heat of the sun, in Shelby street, near the Gayoso House, about two o'clock yesterday afternoon. He was conveyed immediately to the Front Row station-house, where he died last evening. The deceased was employed recently at the wharfboat of Messrs. J. J. Smith & Co. as a freight clerk. He was a native of Canada and was about twenty-eight years of age....Memphis Daily Appeal, 7/23/1859.

Died—At the Central Hotel, in this city on the night of Sunday last, Mr. Samuel D. **WILSON** of Marshall county, Miss., and formerly of Williamson county, Tennessee. Mr. W. arrived here but three or four days before his dissolution, from New Orleans, being far from well at the time of leaving that city. The deceased left an interesting family.....The Appeal, Fri., 5/24/1844.

Tribute of Respect. At a meeting of the Trustees and patrons of Centre Hill Male and Female Academies helf at Centre Hill, De Soto county, Miss., August 3d, 1855, the following preamble and resolutions were unanimously adopted: By an inscrutable dispensation of Providence, one of our associates and _____ has been removed from our midst. Shimael **WILSON** is no more. He died after a short but painful illness at his residence in Marshall county, Mississippi, July 21st, 1855....In the relation of husband, father, neighbor and friend....North Carolina papers please announce. Memphis Daily Appeal, 8/14/1855.

Married, In this city on the 18th(?) instant, by Rev. J. _. **MERRIWETHER**, Mr. Taylor **WILSON** to Miss Anna S.(?) **ADDYMAN**, all of this city. Memphis Daily Appeal, 1/20/1859.

Married, On the 10th instant, by Rev. Robt. L. **ANDREWS**, at the residence of Mr. Wilson **SMITH**, in Lafayette county, Col. Thomas F. **WILSON**, of Panola, and Mrs. Rebecca **SMITH**, of Lafayette. Memphis Daily Appeal, 9/25/1856.

Married, On the evening of the 29th of December, by Rev. J. **WILSON**, Mr. Wm. **WILSON** to Mrs. **McCULLOUGH**, all of Tipton county, Tenn. Memphis Daily Appeal, 1/20/1858.

Strayed From the subscriber, in Memphis, on the 13th inst., a Sorrel Horse...Any information to the subscriber, living 14 miles South East of Memphis, on the Chulahoma road...Osbon F. **WIMBERLY**. Daily Enquirer, 4/18/1847.

Married, On Wednesday morning, 10th instant, at the residence of the bride's father, by Rev. H. **WALSH**, Mr. Wesley A. **WINBERLY**, of Ashley county, Ark., to Miss Mollie L. Hutchenson, youngest daughter of A. R. **HUTCHINSON**, of DeSoto county, Miss. Memphis Weekly Appeal, 3/24/1858.

Married, On the evening of the 16th inst. by Rev. S. W. **SPEER**, D.D., Mr. Richard **WINBORNE** to Miss Maggie Lee **HOWARD**, all of LaGrange, Tennessee. Memphis Daily Appeal, 12/19/1857.

M. B. **WINCHESTER**, Post Master. Daily Enquirer, 3/4/1847. The funeral obsequies of the late Maj. M. B. Winchester will take place on Wednesday morning, 9 ½ o'clock, from his residence on the State Line Road. His body will be interred in Winchester Cemetery….The friends and acquaintances of the late Marcus B. Winchester….Memphis Daily Appeal, Tues., 11/4/1856.

Died, At his residence six miles south of Searcy, White county, on the 7th April, of Pneumonia, Mr. S. H. **WINFORD**; also, on the 19th of April, Mrs. Narcissa Winford, of Pneumonia, consort of Mr. S. H. Winford, leaving four children to mourn the loss of their kind and beloved parents. The children of the deceased have been taken charge of by their uncle, Mr. Martin **SHETTER**, of Des Arc, and kindly provided for. Memphis Daily Appeal, 5/15/1857.

Decision by the Supreme Court of the State. Opinion by Judge Turley. Mayor and Aldermen of Memphis, vs. Wiley **WINGFIELD**. This is a suit brought before a Justice of the Peace by Wiley Wingfield, a free negro, against the Corporation of Memphis, to recover back ten dollars paid by him to the corporation by duress and false imprisonment under an illegal ordinance of the corporation. It appears by the case agreed that on the 18th of March, 1839, the Corporation of Memphis passed an ordinance in the words following: "Be it ordained, That it shall be the duty of the watch-man to arrest any free negro or slave that he or they may find out after ten o'clock and lodge him in the calaboose, there to remain till next morning, unless they have a special pass from their master or mistress if they be slaves, at which time he, she or they, if they be slaves, shall receive ten lashes on their naked backs, and a fine of two dollars be assessed on the owner of said slaves. If a free person of color, he, she or they shall be fined the sum of ten dollars for the use of the corporation." The plaintiff, a resident of the City of Memphis, was quietly and peaceably going along the streets of Memphis, in return from his ordinary employment, when he was arrested by a watchman of the city under this ordinance, imprisoned for the night, and in the morning forced to pay ten dollars for the use of the corporation…We think this ordinance is both unnecessary and oppressive, and enacted without authority, and affirm the judgement of the Commercial and Criminal Court of Memphis declaring it void. Memphis Enquirer, 5/11/1848.

K. J. B. L. **WINN**, Saddle, Bridle, Harness & Trunk Manufacturer, Front Row, between Washington & Adams Streets. Memphis Appeal, 11/20/1847.

Died, In Fayette county, on the 12th instant, Mrs. Martha Ann Winston, wife of Maj. E. **WINSTON**, aged about 33 years. American Eagle Weekly, 9/26/1845.

Married, On Wednesday evening last, by Rev. Mr. Fagg, Dr. Robert **WINSTON**, of Arkansas, to Miss Victoria, daughter of Charles **MICHIE**, Esq., of Fayette County, Tenn. Memphis Daily Appeal, Sun., 4/13/1856.

Married—On the 28th ult., by the Rev. Jeptha **HARRISON**, Mr. John **WINTERS** of Hernando, Miss., to Miss Catherine **PILCHER**, of this city, and late of Fredericksburg, Va. Memphis Enquirer, 5/3/1839.

R. C. **WINTERSMITH**, Cotton Factor, Grocer and Commission Merchant, On Bank Avenue, between Madison and Monroe, Memphis, Tenn….Memphis Daily Appeal, 10/27/1858.

Henrick **WIPPER**'s Residence For Sale. This is a very desirable and convenient Lot, with comfortable House for a small family….This Lot is known as Lot No. 6 on Ed. S. **TODD's** plan of subdivisions of the 100 acre Winchester Tract….G. B. **LOCKE**, Auctioneer and Real Estate Broker. Memphis Daily Appeal, 12/8/1855.

Married – On the 21st inst., by Rev. Dr. Wilkerson, Mr. Henry **WIPPER** to Mrs. Jane **WRIGHT**, both of the vicinity of Memphis. Daily Memphis Enquirer, 3/27/1849.

All persons having claims against the estate of the late Henry **WISE**, deceased, are hereby notified to present the same…for payment…..John A. **COOK**, Executor. Weekly Appeal, 1/29/1847.

Mansion House – Marshall M. **WISE** begs leave to inform his friends and the public, that he has taken the above establishment, situated on Mississippi Row, where he is ever ready to entertain them with the best fare the country will afford…..Memphis Enquirer, 10/27/1838.

Married, On the 21st inst. in the city of Memphis, at the residence of Mr. James **FLAHERTY**, by Rev. Sam'l. Wat__, Mr. A. M. **WISWELL**, of the firm of J. W. Wiswell and Miss Carrie E. **MANN**, of Worcester, Massachusetts. Memphis Daily Appeal, 5/23/1857.

Masonic Funeral. The Funeral…of the late Rev. Bro. George R. **WITT**, will take place at Friendship Church, in Fayette county, six miles West of La Grange, on Sunday next, with Masonic honors.—The Funeral discourse will be delivered by the Rev. Bro. L. H. **MILLIKEN**. The Lodges and transient brethren in all the adjoining counties are respectfully and fraternally invited to attend. Memphis Enquirer, Thurs., 4/19/1849.

Married. At the residence of Mr. Geo. **PENN** by the Rev. Gray, Mr. Simeon P. **WITT** to Miss Caroline H. **WARD**, all of this city. Memphis Eagle & Enquirer, 2/25/1853.

Mr. Tobias **WOLF**, late Wharf Master at this port, has been appointed Naval store keeper at Memphis…Memphis Appeal, 3/3/1852.

Married: On Thursday last at 11 o'clock, A.M., by the Rev. N. **HOWCOTT**, Mr. Benj. T. **WOLFE**, to Miss Louisa **BLACK**, all of this city…Memphis Eagle, Sat., 9/9/1848.

Died, In this city yesterday morning, the 12th inst., of typhoid fever, E. **WOLFE**, in the thirtieth year of his age. The funeral will take place from his late residence, at 169 Main street….This Morning. Memphis Daily Appeal, 8/13/1859.

Married, On the 26th instant by Rev. Wm. Carey **CRANE**, Mr. H. B. **WOLFKILL** and Miss Susan Ann **HIGHTOWER**, all of this city. Memphis Daily Appeal, 4/28/1857.

The funeral of the late Geo. **WOOD** was attended yesterday by a large delegation of the Masonic fraternity, of which he was a member. Memphis Daily Appeal, 8/18/1859.

Died, of Measles, at the Richmond House, on the morning of the 17th inst., Mr. James M. **WOOD**, in the 21st year of his age. The deceased had been a resident of our city but a few months…Memphis Eagle & Enquirer, 5/19/1852.

Died, In this vicinity, yesterday morning, Mrs. Lucinda A. **WOOD**. Funeral from the Episcopal Church, this morning…Memphis Eagle & Enquirer, 2/21/1852. Died, In the vicinity of Memphis, on the 20th ult., Mrs. Lucinda A. Wood, a native of Maryland, but for several years past a resident of this State…May her mantle fall upon her surviving son, her only, her beloved child…Memphis Eagle & Enquirer, 4/27/1852.

John W. **CALDWELL**, who killed Thomas J. **WOOD**, formerly of this city, at Columbus, Ky., last week, had his examination last Tuesday, and was committed to jail on the charge of murder. Memphis Daily Appeal, Sun., 9/4/1859.

The friends and acquaintances of Capt. W. T. and Laura **WOOD** are invited to attend the funeral of their daughter, Laura Bell, from their residence on Union street, near DeSoto, This Morning….Memphis Daily Appeal, 4/9/1857.

Died. Near Brownsville, Haywood county, Tenn., on March 11th, Mrs. Ariadne(?) T. Wood, wife of Wm. Proudfit **WOOD**, Esq., and daughter of the late Linus R. and Julia A. **LEONARD**. Aged 27 years, 3 months and 4 days. She left behind her an affectionate husband, three small children and a large circle of friends...She was a member of the Protestant Episcopal Church...Memphis Daily Eagle, 3/21/1850. Died, Near Brownsville, April 4th, William Proudfit Wood, Esq., son of the late Jonathan **WOOD**, in the 28th year of his age. Memphis Daily Eagle, 4/18/1850.

Married, On the 14th of January, 1857, by Elder N. H. **McFADDEN**, Mr. Louis H. **WOODARD**, of Lauderdale county, and Miss Jane **ANGUS**, of Tipton county, Tenn. Memphis Daily Appeal, 1/24/1857.

Died, In this city on Tuesday morning, Richmond **WOODARD**, age 29 years, second son of the late Col. E_bert and Saludia **WOODARD**. Memphis Daily Appeal, 11/3/1858.

Died, In this city, on the 27th instant, Mr. Thos. S. **WOODRUFF**, of New Albany, Indiana, aged 25 years. Memphis Daily Appeal, 8/29/1855.

Died, In Somerville, Mr. Alsey **WOODS**, of Memphis, aged about 47 years. American Eagle, 9/26/1845.

Died, on the 8th inst., in Randolph, after a painful illness of two months, Ann Eliza Woods, consort of David H. **WOODS**, leaving a loving husband and an infant babe, and a large circle of friends to mourn her loss. Daily Memphis Enquirer, 11/23/1848.

Died. On the 10[th](?) instant at Valley Grove, Ark., of Pneumonia, Mr. Geo. W. **WOODS**. Memphis Daily Appeal, 2/21/1855.

New Store – James **WOODS**, formerly of Philadelphia and late of Nashville, having permanently located himself at this place, respectfully informs his friends and the public that he is receiving and now opening at the store formerly occupied by Dewitt & Sims, Druggists, Mississippi Row.....Memphis Enquirer, 11/3/1838.

Died—On Wednesday, 4th inst., on his way South, Mr. John **WOODS**, Merchant, of this city. The Appeal, 12/13/1844.

The friends and acquaintances of Patrick **WOODS** are requested to attend his funeral This Afternoon at half past 3 o'clock, from the residence of Mr. C. J. **HARGAN**, on Bradford street, east of Winchester avenue. Memphis Daily Appeal, 11/22/1857.

We inadvertently omitted noticing yesterday the death of Plummer **WOODS**, a free negro, who died on Tuesday last. "Plummer" was for years the pressman in this office....By his industry and preseverance he had bought his freedom, and had acquired considerable property for himself and children....He was first attacked by the late prevailing fever....At the time of his death he was engaged as pressman in the *Bulletin* office....in the place of his nativity, Nashville....Memphis Daily Appeal, 10/26/1855.

Died, In this city on Thursday evening last, Mr. Wm. **WOODS**. The deceased was a young man of many sterling qualities...He was attended to his last resting place on yesterday evening by the fraternities of Masons and Odd Fellows, together with a large concourse of citizens. Memphis Daily Appeal, Sat., 1/11/1851.

At a meeting of the returned volunteers...Whereas, information has lately reached us, that our friend and fellow soldier, Lieut. Mathew **WOODSON**, of the Tennessee Cavalry, departed this life on the 7th ult; and whereas, in consideration of his many virtues, kind and gentlemanly deportment, his noble, gallant and patriotic exertion to serve his country in the arduous, bloody and ever memorable twelve months campaign.....H. R. **ROBARDS**, Ch'm. Wm. H. **AXTELL**, Sec'y. Memphis, 10/13/1847. Daily Enquirer, 10/15/1847. Died—At the residence of Richard **LEAKE** in this county, on the 7th inst., Matthew Woodson, aged 37 years, leaving a wife and two children to mourn his loss. His illness was contracted while serving the army in Mexico. Richmond Va. And Huntsville Ala. papers will please notice. Memphis Appeal, 10/16/1847.

Married, At Calvary Church on the 20th inst. by Rev. D. C. **PAGE**, Mr. Achieleus **WOODWARD** to Miss Julia **HAWLEY**, all of this city. Memphis Daily Appeal, 9/22/1855.

Died, At his residence in Crittenden county, Arkansas, at 9 o'clock last evening, Elbert **WOODWARD**, in the 64th year of his age. Petersburg, Va., and St. Louis, Mo., papers please copy. The friends and acquaintances of his family are invited to attend his funeral from the Worsham House at 4 o'clock This Evening. Services by Rev. Dr. Bryan. Memphis Daily Appeal, 3/31/1857.

Married, On the Tuesday evening, 23d instant, by Rev. Knott, Mr. J. Marshall **WOODWARD** and Miss Mary K. **WILLIAMS**, all of this city. Memphis Daily Appeal, 2/25/1857.

...Sir, please publish in your paper the death of private Edmund **WOOLDRIDGE**, a member of the "Memphis Rifle Guards."—He was accidently drowned while bathing in the Rio Grande, 3d inst. The deceased was formerly from Illinois, and had by his good conduct endeared himself to the officers and men of the company. His loss is much deplored...Respectfully, Fred B. **NELSON**, Jr., Lieut. Com'g, Memphis Rifle Guards, 2d Reg. Tenn. Volunteers. Weekly Appeal, 10/2/1846.

Died, Near Memphis, August 24th, 1858, Helen Hoskins Woolsey, only daughter of John L. and Rosa W. **WOOLSEY**—aged four years three months and eleven days. Memphis Daily Appeal, 8/28/1858.

Married—On the 13th inst., at 4 o'clock P.M., by the Rev. Dr. Wm. D. **WILKERSON**, Mr. Edward H. **WORD** of Louisiana, to Miss Martha E. **MORGAN** of this City. Memphis Enquirer, 12/14/1848.

Died, In Holly Springs, on Saturday the 13 th instant, at 7 o'clock, p.m., Mrs. Mary E. Word, consort of Col. T. J. **WORD**. Memphis Eagle & Enquirer, 3/27/1852.

At a meeting of Oakland Lodge No. 136, held February 1st, 1851, the following preamble and resolutions were unanimously adopted: whereas, It has pleased the Almighty Dispenser of human events to summon from our Lodge to the Grand Lodge above, our much esteemed friend, and beloved brother, Wm. L. **WORD**, who died, and was buried at sea on the 29th(?) of August last off Cape _____ Lucas on the Pacific coast, on his way to California...Memphis Daily Appeal, 2/21/1851.

Married, on Tuesday morning, by the Rev. Dr. Riddle, Mr. David P. **WORK** to Miss F. A. **MINER**, both of this city. Daily Memphis Enquirer, Tues., 6/20/1848.

Departed this life, after a short illness, on Saturday, the 1st of August, William Dickinson **WORMELEY**, youngest son of the late John C. **WORMELEY**, in the 24th year of his age.... Memphis Daily Appeal, 8/19/1857.

Married: At the residence of Col. L. J. **DUPREE** on Thursday the 16th inst. by Rev. Dr. Page, Mr. Edward C. **WORSHAM**, of Coffeeville, and Miss Sophie A. **BRIDGES**, of Holly Springs, Miss. Memphis Whig, 8/17/1855.

Married, On the 27th inst. near Collierville, at the residence of Mrs. A. T. **HARE**, by Rev. T. A. **WARE**, Dr. George H. **WORSHAM**, of LaGrange, and Miss Maggie V., daughter of Dr. J. H. **MARSHALL**, of Texas. Memphis Daily Appeal, 5/29/1856.

Married, On the 25th ult., by the Rev. Mr. Weatherby, Mr. J. J. **WORSHAM**, of Memphis, to Miss Martha A., daughter of James **GREER**, Sr., of Holly Springs, Miss. Weekly Appeal, 12/4/1846. Died, yesterday morning at 8 o'clock, John Jennings, youngest child of J. J. and Martha A. Worsham, aged 14 months. Memphis Daily Appeal, 12/27/1856.

Married, In this city by the Rev. S. T. **TONCRAY**, on Sunday evening 28th ult., Mr. William **WOSSON** to Miss Elizabeth **PITT**. The Appeal, 8/2/1844.

Married—On the 4th ins., at the 1st Presbyterian church, by Rev. Coons, Mr. J. Rich **WRAY**, to Miss Harriet C., daughter of Dr. C. E. **REINHARDT**, all of this city. Memphis Enquirer, 1/6/1846.

Died, At Purdy on the 27th ult., after a long and painful illness which was borne with the fortitude of a Christian, Mrs. Martha A. Wright, consort of Maj. Benjamin **WRIGHT**....She had been for many years a member of the Methodist Episcopal Church....She leaves behind her an aged husband and several devoted children to mourn her loss....Memphis Daily Appeal, 3/9/1859.

"Nashoba Springs".—A Summer Retreat. Mr. Editor:--Having occasion to visit the neighborhood of Germantown a few days since, I made it convenient during my stay in that vicinity to gather some definite information relative to those Springs situated upon the plantation of Mrs. Fanny **WRIGHT**, which have within the last eighteen months acquired such favorable notoriety in this division of the District. The Springs in question are situated about two miles from the village above mentioned, on the northern bank of Wolf River, and during the past sultry season they were resorted to daily not only by citizens residing in their immediate neighbor-hood, but by many visitors from a distance...The plantation of Mrs. Wright, including the Springs in question, has recently passed, by lease, into the hands of Mr. Benjamin **MOSBY**...Daily Enquirer, 4/7/1847.

Married, At Eutaw, Greene county, Ala., at the residence of Col. J. W. **WOMACK**, on Tuesday, the 23d(?) inst., by Rev. Mr. Neely, Hon. Jno. V. **WRIGHT**, of Tennessee, to Miss Georgie **HAYS**, of Alabama. Memphis Weekly Appeal, 12/1/1858.

We are authorized to announce Joseph **WRIGHT** a candidate for Alderman of the 3d Ward. Memphis Daily Appeal, 2/23/1848.

Married, In this city on the 18th inst., by Rev. James **YOUNG**, Mr. M. M. **WRIGHT** to Miss Kate **BIRMINGHAM**, all of this city. Memphis Daily Appeal, 1/20/1859.

Married. At the Second Methodist Church on yesterday evening, 2d inst. by Rev. W. C. **ROBB**, Mr. Marcus J. **WRIGHT** to Miss Martha S. **ELCAN**, all of this city. Memphis Daily Appeal, 11/3/1854.

Died, In Tipton county, Tenn., on the 8th of August, Mrs. Margaret **WRIGHT**, aged about 66 years—formerly of York District, S. C. Memphis Daily Appeal, 8/13/1858.

The most deliberate and cold-blooded murder, that has ever shocked the sensibilities of our community, was perpetrated about 2 o'clock yesterday morning upon the person of Mr. Samuel P. **WRIGHT**, who was deliberately shot down at his own door. Mr. W. was a butcher by trade and was engaged in making preparations to attend the market, as was his custom, when the assassin fired from his concealment near by, shooting him in the back, and killing him almost instantly. Circumstances have fixed suspicion upon an individual named Plummer **THURSTON**, who had been for some time associated with Wright in business, as the assassin. Thurston has been arrested, and will be held in custody until Monday 10 o'clock, when an investigation will be had before the examining court. No doubt is entertained of a most wicked and deliberate plot to take the life of Wright, as he had but a few nights before been fired upon by some one in the dark, and we are informed had admonished his family of the existence of a plot to kill him....Daily Enquirer, 9/18/1847.

Married, On Thursday evening last, by J. **WALDRAN**, Esq., Mr. Thomas **WRIGHT** to Miss Juliann S. **JURGESS**, all of this county. Memphis Eagle & Enquirer, Sat., 2/14/1852.

Extract from the minutes of Wesley Chapter, No. 35, at its meeting in March, A.D. 1853. "Whereas, It has pleased divine Providence to remove from this life our esteemed Companion, Thos. L. **WRIGHT**, Esq., a bright ornament of our Chapter....as a Man and a Mason, and that we unitedly extend to his surviving relations our cordial sympathy....Memphis Eagle & Enquirer, 4/9/1853.

Married, In this city, on the 15th inst., by Rev. I. D. (or J. D.) **WILLIAMSON**, Albert C. **WURZBACH** of Memphis, to Margaret Ann, daughter of J. A. **KIMBALL** of New York. American Eagle, 5/20/1847.

Died—In this city, on last Friday night, the 22 instant Lieut. Edwin J. **WYATT**, in the 22d year of his age. The deceased served one year in the late war with Mexico, as a Lieutenant in the 2d Regt. Tenn. Volunteers. His early death is deeply regretted by his numerous friends. Daily Memphis Enquirer, 7/28/1848.

Memphis Emigrants to California—We were yesterday shown a letter addressed to Col. J. C. **McLEMORE**, by Maj. Geo. W. **WYATT**. Maj. W., it will be recollected, was one of a party consisting of Messrs. **KEELING, GOLL, McLEMORE** and others of this city. The letter is dated "Panama, Sept. 13, '49." The party were all in good health, and had crossed the Isthmus with less inconvenience and loss of time than any preceding party. They were to embark on the *California*, on the 17th, for San Francisco.... Weekly Memphis Eagle, 10/18/1849.

Died. In this city, last evening, at the Gayoso House, Col. Peyton S. **WYATT**, of Bowie County, Texas, formerly of Huntsville, Ala.—His friends and acquaintances are invited to attend his funeral from the Gayoso House, this evening at 4 o'clock. Memphis Daily Eagle, 10/25/1847.

Died, on the 12th instant, in this county, of pneumonia, Mrs. Mary Wynne, wife of Peter D. **WYNNE**, formerly of Wake county, North Carolina, and daughter of Samuel and Tabitha **PERSON**, of Moore county, N.C.—in the 48th year of her age. She died with a comfortable prospect of a happy inheritance in eternity. [The Raleigh Register will please copy the above for the benefit of friends and relations in North Carolina.] Daily Memphis Enquirer, 1/26/1848.

Married—On Thursday evening, in this county, by Rev. Gray, Mr. Wm. G. **WYNNE** to Miss Harriet **FEATHERSTON**. American Eagle, Fri., 7/4/1845.

Died—At his residence on the Germantown Plank-road, on Saturday morning, the 9th inst....of chronic diarrhea and dyspepsia, after a lingering illness, William Isham **WYNNE**. Mr. W. was born in Sumner county, Tenn., on the 18th day of September, 1817, and was, therefore, in his 42d year. He was nearly all his lifetime, from the age of 15 years, engaged in mercantile pursuits. He removed from Natchez, Miss., to this place some three years since, and was, at the time of his demise, owner of an extensive flouring mill, near the Charleston Depot. He joined, soon after he attained the age of 21 years, the Masonic fraternity, and was buried by them with all honors. Although a member of no Church, yet he had been raised up by a Christian mother....As a husband, son, father, brother and master, his noble qualities were always displayed. He leaves a wife, three children, mother and two brothers....to grieve his untimely death. Natchez (Miss.) Concordia, La., and Clarksville (Tenn.) papers will please copy. Memphis Daily Avalanche, 4/14/1859.

Information Wanted, of Thomas **YALLOLEE**, who left Memphis in 1837, and stated that he was going to settle in the State of Missouri. If this notice should reach either Mr. Yallolee or any of his relatives or friends, they will find it to their advantage to address the undersigned. Jedediah **PRESCOTT**, Memphis, Tenn. Memphis Daily Appeal, 7/30/1848.

Died. At Germantown, Shelby Co., Tenn., on the 19th ult., Alexander, son of A. L. **YANCEY** in the 3d year of his age. American Eagle, 7/8/1847. I am determined to raise a company of respectable men, to serve in the present war against Mexico. All who are disposed to join me will come forward immediately to Camp Nelson, one mile east of Memphis...A. L. Yancey. Daily Enquirer, 10/12/1847.

It is our melancholy duty to record the death of Mr. James E. **YANCEY**, who departed this life last evening at six o'clock, at his mother's residence in this city. Mr. Yancey was a practical printer, and worked for several years in this city, as well as at St. Louis....His disease was consumption....Memphis Daily Appeal, 5/14/1857. The remains of James E. Yancey will be conveyed to LaGrange to-day for interment in the family burying-ground....Memphis Daily Appeal, 5/15/1857. Owing to the death of Mr. James E. Yancey, brother of Mr. Wm. T. **YANCEY**, one of the editors of the *News*, no paper will be issued from that office this afternoon. Memphis Daily Appeal, 5/14/1857.

Died, In this city yesterday, August 3d, after a short illness, Emma Caroline, youngest daughter of the late R. J. and Mrs. M. W. **YANCEY**, aged thirteen years, six months and five days. The friends and acquaintances are respectfully notified that the funeral of the deceased will take place from the family residence, Vance street, near Main, This Morning....Services by Rev. Dr. Steadman. Memphis Daily Appeal, 8/4/1859.

At a special meeting of La Grange Lodge No. 81, of Ancient, Free and Accepted Masons, at Masonic Hall, in the town of La Grange, on Wednesday, 12th May, A.D. 1852, the following resolutions were offered and unanimously passed: Resolved, That members of this Lodge, in consideration of their esteem for our deceased brother, Robert J. **YANCEY**, formerly a member of this Lodge and for a time its presiding officer, wear the usual badge of mourning for thirty days...Memphis Eagle & Enquirer, 6/8/1852. We are pained to announce the death of Robert J. Yancey, who departed this life yesterday, at his residence in South Memphis, in the 46th year of his age, after a long and painful illness. The deceased was for a great many years connected with the press of this State—having published a paper at Lagrange as early as 1835-6.—He afterwards edited and published the Reporter at Sommerville for a number of years. From Sommerville he removed to Memphis in the spring of 1848, and assumed the editorship of the Enquirer, in which position he remained until the autumn of 1850, when he established the Southerner...Memphis Eagle & Enquirer, 5/9/1852.

Married, On the 1ˢᵗ instant by Rev. Bryan, at the Cumberland Presbyterian Church, Mr. Wm. T. **YANCEY** and Miss Mary L. **DeWITT**, all of this city. Memphis Daily Appeal, 1/3/1857. Wm. T. Yancey, Esq., late one of the editors of the Evening News of this city, has taken the editorial charge of the Corsicanna Times, published At Corsicanna, Navarra county, Texas. We wish him much success in his new home. Memphis Evening Ledger, 12/17/1857.

Prof. L. P. **YANDELL**.—This distinguished Professor of medicine, as we learn from the Louisville *Courier*, has resigned his professorship in the Medical Department of the University of Louisville, with the view of removing to this city. His son, Dr. L. P. **YANDELL**, jr., is already one of our permanent citizens....Memphis Daily Appeal, 5/22/1859.

Married, In this vicinity, on the 19th inst., by the Rev. Coons, Mr. Seth G. **YARBROUGH** to Miss Elizabeth Bettis, daughter of Mr. Tilman **BETTIS** of Shelby county. Weekly Memphis Eagle, 9/27/1849.

Died, On Friday, January 28, 1859....in Louisa county, Va., Mrs. Chas. **YATES**, of this city. The funeral will take place This Afternoon....from the residence of her son, Mr. Meredith **YATES**, on Washington street....The services will be held in the Baptist Church. Mrs. Yates had for some time suffered from ill health and had visited Virginia with the hope of improvement....Putting her arms around the neck of her brother shortly before her death....Memphis Daily Appeal, 2/3/1859. Died, On the 28ᵗʰ January, 1859, at the residence of her relative, Mr. Joseph **COATES**, in the county of Louisa, State of Virginia, Mrs. Chloe Yates, daughter of Meredith **WALTON**, Esq., and widow of the late William **YATES** of the city of Memphis....had recently come on a visit to her near relative in this county, under the care of a very devoted and affectionate brother....Dr. P. B. Pendleton. Louisa Co., Va., Feb. 5, 1859. The deceased was a worthy and highly esteemed member of the First Baptist Church in this city....Memphis Daily Appeal, 2/27/1859.

All persons indebted to the estate of the late William **YATES**, senior, deceased, are requested to call upon the undersigned....Chloe **YATES**, Adm'trix, Meredith **YATES**, Adm'r. Memphis Daily Appeal, 9/10/1853.

Married, On Thursday, the 22ⁿᵈ inst., at the residence of A. **HENDERSON**, by Rev. J. O. **STEDMAN**, Edwin M. **YERGER**, Esq., and Miss Mollie J. **HENDERSON**, all of this city. Memphis Daily Appeal, 10/25/1857.

The members of South Memphis Lodge No. 118, are hereby notified to be at their Lodge Room, on to-morrow (Sunday) afternoon at 2 o'clock, to attend the Funeral of our late brother, James **YERRY**.... Memphis Daily Appeal, 1/27/1855.

Died, At his residence, Hickory Wythe, Tenn., on the morning of the 14th August, 1851, Dr. George M. YOUNG, after a protracted sickness of 2 ½ months.—He leaves a wife and many relations to mourn his loss. Memphis Daily Appeal, 8/19/1851. Masonic Tribute of Respect. At a called meeting of Oakland Lodge No. 136, held August 15th, 1851, the following preamble and resolutions were unanimously adopted: Whereas, It has pleased the Grand Master of the Universe to call from our midst our much esteemed friend and brother, Dr. George M. Young...Wm. CLAMPITT, W. M. Lewis AMIS, Jr., Sec'y. Memphis Daily Appeal, 9/2/1851.

Married, On the 20th day of March by Rev. J. WILSON, Mr. J. YOUNG and Miss FURGISON, both of Tipton county, Tenn. Memphis Daily Appeal, 4/3/1856.

Dr. James YOUNG, Having permanently located in Memphis, respectfully tenders his professional services to the public. Office on Main Street, opposite Court Square. Memphis Enquirer, 11/12/1846.

Married, By the Rev. Dr. Page, on the evening of the 22d instant, at the residence of E. H. PORTER, Esq., Capt. Wm. F. YOUNG to Miss Maria COOK—all of this city. Memphis Daily Eagle, 4/24/1850.

Died, On Sunday morning, 22nd inst., Rachel S., daughter of William W. and J. E. YOUNG. The friends and acquaintances of the family are particularly invited to attend her funeral this morning, 24th inst., at 10 o'clock from her late residence No. 90 Court street. Memphis Daily Appeal, 11/24/1857.

Died, in this city, on the 28th November, in the 25th year of her age, Rebecca K. Younger, wife of Coleman YOUNGER, and daughter of William L. and Constantia D. SMITH. Eighteen months since, warned by the ravages of disease to draw nearer to Him whose final summons she was shortly to hear, she embraced religion, and shortly after joined the Baptist Church, at Little Shoals, Clay co., Missouri...In recording the end and transcribing, for her wide circle of relations in Missouri, in Kentucky, and far away on the Pacific, the last words of a true and gentle-hearted woman...Memphis Daily Eagle, 11/30/1850.

Died, In this city, on the 28th inst., after a few days illness of Gastro-Enteritis, Dr. Caleb B. ZUBER, student in the Botanico Medical College; recently from his residence in Winston Co., Miss. Memphis Daily Appeal, 11/30/1852. (Author's note: Name given as YUBER in list of interrments.)

Married, On Tuesday evening, the 26th inst. by Hume F. HILL, Esq., Mr. Dominick ZWEIFEL, (Proprietor of the German House,) to Miss Ernstine SCHUHMANN, all of this city. Memphis Daily Appeal, 1/28/1858.

....the announcement of the death by accident on Monday of Jacob ZWEIFUL, a member of the Steuben Artillery. The deceased was engaged loading one of the guns during the firing of the salute Monday morning, when the gun was discharged prematurely. By the accident Mr. Zweiful lost a portion of his right arm, and was shockingly burned on other portions of his body. He lingered in great pain until the afternoon, when his suffering ended in death. The deceased was a native of the canton of Claris, Switzerland, and had long been in the employ of Messrs. Joseph Keller & Co., of this city....He was an active member of the Grutlevein Society, of this city, as also of the Independent Order of Odd Fellows. He left a wife and child. The remains of the deceased were followed to their final resting place, in Winchester Cemetery last evening.... Memphis Daily Appeal, Wed., 7/6/1859.

LIST OF DEATHS OF THE TENN. VOLUNTEERS IN THE HOSPITAL AT MEMPHIS:
Wm. HELTON, 5th Regiment Company A; Jas. POLLARD, 4th Reg. Co. A; H. SWANSON, 4th Reg. Co. I; R. HORTON, 5th Reg. Co. L; J. COXE, 3d Reg; Wm. LINES, 4th Reg. Co. I; J. B. CALDWELL, 4th Reg. Co. D; M. HUTCHINS, 3d Reg; E. BECK, 5th Reg. Co. H; R. WILLIAMS, 5th Reg. Co. A; J. GHANT, 3d Reg. Co. E; T. CARPENTER, 4th Reg. Co. C; M. B. GLASS, 5th Reg. Co. L; Wm. MATTHEWS, 4th Reg. Co. C; Thos. LEDDY, 3d Reg. Co. 1; Chas. KELLY, 3d Reg. Co. A; N. NELSON, 5th Reg. Co. I; G. W. JAMES, 4th Reg. John TURNER, 3d Reg. Co. I; L. DAVIS, 5th Reg. Co. H; D. COOPER, 4th Reg.; A. TEMPLE, 4th Reg. Daily Memphis Enquirer, 8/9/1848.

"The Memphis City Guard" met last night at the City Council Chamber – S. P. **WALKER**, Esq., in the Chair. A Constitution was reported and adopted, and the officers elected. The following is a list of the Officers: Jos. R. **WILLIAMS** – Captain, Jno. L. **SAFFARANS** – 1st Lieutenant, Jesse S. **HARRIS** – 2d Lieutenant, C. M. **FACKLER** – 3d Lieutenant, Jno. M. **WILLIAMS** – Orderly Sargeant, P. W. **HUMPHREYS** – Ensign. Memphis Daily Eagle & Enquirer, 5/19/1852.

CITY BUSINESS DIRECTORY, 9/1/1851:
Bankers & Exchange Brokers.
W. H. **CARROLL** & Co., Main st., opposite Odd F's Hall. R. S. **DILL** & Co., Odd Fellow's Hall.
Watchmakers & Jewelers.
F. H. **CLARK** & Co., No. 37, Front Row. C. G. **MERRIMAN**, Corner of Madison st. and F. Row.
Commission Merchants, Wholesale Grocers & Produce Dealers.
A. O. **HARRIS**, No. 25, Front Row. J. M. **PATRICK**, No. 3, Howard's Row. **McCONNELL** & Bro., No. 4, Howard's Row. **CHERRY, TERRY** & Co., No. 10, Howard's Row. J. L. **WEBB** & Co., Madison st., opposite Post Office. I. Y. **GIBSON**, No. 104 Front Row. **TOWNSEND & McMANUS**, No. 55, Front Row. **STRATTON, GOODLETT & McDAVITT**, No. 70, Front Row. **GRIFFING & FORD**, Main st., opposite Odd Fellows Hall. S. & A. **FOWLKES** & Co., corner Main & Adams sts. **TITUS** & Co., No. 1, Exchange Building. Richard E. **ORNE** & Co., Main St., opposite O.F. Hall. **BRADLEY, WILSON** & Co., No. 62 ½, Front Row. Thos. **McKEON**, No. 62, Front Row. G. B. **LOCKE** & Bro., No. 15, Front Row. Q. L. **MORTON**, Main st., between Adams & Jefferson. S. O. **NELSON** & Co., Jefferson st., opposite Com'l Hotel. J. H. **STEPHENSON** & Co., Main st., opposite U. S. Hotel. J. F. **McKINNEY**, Batture, foot of Adams st. W. W. **MILLER**, Batture, foot of Adams st. **McKINNEY** & Co., Main St., Fowlkes Row. **DOUGLASS & GRIDLEY**, No. 8, Howard's Row.
Wholesale Grocer & Dealer in Liquor.
J. **BORO**, No. 20, Front Row.
Saddle Harness & Trunk Maker.
W. P. **LEWIS**, Madison st., opposite Union Bank.
Booksellers & Stationers.
B. C. **CLEAVES**, No. 50, Front Row. S. H. **LAMB**, Madison st., West of Union Bank.
Clothing Stores.
KELLER & SHALLER, No. 35, Front Row. J. R. **MEADE** & Co., No. 62, Front Row. B. **EMANUEL**, No. 82, Front Row. John **HENRY**, East end of Howard's Row.
Merchant Tailors.
SHARPE & WAGGONER, Madison st., opposite U. Bank. A. F. **GIBBS**, Madison st., East of Post Office. John **HENRY**, East end of Howard's Row.
Dry Goods Merchants.
HARBERTS & MAXWELL, No. 9, Front Row. S. **CONDIT**, No. 18, Front Row. G. B. **LOCKE** & Bro., No. 13, Front Row. **STREET & DOHERTY**, Front Row. **FERGUSON & NEILL**, Main st., opposite Odd Fellows Hall. H. G. **BUCKINGHAM** & Co., corner of Madison street & Front Row. F. **FALLY** & Co., corner of Main & Adams sts.
Druggists & Apothecaries.
MANSFIELD & McINTOSH, No. 44, Front Row. B. I. **OLMSTED**, No. 2, Front Row. Dr. W. A. **BOOTHE**, No. 26, Front Row. H. F. **FARNSWORTH**, Madison st., opposite Post Office. T. **McGOWN**, Main st., near U. S. Hotel. H. P. **TOURNER**, corner Madison & Main sts.
Boots & Shoes.
Jno. C. **CLARKE**, No. 75, Front Row. Jos. S. **LOVETT**, No. 47, Front Row. C. **O'CONNER**, Court st.
Insurance Companies.
Mutual Benefit, Life & Fire Insurance, of New Orleans, J. M. **PATRICK**, Agt., No. 3, Howard's Row.
Mutual Protection of Nashville, A. D. **WETHERSPOON**, Agent, Madison st.
Dealers In Tin-Ware & Stores.

RISK & BURNETT, Madison street, near Main. **CHRYSTAL & SMITH**, No. 14, Jefferson st. G. W. **SAFFARANS**, No. 96, Front Row. S. **McMANUS**, No. 43, Front Row.

Milliners & Mantau Makers.

Mrs. Rose P. **THOMPSON**, No. 10, Jeffeson st. Mrs. **CORNWALL**, Madison st.

Music Stores.

P. **FLAVIO**, Jefferson st., under Com'l Hotel.

Plough & Wagon Manufactory.

lsaac **PHELON**, corner Poplar & Second st.

Dentists.

N. **HOWCOTT**, corner Main & Adams st. J. **BORDLEY**, Southside Court Square.

Planeing Mill & Sash Factory.

A. P. **WHIPPLE** & Co., Foot of Madison st.

Foundries.

W. C. **BRADFORD**, Poplar st., near Bayou Gayoso. S. B. **CURTIS** & Co., Batture, West Exchange Square.

Furniture Dealers.

H. M. **GROSVENOR**, No. 10, Exchange Building. J. F. **McKINNEY**, Batture, foot of Adams st. **McKINNEY** & Co., Main st., near U. S. Hotel.

Justice of the Peace.

H. F. **HILL**, Shelby st.

Family Grocers.

A. **COOK**, corner Beale & Shelby sts. J. **CROGER**, Shelby st., between Beale & Linden. J. C. **MORRILL**, Market, east of Main Street. F. **BEAMISH**, Poplar st., between Main & F. Row.

Daguereotypist.

W. G. **ADAMS**, corner Front Row & Court st.

General Land & Collecting Agents.

WILLIAMS & STRAIN, Main st., opposite Odd F. Hall.

Memphis Medical College. Faculty: Hardy V. **WOOTEN**, M.D., Professor of the Theory & Practice of Medicine. Thomas W. **COLESCOTT**, M.D., Professor of Anatomy. Bennet **DOWLER**, M.D., Professor of Physiology & Pathological Anatomy. Ayres P. **MERRIL**, M.D., Professor of Materia Medica & Therapeutics. Howel R. **ROBARDS**, M.D., Professor of Theory & Practice of Surgery. Edward H. **LEFFINGWELL**, M.D., Professor of Chemistry & Pharmacy. Lewis **SHANKS**, M.D., Professor of Obstetrics & Diseases of Women & Children & Dean of the Faculty. George F. **JONES**, M.D., Demonstrator of Anatomy. Memphis Daily Appeal, 9/1/1851.

Memphis Institute....Faculty. H. J. **HULCE**, M.D., Professor of Surgery. D. A. **MILLION**, M.D., Professor of Obstetrics & the Diseases of Women & Children. B. F. **LIDDON**, M.D., Professor of Materia Medica & Medical Botany. J. **GILLMAN**, M.D., Professor of Anatomy. G. **HUTCHINGS**, M.D., Professor of Theory & Practice of Medicine. C. **GILLMAN**, M.D., Professor of Chemistry & Pharmacy. B. **WOOD**, M.D., Demonstrator of Anatomy. H. J. **HULCE**, Dean. Memphis Daily Appeal, 9/2/1851.

The following officers were elected yesterday by the Board of Mayor and Aldermen: Wm. **HOUSTON** – Recorder, City Marshal – J. **HORN**; Assistant do., and "ex officio" – Chief of the Day Police – J. **HALSTEAD**; Tax Collector – Jno. **NEWSOM**; Wharf Master – Tobias **WOLF**; City Sexton – Geo. **FLAHERTY**; Capt. Night Police – J. C. **MORRILL**. The following comprises a full list of the Day and Night Police appointed yesterday by the respective Chiefs: Day Police – J. **HALSTEAD**, Deputy Marshal and Captain of Day Police: John J. **MADDOX**, B. F. **JOHNSON**, W. C. **CAUSEY**, J. C. **DAVENPORT**. Night Police – John C. **MORRILL**, Captain: H. C. **EVANS**, Lieut. J. A. **McCALL**, Eugene W. **MALLORY**, C. M. **NORTON**, James **RILEY**, Enoch **EULOWE**, Maurice **CONWAY**, Wesley

CLEMONDS, Thos. S. CARSON, G. W. GRAY, Thos. MAGUIRE, Jas. C. WILSON. Memphis Daily Appeal, 7/21/1852.

Divine Services, Sunday, July 2, 1854:
First Presbyterian Church, corner of Poplar & Second streets – Rev. J. O. STEDMAN, Pastor.
Second Presbyterian Church, corner of Beale & Main streets – Rev. J. H. GRAY, Pastor.
The Cumberland Presbyterian Church is situated on Court, between Second & Third streets – Rev. Dr. H. S. PORTER, Pastor.
The First Baptist Church is situated on Second street, between Adams & Washington streets – Rev. C. R. HENDRICKSON, Pastor.
Second Baptist Church, on Beale street, east of Bayou Gayoso – Rev. I. D. ISBELL, Pastor.
The Methodist Church is situated on the corner of Second & Poplar – Rev. J. W. KNOTT, Pastor.
The Second Methodist Church (Asbury Chapel) is situated on the corner of Linden & Hernando streets – Rev. J. C. McFARLAND, Pastor.
The Episcopal Church is situated on the corner of Adams & Second streets – Rev. D. C. PAGE, Pastor.
Catholic Church, corner of Third & Adams streets – Rev. T. L. GRACE, Pastor.

City Directory. City officers. R. D. BAUGH, Mayor; L. R. RICHARDS, Register; T. M. EAST, Recorder; J. O. REINHARDT, Marshal; W. J. WHITSITT, Deputy Marshal; E. C. KIRK, Treasurer; S. P. BANKHEAD, Attorney; R. S. JOINER, Inspector; A. H. AVERY, Wharf Master; Frank BYRD, Deputy Wharf Master; Charles MILLER, Street Commissioner; C. A. MALLORY, Jailor; E. CARMICHAEL, G. W. ORR, Assistant Jailor; F. E. STAINBACK, Overseer Work House; J. I. CAIN, Assistant Overseer Work House. Aldermen: 1st Ward – Daniel HUGHES, J. S. IRWIN. 2d Ward – A. STREET, W. O. LOFLAND. 3d Ward – R. S. JONES, J. A. WOODRUFF. 4th Ward – T. J. FINNIE, I. M. HILL. 5th Ward – T. A. HAMILTON, F. M. E. FAULKNER. 6th Ward – John MARTIN, F. M. COPELAND. Policemen: J. F. JOHNSON, Captain Day Police; S. A. MOORE, Lieutenant Day Police; J. C. WILSON, J. A. WISE, J. COPELAND, C. VAN CAMPEN, L. HESS, Sam. LOGAN, R. G. TUCKER, Wm. G. McILVAINE, T. HICKEY, J. P. WORTHAM, B. G. GARRETT, Captain Night Police; S. M. THOMAS, Lieut. Night Police. F. G. BUTLER, G. N. ROBINSON, H. REED, John MAGEVENY, Wm. VIERS, B. A. CARTER, G. NICHOLAS, J. T. COLLIER, G. ORR, W. BARNES, D. T. PORTER, J. J. McMURRAY, Isaac DAY, W. S. TUCKER. Constables: 5th Civil District – John W. TAYLOR; 14th Civil District – John W. HAWTHORN. Sheriff – James E. FELTS, Principal. Deputies – George R. POWELL, James T. CROFORD, John E. BRANCH. Memphis Evening Ledger, 10/16/1857.

DIVINE SERVICES: St. Peter's Catholic Church...Priest, Rev. T. L. GRACE; First Baptist Church...Elder T. J. DRANE, Pastor; Grace Church...Rev. G. P. SCHETSKY; Cumberland Presbyterian Church...Rev. A. M. BRYAN, Pastor; Christian Church...Rev. W. J. BARBEE, Pastor; Second Presbyterian Church...Rev. R. C. GRUNDY, Pastor; Wesley Charge...Rev. J. T. C. COLLINS, Pastor; Second Baptist Church...Rev. Mr. ISBELL, Pastor; Lutheran Church...Rev. BEYER, Pastor....Memphis Evening Ledger, 12/5/1857.

Report of the Board of Health. The following deaths have occurred during the past week: Wm. BLOCKMAN's child, aged 6 months, cholera infantum; G. F. WRIGHT's child, aged 2 years; Wm. MORRISON, aged 54 years, chronic disease of the liver; Mrs. GRIFFIN, aged 30 years, fever; Mr. C. BARBER's child, aged 2 years; Miss BREIL, aged 12 years, congestion of the brain; Mr. T. M. HILTON's child, aged 4 years, inflamation of the brain; Wm. HAUCY, aged about 22 years, cholera; Mrs. O'BRIEN, aged 20 years, cholera....Memphis Daily Appeal, 6/5/1851.

The following deaths have occurred during the past week: Leah **DAVIS**, negro woman, aged 40 years, of cholera; Wm. **HUGHES**, aged 4 years, do; Jas. **HOLCOMB**, aged 22 years, do; Phoebe **GRAHAM**, 22 years, negro woman, do; John **TAYLOR**'s son, 18 months, do; M. C. **McNINCH**, 47, do; Wm. **SLAUGHTER**, 9 months, cholera infantum; Edward **BROOMACHE**, 2, dysentery; Martin **O'BRIAN**, 2, diarrhea; Charles E. **BARRY**, 5, typhoid fever; Wm. **BURNS**, 2, cholera infantum; Mr. **CHRISTY**'s child, 2, diarrhea; H. D. **HIESTAN**'s child, 6 mos., cholera infantum; Capt. J. C. **CARR**, 47, diarrhea. Memphis Daily Appeal, 6/11/1851.

LIST OF INTERMENTS FOR 1851:

7/20–Mr. Patrick **O'BRIEN**, Ireland, 27, cholera; Male child of Jno **CUBBING**, 15 mos, disease unknown. 7/21-Mary **O'LEARY**, 10 days, of spasms; Infant child of Jacob **WELLER**. 7/22-Mary M. **BROWN**, 22 mos, disease unknown; Jno **LANE**, 30, consumption. 7/24-Mr. Patrick **MAHAR**, 27, Ireland, cholera; Mr. Michael **McMAHON**, Ireland, 30, Bilious Fever; Mr. Jno **RYAN**, 27, Ireland, consumption. 7/25–Mr. Jas. **CLIFFORD**, 36, Ireland, cholera; Sarah H. **MANNING**, 43, chronic diarrhea; Mary **DENNESSEY**, 2, diarrhea; Henry **BIGGS**, 13 months, teething. 7/29–Alecia **HENDERSON**, 11 mos., Whooping cough; infant child of Carolina **ROTHEN**, 2 hours old; Margaret **COPPEN**, 30, fever
8/1-James **ROSS**, 21, Billious Fever. 8/3-Andrew **ROGERS**, 22, congestion of the brain. 8/7-W. S. **PRUETT**, 48, congestive chills; Jno. **ROSS**, 2, Whooping Cough; Elizabeth **MORRIS**, 43, Inflamation of the Stomach; Caledonia **WILKERSON**, 9 mos., Diarrhea. 8/8-Mrs. **SAXON**, 25, Child-Birth; Thos. **SHEA**, 36, shot in a fight. 8/9-Robert **GRAY**, 50, Cramp; Sarah **CONSTANTINE**, 18 mos., Diarrhea. 8/11-John T. **HOOPER**, 30, congestive fever; Edmund **BRIEN**, Ireland, 22, congestive fever. 8/12-John **BUER**, 19, congestive fever; Mrs. Mary **FENNESSEY**, Ireland, 30, bilious fever; Mrs. S. A. **SLAUGHTER**, 20, consumption. 8/13-Thos. **CONSTANTINE**, 4; Michael **MARONEY**, Ireland, killed; Willis **WEEMS**, 35, Diarrhea. 8/14-Mrs. Catharine **FOY**, Ireland, 24. 8/15-Son of H. **GLENGARY**, 2 days old. 8/16-Mr. Thomas **BUTLER**'s son, 8 mos., croup. 8/18(?)–Richard **JORDAN**, 40, cramp; John **BURKE**, 26, intermittent fever; J. R. **HADDEN**, 3__ years, typhoid fever; Dennis **DEWIRE**, 28, billious fever. 8/19-Mr. M. **FINLAND**, 40, Ireland. 8/24-Sarah J. **DONNEVAN**, 9, congestive chills. 8/25-Son of Mr. John **McSAUNLEY**, 2. 8/27-Mrs. **KEATON**, 30, billious fever; Mr. James **TAIT**, 51, fever; Mrs. **BANNON**, 30, fever; Mrs. **COFFEE**, 40, congestive chill. 8/29-Infant child of Thos. B. **CARROLL**, Esq. 8/30-Mary **LEVY**, 8, brain fever.
9/1-John W. **BURKE**, 2, inflammation of the bowels; Patrick **SHEA**, 37, fever. 9/4-Mary Ann **MARSH**, 34, congestion. 9/6-Michael **GILLIGAN**, 30. 9/7-John **PORTELL**, 35, consumption; James **HICKEY**, 35, dropsy. 9/8-Garnet **BYRN**'s child, 14 mos., bowel complaint; Joseph **WEBBER**, 12, consumption; Barney **KING**, 35, congestion; Patrick **ROACH**, 32, chills; Daniel **McCARTY**, 50, unknown; Mrs. **STAFFORD**'s son, 9; James **ELLISON**'s son, 14, congestive chill. 9/11-Mr. **STAPLE**'s child, 18 mos. 9/12-Margaret **O'BRIEN**, 10, billious fever; Margaret **McMAHAN**, 30, disease of the heart; Wm. **GARY**, 30, congestion; Robert **MALLORY**, 30, chronic diarrhea. 9/13-Martin **FURLONG**, 27, bowel complaint; Mary **McCARTHY**, 46, billious fever; Rosanna **McCONNELL**, 41, accouchment. 9/14-E. **KEEFE**, 35, consumption. 9/16-Henrietta **IRBY**, 19, billious fever; Thomas F. **SAUNDERS**, 46, consumption. 9/17-Ann **KELLY**, 27, congestion. 9/18-Nicholas **RIESTH**(?), 58, asphyxia; Chas. S. **SEALFASS**, 28, diarrhea; Ed. **CUSACK**, 21, congestion. 9/19-John **McCORMICK**, 30, intermittent fever. 9/20-John **RYAN**, 30, intermittent fever. 9/27-Wm **MARSH**, 21(?), inflammation of bowels; P. **FRANK**, 44(?), congestion. 9/28-Mr. **GALDEN**, 60, congestive chills. 9/29-Edward **McGRATH**, 30, fit; Mrs. **FRENCH**, 32, typhoid fever; Dr. F. R. **NEAL**, 32, dropsy and affection of the lungs; infant of Robert **GIFT**; William, son of W. **WALDRAN**, 16 mos., inflammation; J. C. **CLARK**, effects of burn. 9/30-Mrs. Mary **KITSON**(?), 33, billious fever
10/1-Child of W. O. **LOFLAND**, 6 mos. 10/2-Patrick **CARY**, 35, congestion; James **GORMERLY**, 60, congestion. 10/3-Geo. B. **VINCENT**, 26, hydrocephalia; John **COSHTER**(?), German, 60, congestive chills. 10/4-Mrs. **HILTON**, 40(?), bowel complaint; Ellen **GREEDY**, 18 mos., diarrhea; son of D. M. **GILL**, 16; Mrs. Mary **KAIN**, 30, chills. 10/5-Ellen **TWOHILL**, 18 mos., diarrhea; Maurice **DRADDY**, 33, congestion; Jackson **CAMPBELL**, 7, worms. 10/6-John **McGOWEN**, 45, congestion; Mrs. Eve **RAPP**, 71. 10/7-F. D. **BROWN**, 25, congestive chill; E. M. **DRIVER**, 55, consumption; Catharine

JUNGLASS, 9, billious fever; Henry **DIEUS**, 28, mania potu; Samuel **BURKE**, 18, diarrhea. 10/8-Thomas **CAMPBELL**, 50, billious fever. 10/9-Patrick **RYAN**, 30, euteritis. 10/10–Mrs. John **GORMAN**, accouchment; Catharine **MAHER**, 2 ½, fever; Mary **O'BRIAN**, 1, fever. 10/11–Chas **McGUIRE**, 39, mania potu; Samuel **MANGRUM**, 22, congestion. 10/11-Morris **McNAMARA**, 30, congestive chill. 10/14-G. W. **VINCENT**, 6, fever. 10/16-Merritt R. **BROWN**, 42, congestive chills; Fleury **McCARTHY**, 25, chronic diarrhea. 10/17-Philip **TOLAND**, 22; John **FAINE**, 55, dropsy; John **O'BRIEN**, 20, killed. 10/18-J. H. **LIVELY**, 8 mos, fever; Isabella **McNAMEE**, 2, chronic diarrhea; Mrs. Alice **GREEN**, 50, int. fever. 10/19-Dennis **MULLINS**, 28, dysentery; Mr. **HEMMINGWAY**, 40; Asa **ROLLINS**, 29, diarrhea. 10/20-Mrs. **GRADY**'s daughter, 4, diarrhea; John **GRAIP**, 35, int. fever; Michael **DONNELLY**, 35, congestive chill. 10/23-John L. **WHITE**, 21, erysipelas. 10/24-Boy of est. of Dr. G. W. **MURPHY**; Thos **FITZGERALD**, 30, chronic diarrhea; Mrs. Michael **LISTON**, 33, accouchment. 10/25-Joseph **RAPP**, 73, diarrhea. 10/27-C. **ACCRAMAN**, 46, congestive fever. 10/28-Mrs. Anthony **STREET**'s child, still-born. 10/29-Mrs. Caroline **ISBELL**, 28, typhoid fever; David **ARMOUR**, 56, infla. Bowels; Mrs. **PIERCY**'s child, 5, typhoid fever. 10/30-E. F. **RODGERS**, 55, consumption. 10/31-Miss Ann **WARRINGTON**, 17, congestion of the brain; John **McMAHON**, 35, diarrhea; L. D. **HENDERSON**, 4 ½, euteritis.
11/1-Mrs. **MANNG**'s child, 5, diarrhea; Mrs. **COOK**, 50, consumption. 11/2-Henderson **CARTER**, 44, inflammation bowels; Mary **SULLIVAN**, 25. 11/3-Wm **BUGG**, 18, dysentery; Christopher **TAYLOR**, 24. 11/5-Joseph O. **SHULLMENT**, 40, pleurisy; daughter of G. H. **LOCKE**; A. T. **PEARSON**, 28, cholera morbus. 11/6-Johanna F. **THUNNEL**, 71, old age; Gen. **WILBURN**, 70, pneumonia. 11/7-Lida **BUCKINGHAM**, 1. 11/8-son of A. H. **AVERY**, 9 mos. 11/9-John W. **LAMBENIS**(?), 1, chicken pox. 11/10-Child of Mrs. J. **McDONALD**, 4 days; Mr. **TANNER**'s child, 3. 11/11-Timothy J. **WRIGHT**, 59, congestion. 11/14-Mrs. Maria **THOMAS**, 24, consumption. 11/15-Frederick **BRUNS**, 37, drowned. 11/15-Jas **CHANDLER**, 7, auteritis. 11/16-Margaret **BROOKS**, 40, exposure. 11/17-John **BOGARD**, 5, typhoid fever; Joseph **IRBY**, dysentery. 11/21-Mrs. **POWELL**, 38, general depraved health. 11/22-S. **JOHNS**, 25, dropsy.
12/1-Joseph **WRIGHT**. 12/2-George W. **MORRIS**, 36, diarrhea. 12/3-Jas S. **GLASS'** child, 2, dysentery. 12/4-Malinda **COMSTOCK**, 33, excessive diarrhea; Naomi E. **DAVIS**, 2, diarrhea. 12/5-Martha A. **WILLIAMS**, 39, diarrhea. 12/28-Valentine **KIME**, 10, typhoid pneumonia. 12/29-Wm **CARR**, 26, inf. of bowels; Cornelius **GODDARD**, 18 mo., dentition; W. **MOODY**, 33(?), bilious fever. 12/30-Cyrus A. **DOEBLAR**, 24, excessive diarrhea; Charles **GRIMM**, 63, old age. 12/31- J. W. **CONNELL**, 28, consumption; Jas **CLEARY**, 28, cholera morbus.

LIST OF INTERMENTS FOR 1852:

1/1-Mrs. **SWEETLAND**, 23, consumption. Jan. 2-Andrew G. **BOYD**, 43, apoplexy of the lungs. 1/3-Mrs. James **WALDRAN**, 18. Jan. 4-Mary **BELL**, f.w.c., 19, typhoid fever; Mrs. Ann **HART**, 30, child bed; Dilsey **DOUGHERTY**, f.w.c., 60, pneumonia. 1/7-Thomas **SHAUGHNESSY**, 21, chronic diarrhea. 1/10-Mary Elizabeth **BRITTINGHAM**, 19, chronic diarrhea. 1/12-George **GRAHAM**, 28, congestive fever, 1/13-Solomon **PICTKINS**, 55, phtisic pulmonatis. 1/14-Mrs. Sarah **SPAULDING**, 73, pneumonia. 1/16-Son of J. P. **WRIGHT**, 2 weeks, convulsions; Miss **LOWREY**, 13, dropsy. 1/18-Daughter of N. **STREHL**, 14 mo., croup; Mrs. Isaac **PHELON**, 39. 1/21-John **COOK**, 35, congestive chill; Thomas **YAMBRICK**, 14, pleurisy. 1/24-Donora **McMAHON**, 55, billious fever. 1/25-Mrs. **MAUS**, 23, consumption; Mary E. **WILLIAMSON**, 2, pneumonia. 1/26-James F. **DOFFIN**, 32, pneumonia. 1/27-Son of George **GRANT**, 14 mos; Martin **SUMNERS**, 16, congestive chill. 1/29-James **DEVINNY**, 38, congestive chill.
Week ending 2/7: W. F. **BROTHERLIN**, 38, consumption; Jas **CLIFFENSON**, 8 days; Mrs. **NEAGLE**, 45; Jno **McMAHON**, 30; Rev. Littlebury **STARK**, 60. 2/8-Child of Henry **BARGER**, 2; Child of Isaac **PHELON**, 1 mo. 2/9-Mrs. **FRITZ**, 28, accouchment; Henry **NOILES**, 35, Diarrhea. 2/10-Mrs. Abby **PRESCOTT**, 41, Dysentery. 2/12-Alexander **WORTHINGTON**, 35, Pneumonia. 2/13-Benj F. **JAMES**, 21, Congestive chill; Sally **HERRING**, w.c., 70, Pneumonia. 2/16-Michael **McCARTHY**, 9, Phthisis Pulmonalis. 2/18-Eugene **RACINE**, 8 days, Erysipelas. 2/19-Charles H. **HOLST**, 10, Inflammation of the Brain. 2/22-J. C. **ALLEN**, 2. 2/24-Mrs. Stephen **WEST**, 45, disease of the _____ Kidneys; Son of F. E. **STAGG**, Convulsions. 2/26-Isaac **MORDECAI**, 32, Gangrene. 2/27-Miss Margaret **PATTEN**, 30, Consumption.

3/2-Mary **WHELAN**, 35, Typhoid Fever; Martha **YATES**, 16, Typhoid Fever. 3/6-Charles **DOWNING**, 18(?), Pneumonia. 3/12-Margaret **SPRATT**, 13, Pneumonia; Matilda **CONWAY**, 2, Diarrhea. 3/15-Martha M. **MULVANY**, 33, Consumption. 3/18-Mrs. **McSORLEY**, 43, Consumption. 3/19-Margaret **BRUNER**, 26, Convulsions. 3/21-Nancy Ann **STILL**, 40, accouchment; Geo W. **SCHABEL**, Wound; Louisa **MONTGOMERY**, 28, accouchment. 3/22-Infant of M. E. **WOLFFE**, 8 days. 3/23-Infant of L. **MALLURE**, 4 mo. 3/25-Mary **MITCHELL**, 2, dropsy. 3/27-Timothy **McGRATH**, 45, Congestive chill. 3/27-Michael **MAHAN**, 22, Injury.

4/1-John **ROFF**, Injury. 4/2-Daughter of Andrew **ZIEGEL**, 3 ½ mos, convulsions. 4/4-Wesley **DEW**, 42. 4/5-Geo **IRVING**, 36, Phtisis Pulmoralis. 4/7-James **MAHAN**, 21, Phtisis Pulmoralis. 4/8-W. W. **MILLER**, 35. 4/9-Rebecca **LINNEY**, 22, accouchment. 4/11-Son of J. P. **HUME**, 7 mos, Cholera Infantum; Sam'l C. **PAINTER**, 40, Chronic Diarrhea. 4/14-James **McALLISTER**, 30; Shelby **WHITINGTON**, 25, Intemperance. 4/16-James G. **BELL**, 50, Inflammatory Rheumatism. 4/17-J. L. **WHEATLEY**, 27, typhoid fever. 4/19-Martha **CHITWOOD**, 20, congestive chill. 4/22-John **SULLIVAN**, 26, accidental death. 4/23-Mary **BROOKS**, 36, pneumonia. 4/26-Child of John **GRIFFIN**, 2, Enterites; Michael **CONWAY**, 27, Pleurisy. 4/29-Child of James **GLASS**, 15 mos, convulsions. 4/30-James **TOBIN**, 26, killed.

5/1-Infant of R. C. **HITE**. 5/2-Mrs. Asa **SMITH**, 24, Infl of the Brain. 5/6-H. **McMULLEN**, 21, Diarrhea. 5/7-John **SMITH**, 5, Diarrhea. 5/8-Mary **SMITH**, 3, Diarrhea; Mrs. _____ **MALLORY**, 22, Phthisis Pulmoralis. 5/8-R. J. **YANCEY**, 46, Consumption. 5/11-H. **SCHAFFER**, 35, consumption. 5/12-Wm **WALLACE**, 35. 5/13-J. C. **BELL**, 5, Infl of Brain. 5/16-James M. **NETTLE**, 10, pneumonia. 5/17-Infant of Joseph **ANDERSON**, 7 mos. 5/18-Joseph **JACKMAN**, 32, colliquative diarrhea; Infant of Wm **GRAFF**, 14 mos. 5/19-Infant of John **GREEN**, 2 weeks, convulsions. 5/20-Infant of Ben **O'HAVRE**, 1, measles. 5/21-Joseph B. **DUNCAN**, 21; Infant of Jacob **BRUST**. 5/22-Child of _____ **HANDWERKER**, 2 ½, diarrhea; David **HUMPHREYS**, 17, cholera morbus. 5/23-Mrs. **DANIELS**, 63, Colitis. 5/24-Son of W. C. **CAUSEY**, 3, Measles. 5/25-Infant of R. B. **HAWLEY**, 5 mo. 5/27-Isaac **COCHRAN**, 42, Diarrhea; Anthony **KELLY**, 30, Intemperance; G. W. **STAFFORD**, 52, Colliquative Diarrhea; Daughter of J. G. **LONSDALE**, 18 mos, Congestive Chill. 5/28-John **WALSH**, 44, Consumption. 5/29-Infant of J. N. **WORMLEY**, Premature Birth; Infant of D. C. **WILDER**, 9 mos. 5/30-Daughter of Moses **NEAL**, 20 mos, cholera; Son of Peter **MAINGAULT**, 1, measles; August **REMPLE**, 53, Cholera.

6/1-Benjamin **WITHERS**, 28, Cholera; John **GARVEY** 4. 6/2-Infant of Wm **GOYER**. 6/3-Daughter of Wm H. **CARROLL**, 8, Gastro-Enteritis; Mrs. James **DICKINSON**, 31; J. N. **STAFFORD**, 10, Measles; Lucy **HOLMES**, 32, Gastro-Enteritis; H. J. **POLLOCK**, 11, Dysentery; Josephine **POLLOCK**, 1, Cholera. 6/4-Wm **McBRIDE**, 30, Cholera; Hiram **DAVIS**, 27, Bilious Fever, D. M. **WAYBURN**, 25; Jane **GARVEY**, 31(?), Cholera. 6/5-John **FORD**, 26, Cholera; Child of Wm **BANGIS**, 15 mos, Infl. of Brain. 6/6-Wm **HARRIS**, 45, Intemperance; Child of G. R. **REDFORD**, 2, Measles. 6/7-Rowena **WILLIAMS**, 2 ½, Diarrhea; Franklin **HEIN**, 2, Measles; J. R. **KEEL**, 19, Cholera. 6/8-J. **NEWMAN**, 55, accidental death; Nancy **STAFFORD**, 2, Measles; Mrs. _____ **HARDIN**, 55, Cholera; Michael **COFFEY**, 4, Measles. 6/9-Andrew **LIVELY**, 25, Typhoid Fever. 6/11-Mary M. **GIVNEY**, 18, Diarrhea; Mary Ann **STAFFORD**, 8, Measles; Infant of T. H. **APPLETON**, Still-born; Thomas **MARONEY**, 30 mos, Cholera. 6/12-Mary **WARREN**, 3, Measles; Justice **BRADHAVEN**, 44, Cholera; Child of G. S. **DENEGRI**, 4 mos. 6/13-Sarah M. **APPLETON**, 24, Inflammation of the bowels; Caroline **BELTON**, 27, Cholera; Jane **BELTON**, 7 ½, Measles. 6/14-John **CULLAN**, 50, Cholera; Michael **McGRATH**, 24, Cholera; Washington **HAWLEY**, 37, Cholera. 6/15-Wm **POLLOCK**, 8 ½, Inflammation of the Bowels; E. T. **CHESTER**, 8, Dysentery; Elizabeth **STAFFORD**, 18, Measles. 6/16-Mary **KERNS**, Dropsy; J. B. **SMITH**, 42, Typhoid Fever; Morgan B. **COOK**, 30, Consumption; Wm **BRADSHAW**, 17, Cholera. 6/17-Edward **CULLEN**, 13, Cholera; John **ARCHIBALD**, 25, Billous Fever. 6/18-Cajeton **LEVESQUE**, 42, Inflammation of the Bowels, Aleck **WILLIAMS**, 33, Gastro-Enteritus. 6/20-Michael G. **TATE**, 1 yr 4 mos, chronic diarrhea; Son of Rueben **ALEXANDER**, 1 yr 5 mos, inflammation of the brain. 6/21-Louisa **EPPERSON**, 5, worms; Child of William J. **SMITH**, 20 mos, measles; Gustave **KRAFFT**, 15 mos, diarrhea; Margaret **TIGGS**, 25, diarrhea. 6/23-Mrs. Ann **REARDON**, 28, brain fever. 6/24-A. J. **WILSON**, 5, brain fever; Mrs. M. **PARKER**, 65, measles; Reuben **GARNETT**, 32, cholera. 6/25-John T. **MILLER**, 2, measles; Daughter of H. F. **FARNSWORTH**, 16 mos, measles; Michael **COOLY**, 22, sun struck; Wm **NICHOLS, 27**, cholera.

List of interments for the week ending July 3, 1852: Adolphus **BEATY**, 28, Cholera; Elizabeth **BEATY**, 1 ½, Cholera; Mary A. **BEATY**, 24, Cholera; Wm __ **BEATY**, 3, Cholera Infantum; Cato **BREWER**(?), 6,

Chronic inflam of the bowels; Francis **THOMPSON**, 13, Diarrhea; Henry **BETTON**, 4, Cholera; Mary **FRANTZ**, 48, Fever; Mary **BRAVER**, 6, Cholera; Jere **SCHROK**, 80, Typhoid fever; Child of Mrs. E. E. **ALEXANDER**, 3 mos, Diarrhea; Wm **APPLEWHITE**, 10, Ascarides(?); Mrs. M. **BROWN**, 35, Consumption; Miss Elizabeth **ROACH**, 22, Infl of the bowels; Green C. **WARD**, 2 yrs 2 mos, Typhoid Fever. List of interments for the week ending 7/10/1852: Catharine **PAINTER**, 42, Cholera; Sarah E. **WILEY**, 4, Cholera; Wm J. **WILEY**, 2, Cholera; Maria **THIMES**, 22, Cholera; Butler **ROACH**, 5, Cholera; Sarah **SAXON**, 8, Cholera; James **WALCH**, 32, Cholera; B. **TYSON**, 35, Cholera; Wm **WILLIAMS**, 25, Consumption; James **WOODS**, 38, Disease of the lungs; John F. **DAVIS**, 5 yrs 9 mos, Gangraena Oris; James **MAHONEY**, 35, Cramp; John **SMART**, 27, Enlargement of the Liver; Mrs. **SULLIVAN**, 30, Congestive Fever; T. **RYAN**, 28; P. **HEALY**, 30, Brain Fever; Anna **STOKES**, 20, congestive chill; Jas D. **KERR**, 28, Fever; Catharine **NEIL**, 16, Over Heated; Mary **GEON**(?), 40, Spasms. List of interments for the week ending 7/17/1852: J. L. **LANE**, 7, unknown; Andrew **BREEN**, 21, intermittent Fever; Mrs. **RACHAEL**, 45, Consumption; Richard **DRIVER**, 25, Cholera; Adelaide **WOOD**, 8, Congestive Chill; Sarah **SAXON**, 45, Cholera; Joseph **PERSANTA**, 10, Aprea; Caid **LEVSK**(?), 32, chronic Diarrhea; Nancy **JONES**, 16, Typhoid fever; Mrs. **GRAVES**, 35, Diarrhea. List of interments for the week ending 7/24: James H. **ROGERS**, 37, Diarrhea; George **MOONEY**, 8, Fracture of the Arm; Patrick **MURPHY**, 20, Congestive Chill; Mrs. Lucy **SEGUR**, 51, Typhoid Fever; W. S. **DOUGLAS**, 5, Enteretis & infla. of the Brain; Patrick **GALLAGER**, 4, Brain Fever; W. G. **SMITH**, 5, Infla. Diarrhea; Mrs. D. G. **JAMES**, age unknown, Infla. of the Stomach & Bowels; Child of Robert **GIFT**, 4, Congestive Chill. List of interments for the week ending 7/31: Mrs. Albert **LAVELLETTE**, 25, gastroenteretis; H. C. **HIDLE**, 19, consumption; Mrs. Wm **BAVIN**, cholera morbus; Margaret **McMORROUGH**, 25, billious fever; Mrs. **MALONEY**, 35, int. fever; Mrs. H. **CAHILL**, 75; Daughter of P. **BURKE**, 3, diarrhea; John P. **GARVIN**, __, measles; P. **DOYLE**, 30, coup de soleil; James **PURNELL**, 18, congestive chill; John **MOORE**, 101 & 18 days, old age.
List of interments for the week ending 8/7: John **LUISMAN**, 6, diarrhea; Wm **O'BRIAN**, 18, injury; Wm **WRIGHT**, 5, scrofula; Son of Martin **SLAUGHTER**, 18 mos, measles; James **PATE**, 26, convulsions; J. P. **BARNHILL**, 25, chronic diarrhea; Maria **MORGAN**, 20, gastris enterestes. List of interments for the week ending 8/14: Miss Caroline **JONES**, 15, Consumption; Mr. **FLEMING**, 30, Unknown; Son of E. F. **RISK**, 11 mos, Cholera; James **RHODES**, 34, unknown; Mr. J. T. **BROWN**, (stranger) 25, Typhoid Fever. 8/14-Mr. Geo M. **OTT**, 42, Congestive Chill. 8/15-Wm **MORTON**, 2 yrs 2 mos, Measles; Michael **OMELIA**, 30, unknown. 8/16-Mr. W. **MORRISON**, 37, Typhoid Fever, Henry **POLMIER**, 24, Billious Fever. 8/19-Mrs. **DOWNE**, 65, unknown. 8/20-Mr. A. **McKINNEY**, 30, Chills & Fever; Mr. P. **MURRY**, 35, Typhoid Fever; Tildon **SNELL**, 12, unknown. List of interments for the week ending 8/28: Mrs. Catharine **ADAMS**, 35, Typhoid Fever; Samuel **CREIGHTON**, 13, Typhoid Fever; Michael **SHANNAHAN**, 43, Typhoid Fever; Dr. A. D. **WILDS**, 45, Consumption; Mr. P. **QUINN**, 75, Consumption; Mr. G. M. **PENN**, 50, Ulcer on leg.
List of interments for the week ending 9/4: Wm F. **ALLEN**, __ years, Typhoid Fever; E. **LYNCH**, 32, Consumption; Wm **COCKRELL**, 39, Typhoid Fever; J. **WHEMEAR**, 30, Typhoid Fever; F. **BARTLETT**, 36, Congestive Chill; V. **HAMMON**, 24, Billious Fever; Wm **MORGAN**, 24, Consumption. List of interments for the week ending 9/11: Mrs. Mary **MALONEY**, 50, Congestive Chill; Johana **HARRIS**, 23, Conges. Fever; Wm **FOHERAT**, 8, Conges. Chill; D. **BOTTO**, 32; R. F. **SORDAN**, 33, Cholera Morbus; J. L. **ESKIN**, (stranger) 21, Jaundice; Henry **RAILING**, 27; F. M. **SAUNDERS**, 10, Flux; Boy of W. **LAWRENCE**, 5, Worms; Daughter of S. **MILLER**, 1 day; Ed **GANNON**, 25, Chills & Fever; Infant of D. C. **CAMPBELL**, 15 days; F. W. **BRUNS**, __ ½ yrs, Chronic Diarrhea, N. E. **HARDIN**, 2 ½, Brain Fever. List of Interments for the week ending 9/18: Mary E. **APPLETON**, 2, Congestive Brain; Sam **WARD**, 23, Cholera; Thos **BRADSHAW**, stranger, 23, Sudden death, unknown; Isaac **LOW**, 39, Cholera; Mary **WEABER**, 4, Congestive Fever; L. **BOTTO**, 56, Unknown; Col. D. **MORRISON**, 60, Chronic Diarrhea; Mr. Anthony **HUNT**, 36, unknown; Andrew **SILON**, stranger, 24, General Dibility; Michael **HURLEY**, 20, Consumption; C. **BRIZENTINE**, 54, Cholera; F. **DUPRIVI**, stranger, 23, Ilietis; Son of H. T. **FOX**, 6 days, unknown. List of interments for the week ending 9/25: Mrs. E. **BREZENTINE**, 48, Cholera; Miss E. **BREZENTINE**, 21, Cholera; John **BURNS**, 58, Billious Fever; Anna **BREZENTINE**, 6, Cholera; Mary Jane **CRAVENS**, 13(?), inflammation; John **MORRISON**, 9, Consumption; Child of C. W. **COOPER**, 14 mos, Diarrhea; Mary H. **CANNON**, 4 Fright.
List of interments for the week ending 10/2: Michael **MALONE**, 25, Diarrhea; Miss **ATWOOD**, 9, Congestive Chill; Thos **HARNET**, 27, Consumption; Geo A. **HAYS**, 24, Consumption; Samuel **HOLLINSWORTH**, 8, Dropsy; Son of S. A. **NORTON**, 4, Inflammation of bowels; Mrs. **MARONEY**,

28, Congestive Chill; P. O. **SULLIVAN**, 23, Diarrhea; Catharine **PIKE**, 14, Measles; Mrs. J. J. **RAWLINGS**, 25(?), Inflammation of bowels; Patrick **DIVINE**, 23, Unknown; Wm L. **EYRICK**, 32, Inflammation of the bowels. List of interments for the week ending 10/9: Wm **FINNEY**, (stranger), 24, Chronic Diarrhea; John **DONOHO**, 45, Chronic Diarrhea; Robt J. **PRITCHARD**, 12(?), Chronic Diarrhea; John **RYAN**, 35, Congestive Chill; John **WILLIAMS**, 50, Cholera; J. **FERN**, unknown; John **WOTHINS**, (stranger) 25, died on wharf-boat of Cholera; Miss Mary **TOBIN**, 15(?), Consumption; Mrs. M. L. **McGEE**(?), 34, Typhoid Fever; James **GLEESON**, 23, Cholera morbus. List of interments for the week ending 10/16: Mr. G. **DOLBEAR**, 20, consumption; H. **HUBERS**, 28, brain fever; E. T. **APPERSON**, 11, cong. Chill; Son of Mrs. **APPERSON**, 4, unknown; Child of Mr. **BRENNER**, 2 yrs 6 mos, unknown; Two sons of Mr. **GRIDLEY**, 5 & 2, croup; T. **SHROYER**, 25, chronic disease of lungs; H. **BENTZ**, 35, cholera morbus; W. B. **TERRY**, 51, typhoid fever; Child of J. **BOYD**, 2, unknown; Child of J. B. **GUTLAW**, 5, unknown; Constantine **MOETRI**, 3, brain fever. 10/21-Babel **WEIL**, 21, consumption. 10/22-F. **FRANSIOLI**, 25, cong. of brain. 10/24-H. **HYNES**, 6, consumption. 10/26-Wm **RYAN**, 7, chills; Wm **NASH**, 30, consumption; Mrs. **GABBERT**, 50, unknown; Child of W. **GADSBY**, 10, typhoid fever. 10/27-Joseph **PHLUM**, 25, chron. Diarrhea. 10/30-Ambrose **HOGG**, 35, cholera. 11/2-Mary **HEFFERAN**, 2, cholera infan.; Davis **SHEA**, 20, cholera. 11/3-John **HEFFERAN**, 6, cholera. 11/4-Wm **HEFFERAN**, 26(?), cholera; B. **DONNELLY**, 25, congestive chill; Richard **OGLESBY**, 18, dysentery. 11/6-Calvin **JOHNSON**, 4, diarrhea; Philip **BURKE**, 27, typhoid fever; Jno **McNAMARA**, 26, cholera; Mrs. Robert **GIFT**, 50, typhoid fever. 11/14-A. **McIVER**, 14, typhoid fever; Nancy **FARREL**, 21, cholera morbus; Adolph **NUTHER**, 30, cholera morbus. 11/15-A. H. **SOMMERVILLE**, 25, cholera morbus; J. G. **BESSENGER**, 34, consumption; Child of Mrs. **READ**, 4, chol. Morbus. 11/17-Michael **NASH**, 29, dysentery; T. **O'BRIAN**, 34, diarrhea. 11/18-Dominic **DORSON**, 28, cholera; Sarah **GIBBINS**, 5, death from burn. 11/19-C. **DADIA**(?), 30, typhoid fever; J. A. **PRICE**, 47, unknown; Dr. M. B. **SAPPINGTON**, 50, con. Brain. 11/20-Mrs. **ELSBURY**, 50, cholera morbus; J. **CLACKSTON**, 67, consumption; Mr. **BELLAMY**, 40, diarrhea. 11/25-John **BREMER**, 50, dysentery; Hon. J. W. **CROCKETT**, 45, Pneumonia. 11/26-James **McCABE**, 27, Consumption. 11/21-Mrs. **DIVINE**, 29, Pleurisy. 11/23-J. B. **HOWCOTT**, 35, Pleurisy. 11/28-Dr. C. B. **YUBER**, 24, gast. Enter.; Wm **BIBEON**, 45, pneumonia; S. **TUBBS**, 47, con. Chill. 11/29-T. J. **PARKER**, 21, dyspepsia. 11/30-M. **RYAN**, 25, pleurisy; Catharine **BUTLER**, 3, cholera mor. 12/2-M. **DELANEY**, 30, chills; Mrs. J. D. **GOFF**, 38, pneumonia. 12/3-C. **CARR**, 70, unknown. 12/4-Inf. son of B. C. **CABLE**, 3 days, consulvions. 12/5-Mrs. **VINING**, 28, puerperal fever. 12/6-Elizabeth **WILSON**, 21, diarrhea. 12/7-E. **DICKSON**, 13, typhoid fever. 12/8-Helen A. **MILLS**, 19, consumption; Elizabeth **YOTT**, 24, cholera. 12/9-Woman Adeline, 20, cholera. 12/10-Sam'l T. **COBB**, 47, Infla. of bowels; Child of F. **PENNY**, 1, dis. Unknown; Child of Mr. **VINING**, 10 days, in. of bowels. 12/11-Mr. Sampson **LANE**, 82, old age; L. **CARDES**, 24, dis. not known. 12/?-Mrs. Margaret **ENGLISH**, 45, Consumption. 12/13-____ **PENNY**, 18, Typhoid Fever. 12/14-Mrs. M. G. **CHAMP**, 35, Pneu.; J. P. **DONNELL**, 46, Pneu. 12/16-Infant son of Willis **PRUETT**, 3 mo, croup. 12/17-Wm **WILSON**, 20, gun shot wound.

LIST OF INTERMENTS FOR 1853:

1/3-John **MURA**, 18, death from wound; Wm **HANSELL**, 3 ½, bronchitis. Jan 4-Daughter of F. **DOOLEY**, 4, pneumonia. 1/6-Jas R. **BEATY**, 37, Pneumonia; Child of I. **ELLIOTT**, 5 mos, unknown. 1/9-Dan'l **SULLIVAN**, 32, diarrhea. 1/12-Michael **MORTON**, 57, dropsy; Mrs. A. **McKINNAN**, 42, not reported. 1/13-Mr. G. W. **BLACK**, 25, pneumonia. 1/17-Michael **POWERS**, 23, pleurisy. 1/18-Martha **GIVENS**, 4, unknown. 1/19-Richard **GREEN**, 33, consumption; Mrs. **McALLANEY**, 21, puerperal fever; Geo **ROBINSON**, 12, congestive fever; Dorothea **LANGBEIN**, 8 ½, pneumonia. 1/20-John **SULLIVAN**, 32, pneumonia; James **LEACHY**, 26, from wound. 1/22-Mary **BRILEY**, 10, jaundice; Patrick **KENNEDY**, 23, chills; Boy of A. T. **WELLS**, 13, dysentery. 1/23-Thomas **MILLER**, 35, death from wound. 1/24-Rev. T. W. **PRITCHARD**, 28, not reported. 1/26-Mrs. Julia **TOOMEY**, 54, Pue Fever; Wm **YATES**, jr, 28, Jaundice. 1/27-Mrs. **DUNCAN**, 36, Consumption; Son of Michael **RUSH**, 1 ½, Infl. Throat. 1/28-Mrs. **GRUBER**, 32, Diarrhea. 1/30-G. J. **JOHNSON**, 26, infla. of brain; Mrs. Bridget **BUTLER**, 32, diarrhea. 1/31-Mrs. Mary **BRYLEY**, 60, typhoid fever; Mrs. Mary **HASSET**, 35, puerperal; Mrs. Alech **GREGOR**, 27, dis. of heart. 2/2-Miss M. A. **PARKER**, 17, dis. of brain; Child of R. H. **JONES**, 2 ½, measles; Son of Marcus **JONES**, 2 ½, scarlet fever; Michael **HURT**, 32, diarrhea. 2/3-Mrs. Mariah **MARSHAM**, 26, consumption. 2/6-

Mrs. Dr. **BERRY**, 50, nervous affection. 2/9-E. **HENSON**, 21, typhoid fever. 2/10-Dr. A. D. **HAMMOND**, 53, pleurisy. 2/14-Child of Mr. A. **SEIGEL**, 3, not reported; Mr. Dennis **GRIFFIN**, 40, effects of a fall. 2/19-R. **WHELLY**, 10, Typhoid Pneumonia. 2/21-Miss Josephine **MATTISON**, 8, Pneumonia; Virgil **MATTISON**, 5, Pneumonia; Jas. **O'NEAL**, 18, Convulsions. 2/22-Infant of Mr. N. **OWENS**, 3, Erysipelas. 2/24-Mrs. **MALLORY**, 57, Consumption.

3/5-W. **WALDRAN**, 25, congestive chill. 3/6-Robert **HANNA**, 45(?), nervous affection. 3/9-W. **BRUM**, 25, pneumonia; Peter **HAHN**, 26, brain fever. 3/12-Wm **BOONE**, 15, pneumonia. 3/14-N. S. **HARDENS**, 53, Jaundice. 3/16-Mrs. S. J. **GARARD**, 26, infla. of Lungs. 3/18-J. **LEWIS**, 21, Pneumonia. 3/22-Judith Scott **MOSELY**, 5, measles. 3/23-Wm S. O. **KOLLEY**, 32, pneumonia. 3/25-Joseph **COOPER**, 60, paralysis. 3/31-R. **KIRTLAND**, 33, con. of brain; Miss M. J. **CROSS**, 18, consumption; Child of W. **RINGWALD**, 18 mos.

4/1-Son of Rev. R. H. **JONES**, 12, disease of the heart. 4/5-Augustus **PIERCE**, 30, consumption; Child of G. R. **REDFORD**, 8 mos, pneumonia. 4/6-Son of M. **LAWSON**, 10, pneumonia. 4/8-Samuel **MORGAN**, 43, consumption. 4/13-J. **DEALY**, 60, Disease of the Heart; Son of Mr. **HEFFERAN**, 3, pneumonia. 4/14-Geo W. **ROLAND**, 60, congestive fever. 4/17-F. **COMBE**, 30, consumption. 4/18-John **SMITH**, 37, dropsy. 4/23-T. **CASTILO**, 55, death from wounds. 4/29-V. D. **BARRY**, 57, pneumonia.

5/1-Child of W. C. **EVANS**, 17 mos, dysentery. 5/2-Wm **PITT**, 23, pneumonia. 5/5-Miss **SHELL**, 16, pulmonary appoplexy. 5/12-Mrs. Mary **FITZMANNIE**, 24. 5/13-Miss T. M. **COLLINS**, 15, measles. 5/16-Mrs. Virginia E. **ROBINSON**, 24, consumption. 5/18-Son of J. J. **DAVIS**, 14, inflammation of brain; Son of Thomas **COWE**, 6, worms. 5/20-Mrs. Mary S. **RUFFIN**, 40, congestive fever. 5/24-Mary **MAHONEY**, 8, infla'n brain. 5/25-Mrs. Eliza **NORMAN**, 28, consumption; Peter **BAKER**, 4, congestive fever. 5/27-Infant son of T. R. **SMITH**, 2 days, inflammation of brain. 5/30-Child of F. **GRUBER**, 7 mos, diarrhea. 5/31-Child of J. M. **SACKETT**, 14 mos.

6/1-Mrs. Ellen **HIGGINS**, 60, pleurisy. 6/13 – J. **KENNEDY**, 26, death from wound; Lizzie A. **ARMOUR**, 2, Dysentery. 6/15 – P. **COCKRAM**, 30, Congestive Fever. 6/16 – Son of A. **ANDERSON**, 6, Measles. 6/17 – G. **HENRY**, 24, Sun Stroke; Infant of Peter **BAKER**. 6/22-Mrs. J. **AULT**, 52, consumption; Child of J. H. **JAMES**, 3, inflamation of the brain. 6/25-Mr. L. W. **DAVIS**, 32, effects of wounds.

7/3-Mary T. **BARRY**, 6, inflammation of brain. 7/5-D. **RYAN**, 50(?), diarrhea. 7/7-H. **PLUNKETT**, 24, consumption. 7/9-Miss Mary A. **PATILLO**, 40, typhoid fever. 7/11-Child of Chas **HIDEL**, 13(?) mos, convulsions. 7/12-Ellen **INGLE**, 9, congestion of the brain. 7/13-Mildred **FOSTER**, 28, Dysentery. 7/15-F. **BROWN**, 33, chronic diarrhea; Child of E. **GRIDER**, 3 days, convulsions. 7/20-H. C. **JACKSON**, 11, inflammation of brain. 7/21-Mrs. **CROSBY**, 45, convulsions; Mr. **KING**, 20, effects of a fall; C. W. **CRANNES**, 45, apoplexy. 7/22-W. A. **STREET**, 3, convulsions. 7/25-P. **ARCHARD**, 26, inflammation of lungs. 7/28-Mrs. B. **HENEY**, 65, cancer.

9/12-A. **GRIFFIN**, 12, not reported. 9/13-Mrs. **HABBWECHS**, 20, not reported. 9/16-Mr. G. W. **THOMPSON**, 41, consumption; John J. **SPICKERNAGLE**, 15, Inflamation of the Brain. 9/17-Charles **HOFFMAN**, 37, Jaundice.

10/8-Wm **GRAHAM**, 11, Remittent Fever; John **CUNNINGHAM**, 50, Intemperance. 10/9-Joseph **EMERSON**, 52, gravel; Ann **BADGER**, 10, dysentery; L. C. **HEZEKIAH**, 27, disease of the brain. 10/13-John **CAIN**, 25, consumption; Mrs. F. **JEGGITS**, 24, inflammation of brain. 10/15-Mrs. Narcissa **JOHNSON**, 23, gastro entertis; Joseph **CALEY**, 30, consumption. 10/17-R. **COLEMAN**, 45, pneumonia. 10/19-Mrs. **O'BRIEN**, 60, congestive fever. 10/21-Mrs. Johnanna **AUGAR**, 23, inflammation of brain.

11/15-Mr. **CASTLEMAN**, 29, chronic diarrhea. 11/17-Daniel **FOLEY**, 35, pneumonia; Mrs. E. **HARDIN**, 55, debility. 11/18-Mannie **CONDON**, 60, old age; John **BUCKLEY**, 20, infla. of brain. 11/21-John **KINSEY**, 33, consumption. No date-Thomas **GRAHAM**, 29, typhoid fever.

12/2-Michael **McNAMARA**, 38, pneumonia. 12/18-Infant son of Mr. **McALANY**, 1 day. 12/19-Mr. John **FITZGERALD**, 28, dropsy. 12/21-Mrs. Sarah **WALTHROPE**, 22, pneumonia. 12/25-Mrs. B. **DOYLE**, 27, consumption. 12/26-Mrs. **GOLDSMITH**, 25, consumption. 12/27-Mr. D. **WINE**, 28, inflammation of the Brain. 12/31-Mary E. **SWARENGIN**, 7, winter fever; Timothy **CHAMBERS**, 22, tetanus.

LIST OF INTERMENTS FOR 1854:

1/5-Mrs. C. J. **WARD**, 29, childbirth. 1/8-Mr. W. **JONES**, 30, pneumonia. 1/9-Fanny **WHITE**, 4, congestive fever; Mary **STAFFORD**, 19, intermittent fever. 1/10-T. **MITCHELL**, 30, drowning. 1/11-Child of J. L. **KRAFT**. 1/13-Mrs. C. **RIVES**, 63, diarrhea; Mrs. **EWING**, 25, typhoid fever. 1/14-Mrs.

Martha **JERRY**, 45, typhoid fever. 1/16-James **KINGSTON**, 18, pneumonia. 1/18-Patrick **HANNEGAN**, 30, convulsions. 1/19-Mrs. **DUFFY**, 35, dropsy. 1/20-Mr. **BRADFORD**, 40, gun shot wound.

2/6-H. J. **NORVILL**, 41, diarrhea. 2/9-Mrs. Elizabeth **GALLAGHER**, 65, dropsy. 5/21-J. **SANTAG**, 45, Cholera. 5/22-Mrs. M. **RICHARD**, 46(?), Pleurisy; Mrs. **HARRIS**, __, Cholera. 5/23-J. D. **CLARK**, __ mos., Bronchitis; Mrs. **HENDRICKSON**, 28, Cholera; Mr. **READER**, 50, Congestion of the Brian. 5/24-J. **VOGT**(?), 25, death from gun-shot wound. 5/26-Son of W. **ARRINGTON**, 2 mos, Diarrhea. 5/27-W. H. **TRIGG**, 36, Cholera; Mrs. A. **DWIGHT**, 54, Cholera; Amanda **BOTTO**, 4, Cholera; James **BROWN**, 22, Cholera. 5/29-Mrs. Susan **MUNCH**, 42, Cholera. 5/31-Margaret **FITZGIBBONS**, 1, Scarlet Fever; Dr. S. S. **SMITH**, 34, Cholera.

6/2-B. **SAUNDERS**, 3, Chronic Diarrhea. 6/3-Reuben T. **CROCKETT**, 33, Cholera. 6/6-Marcus **TAYLOR**, 3 Effects of Measles; E. T. **HAMNER**, 12, Cholera. 6/10-Nancy **PHIPPS**, 50, Diarrhea. 6/17-Mrs. J. **DOOLAN**, 27, Cholera Morbus. 6/18-W. S. **SMITH**, 25, Consumption. 6/19-S. **SENN**, 21, Diarrhea; Mrs. J. **PAUL**, 60, Cholera; A. **BALLENTINE**, 4, Cholera; Son of H. **WHITEHORN**, 10 mos, Dysentery. 6/20-P. **LEARY**, 40, Convulsions. 6/21-T. **McDONALD**, 36, Affection of Heart; Jno **SENN**, 25, Cholera Morbus. 6/22-P. **LANE**, 40, Pneumonia; S. K. **OATES**, 53, Pneumonia; Michael **RUSH**, 30, Cholera Morbus. 6/23-Wm **YATES**, 32, Billious Fever; Mrs. **CORDER**, 63, Diarrhea. 6/24-Sennicia **THOMPSON**, 3, Diarrhea; Peter **QUIN**, 1 ½, Spasms; William **KEIGHTON**, 32, Cholera. 6/25-Richard **HEFFERAN**, 28, Jaundice. 6/26-Fanny **FORREST**, 6, Flux; Mrs. Ann E. **LUMPKIN**, 36. 6/28-Terena **HENENSTEEN**, 3, Fever. 6/29-Mrs. S. E. **DONALDSON**, 29; Mr. B. **CICHMONE**, 24, Apoplexy; Mrs. F. **SHEINDLER**, 34, Fever; Charles W. **DAVIS**, 37, Collapsing Stomach; Mrs. A. E. **WELLER**, 30, Dysentery. 6/30-Walter **HITCHCOCK**, 1; Mary **KATEING**, 35, Cholera Morbus.

7/3-Mr. E. L. **EVANS**, 38, Apoplexy; Mrs. S. **TUCKER**, 76, Inflam Bowels. 7/4-Dercher **BEADHART**, 6, Measles; Caroline **MULENBERG**, 6, Brain Fever. 7/5-Mrs. J. H. **FENTON**, 28, Puerperal Convulsions. 7/6-Mr. Octavio **ALVAREZ**, 20, Pistol shot wound; Mrs. Susan **WEDGEWOOD**, 45, Uterine disease. 7/7-Thos **LISTON**, 10, Inflam Bowels. 7/11-Mr. Henderson **McGOWAN**, 30, Chron Diarrhea (rest of page torn off). 7/17-Rev. J. W. **McFARLAND**, 50, Congestive Fever; Jane **TIPPER**, 12, Congestive Chill. 7/19-Charlotte **BROWN**, 37, Cholera Morbus. 7/22-Child of W. P. **CORBIN**, 2 mos, Diarrhea; Elizabeth **McLEAN**, 6, Typhoid Fever; Michael **BRADY**, 21 mos, Teething. 7/23-Polly J. **OATES**, 11, Spinal disease; T. W. **RODGERS**, stranger, 54, Chronic Diarrhea; Child of Mrs. J. **JOICE**, 1 day, Convulsions; Infant of J. S. **LEVETT**, 3 days, Convulsions; Child of Mrs. **BRATT**, 1, not reported. 7/26-Child of Mr. **WAGGENER**, 14 mo, Convulsions; John **PEARCE**, 35, Coup de Soleil.

8/13-Daughter of G. W. **ACREE**, 9, Dysentery; Patrick **TOOL**, Sun-stroke; Child of W. **RICHARDS**, age & disease not reported; Mr. C. **HAYWINKLE**, 32, Bilious Colic. 8/14-Richard **STEGALL**, 13 mos, Dropsy. 8/15-C. O. **NEIL**, 37, Disease of the Heart. 8/16-Son of Richard **NORRIS**, 3, Dysentery. 8/17-Francis **BURTON** (colored), 24, Dropsy; Infant of Mrs. **VACCARO**, 1, Convulsions. 8/21-Mrs. E. **SMITH**, 70, congestion of the brain. 8/22-Theresa D. **AUBITY**, 6, effects of measles. 8/24-John **SUEROLLO**(/), 32, convulsions; Miss Mary M. **SMITH**, 10, congestive chill. 8/25-Infant of B. **O'HAVER**, 1 day, convulsions. 8/26-Son of Mr. **BANAGIN**, 8, typhoid fever.

9/3-Mrs. M. **BYAGER**, 47, Inflammation of Bowels; Eliza **SAUNDERS**, girl of F. **TITUS**, 20, Peritonitis. 9/5-Michael **RYAN**, 40, Consumption. 9/8-Son of E. L. **SMITH**, 13 mos., Teething. 9/9-John **FULSON**, 40, Brain Fever. 9/11-Daughter of I. **PHELON**, 8, congestion of the brain. 9/15-W. **REYNOLDS**, 60, nervous affection; James **WEAVER**, 13, congestive fever; Mary B. **DELAUNEY**, 16, congestive chill. 9/17-Son of J. **BALLENTYNE**, 18 mos, marasmus(?). 9/19-Daughter of A. S. **DORSAY**, 14, Congestive Fever. 9/20-Betty **GRINNELL**, 8, measles. 9/23-Thomas **CONWAY**, 80, old age; Child of Thomas **ROBINSON**, 2, Chronic Diarrhea. 9/24-Mrs. Sidney **HOBDY**, 52, convulsions; Martin **MOONEY**, 50, unknown; Green **CARPER**, 41, liver complaint. 9/29-Child of Wm. **CARR**, 3, unknown. 9/30-James **BALLENTYNE**, 7, disease of the liver.

10/1-Hugh **WALSH**, 29, bowel complaint. 10/3-Mrs. **BUCKLEY**, 28, cholera; Child of Mrs. **HUGHES**, 5, cholera. 10/5-F. M. **GLANVILLE**, 29, bilious congestive fever; Child of Mr. **HOGAN**, 5, cholera. 10/6-Child of John **O'CAIN**, 7, cholera. 10/8-John **HOUGHMAN**, 17, diarrhea; Son of K. **TEUFUL**, 12 days, convulsions. 10/9-J. R. **FERGUSON**, 33, Apoplexy. 10/10-Alice **STIMSBURY**, 2, consumption; J. **McCAUGH**, 18, Bowel Affection. 10/11-R. H. **DeWITT**, 33, Congestion of Brain; Infant son of Mrs. **STANTON**, 8 mos, convulsions. 10/12-J. M. **LOTT**, 2, Congest. of Brain. 10/13-T. **BEATTIE**, 21, Consumption. 10/17-John **HOGAN**, stranger, just from St. Louis, cholera. 10/18-Patrick **BAYLIE**, stranger, cholera; Child of Isaac **HARRISON**, 3, dysentery; Mrs. Ellen **CONWAY**, 23, Consumption;

Infant son of Mrs. **WARRICK**, 1 day, Convulsions; Peter **GRIFFIN**, 11 mos, Consumption. 10/20-D.
LOONY, pauper, 25, not known. 10/22-John **MONOUGH**, 40, Cholera; John **CONDER**, Cholera; John
PETERS, Bowel Affection; T. **FITZPATRICK**, not reported. 10/23-Stephen **BOYLER**, 25, Billious
Fever; Thos. F. **McMANUS**, 3, Croup; Sonora **BEADLE**, 3 yrs 6 mos, Inflammation of Brain; P.
PHILLIPS, 45, Cholera Morbus; W. **RUGG**, 2, Dropsy. 10/24-Child of Mrs. **HUFFANY**, 2, Diarrhea.
10/25-Mrs. **MUIRAHILL**, 22, Diarrhea. 10/28-Thos. **RYAN**, 27, death from pistol shot. 10/29-Nicholas
HANAGAN, 26, cholera; W. D. **HOPKINS**, 6 mos., diarrhea. 10/30-Wm. **BOYD**, 25, not known. 10/31-
James **McGRATH**, (stranger), 30, cholera.
11/2-Martin **DERMODY**, 23, cholera; P. **KANNY**(?), 25, cholera. 11/3-J. **PHILLIPS**, 10, cholera. 11/4-
John **McDONOHOO**, 23, Bowel Affection. 11/5-P. **RYAN**, 40, Consumption. 11/6-Ellen **REAGEN**, 9
mos., Teething; Mary E. **KEISACKER**, 11 mos., Diarrhea. 11/7-Mrs. **ERWIN**, 30, not reported; Son of
Marcus **JONES**, 2, Inflammation of Stomach. 11/8-Martin **LEE**, 27, Diarrhea; Joseph P. **HULBERT**, 2,
Diarrhea; Miss Alice **ORNE**, 21, Typhoid Fever. 11/9-Alex. **ACHEY**, 21, Typhoid Fever. 11/10-Child of
Geo. L. **HOLMES**, 1 week, not reported. 11/12-Martin **MANNING**, 30, Affection of the bowels; James
WARD, 55, intemperance. 11/13-James **WELCH**, 19, diarrhea; Michael **O'CONNER**, 25, diarrhea.
11/17-Mr. **LEVERETT**, 32, bilious fever; Mrs. Susan H. **WILKINSON**, 57, bilious fever; Wm.
CHILDRESS, 30, death from pistol wound. 11/19-John **KEHOE**, 29, consumption. 11/20-Mrs. Littleton
HENDERSON, 65, not reported. 11/21-Mrs. **ELLISON**, 47, diarrhea; Stephen **RIDLEY**, 40, not
reported. 11/23-Infant of John **DUNCAN**, 2 days, not reported. 11/24-Mrs. **BECK**, 30, cholera. 11/26-
Dennis **BAGLEY**, 30, cholera; T. **FITZGERALD**, 23, cholera; W. **CAMDEN**, 35, cholera. 11/27-James
DOYLE, 33, pneumonia; J. **O'NEAL**, 18, cholera; Owen **CONWAY**, 40, cholera; E. **MANNING**, 61,
consumption; Mrs. M. **THOMAS**, 23, dysentery. 11/28-Thos. **CONWAY**, 30, cholera. 11/29-Miss B.
RYAN, 28, cholera.
12/1-Child of Joseph **PRIMM**, 4, death from burn. 12/13-Child of Hannah G. **RAINEY**, 3, disease of the
Kidneys. 12/14-Infant son of R. **COAL**, 2, not known; Mrs. **SCHMITZER**, 31, cholera morbus; F.
LONG, (stranger), 36, cholera morbus; Columbus **TAYLOR**, 10, Typhoid Fever. 12/18-Charles **LONG**,
4, Ship Fever; Mrs. M. J. **SMITH**, 25, Pneumonia. 12/20-Wm. **BARTLETT**, 54, Dropsy. 12/22-Child
of J. **THILL**, 3, Ship Fever; Infant of S. W. **NOEL**, 3 mos., Convulsions. 12/24-Mr. **CONLY**, 40, chronic
diarrhea; Son of W. **HOWARD**, 4, pneumonia. 12/26-Son of J. P. **TOMKINS**, 4, typhoid fever. 12/27-
W. M. **MADDOX**, 40, pneumonia. 12/28-F. **SMITH**, 4_, ship fever; Stephen **JENNINGS**, 25, dysentery.
12/29-Emma W. **WHITFIELD**, 20 mos., croup. 12/30-Daniel **JONES**, colored man, 30, consumption.

LIST OF INTERMENTS FOR 1855:

1/26-Child of J. T. **LYNN**, 10, disease not known; James W. **YERRY**, 30, Cholera, died at wharf-boat, just
from Texas. 1/27-P. **CONWAY**, 5, Congestive Chill.
2/1-Lawrence **ROACH**, 25, Disease of Liver. 2/2-Mr. **TIPTON**, 35, Consumption; Brice A. **COLLINS**,
35, Intemperance. 2/12-Miss Ann E. **WALDRAN**, 33, Dropsy; Wm. Henry **MOSBY**, 4 mos,
Inflammation of Brain; Mrs. E. **SMITH**, 40, Cholera Morbus; Mrs. J. **RYAN**, 30, Typhoid Fever. 2/13-
Mr. **COLE**, 50, Consumption. 2/15-David **BURNS**, 50, Inflammation of Bowels. 2/16-Wm. **McCALE**,
33, sudden death. 2/22-Mrs. E. B. **BROOKS**, 26, Consumption. 2/24-Daniel **O'BRYAN**, 30, Cholera.
2/27-Jacob **DECKER**, 30, pneumonia.
3/1-Daughter of J. **PENDERGRAST**, 7 days, convulsions. 3/3-Marshall **THOMPSON**, 7 mos,
Pneumonia; Robert C. **REID**, 13, Chronic Diarrhea. 3/4-Mrs. **ENGLISH**, 60, Consumption; Z. N.
GARBUTT, 34, Measles. 3/5(?)-Daughter of D. O. **DOOLEY**, 2(?), Pneumonia. 3/7-Mrs. A. **COX**, 38,
Dysentery. 3/8-Charles **LEBER**, 9, Consumption. 3/11-Mrs. Adelia **WHEATON**, 36, consumption; Mary
MADINA(?), 2, diarrhea; Mrs. S. S. **JONES**, 40, pneumonia; Z. **BENEDICT**, 40, cholera. 3/12-Daughter
of H. R. **PUGH**, 11 mos, pneumonia. 3/13-Son of G. F. **JOHNSON**, 7 mos, not known. 3/18-Robert
BELL, 50, Consumption; Mrs. Julia **MAYFIELD**, 33, Consumption; Mrs. B. W. **JOHNSON**, 30, not
reported; Child of Robert **WALLACE**, 4 mos, not reported. 3/19-Dr. Henry M. **GRANT**, 45, Pulmonary
Apoplexy; N. G. **POWERS**, 29, Disease of the Heart; Jno. **McNAMARA**, 53, Congestion of the Brain.
3/27-Infant son of Capt. **WHITSETT**, 1, hydrocephalus. 3/28-Mary L. P. **SMITH**, 13, typhoid fever; John
KLINE, 18, hip disease; John **BUCHANAN**, 80, old age. 3/29-Patrick **SINNETT**, 45, pneumonia.
4/9-John **GREEN**, 30(?), Pneumonia; E. S. **TODD**, 35, effects laud'm. 4/11-Mrs. Margaret **SPIGEL**, 27,
congestive chills. 4/12-J. M. **HOWARD**, 40, consumption; Infant of S. T. **HOFFMAN**, 1 day, not
reported. 4/13-Mrs. **KIRK**, 24, pneumonia; M. **LEONARD**, 60, consumption. 4/14-Capt. D. W. **DILL**,

33, effects of burn. 4/15-John **KENNY**, 69(?), consumption. 4/16-Infant of R. F. **BRADSHAW**, 1, brain fever. 4/18-S. S. **SUMLER**, 45, pneumonia. 4/21-Edward **CUMMINS**, 40, disease of the heart. Week Ending 5/12 – J. A. **STEWART**, 24, Cholera; Mrs. E. **McQUENY**, 28, Cholera; Mr. P. **HINES**, 34, Cholera; Susan **BROWN**, 30, Consumption; Mr. J. **GRIFPHIS**, 25, Cholera; Mr. John **DEAN**, 35, Cholera; Robert E. **BEDFORD**, 2, Cholera; W. T. **BAKER**, 20, Consumption; Son of Mr. **SMITHER**, 4, Fits; Wm. **MATTLY**, 32, Cholera; Mary **LUDLY**, 14, Cholera; Patrick **FULTON**, 30, Cholera; John **KENNEDY**, 45, Cholera; Mr. S. **BAUM**, 30, Cholera; Thos. **CREIGHTON**, 48, Pneumonia; Mrs. E. **NUSS**, 31, Cholera; Mary **REINACH**, 5, Cholera; Mrs. Matilda **PECK**, 24, Cholera; John **NUSS**, 5, Cholera; _____ **REINACE**, 28, Cholera; _____ **REINACH**, 4, Cholera; Daughter of O. S. **TENNY**, 19 mos., Dysentery. 5/28-Mr. W. **CASEY**, 37, intemperance. 5/29-Andrew B. **SHAW**, 11, scarlet fever; Child of Thomas **ATHERTON**, 20 mos., bowel affection; Mary **LUSTER**, 10, typhoid fever. 6/2-Michael **O'HARA**, 40, dropsy; Thomas J. **STEELE**, 24, consumption; Edward J. **KELLY**, 33, typhoid fever.
7/1-Mrs. M. **HIGGINS**, 40, Dropsy. 7/2-Mrs. **SMACHZER**, 30, Cholera; Daniel **QUINLIN**, 27, Congestive Fever; Jesse **WILLIAMSON**, Esq., 45, Cholera. 7/3-Child of W. B. **ADAIR**, 4, Cholera. 7/4-Jno. **STEENBACH**, 23, Cholera; Mrs. A. **LYONS**, 55, Chronic Diarrhea. 7/5-Child of Thos. **VAUGHAN**, 14 mos., Diarrhea. 7/6-W. W. **MORROW**, 25, Inflammation of Brain; 7/7-Child of F. M. **STEWART**, 2, Diarrhea; Child of J. B. **SCRUGGS**, 17 mos., Diarrhea; Child of A. B. **ADAIR**, 2, Diarrhea; Wm. **COLLINS**, 40, Typhoid Fever. 7/8-Child of Michael **BURK**, 17 mos., Diarrhea; Child of Michael **KEMP**, 6 weeks, Convulsions. 7/10-Mrs. **JONES**, 60, Cholera; John **RANDLE**, 40, Cholera Morbus. 7/12-Lewis **HENRY**, 6, Cholera; Susan **REEDER**, 4, Congestion of the Brain; Hardin **POWELL**, 65, Consumption. 7/13-Mrs. Margaret **BURKE**, 50, Billious fever. 7/14-Mrs. Julia **TALLY**, 27, Inflammation of Bowels; Letitia **LUCAS**, 20 mos., Brain Fever; Mary Ann **DINGHAR**, 2, Diarrhea. 7/15-Mrs. **PIMM**, 23, Cholera; Maria **LEGROS**, 27, Diarrhea. 7/16-Mrs. Irabella **McCALISTER**, 20, Congestive Fever. 7/17-Child of Jno. C. **LANIER**, 18 mos., not reported. 7/18-Mr. Dennis **LACY**, 35, Congestion of Brain. 7/19-James R. P. **FISHER**, 10, death from accidental gun shot. 7/20-Child of Robert **SPITTLE**, 10 mos., Congestive Chill. 7/22-Patrick **HEFFERAN**, 24, sun-stroke. 7/23-Harvey **MERRILL**, 16, convulsions. 7/24-Mrs. B. **KING**, 51, disease of the heart. 7/27-Michael **KANNA**, 12, tetanus or lock-jaw; E. **KATTMANN**, 35, hydrothrax; Son of Mr. **GRAHAM**, 5, congestive fever. 7/28-Thomas **MURPHY**, 36, diarrhea. 7/30-Jane **MASON**, 4, Whooping Cough.
8/1-Judge B. F.(?) **CARUTHERS**, 46, Congestion of the brain. 8/4-Child of C. H. **TYLER**, 18 mos., scarlet fever; Patrick **CHARGE**, 26, Bilious Fever. 8/5-Son of E. **WELBORNE**, 2, cholera infantum. 8/6-Mary Ann **LEWIS**, 18 mos. 8/9-William **WAMBLE**, (stranger) 45, bilious fever; Mr. S. **SULLIVAN**, 65, consumption. 8/11-Mrs. Isabella **NUGENT**, 26, consumption. 8/12-Mr. G. _. **BA_UTER**(?), 24, bilious fever; William **JOHNSON**, (stranger) 36, not reported. 8/13-John **MOYLAN**, 24, typhoid fever; Mr. H. **FURMAN**, 42, typhoid fever. 8/14-William **ALEXANDER**, 8 mos., dysentery; John **LEAHY**, 28, yellow fever; T. **RICHARDS**, 73, ____ disease of the heart; William L. **DAUGHERTY**, 27, yellow fever. 8/15-Mrs. Virginia **CLARK**, 32, consumption. 8/16-Emma **BARNET**, 14, yellow fever. 8/17-Charles **NORTON**, 37, consumption. 8/18-T. M. **RHODES**, 16, congestive chill. 8/19-Johanna **COLLINS**, 1, teething. 8/20-Mrs. O. C. **JONES**, 47, inflammation of stomach; H. **HENNY**, stranger, yellow fever on a steamboat. 8/21-Edward **BRANNON**, 28, sun-stroke; Mrs. J. D. **ARMOUR**, 26, sudden death. 8/22-Patrick **KEHOE**, 3, teething; Two infant daughters of A. B. **CRANE**, 1 day, not given. 8/23-J. H. **HARRISON** (on the steamer Harry Hill), 23, yellow fever; John **MEACHAM**, 9, dropsy. 8/24-Miss Martha **THOMAS**, 22, inflammation of bowels. 8/26-Thomas **HAMILTON**, 28, yellow fever, on steamer Harry Hill; Julia **SULLIVAN**, 8, whooping cough. 8/27-Child of Thomas **TALLY**, 3, diarrhea. 8/28-George **HAWKINS**, 36, yellow fever, on steamer Ingomar; George **NEWELL**, 21, yellow fever, on steamer Harry Hill; Thomas **EBERTSON**, 22, yellow fever, on steamer Ingomar; Mr. T. F. **WOODRUFF**, 28, yellow fever. 8/29-James **KITTS**, ten mos., teething. 8/30-Child of J. **QUINBY**, 5 days, convulsions. 9/2-James P. **MERCER**, 45, pistol shot. 9/3-Everett B. **FLEMING**, 40, yellow fever; John **SHEEY**, 23, death from wound; Mrs. W. **TAIT**, 45, consumption; Wm. T. **SPICKERNAGLE**, 18, yellow fever, from steamer Bluff City. 9/4-Hardy **LATHAM**, 13(?), yellow fever. 9/6-Patrick **HOGAN**, 10 mos, teething; Daughter of J. **GNESHARVER**, 16 mos, teething; Child of J. **BLACK**, 9 mos, inflammation of brain; Mr. **McGINNIS**, from steamboat, 35, jaundice. 9/7-W. M. **CROSBY**, found dead; supposed to be from exposure and intemperance. 9/8-Catherine **FUNDLE**, 15 mos, not reported; Ellen **SULLIVAN**, (infant) 1, teething. 9/9-Arabella M. **SMITH**, 2, teething; Honora **SULLIVAN**, 5, teething; Caroline **PANESI**, 55, congestive fever; Wm. **HOSKINS**, 20, yellow fever. 9/10-Mr. Robert **SANGSTER**, 25, yellow fever.

9/11-So_n **WALLACE**, 37, congestion of the brain; Mrs. William M. **JONES**, 30, consumption. 9/12-Mrs. **WILSON**, 90, old age; James **FORBES**, (on the river), 25, yellow fever; O. B. **VANMETER**, 33, congestive fever. 9/13-James E. **WILLIAMSON**, 2, consumption; Infant of Thos. **STIRK**, 11 mos, dysentery; Miss Catherine J. **BOLFES**, 15, yellow fever; Jacob **BERTHALD**, 27, yellow fever. 9/14-Henry **HERBERS**, 11 mos, consumption. 9/14-James H. **RODGERS**, 17, bilious fever; Miss Sarah J. **PORTER**, 25, yellow fever. 9/15-Negro man of W. F. **BARRY**, 30, death from wound; Ambrose **MEADOW**, 29, yellow fever; Ambrose **MADDEN**, 29, yellow fever. 9/16-Benj. **POLK**, 18, congestive chills; Capt. S. **WELLS** (from river), 45, bilious fever. 9/17-Rev. T. B. **CLARY**, 39, yellow fever (**CLEAREY** in another place). 9/18-Mrs. M. A. **HUTCHISON**, 20, bilious fever; Mrs. M. M. **MAY**, 33, bilious fever (name Mary S. **MAY** in another paper); John **NEWELL**, 18, yellow fever. 9/19-Miss **TRESBOURN**, 23, congestion of brain (**TRESBUN** in another paper); Mr. Aleck **FLEMMING**, 39, yellow fever; Chas. **WHEATON**, 38, typhoid fever; Mary **SAVAGE**, 5, billious fever. 9/20-John **THIESS**, 24, typhoid fever; Miss Lucinda **ROBINSON**, 18, typhoid fever; John **MOORE**, 19, yellow fever; Roger **CONWAY**, 52, billious fever. 9/21-Mr. **WALTZ** (stranger), 21, brain fever; Mr. Jacob **GATEKURST** (a German), 22, congestion of brain; R. **CONLEY**, 52, (yellow fever, off the Batture near river.) 9/24-**SOLARI** (Italian), 32, found dead—supposed by coroner to be apoplexy. 9/25-Mr. Ira **ROBINSON**, 59(or 69), debility and old age; Frederick **BIEROT**, 19, typhoid fever; Mr. J. L. **FULLERTON**, 37, intermittent fever. 9/26 & 9/27-Mr. Elijah **WILLIAMS**, 40, yellow fever; Son of John **MECASSAR,** 10, Congestion of the brain; Daughter of B. F. **GOOD**, 11 mos, diarrhea; Daughter of E. B. **FLEMING**, 6(?), yellow fever; Miss Martha **BELOAT**, 10, congestion of stomach; Mr. John **GAMBLE**, 30, bilious fever; Albert **PALMER**, 28, yellow fever; Child of Dr. Z. **HARRIS**, yellow fever; Mrs. **BURKE**, 32, consumption; Mrs. **WATSON**, 36, bilious fever. Mr. **WILLIAMS**, who died of yellow fever this morning, contracted the disease in the unhealthy locality in which the two Mr. **FLEMINGS** died of same disease, some week or two since. We regret to report that there still continues to be much sickness in a portion of South Memphis....Memphis Whig, 9/27/1855. 9/28-Mrs. Martha C. **POWERS**, 24, yellow fever; Mrs. Matilda **PARKER**, 41, yellow fever; Mrs. **McNAMEE**, 45, yellow fever; Mr. Stephen **KEITH**, from the river, 26, yellow fever; Mr. N. **WEBBER**, 42, yellow fever. 9/29-Mrs. **CADWALADER**, 30, yellow fever; Dr. Zeno **HARRIS**, 26, yellow fever; Mr. John L. **McNAMEE**, 23, yellow fever; Miss Eliza **HOFFMAN**, 38, yellow fever; Mr. Ira **ROBINSON**, 28, yellow fever; Miss Sallie E. **WELLS**, 60, congestive chill. 9/30-Kate **ROACH**, 12, typhoid fever; Mrs. **BEHERE**, 25, yellow fever; Jacob **KLIENER**, 22, yellow fever.

10/1-Mr. E. **CADWALLADER**, 38, yellow fever; John **BRYANT**, 68, hemorrhage of the lungs; Mattie **SMITH**, daughter of the late Mrs. S. S. **SMITH**, 15 mos, not yellow fever; Sam'l **CARSON**, 25, inflammation of the bowels; John **WRIGHT**, 29 (or 39), yellow fever; Mrs. **GIBSON**, 35, yellow fever. 10/4-Lulu, daughter of W. G. **WINSTON**, 4 mos, billious fever; Mrs. Henrietta V. **WALLACE**, 42, congestion of bowels; James **MAY**, 29, yellow fever; Cornelius **SHOTZ**, 25, yellow fever; Philip **DIRK**, 18, yellow fever; Mrs. **LEACH**, 17, yellow fever; Mrs. Catherine A. **CONLAN**, 30, yellow fever; Mrs. P. **DUNN**, 24, yellow fever; Mrs. Sarah A. **ROBINSON**, 35, typhoid fever. 10/5-Rev. H. S. **PORTER**, 39, bilious intermittent fever; Mr. Geo. 1. **McMAURY**, 29, yellow fever; Lewis **GRAHAM**, free colored man, 38, not reported; Joseph Jesse **RILEY**, 6, yellow fever; Mr. Thos. **CONWAY**, 45, dropsy; Mrs. **FRICK**, 45, disease not yellow fever. 10/6-Miss Amanda **McGINNIS**, 16, bilious fever; Martin **CONNELLY**, 33, not reported. 10/7-Amy **SMITHERS** (colored woman aged 90 years), yellow fever; James **DALSON**, 39, yellow fever; Mrs. H. P. **HILL**, 32, congestive chill; Henry **BEASLEY**, 10, congestive chill; Mrs. B. S. **GARRISON**, 40, yellow fever; Mrs. **ELAM**, 60, yellow fever. 10/8-Dr. Thomas **KEEFE**, 35, congestion of brain; Melissa **KNEELAND**, 48, not reported; Robert **BENDER**, 26, consumption; Ellen **McDERNUTT**(?), 34, bilious fever; Joseph **VERHOUSCHK**, 34, inflamation of bowels. 10/9-Mr. James **McCLOUD**, 30, yellow fever; Mr. John **KING**, 67, bilious fever. 10/10-Hiram **HAMLIN**, 5, chronic diarrhea; Dr. M. **GABBERT**, 56(?), inflammatory bilious fever; A. **McGINNIS**, 45, yellow fever; Mrs. Amelia **REINHARDT**, 33, yellow fever; Mr. Chas. **KONCHLER**, 25, yellow fever; John **McCARTY**, 40, death from an injury; Thos. **KAIN**, 30, colic; Mrs. **RUDISILL**, 58, yellow fever. 10/12-Miss E.(?) S. **SMITH**, 22, yellow fever; Child of F. **REINHARDT**, 4 mos, yellow fever; Miss Bridget **MEADE**, 26, yellow fever; Mrs. **POWERS**, 50, yellow fever; A. J. **SIGNAIGO**, 30, yellow fever; Michael **BURKE**, 30, yellow fever; James **BRADY**, 35, chills; Georgiana **HAYDEN**, 6 weeks, croup; Miss **LEARY**, 22, diarrhea; Mrs. **SCRUGGS**, 21, yellow fever. 10/13-Mr. E. R. **RACINE**, 34, yellow fever; Mrs. P. **McCARTY**, 22, puerperal; Mr. J. M. **BULKLEY** (from the country), congestive chill; Mrs. Ann **HEFFERON**, 35, yellow fever; Mr. Geo. **HEROLD**, 22, yellow fever; Mrs. M. C. **SMALL**, 37, yellow

fever. 10/14-Mrs. Eleanor **DELANO**, 32, yellow fever; Miss Emily **STEWART**, 23, yellow fever; Mrs. **HUME**, 37, yellow fever; Mrs. **ROACH**, yellow fever; Mr. James B. **McMURRAY**, 25, yellow fever; Mr. **BARRY**, 23(?), diarrhea; Mrs. Eliza O. **PAGE**, 51, yellow fever; Charles **WATKINS**, 49, diarrhea; Mrs. E. **THORN**, 40, yellow fever. 10/15-Mrs. Ella **MURRAY**, 60, consumption; Mrs. J. W. **SMITH**, yellow fever; P. **CODILEY**, 10, yellow fever; Daughter of Thos. **McGRATH**, 2 mos, spasms. 10/17-Mr. W. **GREATHOUSE**, (stranger), 26, erysipilas; Mr. Jno. M. **CARROL**, 29, yellow fever. 10/18-Mr. W. **OVENS**, 41, yellow fever; Mrs. Emily **OVENS**, 35, yellow fever; Mrs. E. **POTTER**, 37, yellow fever; Mrs. A. B. **TAYLOR**, yellow fever. 10/19-Mr. J. Watt **SMITH**, 36, yellow fever; Mr. Thos. **McPHERSON**, 49(?), jaundice; Mr. James **FLANAGAN**, 25, yellow fever. 10/20-Mrs. Catherine C. **DONNELL**, 30, yellow fever; Mr. John H. **HOFFMAN**, 30, yellow fever; Mrs. **MAGINNIS**, 40, yellow fever. 10/21-Mr. G. **BREADEN**, 26, yellow fever; Miss R. **FOLTY**, 18, yellow fever. 10/22-Miss Jetta **FRANK**, 18, yellow fever; Samuel **REED**, 20, yellow fever; Bridget **O'DONNELL**, 1, yellow fever; Mrs. Nancy **BOYD**, yellow fever. 10/23-Mrs. Mary **FLANRY**, 30, puerperal disease; Norman P. **WILCOX**, 30, yellow fever; Michael **BURNS**, 27, yellow fever. 10/24-Colored man, Plummer **WOODS**, yellow fever. 10/26-Miss Barbara **HOFFMAN**, yellow fever; Andrew **KETHEN**, 35, killed by fall of dirt. 10/27-Mrs. M. A. **PORTER**, 34, yellow fever; Capt. E. W. **BOOKSHEER**, 72, yellow fever; Son of Mr. **KNOWLES**, 2, croup; Child of Mr. **KNOWLES**, 5, brain fever; Negro woman of C. W. **CHERRY**, 75, consumption. 10/28 & 10/29-Infant boy of L. E.(or R.) **ORSBURN**, 1, convulsions; Anthony **DECKERS**, 28, yellow fever. 10/29-W. B. **McKEON**, 11, yellow fever; R. A. **DICKINS**, 28, yellow fever; W. H. W. **McKEON**, 11, yellow fever; A. R. **AIKEN**, 34, yellow fever; S. **PFISTER**, yellow fever; M. M. **JOHNS**, 23, yellow fever; Mrs. **ALGEO**, 28, congestion of the Lungs; Infant son of J. W. **SCRUGGS**, 3 weeks, yellow fever; S. P. **WEANER**, 22, yellow fever; Miss **WILEY**, 17, yellow fever; Child of F. G. **BUTLER**, 18 mos, dysentery. 10/31 – Mr. Daniel **RYAN**, 22, yellow fever; W. H. **NEPLER**, 40, consumption. 11/1 – Thomas **WHITFIELD**, 41, inflammation of the brain. 11/2 – Son of Mr. J. **LLOYD**, 3, yellow fever. 11/5 – Owen **BURKE**, 25, congestive fever. 11/6 – Miss Agnes M. **WILLIAMSON**, 18, yellow fever. 11/8 – Mrs. Eunice **WILLIAMSON**, 58, yellow fever; Edwin W. **HILL**, 9, yellow fever. 11/9 – Mr. G. **RAMISOTE**, 21, yellow fever. 11/10 – Dr. R. B. **BERRY**, 55, yellow fever; Adrian G. **NOEL**, 3, consumption. 11/12 – Miss Johanna **KENNEDY**, 23, bilious fever; Mr. J. **BURNS**, yellow fever. 11/14 – Mr. Samuel **EWING**, 61, yellow fever; Mrs. Louisa **BEHKUFF**, 52, dropsy; Lawrence **KENNEDY** (stranger from Natchez), 23, yellow fever. 11/16 – David **PORTER**, 25, bronchitis; Mr. Jno. **McGUIRE**, 56, accidental fall; Michael **TREVINS**, 25, diarrhea.
12/2 – Mrs. Susan W. **MORTON**, 34, consumption. 12/5 – Son of Jacob **STEHAR**, 10, typhoid fever. 12/13 – Charles **BOWLES**, 3, not reported. 12/16 – George L. **RISK**, 1, scarlet fever; Thomas C. **RYAN**, 60, chronic diarrhea. 12/17 – Sam'l. **McGLAUN**, 31, pneumonia. 12/22 – Joseph D. **WISE**, 29, chronic diarrhea; Negro man, Reuben, servant of John D. **RAWHIS**, 40, bilious fever. 12/25 – Child, Thos. **WRIGHT**, 3 weeks, croup; Wm. T. **GOFF**, 7 mos., scarlet fever; Sarah **GOFF**, 4, scarlet fever. 12/26 – Jno. **HAYDEN**, 47, consumption. 12/29 – John **DUFFY**, 38, death from intemperance and exposure

LIST OF INTERMENTS FOR 1856:

1/1 – H. R.(?) **HARRELL**, 42, intemperance. 1/3 – G. W. **MURRAY**, 30, murdered with knife. 1/20 – Debora, daughter of Holloway **MORRIS**, 5 mos., pneumonia. 1/21 – John **CORBIT**, 27, chills and fever; Negro Daniel, of A. **STREET**, 30, pneumonia; Mrs. J. F. **LAUDERDALE**, 62, consumption. 1/22 – Henry **LAW**, 21, typhoid fever. 1/23 – Charles Anna **GERMAIN**, 7, died from being burned. 1/25 – D. H. **SCHAFFER**, 28, pneumonia. 1/26 – Mary Ann **SHEPHERD**, 12, disease of the lungs. 1/27 – Child of J. L. **WARD**, 8 mos., disease of the brain; Child of John **CAUSEY**, 11 mos., disease of the brain. 1/28 – Mrs. Jane C. **DRUMMOND**, 32, consumption. 1/29 – Mr. **LUCKMAN**, 36, pneumonia.
2/4 – Hugh **HENRY**, 17, consumption; Ernest J. **WILLIAMS**, 16 mos., scarlet fever; Conway **QUIGLEY**, 36, pneumonia. 2/8 – Martin **KENNEDY**, 29, consumption. 2/19 – Mr. **PASQUERO**, 35, unknown; Wm. **KEMPLE**, 12, accidental discharge of pistol. 2/21 – Miss Eliza **LESTER**, 10, disease of the liver. 2/22 – Alex C. **HOYLE**, 3, scarlet fever. 2/23 – Mrs. **HOYLE**, 35, congestive fever. 2/24 – Mrs. Delia **BUSEKAMP**, 37, epilepsy. 2/27 – Henry **ABBOT**, 25, consumption. 2/28 – Mrs. M. A. **LEVY**, 25, scarlet fever.
3/10 – Robert J. **CREIGHTON**, 4, scarlet fever. 3/11 – Alison **DAVIS**, 26, consumption. 3/12 – Joseph B. **MEACHAM**, 40, hemorrhage of the lungs. 3/14 – Mrs. **PARTEE**, 40, consumption; Casper

FRANSIOLA, 54, consumption. 3/26 – Jno. W. **PHILLIPS**, 55, consumption. 3/27 – Willis **DUKE**, 22, congestive chill. 3/29 – Bratley **BOYETE**, 53, consumption.
4/1 – John **CURRY**, 50, bilious fever. 4/2 – Miss Julia **HENKEL**, 13, scarlet fever. 4/3 – Mrs. Mary **FITCH**, 21, inflammation of stomach; Molly **MONTGOMERY**, 11 mos., pneumonia; Frederick **BOWEN**, 3, drowned by accident. 4/4 – Child of Mr. H. G. **FOX**, 2 mos., inflammation of Brain. 4/5 – Patrick **HULSHAN**, 33, convulsions. 4/7 – Wm. **HENRY**, 2, Measles. 4/8 – Miss Louisa **LAWRENCE**, 20, Consumption. 4/9 – Abraham **VANDYKE**, (of Ohio) 34, Pneumonia. 4/10 – Joan **ENLOE**, 4, Chronic Diarrhea; R. M. **JONES**, 23, Consumption. 4/13 – Ellen **NEUGENT**, 16, pneumonia; Child of M. B. **JOHN**, 4 mos., disease of the brain. 4/14 – Child of A. D. **HINKEL**, 8 mos., scarlet fever. 4/15 – Mrs. America **BROWN**, 18, disease of the stomach and bowels. 4/16 – P. **MALONEY**, 30, death from accidental fall from a railroad car. 4/17 – A. B. **BAUGH**, 35, consumption; John A. **CARVILL**, 20, consumption; Miss S. **DOUGLASS**, 50, consumption; Bennett **REPETTE**, 45, consumption; Miss Lucinda **MURPHY**, 21, consumption; Magnolia **KEESACKER**, 1, not reported. 4/18 – John **SIMONDS**, 48, hemmorage of the lungs; Child of John **YERBY**, 1 day, convulsions. 4/19 – Amelia **TEUFEL**(?), 4, scarlet fever. 4/23 – Wm. **MAJORS**, 37 (47 in another paper), hemorrage of the lungs. 4/26 – Franklin **BOONER**, 3, scarlet fever. 4/30 – Calvin C. **MATTHEWS**, 27, death from wound.
5/5 – Child of B. F. **SAMPLE**, 2, brain fever; John **DOOLIN**, 26, pleurisy; J. **WILLIAMS**, 26, death from wound; Mary **CALDWELL**, 30, inflammation of brain. 5/6 – Conner **LAHEE**, 22, disease of the lungs; Child of B. F. **JONES**, 20 mos., inflammation of brain; Julia **ENGLISH**, 3, convulsions. 5/9 – Mrs. Elizabeth **HENNEGER**, 65, Chronic Rheumatism. 5/12 – Mrs. **WILDER**, 27, disease of the heart. 5/13 – Child of A. **McCALLISTER**, __ mos., teething. 5/14 – Mrs. E. **GAUDEN**, 25, inflammation of stomach. 5/16 – Colored man, J. **WHITSON**, 27, intemperance. 5/21 – Michael **RILEY**, 35, consumption. 5/22 – John **BENDER**, 46 (or 48), consumption. 5/23 – Sarah **WOLF**, 17, dysentery. 5/24 – Mary **O'HARA**, 3, Congestive chill. 5/25 – Daughter of Dr. A. **DAYTON**, 7 mos., dysentery. 5/26 – Daughter of Thomas **ROBINSON**, 4, sun stroke; Patrick **DALY**, 40, disease of the heart. 5/27 – Daughter of John **FRICK**, 2, euteritis. 5/28 – Daughter of Daniel **CURLEY**, 3 weeks, vomiting; Child of B. F. **MILLER**, 18 mos., scarlet fever. 5/31 – Son of Jasper N. **JONES**, 6 mos., pneumonia.
6/2 – Mrs. A. M. **CRAWFORD**, 54, pneumonia; Eddie C. **BOOKER**, 2, scarlet fever. 6/4 – Mrs. E. M. **YERGER**, 2_, inflammation of the bowels. 6/6 – Harry B. **KING**, 3, dysentery. 6/7 – Michael **MOORE**, 38, not reported. 6/9 – Son of Mr. **HURTEG**, 10, convulsion; A. Byron **SHAW**, 10 mos., ____ infantum; Michael **DOWD**, 35, disease of the heart; Child of Capt. F. **HICKS**, 16 mos., disease of the bowels. 6/10 – Emma **BRYAN**, 2, inflammation of the stomach. 6/11 – Michael **MADDEN**, death from an injury; Mrs. Juliet H. **THOMPSON**, consumption. 6/13 – Mr. John **RIDDING**, 34. 6/14 – Son of J. F. **FRANK**, 20 mos., diarrhea. 6/15 – Daughter of A. S. **LEVY**, 3 mos., chronic diarrhea. 6/16 – Mary J. **GRIFFING**, 4, convulsions. 6/17 – Annie A. **GROVES**, 2, scarlet fever. 6/19 – Mr. Jas. T. **MAHAFFY**, 41, dysentery. 6/20 – Daughter of Thos. **HARDIN**, 15 mos., marasmus; Child of Charles M. **ULLMAN**, 6 mos., bowel complaint. 6/21 – Cincinnatus **FARRIS**, 8, typhoid fever; Miss L. **GUNBERT**, 28, dysentery. 6/22 – Margaret **McKNIGHT**, 9, scarlet fever; Margaret **SULLIVAN**, 5, consumption; Alice **MAHAFFY**, 3, measles; Elizabeth **SEWLER**(?), 6, cholera morbus. 6/23 – Mr. **GRIFFING**, 27, died from wound; Peter **TULLEY**, 7 mos., dyspepsia; Thos. **DALTON**, 30, knife wound; Mrs. Mary **NOBLY**, 55, consumption; Mrs. **CURRY**, 72, inflammation of bowels; John **MURRY**, 33, sunstroke; Thomas S. **LAWLESS**, 21, drowned. 6/25 – Mrs. Rose Ann **STREET**, 30, consumption; Mrs. **CLEMENT**, 22, consumption; Martin **READER**, 33, fits. 6/27 – A. K. **AYRES**, 35, typhoid fever; Mrs. **GRIFFING**, 65; Mrs. Jane **QUINAN**, 80, consumption. 6/28 – Infant son of Mr. C. H. **WHITTMORE**. 6/29 – Cornelius **LYNCH**, 28, inflammation of the bowels. 6/30 – Abner L. **FRAZIER**, 1 mo., marasmus; Chas. D. **JONES**, 16 mos.; Caroline **RODGERS**, 21 mos., convulsions; Son of C. **WHITEMORE**, 13, dysentery. 7/1 – Miss Rhoda **HART**, 56, disease of the brain; Mrs. **ANDERSON**, 62, inflammation of the bowels. 7/2 – Mrs. **KELLY**, 25, puerperal. 7/3 – P. **HEIN**, 38, sun stroke. 7/4 – Mrs. Catharine **FOY**, 27, chills; Mr. O. G. **TENNY**, 35, disease of the heart; Mrs. John W. **MAPLES**, 31, congestive fever; D. **CHURCHMAN**, 37, sun stroke; Michael **HACHET**, 30, sun stroke; James **WILLIAMS**, 30, drowned; Alexander **DEWITT**, 30, chronic diarrhea. 7/5 – John **TURLEY**, 3 mos., measles; James **CAIN**, 35, sun-stroke. 7/6 – Mrs. Susan M. **WEIR**, 35, bowel affection. 7/9 – Michael R. **CANTWELL**, 2, scrofula; Ida **MAGUIRE**, 3, diarrhea; Mrs. **BURKE**, 33, bilious fever; C. T. **SIMMS**, 20 mos., bronchitis. 7/10 – Alex. **HOWARD**, 28, drowned. 7/12 – Mary A. **KEENAN**, 11 mos., convulsions; Mr. John **CONLEY**, 30, bilious fever. 7/15 – Joseph L. **HAULEY**, 6, disease of the heart; Mr. P. **BOWS**(?), 24, sun-stroke. 7/16 – Daniel **CONNEL**, 22, bilious fever; Mary L. **HICKS**, 18 mos., diarrhea. 7/17 – Mrs. **HAMPSON**, 45, consumption; Wm. A.

JOHNSON, 9 mos., congestion of the brain. 7/18 – Child of F. M. **CASH**, 17 mos., typhoid fever; John L. **HOFFMAN**, 1 mo. 7/19 – Mrs. **LANE**, 22, chronic affection. 7/20 – Mrs. Elizabeth **BRUNS**, 71, diarrhea; Mrs. **MORRELL**, 77, intermittent fever. 7/21 – Mrs. Margaret **BURGENER**, 44, apoplexy. 7/27 – Mrs. Johanna **BACK_RT**, 28, bilious fever; Godfrey **GRIMM**, 40; Daughter of E. W. **CALDWELL**, 10 mos., effects of measles; Con **RYAN**, 28, death from a fall. 7/28 – Infant daughter of R. **DICKSON**, 15 years, convulsions; Infant son of C. **BORNER**, 2, chronic diarrhea. 7/29 – Mrs. M. **GRIDLEY**, 38; Walter (or Walker) **CRAWLEY**, 50, consumption; Joseph P. **GARVIN**, __ mos., whooping cough. 7/30 – Miss Alice E. **ARMSTRONG**, 26, typhoid fever. 7/31 – Thos. W. **HUNTER**, 28, inflammation of brain and paralysis.

8/1 – Michael **MALONE**, 26, bilious fever; Thomas **HESS**, 37, inflammation of the bowels. 8/2 – James **TABOR**, 20, consumption. 8/4 – F. **SEITZ**, 29, consumption; Catherine **KENDALL**, 7, congestive fever; H. **WARD**, 28, death from injury on Railroad. 8/6 – Child of Jas. **PEARCE**, 8 mos., intermittant fever; Daughter of R. **WHITNEY**, 17 mos., chronic diarrhea. 8/7 – Mr. John **ALGEO**, 30, abscess of the liver; Elizabeth **JOYCE**, 10 mos., dysentery. 8/8 – W. A. **HICKS**, 5, fever. 8/9 – Mrs. Mary **WHALAND**, 50; Miss Jane **DAVIS**, 17, typhoid fever; W. C. **BRYAN**, 6, pneumonia; Charles **FRANCEVILLE**, 11 mos., not reported. 8/10 – John **McDONALD**, 22, consumption; Sarah A. **HOFFMAN**, 19 mos., congestive fever; E. Jane **DYER**, 5, congestive fever; Son of M. **JACK**, 20 mos., drowned by accident. 8/11 – Daughter of M. G. **BELL**, 1 week, diarrhea. 8/12 – Child of J. **GRIFFITH**, 1, not known; Daughter of O. P. **NEWBY**, 3 mos., pneumonia. 8/15 – Child of Wm. **WASHINGTON**, 1, not known. 8/14 – Mary A. M. **PAGE**, 1, convulsions. 8/16 – Child of E. **CROSBY**, 11 mos., Teething; W. H. **SHELTON**, 35, Dropsy; Mary F. **SMITH**, 19 mos., dysentery. 8/18 – Catherine **McMAHON**, 1 mo., maramus; J. L. **SANDERS**, 11 mos., bowel affection; Mr. W. H. **PATTISON**, 37, consumption. 8/20 – James **FLORENCE**, 2 mos., intermittent fever. 8/21 – Mary **HENNESSAY**, 1, teething; Thos. **GARRETT**, 27, Hemorhage of Lungs; Jessy A. **STRANGE**, 58, consumption; Child of W. P. **WAREFIELD**, 9 mos., teething; Wm. **PROUDFIT**, Jr., 10 mos., inflammation of the bowels. 8/22 – Mr. Timothy **LEANNEL**, 36, consumption. 8/23 – Mr. John **GRIFFIN**, 27, consumption; Thos. **HOLLERAN**, 1, diarrhea. 8/24 – Emily **PILLS**(?), 40, inflammation of stomach and bowels. 8/26 – Mrs. Mary **FRANKLIN**, 21, not reported. 8/27 – Mrs. Eliza **JONES**, 43, inflammation of stomach and bowels. 8/28 – Antonia **CARDONA**, 5, inflammation of brain. 8/29 – Nancy **BANE**, 6, typhoid fever; Adopted child of J. M. **STOCKDEN**(?), 6 mos., inflammation of bowels. 8/30 – Mrs. Margaret **McCORMACK**, 27, consumption; James H. **CORBETT**, 19, consumption. 9/1 – Mrs. E. O. **HERRON**, 18, puerperal fever; Sebastian **STREGHL**, 24, death from a wound. 9/2 – Mrs. Fanny **DOWNS**, 50, affection of the heart; Infant of R. **SULLIVAN**, 5 mos., bilious fever. 9/3 – Lewis W. **MORGAN**, 8, congestion of the brain; Child of J. **GRUMMER**, 3 days, convulsions; Infant daughter of J. **BRUST**, 3 mos., diarrhea. 9/4 – Miss Alice **LAWLER**, 20, effect of over-dose of laudadum; Infant of Thos. **STARK**, 4 days, not reported. 9/6 – Child of S. **CARMICHAEL**, 3, congestive fever. 9/7 – Bettie **WALKER**, 13 mos., teething. 9/8 – Francis B. **MITCHELL**, 3, scarlet fever; Son of H. **BONNER**, 14 mos., pneumonia. 9/9 – Mary **CRAVLEY**, 14 mos., not known; Infant son of S. M. **STROUD**, 1 mo., croup. 9/11 – Edward **HINCHEE**, 2, inflammation; Mrs. **MAHAN**, 42, bilious fever; Son of Wm. J. **SMITH**, 5 mos., not reported; Miss B. **HENSLER**, 22, dropsy. 9/12 – Joseph **MITCHELL**, 6 mos., brain fever. 9/14 – Michael **DONOHO**, 35, bilious fever; Paul F. **FLETCHER**, 15, drowned accidentally; Child of John **VANNESS**, 14 mos., not known. 9/15 – Nelson **BOND** (colored) 60, exposure. 9/16 – John **RYAN**, three, bowel affection; Olive A. **LEE**, 2, cholera infantum; James **DANNEY**, 6 days, convulsions. 9/18 – Michael **KENNEDY**, 35, dysentery. 9/19 – Child of J. **GRIFFITH**, 13 mos., not known. 9/20 – Theresa, daughter of Mr. T. Y. **BINGHAM**, 7 mos., bowel disease. 9/21 – Bridget **GORMAN**, 4 days, convulsions; Wm. **BOOTH**, 16, death by accident. 9/22 – Joseph **WITT**, 2, sudden death; Child of M. **ARCHARD**, 2 mos., brain fever; Mrs. Elizabeth **ENGLEBACH**, 57, nervous fever. 9/23 – John **WALSH**, 4 mos., inflammation of bowels. 9/24 – Martin **DERINE**, 1 day, convulsions; Ann **WATSON**, 2, teething; Martin **O'NEIL**, 2, diarrhea. 9/25 – Infant of H. W. **BARROW**, 1 day, convulsions. 9/26 – Maurice **O'NEIL**, 5, inflammation of brain. 9/30 – Son of Mr. W. **BENDER**, 3 mos., brain fever; Daughter of Dennis **TOOLE**, 2 days, convulsions.

10/2 – John C. **ADAMS**, 20, typhoid fever; John **BRADY**, 24, typhoid fever. 10/3 – Brooks R. **TREZEVANT**, 47, consumption; Son of Mr. **FINNEY**, 3 ½, old complicated disease. 10/4 – Luella Blanch **METCALF**, 8 mos & 2 days, disease of the bowel. 10/6 – Mrs. Ellen **HANNEGAN**, 80, old age. 10/7 – Reid B. **BROWN**, 13, disease of the heart; Jeremiah **PORTER**, 18 mos., congestive fever; Catherine **OWEN**, 11 mos., not reported. 10/8 – Thomas **BROWN**, 17, disease of the heart; Margaret

LACY, 7 days, convulsions; Child of B. **CARTER**, 13 mos., not known. 10/12 – Son of H. **BENHAM**, 3, killed by accident; Jeremiah **MARCH**, 18 mos., bowel complaint. 10/13 – Elizabeth **McKIM**, 8 mos., croup. 10/15 – Mrs. Maria M. **HENRY**, 47, chronic diarrhea. 10/16 – Son of J. F. **WOLF**, 3, marasmus. 10/17 – Michael **GARNER**, 60, dropsy. 10/27 – William **HARVER**, 16, death from pistol shot. 10/29 – William **MURRAY**, 49, inflammation of stomach and bowels. 10/30 – Ann Elizabeth **BURNS**, inflammation of lungs.
11/2 – Michael **McKEON**, 8, inflammation of the brain; Major M. B. **WINCHESTER**, 55, paralysis. 11/3 – Thos. **RYAN**, 35, inflammation of stomach and bowels. 11/5 – Mrs. Sarah **BORO**, 24, consumption. 11/6 – Mrs. W. **O'CONNER**, 30, consumption. 11/7 – Calvin C. **CLEAVES**, jr., 2, death from burn; Dr. N. **HOWCOTT**, 19, dropsy. 11/8 – John **CORCORAN**, 30, inflammation of bowels; M. **DORINCAMP**, 33, exposure; Daughter of John **WINTER**, 2, merasmus. 11/11 – Valentine **AUSTIN**, 37, death occasioned by accidental discharge of cannon. 11/12 – Child of E. **SULLIVAN**, 2, diarrhea. 11/13 – Fridel D. **ARAGON**, 18, typhoid fever. 11/14 – Son of J. **TWIFEL**, 16 mos., consumption. 11/15 – Joseph P. **McKEON**, 7, death by fall from a horse. 11/17 – Mary **LYNCH**, 1, consumption; J. Gray **HARDEMAN**, 16 mos., not reported. 11/18 – Amanda **EDWARDS**, 1, whooping couch. 11/21 – O. J. **SMITH**, 27, chronic diarrhea; Jacob **NEFFE**, 26, consumption. 11/22 – Major J. M. **WILSON**, 63, pneumonia; Mrs. **WATKINS**, 30, not known; Elizabeth **ALEXANDER**, age and disease not known. 11/23 – David **BROWDER**, 4, croup; Emily J. **CLARK**, 2 mos., inflammation of the lungs; Robert F. **LOWERY**, 56, pneumonia; E. **McCOMBS**, 14 mos., chronic dysentery; Dorothy **SIMISTER**, 16 mos., scarlet fever. 11/28 – W. J. **McLEAN**, 42, inflammation of the stomach.
12/4 – Mrs. Jane E. **TAYLOR**, 26, consumption. 12/8 – Jenny **SHAY**, 30, Consumption. 12/12 – Mrs. Martha **WATSON**, 27, chronic diarrhea; Christy **O'NEAL**, (stranger) 24, fever. 12/15 – Mr. **MORRIS**, 23, diarrhea. 12/16 – Robert **HAYS**, 3, whooping cough. 12/23 – Mrs. Charlotte E. **FINNIE**, 33, debility. 12/24 – James **MATH**, 28, disease of the Spleen; Patrick **O'BRIEN**, 30, inflammation of the lungs; Child of L. __. **DUPREE**, 5 mos., spasms. 12/27 – Isaac **NEVIN**, 38, pneumonia; James **MANNAGAN**, 70, pneumonia; Child of J. J. **WORSHAM**, 14 mos., scarlet fever. 12/28 – Michael **MAHER**, 26, death from accident on the railroad. 12/29 – Child of E. **ENLOE**, 3 weeks, Croup. 12/30 – Joseph **BOAGALUPO**, 35, Pneumonia.

LIST OF INTERMENTS FOR 1857:

1 / 4 – Mrs. **BUSHBY**, 33, consumption. 1/5 – Child of Mrs. J. H. **ATKINSON**, 22 mos., not known. 1/6 – Mr. J. M. **STRANGE**, 21, consumption. 1/10 – Jno. **HERMANS**, 22, effects of cold. 1/19 – Patrick **KELLY**, 25, inflammation of the lungs. 1/21 – Gus **ROBERTSON**, 36, effects of laudnum and whisky. 1/22 – Child of Jacob **GRUBER**, 6, scarlet fever. 1/24 – George **CROFFORD**, 50, dysentery. 1/25 – Louisa **FUSSELL**, 3, typhoid fever; Mr. L. W. **FUSSELL**, 38, inflammation of the stomach. 1/26 – Child of T. S. **CRAIG**, 4 weeks, convulsions; Mrs. **MANNING**, 30, consumption. 1/27 – James H. **PRITCHEL**, 21, consumption. 1/28 – Mrs. **HENSLEY**, 37, puerperal; Emma **FRY**, 19 mos., scarlet fever. 1/29 – Mrs. J. D. **JONES**, 30, exposure; C. P. **SMITH**, 4, croup; Mrs. **LOYD**, 86, old age; Mrs. Elizabeth **JAMES**, 32, puerperal fever. 1/31 – Emma **DAVIS**, 3, not reported.
2/1 – James **MONTGOMERY**, 44, Congestion of the Lungs. 2/2 – Emma **SPICKERNAGLE**, 20 mos., Inflammation of the Brain; Child of Patrick **TOOL**, 7 days, convulsions; Mr. John A. **GARRISON**, 21, Consumption. 2/3 – Mrs. C. **ARRINGTON**, 28, Rheumatism. 2/4 – Son of Louis **BISA**(?), 1, Scarlet Fever. 2/5 – Child of Joseph **ELLIOTT**, 2, Scarlet Fever; Child of Charles R. **STEWART**, 18 mos., injury from fall. 2/6 – Child of Jacob **GURBER**, 22 mos., Scarlet Fever; Mrs. Mary **CAMPBELL**, 46, Pneumonia. 2/9 – Miss Mary C. **TULEY**, 18, Consumption; W. G. **TANNER**, 24, death from assassination. 2/11 – J. **THORNHILL**, 37, Intemperance; Mrs. Carolina **KATTMAN**, 33, Consumption. 2/14 – Thos. **BURKE**, 24, inflammation of the stomach and bowels. 2/18 – Mr. T. G. **ASHBRIDGE**, 24, death from accident on railroad; Mr. S. M. **SAMUELS**, 56, dropsy. 2/21 – Child of C. **HORNE**, 3 mos, bowel affection. 2/22 – Thomas **CARR**, 58, death from a fall; John **NEWLAND**, 27, erysipelas. 2/23 – Son of Mrs. **GALBAUGH**, 2, disease of the brain. 2/26 – Mrs. **GARRY**, 45, pneumonia. 2/27 – Mary J. **PALMER**, 22, consumption.
3/2 – Son of S. **MOSBY**, 4, whooping cough; Son of H. **LEVY**, 3, scarlet fever. 3 / 4 – Infant daughter of Patrick **KIRWAN**, 1 day, convulsions; Mary A. **McKINNEY**, 5, scarlet fever. 3/5 – Mrs. Mary H. **ROWAN**, 70, old age. 3/6 – Caroline **DOWDY**, 27, pneumonia; Thos. **FENLY**, 23, not known. 3/7 – Joseph L. **BORO**, 5 mos, marasmus. 3/9 – R. M. **HORSELEY**, 42, wound; Mary Ann **KANE**, 6 mos,

measles. 3/11 – Michael **RYAN**, 25, effects of wound. 3/12 – J. H. **MOORE**, 17 days, marasmus; Mrs. **DAVIDSON**, 23, pneumonia. 3/13 – Q. L. **MORTON**, 50, dropsy. 3/15 – Infant daughter of J. P. **STRANGE**, 10 days, not reported. 3/16 – Mrs. **McCARTY**, 29, Consumption; Henry D. **PARHAM**, 8, Scarlet Fever; Robert M. **PARHAM**, 6, Scarlet Fever; John P. **FERGUSON**, 7, Congestion of Brain; Susan **STOCKSLAGER**, 21, Consumption. 3/17 – Lizzie **CARROLL**, 2 yrs & 9 mos, effects of Measles; Mary **HENESSES**, 11, Croup. 3/18 – Mrs. Mary J. **STRANGE**, 27, Erysipelas; Mary R. **TEST**, 5, Scarlet Fever. 3/21 – Lard(?) **MYNATT**, 19, Scrofula. 3/22 – Francis **SPINETTO**, 45, Inflammation of the Bowels; Mr. W. H. **RAY**, (stranger) 25, Inflammation of Throat. 3/23 – Malina **ARMOUR**, (colored woman), 43, chronic disease of Lungs; Child of B. **DAVIDSON**, 1 mo., Convulsions; Miss M. J. **BRYAN**, 55, Bronchitis; Chas. S. **HARRIS**, 16 mos., Measles. 3/24 – Mrs. **STROND**(?), 22, Measles. 3/2? – J. W. **MILLER**, 48, Pneumonia. 3/25 – Wm. S. K. **McDONALD**, 11 mos., Croup. 3/26 – Mr. A. M. **JACKSON**, (of Des Arc, Ark.) 40, Typhoid Fever. 3/27 – Mrs. W. J. **ADAMS**, 42, apoplexy. 3/28 – Joanna **SULLIVAN**, 3 yrs & 4 mos., scarlet fever; Prentiss **MARABLE**, 14 mos., Scarlet Fever. 3/30 – G. W. **DYER**, 3, scarlet fever. 3/31 – Child of Mrs. **BURKE**, 6, scarlet fever.

4/1 – J. **SULLIVAN**, 1, scarlet fever; Mary **KENNEDY**, 2, scarlet fever; Mrs. A. **HOWCOTT**, 46, inflammation of bowels; Georgiana **KELLER**, 2 yrs & 6 mos, scarlet fever; J. B. **HARRIS**, 4, effects of measles. 4/3 – Child of C. C. **CLEAVES**, 9 mos., dysentery; Infant of Mrs. J. **HITCHLER**, 1 day, not reported; John **GALLAGER**, 25, congestion. 4/5 – Mrs. Mary _ . **HENRY**, 17, consumption. 4/6 – Col. Lyttleton **HENDERSON**, 66, pneumonia. 4/7 – Louisa R. **BRYAN**, 6(?), congestion of the lungs; Mr. P. W. **HUMPHREYS**, 36, disease of the heart; Mrs. Catherine **NORMY**(?), 27, consumption; Virginia Cary **THOMAS**, 4, congestive fever; Wm. **MYNATT**, 32, typhoid fever; John **KELLER**, 5, dropsy of the heart. 4/8 – Mr. Philip **DEVISE**, 29, erysipelas; Laura B. **WOOD**, 6, scarlet fever. 4/11 – Geo. **MINDERMAS**, 56; Fred **SCHOR**, 5 years 2 mos., Diarrhea; Mary C. W. **COOPER**, 8, Scarlet Fever; James **RYAN**, 35, Congestive Chill. 4/14 – W. B. **TAYLOR**, 23, Typhoid Fever; Child of Dr. **CHIDSEY**, 3 days; Ed **RYAN**, 11 mos., Measles. 4/15 – Cornelius **DALY**, 33, Consumption. 4/16 – James **DALY**, 7 mos., Brain Fever. 4/17 – Bridget C. **GRIFFIN**, 1 yr. 4 mos., Hooping Cough; Samuel **SWEETLAND**, 37, Hemorrhage. 4/19 – Mary **YOUNG**, 6, scarlet fever. 4/21 – Catharine **GRIFFIN**, 9, measles; Lammy **STEWART**, 4, scarlet fever; Mrs. Livily(?) **BRUMLEY**, 35, measles & pneumonia; Oscar D. **JOHNS**, 22, congestion following measles. 4/23 – Katy **APP**, 3, pneumonia. 4/24 – Mildred **SIKES**, 32, not reported. 4/25 – Miss **BLACK**, 16, measles; A. G. **WRIGHT**, 28, unknown; Mrs. **SCROGGINS**, 60, cancer; John, negro of W. D. **FERGUSON**, 22, death from pistol shot; Mary J. **FENNER**, 2 years & 7 mos., scarlet fever. 4/27 – Eliza **CHUBB**, 40, angiora pectoris. 4/28 – Francis M. **MERRIMAN**, 10, scarlet fever. 4/29 – Mrs. **BRADLEY**, 75, inflammation of liver. 4/30 – Thos. B. **CARROLL**, 38, gastric fever.

5/2 – Mrs. Mary W. **FENNER**, 68, chronic diarrhea. 5/10 – John T. **MOORE**, 14, disease of the brain. 5/11 – Wm. **PEACH**, 25, winter fever. 5/12 – Percy **POPE**, 13, scarlatina; Daughter of J. **HICKMOTH**, 15 mos., convulsions. 5/13 – Daughter of A. **PLISCHKE**, 8 mos., no physician; John Bleakley **MURPHY**, 8, scarlet fever; James E. **YANCEY**, 25, consumption; Child of R. B. **HIGGINBOTHAN**, measles. 5/15 – J. D. **SPAIGO**, 50, congestive fever. 5/17 – Mrs. Emmeline S. **MERRIMAN**, 37; Mrs. V. **MAY**, 21, puerperal convulsions. 5/18 – Thomas **CAMPBELL**, 10 mos., pneumonia; William **CAMBY**, 56, disease not reported. 5/19 – Mary **GIDDINGS**, 11, measles. 5/20 – J. W. T. **CAMPBELL**, 3, pneumonia. 5/21 – Wm. **CARR**, 33(?), abscess of livers; Patrick **BREEN**, 42, pneumonia; Daughter of Chas. **WIESNER**, 1 year & 3 mos., convulsions. 5/22 – Son of S. **LEVY**, 2 years & ten mos., inflammation of the brain.

6/6 – Ellen **BUCKLEY**, 40, remittent fever. 6/9 – Wife of Dr. B. F. C. **BROOKS**, 30, puerperal fever. 6/10 – Child of Dr. **HEWETT**, scarlet fever; Mr. **PLUNKETT**, 52, pneumonia. 6/11 – Richard **MURRAY**, 35, pneumonia; Jacob **STEEG**, 13 mos., cholera morbus. 6/12 – F. **RINGWALD**, 48, apoplexy; Eliza **ALBERT**, 40, effects of fall. 6/29 – J. P. **SPICER**, 3 mos, whooping cough; John **McMAHON**, 45, apoplexy. 6/30 – Son of T. **NUSS**, 7 mos, inflammation of the brain.

7/1 – William **MILLION**(?), 18, dysentery. 7/2 – Mrs. Sarah **NORMAN**, 52, chronic diarrhea. 7/26 – Margaret A. **MOORE**, typhoid fever; Cynthia A. **HENDRICKSON**, 1 year & 6 mos, inflammation of the brain. 7/27 – Son of H. T. **HULBERT**, 1 year & 10 mos, measles. 7/29 – Mrs. R. **HOFFMAN**, 23, puerperal fever. 7/30 – Olivia **HOWARD**, 10 mos, inflammation of the bowels; Edwin **FELLOWS**, 1 yr & 2 mos, congestion of the brain; Ellen **CROWLEY**, 40, jaundice. 7/31 – Daughter of A. B. **MUELER**, 10 mos, teething.

8/1 – W. D. **WORMELEY**, 24, dysentery. 8/10 – Elizabeth **CLARK**, 43, intermittent fever; Son of C. **BONER**, 16 mos, diarrhea. 8/12 – Rachel H. **GRIDER**, 19, consumption; Duff **McPHERSON**, 17 mos, marasmus. 8/14 – George W. **ROBERTSON**, 43, consumption; Son of Joseph **TEUFEL**, 19 mos, brain fever. Week Ending 8/15 – Mrs. M. **POWERS**, 68(?), congestive fever; George **SYPERT**, 25, fall; Miss M. **BROWN**, 17, congestive chill; Mary **SHOBY**, 30, typhoid fever. 8/17 – James **CHAUNCEY**, pauper, 40, sunstroke. 8/24 – Mrs. B. **DOYLE**, 30, consumption; Samuel **BRADY**, 6 mos, consumption; Daughter of Mrs. C. **RAWDY**, 8 mos, marasmus. 8/25 – G. S. **WILLIAMS**, 18, bilious fever; Child of W. E. **CHATMAN**, 5 days, convulsions; Ephraim **BURGET**, 41, dropsy. 8/26 – Infant daughter of Mrs. **MANAHAN**, 2 days, not known; Joanna **KENNEDY**, 5 mos, spasms. 8/27 – Martin **SCANTLAN**, 70, old age; Infant of Mrs. S. E. **LEESER**(?), 18 mos, bowel affection; Walter D. **JOHNSON**, 4 mos, bowel affection. 8/30 – Olivia B. **BARKER**, 2, chronic diarrhea. 8/31 – Mary **MADDEN**, 40, consumption.
9/1 – Dr. G. W. **BANKS**, 30, chronic affection; Henry C. **SPIVEY**, 2, congestion of the brain; Jesse **TEGUE**, 2, worms. 9/2 – W. C. **PAYNE**, 26, de_rium tremens; Wm. **TOLES**, 77, old age. 9/5 – Wm. **DEMPSEY**, 15, inflammation of stomach. 9/6 – John **HICKEY**, 22, inflammation of the bowels; Mr. E. R. **THRALL**, 22, typhoid fever. 9/7 – Lizzie **FLOYD**, 5, inflammation of brain; Thomas **GRAHAM**, 25, congestive chill. 9/9 – Mr. Wm. **KEEFE**, 38, congestive fever. 9/10 – Jas. T. **TURNAGE**, 1, teething. 9/11 – Mr. John H. **BARTON**, 72, consumption. 9/14 – Wm. M. **FORD**, 26, typhoid fever; Son of J. **DUTLINGER**, 14 mos, purpura hemorrhage; Child of F. M. **JOLLEY**, 2 days, convulsions; Enoch **ENLOE**, 38, consumption. 9/15 – Wade **TREADWELL**, 1, congestion of brain. 9/17(?) – George **SCOTT**, 27, sunstroke. 9/18 – Ellen **MAURY**, 40, bilious fever; Joseph **BOTTO**, 3 yrs & 4 mos, brain fever; Mrs. Emma L. **HARBERER**, 24, puerpural fever. 9/19 – Michael **HARTAGAN**, 1, bowel affection. 9/20 – Mary **VACCARO**, 20 mos, chronic diarrhea; Child of F. M. **JOLLY**, 8 days, spasms. 9/22 – John **ROACH**, 22, debility; Geo. **ORR**, 7 mos, dysentery. 9/23 – Wm. **SHERIDAN**, 2 yrs 8 mos, diarrhea. 9/25 – Patrick **NEEDHAM**, 2, bowel affection; Samuel **HALSTON**, 25(?), consumption. 9/26 – Frederick **KELLERMAN**, 36, bilious fever; Infant son of Dr. S. C. **GRAY**, 2 mos, marasmus. 9/29 – Andrew F. **NEAGLE**, 1, bowel affection. 9/30 – Infant of T. **ROACHFORD**, 1 mo, spasms; Michael **FARVEY**, 30, chronic diarrhea; Mrs. Allen **WOOD**, 56, chronic diarrhea.
10/2 – Mrs. Sarah **JONES**, 29, consumption. 10/11 – Mrs. N. R. **WILLIAMS**, 36, puerperal fever. 10/13 – Son of Dr. W. **WANT**, 10 days, affection of stomach; Joseph **CRAWFORD**, 54, inflammation of stomach. 10/14 – Mrs. **FLYNN**, 40, pneumonia. 10/15 – Miss Catherine **PENDERGRAST**, 25(?), consumption; Wiley B. **FORA**(?), 42, congestive fever. 10/17 – Lucinda **RADFORD**, 40, typhoid fever. 10/18 – Mary **McDONALD**, 50, inflammation of stomach & bowels. 10/19 – Mrs. **FARMER**, 55, dysentery; Leroy S. **FITZPATRICK**, 6, bilious typhoid fever; Miss Julia **BRYANT**, 16, typhoid fever; Joanne **CANTRELL**, 22, consumption. 10/20 – Kate Louise **VIRGESON**, 11 mos, consumption; Mrs. **VANHAMBURG**, 50, convulsions. 10/21 – T. G. **KIEN**, (stranger) 32, death from wound. 10/22 – Dennis **LILLY**, __, croup. 10/23 – Dennis **KENNEDY**, 30, miasmatic fever. 10/24 – Miss C. **DORFINGER**, 23, typhoid fever; Cecila E. **MORRIS**, 14, congestive chill. 10/26 – Mrs. **RODGERS**, 45, dropsy. 10/28 – Mr. W. S.(?) **KEITH**, _6, larangitis.
11/3 – Andrew **SPAIN**(?), 23, wound in hand. 11/4 – Dennis **FILMN**, 50, death from fall. 11/6 – Phillip **LILLY**, 23, typhoid fever. 11/10 – Maj. Thos. **MULL**, 43, pistol shot; Son of Thos. **HORNE**, 9 mos, Congestion of the Lungs. 11/12 – Michael **McCARTY**, 30, exposure. 11/14 – Edward **INWOOD**, 23, death from a fall. 11/15 – W. F. **GRAY**, 35, pneumonia. 11/17 – Daughter of R. R. **PITTMAN**, 2, congestive chill. 11/22 – Wm. H. **VAUGHN**, 38, consumption; Miss Rachel **YOUNG**, 41, consumption; Daughter of W. B. **FULTON**, 2 years & 4 mos, sore throat. 11/23 – Patrick **WOODS**, 28, dropsy. 11/24 – Phillip H. **RICHARDSON**, 4 years & 1 month, _____. 11/25 – John **CARR**, 24, jaundice. 11/26 – A. P. **BLOOD**, 15, injured on railroad. 11/28 – Z_ek **VAL_SON**, 22, hemorrhage of lungs. 11/29 – Mrs. M. **MIRGERD**, 19, cerebr___. 11/30 – Son of C. **BONNER**, 5, congestion of the Brain.
12/1 – Mrs. Ellen **CRANE**, 36, consumption. 12/3 – Son of W. S. **FULTON**, 5 weeks, inflammation of the bowels; Percy **AYDLETTE**, 6, fever. 12/4 – Benjamin **TIPPETT**, 12, fever. 12/5 – Mr. Dennis **KENNA**, 40, pneumonia. 12/6 – Willie **TIPPET**, 7, fever; Catharine **CONWAY**, 6, erysipelas. 12/8 – Mr. Mark M. **TAYER**, 63, congestion of brain. 12/9 – J. L. **McDONALD**, 24, typhoid fever, stranger. 12/12 – Lawrence **McNAMARA**, 3_, cholic. 12/17 – W. L. B. **COOK**, 6 mos, cholera infantum. 12/18 – C. **MEIGHER**, death from accidental discharge of pistol. 12/25 – James H. **TIPPETT**, 14, Congestion of the Stomach. 12/26 – Lawrence **GARVEY**, 45, pneumonia.

MORTALITY OF THE CITY FOR WEEK ENDING:

1/2/1858 – Wm. S. **STOUT**, 23, consumption; J. **FLINN**, 32, pneumonia; B. **RYAN**, 1, congestion of stomach; Miss Ann **SMITH**, 42, hepatitis; J. C. **WILROY**, 45, epilepsy; daughter of L. **HERMAN**, 2 weeks, marasmus. 1/28/1858 – Walter **RICHMOND**, Abscess; Ishana **MARONEY**, Croup; John **DUNN**, Bilious Fever; F. M. **EPSEY**, Consumption; Mrs. M. M. **STRATTON**, Inflammation of stomach and bowels; Daughter of R. **BRYSON**, Croup.

LIST OF INTERMENTS FOR 1858:

1/25 – Elizabeth **FARRELL**, 4 mos, congestion of stomach; Mrs. Helen **CICILLA**, 18, inflammation of stomach. 1/26 – Dr. Benj. **WALKER**, 44, typhoid fever. 1/27 – John R. **BOOKER**, 30, bilious pneumonia; George **HELMS**, 24. 1/29 – Mrs. Johana **DUGGAN**, 50, pneumonia; John **GLIDEWELL**, 30, consumption; Mrs. Catharine **BREWER**, 2_, puerperal fever. 1/30 – John **McCARTHY**, 1 day. 1/31 – Edward E. **HOLST**, infant, pneumonia.
2/9 – Child of J. G. **YANCEY**, 10, consumption. 2/10 – Daniel **CONNER**, 35, pneumonia; Jas. **CONNELLY**, 1, effects of cold. 2/11 – Jas. **CLARK**, 36, intemperance; Avis C. **HAWKS**, 2, scarlet fever. 2/12 – Daniel **FOLEY**, 2 yrs 7 mos, effects of burn; David **ADAMS**, 38, consumption. 2/14 – W. S. **JONES**, 49, injury from fall. 2/18 – Charles **NORMENT**, 7, inflammation of brain. 2/19 – John **DESMOND**, 38, Erysipilas. 2/23 – Son of H. B. **HOWELL**, 12 days, convulsions. 2/25 – M. **REED**, 35, consumption. 2/26 – Jacob **HARMON**, 24(?), consumption; Mr. **SWATTS**, 60, dropsy. 2/27 – Matthew **CONNER**, 6, scarlet fever.
3/16 – Austin **FARRIS**, 28, pneumonia. 3/20 – Martin **LEARY**, 30, congestive chill. 3/30 – Robert **HOLT**, 10, pneumonia.
4/1 – A. E. **HUNTSMAN**, 22, inflammation of the stomach and bowels. 4/3 – Mrs. C. B.(?) **CHURCH**, 40, inflammation of stomach. 4/5 – Mrs. M. **HAWKINS**, 3_, dropsy. 4/7 – James **STEWART**, 62, congestive chill. 4/8 – S. B. **WILLIAMS**, 35, death from wound. 4/9 – Wm. M. **MOODY**, 26, erys_ph_ _. 4/10 – A. M. **YOUNG**, 3_, affection of throat. 4/18 – Mrs. Margaret **FORD**, 33, pneumonia. 4/19 – Wm. **FARRELL**, 22, drowned; Wm. **LANDEY**, 19, drowned. 4/20 – Mrs. **MORIARTY**, 19, puerperal; Wm. **BRAYDEN**, 24, typhoid fever. No Date – Daughter of W. A. **WILLIAMS**, 8, Typhoid pneumonia.
5/17 – Jno. **CUSACK**, 25, Hemorrhage of Lungs. 5/18 – Joanna **LANDE_GIN**, 38, Pneumonia. 5/23 – Powhattan **LOWNES**, 8 mos, Whooping Cough. 5/24 – Daniel **GRIFFIN**, 10, Congestive Chill. 5/25 – James **MARTIN**, 26, Consumption. 5/28 – Child of W. V. L. **COOPER**, 19 mos, Diarrhea. 5/29 – Michael **RYAN**, 30, Plurisy; Wm. **O'NEILL**, 23, Consumption. 5/30 – John **RYAN**, 7, Croup; Child of W. **MILLER**, 3 mos, Marasmus.
6/? – Wm. **SADDLER**, 5, drowned. 6/1 – Child of Ann **APPLETON**, 5, Croup; Mrs. **DUDLEY**, 44, Dropsy. 6/3 – Ann M. **McGRATH**, 5 mos, Inflammation of the Bowels. 6/4 – Son of A. O. **LYDE**, 22 mos, Spinal Disease. 6/5 – Thomas B. **DAY**, 17, Pleurisy. 6/7 – Daughter of Mr. **SCHNEL**, six mos, Cholera Infantum. 6/9 – Son of Ernest **VISS**, 8 mos, Marasmus. 6/10 – Alber. **SAMPSON**, 5 mos, Brain Fever. 6/11 – Child of R. **ARMSTRONG**, 4, Putrid Sore Throat. 6/14 – Lucas **BREMISH**, 34, Dropsy. 6/15 – Sophronia **BUTLER**, 53, Disease of the Heart. 6/16 – Mrs. E. **ROBINSON**, 25, Chronic Diarrhea. 6/17 – Son of W. **ROBINSON**, 3, Tabes Misentenis(?); J. H. **CAMPBELL**, 35, death of wounds on Pennsylvania. 6/18 – Geo. **MORRISON**, 3, Diarrhea; Son of Chas. **NESTLE**, 4 mos, Chronic Diarrhea. 6/20 – H. **CLEMENTS**, 23, Death from explosion of the Pennsylvania. 6/21 – Thos. **McGEHEE**, 30, Death from the explosion of the Pennsylvania; Child of T. W. **BARNES**, 3 mos, Chronic Diarrhea; Frank R. **JONES**, 26, Death from steamboat explosion; Margaret **TRACEY**, 18, drowned. 6/24(?) – Jos. **HOWARD**, 41, Chronic Diarrhea; Child of W. **HARRIS**, 2, Pneumonia; Thos. A. **ROGERS**, 23, Consumption. 6/25 – Martin **McGRATH**, 22, Consumption. 6/26 – L. **BARDINELLA**, 43, Affection of Bowels. 6/27 – Indian, **CHOKOOLOETA**, 80, Old age; Ulick **BURK**, 60, Effects of Cold. 6/28(?) – Mrs. **ISBELL**, 35, Consumption; James **HOPPER**, 22, not reported; Infant of S. W. **VERNON**, 3 days, Spasms; Margaret **SWAN**, 1, Convulsions; John **LEDGE**, 28, death from explosion of Pennsylvania. 6/29 – H. M. **EMORY**, 4 mos, Diarrhea; Patrick **FLANEGAN**, 45, Congestive Chill. 6/30 – James **LOVE**, 30, Inflammation of Stomach.
7/2 – Wm. F. **COULTER**, 9 mos, Teething; James O. **TOMES**, 4, Disease of the Bowels; Patrick **TARPEY**, 42, Pistol Shot. 7/3 – Son of C. **BONNER**, 5 mos, Chronic Diarrhea. 7/4 – Geo. B. **GREGORY**, 1, Cholera Infantum. 7/5 – Child of T. E. **CLARK**, 1 mo, Teething; Child of H. **NEFF**, 2,

Bowel Affection; E. T. **CALLAN**, 23, Congestive Fever; Wm. D. **HOWARD**, 30, Scalds on steamer Pennsylvania. 7/7 – Bridget **GLENN**, 28, Apoplexy. 7/10 – Henry H. **REDFORD**, 24, Typhoid Fever; John **LARKIN**, 24, Intermittent Fever; Margaret **CONWAY**, 4_, Consumption. 7/11 – Child of J. J. **ROBINSON**, 4 mos, Pneumonia. 7/12 – Melvin **FIELDS**, 12, Bilious Fever. 7/13 – Henry **LAKE**, 1, Congestion of the Brain; Mr. **MOONEY**, 42, Pneumonia; John **WELSH**, 40, Insanity; Mrs. A. **CLIFTON**, 53, Erysipelas. 7/15 – Robt. **WILMAN**, 3 mos, Spasms. 7/16 – David **JONES**, 48, Bilious Fever. 7/19 – Wm. **O'MERA**, 60, Inflammation of the Bowels; Timothy **LEARY**, 27, Sun Stroke; Child of J. B. **PARK**, 5, Congestion Brain. 7/21 – Daniel B. **JOINER**, 2, Croup. 7/22 – Joanna **NUNAN**, 70, Intermittent Fever. 7/24 – Francis P. **DALE**, 22 mos, Inflammation of Bowels; Daughter of P. **PHELON**, 7 mos, Brain Fever; Edmund **BUCKLEY**, 24, Convulsions. 7/25 – Dennis **COLLINS**, 6 mos, Whooping Cough; Mrs. A. A. **SMITHWICK**, 27, Puerperal Fever. 7/26 – Infant of D. **MORIARTY**, 3 mos, Cholera Infantum; Isham **BRIDGE**, 50, disease of the liver; Andrew **HESSION**, 40, death from accidental injuries; Mrs. Lucy L. **POWERS**, 19, Puerperal fever; David **PHELON**, 7 mos, Whooping cough; Infant of W. **LEATH**, age half day. 7/27 – Child of Mrs. **FINN**, 4, Bilious fever. 7/28 – Mrs. **KIRK**, 27, Consumption. 7/31 – Child of A. **NUTALL**, 5 mos, Inflammation of bowels; Ann **FITZGIBBENS**, 25, pneumonia.

8/2 – Patrick **FOGERTY**, 30, bilious fever. 8/3 – Mrs. **DUNIGAN**, 24, consumption; James **PERRY**, 21, congestive fever. 8/4 – Mary **CONNELLY**, 50, bilious fever; Eliza R. **BURKE**, 11 mos, teething; Child of Mrs. **McSEE**, 11(?) mos, teething. 8/5 – Mary R. **IRVIN**, 19 mos, chronic diarrhea; John **BREDIS**(?), 9, congestive fever; Alex. **BOWEN**, 30, consumption. 8/6 – Infant of J. **EDGERLY**, 8 days, convulsions; Richard **KEHO_S**, 25, bilious fever; James **DAVERN**, 35, sun stroke; James **FITZGERALD**, 39, drowned. 8/7 – Henry **NEUMAN**, 6 weeks, Bilious Fever. 8/9 – Theo W. **CURTIS**, 21, hemorrhage of lungs; Infant of R. C. **COBB**, 8 days, Spasms. 8/10 – Child of R. **NICHOLSON**, 3 mos, Marasmus; Mrs. W. **JAMES**, 42, Congestive Chill; R. B. **MILLER**, 5 mos, Fever. 8/11 – Hugh **ELLIS**, 30, death from accident on railroad. 8/13 – Henry C. **CORDONA**, 5, Brain Fever; Jacob **McGLACHLEN**(?), 34, Inflammation of Bowels; B. Ann **KENNY**, 17 mos, Chronic Diarrhea. 8/14 – John **MITCHELL**, 34, Consumption; Daughter of Dr. A. W. **WRIGHT**, 18 mos, Inflammation of the Stomach; Dennis **LYNCH**, 25, Effects of Heat. 8/16 – Kat **OWEN**, 6, Bilious Fever; Dennis **SULLIVAN**, 30, Inflammation of the bowels. 8/17 – Mrs. **THOMAS**, 45, Congestive Chill. 8/18 – Mary **McCORMICK**, 40, Pneumonia; Jas. **POWERS**, 40, Dropsy; Lieutenant **RADZIMISKY**, U.S. Navy, 45, Consumption. 8/20 – Michael **BORDEN**, 2, Congestive chill; Laura **PAILLARD**, 15 mos, Congestive Chill; John H. **SMIDT**, 26, bilious fever; Mrs. Mary E. **BUCHANAN**, 32, not reported; Henry **BUCHEL**, 69(?), dropsy. 8/21 – Harrison **INGALLS**, 52, Intermittent Fever. 8/23 – Patrick **MALONE**, 25, death from fall. 8/24 – Mary **BELL**, 30, Hemorrhage; Child of Dr. **ROWLAND**, 1 day, spasms; John **SHIELDS**, 35, Congestive Fever. 8/25 – Margaret **MANN**, 2_, Bilious Fever; Thos. **LANNIN**, 45, Bilious fever; John **LOM__AIRE**, 61, Typhoid Fever. 8/26 - _. **McNAMARA**, _6, Apoplexy; W. H. **BALDWIN**, 6 weeks, Marasmus. 8/27 – E. D. **HOFFMAN**, 10, Congestion of the Brain. 8/28 – Patrick **COURREY**, 30, Convulsions. 8/29 – Wm. **McCLURE**, 85, old age; Francis **SLOAN**, 2, spasms; G. W. **POWERS**, 32, congestive chill. 8/30 – T. C. **NEWSOM**, 3, inflammation of bowels. 8/31 – Samuel **RAGAN**, 7, congestion of brain; Wm. **WOODS**, 30, disease not known.

9/1 – Thomas **MAHONEY**, 18, inflammation of bowels; Anthony **STROP**, 25, death from wounds. 9/3 – Frederick **STRABLER**, 34, congestion of brain; Howard **MALLORY**, 28, consumption. 9/4 – P. Y. **LUND**, 22, consumption. 9/5 – Geo. **FLAHERTY**, 46, consumption. 9/7 – Child of Matthias **HANSON**, 3, dropsy. 9/10 – Mr. **KEATING**, 37, bilious fever. 9/11 – John **THOMAS**, aged – years, death from wounds. 9/12 – Michael **GANNIN**, 30, diarrhea. 9/13 – John **MADDOX**, 40, consumption. 9/17 – Mrs. A. **HORNE**, 45, dysentery; Joseph **COOPER**, 33, pneumonia. 9/19 – Peter **QUINN**, 35, congestion of the brain; Francis **GLANCY**, 38, delerium tremons. 9/20 – Florence **GROVE**, 1, intermittent fever; Patrick **MALONE**, 48, consumption; Mr. **OTIS**, 26, congestion of the brain; Hugh **ARCHIBALD**, 25, death from exposure. 9/21 – Jas. **ARNOLD**, 26, congestive chill. 9/22 – Miles **PAYNE**, 3 weeks, spasms; John **McELEER**(?), 36, mania par_.

10/3 – Andrew **WILSON**, 20 mos, Teething; Margaret E. **PHILLIPS**, 24, Consumption. 10/4 – John **STOKES**, 55, Congestive Chill; George **NEEF**, 25, Congestive Chill; Henry **SNICK**, 28, Congestive Chill. 10/5 – Joanna **LONDERGIN**, 19 mos, disease not reported; Antonia **MASSA**(?), 31, disease not known. 10/6 – Morris **KAIN**, 4_, Bilious Fever; Charles **McCARTY**, 75, Old age. 10/10 – Owen **CORBIN**, 35, Bilious Fever; Michael **MAHON**, 25, not reported. 10/12 – Thomas **HIGGINS**, 40, Congestive Chill; Patrick **FOGERTY**, 43, Death from exposure; M. **SHALLER**, 45, Sudden Death, disease unknown. 10/13 – Christopher **HAYS**, 17, Congestive Chill. 10/15 – Michael **DUNN**, 25,

Congestive Chill; Thomas **CHESTER**, 23, Bilious Fever; Martha J. **BALL**, 30, Dysentery; John
COLEMAN, 25, Congestive Chill; Chas. **SPIDE**, 22, Bilious Fever. 10/16 – Mrs. **HORN**, 36(?),
Dysentery. 10/17 – Mrs. Martha A. **HILLIARD**, 49, jaundice. 10/18 – Child of J. **HARMAN**, 6, dropsy;
Bias **PITTMAN**, 12, death from accident on railroad; Child of Michael **DAY**, 6 weeks, spasms. 10/19 –
Mrs. Felicity **DENIE**, age & disease not reported; Carl **HOFFMAN**, 23, bilious fever. 10/20 – A. I.
DOYLE, 27, hemhorage of lungs; Mrs. A. **COPELLO**, 30, acute enteritis; Child of Harris **BELL**, 2,
congestive chill; James **NICHOLS**, 23, cramp colic. 10/21 – Mary **COTHLIN**, 44, intermittent fever;
Mrs. Catharine **O'DONNELL**, 28, consumption; Wm. G. **MILLER**, 7 mos, dysentery; Child of S.
REECE, 1 mo, spasms. 10/22 – Peter **DUMPY**, 40, consumption. 10/23 – James **DORSEY**, 60, effects
of old age; Isaac **HOLMES**, 28, death from fall. 10/24 – A. **HENDERSON**, 56, dropsy of chest; A. S.
DANCY, 49, debility. 10/25 – J. **BRIZZOLARI**(?), 26, consumption; G. H. **COWAN**, 25, typhoid fever.
10/28 – Mrs. E. S. **JONES**, 31, abscess; V. **BORO**, _7, gangrene of lungs; Charles **GARGIN**, _5,
intemperance. 10/30 – Thos. **HAYS**, 33, congestive chill.
11/7 – C. M. **HORTON**, 31, dysentery and pneumonia. 11/8 – Peter **CONLY**, 20, disease unknown.
11/10 – W. **YANCEY**, 40, intemperance. 11/11 – Mrs. **TRAVIS**, 22, pneumonia. 11/13 – Eben
HALLENBACK, 43, pneumonia; Robert **SHELAN**, 21, dropsy; John **GRIFFIN**, 31, dysentery; Geo.
FRITZ, 53, bronchial congestion. 11/14 – Daughter of Chas. **WINTERS**, 5, Marasmus. 11/15 – Michael
HARLY, 30, fractured limb; Kate **McDONALD**, 18, Typhoid Fever; Emma C. **HORNE**, 7, Typhoid
Fever; Michael **DUNN**, 39, Consumption. 11/16 – Mrs. T. **KEINACH**, 56, Typhoid Fever; M. H.
TROTT, 65, death from a fall. 11/17 – M. W. **ASHLEY**, 35, Typhoid Pneumonia; S. R. **GARNER**, 33,
Pneumonia. 11/19 – Michael **MALONEY**, 55, disease not known. 11/20 – T. O. **CRENSHAW**, 45, death
from a fall; Nannie **COLEMAN**, 3, Croup; Bryan **CONNER**, 25, Pneumonia; F. B. **HOLLOWAY**, 7 mos,
inflammation of brain. 11/21 – Thomas **CONNELL**, 22, congestive chills. 11/22 – John **CONNER**, 25,
typhoid fever. 11/23 – Cath. **BUTLER**, 55, not reported. 11/24 – Thos. **FITZGERALD**, __, pneumonia.
11/26 – Wm. **McMAHON**, 50(?), consumption; David **McGAUGH**, 23(?), consumption. 11/27 – Hugh
MANNING, 30, pneumonia; James A. **DUNTO**(?), 34, typhoid fever. 11/28 – Julius **RANER**, 5,
pneumonia; Mrs. Martha **TUFTS**, 40, chronic disease.
12/1 – Miss A. C. L. **ARMOUR**, 20, dysentery. 12/3 – Wm. **FOY**, 50, consumption. 12/4 – C. F.
PITTMAN, 30, consumption; Mrs. **BANBER**, 27, puerperal fever; Thos. **WAGENER**, 21, congestive
chill; B. **D_TLINGER**, 64, old age and debility. 12/7 – W. **DAVID**, 31, pneumonia. 12/10 – Ellen
LONY, 22, inflammation of lungs; Sarah J. **SWAN**, 30, consumption. 12/12 – Daughter of J. **BEER**(?),
10, scarlet fever. 12/13 – Ann M. **DUNCAN**, 18 mos, convulsions; James **CARR**, 6 mos, diarrhea; Mary
B. **GIVENS**, 4 mos, spasms. 12/14 – David **MURRAY**, 23(?), congestive chill; Andy **HUSSY**, 38,
pneumonia. 12/16 – John **ELY**, 32, disease not known. 12/17 – Son of M. **GRAFF**, 5, disease of the
brain; John **CULLY**, 35, complication of disease.

LIST OF INTERMENTS FOR 1859:

1/8 – Mrs. E. A. **RICHARDSON**, 56, disease not reported. 1/10 – Thos. **BAKER**, 4, scarlet fever. 1/12 –
Margaret E. **BOLGER**, 8, pneumonia; A. J. **HENRY**, 50, pneumonia; Mrs. **MANDRITZ**, 30, pneumonia.
1/14 – John W. **NORMENT**, 3, pneumonia; Alexander **PUCKET**, 52, erysipelas. 1/18 – Conrad
HALTENBACH, 51, Intemperance. 1/20 – W. J. **STEWART**, 26, death from wound. 1/21 – Angeline C.
BACKUS, 22 mos., congestive fever. 1/22 – M. O. **DONNELL**, 27, typhoid fever. 1/30 – Chas. **BANER**,
26, consumption.
2/1 – Ada **BENSON**, 6(?), scarlet fever; Frank **BENSON**, 4, scarlet fever; Michael **MANNING**, 15
months, scarlet fever. 2/2 – Israel **HAINE**, 43, tetanus; Mrs. A. **STILES**, 28, pneumonia; B. F. **ELMER**,
age ---, congestion of Liver. 2/3 – Robert **COMPERRY**, 50, intemperance. 2/7 – Joseph **HUNTER**, 13,
erysipelas. 2/8 – Mrs. D. W. **SHANKS**, 25, puerperal fever. 2/10 – Child of D. W. **SHANKS**, 2,
pneumonia. 2/11 – Henry **TEST**, 53, inflammation of brain. 2/14 – Mrs. **HARRIS**, 60, consumption;
Child of F. **MELLISH**, 11 months, scarlet fever; H. **McGEE**, stranger, 35, disease not known. 2/15 – J.
QUAMBY, 26, pneumonia; John **MACK**, 41, pneumonia; Isaac **ZIMILEY**, 34, disease not known. 2/17
– Soloman **McMAHON**, 33, typhoid fever. 2/19 – Dr. Jas. S. **PEACOCKE**, 38, acute bronchitis. 2/21 –
Mary L. **MATTHEWS**, 4 months, pneumonia. 2/22 – Eliza J. **SHIPWAY**, 8 months, teething; Bernard
DUNN, 16 months, croup. 2/23 – L. D. **HENDRIX**, 37, pneumonia; Child of John **HALAND**, 2 months,
convulsions; G. W. **SKELTON** (stranger), 38, congestive fever. 2/28 – Emanuel **MONROE**, 51,
inflammation of brain.

3/2 – John **HOWARD**, 5 weeks, croup; Judge H. **HAWLEY**, 77, old age. 3 / 4 – John **GERMAN**, 10 months, spasms. 3/6 – Jacob **BACKTOLD**, 45, rheumatism. 3/7 – John **BOHLEN**, 51, consumption. 3/9 – Matthew **JACOB**, 55, erysipelas; Jerry **WAHEN**, 26, erysipelas; O. P. **NEWBY**, 43, consumption; Mrs. Mary **BLACK**, 67, pneumonia. 3/11 – Ernst **LAUGHRIN**, 17, congestion of brain. 3/12 – Mahala **LANE**, 38, consumption; Infant daughter of J. H. **HAIGHTON**, spasms; John M. **JENNY**, 25, consumption. 3/14 – Timothy **CONNER**, 40, pneumonia. 3/15 – F. W. **NEVIL**, 20 months, diarrhea; Dennis **FOCKEN**, convulsion. 3/16 – Mrs. B. **BRANNIN**, 30, typhoid fever; John **DUGAN**, 3, pneumonia; Benj. **REID**, 54, inflammation of stomach and bowels. 3/20 – John **DESMOND**, 28, pneumonia. 3/22 – Sarah S_**ERK**, 33, pneumonia; John Z. **BECKTOLD**, 3, convulsions. 3/24 – James **BARRY**, 30, pneumonia; Infant of J. W. **ARMSTRONG**, 10 days, spasms. 3/25 – Patrick **FITZGIBBONS**, 56, bowel affections. 3/26 – John **RILEY**, 20, congestive chill. 3/28 – John **McNAMARA**, 32, gangrene of bowels; John **JACOBS**, 25, consumption; John **GLESON**, 40, congestion of lungs; Barney **SPALDING**, 35, consumption. 3/29 – Jasper **FRANSIOLI**, 28, effect of wounds. 3/30 – Eliz **ANDERSON**, 4 months, croup; Michael **SHAY**, 35, inflammation of lungs.

4/1 – George T. **HUNTSMAN**, 26, congestive fever; Andrew **LAHIFF**, 26, death from wound. 4/4 – Mr. **FRANK**, 35, mortification. 4/5 – David **COOK**, 5, congestive chill. 4/6 – Robert H. **DEARING**, 26, inflammation of Stomach; S. R.(?) **DAVIDSON**, 28, typhoid fever; Albert **BROWN**, 34, congestive chill. 4/7 – Robert **GIBBONS**, 6 months, inflammation of lungs. 4/8 – Daughter of Mrs. **FILSON**, 3 months, disease not known. 4/16 – D. **BENDEL_UBER**, 18, rheumatism. 4/18 – John **GANNON**, 28, death from fall; Mrs. Eugenie **SAWTELLE**, 23, consumption. 4/19 – Emma **KRAFT**, (col.) 35, inflammation of the bowels; Patrick **SHEA**, 8 months, marasmus. 4/20 – John **ROBARDS**, 75, typhoid pneumonia. 4/22 – Wm. **LEACH**, 4, pneumonia. 4/23 – Thomas **LOFTON**, 23, jaundice; Miss **GURLEY**, 14, inflammation of the bowels. 4/24 – Mr. C. **GREEN**, 50, rheumatism. 4/27 – Alice **TEAGUE**, 4 weeks, spasms. 4/28 – Kate **KELLY**, 1, not reported; H. **BECKEL**, 45, pneumonia. 4/29 – Michael **SHAY**, 19 months, pneumonia; Jno **LAUGHIN_**, 17, death from burn; Jas. **ELLIS**, 10, unknown. 4/30 – Mr. E. D. **ORWAN**, 28, consumption.

5/8 – Maggie **ROBINSON**, 13 months, affection of the brain; A. H. **AVERY**, 36, consumption; Wm. **MAHARA**, 37, brain fever. 5/9 – Robert **WILKINSON**, 1, cholera infantum; B. B. **STUART**, 23, death from burn on the *St. Nicholas*. 5/10 – Louise **RAJOUX**, 11 months, inflammation of brain; E. **MYERS**, 29, consumption. 5/13 – Thomas **MURPHY**, 28, consumption. 5/15 – Child of W. W. **GRANT**, 1 week, spasms; Mrs. Theresa **SIGNAIGO**, 16, puerperal fever. 5/16 – W. R. **JAMES**, 43, accidental drowning. 5/17 – Robert **BOYD**, (colored) 29, from wounds. 5/21 – Jas. **FINNEY**, 3, dropsy. 5/27 – Frederick **MYERS**, 11 months, croup. 5/28 – Markin **HAWK**, 36, inflammation of stomach; R. **VIRGESON**, 32, inflammation of brain. 5/31 – John **SWEANEY**, 35, billious cholic; Thomas **COPPERWAIT**, 39, disease not reported; John **WINTERS**, 2 months, disease not reported.

6/1 – Crisp **RILEY**, 32, inflammation of stomach and bowels. 6/2 – Chas. **HARPER**, 34, chronic rheumatism. 6/3 – Rosalin **AMORETTE**, 6 weeks, cholera infantum. 6/4 – Elizabeth **COPELAND**, 24, dysentery. 6/26 – Wm. **HIGGENBOTTOM**, 1, teething; Geo. R. **FROST**, 24, congestive chill; Son of Geo. **GARIRS**, 12 months, teething. 6/27 – Charles **PNACH**, 16 months, teething; Child of R. H. **NORRIS**, 7 months, cholera infantum. 6/28 – Mary **O'HERREN**, 1 month, spasms; Fred. **WIND**, 8 months, teething. 6/29 – Infant of P. **FLAHERTY**, 1 week, spasms. 6/30 – Daniel **SULLIVAN**, 35, sun stroke; Lewis **BRUEL**, 25, brain fever.

7/1 – Infant of F. H. **WILLIAMSON**, 3 days, spasms; James **McDONALD**, billious fever; Mr. **COLLINS**, 16, fever and ague. 7/2 – L. M. **VINCENT**, 5 days, hives; Jos. **WHITE**, 2 ½, effects of nitric acid; Joseph **HOUSER**, 14 months, chills and fever. 7/3 – Margaret **CLIFFORD**, 2, bowel complaint; Frederick **MANSTRAUSEN**, 42, sun-stroke. 7/4 – Mary A. **KAGAN**, 1, teething; E. R. **GAILOR**, 17, typhoid fever. 7/5 – Jacob **ZWEIFUL**, 29, accidental discharge of cannon. 7/7 – Mary **DONAHO**, 11 months, teething; Child of Robert **MILLER**, 4 ½, effects of morphine. 7/8 – Zulieka **DICKSON**, 9 months, disease not reported; Michael **CONNELLY**, 30, billious fever; Mariantha **MONTAGUE**, 9 months, cholera infantum. 7/9 – A. **McELHERAN**, 26, typhoid fever. 7/11 – John **DOUGHERTY**, 45, exposure. 7/13 – John **BURKE**, 26, intermittent fever; Elizabeth **CANNAUGHT**, 3, billious fever; Child of Mr. **OILMAN**, 3 months, intermittent fever; Child of E. **HUMPHREYS**, 2, cholera infantum. 7/14 – Wm. **POST**, 32, typhoid fever; M. **HARAGAN**, 35, injuries from fall; Thos. **LUBY**, 45, bilious fever; Child of J. L. **HUDSON**, 1, teething. 7/15 – John J. **SHAW**, 12, injuries from fall; Margaret **CUMMING**, 15 months, teething; Daughter of J. **GEUGEL**, 2, inflammation of brain; Child of J. I. **POLLARD**, 18 months, affection of bowels; Child of M. A. **HOUSTON**, 17 months, affection of Bowels. 7/17 – Louis

LALEMAND, 15 months, teething; Henry **BENNET**, 25 years 6 months, sunstroke; Daughter of A. **GRIESHABER**, 7 months, not reported. 7/18 – Margaret **METARE**, 29, consumption; Frank **MORGAN**, 33, sun stroke; Daughter of M. D. **VANCE**, 5, typhoid fever; John **DENCY**, 30, sun stroke; F. C. **NEWSOM**, 50, sun stroke; Wm. **McCABE**, 40, sun stroke; Daughter of Mrs. **HARKINS**, 2, cholera infantum. 7/19 – David **McLORLY**, 18, sun stroke; Wm. **MANNING**, 12 months, teething; John **STAUNTON**, 2, intermittent fever; Mrs. M. **GORMLEY**, ---, not reported; Mrs. **FOX**, 20, disease not known; Frederick **BREES**, 28, sun stroke; Daughter of L. **DUTLINGER**, 10 months, diarrhea. 7/20 – Catherine **BURKE**, 50, diarrhea; John **KEY**, 23, not reported; Mary **CONNELLY**, 2 months, teething; Ann **CAVIL**, 27, sun stroke; Pat **FANECA**, 30, sun stroke; M. **O'CONNER**, 35, sun stroke; Mrs. L. **WEADLEY**, 30, sunstroke. 7/21 – Mary **DWIRE**, 55, sun stroke; M. H. **McGARRY**, 20 months, teething; Mrs. B. **JONES**, 45, sun stroke; Mary **COSGROVE**, 14 months, teething; John **MALER**, 20, typhus fever; Miss M. **PARSONS**, 16 months, chronic diarrhea; Jos. **BRITISEH**, 45, consumption; Daughter of Thomas **CALLEN**, 3, spasms; John **MAHONEY**, 38, sunstroke; Son of J. W. **LU_HWIG**, 2, typhus fever; Jas. J. **MORGAN**, 27, consumption. 7/22 – Mrs. **O'BRIEN**, 26, not reported; Robt. **WILSON**, 32, sun stroke. 7/23 – Mr. **WILLIAMS**, 55, not reported; Child of Mr. **FLINT**, 9 months, not reported; Thomas **KEAN**, 1 week, convulsions. 7/24 – Jacob **SHALL**, 75, old age. 7/25 – A. M. **FRECK**, 51, chronic diarrhea; Charlotte M. **FLETCHER**, 1, whooping cough. 7/26 – Henry D. **LOGWOOD**, 2 months, convulsions. 7/27 – Child of L. G. **FARMER**, 19 months, cholera infantum. 7/28 – Wm. **KEEFES**, 20 months, diarrhea. 7/30 – Daughter of P. **WINTER**, 16 months, teething.
8/21 – Mrs. **LAUGHLIN**, 25, erysipelas; Kate **COTTER**, 4, bilious fever; Infant son of J. **RINGWALD**; Mrs. T. A. **STEPHENS**, 26, enteritis. 8/22 – Mary O. **LAUGHLIN**, 2, diarrhea; Mrs. H. **RYAN**, 27, consumption; Jane **ROBERTS**, 60, congestive chill. 8/24 – H. R. **WARD**, 23, inflammation of bowels; John **RYAN**, 28, pneumonia; Mrs. L. **CROSBY**, 24, general debility. 8/26 – Thomas **HANNAGAN**, 45, pneumonia. 8/27 – John **MALONE**, 27, fall. 8/28 – Martin **DONNELLY**, 44, diarrhea. 8/29 – Patrick **LUDIN**, 19, bilious fever; Dennis **McMAHON**, 55, diarrhea. 8/31 – Patrick **DORNEY**, 30, pneumonia. 9/1 – Wm. **WHITE**, 19, congestion of brain; Mrs. Sarah G. **PATTISON**, 48, dyspepsy. 9/2 – C. B. **ABBOTT**, 36, convulsions; Child of Jos. C. **WILSON**, 18 months, teething. 9/4 – Geo. Otto **REICHENBACKER**, 20 months, diarrhea. 9/5 – John **TAYLOR**, 22, consumption. 9/6 – Mrs. Augusta B. **PRICE**, 22, gastroenteritis; Bernard **HARMAN**, 24, dysentery. 9/7 – Jno. **CURRIN**, 23, consumption. 9/8 – Robert **JOHNSON**, 25; Mrs. John **DAVIS**, 48, typhoid fever; Chas. **CURTAIN**, drowned. 9/11 – Michael **GRADY**, 45, decline; Wm. **AXTEL**, 33, congestion of lungs; Mary A. **FLYN**, 14, typhoid fever. 9/12 – Michael **DOLAN**, 40, diarrhea; Wm. **SHERRIDAN**, ---, mania-a-po_n; Martin **GLANCY**, 28, ____ maligna; Jas. **WHALEN**, ---, disease of brain; M. **DONE**, 30, not reported. 9/13 – Sarah **RYAN**, 50, consumption. 9/14 – Michael **HOFFMAN**, 37, congestive fever. 9/15 – Fannie S. **POWERS**, 2, inflammation of brain; Frederick **ECKERT**, 2, diarrhea; Child of John **MURPHY**, 3, disease of brain. 9/16 – Daughter of Robert **LEARY**, 1, not reported. 9/17 – Child of H. G. **FOX**, 2, ____ tonsillaris; Jas. **PEEL**, 25, congestive chill; Michael **COLEMAN**, 26, dysentery. 9/18 – Son of Dennis **O'BRYAN**, 2 months, debility; G. **PITMAN**, 30, consumption. 9/19 – Julius **RYNOR**, 35, consumption; Son of F. **ECKERT**, 7 months, debility. 9/22 – Mrs. Jas. **HAMILTON**, 23, gastro-enteristis; Wm. **FORSITH**, 26, injuries from fall. 9/23 – John K. **FARMER**, 30, injuries from fall. 9/24 – Mrs. C. **MAHLER**, 52, puerperal peritonistis. 9/25 – W. B. **GREEN**,---, typhoid fever; Eliza **JUKES**, 50, typhoid fever; Daughter of T. **CACEY**, 2, congestive fever. 9/26 – Mrs. R. L. **CRANE**, ---, consumption; E. C. **ZUGLER**, 5, pneumonia. 9/27 – Fannie M. **REDFORD**, 5, inflammation of brain; Mrs. S. J. **COOK**, 24, dropsy; Edward **CHURCH**, 3, convulsions; child of Mr. H. **HORNE**, 1, disease of the throat. 9/29 – Mat L. **BALL**, 3, appoplexy; Denis **McMARRAH**, 26, typhoid fever; J. **KEUTER**, 50; John **WOMKE**, 26, typhoid fever; Mrs. Susan **FLOYD**, 38, consumption. 9/30 – Marcellus A. **FOUTE**, 3, cynance maligna. 10/1 – Mrs. Mary S. **LOGWOOD**, 23, consumption; James **KELLY**, 42, chronic diarrhea. 10/2 – Edward **HENDRICK**, 6 months, hydrocephalus; Ellen **MURPHY**, 1, gastritis; Julia G. **SMITHER**, 19, consumption; Martin **MARRINER**, 25, dropsy. 10/3 – Thomas **NESBITT**, 33(?), dysentery. 10/7 – Mrs. Florida **WOOLFOLK**, 25; Bridget **FLANNERY**, 15 months, teething; Sarah **DOROSSET**, 3, not reported; Sarah J. **McCARTY**, 15 months, teething. 10/8 – Joseph **BOTTO**, 56, dropsy; B. B. **VERNON**, 9, bronchitis; Julia B. **FORSYTH**, 19 months. 10/10 – M. **BARTH**, 33, bronchitis; Wm. **DOUGHER**, 3, effects of fall. 10/12 – Jno. **CROPLEY**, 3, debility. 10/13 – Hazelhurst **FOUTE**; Thos. J. **PARDUE**, 40, consumption; Patrick **KELLEY**, 28, typhoid fever; Miss M. G. **PATTERSON**, 13, congestive fever. 10/14 – Mrs. R. **RIESER**, 39, consumption; Mrs. E. **RIELY**, 35, consumption; Wm. **COCKLIN**, 40. 10/15 – John **SIPLES**, 27, swamp fever; Alexander W. **CLINE**, 34, suicide by strychnine. 10/16 – Lewis

MALLICK, 40, dropsy. 10/18 – Mrs. Margaret O'HARA, 55, debility. 10/19 – Patrick KELLY, 27, unknown; Mrs. Margaret SAMUELS, 60, paralysis; Mrs. Ann _. ORGAN, 50, not reported; Mrs. Mary J. WRIGHT, 21, congestive fever. 10/20 – F. B. WILLIAMS, suicide by pistol shot. 10/22 – Henry LONG, 40, not reported. 10/24 – Daughter of H. HINKLEMAN, 15 months, teething; Benhart WIMMER, 69, old age; John GREENLACH, 40, typhoid fever; Anna CHURCH, 11 months, not reported; W. KING, 45, not reported; Jno. MONAHAN, 23, intermittent fever. 10/25 – Mary EVANS, 4, congestive fever; --- BRUMLY, 44, consumption; T. T. ARMSTRONG, 41, fever. 10/26 – Ellin HARRINGTON, 29, dysentery. 10/27 – Geo. W. HAYNES, 14, consumption; Mary WHELON, 39, congestive fever. 10/28 – Mary O'CONNER, 30, apoplexy. 10/30 – John F. TOMPKINS, 33, consumption; Mr. VAUGHAN, 40, casualty. 10/31 – W. D. MAY, 31, gastritis.
11/1 – Samuel C. SUIT, 39, cystitis. 11/2 – Thomas BRUSHMAN, 35, congestive fever; Mr. GASTON, 30, congestive fever. 11/4 – Lucas ROCK, 50, entritis; Miss Julia VADEN, 26, gastritis; W. STEVENSON, 45, consumption. 11/5 – Oscar FINLEY, 20, typhoid pneumonia; Edmond CARTER, 31, casualty; Joseph DAVIS, 35, consumption; Child of Fred CLUTE, 2 months, marasmus. 11/6 – Patrick McQUINLEY, 42, fracture of skull. 11/8 – Thos. SHEAHAN, 30, billious fever; Martin KELLY, 20 months, intermittent fever. 11/11 – Timothy HARLEY, 34, consumption; L. P. FOWLKES, 35, consumption. 11/12 – Son of James GILLOOLY, 19 months, disease of the brain. 11/19 – Wm. FAUG_MAN, 23(?), billious fever; Dennis McCARTY, ---, intemperance. 11/21 – Henry CARROLL, 31, disease of heart; Gilbert BACHELDOR, 2 months, gastro enteritis; J. M. CABE, 30, erysipelas. 11/22 – John GLEASON, 35, disease of heart. 11/23 – Frank FARMER, 3 months, congestion of bowels. 11/24 – Martin CAYN, 1 week, frismus nascentium. 11/26 – James HACKEY, 32, congestive chill; Mrs. Sarah J. STELL, 38, gastritis; H. CHANDLER, 14. 11/27 – Ambrose PIERCE, 28, pneumonia; Hannah ST. CLAIR, 5 months, dysentery. 11/28 – Shoemake DONOHO, 6, disease of heart; Joseph STONSON, 21, consumption. 11/29 – L. SCEULWICK, 24, death by laud.
12/3 – Alfred CAUGHEY, 18, gastro enteritis. 12/4 – Patrick BOREN, 36, consumption. 12/5 – Mrs. Mary CALBRAN, 45, disease of stomach. 12/6 – Chas. ROACH, 25, intermittent fever. 12/7 – Julia O'BRYAN, 17 months, cholera infantum. 12/8 – J. RADCLIFF, 45, unknown. 12/9 – Lizzie HUGHES, 3, burn; Thomas F. GIBBS, 64, disease of heart. 12/10 – Michael SHANNON, 2, inflammation of brain. 12/12 – Bridget LAREY, 3, burn. 12/13 – Margaret HENRY, 9 months, effects of laudanum. 12/14 – Mrs. Kate WILLIAMSON, 25, puerperal fever. 12/15 – John DONNELLY, 18 months, convulsions. 12/18 – Geo. M. PATTISON, 25, consumption. 12/19 – Ellen W. CARROLL, 2 years, 10 months, croup. 12/20 – Mariana WELLER, debility; G. KRANCHI, 45, not reported. 12/21 – Ellen MURRAY, 3, congestion of brain; Almeda BOYCE, 12, chronic diarrhea. 12/22 – Mrs. Frederick ENGEL, 28, burn. 12/24 – Ann Margaret ECKERT, 34, chronic diarrhea; Mrs. H. W. REED, 47, consumption.

REV., 52
BOTELER
  MARCUS A., 31
BOTTO
  AMANDA, 328
  D., 325
  HATTY, 239
  JOSEPH, 337, 342
  L., 325
  ROSA, 239
BOUCHER
  GILBERT B.(?), 31
BOUGH
  W.R., 31
BOULTON
  JNO., 23
  JOHN, 23(2)
BOUNDS
  G.W., LIEUT., 130
BOURNE
  JAMES T., 31
BOWDEN
  B.T., 31
  GIDEON, 31
BOWDOIN
  EMILY S., 11
  WALTER, 11
BOWEN
  ALEX., 339
  ELIZABETH, 32
  EPAPHRODITUS, 31
  F., 69
  FREDERICK, 333
  G.A., 32
  JOHN H., 32
  POSTON, 32
  W.P., 32
BOWERS
  B., MAJ., 32(2)
  BILLY, 32
  GEO., MAJ., 32
  HENRIETTA L., 32
  JAMES, 196
  JAMES [_.], 32
  SUTHERLAND, 32
  THOMAS CASWELL, 32
  WILLIAM P., 32(2)
  WILLIAM PRIDDY, 32
  WM. E., 126
BOWES
  MR., 119
BOWLES
  CHARLES, 332
  JOHN, 115(3)
  MR., 120
  THERESE C., 127
  TIMAXENA, 127
  WILLIAM, 32
  Z.P., 32
BOWLES & SMITHER, 32
BOWLIN
  J.C., 33
BOWLING
  ELIZABETH C., 33
  GEO. W., 33
BOWLS
  RICHARD, 33
BOWMAN
  [BLANK], 249
BOWNDS
  MARGRET, 33
  MILTON FAIRCHILD, 33
  THOMAS, 33
BOWS(?)
  P., 333
BOYCE

ALMEDA, 343
EDWARD, 33
J.K., REV., 192, 195
MRS., 205
BOYD
  ANDREW G., 323
  J., 326
  JAMES, 33
  JAMES J., 33
  JOHN C., 33
  MARY, 233
  NANCY, 332
  ROBERT, 341
  ROBERT M., 33
  ROBERT _., 33
  SUSAN ANN, 33
  WILLIAM, 33
  WM., 329
BOYER
  S.W., 33
BOYET
  BARTLEY, 33
BOYETE
  BRATLEY, 333
BOYKIN
  CHARLES E., 34
BOYLER
  STEPHEN, 329
BRACKINRIDGE
  ADELINE, 248
BRADBURY
  GEORGE W., COL., 34
BRADEN
  GABRIEL, 34
  J.P., 34
  MARTHA E., 34
BRADFORD
  A.B., GEN., 307
  ANNE CHAMBERS, 153
  ANNELIJAH, 34
  CARROLL, 298
  DARTHULA O., 307
  J.W., 34(3)
  JOHN D., 5
  JULIA B., 298
  KING, 34
  M.A., 192
  MARY, 34
  MOLLIE C., 155
  MR., 328
  ROBERT P., 34
  W.C., 34, 320
  WATT C., 155
BRADHAVEN
  JUSTICE, 324
BRADLEY
  MRS., 336
  SUSAN S., 34
  WM. T., 34
BRADLEY, WILSON & CO.,
  319
BRADSHAW
  JOSEPH J. FRANCIS,
  34
  R.F., 330
  RICHARD F., 34
  SARAH F.(?), 34
  THOMAS, 34
  THOS., 325
  WM., 35(2), 324
BRADY
  JAMES, 331
  JOHN, 334
  MICHAEL, 328
  SAMUEL, 337
BRAHAN

JOHN C., COL., 13
SILAS, 35
BRAMLETT
  ELIZA JANE, 161
  JUDGE, 161
  L.M., 161
BRANCH
  J.K., 66
  JOHN E., 321
BRANDON
  WM., 35(2)
BRANNIN
  B., MRS., 341
BRANNON
  EDWARD, 330
BRANSON
  NATHAN, 304
BRATT
  MRS., 328
BRATTON
  S.E., DR., 35
BRAVER
  MARY, 325
BRAY
  E., 278
  E.D., 35
BRAYDEN
  WM., 338
BREADEN
  G., 332
BREATHITT
  EDWARD, 35
  EDWARD, DR., 35(2)
  JOHN EATON, 35
  MARY P., 35(2)
BRECKINRIDGE
  ROBERT, 35
BREDIS(?)
  JOHN, 339
BREEN
  ANDREW, 325
  PATRICK, 336
BREES
  FREDERICK, 342
BREIL
  MISS, 321
BREMER
  JOHN, 326
BREMISH
  LUCAS, 338
BRENNER
  MR., 326
BRET
  M.C., 306
BRETT
  JAMES, JR., 35
BREWER
  CATHARINE, 338
  HERRING, 36
  MOREAU, 36
BREWER(?)
  CATO, 324
BREZENTINE
  ANNA, 325
  E., 325
  E., MRS., 325
BRIAN
  MARTIN C., DR., 36
BRICE
  JOHN, REV., 241
BRICK
  DENNIS, 36
BRIDGE
  ISHAM, 339
BRIDGERS
  SOPHIE A., 294

BRIDGES
  B.H., 36
  MRS., 36
  SOPHIE A., 314
  THOMAS, 36
  WM. H., 36
BRIEN
  EDMUND, 322
BRIGANCE
  MARTHA FREDONIA, 92
BRIGHT
  J.E., REV., 60, 135,
  206, 217
  MARY C., 301
  REV., 67
BRILEY
  MARY, 326
BRINKLEY
  ANN C., 36
  G.A., 36
  GEO., 36
  GEO. A., 263
  GEORGE, 36
  JOHN, 37
  R.C., 37
BRITISEH
  JOS., 342
BRITT
  B.W., 37
BRITTINGHAM
  ELIZABETH, 323
  MARY E., 37
BRIZENTINE
  C., 325
BRIZZOLARI(?)
  J., 340
BROADERS
  EDWIN R., 37
BROCCHUS
  E.F., 111
BRODHEAD
  S.A., 37
BRONAUGH
  ANNA LOUISA, 37
  JEREMIAH, 37(2)
BRONSON
  DAVID, 37
BROOKLYN, L.I., 304
BROOKS
  B.F.C., DR., 37(3),
  336
  BENJAMIN W., 37
  E.B., MRS., 329
  E.W., 37
  ELIZABETH, 213
  EVELINA E., 37
  F.W., 37
  HUGH M., 37
  ISAAC, 37
  L.A.E., 296
  LEWIS, 38
  MARGARET, 323
  MARY, 324
  MOLLIE T., 307
  MR., 213
  ROBERT, 35
  W.J., 38
  WM., 38
BROOKSHAW
  ANN ELIZA, 196
BROOM
  A.H., REV., 70
  ELIZABETH, 300
BROOMACHE
  EDWARD, 322
BROT_EPE

JACOB, 38
BROTHERLIN
  W.F., 323
BROWDER
  DAVID, 335
BROWN
  A.G., 39
  A.H., 38
  ALBERT, 341
  ALETHEA, 38
  AMERICA, 333
  AMERICA C., 40
  AMERICA E., 40
  AMERICA FORREST, 40
  ANN M., 63
  ANNA HERSCHELL, 40
  ANNE M., 40
  B.C., 133
  B.J., 38
  BEDFORD, 38(2)
  CHARLES EMMERSON, 39
  CHARLOTTE, 328
  COL., 75
  DAVID S., 38
  E.M., 38
  ELIZABETH, 39
  F., 327
  F.D., 322
  FANNIE, 173
  FRANCES CATHERINE,
  162
  FRANCIS E., 162
  G.Y., 216
  HARRIET, 83
  HONOR, 38
  J. TURNER, 39
  J.H., REV., 93
  J.N., DR., 38
  J.N., LIEUT., 38
  J.T., 325
  J.W., DR., 39
  J.W.S., 155
  JAMES, 328
  JAMES, COL., 254
  JANE B., 39
  JENNETT T., 39
  JOHN, 39, 71, 163
  JOHN L., COL., 39
  JOHN T., DR., 39
  JOHN W., 245
  JOSEPH, 39
  JOSEPHINE, 106
  JULIA M., 254
  L.M.(?), DR., 39
  LUCINDA, 231
  LUCY ANN, 39
  LYDIA H., 232
  M., 337
  M., MRS., 325
  MARTHA A., 163
  MARTHA E., 160
  MARY A., 81
  MARY E., 75
  MARY M., 322
  MERRITT R., 323
  MINNIE L., 173
  MR., 19
  NANCY, 39
  R.A., DR., 160
  R.B., 39
  R.F., DR., 39
  R.H., DR., 39
  REBECCA, 83
  REBECCA E., 48
  REID B., 334
  ROBERT A., 39

JULIET, 307
JUSTICE, 175
LAFAYETTE, M.D., 130
LIZZIE B., 38
LUCIEN W., 130
MARY T., 129
MATILDA E., 130
MATILDA W., 130
MOLLIE, 226
NAPOLEON, 130
ROBERT, 93
S. FRANK, 49
SAMUEL, 129
SARAH ANN, 130
SARAH ISABEL, 130
T.B., 130
THOS., 295
W.B., 130
WILLIAM S., 130(2)
WM., 130
WM. B., 77, 130
WM. KENAN, 130(2),
    307
HILL & HAYLEY, 130
HILLIARD
    K.W., 179
    MARTHA A., 340
HILLIS
    JOS. B., 130
HILTON
    MRS., 322
    T.M., 321
    WARD H., 131
HINCHEE
    EDWARD, 334
HINDMAN
    JAMES, 131
    T.C., COL., 131
HINEMAN
    D.G., 131
HINES
    P., 330
    REV., 300
    RICHARD, REV., 285
HINKEL
    A.D., 333
HINKLEMAN
    H., 343
HINNANT
    NANCY, 131
    STEPHEN, 131
HINTON
    EUGENE J., GEN., 131
    FRANCIS E., 93
    LEWIS R., 93
HIRCH
    SAML., 131
HIRSCH
    AARON, 131
HISSKELL
    ELLEN MARY, 132
    THOMAS, 132
HITCHCOCK
    SOPHIA, 131
    WALTER, 131, 328
    WILLIAM, 131
HITCHLER
    J., MRS., 336
    JOHN, 131(3)
HITE
    MARY ELIZA, 131
    MARY S., JR., 131
    R.C., 324
    WM. H., 131
HOBDY
    SIDNEY, 328

HOBGOOD
    JOSEPH F., 131
HODGE
    REV., 277
    SAMUEL, REV., 25
    W.W., 131
HODGES
    JOHN T., 132
    JOHN W., 132
HOFFMAN
    BARBARA, 332
    CARL, 340
    CHARLES, 327
    E.D., 339
    ELIZA, 331
    ELIZABETH D., 132
    J.P., 132
    JNO. H., 132
    JOHN H., 332
    JOHN L., 334
    MICHAEL, 342
    R., MRS., 336
    S.T., 329
    SARAH A., 334
HOFTER
    THOMAS, 38
HOGAN
    JOHN, 328
    MR., 328
    PATRICK, 330
HOGE
    REV., 264
HOGG
    AMBROSE, 326
HOKE
    DANIEL, 194
HOLCOMB
    B.L., COL., 89
    J., 191
    JAS., 322
HOLCOMBE
    H.L., COL., 308
HOLDEN
    MR., 244
HOLDER
    W.D., 127
HOLLAND
    GEO. B., 132
    JANE M., 132
    JOHN, 132
    JOHN M., 132
    LUCY, 132
    MR., 122
    SARAH P., 234
HOLLENBECK
    JOHN H., 132
HOLLERAN
    THOS., 334
HOLLINSWORTH
    SAMUEL, 325
HOLLOWAY
    A., 4
    F.B., 340
    MARGARET, 48
HOLLY SPRINGS, 19, 20,
    27, 67, 85, 112,
    133, 144, 189,
    194, 201, 255,
    259, 294, 302,
    307
HOLMES
    ELIZABETH, 271
    ELIZABETH MARTHA,
        132
    ELIZABETH P., 132
    EMMA, 67

FINDLEY, 132
FINLEY, COL., 132
FINLY, COL., 7
G.L., 301
GEO. L., 16, 329
GEORGE C., 132
ISAAC, 132, 340
J.H., DR., 166
JAMES, 132
JAMES D., 132
JAMES, REV., 147,
    275
JAS., REV., 114, 212
JOHN B., 144
LUCY, 324
LUCY ANNA, 132
MARY E., 132
NANCY W., 232
WILLIAM, 132
WM., 132
HOLOWAY
    R., REV., 83
HOLST
    C.K., 132(2)
    CHARLES H., 132, 323
    EDWARD E., 338
    MARY ANN, 132
    MR., 230
HOLT
    NEIL B., 132
    ROBERT, 338
HOLYOAKE
    THOMAS, 132
HOLYOAKE, LOWNS & CO.,
    208
HOMES
    A.C., 133
    L., DR., 132
    MARY EMILY, 132
    SALLIE _., 132
HOOD
    JAMES H., 133
HOOKER
    JOHN R., 133
    M.A.V., 116
    MATTIE, 154
    R.B., 133
HOOKS
    MALCUS, 133
HOOPER
    JOHN T., 322
    NICHOLAS, 133
HOOVER
    CHRISTIANA, 20
    EPHRAIM, 20
HOPEFIELD, 79
HOPKINS
    A.M., 130, 153
    W.D., 329
HOPPER
    A.C., 133
    JAMES, 338
    [BLANK], 133
HOPSON
    A.M., 130
    H.R., DR., 54
HOPTON
    A., 66
    ABNER, 133
    ABNER, M.D., 66
HORN
    J., 320
    JESSE, 133
    MRS., 340
HORNE

A., MRS., 339
C., 335
CORONER, 3, 113,
    274, 293
EMMA C., 340
ESQ., 28, 60, 115,
    170, 244, 282(2)
ESQUIRE, 38, 58, 63,
    135, 150, 183(2),
    244
H., 342
J., 85, 219, 300
J.G., 133
JOSIAH, 53, 133,
    157, 218
THOS., 337
HORSELEY
    R.M., 133, 335
HORTON
    C.M., 340
    H., REV., 232
    H.C., REV., 159
    M.M., 111
    R., 318
    REV., 224, 243
    _. C., REV., 134
HORTON & HUNTER, 137
HOSKINS
    NANNIE, 149
    WM., 330
HOTCHKIS
    JANE T., 217
HOTCHKISS
    E.B., 134
HOTTER
    J., 134
HOUGHMAN
    JOHN, 328
HOUGHTON
    G.N., REV., 132
HOURCEIGT
    MRS., 72
    OCTAVIA, 72
HOUSE
    FRANK _., REV., 65
    H., 134
    HENDERSON, 134
HOUSER
    JOSEPH, 341
HOUSTON
    E., 166
    ELIZA L., 134
    JNO., 134, 164
    JOHN, 254, 281
    LAURA AMARYLLIS, 164
    M.A., 341
    MAJ., 178
    MARY, 221, 310
    MARY JANE, 254
    MR., 102
    PRESIDENT, 193
    WILLIAM, MAJ., 221
    WM., 320
    WM., MAJ., 134
HOWARD
    ALEX., 333
    ALEXANDER, 134
    CHAS. T., 279
    DANIEL J., 134
    ELIZABETH ANN, 279
    FREAK C., 134
    J.C., 69
    J.M., 329
    JAMES M., 134(2)
    JAS. M., 134
    JOHN, 341

JOS., 338
JOSEPH J., 134
JOSEPHINE, 221
MAGGIE LEE, 311
MARY JANE, 182
MRS., 182
OLIVIA, 336
REV., 47
W., 90, 329
W.R., 135
W.T., 134
WARDLOW, 135
WM. D., 339
HOWARD & LAIRD, 134
HOWCOTT
    A., MRS., 135, 336
    H., 320
    H., DR., 160
    J.B., 326
    JOHN, 135
    MARY LOUISE, 158
    N., 135
    N., DR., 135, 335
    N., REV., 235, 312
    NAT., DR., 158
HOWELL
    H.B., 338
    JUNIUS H., DR., 135
    LUCY DUNCAN, 80
    M., REV., 90
    MARIA L., 191
    MARY JANE, 42
    R.B.C., REV., 224
    W.E., 135
HOWERTON
    JOHN, 26
HOYLE
    ALEX C., 332
    ALEXANDER
        CREIGHTON,
        135
    ALLEN, 135
    ALLEN, MRS., 135
    MRS., 332
    P., REV., 11
    WM. ALLEN, 135
HUBBARD
    ALICE, 157
    DAVE A., 135
    E.H., REV., 135
HUBER
    JOHN, 135
HUBERS
    H., 326
HUCKELBY
    MR., 135
HUDSON
    CAPT., 135
    HALL, 135
    J.L., 341
    KATE, 8
    MARY SMITH, 231
    MR., 202
    THO'S W., 135
HUDSONVILLE, 162
HUDSPETH
    SEATON, COL., 135
HUFFANY
    MRS., 329
HUGGINS
    L.M., 136
HUGHES
    DANIEL, 136, 321
    LIZZIE, 343
    MARY, 185
    MARY P., 183

VIRGINIA A., 139
WILLIAM L., 169
WM. L., DR., 169
LUNSFORD
JOHN, 34(2)
LURRY
SARAH, 309
WILSON, 309
LUSHER
HENRY M., 169
N.P., 169
NATHANIEL PEARSON, 169
LUSK
ROBERT, MAJ., 169
LUSTER
MARY, 330
LUTER
JOSEPH, 170
LU_HWIG
J.W., 342
LYDE
A.O., 338
LYLE
MR., 69
LYLES
ARCHIBALD M., DR., 170
LYNCH
CORNELIUS, 333
DENNIS, 339
E., 325
J.D., 282
JOHN, CAPT., 157
MARY, 335
OLIVE G., 254
REV., 202
LYNES(?)
ELIZABETH, 63
LYNN
ELIZABETH, 203
FRANK W., 170
J.N., 233
J.T., 329
JOHN T., 170
MARY ADELA, 170
MINERVA, 170
SARAH, 131
LYON
JAMES A., REV., 183
LIZZIE, 242
MARGARET E., 207
MR., 244
S.H., 170(2)
LYONS
A., MRS., 330
LYTLE
JAMES S., 170
LYTLE (OR LYDE)
O.H., 20

-M-

MABRY
J.C., DR., 170
JNO. C., DR., 170
OVID, 170
MABSON(?)
ARTHUR, 82
RACHEL, 82
M'ADOO
W.H., 179
McADOO
WM. G., LIEUT., 130
McALANY
MR., 327

McALEAR
MICHAEL, REV., 98
McALEER
MICHAEL, REV., 150
REV., 157, 244
McALEXANDER
SAMUEL R., 179
McALISTER
JOHN W., 179
McALLANEY
MRS., 326
McALLISTER
JAMES, 324
M'ALPIN
R.C., 179
ROBT. C., 131
McASH
ELLA, 179
JUDGE, 179
M'ATEER
WM., 179
McBRIDE
CASPER, 271(2)
WM., 324
McCABE
JAMES, 326
WM., 342
McCAIN
ELIZA H., 310
H. CONNOR, 179
JAMES M., 179
W.R., 179, 310
McCALE
WM., 329
McCALISTER
IRABELLA, 330
McCALL
ANN, 170
J.A., 127, 320
McCALLISTER
A., 333
McCALLUM
MALCOLM, 179
MARY, 179
MARY MALCOLM, 179
McCAMPBELL
MR., 215
McCANN
AGNES, 281
McCARGE
LUCY A., 180
WM. H., DR., 180
McCARGO
WM. H., DR., 180
McCARNON
D., 180
McCARTHY
FLEURY, 323
JOHN, 338
MARY, 322
MICHAEL, 323
McCARTY
CHARLES, 339
DANIEL, 322
DENNIS, 343
JOHN, 331
MICHAEL, 180, 337
MRS., 336
P., MRS., 331
SARAH J., 342
McCAUGH
J., 328
McCAUGHAN
K.A., 180
L.C., 180
McCAUGHEY

ELIZA F., 46
McCAY
JANE C., 231
McCLAIN
A.L., 39
McCLANAHAN
HAMPDEN, 180
HAMPTON, 180
JOHN D., 180
LOUISA, 180
LUCY, 180
NELSON, 180
ROBERT, 180
SAMUEL, 180(2)
McCLANE
WM. J., 181
McCLAREN
JULIA F., 222
M'CLEARY
JAMES A., 179
NEWTON, JR., 179
McCLELLAN
I.B., 63
ISABELLA C., 181
JAMES D., 181(2)
T.D.G., M.D., 181
WILLIAM B., 181
M'CLEVAIN
R.G., 179
McCLOSKY
MARTHA, 297
McCLOUD
JAMES, 331
McCLUER
JACKSON, 181
McCLUNG
JAMES W., 216
McCLURE
ED., REV., 181
WM., 339
McCLUSKIN
M.J., 197
McCODE
JAMES, 181
McCOLLUM
MALCOLM, 181
McCOMBS
E., 335
ELIZABETH W., 181
HARRY SYLVESTER, 181
J.M., 181, 284
JAS. M., 181
McCONNEL
P., 181
McCONNELL
JAMES, 181
ROSANNA, 322
McCONNELL & BRO., 319
McCOOL
JAMES, 181
McCORKLE
JOSEPH M., 181
MARY JANE, 97
SARAH E., 5
McCORMACK
MARGARET, 334
McCORMICK
JOHN, 322
MARY, 339
McCORRY
S., 49
THOMAS, 49
M'COULEY
JOHN C., 179
McCOULL
ANN MARIA, 176

DR., 170
FREDERIC A., 181
J.M., DR., 182
JOHN, 176
McCOY
R., REV., 51
REV., 109
McCRACKEN
J.W., 182(2)
MARY ANN, 182(2)
McCRAKEN
DAVID J., 182
McCRAW
WILLIAM, 182
McCREADY
ALEXANDER, 182
M'CREIGHT
JOHN R., 179
M'CULLOCH
ALEXANDER, 71
McCULLOCH
REV., 286
McCULLOUGH
MRS., 310
REV., 32
McCULLY
THOMAS, 182
McCULL_H
M., 182
McCURE
CORNELIUS, 182
McDANIEL
_. A., 182
McDAVITT
E., 105, 256
ROSELLA C., 105
McDERNUTT(?)
ELLEN, 331
McDONALD
A.C., DR., 182
ANN B., 266
EDWARD, 182
J., MRS., 323
J.L., 337
J.R., 183
JAMES, 183, 341
JOHN, 334
KATE, 340
MARY, 337
MATILDA JANE, 177
R.R., 175
T., 328
WILLIE, 183
WM. S.K., 336
McDONOHOO
JOHN, 329
McDONOUGH
CAPT., 64
McDOWELL
ANDREW, 183
M'DOWELL
J., 35
McDOWELL
MATTHEW, 183
THOMAS J., 183
McELEER(?)
JOHN, 339
McELHERAN
A., 341
ALEX., 183
McELWEE
S.J., 3
McEVOY
HENRIETTA, 116
J.A., 183
McEWEN

T.B., 183
McFADDEN
N.H., 313
N.H., REV., 281
REV., 121
McFARLAND
J.C., REV., 321
J.W., REV., 183, 328
McFERRAN
J., REV., 73
REV., 118
McFERRIN
JOHN H., 183
WM. M., REV., 253, 304
McGARRY
M.H., 342
McGAUGH
DAVID, 340
McGAVOCK
E., 56
EDWARD J., 183
R., 56
McGAVROCK
HARRIET R., 106
R., 106(2)
McGEE
H., 340
JAMES, 183(3)
MARY ANN, 183
PHILIP, 183
R.G., 184
THOS., 184
McGEE(?)
M.L., MRS., 326
McGEHE
JOHN C., 294
MARTHA A.E., 294
McGEHEE
ABNER, 184
E., 184
EDWARD, 184
HUGH, 184
J.O., 184
JOHN S., 87, 305
KATE, 305
THOS., 338
McGINNIS
A., 331
A.B., 230, 288
AMANDA, 331
MR., 330
McGLACHLEN(?)
JACOB, 339
McGLAUN
SAM'L, 332
McGOWAN
HENDERSON, 328
MOLLIE I., 215
Z.A., 208
McGOWEN
JOHN, 322
MARY E., 307
McGOWN
G.W., CAPT., 130
HENDERSON, 184
T., 319
McGRATH
ANN M., 338
EDWARD, 322
JAMES, 329
JOHN, 184
MARTIN, 338
MICHAEL, 324
THOS., 332
TIMOTHY, 324

MR., 339

OTT
GEO. M., 325

OUSLER
JOHN, 209

OUTLAW
JOSEPH B., DR., 209

OVENS
EMILY, 332
W., 209, 332

OVERTON
ARCHIBALD W., 35

OWEN
ANNIE M., 183
CATHERINE, 334
ELIZABETH H., 209
F.A., REV., 134, 209, 236
HELLEN, 209
HENDERSON, 29
HENRY, 62
IDA, 210
JABEZ, 209
KAT, 339
L.V., 37
MARGARET, 210
MARTHA A., 209(2), 210
MARY E., 62
MELISSA, 210
MILES, 209(2), 210(2), 223, 251
MOLLIE E., 62
NARCISSA E., 210
P.A., 210
REBECCA R., 29
RICHARD, 209
SAMUEL P., 210
THOMAS, 23
THOMAS B., 210
VIRGINIA L., 210
WILBER FISK, 209
WILLIAM, 209
WILLIAM E., COL., 210
WILLIAM L., 210

OWENS
GEORGE J.(?), 210
HENRY, 210
N., 327

OXFORD, 107, 163

OZMONT
V., 210

-P-

P. H. GOODWYN & SON, 107

P.M. PATTERSON & BRO., 214

PACE
S.D., 3

PADGETT
CALVIN, 210
WESLEY, 210

PADUCAH, 75

PAGE
D.C., REV., 13(2), 50, 119, 120, 158, 210, 240, 276, 288, 294, 314, 321
DAVID C., REV., 210(2)
E.O., 210
ELIZA O., 332

ELIZA ORMSBY, 210
MARY A.M., 334
REV., 8, 9, 15, 41, 47(2), 52, 54, 64, 65, 75, 86, 89, 96, 108, 110, 121, 136, 138, 144, 159, 174, 191, 198, 216, 229, 233, 257, 261, 302, 314, 318
ROBERT ORMSBY, 210

PAILLARD
LAURA, 339

PAINE
JAMES A., 211
JOSEPH N., 211
REV., 285
REV. BISHOP, 67

PAINTER
CATHARINE, 325
SAM'L C., 324
W.D., 211

PALMER
ALBERT, 331
FRANCES, 211
MARGARET, 211
MARY J., 335
STEPHEN, 211
WILLIAM, 211

PALMORE
JOHN STEPHEN, 211
SUSAN E., 211

PAMPLIN
WILLIAM S., 282

PANESI
CAROLINE, 330

PANOLA, 310

PAPA
GABRIEL, RV., 23

PARAM
WM., 218

PARDUE
THOS. J., 211, 342

PARHAM
HENRY D., 336
JOS. J., 211
MARTHA A., 172
R.S., 172
ROBERT M., 336
S., REV., 290

PARIETE
IRABELA, 211

PARIS, 33, 65, 66

PARISH
F.H., 211

PARK
A.G., 211
ANDREW, 211
ANN E., 211
DAVID, 85, 211(2), 212
J.B., 339
JAMES B., 211
JANE, 211
JENNIE R., 72
JNO., 212
JOHN, 212
REBECCA, 212
WM., 86, 212(2)

PARKER
D.J., REV., 241
DANIEL E., SR., 212(2)
ELIZABETH, 212

GEO. H., M.D., 212
GEORGE L., COL., 212
J.G., 86
JOHN G., REV., 309
LINAS, REV., 282
M., MRS., 324
M.A., 326
MARTHA, 212
MARTHA ANN, 212
MARY ANN, 99, 212
MARY J., 58
MATILDA, 331
R.A., 94, 212(4)
R.A., JR., 212
SAMUEL W., 212
T.J., 326
THOMAS, 212

PARKS
E.M., DR., 213

PARR
JIMIE BAILEY, 213
LOU., 213
WILLIAM, 213

PARRAN
THOMAS A., 213
THOMAS O., 213

PARRISH
DAVID M., 213
LUCINDA, 213
WILLIAM S., 213(3)

PARSONS
M., 342

PARTEE
DAVID M., DR., 213
HIRAM, COL., 213
LOUANNA, 213
MARIA, 104
MRS., 332

PARVIN
R.T., REV., 209

PASAVANT
W.A., REV., 5

PASCHALL
A.S., 213
J.M., 213
KATE, 213
PAULINA, 213

PASLEY
AUSTEN, 213
R.H., 213

PASQUERO
MR., 332

PATE
JAMES, 325

PATELLO
R.H., 215

PATILLO
MARY A., 327
P.C., 220
R.H., 213
ROBERT H., 213

PATRICK
E.M., 213
FREDONIA O., 12
GEO. C., 213
HARRIET A., 239
J.M., 44, 213(2), 319(2)
L., 213
LEONIDAS KNOX, 213
M.K., 213
ROBERT GREENVILLE, 213

PATRIDGE
ISAAC M., 214

PATTEN

MARGARET, 323

PATTERSON
B.M., JR., 214
BERNARD M., JR., 214
BILLY, 214
ISABELLA, 238
JOHN, 154
KATE, 41
M.G., 342
NANCY M., 281
OCTEVE S., 108
PUGH T., 214
TEMPE, 214
WILLIAM M., 214
WM., 214
[..] C., REV., 41

PATTISON
ALEX., JR., 214
ANNIE E., 194
GEO., 214
GEO. M., 343
GEO., COL., 194
GEO., JR., 214
GEORGE, 214
GEORGE, COL., 214(2)
SALLIE G., 214
SARAH G., 342
W.H., 334
WM. H., 214

PATTON
SUE, 35

PAUL
FRANC M., 43
J., MRS., 328
LUCY H., 214
W.P., 214

PAYELLE
G., 59

PAYNE
C.B., 215
EDWIN A., 215
ELIZA F., 180
FRANCES K., 180
M., MRS., 59
MARIA S., 215
MARY, 59
MILES, 339
REV., 211
ROBERT, 180, 215
ROBERT, REV., 94
ROBT., 215
W.C., 337

PAYNTER
H.H., 48

PEACE
ELENOR F. S., 149

PEACH
WM., 336

PEACOCK
MARIA B., 90

PEACOCKE
JAMES S., DR., 215
JAS. S., DR., 340

PEAK
FANNIE A., 90

PEAKE
CONDICE, 215
JULIA ANN, 215
SAMUEL H., 215

PEARCE
A., 215
BENJAMIN, 215
J.A., DR., 215
J.T., REV., 39
JAS., 334
JOHN, 328

SUSAN P., 215
WALTER BENJAMIN, 215

PEARSON
A.T., 323
J.S., DR., 215
MOSES, 215
NATHANIEL, 169
SARAH, 205

PECK
DR., 6
MATILDA, 330
REV., 83, 101
WILEY B., REV., 163

PEEBLES
BURLIN, 215
ETHELDRED D., 215
GEORGIANA M., 215

PEEL
CHARLOTTE, 216
JAS., 342
THOS. J., 216

PEGUE
A.T., 282

PELL(?)
H.D., 216

PENDER
J.W., REV., 52, 108, 184

PENDERGRAST
CATHERINE, 337
J., 329

PENDLETON
P.B., DR., 317

PENLAND
N.A., REV., 218

PENN
G.M., 325
GEO., 312
GEO. M., 216
J.L., 216
JAMES, 128
JAMES L., 216
JAMES LYTTELTON, 216
JAMES LYTTLETON, 216
JAMES, MAJOR, 38
JAS., MAJ., 159
MARIA WEST, 172
MARY B., 38

PENNINGTON
JOHN B., 216

PENNSYLVANIA
ALLEGHANY CITY, 44
ALLEGHENY CITY, 267
BLAIRSVILLE, 277
HARRISBURG, 202
PHILADELPHIA, 132, 163
PITTSBURG, 162
POTTSVILLE, 283
YORK, 277

PENNY
F., 326
[BLANK], 326

PEOPLES
S.T., 83

PEPPER
CAPT., 209
JAMES H., CAPT., 217
JIM, CAPT., 217

PERCIVAL
ROBERT D., 217

PERES
J.J., REV., 100

PERKINS
ANGELINA MARIA, 217
BENJAMIN F., 217

386